VOTE

STATE & LOCAL POLITICS

Institutions & Reform
The Essentials

Todd Donovan

Christopher Z. Mooney

Daniel A. Smith

D0071293

State	Abbreviation	State Capital	Current Governor (party)[a]	Legislative Majority (Senate/House)[b]
Alabama	AL	Montgomery	Robert Bentley (R)	R/R
Alaska	AK	Juneau	Sean Parnell (R)	tied/R
Arizona	AZ	Phoenix	Jan Brewer (R)	R/R
Arkansas	AR	Little Rock	Mike Beebe (D)	D/D
California	CA	Sacramento	Jerry Brown (D)	D/D
Colorado	CO	Denver	John Hickenlooper (D)	D/R
Connecticut	CT	Hartford	Dan Malloy (D)	D/D
Delaware	DE	Dover	Jack Markell (D)	D/D
Florida	FL	Tallahassee	Rick Scott (R)	R/R
Georgia	GA	Atlanta	Nathan Deal (R)	R/R
Hawaii	HI	Honolulu	Neil Abercrombie (D)	D/D
Idaho	ID	Boise	C.L. "Butch" Otter (R)	R/R
Illinois	IL	Springfield	Pat Quinn (D)	D/D
Indiana	IN	Indianapolis	Mitch Daniels (R)	R/R
Iowa	IA	Des Moines	Terry Branstad (R)	D/R
Kansas	KS	Topeka	Sam Brownback (R)	R/R
Kentucky	KY	Frankfort	Steve Beshear (D)	R/D
Louisiana	LA	Baton Rouge	Bobby Jindal (R)	D/R
Maine	ME	Augusta	Paul R. LePage (R)	R/R
Maryland	MD	Annapolis	Martin O'Malley (D)	D/D
Massachusetts	MA	Boston	Deval Patrick (D)	D/D
Michigan	MI	Lansing	Rick Snyder (R)	R/R
Minnesota	MN	St. Paul	Mark Dayton (D)	R/R
Mississippi	MS	Jackson	Haley Barbour (R)	D/D
Missouri	MO	Jefferson City	Jay Nixon (D)	R/R
Montana	MT	Helena	Brian Schweitzer (D)	R/R
Nebraska	NE	Lincoln	Dave Heineman (R)	Nonpartisan
Nevada	NV	Carson City	Brian Sandoval (R)	D/D
New Hampshire	NH	Concord	John Lynch (D)	R/R
New Jersey	NJ	Trenton	Chris Christie (R)	D/D
New Mexico	NM	Santa Fe	Susana Martinez (R)	D/D
New York	NY	Albany	Andrew Cuomo (D)	R/D
North Carolina	NC	Raleigh	Beverly Perdue (D)	R/R
North Dakota	ND	Bismarck	John "Jack" Dalrymple (R)	R/R
Ohio	OH	Columbus	John Kasich (R)	R/R
Oklahoma	OK	Oklahoma City	Mary Fallin (R)	R/R
Oregon	OR	Salem	John Kitzhaber (D)	D/tied
Pennsylvania	PA	Harrisburg	Tom Corbett (R)	R/R
Rhode Island	RI	Providence	Lincoln Chafee (I)	D/D
South Carolina	SC	Columbia	Nikki Haley (R)	R/R
South Dakota	SD	Pierre	Dennis Daugaard (R)	R/R
Tennessee	TN	Nashville	Bill Haslam (R)	R/R
Texas	TX	Austin	Rick Perry (R)	R/R
Utah	UT	Salt Lake City	Gary R. Herbert (R)	R/R
Vermont	VT	Montpelier	Peter Shumlin (D)	D/D
Virginia	VA	Richmond	Bob McDonnell (R)	D/R
Washington	WA	Olympia	Christine Gregoire (D)	D/D
West Virginia	WV	Charleston	Earl Ray Tomblin (D)	D/D
Wisconsin	WI	Madison	Scott Walker (R)	R/R
Wyoming	WY	Cheyenne	Matthew Mead (R)	R/R

Sources:

[a] National Governors association website (http://www.nga.org)—as of December 15, 2010

[b] National Conference of State Legislatures website (http://www.ncsl.org/documents/statevote/2010_Legis_and_State_post.pdf)—as of December 15, 2010

State	Population (1000's in 2008)[c]	Per Capita Personal Income (2007)[d]	Obama/McCain vote 2008 (%)[e]	Conservatism (rank)[f]
Alabama	4,662	$32,401	39/61	8
Alaska	686	$39,934	36/62	22
Arizona	6,500	$32,900	45/54	28
Arkansas	2,855	$30,100	39/59	6
California	36,757	$41,580	61/37	43
Colorado	4,939	$41,019	53/46	36
Connecticut	3,501	$54,984	62/36	47
Delaware	873	$40,058	61/38	42
Florida	18,328	$38,316	51/49	31
Georgia	9,686	$33,416	47/52	18
Hawaii	1,288	$39,060	72/27	48
Idaho	1,524	$31,703	36/62	12
Illinois	12,902	$40,919	62/37	40
Indiana	6,377	$33,152	50/49	16
Iowa	3,003	$34,796	54/45	23
Kansas	2,802	$36,483	41/57	10
Kentucky	4,269	$30,787	41/58	19
Louisiana	4,411	$35,770	40/59	7
Maine	1,316	$33,962	58/40	37
Maryland	5,634	$46,646	61/38	41
Massachusetts	6,498	$49,142	62/36	49
Michigan	10,003	$34,342	57/41	32
Minnesota	5,220	$40,969	54/44	38
Mississippi	2,939	$28,527	43/57	1
Missouri	5,912	$33,984	49/50	20
Montana	967	$33,145	47/50	17
Nebraska	1,783	$36,189	41/57	14
Nevada	2,600	$39,649	55/43	21
New Hampshire	1,316	$41,444	55/44	39
New Jersey	8,683	$49,238	57/42	45
New Mexico	1,984	$30,604	57/42	35
New York	19,490	$46,664	62/37	46
North Carolina	9,222	$33,663	50/49	15
North Dakota	641	$35,955	45/53	2
Ohio	11,486	$34,509	52/47	26
Oklahoma	3,642	$34,910	34/66	3
Oregon	3,790	$35,027	55/43	33
Pennsylvania	12,448	$38,740	55/44	30
Rhode Island	1,051	$39,712	64/35	43
South Carolina	4,480	$31,048	45/54	9
South Dakota	804	$35,664	45/53	4
Tennessee	6,215	$33,373	42/57	13
Texas	24,327	$37,006	44/55	10
Utah	2,736	$30,090	34/63	5
Vermont	621	$37,446	67/31	50
Virginia	7,769	$41,561	52/47	24
Washington	6,549	$41,062	58/41	34
West Virginia	1,814	$29,293	43/56	27
Wisconsin	5,628	$36,241	56/43	25
Wyoming	533	$47,038	33/65	29

Sources:

[c] Morgan and Morgan 2009, p.455

[d] Morgan and Morgan 2009, p.100

[e] CNN Election Center 2008 website (http://www.cnn.com/election/2008/results)—as of November 15, 2008

[f] Adapted from: Erikson, Robert S., Gerald C. Wright, and John P. McIver. 2006. "Public Opinion in the States: A Quarter Century of Change and Stability." In *Public Opinion in State Politics*, ed. Jeffrey E. Cohen. Stanford, CA: Stanford University Press.

STATE & LOCAL POLITICS

STATE & LOCAL

POLITICS
Institutions & Reform
The Essentials

2e

VOTE

Todd
Donovan

Christopher Z.
Mooney

Daniel A.
Smith

WADSWORTH
CENGAGE Learning

Australia • Brazil • Canada • Mexico • Singapore • Spain • United Kingdom • United States

State and Local Politics: Institutions and Reform, The Essentials, Second Edition
Todd Donovan, Christopher Z. Mooney, Daniel A. Smith

Publisher: Suzanne Jeans

Executive Editor: Carolyn Merrill

Associate Development Editor: Katie Hayes

Editorial Assistant: Angela Hodge

Media Editor: Laura Hildebrand

Production Manager: Suzanne St. Clair

Art Director: Linda Helcher

Rights Acquisition Specialist-Text:
Shalice Shah-Caldwell

Rights Acquisition Specialist-Image:
Amanda Groszko

Print Buyer: Fola Orekoya

Manufacturing Manager: Denise Powers

Manufacturing Director: Marcia Locke

Sr. Marketing Communications Manager:
Heather Baxley

Marketing Manager: Lydia Lestar

For product information and technology assistance, contact us at
Cengage Learning Customer & Sales Support, 1-800-354-9706

For permission to use material from this text or product,
submit all requests online at **www.cengage.com/permissions**
Further permissions questions can be e-mailed to
permissionrequest@cengage.com

Library of Congress Control Number: 2010940911

ISBN-13: 978-0-495-90810-4

ISBN-10: 0-495-90810-X

Wadsworth
20 Channel Center Street
Boston, MA 02210
USA

Cengage Learning is a leading provider of customized learning solutions with office locations around the globe, including Singapore, the United Kingdom, Australia, Mexico, Brazil and Japan. Locate your local office at
www.cengage.com/global

Cengage Learning products are represented in Canada by
Nelson Education, Ltd.

To learn more about Wadsworth, visit **www.cengage.com/wadsworth**

Purchase any of our products at your local college store or at our preferred online store **www.cengagebrain.com**

Printed in the United States of America
1 2 3 4 5 6 7 14 13 12 11

To our families, with love: Deborah, Fiona, and Ian; Laura, Allison, and Charlie; and Brenda, Eliot, and Safi.

Brief Contents

Contents

TODD DONOVAN (Ph.D. University of California, Riverside) is a professor of political science at Western Washington University, where he teaches state and local politics, American politics, parties, campaigns and elections, comparative electoral systems, and introductory research methods  and statistics. His research interests include direct democracy, election systems and representation, political behavior, subnational politics, and the political economy of local development. He has published extensively in academic journals, written a number of books on direct democracy, elections, institutions, and reform, and has received numerous grants and awards for his work. With Ken Hoover, he is the co-author of *The Elements of Social Scientific Thinking*, also with Cengage.

CHRISTOPHER Z. MOONEY (Ph.D. University of Wisconsin, Madison) is professor of political studies at the University of Illinois at Springfield, and research fellow at the Institute of Government and Public  Affairs at the University of Illinois. He is the founding editor of *State Politics and Policy Quarterly*, the official journal of the State Politics and Policy section of the American Political Science Association. He has published many books and articles on legislative politics, morality policy, and research methods. He can be heard each week as a regular panelist on *State Week in Review*, an NPR radio program broadcast state-wide in Illinois.

DANIEL A. SMITH (Ph.D. University of Wisconsin, Madison) is professor of political science at the University of Florida and the Director of the M.A. Political Campaigning Program. He teaches courses on state and local  politics, political parties, interest groups, campaign finance, and direct democracy. He has published numerous articles on direct democracy, political parties, interests groups, and campaign finance, as well as two books on the politics and processes of ballot initiatives. Smith, a former Fulbright Scholar, serves on the Board of Directors of the Ballot Initiative Strategy Center Foundation (BISCF) and is a Senior Research Fellow at the Initiative and Referendum Institute.

Studying State and Local Government

American state and local governments provide perhaps the best opportunity to study political phenomena in the world. They give political scientists a manageable number of cases similar enough in social structure, economics, politics, and government to make meaningful comparisons of them without becoming overwhelmed by extraneous variation. But they are also different enough from one another in theoretically and substantively important ways to allow us to test a wide range of questions concerning political behavior and policymaking central to our understanding of politics. For example, what is the best way to choose our leaders? How should we make public policy? What are the impacts of public policy on policy problems, people, businesses, the economy, or anything else? These and other fundamental questions can not only be explored more productively by studying the American states and communities, they can be explored best there.

The study of state and local government can be just as productive and interesting for students as it is for political scientists. But as we all know, an undergraduate state and local government class is usually not the highlight of a student's college career. It is often taught as a large service course required by a variety of majors—everything from education to journalism to social work—or as a social science general education course. Ironically, state and local governments will have a greater impact on most students for the duration of their lives than almost any other topic they study in a political science class. For example, teachers and social workers will be working for these governments, and many journalists will at least begin their careers by covering them. Even American college students not pursuing these majors will be deeply affected by the politics and government of the states and local communities. Laws, ordinances, and regulations about their driver's licenses, the clubs and restaurants where they work and play, landlord-renter relationships, and even the large state universities many of them attend are all in the bailiwick of these governments. Furthermore, college students tend to move more often than the average American, and in going from place to place for college, a new job, or just spring break, they are frequently exposed to the diversity of state and local government laws around the country—the differing speed limits, gambling laws, alcohol sales regulations, tax structures, and so forth. For the untrained person, these variations can be just confusing annoyances, but for those students who have taken a good state and local government class—and for those students who have read this book— the exposure to these variations are teachable moments. Such students are more likely both to notice and to understand these differences, making them better citizens in the process and for the long run.

Approach of the Book

We wrote this essentials edition with these teachable moments in mind, packing each chapter with lively and wide-ranging examples pulled from headlines across the nation to illuminate our points. From the outset, we have made every effort to engage, excite, and inform students about American state and local government and politics and to help them develop the critical thinking skills needed to make them better political scientists and better citizens. Our aim with this essentials edition is to provide an affordable and flexible alternative, without compromising on substance, scholarship, or style.

Theme

To accomplish this task, the book's central theoretical theme is **Comparisons Help Us Understand the Political World.** This is our central methodological theme. We continually return to the questions of how politics and government differ among the states and communities and the causes and effects of this variation.

Approaches

Up-to-Date Scholarship Since 1990, there has been a renaissance in political science scholarship using the states and communities to understand political processes and behavior. We have integrated the insights of this literature throughout the book so that students and instructors have access to the most current research available on the subject. We have meticulously documented our sources to assist students working on class assignments, as well as to help instructors wanting to keep abreast of this important and extensive literature.

Political Science Methods This is a political science textbook, not a government textbook. We very self-consciously show students how to use the variation among the states and communities to develop and test hypotheses about political behavior and policy making. Rather than simply describing how things are, we expose students to a multitude of differences among the states and communities and ask them to think about their causes and effects. In doing so, students will not only learn much about American states and communities, but they will also learn how to think like political scientists—a skill that will help them in any

college course they take thereafter, as well as throughout the rest of their lives.

Unique Chapter on Direct Democracy Not only have ballot measures been at the center of some of the most significant political battles in the country in recent years, but they have also recently generated a great deal of high-quality scholarship and are sure to engage student interest. Direct democracy—which represents one of the major institutional differences between states—has been used by citizens to pass laws cutting taxes, increasing funding for public education, banning smoking in public places, prohibiting same-sex marriage, providing funding for stem cell research, and raising the minimum wage. Because of its increasing relevance to the lives of millions of Americans, we devote an entire chapter to the study of direct democracy in the American states and communities.

Plan of the Book and What's New to This Edition

We try to convince students that state and local politics have important consequences for their own lives. The book begins with an introduction to some of the major questions asked when we study state and local politics and a discussion of some of the methods we use to answer such questions. It includes a completely new opening vignette comparing the diverging public policies of two states (New Hampshire and Vermont) with similar political histories and cultures and updated data from the most recent elections. The second chapter places states and localities in the larger context of the American federal system and introduces students to how other models of federalism compare with "progressive federalism" under the Obama administration. It opens with a new vignette on the protracted controversy over President Obama's federal stimulus package.

Subsequent chapters introduce students to various state and local political institutions, with a particular emphasis on how different institutions, in different places, may produce different outcomes. Chapter 3, which contains a new vignette about the local-level mobilization of anti-tax protesters after the election of President Obama, has been completely updated to reflect the most recent elections and examines rules that affect elections and participation. Chapter 4 covers the unique institutions of direct democracy. It highlights the latest battles over ballot initiatives, an update on initiative use and spending in the 2008 election, discussion of local recall efforts from 2009, and a new normative discussion on the impact of ballot measures on minorities. Chapter 5 covers political parties and interest groups at the state and local levels. It includes new discussions on the blanket primary system, party fusion voting, barriers to third-party access, and expanded coverage of interest group contributions to state party committees. Chapters 6, 7, and 8 examine the core institutions of American state politics: legislatures, governors, and courts, respectively. They each have completely new opening vignettes and boxed features. Chapters 6 and 7 have new data and discussion of the 2007, 2008, 2009, and 2010 elections. Chapter 6 includes an enlarged discussion of bureaucratic oversight by the state legislature. Chapter 7 includes increased coverage of the bureaucracy and independently elected executives. Chapter 9, which tackles issues facing various forms of municipal government, has been updated to reflect the most recent estimates from the U.S. Census Bureau. Chapter 10 is devoted to state and local fiscal politics, including a discussion of tax and spending political decisions affect public policy. It has been updated to include the most current Census of Government data on state and local finances and is re-cast to highlight the difficulty of budgeting during one of the nation's most severe economic recessions.

Special Features and Pedagogy

Comparisons Help Us Understand. These boxes use comparative data from the states to test different hypotheses about the political process. For example, in Chapter 4, this feature examines the question of whether direct democracy or representative democracy results in better outcomes for minority groups; in Chapter 5, it describes the existence of factions of dissent within political parties; and in Chapter 13, it lays out variations in policies on same-sex marriage in a number of different states.

Design Vivid tables, maps, graphs, and photographs throughout the book provide the visual tools students need to process detailed comparative data on the states.

Endpapers The inside front and back cover of the book provide basic information on state and local governments for convenient reference.

Other Pedagogical Features Each chapter includes a full set of study aids including a chapter outline, a chapter summary, and key terms. The chapter outlines list the major sections of the material presented so students can get a general sense of the topics to be covered, and the summaries provide a recap of the most important ideas of the chapters. A glossary of key terms and definitions provides an opportunity for students to check their mastery of the terminology. For those students who wish to further explore a topic, the companion website provides a list of suggested readings and a list of annotated websites for each chapter.

Instructor Resources:

The PowerLecture for *State and Local Politics: The Essentials* CD-ROM contains:

- A test bank in Microsoft Word and ExamView® computerized testing, created by the authors of the book, offers a large array of well-crafted multiple-choice and essay questions, along with their answers, page references, and learning objectives.

- PowerPoint lectures bring together text-specific outlines, tables, and figures from the book for each chapter.

- An Instructor's Manual with chapter summaries, learning objectives, discussion questions, suggestions for stimulating class activities and projects, and tips on integrating media into your class.

Student Resources:

- A companion website for *State and Local Politics: The Essentials* gives students access to tutorial quizzes, learning objectives, web links, suggested readings, and more. http://www.cengage.com/politicalscience/donovan/stateandlocalessentials2e.

Acknowledgments

This book, which condenses our fuller study of state and local politics, represents the tangible expression of the work of dozens of people. Fortunately for us, we have the honor of putting our names on the spine. We would like to express our deepest gratitude to all those who offered countless hours of their valuable time to help us in our efforts on this project. First, some of the nation's top political scientists gave us detailed feedback on early drafts of the chapters in their areas of expertise: Thad Beyle (University of North Carolina at Chapel Hill), Chris Bonneau (University of Pittsburgh), Tom Carsey (University of North Carolina at Chapel Hill), Susan Clarke (University of Colorado-Boulder), Richard Clucas (Portland State University), Chris Cooper (Western Carolina University), Peter Eisinger (New York University), Margaret Ferguson (Indiana University at Indianapolis), Peter Francia (Eastern Carolina University), Don Haider-Markel (University of Kansas), Zoltan Hajnal (University of California, San Diego), Melinda Gann Hall (Michigan State University), Jennifer Jensen (SUNY-Binghamton), Lael Keiser (University of Missouri-Columbia), Gary Moncrief (Boise State University), Karen Mossberger (University of Illinois at Chicago), Dometrius Nelson (Texas Tech University), Adam Newmark (Appalachian State University), Steve Nicholson (University of California, Merced), Tony Nownes (University of Tennessee), Elizabeth Oldmixon (North Texas University), David Paul (Ohio State University-Newark), Marvin Overby (University of Missouri-Columbia), Eric Plutzer (Penn State University), Mark Rom (Georgetown University), Beth Rosenson (University of Florida), Richard Scher (University of Florida), Joe Soss (University of Wisconsin-Madison), Don Studlar (West Virginia University), Ray Tatalovich (Loyola University, Chicago), Bob Turner (Skidmore College), Craig Volden (Ohio State University), Carol Weissert (Florida State University), Dick Winters (Dartmouth College), Gerald Wright (Indiana University at Bloomington), and Joseph Zimmerman (SUNY-Albany).

We would also like to thank those scholars and teachers who reviewed the book for this second edition:

Matthew Beverlin	Rockhurst University
Robert E. Breckenridge	Mount Aloysius College
Frank J. Coppa	Union County College
William Cunion	Mount Union College
Alesha E. Doan	University of Kansas
Margaret Gonzalez-Perez	Southeastern Louisiana University
Janet Raup Gross	Columbus State Community College
Eric T. Kasper	University of Wisconsin-Barron County
William J. Lipkin	Kean University
Bryan McQuide	University of Idaho
Cynthia E. Newton	Norwich University
Kevin Parsneau	Minnesota State University

William Pierros   Concordia University-Chicago
Sherri Thompson Raney   Oklahoma Baptist University
Jesse Richman   Old Dominion University

First Edition Reviewers:
Robert Alexander   Ohio Northern University
Ross C. Alexander   North Georgia College & State University
David Bartley   Indiana Wesleyan University
Jack M. Bernardo   County College of Morris
Scott E. Buchanan   Columbus State University
Thomas M. Carsey   University of North Carolina-Chapel Hill
Nelson Dometrius   Texas Tech University
Donald P. Haider-Markel   University of Kansas
Amy E. Hendricks   Brevard Community College
Paula M. Hoene   Walla Walla Community College Clarkston
Pressley Martin Johnson   University of California, Riverside
Andrew Karch   University of Texas at Austin
Christine Kelleher   Villanova University
Kenneth Kickham   University of Central Oklahoma
Junius Koonce   Edgecombe Community College
Adam Newmark   Appalachian State University
Anne Peterson   University of Washington, Bothell
Sherri Thompson Raney   Oklahoma Baptist University
John David Rausch, Jr.   West Texas A&M University
Scott Robinson   University of Texas at Dallas
David L. Schecter   California State University-Fresno
John A. Straayer   Colorado State U.
Paul Teske   UCDHSC, Graduate School of Public Affairs
Caroline Tolbert   University of Iowa
Susan Peterson Thomas   Kansas State University
Jeff Worsham   West Virginia University

We would like to express special appreciation for three scholars who helped us by testing an early draft of the book in their state and local government courses, giving us thoughtful and detailed comments about the manuscript and their students' reactions to it: Caroline Tolbert (Kent State University and University of Iowa), Carolyn Cocca (SUNY-Old Westbury), and Richard Scher (University of Florida). For their invaluable (and frank) feedback, we also thank their students, including: Kathryn N. Domanico, Numan Imtiaz, Jason Von Buttgereit, Thomas Mastrocinque, and Michele Ricero, as well as many others who preferred to remain anonymous. Three scholars helped us by providing some of the data we have included herein: Tim Storey (National Conference of State Legislatures), Laura Langer (University of Arizona), and Barbara Van Dyke-Brown (University of Illinois at Springfield). Several of our own students helped us copyedit the manuscript and worked on the ancillaries, including Brian Bartoz (University of Illinois at Springfield) and Brittany Rouille, Leah Rose Cheli, and Aaron Retteen (University of Florida). We would also like to thank those wonderful people at Cengage who helped us turn the manuscript into this book and get it into your hands: Carolyn Merrill, executive editor; Rebecca Green, development editor; Lydia LeStar, marketing manager, and Katie Hayes, associate development editor. Finally, we would like to give a special thanks to Caroline Tolbert, not only for her extensive and valuable comments on the manuscript at various points in its development, but for her tremendous support, encouragement, and friendship from the beginning of this project to the end.

STATE & LOCAL POLITICS

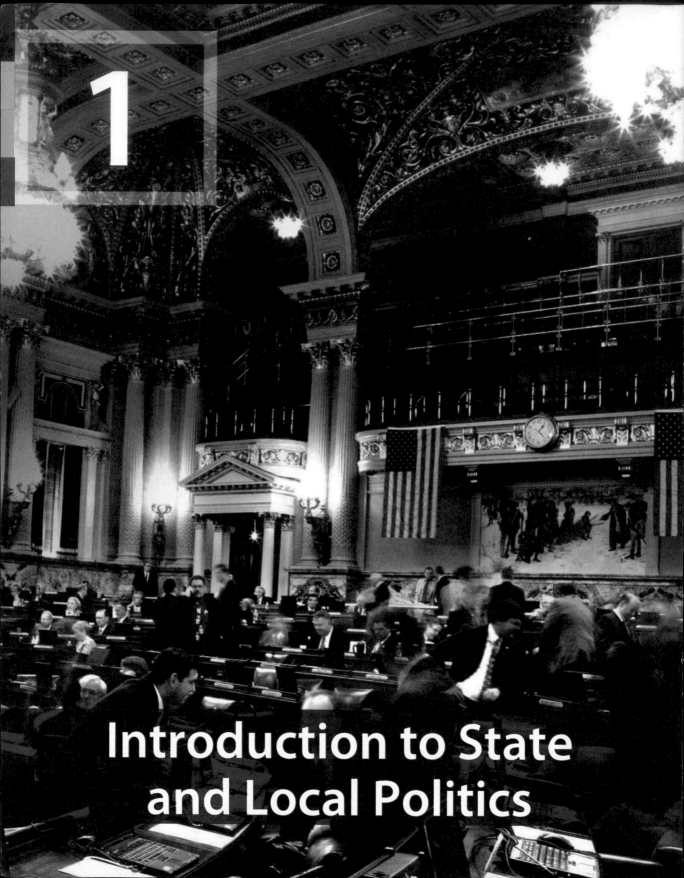

1

Introduction to State and Local Politics

INTRODUCTION

Welcome to the study of perhaps the most important thing you have never thought much about before—American state and local government. In every chapter of this book, we focus on four important points that we hope will not only enlighten you about state and local government, but will also show you how the study of this aspect of American government will help you think and learn about politics and people more generally.

First, state and local governments are vitally important to all Americans in countless ways. In addition to their impacts on "politics" and "the economy," concepts that may seem rather vague and general to you, state and local governments have significant impacts on you, personally, in dozens of practical ways every day. Twenty-four hours a day, seven days a week, fifty-two weeks a years, every year of your life, these governments are busy affecting the quality of your life and the choices you can make. In fact, state and local governments have a far greater impact on your daily life than the federal government does—unless you are serving in the U.S. armed forces. On virtually every page of this book, you will see just how state and local governments affect you and everyone you know in a multitude of ways every day.

Our second major theme is that **political institutions** matter. Political institutions are the rules, laws, and organizations through which government functions. These are enduring mechanisms designed to translate the principles and values of public policy into reality. They often define consequences for policy makers' and citizens' choices, encouraging some and discouraging others. For example, a state's sales tax system is an institution that has a wide range of consequences, many of them only indirectly related to government revenue generation. This is just one example of how the institutions with which we organize government can have important, complex, and often unintended consequences. We will discuss many more such examples in some detail.

Reform is the third theme of this book. Among all the broad forces that affect people's lives, it is often political institutions that can be changed—or **reformed**—most readily. Government cannot easily alter many of the social forces that influence peoples' lives. A state or community's partisan makeup, demography, and economy have major political and personal impacts, but the government can do little about them in the short term, even if it so desired. But virtually any political institution or policy can be reformed if the people want it to be. States and communities are constantly tinkering with their institutions and changing their policies. Throughout this book, we will discuss both the causes and effects of many such reforms.

Our final theme is that states and communities and their governments differ from one another in countless ways, and comparisons of these differences can help us understand much about politics and government in general, both in the United States and beyond. Despite the homogenizing effects of television, the Internet, big box stores, and chain restaurants, the United States is still very much a big, diverse country. States and communities differ in their history, economy, people, and geography. State and local governments differ in how they are organized, the policies they pursue, and the institutions they establish. Even two states like New Hampshire and Vermont, or like Arizona and New Mexico, which to outsiders might at first blush seem like two peas in a pod, differ in many ways. Because of these differences, it matters what state and community you live in, no matter whether you're a student, parent, consumer, businessperson, retiree, or anything else. This diversity can be baffling and, at times, frustrating. This is especially true for governmental and political differences, because they can seem so arbitrary. For example, you may know someone who attends a public university in another state where the tuition is much higher or lower than yours—why is that the case? Other differences can be equally confusing and troubling to other people. Why are cigarette taxes so much higher in Michigan than across the border in Indiana? Why do people in Vancouver, Washington, pay no state income tax, while those just across the Columbia River in Portland, Oregon, pay no sales tax? Why does the public high school in one town have a beautiful swimming pool and a large auditorium, while the school in a nearby town cannot even afford to offer its students music or art classes? Why are the rivers cleaner and the parks nicer in some states than in others? And on and on the questions go.

The countless differences among states and communities are especially relevant for this book and the course for which you are reading it. While these differences may cause some people to scratch their heads or pound the table, political scientists see this diversity as a wonderful opportunity to extend our understanding of how people work together to survive and thrive, that is, to extend our understanding of government, politics, and policy. Because of this diversity, the study of state and local government not only raises important and interesting questions, but it also offers an extraordinary way to answer them—*the comparative method*. In short, we use the variation among the states and communities to explore the forces at work in politics and government in the United States today. For example, if we want to explain government support of higher education, we can identify states that charge different college tuition rates at their universities and compare those states on other characteristics to find clues to explain this difference. Maybe states that charge lower tuition are wealthier, have more diverse economies, or have a more liberal **political culture** than do other states. Maybe these factors have subtle and complex relationships that are not obvious. With over 87,000 state and local governments in the United States,[1] political scientists working in this field have a vast and rich laboratory. The comparative method allows us to tease out and demonstrate often quite intricate patterns of relationships.

In this chapter, we demonstrate the importance of studying American state and local government, and we explain our approach to doing so. By the time you have finished this book, we hope that you won't be able to read or hear a news story about government or politics without asking yourself: Why has that government dealt with that public problem in that way? How have other governments dealt with that problem? Why have these governments adopted these different approaches to solving that problem? Which approach to that problem is better?

In other words, you will become an amateur political scientist. But more important,

---

[1] U.S. Census Bureau, *Census of Governments*, GC02-1(P) (Washington, DC: U.S. Government Printing Office, 2002).

you will become a better and more intellectually active citizen with the tools to understand politics and government at all levels much more deeply.

State and Local Government: At Your Service All Day, Every Day

Even though you may never have thought about it before, state and local governments are intimately connected to your life every day in more ways than you can count. Just walk through your day and see how they affect you. Your alarm clock rings—the state government determines whether you will fall back and spring forward for daylight-saving time.[2] Even before you're ready to get up, trash collectors bang cans in the street and the bus or mass transit train rumbles by—each of these is a local government function or responsibility. You turn on the light—an extraordinarily complicated set of state and local regulations keeps electricity generation safe, affordable, and not unduly damaging to the environment. You may even live in one of those communities—like Springfield, Illinois, and Orlando, Florida—where the local government actually generates and sells its own electricity.

Next, you eat breakfast—the organic milk on your cereal is regulated and inspected by state officials. You take a shower—the water is probably provided by your local public utility. You drive to school—the roads are built and maintained by state, county, and local employees, and police officers from these same governments ensure their safety. You sit down in class—if you attend a college run by a state or local government (as the vast majority of

American college students do), then your entire education is controlled by employees of these governments. Your college's admissions requirements, tuition and fees, degree requirements, course catalogue and schedule, the topics that are covered in each class (even the fact that you have been assigned to read this book) are all determined by state or local government officials.[3]

Even beyond college, state and local governments affect your life and those of your family and friends in innumerable other ways. They regulate restaurants, doctors, dentists, and nurses—and even hair, fingernail, and tanning salons—to watch out for your health and safety. They regulate major parts of the insurance and banking industry to watch out for your financial well-being. Do you want to smoke a cigarette? State and local governments tax you heavily for the privilege, and then they tell you where and when you can do it. Do you want to go to a dance club? State and local laws regulate how loud the music can be, how much tax you pay on your food and beverage, who can serve you, how late the club can stay open, and how many people can enter. Do you want to build a house or start a business? Buy insurance or drive a car? Get married or get divorced? All these and many more of life's regular activities are regulated, encouraged, discouraged, modified, or monitored by state and local government. They even closely regulate funeral homes and cemeteries—perhaps your last connection with state and local government.

Maybe this sounds like some insidious plot straight out of George Orwell's *1984*, but it is not these governments that are trying to take over your life, per se. Virtually every one of these government activities has been demanded by some group of citizens or businesses. Typically, people in the government

---

[2] Residents of Arizona and Hawaii do not change their clocks. Daylight-saving time was a highly controversial political issue in Indiana before it was settled in 2005. See Joseph Popiolkowski, "Daylight-Savings Time Dawns in Indiana," *Stateline.org*, 20 September 2009, online edition.

[3] Private colleges are also affected heavily by the governments of the states and communities in which they are located, through various laws and regulations, monetary incentives, and so forth.

are too busy to be out looking to take over more aspects of your life. Rather, we want and ask government to do many things for us—to educate us well; to build good roads; to keep us safe from crime; to ensure that the various industries and professions we rely on are safe, reliable, and honest; and so forth. In our modern, complex society, we want and need government both to encourage the things we want and to discourage those things that are unsafe or undesirable. And throughout American history, we have turned to state and local governments for help first. Washington, DC, and the federal government are far away from most of us, both physically and psychologically. State and local governments are literally as close as the sidewalk in front of our house, the cop on the corner, and the school down the block. In fact, aside from international relations and national defense (no small things, of course), the national government has very little to do with the public services you receive every day.

These days, as has been true throughout most of U.S. history, state and local governments control virtually all domestic government policy in the country. Thus, it should be no surprise that service in these governments is extremely attractive today to high-powered individuals who are smart and want to make a difference in the world. The most obvious examples of these are Mayor Michael Bloomberg of New York City and former Governor Arnold Schwarzenegger of California. Bloomberg made billions on Wall Street and in the communications industry before searching for—and finding—a greater challenge running the Big Apple. He did this so successfully that the city council repealed mayoral term limits in 2008 so that he could run for his third four-year term. Schwarzenegger not only starred in dozens of box office hits, but he also ran his own very successful production company before winning the extraordinary 2003 recall election that ousted sitting Governor Gray Davis. Beating 136 candidates in the process, Schwarzenegger took on perhaps the most difficult challenge in government, running a state that some argue is "ungovernable" due to its seemingly intractable fiscal, social, and environmental problems.[4]

These two larger-than-life characters, the "New Action Heroes" as *TIME* magazine called them,[5] are just the most visible of a new generation of highly talented men and women, successful in a variety of endeavors of life, who were looking for a challenge and an opportunity to give back to their communities and found them in state and local government service. People like Bobby Jindal, governor of Louisiana, Corey Booker, mayor of Newark, New Jersey, and Jennifer Granholm, governor of Michigan, have all taken on great challenges with hard work, intelligence, and new ideas, and they have made a significant difference in their states and communities. When Barack Obama—who served in the Illinois State Senate longer than he served in the U.S. Senate—looked around the country to staff his first cabinet, he found almost half of them serving (or having recently served) in state and local government—four governors (Tom Vilsack, Iowa; Gary Locke, Washington; Kathleen Sebelius, Kansas; and Janet Napolitano, Arizona), two local government officials (Arne Duncan, CEO of the Chicago Public Schools; and Shaun Donovan, director of the New York City Department of Housing Preservation and Development), and a state agency director (Lisa Jackson, New Jersey Commissioner of Environmental Protection). Thus, state and local government not only have major influences on your life every day, but they are also where the action is for public service.

[4] "The Ungovernable State," *The Economist*, 19 February 2009, online edition.

[5] Michael Grunwald, "The New Action Heroes," *TIME*, 25 June 2007, 32–38.

Government, Politics, and Public Policy—Definitions

To start this book, we must describe three basic concepts that are at the center of our discussion: government, politics, and public policy. Although you surely have some idea about what these are, we start with an explicit definition of each to give a clear and common understanding as we move forward.

Government

Government can be thought of as the set of authoritative institutions by which a geographically defined group of people organizes itself to achieve their common goals. As individuals, humans' abilities and capacities are very limited, but working together, people can do much more than they can do alone. This is something that our species—and its predecessors—learned in the distant evolutionary past. Alone, no person could hunt a mastodon or even survive long in a hostile environment, much less build a dam, use stem cells to develop a cure for diabetes, or protect the environment from toxic waste dumping. Personal economic rewards can motivate people to work toward some common goals voluntarily. Microsoft was organized to make computer software, and Federal Express was organized to deliver packages; those people working together to accomplish those goals do so because they either earn a salary or a return on their investments. But it is very difficult to organize building a dam, studying stem cells, or monitoring the amount of waste that companies produce in such a way that an immediate profit can be made from them. Sure, towns are protected from floods, people are cured of disease, and the environment is improved. But ironically, when *everyone* benefits from the actions of a group, and when there is no way to stop those

who don't help from gaining this benefit, *no one* has an incentive to contribute individually.[6] This is what economists and political scientists call a **collective action problem**—the problem of coordinating a group of people to achieve a common goal. Think about group projects you have done for college classes; the same principle applies here. No person or company will take the initiative to complete a major project alone, no matter how meritorious, when the benefits are widely dispersed, noneconomic, and/or received over a very long period of time—the Red Cross and Doctors Without Borders notwithstanding.

So over the past 10,000 or more years, we human beings have enhanced the lot of our species by developing government as a way to solve problems and complete tasks with widely dispersed, long-term benefits where the potential for short-term, private profit is limited. By paying taxes and following laws, we all help to achieve these **public goods** that benefit the entire community but that no one would or could accomplish alone. Government, then, consists of the people who are hired and the institutions that are established to accomplish these common tasks that help us all.

Politics

Politics is the process that a group of people uses to determine what its government ought to do. We use politics to decide which public goods our government should provide, how it should do so, who should benefit, and how we are going to pay for them. Politics consists of elections, campaigns, lobbying, lawmaking, and much else that we see daily in the news, and each of these affects these important decisions about government action. This is most obvious in election campaigns. For example, one candidate for mayor wants to encourage economic growth in her city, while the other one focuses on preserving the environment and lowering the crime rate. In their campaigns,

---

[6] Mancur Olson, *The Logic of Collective Action*, rev. ed. (Cambridge, MA: Harvard University Press, 1971).

these candidates tell voters what they want to do and why, and then people vote for the candidate with the plan and ideas that most closely agrees with their values and beliefs. But politics is also at work, if less directly, when groups of citizens and businesses contact that winning mayor and present their arguments about what city government ought to do. The mayor then considers the values and information she hears during this lobbying process, weighs it against her own knowledge and judgment, and then makes policy decisions. This aspect of politics is different than what you see in campaign commercials and debates on television, but it remains an important part of the process by which government decisions are made.

Public Policy

Public policy consists of a government's decisions and actions that are designed to accomplish the common goals identified through the political process for that **jurisdiction**. Any official or regular action of a government or its officers is a policy, including its institutions, laws, and regulations. But the norms and traditions that help determine its officers' actions are also public policy, even if less formal and less explicitly stated. At root, every policy is designed to help provide some public good. For example, a road's speed limit is set at 15 miles per hour in a school zone because the city's residents have a common interest in protecting its young children from harm. Sometimes a government worker's action may not seem like a public policy, and sometimes the public good behind a policy is hard to see. For example, professors at the University of Iowa are required to give a final exam in every undergraduate class. This is a public policy because it is a regulation established by a government official—the university's provost (who works for the state of Iowa). What is the common goal behind this final exam requirement? It is

probably meant to enhance the education of Hawkeye students by (1) motivating them to study, (2) forcing professors to give them that motivation, and (3) encouraging professors to teach well (because poor teaching may translate into poor performance on the exams). Educating college students well is a public good that the university produces for the people of Iowa—and beyond.

There are, then, two distinct reasons for opposing a public policy: (1) you believe that government should not pursue the common goal that the policy is meant to achieve; and (2) you think that that policy will not help reach that common goal. For example, a state senator in New Jersey recently advocated legalizing sports betting in the Garden State with the intention of allowing the state to beef up its sagging coffers by taxing some of the billions of dollars that are now bet illegally each year through off-shore Internet sites and other ways.[7] You might oppose this policy, first, based on its efficacy in attaining its goal. That is, you may think that people would avoid the taxes by continuing to bet on sports using the illegal means they use today. But, second, you might also oppose this policy because you don't like its goal. That is, you may not think that the state should be in the business of sports gambling, either for moral reasons or because you think it could lead to social problems. As a policy debate develops, different goals may be pursued and different approaches to meeting those goals may be tried. In this way, public policy is constantly evolving through the process of political reform.

Government, politics, and public policy are all about people working together in groups to accomplish what they cannot accomplish alone. In this book, we explore how government, politics, and public policy interact with the various social and economic conditions in different parts of the United States to yield the

---

[7] Pamela M. Prah, "Sports Betting Next Target for Some States," *Stateline.org*, 7 May 2009.

marvelous tapestry of public life that exists today in our states and communities.

Differences in Government, Politics, and Public Policy—Three Examples

American states and communities differ in a wide range of ways, including in their governments, politics, and public policy. Not only are these differences inherently important, but also, political scientists can use them to help explain why people and groups behave as they do in the political world. You will read about dozens of these differences throughout this book, but here are three examples to whet your appetite.

Differences in Government: Choosing State Judges

All federal judges are nominated by the president and confirmed by the U.S. Senate. All governors are elected, as are all state and federal lawmakers. All secretaries of state senates are appointed by the leaders of those bodies. State judges, however, who preside over 98 percent of American court cases,[8] come to the bench in a variety of ways (see Chapter 8). In 12 states, judges for at least some courts are elected on a partisan ballot. So just like governors and state legislators, someone wanting to be a judge in these states runs for a party's nomination in a primary election or convention and then faces an opponent from the other party (or parties) in a general election. Twenty-one states use nonpartisan elections

to fill at least some of their judgeships. Candidates for these judicial seats run without declaring a party label, something that is done in many elections for local legislators and executives (see Chapter 9). In five states, judges are simply appointed by either the legislature or the governor. Finally, 24 states use a hybrid of appointment and **retention election**, where at the end of a judge's term, voters decide simply whether he or she should keep the job, that is, be retained.[9] Figure 1.1 shows how each of the states selects their Supreme Court justices.

At this point, two questions may have occurred to you: (1) Why do states select their judges differently? and (2) What difference does it make that they do? These two questions will be discussed throughout the book regarding a wide variety of differences among the states and communities, and we'll talk about this particular difference at greater length in Chapter 8. For now, let's say that, first, the states tend to differ from one another on judicial selection because (1) Americans have been ambivalent about exactly what they want their judges to do, and their values about this have evolved over the years; and (2) the selection method chosen by a state largely reflects the values that were in vogue about judges at the time it gained statehood or made major changes to its **constitution**. And what difference does judicial selection method make? That is a tougher and, in the end, a more important question, but scholars have recently made some headway in answering it. For example, one study has shown that elected judges reflect the values of the state's citizens better than appointed judges do.[10] This sounds great, but maybe not if you are convicted of a crime—another study showed that as judges

[8] For data on the number of cases in federal and state courts, see the websites of the U.S. Bureau of Justice Statistics (http://www.ojp.usdoj.gov/bjs/) and the National Center for State Courts (http://www.ncsconline.org), respectively.

[9] You may have noticed that the number of states mentioned here as having these selection methods does not add up to 50. That is because several states use different methods for selecting judges on different courts.

[10] Paul Brace and Brent D. Boyea, "State Public Opinion, the Death Penalty, and the Practice of Electing Judges," *American Journal of Political Science* 52(2008):360–72.

Figure 1.1

State Supreme Court Judicial Selection

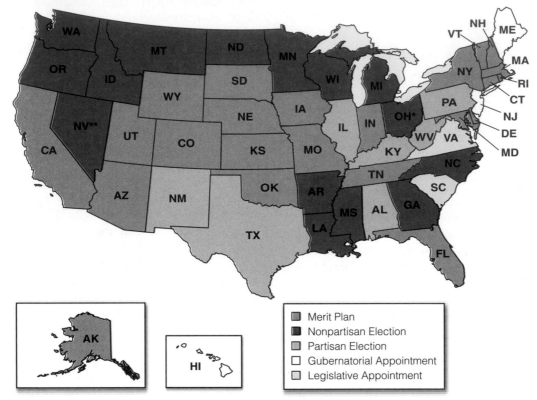

Merit Plan
Nonpartisan Election
Partisan Election
Gubernatorial Appointment
Legislative Appointment

*In Ohio, party affiliations do not appear on the ballot, but candidates are chosen through partisan primaries.

**In 2010, voters in Nevada will decide whether to change from a system of nonpartisan elections for selecting their state supreme court justices to the Merit Plan.

Source: Audrey S. Wall, *The Book of the States 2008*, vol. 40 (Lexington, KY: Council of State Governments, 2008), pp. 277–278. See the source for details.

approach reelection, they sentence defendants to noticeably longer sentences.[11] Perhaps more disturbing, one study finds that elected judges may favor defendants whose attorneys have contributed to their (the judges') election campaigns.[12] This is just one of the scores of examples we will discuss of how the institutions with which we organize government can have important, complex, and not always intended consequences.

Differences in Politics: Political Parties and Competition

American political parties are not nearly as ideologically pure or well organized as those in most other democracies, but they still serve an essential role in our political process (see Chapter 5).[13] Among the most important functions of parties are those that they serve in the policy-making process.

---

[11] Gregory A. Huber and Sanford C. Gordon, "Accountability and Coercion: Is Justice Blind when It Runs for Office?" *American Journal of Political Science* 48(2004):247–63.

[12] Damon M. Cann, "Justice for Sale? Campaign Contributions and Judicial Decisionmaking," *State Politics and Policy Quarterly* 7(2007):281–97.

[13] Malcolm E. Jewell and Sarah M. Morehouse, *Political Parties and Elections in American States*, 4th ed. (Washington, DC: CQ Press, 2001).

Comparisons Help Us Understand

American states and communities vary on a multitude of factors—social, economic, political, and more. This diversity not only makes life here exciting and interesting, but it can also help us understand how politics and policy work. When a political scientist sees a difference between communities or states, two big questions immediately come to mind: (1) What caused these differences? and (2) What are the effects of these differences? The cause-and-effect relationships behind the answers to these questions often help explain both the narrow differences being observed at the time and enlighten us on more general processes of politics and policy making. Throughout this book, we compare and contrast states and communities and their governments to enhance our appreciation of American political life. In addition, we include a "Comparisons Help Us Understand" sidebar in each chapter highlighting how these differences can be used in this way.

Almost all[14] governors and legislators are elected with a party affiliation, as are many local government policy makers. These party affiliations allow policy makers to organize themselves as to their general beliefs about policy and government action. By and large, this means that Republicans tend to agree more among themselves on many important issues than they do with Democrats, and vice versa. This process of sorting out and choosing up sides facilitates lawmaking, since it limits and defines the values that need to be reflected in policy and the conflicts that need to be resolved in the process. We will talk about this at length with regard to the legislative process in Chapter 6.

The states' party politics vary in a variety of ways. Some states are predominately one party or another. For example, politics in Massachusetts and Hawaii is dominated by the Democratic Party, while Republicans tend to control government in South Carolina and Idaho. States also vary on the stability of this party control. Some states have had the same partisan makeup for decades, while others have had significant changes in recent years.

In particular, for over 100 years after the Civil War, the states of the old Confederacy in the southeastern part of the country were known as the "Solid South" because of Democrats' supremacy in the region. In the last quarter of the twentieth century, however, the region, whose voters have always tended to be very conservative, began to swing toward the party that better represented its values and ideology (the Republicans) to the point where much of the South is now "solid" in the other direction—for the GOP.[15]

Another aspect of political party variation among the states that has serious implications for government and policy is the extent to which a state's legislature and governorship are controlled by the same or different parties, that is, whether the state has unified or **divided government**. Lawmaking in states where the governor and majority of both chambers of the legislature are of the same party is much different than where each party controls at least one of these three legs of the process. With divided government, a much wider range of values and opinions must be taken into account in policy making, which makes compromise and finding

[14] Nebraska's lawmakers are elected on nonpartisan ballots.

[15] Danny Hayes and Seth C. McKee, "Toward a One-Part South?" *American Politics Research* 36(2008):3–32.

a balance among these values and opinions both necessary and more difficult. This is especially true when the two chambers of the legislature are divided.[16] In Figure 1.2, we show which states have divided and unified government and, of those with the latter, which are controlled by which party.

Differences in Public Policy: Capital Punishment

Since there is so much variety in government and politics around the country, it should be no surprise that public policy also varies tremendously. One of the most extreme ways

in which the states' policies differ from one another is on capital punishment, that is, whether and under what conditions a state government is allowed to execute a person convicted of a crime. Execution is the ultimate impact that a government can have on a person. Early in U.S. history, the states executed people for a wide variety of crimes, primarily because there was no practical alternative to punish those who committed severe offenses. For example, in New York around the time of the American Revolution, 20 percent of all the sentences handed down by state courts were for hanging.[17] Over the years, as penal options expanded, public opinion changed, and the

Figure 1.2

Divided and Unified Party Government in the States

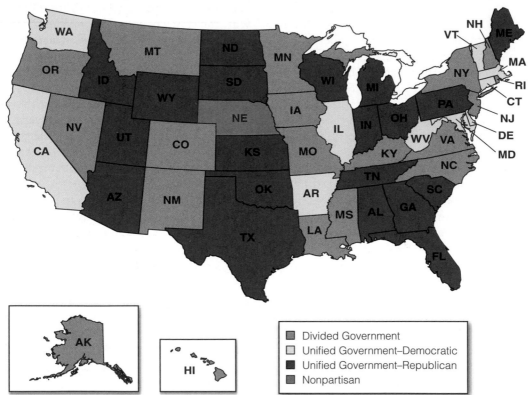

Source: National Conference of State Legislatures (http://www.ncsl.org/default.aspx?tabid=19488) and National Governors Conference (http://www.nga.org/).

[16] James R. Rogers, "The Impact of Divided Government on Legislative Production," *Public Choice* 123(2005):217–33.

[17] Walter Berns, *For Capital Punishment: Crime and the Morality of the Death Penalty* (New York: Basic Books, 1979), pp. 43–44.

courts interpreted the U.S. Constitution differently, executions have become rare and only used as punishment for some of the most heinous murders.[18]

The states vary in two important ways in their capital punishment policies. First, and most obviously, 35 states allow executions for some crimes and 15 never do. And the ranks of the non–capital punishment states appear to be growing.[19] Most of the 15 non-death penalty states abolished the practice in the nineteenth century, but since 2007, New Jersey, New Mexico, and New York have done so, and Colorado and Maryland came close to doing so in 2009.[20] Many states have had rancorous debate on the issue for years. Religious and civil liberties groups argue that it is immoral for a government to take a life as punishment for a crime, regardless of the nature of that crime; victims' rights and law enforcement groups argue that victims deserve justice; both sides debate the deterrent effect of capital punishment. One of death penalty's opponents' more recent—and effective—arguments has been that, with all the court cases and extra costs of maintaining a death row, executions are actually more expensive than life imprisonment.[21]

Among those states that allow executions, there is also great variation in how often they actually put criminals to death. Many states have capital punishment on the books more as a symbol than as a criminal justice option that is actually used much in practice. For example, Kansas and New

Hampshire have not executed anyone since a key U.S. Supreme Court decision in 1976,[22] while Connecticut, Colorado, Idaho, South Dakota, and Wyoming have each only executed one person. On the other hand, in that same time period, Texas has executed 456 people and Virginia 106.[23] In addition, this difference is not simply a function of a state's size; Oklahoma, a state with fewer residents than Colorado and almost exactly as many as Connecticut, has executed 92 people since 1976. Figure 1.3 shows which states do and do not allow capital punishment, and among those that do, the number of executions since 1976.

Diversity across the States and Communities

As anyone knows who has ever traveled more than 20 miles from home, American states and communities differ from one another in many ways besides their governments, politics, and public policy. The United States is heterogeneous in so many ways that its diversity in government, politics, and public policy is not only less noticeable but also perhaps even less significant than its diversity in other ways. In fact, the variation in the social, economic, and even geographical characteristics of this country goes a long way toward explaining some of its political and policy variation. We don't have space to describe the diversity of this country fully, but we can consider some

[18] Christopher Z. Mooney and Mei Hsein Lee, "Morality Policy Re-Invention: State Death Penalties," *Annals of the American Academy of Political and Social Science* 566(1999):80–92. **Statutes** in seven states also allow for capital punishment for the rape of a child; nine states allow it for treason; and seven states allow it for various other extreme crimes. But in 2008, the U.S. Supreme Court ruled that execution for such non-murder crimes was cruel and unusual and therefore violated the 8th Amendment to the U.S. Constitution (*Kennedy v. Louisiana* 554 U.S. ___ [2008]).

[19] Every year, bills are introduced to repeal and/or reinstate the death penalty in some states. To keep up to date on legislative and executive action on this issue, see the Death Penalty Information Center's website: http://www.deathpenaltyinfo.org.

[20] Kirk Johnson, "Death Penalty Repeal Fails in Colorado," *The New York Times*, 5 May 2009, online edition.

[21] John Ingold, "Death Penalty Dealt Blow," *The Denver Post*, 22 April 2009, online edition.

[22] *Furman v. Georgia*, 408 U.S. 238 (1972).

[23] For all these states, these are the numbers of executions as of May 20, 2010.

Figure 1.3

Capital Punishment and Executions in the States Since 1976

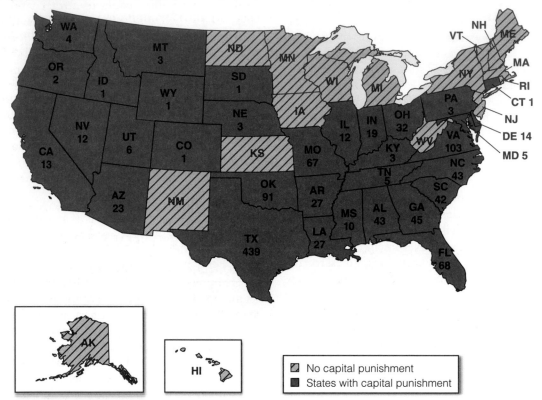

WA 4
MT 3
ND
MN
VT
NH
ME
OR 2
ID 1
SD 1
WI
MI
NY
MA
RI
WY 1
NE 3
IA
PA 3
CT 1
NV 12
UT 6
CO 1
KS
MO 67
IL 12
IN 19
OH 32
WV
VA 103
NJ
DE 14
MD 5
CA 13
AZ 23
NM
OK 91
AR 27
KY 3
TN 5
NC 43
SC 42
TX 439
LA 27
MS 10
AL 43
GA 45
FL 68

AK

HI

▨ No capital punishment
■ States with capital punishment

Note: New Mexico eliminated capital punishment in 2009, but prior to this, it had executed one person since 1976.

Source: The Death Penalty Information Center (http://www.deathpenaltyinfo.org/). This information is up to date as of May 20, 2010.

of it. Much of this diversity will be familiar to you, but maybe you never thought about it systematically before or in relation to politics. As we describe these characteristics, think about how they could help explain the diversity of policy and politics among the states and communities.

Geography and History

Some of the differences among the American states and communities are rooted in their oldest characteristics. The very geography and geology of a place can affect its politics and policy. For example, since Florida's sunshine and beaches attract so many tourists, the state can easily "export" some of its tax burden by

relying heavily on the sales tax to fund its governments (Chapter 10). Likewise, Louisiana, Alaska, and Texas get outsiders to help pay for their public services by taxing oil and natural gas extraction. Indeed, any area's geography has a big effect on its economy, which in turn has a big effect on its politics and public policy. For example, the climate and soil of the Southeast were especially suited for cotton and tobacco farming, a type of agriculture that led to big plantations, slavery, Jim Crow laws, and conservative politics, while the flat and fertile land of the central part of the country led to a type of agriculture that led to independent homesteading by immigrants in the nineteenth century and a shift to large-scale commodity farming and the depopulation of the region with agricultural mechanization in the twentieth and twenty-first centuries. On the other hand, New England's many rivers gave it the hydro-power needed to develop the first manufacturing economy in the country in the nineteenth century, which led to urban living, labor unions, and political machines. Even within a single state, geographic variation can define politics and policy.[24] For example, political conflict in Mississippi often divides those who live in its northern hills from those who live in the Delta region and those who live along the Gulf Coast. Many states' internal politics are defined by conflict between their coastal and inland areas, their mountainous and plains regions, or their rural and urban regions.[25]

Early U.S. political history can also explain much of the variation in our politics and policy that we see today. During the Civil War, 11 states seceded from the country,[26] and the politics of these states still have unique qualities that can be traced back to that war and its aftermath.[27] The residual resentment for the humiliations of Union occupation during the Reconstruction era has instilled in these states a special antagonism toward the national government, an attitude that affects federalism in these states (see Chapter 2) and has made the region fertile ground for the anti-government Tea Party movement. Politics and policy in the West still reflect traces of their years as frontier territory, such as women being more likely to be elected to office there than in most states in the East (see Chapter 7). On the frontier, everyone worked hard to survive, and so gender equality was more the norm than elsewhere in the country. In addition, these states simply needed to do whatever they could to attract women since relatively few of them wanted to endure the privations of the frontier. These two forces led to the region empowering women politically to a greater extent than elsewhere in the country. For example, women could vote in Wyoming in 1869, 50 years before the 19th Amendment to the U.S. Constitution recognized that right for them throughout the country.

Social Forces

States and communities also differ on a wide range of social characteristics that can affect their politics and policy. For example, a recent poll documented how the states vary on their residents' emotional and physical well-being, or "happiness," from the most happy states of Utah and Hawaii (of course) to the least happy states of West Virginia and Kentucky.[28] States also vary dramatically on the extent to which their adult residents have college degrees, from over 35 percent in Colorado, Massachusetts, and Maryland to less than 20 percent in Kentucky, Mississippi, Arkansas, and West Virginia. You might be able to conceive of many ways in which happiness and education could affect, or be affected by, politics and policy. In this section we focus on two social characteristics whose political impacts scholars have explored at some length—race/ethnicity and religion. As a country of immigrants, much of these features of Americans' social heritage has been

[24] James G. Gimpel and Jason E. Schuknecht, *Patchwork Nation: Sectionalism and Political Change in American Politics* (Ann Arbor, MI: University of Michigan Press, 2003).

[25] Shanna Pearson-Merkowitz and John Michael McTague, "Partisan Mountains and Molehills: The Geography of U.S. State Intraparty Factionalism," *State Politics and Policy Quarterly* 8(2008):7–31; V.O. Key, Jr., *Southern Politics* (New York: Vintage, 1949).

[26] The 11 states that made up the Confederacy were Virginia, North Carolina, South Carolina, Georgia, Florida, Tennessee, Alabama, Mississippi, Louisiana, Arkansas, and Texas. Delaware, Kentucky, Maryland, and Missouri were known as Border States, since they had both slavery and significant pro-Confederacy public sympathy during the Civil War, but they never seceded from the United States. Interestingly, West Virginia began the war as a section of Virginia, but in 1863, it split off to become a separate state that supported the Union. After the war, Virginia unsuccessfully disputed the legal sleight-of-hand involved in the split (*Virginia v. West Virginia*, 78 U.S. 39 [1870]), which irritated Virginia for over 100 years. See Richard Orr Curry, *A House Divided: A Study of Statehood Politics and Copperhead Movement in West Virginia* (Pittsburgh, PA: University of Pittsburgh Press, 1964).

[27] Key, op. cit.

[28] Associated Press, "Utah, Hawaii, Wyoming Top 'Happiness' Poll," *MSNBC.com*, 11 March 2009, online edition.

brought from elsewhere in the world in the past several generations. And just as important for understanding state and local politics in the United States, our social heritage is not evenly distributed around the country.

Historically, immigrants from the same place tended to enter the country at the same place and stay near their point of entry, at least a few generations. As a result, big cities in the Northeast and Midwest have many people of eastern and southern European descent living in them, whose ancestors arrived there in the late nineteenth and early twentieth centuries, and the South has lots of African Americans because many of their ancestors were enslaved there until 1865. Immigrants from Latin America often came to the United States from or through Mexico and the Caribbean, so Florida, Texas, Arizona, and California have many Latino residents; immigrants from Asia often entered the country in the West, so Washington, Oregon, and California have many Asian Americans.

Internal migratory patterns that developed over the years also have helped shape our current ethnic and racial makeup. For example, as political oppression and agricultural mechanization forced many African Americans to leave the South, they moved to the big cities where manufacturing jobs were plentiful, such as Los Angeles, Chicago, Detroit, and New York, especially during the two world wars. As a result, African Americans living in the Northeast, Midwest, and West tend to be concentrated in urban areas more than are those who live in the South. More recently, Latinos

also have moved north in larger numbers. But even though many Latinos are also attracted to big cities (as are Americans of all racial and ethnic backgrounds), they are settling more frequently than blacks in smaller towns and rural areas of the Midwest and West, where many have found jobs in food production.

A state or community's racial and ethnic composition can affect its politics and policy in a variety of important ways.[29] For example, despite the fact that they comprise a lower percentage of the population in the Midwest and Northeast than in the South, African Americans began to be elected to political office earlier in the former than the latter because their concentration in the cities more often led to their having majorities in political districts.[30] And even just the amount of racial and ethnic diversity in an area—regardless of which groups are in the majority or minority—can affect such things as public attitudes toward government and the outcomes of certain government programs.[31] One potential voting phenomenon that has been heavily studied (and debated) in the states and communities over the years is called "racial backlash."[32] This is the idea that, the larger a racial minority is, the more likely it is that people in the majority will vote against the interests of those in the minority. This helps explain the anti-democratic phenomenon of African Americans' interests being less well represented in the South (before the changes wrought by the civil rights movement), even though they lived there in larger numbers than in the North.

[29] Rodney E. Hero, *Faces of Inequality: Social Diversity in American Politics* (Oxford: Oxford University Press, 1998); Rodney E. Hero and Caroline J. Tolbert, "A Racial/Ethnic Diversity Interpretation of Politics and Policy in the States of the U.S.," *American Journal of Political Science* 40(1996):851–71; and Regina P. Branton and Bradford S. Jones, "Reexamining Racial Attitudes: The Conditional Relationship between Diversity and Socioeconomic Environment," *American Journal of Political Science* 49(2005):359–72.

[30] Of course, African Americans' underrepresentation in political offices in the South before the end of the twentieth century was also caused by the institutionalized racism in those states that routinely denied them their political rights.

[31] Michael Rushton, "A Note on the Use and Misuse of the Racial Diversity Index," *Policy Studies Journal* 36(2008):445–59; David W. Pitts, "Diversity, Representation and Performance: Evidence about Race and Ethnicity in Public Organizations," *Journal of Public Administration and Research* 15(2005):615–31.

[32] Caroline J. Tolbert and John A. Grummel, "Revisiting the Racial Threat Hypothesis: White Voter Support for California's Proposition 209," *State Politics and Policy Quarterly* 3(2003):183–202; Michael W. Giles and Kaenan Hertz, "Racial Threat and Partisan Identification," *American Political Science Review* 88(1994):317–26.

Along with race, religion is perhaps the most important social characteristic differentiating U.S. states and communities and their politics and policy. There is a deep irony in the role of religion and politics in this country. While the U.S. Constitution guarantees freedom of and from religion, and while the United States was the first country to recognize such rights, today, we are probably the most religious country in the Western world.[33] Many of our earliest immigrants came here to escape religious persecution in Europe, but once they arrived, they frequently set up religiously oppressive regimes of their own.[34] People of different religions established settlements in different parts of the Eastern Seaboard. Puritans established a colony in what is now Massachusetts, Roman Catholics did so in Maryland, Quakers in Pennsylvania, French Protestants in South Carolina, and so on. American states and communities continue to vary significantly in the proportion of different religious denominations' adherents that live in them.[35] In addition to denomination, the general propensity to be religious also varies from place to place. A 2008 Gallup poll of 350,000 Americans found that while fully 85 percent of Mississippians responded affirmatively to the question "Is religion an important part of your daily life?" only 42 percent of Vermonters did so.[36]

Not surprisingly, such large variation on this important social force can lead to significant differences in politics and policy around the country. Perhaps most obviously, we know that a state or community's religious makeup influences policies that have a strong moral dimension, such as abortion regulation and same-sex marriage.[37] But religion can also have unexpected effects, such as the Roman Catholic Church's strong influence on education policy in some places due to its long tradition of running parochial schools. In fact, in big cities with many Catholic residents, like New York, Los Angeles, and Chicago, the Catholic school system can rival the public school system for students and resources. As a result, even state-level education policy is affected.

Economic Characteristics

Certainly, the geographic, historical, and social characteristics of a state or community help shape its economy, but how people earn their living and the types of businesses and industries that exist in a place can also have significant independent effects on its government, politics, and public policy. This becomes especially obvious in a time of great economic strife, as the country experienced since the end of 2008. States that rely on manufacturing and exports, such as California, or where the real estate boom of the 1990s and 2000s was especially strong, such as Nevada and, again, California, have been especially hard hit by the current recession, so their state and local government budgets have been decimated to an even greater extent than those of other states. In one month (February 2009), one in every 60 homes in Las Vegas was in some stage of foreclosure, more than seven times the national average.[38] Under those conditions, a city both has the greatest need for revenue to help those in need and the least ability to generate it, since local governments

[33] Pippa Norris and Ronald Inglehart, *Sacred and Secular: Religion and Politics Worldwide* (New York: Cambridge University Press, 2004).

[34] James A. Morone, *Hellfire Nation: The Politics of Sin in American History* (New Haven, CT: Yale University Press, 2003).

[35] Clifford Grammich, *Many Faiths of Many Regions: Continuities and Changes among Religious Adherents across U.S. Counties*, WR-211 (Santa Monica, CA: RAND Labor and Population working paper series, 2004).

[36] Frank Newport, "State of the States: Importance of Religion" Gallup Poll Report, 28 January 2009 (http://www.gallup.com/poll/114022/State-States-Importance-Religion.aspx).

[37] Raymond Tatalovich and Byron W. Daynes, eds., *Moral Controversies in American Politics*, 3rd ed. (Armonk, NY: M.E. Sharpe, 2004); Christopher Z. Mooney, ed., *The Public Clash of Private Values: The Politics of Morality Policy* (Chatham, NJ: Chatham House, 2001).

[38] Brian Wargo, "Las Vegas Leads Nation in Foreclosures," *Las Vegas Sun*, 11 March 2009, online edition.

rely heavily on property taxes (see Chapter 10). By one estimate, all but four state governments were projected to have a budget deficit in 2010.[39] The states that are in the best fiscal shape—Alaska, Montana, North Dakota, and Wyoming—have small populations and significant mineral resources that have helped them through the recession. On the other hand, Michigan, whose economy has long been focused on the recently decimated automobile manufacturing industry (Cash-for-Clunkers, notwithstanding), continues its downward track from a rich industrial state to an impoverished state losing population and searching for a way forward.

Public policy is influenced in many ways by the shape of a place's economy. Everything from education funding and environmental regulation to infrastructure needs and taxation is influenced by the sort of economic activity a state or community has. One important economic characteristic that Michigan's plight suggests is the extent to which a state has moved from an economy based on the production of goods to one based on services, especially in the high-tech sector of the economy. The "digital divide" not only distinguishes between people who use and are comfortable with technology from those who are not, it also distinguishes states that have a strong technology sector in their economy from those that do not.[40]

Finally, a state or community's wealth can have wide-ranging political effects. Places with more money can certainly afford to provide better public services to their citizens. But less obviously, and sadly, wealthy places actually need to tax their citizens at a lower rate than poorer places. When a government has more wealth to tax, doing so at a lower rate yields plenty of resources for its residents' needs. For example, 10 percent of $100 is the same as 1 percent of $1,000. Furthermore, wealthy states and communities typically need fewer resources overall because well-off people need less of certain expensive government services (such as social welfare programs and police and fire protection) than do poor people. This is why people find that their property taxes sometimes go down when they move to the suburbs from the city, even though their schools and other services may seem better. On the other hand, people with more money often demand higher-quality government services and are willing to pay for them. For instance, they may be willing to pay higher taxes for high schools that offer several foreign languages and have a swimming pool, whereas these may be luxuries that a poor community simply cannot afford, no matter how much they may want them, since they have fewer resources and a greater need for remedial classes in reading and math, counselors, security, and so forth.

Political Values

Last, but probably most obviously, another set of potential explanations for the political differences among the states and communities is the thoughts, ideas, and values of the people who live there. Of course, in a democracy, we believe that what voters want and believe should determine the form of government they have and the policies that their government pursues. And in broad terms, scholars have found that this is indeed the case in the American states and communities.[41]

First, consider people's most deep-seated ideas and values about politics, the proper role

[39] Elizabeth McNichol and Nicholas Johnson, "Recession Continues to Batter State Budgets; State Reponses Could Slow Recovery," Center on Budget and Policy Priorities report, 25 February 2010 (http://www.cbpp.org/cms/?fa=view&id=711).

[40] Karen Mossberger, Caroline J. Tolbert, and Mary Stansbury, *Virtual Inequality: Beyond the Digital Divide* (Washington, DC: Georgetown University Press, 2003).

[41] Robert S. Erikson, Gerald C. Wright, and John P. McIver, *Statehouse Democracy: Public Opinion and Policy in the American States* (New York: Cambridge University Press, 1993); and Robert S. Erikson, Gerald C. Wright, and John P. McIver, "Public Opinion in the States: A Quarter Century of Change and Stability," in *Public Opinion in State Politics*, ed. Jeffrey E. Cohen (Stanford, CA: Stanford University Press, 2006); Charles Barrilleaux, Thomas Holbrook, and Laura Langer, "Electoral Competition, Legislative Balance, and American State Welfare Policy," *American Journal of Political Science* 46(2002):415–27.

of government, and other people. These beliefs do not change quickly over time, either for an individual or a community, and they are not evenly distributed around the country.[42] The most common way Americans think about general political values is along a one-dimensional continuum of **political ideology**, from liberal to conservative. Although most Americans—and even political scientists—would be hard-pressed to define these terms clearly, people have a general understanding about what they mean, and

they are willing to tell a pollster where they fall on this continuum. Those places in the United States that are more conservative tend to elect more Republicans and have policies that we associate with that ideology and that party, such as stricter abortion and gambling regulations, less spending on education and welfare, stricter criminal laws, and tax rates that are harder on the poor.[43] There is a similar correlation between policy, party, and ideology in the more liberal and Democratic places around the

Figure 1.4

Political Values: Conservatism versus Liberalism

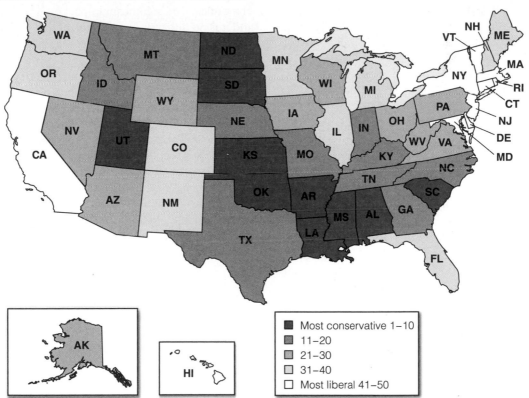

Note: These data represent the average of hundreds of public opinion polls undertaken from 1996 to 2003. In this map, the darker the state, the more conservative are its residents.

Source: Adapted from: Erikson, Robert S., Gerald C. Wright, and John P. McIver. 2006. "Public Opinion in the States: A Quarter Century of Change and Stability." In *Public Opinion in State Politics*, ed. Jeffrey E. Cohen. Stanford, CA: Stanford University Press.

[42] Paul Brace, Kevin Arceneaux, Martin Johnson, and Stacy G. Ulbig, "Reply to 'The Measurement and Stability of State Citizen Ideology,'" *State Politics and Policy Quarterly* 7(2007):133–40.

[43] This was not always the case, since the very conservative South tended to vote Democratic for more than 100 years after the Civil War out of animosity for the party of Lincoln, which defeated the Confederacy. In the past generation, partisan politics in the South has become much more reflective of the values of the parties nationwide (see Chapter 5).

country. Although this may not surprise you, only recently have scholars been able to find solid evidence that, in fact, Americans' values are translated fairly accurately through political parties into public policy.[44] Scholars were able to do this by taking advantage of the variation found on these factors among the U.S. states and communities (see Figure 1.4).

The Rules of the Game Have Consequences: Political Institutions and Reform

As you can see, even in the twenty-first century, the United States is a highly diverse country. Television, the Internet, and Americans' penchant for peripatetic movement have homogenized the country to some degree, but, for examples, Arizona is still not Ohio, and New York City is still not Los Angeles. And despite their similar situations as mid-sized, Midwestern state capitals, Madison is still not even Springfield. You have already seen how some of the fundamental differences among people and places can go a long way toward explaining some of the differences we see in politics and policy around the country. But just as people's lives are not completely determined by the circumstances into which they were born (like their race, their parents' income, and where they live), people in the states and communities make choices about their governments that affect their politics and policy for good or ill. That is, we can establish the political institutions that we want, and these institutions can affect the way we live and how our governments work. Just as important, if we want to change our policies or politics or any other aspect of the world we live in, we need to concentrate on the features of civil society that we are *able* to change. Someone

who wants to ban capital punishment cannot suddenly make her state more liberal. Nor can someone who wants to spend more money on state universities easily make his state wealthier. But people can reform their state's political institutions to facilitate the enactment of the policies they would like. Therefore, political institutions take on a special importance in the study and explanation of the political differences among the states and communities.

A major theme of this book is that *political institutions influence politics and public policy.*[45] As anyone who has ever played volleyball, Dungeon and Dragons, or Halo knows, the rules of a game have a significant impact on who wins, and it is no different in government and politics. Political institutions are the rules that define how the game of government and politics is played, the end product of that game being public policy. But the rules of this game are far more detailed and complicated than even those of Dungeons and Dragons. Some political institutions are at least somewhat familiar to everyone, like the governor's office, the local school board, and the state's Department of Natural Resources. These institutions have buildings and staff with official titles, some of whom even wear uniforms. These really *look* like institutions. But some political institutions exist simply as sets of rules without physical edifice. For example, there is no building you can point to and say, "That is a primary election system," but a primary election system is a political institution that is both very important and varies from state to state (Chapter 3). Direct democracy (Chapter 4), political parties, and interest groups (Chapter 6) are also this type of institution.

More important than any outward trappings, a political institution consists of a more or less elaborate set of rules, some of which are laws, some official regulations, and some merely procedures and customs. Such rules determine, for example, when the governor

[44] Robert S. Erikson, "The Relationship between Public Opinion and State Policy: A New Look Based on Some Forgotten Data," *American Journal of Political Science* 20(1976):25–36.

[45] Douglass C. North, *Institutions, Institutional Change and Economic Performance* (New York: Cambridge University Press, 1990); Elinor Ostrom, *Governing the Commons: The Evolution of Institutions for Collective Action* (New York: Cambridge University Press, 1990).

can veto a bill, how much discretion the school board has in setting high school graduation requirements, and what a game warden must do to arrest someone for poaching. The rules that define and empower political institutions in U.S. states and communities are almost countless and incredibly diverse, even in a single state or community. Not surprisingly, these institutions can also be quite different among jurisdictions. For example, the mayor's offices in Indianapolis and Dallas are very different institutions because the rules that define their powers are very different. Judges in New York and California are selected in different ways, and their courts are organized differently. Such variation in political institutions can lead to a whole gamut of political and policy differences among these places.

Those who work in and around politics and government understand the importance of institutions and institutional reform only too well. State and local governments are constantly tinkering with their rules about their officials' powers, how people vote, what is taxed, and every other government function and political activity imaginable. Changes in these institutions take up much of the time of policy makers and those trying to influence them. Those advocating a given change call it a "reform," since that word has a positive connotation. Of course, not all reforms have their intended effects. For example, in 1999, then-Governor George Ryan of Illinois issued an executive order that governors and other statewide officials in the state could not take campaign contributions from their employees, and his successor, Governor Rod Blagojevich, followed suit with even tighter restrictions in 2008. But these reforms did nothing to stop these men from being arrested and convicted of felonies[46] for corruption related to campaign contributions. Throughout this book, we describe a wide range of political institutions and show how they affect who gets what from government and what happens when you change them.

The Political Science of State and Local Government: Using the Comparative Method

Another central theme of this book is that we can use the **comparative method** of political analysis in the states and communities to help explain how politics and public policy work. The diversity among the states and communities often both suggests propositions—or **hypotheses** about political behavior and policy making and allows us to test them. For example, why do women comprise 30.4 percent of the New Mexico legislature, while only 16.4 percent of the West Virginia legislature is female? Are there social or economic reasons for this difference, or does it come down to difference in political values? If the latter, why do these states differ in their values? Why does New York City have such an extensive and efficient mass transit system, while Los Angeles does not? Does it have to do with history, geography, political culture, or something else? Why does Texas execute a dozen or more murderers every year, while Wisconsin didn't even execute serial killer Jeffrey Dahmer? Is this perhaps due to political ideology?

More important than just trying to explain any specific difference we observe, political scientists use this variation among the states and communities to test many of our most general theories about political behavior and policy making.[47] Science consists of developing general theories about how the world works and then

---

[46] At press time, Ryan is serving a six-and-a-half-year sentence in the Federal Correctional Complex in Terre Haute, Indiana, for corruption offenses. In August 2010, Blagojevich was found guilty on one felony charge of lying to the FBI; at press time, he is awaiting a new trial on the 23 other federal corruption charges on which the first jury failed to reach a decision.

[47] Christopher Z. Mooney, "*State Politics and Policy Quarterly* and the Study of State Politics: The Editor's Introduction," *State Politics and Policy Quarterly* 1(2001):1–4.

observing the world to see if hypotheses derived from those theories seem to be correct. In this way, political science is no different than biology or chemistry.[48]

But a significant difficulty for political scientists in this respect is that our **units of analysis** are often so diverse that a particular phenomenon may have many possible explanations. So since two pieces of iron can be assumed (or tested) to be exactly the same before placing one of them into an experimental solution, any difference in them observed later can be safely attributed to that solution. But it is not that easy to test for cause and effect in politics and government. Suppose you wanted to understand the influences on women's representation in democratically elected legislatures. You might hypothesize that a more educated citizenry would be more likely to elect women to office because education would weaken traditional negative stereotypes and biases about a woman's role in society. You might think about testing this **hypothesis** by comparing national lawmaking bodies, seeing if more educated countries tended to have more women lawmakers. But the problem with this would be that the multitude and magnitude of other differences among countries would overwhelm your ability to find any influence of education. For example, the fact that there are more women in the Norwegian Storting than the Spanish Cortes Generales might have something to do with the higher level of education in Norway than Spain, but it might also have to do with the huge differences between the two countries' other historic, social, and economic characteristics or their very different political institutions. On the other hand, while the states also differ in these ways, as we have shown, the differences are much more constrained, so that tests of this hypothesis could be more valid and less confounded by these other factors.[49] Even Alaska and South Carolina are much more similar to one another than are Norway and Spain, in many ways. This makes the states and communities an ideal place to test general theories about political behavior and policy making.

In this book, we focus on using the comparative method to evaluate *the effects of political institutions on politics and public policy*. Reformers who promote institutional change are essentially posing a hypothesis. For instance, as you will read in Chapter 8, the American Bar Association argues that state judges should be appointed to the bench, in part, because voters don't know enough about the law and the courts to select judges who will reflect their values and expectations well.[50] By using the comparative method, scholars have been able to test whether this and other reforms of state and local government institutions have the effects that their advocates hypothesize.[51] Just as important, this approach also allows us to see if these reforms have had any of the undesirable effects that their opponents hypothesized or even any effects that no one predicted. Thus, the comparative method not only allows us to develop and test theory about political behavior and policy making, it also helps us evaluate policies and institutions so that those with the best outcomes can be implemented in other states and communities.

[48] Jon R. Bond, "The Scientification of the Study of Politics: Some Observations on the Behavioral Evolution in Political Science," *Journal of Politics* 69(2007):897–907.

[49] John F. Camobreco and Michelle A. Barnello, "Postmaterialism and Post-Industrialism: Cultural Influences on Female Representation in State Legislatures," *State Politics and Policy Quarterly* 3(2003):117–38.

[50] Kent A. Lambert, "Judicial Elections Continue under Fire," *Litigation News* (Washington, DC: American Bar Association), 27 March 2009 (http://www.abanet.org/litigation/litigationnews/top_stories/judicial-elections.html).

[51] For recent examples of this sort of analysis of government reforms, see Chris W. Bonneau and Melinda Gann Hall, *In Defense of Judicial Elections* (New York: Routledge, 2009); and Karl T. Kurtz, Bruce Cain, and Richard G. Niemi, eds., *Institutional Change in American Politics: The Case of Term Limits* (Ann Arbor, MI: University of Michigan Press, 2007).

Summary

State and local governments have a major impact on your everyday life, whether you know it or not. All day, every day, in dozens of ways, these governments affect your pocketbook, your quality of life, your family, and your future. The more you know about state and local government, the more control you can take over your own life.

American states and communities differ from one another in myriad ways, including their histories, social structures, economics, and political values. Political institutions—the rules, laws, and organizations through which and by which government functions—are enduring mechanisms designed to translate the principles and values of public policy into reality, and these also differ around the country. Political scientists use the variation of these characteristics and institutions to describe how, and understand why, we choose to organize ourselves

and our governments and what impacts these choices have. Throughout this book, we examine a variety of public policy and institutional reforms, considering why they developed and what impacts they had, both expected and unexpected.

In this chapter, we laid out the four basic themes that will guide this book:

- American states and communities *vary widely* in their politics, policy, and governments and the factors that affect those things.
- *Political institutions* can affect politics and public policy.
- Public policies and political institutions can be *reformed*.
- *Comparisons* of the states and communities provide a tremendous opportunity to understand politics and policy making.

Key Terms

Comparative method

Collective action problem

Constitution

Divided government

Hypothesis

Individualistic political culture

Jurisdiction

Libertarianism

Moralistic political culture

Political culture

Political ideology

Political institution

Public goods

Reform

Retention election

Statute

Traditionalistic political culture

Unit of analysis

Suggested Readings

Connor, George E., and Christopher W. Hammons, eds. 2008. *The Constitutionalism of American States*. Columbia, MO: University of Missouri Press.

Erikson, Robert S., Gerald C. Wright, and John P. McIver. 1993. *Statehouse Democracy: Public Opinion and Policy in the American States*. New York: Cambridge University Press.

Gimpel, James G., and Jason Schuknecht. 2003. *Patchwork Nation: Sectionalism and Political Change in American Politics*. Ann Arbor, MI: University of Michigan Press.

Gray, Virginia, and Russell L. Hanson, eds. 2008. *Politics in the American States: A Comparative Analysis,* 9th ed. Washington, DC: CQ Press.

Hero, Rodney E. 1998. *Faces of Inequality: Social Diversity in American Politics*. New York: Oxford University Press.

Johnson, Janet Buttolph, H. T. Reynolds, and Jason D. Mycoff. 2008. *Political Science Research Methods,* 6th ed. Washington, DC: CQ Press.

Key, V.O., Jr. 1949. *Southern Politics: In the State and Nation*. New York: Knopf.

Morgan, Kathleen O'Leary, and Scott Morgan, eds. *State Rankings 2010: A Statistical View of America*. Washington, DC: CQ Press.

Orfield, Myron. 2002. *American Metropolitics: New Suburban Reality*. Washington, DC: Brookings Institution.

Peterson, Paul E. 1981. *City Limits*. Chicago: University of Chicago Press.

Wall, Audrey S., ed. 2010. *The Book of the States 2010*, vol. 42. Lexington, KY: Council of State Governments.

Websites

Council of State Governments (http://www. csg.org): The CSG is a nonprofit association of state governments doing research, training, and advocacy for all branches of state government.

National League of Cities (http://www. citymayors.com/orgs/natleague.html): As the oldest organization representing municipal governments in the United States, NLC works with 49 state municipal leagues to strengthen cities.

Stateline.org (http://www.stateline.org): Staffed entirely by professional journalists, Stateline.org was founded by the Pew Research Center as a nonprofit resource for journalists covering state governments. It offers in-depth and timely news stories on public policy in the states and communities, both from a single-state and comparative perspective.

Statistical Abstract of the United States (http://www.census.gov/compendia/statab/): The U.S. government gathers an enormous amount of data about U.S. states and communities and their residents. The Statistical Abstract is the Census Bureau's consolidation report of a wide range of these data.

2

Federalism: State and Local Politics within a Federal System

INTRODUCTION

"**I** think we just have a fundamental disagreement here," Louisiana Governor Bobby Jindal cautioned on NBC's *Meet the Press*. If all the Obama administration does "is borrow federal money and give it to the states," the Republican continued, "all we're really doing is delaying the inevitable." Less than a week after President Barack Obama signed into law the economic stimulus package—the American Recovery and Reinvestment Act of 2009—Governor Jindal and several of his fellow conservative governors publicly announced that they would reject portions of Congress' $787 billion stimulus package that was earmarked to their state governments.[1]

The federal government's rapid response—providing billions of stimulus dollars to the states following the collapse of the U.S. economy—once again altered the terms of agreement between the federal government and state and local governments. By reexerting its power over the subnational governments, the federal government elevated the stature of the powerbrokers operating in the nation's capital, Washington, DC. Such is the contemporary flow of American federalism, continual waves of ideology infused with pragmatism, devolving power to the states and recentralizing it back to the national government.

In this chapter, we examine the dynamic relationship between the federal and state governments. The ambiguity in the demarcation of state and national (or federal) institutional powers inherent in the U.S. Constitution has defined the way Americans have thought about government and politics and how we have designed our government institutions. After defining federalism and placing the American federal system in a broader comparative context, we investigate the ambiguities inherent in the U.S. Constitution. In discussing the historical trajectory and evolution of American federalism, we discuss the roles that Congress and the federal courts have played in delineating the relative powers of the national and state governments. We conclude by discussing how power has become more centralized in Washington following 9/11 and the downturn in the U.S. economy. What should become apparent in this story of American intergovernmental relations is the gradual, if at times punctuated, expansion of federal powers over the past century.

---

[1] Shaila Dewan, "6 Governors May Reject Portions of Stimulus," *New York Times*, 21 February 2009. Available: http://www.nytimes.com/2009/02/21/us/21govs.html?_r=1; J. David Goodman, "Governors' Fight over Stimulus May Define G.O.P.," *New York Times*, 22 February 2009. Available: http://www.nytimes.com/2009/02/23/us/politics/23governors.html?hp; Associated Press, "S.C.'s Sanford Makes It Official, Rejects $700 Million Stimulus," *Miami Herald*, 13 April 2009.

What Is Federalism?

The 50 American state governments constitute semisovereign political systems. Governmental powers in the United States are split geographically between national, state, and local governments. **Federalism** is the structural (or constitutional) relationship between a national government and its constitutive states. **Intergovernmental relations**, on the other hand, are the interactions among the federal government, state governments, and local governments. A Federalist system of intergovernmental relations conjoins a national government with semiautonomous subnational governments, but allows each to retain, to some degree, its "own identity and distinctiveness."[2] Although maintaining separate and autonomous powers, each layer of government is responsible for providing for the social and economic welfare of the populations living within its jurisdiction.[3] As we discuss below, the structure of a Federalist system is different from those of unitary and confederal systems of governance.

How does a Federalist system work? In theory, federalism combines the unifying powers of the national government with the diversity of subnational governments. The American states are not mere administrative appendages or extensions of the national government. Rather, they have discrete powers that are derived from the federal Constitution as well as their own constitutions and laws. Each layer of government has some autonomy, but there is much overlap in the powers held by the national and state governments.[4] It may seem somewhat ironic, then, that although many countries—including Australia, Brazil, Canada, Germany, India, Italy, Mexico, Nigeria, Russia, Spain, and even Iraq—have adopted an American system of federalism, the term *federalism* is not mentioned in the U.S. Constitution.

Sovereignty and State Variation in a Federalist System

In theory, under federalism, states retain a broad swath of sovereign powers, subject to the will of their own citizens. "In establishing this system," writes historian Samuel Beer, "the American people authorized and empowered two sets of governments: a general government for the whole, and state governments of the parts."[5] Such is a system of dual federalism, whereby governmental functions are apportioned so that, in the words of Founding Father James Madison, the states are "no more subject within their respective spheres to the general authority than the general authority is subject to them within its own sphere"[6] (see Figure 2.1). Though sometimes pictured as a "layer cake," dual federalism does not necessarily imply that the national and state governments never encroach upon each other's territory. Rather, if a confectionary metaphor is to be used, the American system might be more aptly described as a "marble cake."[7]

Unitary Systems: Centralized Power

In contrast to a Federalist system of governance, some countries have **unitary systems** of governance, with all governmental power

---

[2] Ronald Watts, "Federalism, Federal Political Systems, and Federations," *Annual Review of Political Science* 1(1998):117–37.

[3] Paul Peterson, *City Limits* (Chicago: University of Chicago Press, 1981), p. 67.

[4] David Walker, *The Rebirth of Federalism* (Chatham, NJ: Chatham House, 1995).

[5] Samuel Beer, *To Make a Nation: The Rediscovery of American Federalism* (Cambridge, MA: Harvard University Press, 1993), pp. 1–2.

[6] James Madison, "The Federalist No. 39: Conformity of the Plan to Republican Principles," *Independent Journal* 16 January 1788. Available: http://www.constitution.org/fed/federa39.htm.

[7] Morton Grodzins, "The American System," in Robert Goldwin, ed., *A Nation of States* (Chicago: Rand McNally, 1969); and Morton Grodzins, *The American System* (Chicago: Rand McNally and Company, 1966).

Figure 2.1	Figure 2.2
Models of Federalism	Systems of Government

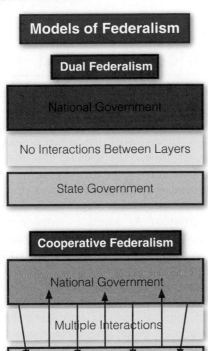

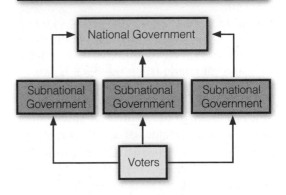

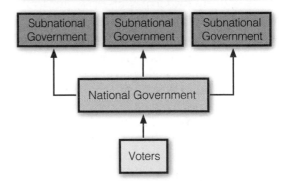

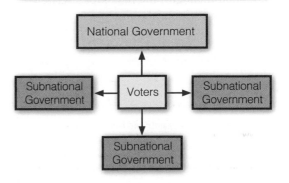

vested in the national government. As Figure 2.2 shows, a unitary system has a strong central government that controls virtually all aspects of its constitutive subnational governments (be they regional, territorial, state, or local units). Unitary systems, such as those in France, Israel, and China, consolidate all constitutional authority in the national government. In a sense, subnational divisions of the country are mere administrative appendages of the national government; that is, policy is made at the national level, and the subnational units simply carry out that policy. There is far less regional diversity in terms of subnational electoral systems, governance structure, and public policy in countries with unitary systems of governance. By contrast, in the United States, policy decisions concerning criminal justice, public education, social welfare, health care, and transportation are often left to the states.[8]

Confederal Systems: Decentralized Power

In terms of a spectrum of the balance of power between national and subnational levels of government, a **confederal system** is located at the opposite pole from a unitary system. A confederacy, as Figure 2.2 shows, is a system of governance whereby the national government is subject to the control of subnational, autonomous governments. In a confederacy, the constituent subnational governments enter into a covenant with one another and derive the bulk of their sovereign powers not from the central government, but from their own constitutions.[9] As we discuss below, in the history of the United States there have been two confederacies: the Articles of Confederation (1781–89) and the Civil War–era Confederate States of America (1861–65).

Although defenders of confederal systems of shared governance argue there are several advantages when governmental powers are devolved to subnational units, the decentralization of political power can lead to asymmetrical relations among the states. In the United States, not all states have the same degree of power within the Federalist system. Although all states are afforded the same protection and authority under the U.S. Constitution, some states have more clout within the federation because of the relative size of their economies and populations, differences in their socioeconomic and demographic makeup, and disparities in their social and cultural environments. These variations have led to differential power

relations among the states, as well as between each state and the federal government.[10]

Why Federalism? America's Founding

One of the most fundamental struggles in American political history has been the turf battle for political power waged between the states and the national (or, as mentioned, federal) government. The cyclical ebb and flow of this tension between the national and state governments has been continuous for over two centuries, and is rooted in the founding of the country. As Martha Derthick writes, "American federalism was born in ambiguity, it institutionalizes ambiguity in our form of government, and changes in it tend to be ambiguous too."[11] The inherent, ambiguous tensions of the American Federalist system can be traced back to the late eighteenth century. In developing a Federalist system, the founders had no working model on which to draw.[12] So, why did the United States end up adopting a Federalist system of governance?

The Articles of Confederation

The United States has not always had a Federalist system. The American colonies were originally chartered as independent settlements, under the control of European colonial powers. Settlers identified themselves not as Americans, but as subjects of a colonial power. By the late eighteenth century, though, citizens of several of the original 13 colonies—frustrated by the dictates of the British Parliament and the monarchy of King George III—began

---

[8] Mitchell Pickerill and Paul Chen, "Medical Marijuana Policy and the Virtues of Federalism," *Publius* 38(2008):22–55.

[9] Daniel Elazar, *American Federalism: A View from the States,* 3rd ed. (New York: Harper & Row, 1984); Daniel Elazar, "Contrasting Unitary and Federal Systems," *International Political Science Review* 18(1997):237–52.

[10] Charles Tarlton, "Symmetry and Asymmetry as Elements of Federalism: A Theoretical Speculation," *Journal of Politics* 27(1965):861–74.

[11] Martha Derthick, "American Federalism: Half-Full or Half-Empty," *The Brookings Review* 18(2000):24–27.

[12] Jack Rakove, *Original Meanings: Politics and Ideas in the Making of the Constitution* (New York: Knopf, 1997), p. 168.

challenging the consolidated power of Great Britain.[13] Rebellious leaders of the colonies convened in September 1774 to establish the First Continental Congress. Proposed jointly by the Massachusetts and Virginia legislatures, 12 of the 13 colonies sent delegates to Philadelphia for the proceedings; only Georgia did not immediately send representatives. The Continental Congress was weak, though, as the states retained the authority to reject or alter its wishes.

After the signing of the Declaration of Independence in 1776, it became apparent to many leaders of the fledging states that they needed a stronger central government, albeit one that would not undermine the sovereignty of the states. In 1777, the Second Continental Congress approved the **Articles of Confederation,** the country's first constitution, and sent it to the states for ratification.[14] As a confederal system, the document delimited the separation of powers between two layers of governments in an effort to make one nation out of 13 independent sovereign entities. Under the Articles, Congress was granted the authority to declare war and make peace, enter treaties and alliances, coin or borrow money, and regulate trade with Native Americans, but it could not levy requisite taxes or adequately enforce its commerce and trade regulations among the states. Members of the Continental Congress, who served one-year terms and were chosen by their state legislatures, acted typically as delegates of their state legislatures. Beholden to the states, the federal government—which lacked an executive branch to enforce laws passed by Congress—was wholly reliant on the states for its operating expenses.

The Federalists

Many founders were appalled by the ineffectualness of the federal government under the Articles. General George Washington, for one, was "mortified beyond expression" that the federal government under the Articles was so emasculated that it could not even defend its citizens from relatively minor internal threats.[15] Tensions between rival sovereigns—the 13 states and Congress—were mounting. In May 1787, Congress called for a Constitutional Convention to amend the U.S. Constitution. Over that summer, delegates to the Constitutional Convention would decide to scrap the Articles, replacing them with a Federalist system. In addition to restructuring the federal government's institutional design, the proposed constitution would alter the relationship between the federal government and the states, having each share power and the representation of their respective constituencies.[16]

Federalists who supported the new constitution argued in favor of a strong central government. But they made it clear that the central government's authority would be checked by the separation of powers among the legislative, executive, and judicial branches, as well as through the division of sovereignty between the states and the federal government.[17] Writing in 1788 under the pseudonym "Publius," James Madison, Alexander Hamilton, and John Jay authored a series of pamphlets that collectively became known as the Federalist Papers. As part of a public relations campaign to generate popular support for the ratification of the Constitution, the authors claimed the new constitution would provide for internal

---

[13] Over a span of a few years, a series of parliamentary acts were handed down from London, including the 1765 Stamp Act, which required the colonies to place revenue stamps on all official documents, the 1767 Townshend Acts, which placed duties on colonial imports, and the 1773 Tea Act, which granted the East India Company a monopoly over the export of tea from Britain.

[14] The Articles effectively served for nearly 12 years as the country's first constitution, despite the fact that it was not ratified until March 1781. Merrill Jensen, *The New Nation: A History of the United States during the Confederation: 1781–1789* (New York: Vintage Books, 1950), 18–27.

[15] Letter from George Washington to David Humphreys, 22 October 1786. The George Washington Papers at the Library of Congress, 1741–1799. Available: http://lcweb2.loc.gov/cgi-bin/query/r?ammem/mgw:@field(DOCID+@lit(gw290023)).

[16] David Brian Robertson, "Madison's Opponents and Constitutional Design," *American Political Science Review* 99(2005):225–43.

[17] Joseph Ellis, *Founding Brothers: The Revolutionary Generation* (New York: Knopf, 2001).

checks and balances in the fledgling nation and would structurally limit the supremacy of the national government by creating competitive (sometimes rival, sometimes cooperative) state governments.[18]

The U.S. Constitution and the Historical Development of Federalism

Following Congress's submission of the U.S. Constitution to the states in 1787 and its subsequent ratification, a vexing question continued to linger: which had more authority, the Union or the states?[19] Federalist sympathizers tried to downplay the power of the federal government in the proposed constitution. Temporally and

territorially, of course, the states clearly preceded the Union. Yet, compared with the failed Articles, the U.S. Constitution laid out clear powers for the federal government. Figure 2.3 displays some of the basic powers held in principle by the national and state governments when the Constitution was first adopted. As we discuss later in this chapter, the division of powers between the states and the federal government today hardly resembles the allocation in the 1790s. The continual fluctuation in the relative authority of the states and the federal government has cumulated in a slow expansion of federal power over time.

Federal Powers under the U.S. Constitution

There are several provisions found in the U.S. Constitution that enhance the power of the federal government, and specifically the authority

Figure 2.3

Original Constitutional Powers of National and State Governments

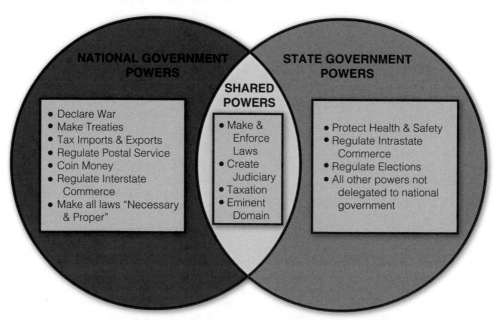

[18] David Epstein, *The Political Theory of the Federalist* (Chicago: University of Chicago Press, 1984); Frederic Stimson, *The American Constitution as It Protects Private Rights* (New York: Charles Scribner's Sons, 1923).

[19] Jack Rakove, *Original Meanings: Politics and Ideas in the Making of the Constitution* (New York: Knopf, 1997).

of Congress. The document grants Congress, the bicameral legislative arm of the national government, several explicit powers. These include the right to declare war; provide for the common defense; lay and collect taxes, duties, imposts, and excises; regulate commerce with foreign nations, among the several states, and with the Indian tribes; establish post offices and post roads; and provide for the general welfare of the United States. These "expressed" or "enumerated" powers of Congress, found in Article I, Section 8, Clauses 1–17 of the Constitution, especially the Commerce Clause, expand Congress's reach.

The National Supremacy Clause

Article VI, Section 2, known as the **National Supremacy Clause,** stipulates that the U.S. Constitution and national laws and treaties "shall be the supreme law of the land…anything in the Constitution or Laws of any State to the Contrary notwithstanding." This means that the federal Constitution and federal laws trump conflicting state constitutional provisions or laws. Thus, when there is no clear delineation of which level of government is to have the dominant role in policy making, or when there is a conflict between national and state public policies, federal laws are superior to state laws. It bears noting that there is no mention of local governments in the U.S. Constitution.

State and local governments, for example, are not permitted to enter into treaties with American Indian tribal nations without authorization from the federal government. Indian nations, which exist in 34 states, are *domestic dependent nations*, a term coined by the U.S. Supreme Court in its 1831 decision *Cherokee Nation v. Georgia.* According to the high court's ruling in *Worcester v. Georgia,* which was handed down the following year, the national government has the authority to enter into agreements with sovereign Indian tribes. However, the federal government occasionally grants states the power to negotiate certain

compacts with the tribes located within their boundaries. Today, one of the most common negotiation areas between the states and Indian tribes has to do with casino gambling. Congress in 1988 passed the Indian Gaming Regulatory Act, which requires tribes to enter compacts with the state governments specifying the types of gaming that are permitted on their reservation lands and any compensation that should be made to the state governments.[20]

The Commerce Clause

The **Commerce Clause** is the third clause in Article I, Section 8 of the U.S. Constitution. The clause gives Congress the power "[t]o regulate Commerce with foreign Nations, and among the several States, and with the Indian Tribes." As we discuss at length below, Congress has interpreted the 16-word clause broadly, greatly expanding its legislative power to intervene in a wide number of facets of the national economy. Beginning in 1824, with its decision *Gibbons v. Ogden,* the U.S. Supreme Court has generally granted Congress broad powers to pass laws dealing with issues only indirectly related to interstate commerce, such as civil rights, environmental regulations, possession of firearms and drugs, and Internet transactions. Congress's broad definition of interstate commerce has even been used to regulate internet sales, racial segregation in restaurants and hotels, and the production of subsistence wheat crops in Kansas. Today, with the increased interconnectivity of human activity, most economic activities extend beyond a state's borders and thus may fall prey to congressional regulations.

The Necessary and Proper Clause

Unlike the Articles of Confederation, the Constitution also grants Congress wide discretion in its interpretation of its powers in Article I, Section 8. Clause 18 of Article I, Section 8, known as the **Necessary and Proper Clause** or the Elastic Clause, has been a key component in the

[20] Institute of Governmental Studies, "Indian Gaming in California," University of California at Berkeley, 2006. Available: http://www.kumeyaay.info/san_diego_indian_casinos/Indian_Gaming_California_HISTORY.pdf.

centralization of power by Congress over time. The clause enables Congress to interpret and expand upon the 17 preceding substantive clauses in Article I, Section 8. Congress's implied powers give the national legislative body authority to make all laws that shall be "necessary and proper for carrying into execution the foregoing powers."

The Full Faith and Credit Clause Enshrined in Article IV, Section 1, the **Full Faith and Credit Clause** stipulates that the states must mutually accept one another's public acts, records, and judicial proceedings. Congress is given the authority to oversee the manner and effect of the reciprocity among the states. Today, the Clause has regained prominence in the controversy over gay marriage, which is legal in five states. In 1996, Congress passed and President Bill Clinton signed into law the Defense of Marriage Act (DOMA). The act gave states the power to not recognize legal same-sex marriages performed in another state. Some social conservatives contend that if the U.S. Constitution is not amended, gay rights activists might be able to successfully challenge DOMA in court, thereby forcing states that have outlawed same-sex marriage to recognize those sanctioned in other states.

Privileges and Immunities Clause Article IV, Section 2 of the Constitution, the **Privileges and Immunities Clause**, ensures that residents of one state cannot be discriminated against by another state when it comes to fundamental matters, such as pursuing one's professional occupation, access to the courts, or equality in taxation.[21] Because of the Privileges and Immunities Clause, a state, for example, may not bar citizens from other states from practicing law in the state, assuming they pass the state's bar exam. Section 2 of Article IV also includes a provision that was upheld by the U.S. Supreme Court's infamous 1857 decision *Dred Scott v. Sanford*. Before it was stricken by

the 13th Amendment in 1865, the third clause of Article IV permitted states to maintain the institution of slavery and required fugitive slaves who had fled to free states to be forcibly returned to their legal slaveholders. The clause continues to be invoked by states wishing to preserve states' rights. In 1978, for example, the high court struck down the "Alaska Hire Law," which had restricted the occupational opportunities of nonresidents interested in working in the state's oil industry. The Court, though, continues to permit what some view as another discriminatory practice: allowing public universities to charge higher tuition for out-of-state students.

State Powers under the U.S. Constitution

Federalists such as Alexander Hamilton, James Madison, and their fellow delegates who supported a strong national government during the proceedings of the 1787 Constitutional Convention in Philadelphia did not prevail on all fronts. Anti-Federalists, as they were known, expressed their discontent over the increased powers of the federal government. The Constitution was unfinished, they contended, as it failed to enshrine the rights of the states. "The Constitution did settle many questions, and it established a lasting structure of rules and principle," writes Herbert Storing. "But it did not settle everything; it did not finish the task of making the American polity."[22] With the ratification of the U.S. Constitution in 1788, the political dialogue was just beginning, as Anti-Federalist concerns and principles became central to the ongoing debate.

The Bill of Rights Joining Thomas Jefferson and George Mason of Virginia, James Madison would eventually moderate his strong defense of the national government, insisting too that a Bill of Rights be appended to the Constitution. In December 1791, three-quarters of the

[21] David Bogen, *Privileges and Immunities: A Reference Guide to the United States Constitution* (Westport, CT: Praeger, 2003).

[22] Herbert Storing, ed., *The Anti-Federalist: Writings by the Opponents of the Constitution* (Chicago: University of Chicago Press, 1985), p. 1.

states ratified the first 10 proposed amendments to the Constitution. A major goal of the Bill of Rights was to ensure the protection of individuals from the national government. But it also protects the autonomy of the states. The 9th and 10th Amendments guaranteed that states were not deprived by the federal government of any rights not explicitly expressed in the Constitution. As many people in the states quickly discovered, though, the Bill of Rights did not immediately prevent state governments from depriving their residents of rights.

The 10th Amendment The 10th Amendment explicitly limits the powers of national government vis-à-vis the states. Known also as the **Reserve Clause**, it gives the states broad authority, stipulating: "The powers not delegated to the United States by the Constitution, nor prohibited by it to the States, are reserved to the States respectively, or to the people." Because there is no mention in the U.S. Constitution of numerous substantive issues, such as those dealing with education, public health, the environment, or criminal justice, it was widely understood by the founders that these policy domains would be left to the states. Despite the centralization of power brought about by the ratification of the U.S. Constitution, the Bill of Rights infused the states with more sovereign powers. Because of the 10th Amendment, in theory at least, the states are not administrative arms of the national government, but rather constituent parts that retain their autonomy from the central government.

Federalism Today

As discussed previously, there are numerous provisions in the U.S. Constitution granting authority to the national government.

Through the various powers granted by the U.S. Constitution, Congress has often asserted its authority over the states, preempting state laws. **Federal preemption** occurs when the federal government takes regulatory action that overrides state laws. Advocates of federal preemption claim that it is necessary to create a uniformity of laws and regulations so as to avoid a confusing and inconsistent patchwork of standards across the states. But preemptive legislation by Congress has created an ongoing tussle between the federal government and the states.[23] According to one count, between 1789 and 2005, Congress passed 529 preemption statutes.[24] Since the mid-1990s alone, Congress has preempted, and thus partially or completely curtailed, state regulatory authority in numerous areas, including food safety, health care, telecommunications, international trade, and financial services. Critics of federal preemption claim that it leads to less flexibility in regulations and the delivery of public services, hurts the ability of states to experiment with and develop best practices, limits the ability of states to coordinate their economic development priorities with their regulatory policies, and diminishes the protections that states are able to craft for their citizens.[25]

The Ebb and Flow (and Gradual Erosion) of Federalism

In 1908, future-President Woodrow Wilson wrote, "The question of the relations of the states and the federal government is the cardinal question" of the American political system.[26] The inherent tension existing between the national and subnational levels of government

---

[23] Joseph Zimmerman, *Contemporary American Federalism* (Westport, CT: Praeger, 1992).

[24] Joseph Zimmerman, *Congressional Preemption: Regulatory Federalism* (Albany: State University of New York Press, 2005).

[25] Raymond Scheppach, "Federal Preemption: A Serious Threat," 17 August 2004. Available: http://www.Stateline.org.

[26] Quoted in Kenneth Vines, "The Federal Setting of State Politics," in Herbert Jacob and Kenneth Vines, eds., *Politics in the American States,* 3rd ed. (Boston: Little, Brown and Company, 1976).

is a defining characteristic of American federalism. The ebb and flow between the states and the national government, which were codified by the ratification of the U.S. Constitution in 1788 and the Bill of Rights in 1791, are a recurrent theme in the study of American politics. Competition or even disharmony between the national and state levels of government, then, is to be expected, with disagreements between the two layers of government being interpreted as a healthy sign that the division of powers is working.[27]

The Shifting Sands of Federalism

Since the country's founding, the locus of political power in the United States has flowed from the federal government to the states and back again to the federal government. These tidal shifts, though, have not been equal in force. Although at any given moment the relative level of power between the states and the national government is refreshingly and predictably fluid,[28] with each wave the federal government has slowly eroded the sovereignty of the states. Many waves of federal encroachment on state power have been the result of crises—from the Civil War, to World War I, to the Depression and the New Deal, to the War on Poverty in the 1960s, to 9/11. In the aftermath of each of these tidal storms, the states did not become mere appendages of the national government, but they did successively lose ground to the federal government.

The reason for this constant shifting and gradual expansion of the power of the federal government stems from the fact that the authority of the federal and state government is not clearly demarcated in the U.S. Constitution. Because of the ambiguities of national and state powers, logical arguments have been made equally forcibly in defense of states' rights or for more centralized power. For example, at one extreme of the spectrum, Vice President John C. Calhoun of South Carolina in the mid-nineteenth century advocated the theory of nullification, arguing that the states held veto power over the actions of the federal government, which included the right to permit slavery and reject national trade agreements. At the other extreme, Alexander Hamilton argued that the United States had the right to establish a national bank that could assist the federal government in meeting its financial obligations, and that the national government could impose tariffs and duties to protect nascent industries that were central to the national interest. Over the long haul, Hamilton's view of a stronger, more centralized federal government has prevailed.

Centralization and Devolution

The American federal system, however, continually cycles through periods of greater centralization and devolution. **Devolution** is the decentralization of power and authority from a central government to state or local governments; **centralization** reverses the flow, empowering a national governing authority with unitary control and authority. Writing in the 1830s, the French observer Alexis de Tocqueville noted that devolution not only had positive administrative effects but also had beneficial political effects, in that it enhanced the civic values and opportunities of citizens.[29] Because the national government does not have monopoly power in the American system, the embrace of **decentralization** has at times led to a tremendous amount of diversity across the states regarding the kinds of laws subnational governments have adopted over time.

In the American context, centralization and devolution are relative terms, denoting the

---

[27] Thomas Dye, *American Federalism: Competition among Governments* (Lexington, MA: Lexington Books Heath, 1990); and D. Kenyon and John Kincaid, eds., *Competition among States and Local Governments: Efficiency and Equity in American Federalism* (Washington, DC: The Urban Institute, 1991). See also, William Riker, *The Development of American Federalism* (Boston: Kluwer Academic Publishers, 1987).

[28] Zimmerman, *Contemporary American Federalism*, 1992.

[29] Alexis de Tocqueville, *Democracy in America*, Book 1, chapter 5. Available: http://xroads.virginia.edu/~HYPER/DETOC/home.html.

distribution of power and the level of policy-making responsibility taken on by the national or state governments. Besides the role of the federal courts, the level of centralization or devolution present in the American Federalist system is dependent on a host of outside factors. In times of war and national crises, such as the aftermath of 9/11, an increasing amount of power tends to become centralized in Washington, DC. Centralization also occurs when people call to redistribute the nation's wealth in an effort to create greater equity in society, perceive a need to establish national standards or policy goals, and make efforts to create more efficiencies in the implementation of public policy. Power tends to flow back to the states when citizens clamor for public policies that are better tailored to fit their specific needs or when there is growing distrust of elected officials in the federal government. Although at times political power devolves to the states, rarely does it completely offset any preceding periods of centralization.

Creeping Centralization: The Political Evolution of Federal Power

Abetted by the power vested in Congress by the federal courts, the authority of the federal government relative to the states grew considerably during the late nineteenth and twentieth centuries.[30] During the mid-nineteenth century, Congress passed several laws that slowly expanded the power of the federal government. For example, in 1862 in the midst of the Civil War, the federal government cleared the way for westward expansion by passing the Pacific Railroad Act, giving charters to companies building a transcontinental railroad. That same year, Congress passed the Morrill Act, which provided territory to establish public schools and land grant universities, and the Homestead Act, which allowed citizens or persons intending to become citizens to acquire 160 acres of public land, and then purchase it after five years for a nominal fee.[31] Following the Civil War, with the Union Army's defeat of the Confederate Army, advocates of states' rights were momentarily silenced, setting the foundation for a stronger federal government and the development of a national grants-in-aid system. In 1913, with the ratification of the 16th Amendment permitting the federal government to tax incomes, the powers of the federal government were dramatically enhanced.

The New Deal, World War II, and Cooperative Federalism

The relative sovereignty of the 50 states was altered during three notable high points of federal governmental power in the twentieth century: the New Deal, World War II, and the Great Society programs of the 1960s.[32] Although there has been much rhetoric about the devolution of power to state and local governments, much of the political power initially grabbed by the federal government vis-à-vis the states during these time periods remains in Washington, DC.

The expansion of national power has been gradual. Although its role increased during the period of Reconstruction,[33] the New Deal programs of the 1930s advanced by the Franklin Delano Roosevelt administration forcefully inserted the federal government into the national economy as never before. In 1933, in an effort to mitigate the Great Depression, Congress passed the Agricultural Adjustment

---

[30] See Stephen Skowronek, *Building a New American State: The Expansion of National Administrative Capacities, 1877–1920* (Cambridge, MA: Cambridge University Press, 1982).

[31] Daniel J. Elazar, *The American Partnership: Intergovernmental Co-operation in the Nineteenth-Century United States* (Chicago: University of Chicago Press, 1962).

[32] Martha Derthick, "Wither Federalism?" *The Urban Institute* 2(1996). Available: http://www.urban.org/UploadedPDF/derthick.pdf.

[33] Kimberley S. Johnson, *Governing the American State: Congress and the New Federalism, 1877–1929* (Princeton: Princeton University Press, 2006).

Act, which created educational programs and protected farmers by providing crop subsidies. The same year, Congress created the Civil Works Administration, which created public works jobs for millions of the unemployed, and also established the Civilian Conservation Corps (CCC), which sent a quarter of a million men to work camps around the country to help reforest and conserve the land. The Works Progress Administration (WPA), created by Congress in 1935, employed more than 8 million workers in construction and other jobs.[34] In 1936, Congress passed legislation creating a joint federal-state entitlement program, Aid to Families with Dependent Children (AFDC), which provided direct aid to families falling below the poverty line. Although these and other unprecedented incursions by Congress into policy areas previously controlled by the states were found to be constitutional, the U.S. Supreme Court struck down several other New Deal programs due to congressional encroachment on the states.

The entry in 1941 of the United States into World War II gave rise to greater federal powers. In addition to asking Americans to make sacrifices for the war effort, the federal government commanded control of several aspects of the economy, rationing foodstuffs and consumer goods and even nationalizing some factories for wartime production. In addition to the dramatic increase in the number of military personnel, the number of civilian employees working in the federal bureaucracy skyrocketed, rising nearly fourfold to almost 4 million workers by 1945. At the same time, as we discuss in Chapter 10 when examining the fiscal effects of federalism, annual spending by the federal government rose tenfold during the war, from $9 billion to more than $98 billion. By the end of the war, political power rested squarely in the hands of the federal government.

The efforts of the Roosevelt administration, with the blessing and support of the Democrat-controlled Congress, to insert the federal government into the economy by way of the states are often characterized as **cooperative federalism**.[35] In such an arrangement, responsibilities for virtually all functions of government are interdependent, shared between the federal, state, and local governments. National and subnational officials act primarily as colleagues, not adversaries.[36] Although traces of such inter-level cooperation existed prior to the New Deal, the collaboration between various layers of government blossomed during the 1930s, with Congress utilizing **categorical grants** to entice the state governments to cooperate.

The Great Society and Coercive Federalism

In the 1960s, Congress further expanded the scope of the federal government by using **block grants** to spread a wide swath of programs across the nation. Following the assassination of President John F. Kennedy, President Lyndon B. Johnson urged Congress to create a "Great Society," one that would bring about many of the social and economic changes unrealized during his predecessor's truncated term in office. Many political observers questioned the ability, as well as the will, of many state officials to provide equal protection of the law and social services to all their citizens. Political scientist John Kincaid has characterized this period of expanding national growth and attendant federal programs, which some scholars date from 1960 to 1972, as **coercive federalism**.[37] With the federal government spearheading and funding

---

[34] William E. Leuchtenberg, *Franklin D. Roosevelt and the New Deal, 1932–1940* (Princeton: Princeton University Press, 1963); and Alan Brinkley, *The End of Reform: New Deal Liberalism in Recession and War* (New York: Knopf, 1995).

[35] Elazar, *The American Partnership,* 1962

[36] Walker, *The Rebirth of Federalism,* 1995.

[37] John Kincaid, "From Dual to Coercive Federalism in American Intergovernmental Relations," in John Jun and Deil Wright, eds., *Globalization and Decentralization* (Washington, DC: Georgetown University Press, 1996), pp. 29–47.

several new programs in its war on poverty, some scholars have referred euphemistically to this period as creative federalism.[38] Congress sought to relieve growing social pressures found across the American states by expanding social welfare programs, including those intended to reduce urban and rural poverty and eradicate public school inequalities. In many instances, the federal government completely bypassed the states, funneling grant-in-aid directly to local governments.

In the 1960s, building on the U.S. Housing Act of 1937, Congress established an array of federal programs to aid citizens in policy areas traditionally left to the states. With the Economic Opportunity Act of 1964, Congress created numerous local antipoverty programs. The following year, Congress established the Department of Housing and Urban Development, which was charged with improving public housing and urban life. In addition, Congress passed the 1964 Civil Rights Act—which enforced the right to vote, extended federal protection against discrimination in public accommodations, and outlawed job discrimination—and the 1965 Voting Rights Act, which guaranteed the right to vote to African Americans. In the mid-1960s, Congress passed legislation creating Medicare, which created a national health insurance program for the elderly, and Medicaid, a joint federal/state-funded health care program for poor people. Each and every one of these programs increased the relative power of the federal government vis-à-vis the states.

The Continued Expansion of Federal Powers during the 1970s

Although many of the programs established during the Great Society era have been either mothballed or transferred in part by Congress to the states, many still exist. The list of programs created by the federal government during the 1960s and early 1970s is impressive and expansive. In each case, state sovereignty over these policy areas was slowly eroded. Created in the 1960s, the Head Start public education program continues to prepare disadvantaged poor children for their first years of school; similarly, the Food Stamps program provides sustenance to those falling below the poverty line. Medicare and Medicaid, two of the largest domestic federal programs today, provide millions of Americans with medical insurance and health care. In addition to continuing to regulate auto emissions and the use of toxic chemicals, the Environmental Protection Agency (EPA), created by Congress in 1970, enforces the cleanup of hazardous waste, monitors the ozone layer, and enforces clean air and water laws.

In the early 1970s, the Nixon administration pushed for more block grants and changes to the way federal grants were administered. The president also pushed for **General Revenue Sharing (GRS)**, a grant-in-aid program whereby the federal government provides financial aid to subnational units, but does not prescribe how those units are to allocate the funding. Congress, however, abandoned the grant-in-aid scheme, as lawmakers were unable to claim credit for projects that the federal government paid for but were implemented by subnational officials.[39]

All of these social welfare programs have undergone restructuring since their creation. Yet, they are very much essential components of the social welfare system expanded by the federal government during the 1960s.[40] Indeed, Great Society programs have had lasting effects on reducing malnutrition, infant mortality, and inequality in obtaining medical services, as well as improving affordable housing, job training, and environmental cleanup efforts.[41]

[38] Walker, *The Rebirth of Federalism,* 1995, p. 25.

[39] Timothy Conlan, *New Federalism: Intergovernmental Reform from Nixon to Reagan* (Washington, DC: Brookings, 1988).

[40] Michael Katz, *The Undeserving Poor: From the War on Poverty to the War on Welfare* (New York: Pantheon, 1989); and James Patterson, *America's Struggle against Poverty, 1900–1980* (Cambridge, MA: Harvard University Press, 1981).

[41] John Schwarz, *America's Hidden Success: A Reassessment of Public Policy from Kennedy to Reagan,* rev. ed. (New York: W.W. Norton 1988), pp. 68–69.

New Federalism during the Reagan Era

In the 1980s, many scholars observed how power seemed to be devolving back to the states. They pointed to the rise of entrepreneurial activities of the American states, with the state governments taking on new responsibilities to energize their economies by creating new jobs and economic opportunities.[42] The creative, self-directed activities of state and local governments conformed to the dominant political ideology of the time, decentralization, advanced most prominently by Republican President Ronald Reagan. In his first inauguration in 1981, Reagan famously pronounced, "Government is not the solution to our problem; government is the problem." Many states' rights proponents felt they had a champion in the White House.

During the Reagan years (1981–1989), Congress aggressively consolidated categorical grants into block grants, cutting or eliminating entirely the funding of existing federal programs in the process. This wholesale transformation occurred despite the fact that the administration never outlined a clear set of principles regarding the proper delineation of federal and state powers. In 1982, the administration went so far as to propose what would become known as the "Big Swap," whereby the federal government would turn over to the states the responsibility to provide for education, social services, transportation, and cash public assistance programs, in exchange for taking over the provision of health services for the poor. To offset their increased costs, the states would receive a portion of the federal tax revenue. Congress rejected the proposal, as members were leery that the state and local governments would be unable to shoulder the financial costs of their new policy responsibilities.[43] The Reagan administration's zeal to lessen the capacity of the federal government was not so much driven by devolution as by an "antigovernmental imperative" of "individualism."[44] Reagan and his top officials calculated that if federal dollars to states and localities were reduced, those governments would necessarily cut back on social programs. But rather than cutting programs, many state and local governments used their own funds to continue the programs. This was not the first time in American history that arguments over federalism were used to try to conceal or advance other political agendas, including the politics of race and social control.[45]

The Political Expediency of Federalism

Despite Reagan's pronouncements that power should be devolved to the states, the federal government continued to exert its authority vis-à-vis the states during the 1980s and 1990s. It is often the case that when federal candidates run for office they tout the devolution line, but when they are elected, they usually—if not always—back off.[46] Many actions taken by Congress in the 1980s were driven by political expediency as much as any ideological commitment to the Reagan doctrine of "New Federalism." Take, for instance, the passage of the Anti Drug Abuse Act of 1988, which came exactly four years after the passage of the Comprehensive Crime Control Act of 1984.

---

[42] Peter Eisinger, *The Rise of the Entrepreneurial States* (Madison: University of Wisconsin Press, 1988); and David Osborne, *Laboratories of Democracy* (Boston: Harvard Business School Press, 1988).

[43] Alice Rivlin, "The Federal Government in a Federal System: Current Intergovernmental Programs and Options for Change," Congressional Budget Office, August 1983. Available: http://www.cbo.gov/showdoc.cfm?index=5067&sequence=0.

[44] Samuel Beer, *To Make a Nation: The Rediscovery of American Federalism* (Cambridge, MA: Harvard University Press, 1993), p. xiii.

[45] Joe Soss, Richard Fording, and Sanford Schram, "The Color *of* Devolution: Race, Federalism, and the Politics *of* Social Control," *American Journal of Political Science* 52(2008):536–53.

[46] Timothy Conlan, *From New Federalism to Devolution: Twenty-Five Years of Intergovernmental Reform* (Washington, DC: Brookings, 1998).

The bills, which created mandatory sentences for federal crimes and revised bail and forfeiture procedures, came just a few weeks prior to the 1984 and 1988 general elections, respectively. Both pieces of legislation were largely the result of Democrats and Republicans trying to outbid each other to look tough on crime at election time.

With the Anti Drug Abuse Act of 1988, Congress felt it needed to respond to the tragic death of Boston Celtics first-round draft pick Len Bias. Bias was a collegiate star at the University of Maryland who died of a cocaine overdose. Then-speaker of the U.S. House of Representatives Democrat Tip O'Neill from Boston worked with Republican leaders to pass mandatory five-year federal sentences for possession of small amounts of illegal drugs favored by the poor (5 grams of crack cocaine, or 10 grams of methamphetamines or PCP) and of larger amounts favored by the wealthy (500 grams of powdered cocaine). The law, which required employers receiving federal aid to provide a "drug-free workplace" or risk suspension or termination of a grant or contract, was adopted without hearings, debate, or expert testimony.

Expanding National Power: Setting National Standards

In the early 1990s, Congress passed numerous laws encroaching on the power of the states. In 1990, Republican President George H. W. Bush signed into law a bill (the Gun Free School Zones Act of 1990) passed by a Democratic-controlled Congress making the possession of guns in or near schools a federal crime. In 1994, President Clinton signed into law bills making domestic violence (the Violence against Women Act of 1994) and failure to run background checks before the sale of weapons (the Brady Bill of 1994) federal crimes. (Both laws were later struck down by the U.S. Supreme Court.) By 1994, Congress had created 50

new crimes that could be prosecuted in federal court, many with possible death sentences.[47] With its "Three Strikes You're Out" legislation, Congress federalized penalties for the possession of marijuana, created mandatory minimum sentence guidelines for federal judges, and allowed the death penalty for certain drug-related crimes. Prior to 1994, many of these crimes were prosecuted in state courts, at the discretion of state prosecutors. With all these laws, Democrats joined Republicans to ensure that their party would not be demonized come election time as being soft on crime.

The Devolution Revolution?

After Republicans took over the U.S. House and Senate in 1994, under the leadership of House Speaker Newt Gingrich, a more conservative Congress did try to tackle the centralization of power in Washington, DC. Led by Gingrich, Republicans pushed forth their Contract with America, which, among other policy goals, called for devolution of power to the states. One of the only pieces of legislation packaged as part of the Contract with America to become law was the Unfunded Mandate Reform Act of 1995. In an effort to mitigate criticism among state and local government officials for the encroachment of the federal government on state powers, Congress agreed to restrict bills containing unfunded mandates. An **unfunded mandate** is a public policy that requires a subnational government to pay for an activity or project established by the federal government. Many state and local governments were upset with regulations handed down by Congress in the 1980s and 1990s with no money with which to implement the legislation. With its 1995 act, Congress must now include a cost estimate for any program including a mandate costing state or local governments at least $50 million. In addition, any mandate costing state or local governments more than $50 million a year can be stopped by a point-of-order objection raised on either the House or Senate floor.

[47] American Bar Association Report, "The Federalization of Criminal Law," 16 February 1999.

A majority of the membership in either chamber is allowed to override the point of order and pass the mandate, but the objection affords the chamber an opportunity for debate.

Despite the flurry of rhetoric urging the decentralization of power to the states since the Republican Party took control of Congress in the mid-1990s, Congress has taken few concrete steps to actually transfer policy responsibilities to the states. As has been the case since the United States' founding, philosophical and ideological arguments over federalism have been trumped by quests for political power. Most notably, Congress passed legislation to "end welfare as we know it" by replacing the long-standing joint federal-state social welfare entitlement program, Aid to Families with Dependent Children (AFDC), with the Personal Responsibility and Work Opportunity Reconciliation Act (PRWORA), signed into law by President Clinton in 1996. The new law required eligible recipients to work in exchange for time-limited assistance, but gave the states wide latitude in determining both the work requirements and the levels of cash and in-kind assistance that recipients could receive.

Despite the rhetoric of devolution, the actions of Congress during the administration of George W. Bush further increased the powers of the federal government. Following the complications of the 2000 presidential election, Congress passed the Help America Vote Act of 2002 (HAVA), a grant-in-aid program that required the states to conform to federal standards concerning registration and voting. That same year, President Bush signed into law the No Child Left Behind Act, which mandated that public schools make "adequate yearly progress" or risk losing federal support. At the urging of the Bush administration, in 2005 Congress passed the National Intelligence Reform Act. In addition to several other provisions that reorganized national security agencies in response to the 9/11 terrorist attacks, the law created national standards for the issuance of state driver's licenses. With the U.S. Department of Transportation overseeing the changes of what is known as the "Real ID" law, states are now required to develop "smart" driver's licenses that have a digital photograph or some other unique biometric identifier, such as a fingerprint or retinal-scan imprint. With each of these laws, Congress greatly expanded its reach into what are traditionally the domains of state or local government.

When Does the Federal Government Become Stronger?

There has been little systematic research investigating the distribution of political power between the American states and the federal government over time. Using a measure of the level of policy centralization between 1947 and 1998, one recent study finds that the authority of the national government in the United States has gradually increased since World War II, diminishing the power of the state governments. But rather than a pattern of stable growth in federal authority during the five-decade period, they find the authority of the national government has come in fits and starts. More significantly, perhaps, efforts to devolve power to the states during the presidential administrations of Republicans Richard Nixon and Ronald Reagan—contrary to their rhetoric of devolving power to the states—did not lead to the states having increased policy-making authority.[48]

Umpiring Federalism: The U.S. Supreme Court

Given the inherent ambiguity in the interpretation and implementation of American federalism, who determines whether the state governments or the federal government has the constitutional authority to make laws? Soon after the founding of the United States, the

---

[48] Ann Bowman and George Krause, "Power Shift: Measuring Policy Centralization in U.S. Intergovernmental Relations, 1947–1998," *American Politics Research* 31(2005):301–25.

federal courts assumed the role of adjudicating disputes between the federal and state governments. As umpire, the federal courts determine who is in the right when disputes between the national and subnational levels of government arise. In particular, the U.S. Supreme Court serves as the ultimate arbiter of the tension existing between the federal government and the states, with the highest state courts deciding the constitutionality of state laws under state constitutions. However, as we witnessed in 2001 with the Supreme Court's controversial *Bush v. Gore* decision that tipped the presidential contest, its decisions on questions of federalism are not always consistent or grounded in historical precedence.[49] In its hasty decision, the five conservative members of the Court ruled against the precedence of states' rights, overturning the Florida Supreme Court's ruling that ordered a manual recount of all under-voted ballots in the state.

Judicial Review of the Power of the Federal Government

In 1819, 16 years after the U.S. Supreme Court ruled that it had the final word on determining whether laws were in conflict with the U.S. Constitution, the high court put the question of national government broadly usurping state power to the test in the case *McCulloch v. Maryland*. The State of Maryland had imposed a tax on transactions, including those of the Second Bank of the United States, on all banks that were not chartered in the state. The Supreme Court, under the direction of Chief Justice John Marshall, ruled that although it was not explicitly granted the right, Congress with its implied powers had the authority to establish a national bank. Under the Commerce Clause, found in Article I, Section 8 of the Constitution, the Court ruled that Congress had the power to lay and collect taxes, borrow money, and regulate commerce. Therefore, the Court ruled that the national bank was a "necessary and proper"

outgrowth of the federal government's powers. Furthermore, the Court ruled that the State of Maryland had no constitutional authority to tax the national bank. The ruling, in tandem with *Gibbons v. Ogden* (1824), which permitted Congress to regulate interstate navigation, greatly empowered the federal government's hold over questions of dealing with interstate commerce.

The Supreme Court and Dual Federalism

For much of American history, not all individuals have been protected equally by the U.S. Constitution's Bill of Rights. Irrespective of one's race, ethnicity, or creed, a person's civil liberties largely have depended on where that person resided. Although perhaps difficult to comprehend today, the civil liberties found in the first eight amendments to the U.S. Constitution did not automatically apply to all citizens. Rather, from the late eighteenth century to the twentieth century (1789–1913), the United States was characterized by a system of dual federalism. In theory, under **dual federalism**, citizens are essentially governed by two separate legal spheres. Every eligible person is a citizen of the national government and, separately, a citizen of the state in which he or she resides.

In a series of early rulings, the U.S. Supreme Court interpreted the Bill of Rights as being applicable only to the actions of the federal government, not the states. In its 1833 decision *Barron v. Mayor and City Council of Baltimore*, the Court ruled that these federal civil liberties provided "security against the apprehended encroachments of the general government—not against those of local governments." The Court ruled that the 5th Amendment to the U.S. Constitution—which limits the taking of private property for public use without just compensation—did not apply to the states, as "each state established a

[49] E.J. Dionne and William Kristol, *Bush v. Gore: The Court Cases and the Commentary* (Washington, DC: Brookings Institution Press, 2001).

constitution for itself, and in that constitution, provided such limitations and restrictions on the powers of its particular government, as its judgment dictated."[50]

Unless specifically limited by their own state constitutions, states were not bound by the restrictions that the Bill of Rights placed on the federal government. Indeed, the states were not obliged to take positive (or affirmative) action to protect their citizens from governmental actions, even those of other citizens. For example, several states in the early nineteenth century had established official state religions; Congregationalism, for example, was Connecticut's official religion until 1818, and until 1833 every man in Massachusetts was required by state law to belong to a church. Other states limited the freedom of their citizens to openly criticize the government.

The Civil War and National Unity

Prior to the Civil War (1861–1865), the American system of dual federalism permitted the states certain latitude to determine their own social and economic relations. In the mid-nineteenth century, there were clear regional divisions in the United States. In addition to deep cultural differences, there were profound disagreements among the states on how to best manage and regulate the national economy, including most notably the question of slavery. Undergirding these questions of human rights and the economy, though, was the ever-present issue of federalism, namely, states' rights.

The Civil War fundamentally changed American federalism. In early 1861, following the election of Republican Abraham Lincoln, seven southern states seceded from the Union. In February, these states, led by South Carolina, created a new government, the Confederate States of America. The state governments seized property—including forts—of the federal government. Soon thereafter, in April 1861, the American Civil War began. Eventually, 11 southern states would secede from the Union; by the end of the war, over 620,000 Union and Confederate soldiers died in action. With the end of the war came the opportunity for the victorious national government to reshape the contours of American federalism.

Incorporating the 14th Amendment in the States

The end of the Civil War fundamentally altered the American system of dual federalism. Most notably, the ratification of the 14th Amendment in 1868 provided for a single national citizenship. In part, the 14th Amendment states,

> No State shall make or enforce any law which shall abridge the privileges or immunities of citizens of the United States; nor shall any state deprive any person of life, liberty, or property without due process of law; nor deny to any person within its jurisdiction the equal protection of the laws.

By extending federal rights through the Due Process Clause and "Equal Protection of the Laws" Clause of the 14th Amendment, the Supreme Court has slowly incorporated the Bill of Rights into the states. The **incorporation of the Bill of Rights** has been gradual, taking place through a series of U.S. Supreme Court decisions. For example, it was not until 1925, when the Court ruled in *Gitlow v. New York*, that the 14th Amendment made the 1st Amendment's protection of freedom of speech applicable to the states. Subsequent rulings by the Court slowly began incorporating other amendments of the U.S. Constitution that protect the civil liberties of Americans into the states.[51] Although this process of incorporation was slow, many states adopted new state constitutions that provided greater rights than the federal Constitution.

---

[50] Harry Scheiber, "Federalism and the American Economic Order, 1789–1910," *Law & Society Review* 10(1975):57–118.

[51] Carl Swidorski, "The Courts, the Labor Movement and the Struggle for Freedom of Expression and Association, 1919–1940," *Labor History* 45(2004):61–84.

Writing in the late 1800s, Lord James Bryce, a trenchant observer of American politics, was duly concerned about the system of American federalism. Bryce, the long-serving British ambassador to the United States, contended that the constitutionally prescribed dispersion of authority between the national and state governments weakened the ability of nationally elected officials to respond to internal and external threats to the nation, or changes in public opinion on domestic policy. For Bryce, the constitutional crisis over slavery that led to the Civil War was "the function of no one authority in particular to discover a remedy, as it would have been the function of a cabinet in Europe."[52]

Fortunately for Americans, Bryce noted, there were centrifugal forces that led toward increasing uniformity among the states, most notably national political parties that advanced coherent policy agendas, a transitory population, modern communications and transport, and a lack of significant physical boundaries between states. These forces, which were not bound by the federal structure, helped to homogenize differences among the states and allow for a more national trajectory in the historical development of federalism.

Establishing Minimum Standards for the States

Through a series of rulings during the 1950s and 1960s, the U.S. Supreme Court aggressively drew upon the 14th Amendment to greatly expand the scope of powers held by Congress to enforce the amendment's guarantees. Under the guidance of Chief Justice Earl Warren, a former Republican governor of California, the Court ruled that state and local governments were required to affirm the equal protection of their citizens. In the landmark decision *Brown v. Board of Education* (1954), the Court overturned the longstanding practice of "separate

but equal" racial segregation of public schools. The Court also invalidated discriminatory electoral practices in several states with a series of decisions anchored by *Baker v. Carr* (1962), which granted the federal courts jurisdiction to hear reapportionment cases dealing with the malapportionment of legislative seats, and required that state legislatures be apportioned on the basis of population.[53]

Between the 1950s and mid-1970s, the Supreme Court extended a broad array of procedural rights to individuals under the 14th Amendment. In its 1963 decision *Gideon v. Wainwright*, the Court struck down a criminal procedural statute in Florida that criminal suspects did not have the right to consult with an attorney. In *Griswold v. Connecticut* (1965), the Court struck down a Connecticut law that forbade married couples from using contraception after Estelle Griswold was arrested and convicted for distributing birth control products from her clinic. In its majority and concurrent decisions, the Court established the "right of privacy," found in the "penumbra" of the 9th Amendment as well as that of the 14th Amendment's Due Process Clause. In 1966, the Court ruled in *Miranda v. Arizona* that state and local police must inform a suspect of his or her 5th and 6th Amendment rights, and that a person under arrest has the right to remain silent and must be clearly informed of his or her right to consult an attorney during a subsequent interrogation prior to being charged with a crime. In *Roe v. Wade* (1973), the Court established that states, such as Texas where the case unfolded, were not permitted to criminalize or wholly thwart abortions, as such actions would violate a woman's right to privacy afforded to her under the 14th Amendment. However, in subsequent abortion-related decisions, such as *Webster v. Reproductive Health Services* (1989), the Court gave the states considerably more room to regulate the procedure.[54]

---

[52] James Bryce, *The American Commonwealth*, vol. 2 (New York: Macmillian, 1893), pp. 358–59.

[53] Gerald Rosenberg, *The Hollow Hope: Can Courts Bring about Social Change?* (Chicago: University of Chicago Press, 1991).

[54] Jean Cohen, "Democracy, Difference and the Right of Privacy," in Seyla Benhabib, *Democracy and Difference: Contesting the Boundaries of the Political* (Princeton, NJ: Princeton University Press), pp. 187–217.

In each of these decisions, the high court established minimal standards—a floor—in terms of incorporating the protections of civil rights and liberties afforded by the federal Bill of Rights and 14th Amendment. In this era of "new judicial federalism," the Court did not curtail the right of the states to go beyond these minimal standards. Indeed, many states have public policies—for example, minimum or living wage laws, environmental regulations, and antidiscrimination laws—that far exceed the standards set by the federal government.[55] Most notably, in 1985, the high court ruled in *Garcia v. San Antonio Metropolitan Transit Authority* that federal wage and hour standards (set by Congress in 1974) were applicable to employees of state and local governments. In other words, the Court agreed that Congress had the authority over the supposedly "sovereign" states regarding how much they had to pay their workers.[56]

Expanding States' Rights

More recently, with its ever-evolving interpretations of the Constitution, several rulings by the U.S. Supreme Court have returned authority back to the states. Before his death in 2005, former Chief Justice William H. Rehnquist took a much narrower view of the scope of the 14th Amendment. With Rehnquist at the helm of a deeply divided bench, the Supreme Court began to crack down on the national encroachment on state government prerogatives, especially those enhanced by an expansive reading of the Interstate Commerce Clause. In *United States v. Lopez* (1995), the Court found that Congress had overstepped its authority when in 1990 it passed the Gun-Free School Zones Act, which made it a federal crime to carry a firearm in a designated school zone. In its narrow 5–4 decision, the Court ruled that Congress did not have the authority under the Commerce Clause to criminalize the possession of a gun in a school zone because there was no evidence that the activity dealt with interstate commerce. It was the first decision in over 50 years in which the Court abrogated Congress' supposed power under the Commerce Clause to regulate an activity.[57]

Two years later, in 1997, the high court ruled again to limit the reach of Congress. In *Printz v. United States*, the Court reaffirmed the principle that the Necessary and Proper Clause does not give Congress the power to compel local law enforcement agents, such as Montana's Ravalli County Sheriff Jay Printz, to conduct mandatory background checks on individuals wishing to buy a handgun. In a 5–4 decision, the Court ruled that Congress stretched the Necessary and Proper Clause too far when it passed the Brady Handgun Violence Prevention Act in 1993. Then in 2000, the Court ruled in *United States v. Morrison* that Congress' 1994 Violence Against Women Act was unconstitutional, as it did not substantially affect interstate commerce. Time and again under the leadership of Rehnquist, the high court limited Congress' authority to invoke the Commerce Clause to regulate in areas that have only an insignificant connection with interstate commerce.[58]

Protecting the States from Lawsuits

Under Rehnquist, the Court also greatly expanded the rights of states by expanding their protection from lawsuits. According to the U.S. Constitution's 11th Amendment, ratified in 1795, the states have "sovereign immunity," meaning they have some protection from lawsuits brought by individuals.[59] In 1996, the U.S. Supreme Court ruled in *Seminole Tribe v. State*

---

[55] John Kincaid, "The State and Federal Bills of Rights: Partners and Rivals in Liberty," *Intergovernmental Perspective* 17(1991):31–34.

[56] John Pittenger, "Garcia and the Political Safeguards of Federalism: Is There a Better Solution to the Conundrum of the Tenth Amendment?" *Publius* 22(1992):1–19.

[57] Cornell Clayton and Howard Gillman, eds., *Supreme Court Decision-Making: New Institutional Approaches* (Chicago: University of Chicago Press, 1999).

[58] Mark Tushnet, *Taking the Constitution Away from the Courts* (Princeton, NJ: Princeton University Press, 1999).

[59] Sanford Schram and Carol Weissert, "The State of U.S. Federalism: 1998–1999," *Publius* 29(1999):1–34.

Comparisons Help Us Understand

TOASTING THE U.S. SUPREME COURT

Have a thirst for a full-bodied Napa Valley Cabernet Sauvignon? How about a California-grown Pinot Noir, Merlot, or Chardonnay? Prior to 2005, if you were at least 21 years old and living in Wisconsin—or any of the other 28 states permitting direct shipments from California wine makers—your thirst could be readily quenched by ordering a bottle either by phone or over the Internet. Direct mailing of wine to consumers is big business, with the more than 3,200 wineries in the country accounting for more than $18 billion in annual sales. But if you were living in Michigan, New York, Florida, or several other states banning out-of-state shipments of wine, you were out of luck. In those states, you were permitted to order wine and have it delivered to your doorstep, but only if it was produced in-state.

In May 2005, in a 5–4 decision, the U.S. Supreme Court ruled in *Granholm v. Heald* that the Constitution prohibited such discriminatory regulation, as the "state regulation of alcohol is limited by the nondiscrimination principle of the Commerce Clause." Although the 21st Amendment to the Constitution gives states tremendous leeway in regulating alcohol, "if a state chooses to allow direct shipments of wine," wrote Justice Anthony Kennedy in the majority opinion, "it must do so on evenhanded terms." The high court indicated that the states remain free to permit or ban the direct sale of wine to consumers, but it ruled that they may not give "preferential treatment" in direct sales to local wineries. Since the ruling, nearly two-thirds of the states now permit direct shipping of wine to consumers, including both Michigan and New York, but more than a dozen states have decided to completely ban all direct mail wine sales.[1]

[1] Linda Greenhouse, "Supreme Court Lifts Ban on Wine Shipping," *New York Times*, 17 May 2005, p. A1; Wine Institute, http://wi.shipcompliant.com/Home.aspx?SaleTypeID=1.

of Florida that the Seminole Indians were not permitted to sue the State of Florida for what the tribe alleged was the state's failure to negotiate in good faith new regulations for casino gaming activities as required by Congress's Indian Gaming Regulatory Act of 1988. The Court's 5–4 decision held that Congress did not have the authority under the Commerce Clause to trump the protections from lawsuits afforded the states under the 11th Amendment.

States' Rights Legacy and the Roberts Court

Following a string of decisions granting more power to the federal government, many court-watchers asked whether the Court's federalism revolution would outlast the Rehnquist Court.

Some asked whether the Court's effort to protect states' rights was more "a revolution of convenience" than driven by some deep ideological commitment to decentralized government.[60] With the appointment of John Roberts as the new chief justice in 2005, it appears that the Court's effort under Rehnquist to bolster states' rights has begun to fade.

Some cracks in the Court's bulwark to protect states' rights were already appearing in the waning days of the Rehnquist Court. Prior to retiring from the bench in 2005, Chief Justice Rehnquist was on the losing side in the case *Gonzales v. Raich*, when the Court ruled that federal law enforcement officials have the authority to enforce a congressional act prohibiting the cultivation and possession of marijuana, even for physician-approved uses. Since the

[60] Linda Greenhouse, "The Rehnquist Court and Its Imperiled States' Right Legacy," *The New York Times* 13 June 2005, p. A3.

mid-1990s, nearly a dozen states have passed ballot initiatives permitting physicians to prescribe medical marijuana to patients to relieve their pain and suffering. The Court's decision allows Congress to preempt state medical marijuana laws, meaning that patients receiving herbal prescriptions can be subject to federal arrest and prosecution. With the decision, some Supreme Court watchers claim that "the federalism boomlet" that devolved responsibilities to the states "has fizzled," as "the court never reached a stable equilibrium" to enable decentralization to take hold for good.[61]

Yet in 2006, the newly constituted Roberts Court ruled 6–3 to uphold an Oregon law allowing physician-assisted suicide and to strike down the federal government's effort in 2001 to punish any doctor prescribing a lethal dose of a federally controlled drug in an effort to terminate a patient's life. The Court's majority in *Gonzales v. Oregon* found that the Department of Justice did not have the authority to use the 1971 Controlled Substances Act to override the Oregon law, which was passed via a citizen initiative in 1994, and then reaffirmed in a 1997 statewide referendum.[62] Rather, the Court ruled that the states—not the federal government—were responsible for the regulation of their own medical practices. The Court's ruling, with Roberts notably joining a dissenting opinion, provided the first evidence that the new leader of the high court was ready to retreat from Rehnquist's states' rights agenda, though some of his fellow justices were perhaps not yet ready to follow.[63]

Because of the inherent ambiguity in the U.S. Constitution, the Supreme Court has a tremendous amount of power in settling interpretive differences between the federal government and the state governments. In one sense, federalism is what five judges with lifetime tenure say it is, and the Court's interpretation evolves as its members come and go. As the recent spate of rulings on federalism suggests—with the Court deciding that Congress has the power

to criminalize the cultivation of marijuana for medical use even though a state allows it, but that Congress does not have the power to criminalize the possession of a handgun near a school or prevent a state from allowing certain citizens to take their own lives—there is some truth to this somewhat cynical interpretation of how federalism plays out in practice. Whether this drastic or not, the American Federalist system has been undoubtedly affected by the legal reasoning, political ideology, and personal preferences of the nine justices on the high court.

Federalism in an Age of Terror and Economic Crisis

As mentioned earlier, the national government's response to the terrorist attacks of September 11, 2001, as well as to subsequent threats to the security of the nation, has created a new set of challenges for the 87,000-plus local and 50 state governments. A hallmark of the "war on terror" waged by the administration of George W. Bush was the centralization of political power in Washington, DC. Yet, much of the war on terror continues to be conducted on the ground at the state and local levels. As such, many subnational governments have been severely affected, and in some cases constrained, by the crush of new federal laws and administrative rulings stemming—however indirectly—from 9/11.

9/11 and Federal Powers

During the first term of George W. Bush, the Republican-controlled Congress passed numerous laws impinging on the authority of the states. The USA PATRIOT Act, passed in 2001 just 45 days after the 9/11 attacks, expanded the federal government's police powers, including the right to access medical and tax records, book purchases, and the borrowing of library books, as well as to conduct secret home searches.

[61] Greenhouse, "The Rehnquist Court and Its Imperiled States' Right Legacy," 2005.

[62] Charles Lane, "Court Hears Case on Suicide Law," *The Washington Post* 6 October 2005, p. A4.

[63] Charles Lane, "Justices Uphold Oregon Assisted-Suicide Law," *The Washington Post* 18 January 2006, p. A1.

President Bush even authorized the National Security Agency to monitor—without preclearance from a judge—phone calls and e-mails of U.S. citizens. In response, nearly 400 local governments and a handful of states passed resolutions denouncing the PATRIOT Act. Some of these nonbinding resolutions urge local law enforcement officials to refuse requests made by federal officials that may violate an individual's civil rights under the U.S. Constitution.[64]

Reverberations from 9/11 have also touched upon substantive policy areas that seem to have little to do with homeland security. Besides concerns voiced by civil libertarians that much of the new federal legislation has curtailed the civil liberties of American citizens, Congress passed legislation increasing federal control over state and local governments in a host of policy arenas. The federal crackdown on foreign threats has impinged directly on areas normally under the control of state and local governments, enabling the federal government to reign supreme over the states. Under the ever-expansive umbrella of homeland security, federal laws regulating public health care facilities, restricting the importation of prescription drugs, nationalizing K–12 education policies, and standardizing state driver's licenses have all encroached upon policy areas traditionally delegated to the states.

The War on Terror and State Militias

One of the areas greatly affected by the post-9/11 landscape concerns the National Guard. According to Article I, Section 8 of the U.S. Constitution, the National Guard is commanded directly by governors during times of peace. Unlike federal troops, which may not enforce civilian laws unless authorized by Congress, the National Guard is permitted to enforce state laws. Immediately following 9/11, many

governors called up members of the National Guard to protect potentially vulnerable airports, nuclear power plants, water treatment facilities, and bridges in their states. In the past, governors have activated the National Guard to deal with natural disasters and civil unrest in their states—providing relief to flood victims and even securing South Central Los Angeles in 1992 when rioters killed 55 people and destroyed more than $1 billion worth of property following the acquittal of police officers on trial for the beating of motorist Rodney King.[65]

Due to the ongoing U.S. military presence in both Iraq and Afghanistan, there are fewer National Guard troops available stateside to help out in emergency situations here in the U.S. Since September 2001, over half-a-million National Guardsmen and -women (along with other "reservists") have been "involuntarily activated"—that is, called into federal service by the Pentagon.[66] Because these erstwhile "weekend warriors" may serve up to two years of active duty overseas, governors have fewer troops to deploy when natural disasters strike. In September 2005, when Hurricane Katrina hit the northern Gulf of Mexico coast, search-and-rescue and disaster relief efforts were hampered in Alabama, Florida, Louisiana, and Mississippi due to the lack of National Guard troops available. At the time, Louisiana Governor Kathleen Blanco and New Orleans Mayor Ray Nagin, both Democrats, as well as many residents of the Crescent City, were understandably angered by the slow response by the federal government.[67] Governor Blanco was so incensed that she initially refused a White House request to turn over control of the National Guard to President Bush. In response to the chaotic response in the aftermath of Hurricane Katrina, Congress in 2006 modified a 200-year-old law, the Insurrection Act of 1807, to empower the president to take

[64] Bill of Rights Defense Committee, "Resolutions Passed and Efforts Underway, By State," 2005. Available: http://www.bordc.org/index.php.

[65] Robert Preiss, "The National Guard and Homeland Defense," *Joint Forces Quarterly* 36(2005):72–78. Available: http://www.ngb.army.mil/media/transcripts/Preiss_JFQ_36_article.pdf.

[66] Lawrence Kapp, "Reserve Component Personnel Issues: Questions and Answers," Congressional Research Service, Library of Congress, 10 January 2005.

[67] Cherie D. Maestas, Lonna Rae Atkeson, Thomas Croom, and Lisa A. Bryant, "Shifting the Blame: Federalism, Media, and Public Assignment of Blame Following Hurricane Katrina," *Publius* 38(2008):609-32.

control of National Guard troops not only to put down rebellions but also for natural disasters and other public emergencies.[68]

Crises and Opportunistic Federalism

The centralization of power in Washington, DC, that followed 9/11 and Hurricane Katrina was not unexpected.[69] After every other national crisis—the Civil War, the Great Depression, and World War II—the federal government has asserted greater authority over states and localities. For over 200 years, in the aftermath of a national tragedy the national government has tried to usurp political power, preempting the authority of subnational state and local governments.[70] The pattern simply reasserted itself after 9/11, as wave after wave of federal power has washed away much of the authority of the American states.

Due to the shock of 9/11 and the public outcry to secure the nation's homeland, former President Bush increased the role of the federal government in the name of defending the homeland, and Congress obligingly followed his lead. Some, though, have questioned the increased role (and spending) of the federal government. For example, in 2005 the Republican-controlled Congress appropriated $825 million in Urban Area Security Initiative grants to the nation's cities. Congress decreased the total amount it spent on the program in 2006, but many of the new grants to combat terrorism were disbursed to cities not typically considered high-risk areas. Ironically, many members of Congress who once heralded the downsizing of the federal government when President Reagan was in office eagerly supported increasing the powers and spending of the federal government, especially if those

dollars were for homeland security programs or newly created federal jobs in their own states. Indeed, after a decade of downsizing the personnel of the federal bureaucracy, with more than 350,000 federal jobs cut during the eight years of the administration of President Clinton, the federal government created more than 100,000 new public sector jobs during Bush's first term in office.[71]

Both Republicans and Democrats use centralization arguments when they advance their policy goals and political opportunism. Backlashes against centralized policy making in the nation's capital—from the abandonment of the First Bank of the United States in 1811, to the collapse of Reconstruction in the 1870s, to the Great Society programs of the 1960s—are as predictable as the cycles of the moon. Indeed, there are growing indications that subnational resistance to contemporary federal policies and the co-optation of power by those inside the Beltway is already taking root. Somewhat hypocritically, it is now the Democrats—who since the 1930s, and especially during the Great Society years of the 1960s, called on the federal government to override states' rights—who are leading the charge to downsize the federal government's reach in many policy realms, especially in areas concerning public education and homeland security. With the American Federalist system, ideological visions of federalism are readily trumped by political considerations.

Economic Crisis and Progressive Federalism

Upon assuming office in January 2009, one of President Barack Obama's first executive orders allowed the states—and specifically, California—more leeway in setting higher standards on greenhouse gas emissions and mileage

[68] Kavan Peterson, "Governors Lose in Power Struggle over National Guard," *Stateline* 12 January 2007. Available: http://www.stateline.org/live/details/story?contentId=170453.

[69] Carmine Scavo, Richard C. Kearney, and Richard J. Kilroy, "Challenges to Federalism: Homeland Security and Disaster Response," *Publius* 38(2008):81–110.

[70] Joseph Zimmerman, "Federal Preemption under Reagan's New Federalism," *Publius* 21(1991):7–28.

[71] U.S. Office of Management and Budget, "The Budget of the United States Government, Fiscal Year 2006, Historical Tables." Available: http://www.gpoaccess.gov/usbudget/fy06/browse.html

standards for vehicles. With a stroke of his pen, Obama signaled that he was willing to give the states greater authority to deal with pressing environmental issues. If the states wanted to pass their own environmental standards and regulations that exceeded those of the federal government in an effort to save energy and clean up the environment, the Obama administration would not stand in their way.

For some, this early executive decision by the Democratic administration indicated a new wave of federalism infused by "a spirit of cooperative federalism." Observers even coined the term **progressive federalism** to describe the Obama administration's early inclination to grant the states the green light to supersede regulations set by the federal government. However, any chance that there would be cooperation between the federal government and the states was short-lived, in large part due to the Obama administration's dogged effort to push health care reform through Congress. The passage in March 2010 of the Patient Protection and Affordable Care Act (PPACA)—derisively dubbed "Obamacare" by Republicans who opposed it—killed any likelihood of bipartisanship and federal-state cooperation during Obama's first term. With conservative media outlets urging Tea Party activists to take to the streets and disrupt townhall meetings, the administration faced charges that it was employing old-school, heavy-handed, coercive federalism, with the federal government calling the shots and mandating standards for the states.

While the debate over health care is far from over, what is clear is that when it comes to regulatory actions on issues such as environmental standards, consumer protection laws, and health care during its first two years, the Obama administration broke from the previous eight years of Republican efforts to use federal powers to deregulate and let the marketplace determine policy outcomes. Some commentators have described Obama's view of intergovernmental relations as having the federal government provide a floor, not a ceiling, albeit a very high floor. States must adhere to federal guidelines and regulations, but they may go beyond them if they see fit. Others more critical of the heightened regulations emerging out of Washington, DC., see it as an open invitation for the states to become too experimental, leading to what some have called "free-for-all federalism" and a "patchwork of laws."[72]

Certainly, Congress's passage of the American Recovery and Reinvestment Act of 2009 has given the federal government more say over a range of issue areas. With over $150 billion going to the state and local governments to help close their budget gaps, the Democratic Congress and Obama administration made sure numerous strings were attached to the money, ensuring that the federal government would have a say on how the money would be spent at the subnational level. The states received an infusion of federal dollars—Medicaid funding for health care, K–12 and higher education funding, unemployment assistance, renewable energy grants, aid to combat homelessness, grants for welfare assistance, and money for thousands of "shovel-ready" transportation projects.

Summary

In his landmark dissent in *New State Ice Co. v. Liebmann* (1932), Louis Brandeis, an associate justice of the U.S. Supreme Court, coined the phrase "laboratories of democracy." Brandeis wrote, "It is one of the happy incidents of the federal system that a single courageous State may, if its citizens choose, serve as a laboratory; and try novel social and economic experiments without risk to the rest of the country." Many commentators have lauded Brandeis's minority ruling, as it highlights the genius of the United States' federal system. With the

---

[72] John Schwartz, "Obama Seems to Be Open to a Broader Role for States," *New York Times* 30 January 2009. Available: http://www.nytimes.com/2009/01/30/us/politics/30federal.html?ref=us.

premium the system places on state and local experimentation as well as competition, in theory the responsibilities for policy making are often devolved to the states.

Despite the gradual erosion of authority caused by wave after wave of federal government power crashing on their shores, the states have retained considerable policy-making discretion. The states have been at the forefront of experimentation in education, social welfare, political economy, criminal justice, and regulatory policies, and are often in competition with one another in crafting and implementing public policies. As Justice Brandeis indicated, competition among the states, as well as between the states and the federal government, encourages policy experimentation and diffusion among the states.[73] But policy experimentation is also a highly political process.[74] In the American system, the states not only do battle with the federal government but also perennially challenge one another over how to implement domestic public policies being handed down from Washington.

Since at least the turn of the twentieth century to the present day, however, the states have had to struggle to maintain their autonomy from the federal government. In addition, states have had to go it alone when the federal government has opted not to become involved in making public policy. Recently, for example, California voters approved a $3 billion bond measure, placed on the ballot via an initiative, for stem cell research. The effort to fund such research was precipitated by cutbacks by the federal government to fund stem cell research. With the State of California functioning within a competitive market, taxpayers there are willing to finance research that will in all likelihood benefit the state's economy.

In this sense, the "quiet revolution" in the states, which Carl Van Horn observed in the 1980s, is still occurring.[75] However, as states have gradually become more powerful actors, increasing their state capacities and becoming more professionalized, so too has the federal government. State governments, with their ambiguous constitutional autonomy, continue to be relegated as semisovereign units in the system of American federalism. The following chapters compare many of the institutional differences found across the states and their localities.

Key Terms

Articles of Confederation
Bill of Rights
Block grants
Categorical grants
Centralization
Coercive federalism
Commerce Clause
Confederal system
Cooperative federalism
Decentralization
Devolution

Dual federalism
Federalism
Federal preemption
Full Faith and Credit Clause
General Revenue Sharing (GRS)
Incorporation of the Bill of Rights
Intergovernmental relations
National Supremacy Clause
Necessary and Proper Clause
Privileges and Immunities Clause
Progressive Federalism

[73] Karen Mossberger, *The Politics of Ideas and the Spread of Enterprise Zones* (Washington, DC: Georgetown University Press, 2000).

[74] Andrew Karch, *Democratic Laboratories: Policy Diffusion among the American States* (Ann Arbor: University of Michigan Press, 2007); Charles R. Shipan and Craig Volden, "Bottom-Up Federalism: The Diffusion of Antismoking Policies from U.S. Cities to States," *American Journal of Political Science* 50(2006):825–43.

[75] Karl Van Horn, *The State of the States* (Washington, DC: CQ Press, 1989).

Reserve Clause

Unfunded mandate

Unitary system

Discussion Questions

(1) The federal government's powers expanded following the September 11, 2001, terrorist attacks. Do you think the federal government's increased powers are warranted? Has the federal government encroached too far on states' rights?

(2) What are the advantages and disadvantages of a Federalist system of government compared to a unitary or confederal system of government?

(3) How did the powers of Congress under the Articles of Confederation compare to those of the 1787 U.S. Constitution?

(4) Has President Obama's 2009 federal stimulus altered the relationship between the states and the federal government? Do you think it constitutes a new form of federalism, what some are calling "progressive federalism?"

Suggested Readings

Beer, Samuel. *To Make a Nation: The Rediscovery of American Federalism.* 1993. Cambridge, MA: Harvard University Press.

Conlan, Timothy. *New Federalism: Intergovernmental Reform from Nixon to Reagan.* 1988. Washington, DC: Brookings Institution.

Elazar, Daniel. 1984. *American Federalism: A View from the States*, 3rd ed. New York: Harper & Row, 1984.

Karch, Andrew. *Democratic Laboratories: Policy Diffusion among the States.* 2007. Ann Arbor, MI: University of Michigan Press.

Walker, David. *The Rebirth of Federalism.* 1995. Chatham, NJ: Chatham House.

Zimmerman, Joseph. *Contemporary American Federalism.* 1992. Westport, CT: Praeger.

Websites

American Enterprise Institute (http://www.federalismproject.org): AEI's Federalism Project provides scholarly research on American federalism and monitors recent developments.

Brookings Institution (http://www.brookings.edu): Brookings' Governance Studies Program provides numerous scholarly reports on the developments of American federalism.

Institute of Federalism (http://www.federalism.ch): An international research center based in Switzerland that focuses on questions of culture and federalism.

Publius (http://publius.oxfordjournals.org): *Publius: The Journal of Federalism* is the leading journal devoted to federalism, with scholarly articles examining the latest developments and trends on federalism and intergovernmental relations.

Urban Institute (http://www.urban.org/center/anf/index.cfm): UI's Assessing the New Federalism project examines federal programs that affect municipalities, documents how children and families are affected by these programs, and provides national survey data on the topic.

3

Participation, Elections, and Representation

INTRODUCTION: IS ALL POLITICS LOCAL?

Thomas Jefferson, who served as a legislator in colonial Virginia, suggested that a healthy democracy depends on having ordinary citizens engaged with local politics.[1] Jefferson's sentiments were shared by Alexis de Tocqueville, an early observer of American democracy. Jefferson and de Tocqueville stressed that people could best learn how to govern themselves and remain true citizens by participating in local politics.[2] Today, many perceive that access to elected officials in Washington, DC, depends on large campaign contributions, whereas state and local officials are a short drive or bus ride away. One might assume that because state and local officials are fairly easy to contact, and because state and local politics are immediately accessible and visible to citizens, more people would participate in local than national politics. Clearly, political participation must be easier, and more common, closer to home.

By one key measure, the opposite is true. The average person is far more likely to vote in national elections than in his or her state and local contests. This chapter examines this paradox of participation: Despite the fact that state and local governments are closest to people, Americans participate more in national than state and local elections.[3] Despite many attempts to increase voter participation in the United States, turnout at state and local elections remains low. The decline in participation, furthermore, has been most dramatic in U.S. central cities.[4]

[1] See Thomas Jefferson, *Notes on the State of Virginia* (1785); see also John Winthrop, "A Model of Christian Charity" (1630).

[2] See Alexis de Tocqueville, *Democracy in America*, 2 vols. (1835–40). See also Robert Dahl, "The City and the Future of Democracy," *American Political Science Review* 61 (1967).

[3] Participation in local elections is also lower than in national elections elsewhere. For Britain, see Collin Rallings and Michael Thrasher, "Local Electoral Participation in Britain," *Parliamentary Affairs* 65(2003):700–715. In the Netherlands, see Henl van de Kolk, "Turnout in Local Elections: Explanations of Individual and Municipal Turnout Differences" (paper presented at the European Consortium for Political Research Joint Workshops, 2003).

[4] Esther Fuchs, Lorraine Minnite, and Robert Shapiro, "Political Capital and Political Participation" (unpublished manuscript).

Forms of Political Participation

Citizens interact with their government in many ways—the most visible is electing their representatives and instructing them on how to behave. Elections are by no means the only manner through which people participate in the political process. Voting and elections are often given disproportionate attention because of their capacity to alter who controls government and to grant legitimacy on those who serve as elected officials. Low rates of participation in elections, then, may be a cause for concern. At some point, turnout at elections might be so low that the actions of elected officials lack legitimacy in the eyes of those who did not participate. But how low is too low? From 1972 to 2000, most Americans over age 18 did not vote in presidential elections. By 2008, turnout in presidential elections increased to the highest level since 1968,[5] but with state, local and congressional elections, the norm seems to be that most people don't participate. As Table 3.1 illustrates, few people vote in "odd year" (that is, not during the year of a presidential election) state elections and even fewer in local elections.

Scholars and democratic theorists offer us limited guidance about how much public participation can shrink before the legitimacy of a democratic government evaporates. It seems clear, however, that fewer are participating now than in previous decades and that there are growing differences between those who do participate and those who do not.[6] If participating citizens were largely similar to nonparticipating citizens, low levels of political participation might not be such a worry. As we see below, however, there is clear evidence of **participation bias**—or differences between those citizens who participate and those who do not.[7]

Table 3.1

Levels of Voter Participation in the United States in Different Races

Voting-Age Population Participating	%
2008 presidential race	56.9
2007 gubernatorial races	38.1 (LA, KY, and MS)
2006 congressional race	37.0
2000 California local races	30.0

Source: Federal Election Commission; Zoltan Hanjal and Paul Lewis, "Municipal Institutions and Voter Turnout in Local Elections," *Urban Affairs Quarterly* 38(5)(2003): 654–68; California, Kentucky, and Mississippi secretaries of state; and United States Elections Project, http://elections.gmu.edu.

Participation Is Much More Than Voting

Voting involves electing representatives, and in many places that use direct democracy (see Chapter 4), voting also involves public decisions to approve or reject policy proposals. There are many other ways, in addition to voting, that Americans are engaged politically. Some of these other forms of political participation may be seen as attempts to instruct elected officials how to act after elections are held. Indeed, all of what governments do—the laws, policies, rules, and regulations they pass—takes place between elections, after we have voted. People participate by joining groups, lobbying, contacting officials, attending meetings, and writing letters, among other activities.

Why Bother? The Stakes Are High Although most Americans do not usually vote in their state and local elections, political engagement at the local level is relatively impressive when compared with the public's engagement with national political campaigns and presidential elections. If public opinion surveys are to be believed, many (and occasionally most) adult

---

[5] In 2008, turnout was 56.9 percent of voting-age population and 62.4 percent of voting-eligible population.

[6] Stephen Macedo et al., *Democracy at Risk: How Political Choices Undermine Citizen Participation, and What We Can Do about It* (Washington, DC: Brookings Institution, 2005).

[7] See, for example, Sidney Verba, Kay Schlozman, and Henry E. Brady, *Voice and Equality: Civic Voluntarism in American Politics* (Cambridge, MA: Harvard University Press, 1995).

Americans show up to vote in presidential elections once every four years, but they spend little time actively engaged working on national political issues. More Americans say that they spend their time working on issues that face their schools and their communities rather than spend time involved with high-profile presidential elections. This makes some sense, given the stakes. In the previous chapter, we discussed the scope of what state and local governments do. Most critically, state and local governments spend about 17 cents of every dollar generated by the American economy (far more than that spent by the federal government). The U.S. Supreme Court has given states wide latitude over many areas of policy. Cities and counties control nearly all aspects of land-use decisions, and state and local courts administer the vast majority of civil and criminal cases. Furthermore, over 95 percent of all elected positions in the United States are at the local level.

Participation at state and local levels, then, is likely to have a substantial impact on what government does. Americans are actually relatively optimistic about their ability to accomplish things at the local level. As Table 3.2 illustrates, nearly three-quarters believed that "people like you" can have a moderate or big impact in making their community a better place to live. Table 3.3 illustrates that although Americans are fairly cynical about politics generally, and most distrust the federal government, people are much more trusting of their local governments and less likely to believe that they have "no say" at the local level compared to the national level.

Yet, the effect of political participation might be understood in terms of the cliché, "The squeaky wheel gets the grease." That is, if we assume that governments respond mostly to those who participate, and less to those who do not, we can understand who gets what from government, at least in part, by considering who participates.

Who Participates? Who Does Not? Political participation in nearly all forms—voting,

Table 3.2

Local Political Efficacy (N = 3,003)

Overall, How Much Impact Do You Think People Like You Can Have in Making Your Community a Better Place to Live?	%
No impact at all	4
A small impact	19
A moderate impact	42
A big impact	35

Source: Social Capital Benchmark Survey, 2000.

Table 3.3

Public Trust and Efficacy in Local and National Government (N = 3,003)

Trust Local or National Government to Do What Is Right	Local (%)	State (%)	National (%)
Always or most of the time	52	33	26
Some of the time/hardly ever	48	66	74

Source: CNN/Opinion Research Corporation, 2010.

People Like Me Have No Say in What Local or National Government Does[a]	Local (%)	National (%)
Agree	35	41
Disagree	62	50

[a]Question to respondents was as follows: "Do you agree or disagree that 'people like me have no say in what the [federal] government does' and 'People running my community don't really care much about what happens to me'?"

Source: National Election Study, 2000; and Social Capital Benchmark Survey, 2000.

attending meetings, contacting public officials, and contributing to political candidates—is not behavior that is randomly distributed across the population. Depending upon the form of participation we are examining, there may be substantial differences between those who participate and those who do not. Consider the forms of participation listed in Table 3.4. There are striking differences across income groups. The wealthy tend to be overrepresented

Table 3.4

Levels of Local Participation in the United States (N = 3,003)

In the Last 12 Months, Did You ...	Overall (%)	Poor (%)	Wealthy (%)
Attend a public meeting to discuss school or town affairs?	45	31	63
Work on a community project?	38	23	60
Attend a PTA or school group meeting?	24	14	34
Participate in a neighborhood or homeowner association meeting?	22	12	41
Participate in a group that took action for local reform?	18	9	30

Note: Poor = household income is $20,000 or less; wealthy = $100,000 or more.

Source: Social Capital Benchmark Survey, 2000.

In the Last 12 Months, Did You ...	Overall (%)	Rent (%)	Own (%)
Attend a public meeting to discuss school or town affairs?	45	36	49
Work on a community project?	38	28	42
Attend a PTA or school group meeting?	24	19	26
Participate in a neighborhood or homeowner association meeting?	22	14	26
Participate in a group that took action for local reform?	18	15	19

Source: Social Capital Benchmark Survey, 2000.

relative to average people and less wealthy people in several forms of local-level political participation. Most wealthy people say they go to public meetings and work on community projects. Most of the least affluent people do not. It is important to note that wealth itself and education alone are not what cause people to participate in politics. Education and wealth lower the costs of becoming engaged with politics. By costs, we mean such things as time and the difficulty of collecting and processing political information.

Voting

When we consider voting, there are clear differences between those citizens who vote and those who do not. One study found that although 55 percent of all American adults earned lower- to middle-level incomes, this majority group represented only 46 percent of voters in national elections, 43 percent of campaign hours volunteered, and just 16 percent of campaign dollars provided to candidates.[8] This participation gap between the affluent and less wealthy may even be greater in state and local elections that have lower levels of citizen participation. The voting population tends to overrepresent the affluent, older voters, people from white-collar professions, people with higher levels of education, and those who have jobs.[9] This said, voters are probably more representative of the general citizenry than other types of participants, such as campaign contributors and members of organized political groups.[10]

Voter turnout in local elections is also significantly higher in cities with a higher social status population and in places with more voters who are over 65 years old.[11] Public opinion surveys suggest that homeownership may have no

[8] Verba et al., *Voice and Equality.*

[9] Jan Leighley and Jonathan Nagler, "Socioeconomic Class Bias in Turnout, 1964–1988: The Voters Remain the Same," *American Political Science Review* 86(3)(1992):725–36; and Jan Leighley and Jonathan Nagler, "Individual and Systemic Influences on Turnout: Who Votes?" *Journal of Politics* 54(3)(1992):718–40.

[10] Verba et al., *Voice and Equality.*

[11] Zoltan Hanjal and Paul Lewis, "Municipal Institutions and Voter Turnout in Local Elections," *Urban Affairs Quarterly* 38(5)(2003):654–68.

impact on whether someone votes in national elections,[12] but the incentives to vote that come with homeownership—being concerned about property values and property taxes—are more likely to be felt in local elections. Records of actual votes cast in a nonpartisan Atlanta mayoral race, for example, demonstrated that homeowners are more likely to vote than renters. The stimulating effect of property tax issues on voter turnout was famously seen in California in 1978, where more people voted on a property tax cut measure (Proposition 13) than voted in the gubernatorial race on the same ballot.

As Table 3.4 illustrates, homeowners are more likely than renters to report many other forms of local political participation. With lower levels of participation, renters and the less affluent might be expected to have less influence in local politics relative to their share of the population.

Contacting and Contributing

The participation gap between rich and poor is even more striking when we look at the "activists"—people who donate their time and money to candidates and who contact government officials. Sixty percent of all reported "contacts" with public officials came from the top 45 percent of income earners.[13] Studies of people who contact local officials suggest that contacting increases with social status and income, although contacts based on needing help from the government may be related to having less income.[14] It's not just income alone that causes contacting. Wealth corresponds with education, with political skills, and with **efficacy**—the sense that political involvement can actually make a difference.

Attending Meetings

State and local politics differ from national politics in that the actions of government are more accessible locally. Many aspects of state and local government require open public meetings that provide for public comment. Individual citizens and people representing organized groups may attend without having to bear substantial travel costs. Mandates that government provide open meetings do not necessarily ensure that officials give full consideration to all citizen comments.

Interest Group Activity

In addition to contributing to groups, citizens join and serve on boards of homeowners' associations, school groups, and many different voluntary political and social groups that work to shape their states and communities. An influential theory of interest group activity, collective action theory, predicts that groups seeking economic benefits from governments (such as tax breaks and public subsidies) are more likely to remain organized and well funded than groups seeking "public" benefits, such as parks and consumer protections.[15] Records detailing which political groups register to lobby the federal government are consistent with this theory. Sixty-one percent of political action committees (PACs)—including those spending the most on lobbying—are affiliated with corporations, trade groups, professional associations, and the health care industry. Only 32 percent were "nonconnected" ideological and public interest groups, and 6 percent were labor groups.[16]

At the local level, the presence of organized suburban neighborhood associations may have

---

[12] Eric Plutzer, "Voter Turnout and the Life Cycle: A Latent Growth Curve Analysis" (paper presented at the Midwest Political Science Association meeting, 1997).

[13] Verba et al., *Voice and Equality.*

[14] Elaine Sharp, "Citizen Initiated Contacting of Local Officials and Socio-Economic Status," *American Political Science Review* 76(1982):109–15; but see Rodney Hero, "Explaining Citizen-Initiated Contacting of Government Officials," *Social Science Quarterly* 67(1986):626–35; and Michael Hirlinger, "Citizen-Initiated Contacting of Local Officials," *Journal of Politics* 54(1992):553–64.

[15] Mancur Olson, *The Logic of Collective Action* (Cambridge, MA: Harvard University Press, 1965).

[16] As of July 2008. See Federal Elections Commission, http://www.fec.gov/press/press2008/20080812paccount.shtml.

an upper-status bias, reflecting that affluent suburbanites have resources to organize and work collectively to protect themselves (and their property values) from unwanted development.[17] Survey data reported in Table 3.4 also show large differences across income groups in who gets involved with local political groups. Compared to those from households in the bottom one-fifth of all incomes, people in the top fifth of all incomes were twice as likely to be involved with parent-teacher association (PTA) groups and other school groups. They were three times more likely to be involved with neighborhood groups and almost four times more likely to be involved with a local political reform group.

Grassroots Political Activity

Many interest groups function by collecting contributions from members to pay for the work of full-time staff. Groups with a broader base of support may rely on rank-and-file members or on the general public to bring attention to their issue. As examples, neighborhood groups may attempt to pack city council hearings with residents worried about the impact of proposed developments, or to promote neighborhood interests. Crime and environmental degradation have prompted grassroots activism at the local level. Grassroots neighborhood groups also organize to fight poverty, promote quality housing, and resist urban renewal. Prominent figures supported by grassroots neighborhood groups have been elected mayor in cities such as Boston, Cleveland, Portland, and Santa Monica, California.

Social Movements and Protest

In addition to joining formal groups, people participate in larger, broad-based social movements. Social movements may comprise many loosely affiliated groups that share a common purpose of sustained, mass-based participation throughout a large number of communities in order to mobilize public opinion and change

public policy. Formal channels of participation in social movements are sometimes difficult to define but may include the forms discussed above as well as lawful protest, public demonstrations, and peaceful civil disobedience.

The American civil rights movement serves as a classic example of a broad, mass-based social movement working in many communities to change the nation's perceptions of racial segregation and voting rights abuses.

How Many Citizens Participate?

Records show low levels of voting at the state and local levels, yet many American adults are politically active at the local level. Between elections, these politically active citizens try to shape policy by attending meetings and testifying at public hearings. In 2000, 45 percent of Americans reported that they had attended at least one meeting in the last 12 months to discuss affairs related to their town or schools. Another 20 percent said they attended at least two such meetings in the previous year. Significant numbers also reported working on community projects and working with groups that promoted social and political change in their communities.[18] Political participation can also take forms such as circulating petitions, attending protests, contacting elected officials, writing letters, and

Participants in the 1965 civil rights march from Selma, Alabama, to Montgomery, the state capital. This march and others brought attention to barriers that kept blacks from voting. Participants were attacked and beaten by police before they reached Montgomery.

Peter Pettus/The Library of Congress

[17] John Logan and Gordana Rabrenovic, "Neighborhood Associations: Their Issues, Their Allies," *Urban Affairs Quarterly* 26(1990):68–94.

[18] Social Benchmark Survey.

the like. Over 50,000,000 Americans belong to homeowners' associations, with over 1 million serving on boards and committees. Although these numbers are impressive, local political participation seems to be declining. By 1990, half as many people reported voting in local elections than did in 1967.[19]

Barriers to Participation at the State and Local Levels

As Figure 3.1 illustrates, there is substantial variation in voter participation across the 50 states, just as there is across American towns and cities.

Minnesota and Maine led the nation in the percentage of adults over 18 who voted in the 2008 presidential election, with over 70 percent of their **voting-age population** (all people over age 18) having participated. Hawaii, Texas, and Arizona rank lowest, with less than half of the adults in these states voting. These vastly different participation rates are a result of many factors. States like Minnesota have far more people with traits known to correspond with interest in politics. A higher proportion of Minnesotans have college degrees and higher income levels than people in states like Texas. Maine and Minnesota also have far fewer noncitizens than Texas and Arizona. Only U.S. citizens can vote in presidential elections, which means we should also think of voter turnout as a percentage of

Figure 3.1

Voter Participation in the 2008 Presidential Election, by State

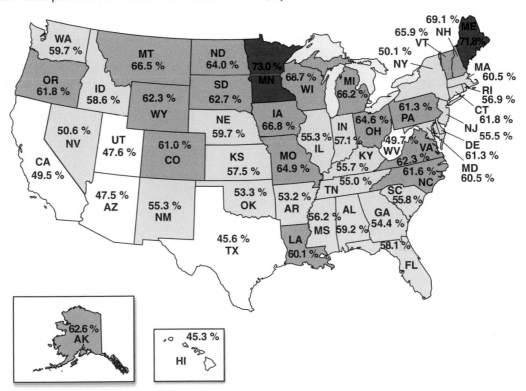

Percentage of all state residents 18 years of age or over voting in the November 2008 general election

[19] Verba et al., *Voice and Equality*, p. 72.

a state's **voting-eligible population**—that is, the proportion of citizens who vote who are not disenfranchised by felony convictions. States differ as to the rules they use to define which citizens are eligible to participate in elections, and they use different rules about when (or if) a person must register to vote prior to an election.

Race-Based and Gender-Based Barriers

States set many rules that affect who votes and who does not. Although the 15th Amendment to the U.S. Constitution (1870) says that the right to vote cannot be denied "on account of race or color," the amendment was substantially meaningless for nearly a century. In the latter half of the nineteenth century, many states erected substantial barriers to the voting process in order to prevent African Americans from voting. Some rules requiring that voters register far in advance of elections were often adopted in response to the perception that corrupt party machines (see Chapter 5) had their supporters "vote early, and vote often." Other barriers were racially motivated, such as racial gerrymandering, closing polling places, not allowing voters to register, implementing **literacy tests** and **poll taxes** (charging a fee to vote), and establishing **grandfather clauses** that allowed whites to vote regardless of whether they paid a poll tax or passed a literacy test. Such rules were used to reverse the expansion of African American voting rights that occurred after the Civil War.[20]

Prior to 1920, states could also deny women the right to vote, and most did. Utah and Washington allowed women to vote briefly in the 1880s, and the Territory of Wyoming gave women the vote in 1869. Idaho (1896),

Washington (1910), and California (1911) were the first states to extend voting rights to women. After the 19th Amendment (1920) was adopted, women won the right to vote in any state, but racially motivated barriers to voting persisted.

Prior to the civil rights movement and Voting Rights Act of 1965, local election officials had the discretion to apply these barriers selectively, in order to disenfranchise blacks but not whites.[21] In some places, blacks who attempted to register faced economic reprisals, physical violence, and even death. In 1964, for example, only 7 percent of blacks in Mississippi were registered to vote, compared to 70 percent of whites. In Alabama, 19 percent of blacks were registered in 1965, compared to 70 percent of whites.[22] At the time the Voting Rights Act was adopted, several southern states required people to pass subjective literacy tests in order to register, and four southern states required voters to pay a tax to vote in state elections.[23] The Voting Rights Act applied to states, counties, and cities that had low minority voter participation. It gave the federal government the authority to enforce the right to register and vote and allowed federal observers to monitor elections. It gave federal authorities the power to review and "pre-clear" any changes to voter registration and election rules in jurisdictions covered by the act in order to restore voting rights. It also ended literacy tests in six southern states with low registration levels (Alabama, Georgia, Louisiana, Mississippi, Virginia, and much of North Carolina).

As late as 1970, 18 states still had literacy tests that prospective voters were required to pass in order to register (these were finally banned in 1975 due to their history of discriminatory application).[24] In 1972, the U.S. Supreme Court moved to end state laws requiring that a person

[20] See Alexander Keyssar, *The Right to Vote: The Contested History of Democracy in the United States* (New York: Basic Books, 2000).

[21] U.S. Department of Justice, http://www.usdoj.gov/crt/voting/intro/intro_c.htm.

[22] Bernard Grofman, Lisa Handley, and Richard G. Niemi, *Minority Representation and the Quest for Voting Equality* (New York: Cambridge Press, 1992).

[23] Chandler Davidson, "The Evolution of Voting Rights Law," in Grofman, Handley, and Niemi, *Minority Representation*.

[24] In *Oregon v. Mitchell* (1970), the U.S. Supreme Court upheld a temporary five-year federal ban on the tests. The ban was made permanent in 1975.

reside in a jurisdiction at least one year prior to registering to vote. In 1975, the act was amended to apply to states and counties with low registration levels and large non-English-speaking populations (all of Alaska, Arizona, and Texas and many areas in other states). The act was also amended to give plaintiffs greater latitude to challenge election practices—including at-large plans—that can be shown to dilute minority representation.

Despite Civil War–era amendments to the U.S. Constitution extending voting rights regardless of race, it took well over a century for the U.S. Congress and the U.S. Supreme Court to strike down the most overt prohibitions on voting.[25] But the gap between white and black registration levels in southern states covered by the Voting Rights Act was nearly eliminated by 1988 as a result of the Voting Rights Act. This does not mean that all barriers were eliminated by the act. Some state and local governments responded to increased minority participation by changing how they conducted their elections in order to dilute the influence of minority voters. The act is still used to guard against such practices. In 2006, Congress voted to reauthorize the act for another 25 years. Whether racially motivated or not, state policies that made it difficult to register and vote are still more likely to be present in states with greater racial diversity.[26]

Comparisons Help Us Understand

TAXATION WITHOUT REPRESENTATION: SHOULD NONCITIZENS VOTE?

The U.S. Constitution stipulates that the right to vote in federal elections extends to citizens, but this clause does not apply to state and local elections. States can determine if legal immigrant noncitizens are eligible to vote. Noncitizens could previously vote in many states, but voting rights were eliminated by the 1920s when America closed its doors to immigration. Immigration was later reestablished, without state and local voting rights. An estimated 20 million legal immigrants now work in the United States and pay taxes. They may also serve in the military, but they cannot vote. Historically, granting the right to vote to immigrants was seen as a method to get people engaged with politics. Advocates of voting rights for noncitizens note that America's noncitizens could vote in colonial times and in many U.S. states until an anti-immigrant backlash in the 1920s. Until 1926, 22 states and territories allowed immigrants to vote in local elections.[1]

Noncitizens are allowed to vote in local elections and or national elections in over 40 nations. A few places in the United States, such as Takoma Park, Maryland, do allow legal immigrants to vote in local elections. New York City and Chicago have allowed legal immigrants to vote in school board elections. Voters in the Massachusetts cities of Amherst and Cambridge passed initiatives that allowed noncitizens to vote in local elections.

Opponents argue that if immigrants want the full rights of citizens, including voting rights, they should become citizens. They also worry that if noncitizens are registered to vote in local races, that it would be difficult to keep them from voting in national elections.[2]

Notes
1. Alexandra Marks, "Should Noncitizens Vote?" *Christian Science Monitor*, 27 April 2004.
2. Brock Parker, "Voting Rights on Agenda: Proposal Gives Say to Immigrants" *Boston Globe*. 30 September 2010.

[25] Chandler Davidson and Bernard Grofman, eds., *Quiet Revolution in the South: The Impact of Voting Rights Act 1965–1990* (Princeton, NJ: Princeton University Press, 1994).

[26] Kim Q. Hill and Jan Leighley, "Racial Diversity, Voter Turnout, and Mobilizing Institutions in the United States," *American Politics Quarterly* 27(3) (1999):275–95; and Shaun Bowler and Todd Donovan, "State-Level Barriers to Participation" (paper presented at the American Political Science Association meeting, September 2005).

Mississippi and South Carolina—which have some of the highest proportions of black residents in the United States—had the longest requirements for preregistration before elections (30 days in 2010). Polls were open for 14 or 15 hours in Connecticut, Rhode Island, Maine, and parts of New Hampshire on Election Day 2008 but for just 12 hours in racially diverse Florida, Georgia, Mississippi, South Carolina, and Texas.

Registration Barriers

Although many of the most egregious barriers to voting are now gone, there are still important differences in registration laws across the states. In 1995, the National Voter Registration Act (also called the "Motor Voter" Act) went into effect, requiring that states accept mail-in registrations for federal elections if postmarked 30 days prior to an election and requiring that public agencies provide voter registration forms. States continue to have discretion to allow voter registration on the same day of the election or to have waiting periods of up to 30 days. States also have the discretion to adopt laws that make it easier (or harder) to vote by mail. States with higher proportions of African American residents continue to have more barriers to registration and easy voting.[27]

Having registration offices open for shorter hours, and having closing dates for registration further from the election, can depress turnout.[28] Conversely, states that allow registration on the day of the election rank highest in voter participation. As of 2010, there were 10 states where unregistered voters could nonetheless vote on election day (Idaho, Iowa, Maine, Minnesota, Montana, New Hampshire, North Carolina,

North Dakota, Wisconsin, and Wyoming). North Dakota does not require voter registration, and Connecticut allows election day registration for presidential elections. One study estimated that turnout in the 2008 election was 7 percent higher in states with election day registration, but these states already had higher turnout so the effect of election day registration was probably lower.[29]

Districting Barriers

A larger institutional barrier to voting may be found in the nature of American elections themselves. Elections for nearly every seat in the U.S. House of Representatives, most state legislatures, and many city and county councils are conducted in single-member districts under **winner-take-all election** rules. This means that the single candidate winning the most votes represents a specific geographical area. Winner-take-all election rules tend to produce two-party systems. That is, because there is nothing to be won for candidates from parties that always place third or fourth, people fear wasting their vote on such parties, and only the largest parties survive.[30] Winner-take-all elections are the main reason why the U.S. Congress, every state legislature, and nearly every local partisan council are dominated by representatives of just one or two political parties.

District boundaries used to elect representatives must be redrawn on occasion, or redistricted, to account for shifts in population. Critics of the redistricting process note that incumbents can have too much influence over how their district lines are drawn, such that elected officials are picking their voters rather than voters picking the officials. Democrat

[27] Bowler and Donovan, "State-Level Barriers to Participation."

[28] Leighley and Nagler (1992); Jan Leighley and Jonathan Nagler, "Individual and Systemic Influences on Turnout: Who Votes?" *Journal of Politics* 54(1992):718–41; Steven Rosenstone and Raymond Wolfinger, "The Effect of Registration Laws on Voter Turnout," *American Political Science Review* 72(1978):22–45.

[29] Stuart Comstock-Gay, Steven Carbo, and Regina Eaton, "Voters with Election Day Registration." Available: demos.org; Michael Hanmer, Discount Voting: Voter Registration Reforms and their Effects (Cambridge, MA Cambridge University Press, 2009).

[30] William Riker, "The Two-Party System and Duverger's Law: An Essay on the History of Political Science," *American Political Science Review* 76(4) (1982):753–66.

incumbents have incentives to make sure that their districts' boundaries include as many loyal Democratic voters as possible, whereas Republican incumbents have incentives to pack their districts with as many Republican voters as possible.[31] In many states, partisan elected officials have near total control over how these districts are drawn. In other states, legislators pick "bipartisan" commissions to make district maps or have the courts settle the issues. Parties keep detailed records of block-by-block voting trends and use sophisticated computer mapping programs to design their preferred districts.

When elections are one-sided, there is less campaign activity. When elections are contested by just one major party, there may be no campaign. Without campaigns, voters are probably less likely to notice that an election is being held. Turnout decline in American congressional elections since 1960 corresponds with a decline in competitive elections, as more districts are drawn to be safe for just one party or the other. Congressional and state legislative races are often uncontested by one of the major parties because they have no chance to win. In recent years, nearly one-third of all state legislative races have not been contested by one of the major parties.[32] When fewer races are contested, fewer candidates campaign, and fewer citizens are likely to be engaged by the election.[33]

Who Is Ineligible?

State governments set rules about who is eligible to vote in their state and local elections.

They have the power to decide if certain groups of people may or may not vote in state and local elections (federal law regulates who may vote in federal contests). Depending on the state, people found to be "mentally incompetent," convicted felons who served their time, people in prison, people on parole, and legal immigrant noncitizens may be banned from voting. Or, depending on the state's laws, they may be permitted to vote.

California, New Jersey, Arizona, Texas, and Florida had more noncitizens per capita in 2008 than any other state. Noncitizens typically cannot vote. Florida, Texas, and Mississippi also have far more inmates, parolees, felons, and ex-felons than the average state and do not allow many of them to vote.[34] Felon voting bans were adopted by states in the late 1860s and 1870s as the 15th Amendment was extending voting rights to African Americans.[35] States with larger nonwhite prison populations were more likely to ban convicted felons from voting than states where more whites were in the prison population. States with more white prisoners in the twentieth century were subsequently more likely to soften or repeal these laws than states with higher African American prison populations.[36] Southern states have been significantly less likely to repeal laws that prevent ex-felons from ever voting again. One of the largest sources in the decline in voter turnout in recent years is the steep increase in the proportion of citizens who are losing their voting rights due to felony convictions, often for drug possession.[37]

[31] Rob Ritchie, *Monopoly Politics (Report by the Center for Voting and Democracy. Washington, DC, 1997)*; and Center for Voting and Democracy.

[32] NCSL report. "Many state legislative races are uncontested." Associated Press. October 30, 2006. Available: http://www.msnbc.msn.com/id/15446775/.

[33] Todd Donovan and Shaun Bowler, *Reforming the Republic: Democratic Institutions for the New America* (Upper Saddle River, NJ: Prentice Hall, 2004).

[34] Over 1 percent of the Texas adult population are felons or ex-felons. The U.S. average is 0.67 percent. See Michael McDonald, Voter Turnout Project, George Mason University. Ex-felons may vote in Texas but parolees, inmates, and probationers may not. Mississippi and Florida also prevent ex-felons from voting.

[35] See Jeff Manza and Christopher Uggen, *Locked Out: Felon Disenfranchisement and American Democracy* (New York: Oxford University Press, 2005).

[36] Angela Behrens, Christopher Uggen, and Jeff Manza, "Ballot Manipulation and the 'Menace of Negro Domination': Racial Threat and Felon Disenfranchisement in the United States, 1850–2002," *American Journal of Sociology* 109(2003):559–605.

[37] Michael P. McDonald and Sam Popkin, "The Myth of the Vanishing Voter," *American Political Science Review* 95(2000):963–74.

Where Are the Greatest Barriers?

Figure 3.2 illustrates which states had the most barriers to voting and registration as of 2005. We identified 10 restrictions that states may place on voting and registration and then assigned a state one point for each restriction the state maintains. Restrictions include requiring that voters register at least 20 days in advance, not allowing polling place registration, not allowing parolees or felons to vote, having shorter than average polling place hours, allowing no early voting, placing restrictions on "no excuse" absentee voting, and other similar rules.

The state with the most of these restrictions on voting is Mississippi (scoring a perfect 10), followed by several other southern states, including Kentucky (9), Virginia and Alabama (8), and Maryland, Florida, Georgia, and Texas (7). Nevada, New York, and Pennsylvania also score high (7). North Dakota places the least restrictions on voting (0.5), followed by Vermont, Oregon, and Maine (2) as well as Utah (2.5), California (2.5), and New Hampshire (3). Other things being equal, states with more of these barriers had lower participation in the 2004 presidential election. On average, every three restrictions that a state maintains were associated with 2.4 percent less voter turnout. Rules requiring advance registration have particularly noticeable effects. Every 10 additional days that a state required for advance registration

---

Figure 3.2

Barriers to Voting in the U.S. States, by State

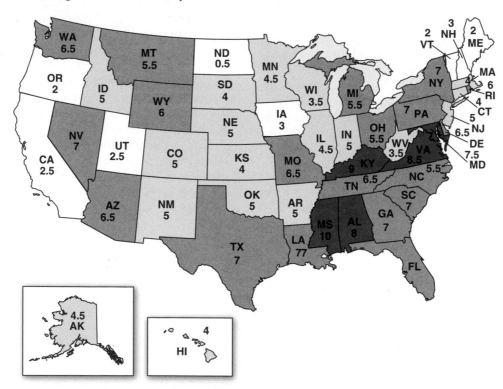

States are ranked on a scale of 0 to 10, with low scores representing few barriers to registration and voting and high scores representing more barriers. The index represents barriers such as long advance dates for registration, a prohibition on absentee voting, a prohibition on early voting, a restriction on parolees and felons voting, and shorter-than-average polling place hours.

were associated with 2.5 percent less turnout in 2004.[38]

Party System Barriers

Local political party organizations traditionally played a large role in mobilizing voters and getting them to participate in politics. Local party "machines" once relied heavily on large numbers of loyal workers to get their supporters to the polls. Some party workers could be rewarded with municipal jobs in exchange for their work on behalf of the party's electoral efforts. Party workers checked the sign-in sheets at polling places to track who had not yet voted, tracked down those who had not yet voted, gave people rides to polling places, and called on neighbors to remind them to vote. It helped if local elections were contested under party labels and held in synch with high-profile national races. Party labels and local party organizations lowered the "cost" that voters faced when voting. Party labels—usually Democrat or Republican—told voters a lot about relatively unknown candidates seeking state and local offices.

Decades of anti-party reform laws passed by state legislatures have changed the role of parties in many states.[39] Civil service reforms make it difficult—if not illegal—for parties to reward their supporters with public sector jobs. Nowadays, nearly 75 percent of local elections are nonpartisan. Nearly all local elections (95 percent) in western states are nonpartisan, whereas most local contests in the northeastern states remain partisan.[40] Turnout remains higher today in local partisan elections. Many places also have their nonpartisan local elections in "off years," out of synch with higher profile contests—further depressing turnout.

Historians demonstrate that many of these anti-party reforms were adopted at the start of the twentieth century to "depoliticize" local politics and ensure that the influence of working-class people and racial and ethnic minorities would be diluted in favor of people who wanted to improve the business climate in their cities.[41] The drop in party mobilization of voters has been found to be one of the largest factors behind low turnout in the United States.[42] With the decline of parties, Americans may now be less likely to have someone knock on their door to encourage them to vote. However, experiments in cities like Columbus, Ohio, and Raleigh, North Carolina, demonstrate that face-to-face visits with voters before a local election can increase participation by about 10 percent.[43] However, few organizations have the resources to mount large-scale, door-to-door canvassing drives.

Noncompetitive Elections

Local elections may be less competitive than in previous decades. This means elections have less ability to get people's attention or provide them with information about local affairs. One study estimated that the number of candidates seeking local office dropped by 15 percent from 1974 to 1994.[44] Another study found that 17 percent of mayoral candidates ran unopposed in California in 2003 and found that seven California cities cancelled their elections that year due to lack of competition.[45]

---

[38] Analysis from Bowler and Donovan, "State-Level Barriers to Participation."

[39] Walter Dean Burnham, *Critical Elections and the Mainsprings of American Politics* (New York: Norton, 1970), chs. 4–5.

[40] Tari Renner, ed., "The Municipal Election Process: The Impact on Minority Representation," in *The Municipal Yearbook* (Washington, DC: International City Managers Association, 2005).

[41] Amy Bridges, *Morning Glories* (Princeton, NJ: Princeton University Press, 1999); and Burnham, *Critical Elections*.

[42] Steven Rosenstone and John Mark Hansen, *Mobilization, Participation and Democracy in America* (New York: Longman, 2003).

[43] Alan S. Gerber and Donald P. Green, "The Effects of Personal Canvassing, Telephone Calls and Direct Mail on Voter Turnout: A Field Experiment," *American Political Science Review* 94(3)(1993):658.

[44] Robert Putnam, *Bowling Alone* (New York: Simon and Schuster, 2000).

[45] *The New York Times*, 21 September 2003, p. 30.

President Lyndon Johnson giving Dr. Martin Luther King Jr. a pen used to sign the Voting Rights Act of 1965.

State laws determine how local elections will be conducted. In many local elections, candidates run at large (that is, citywide). These **at-large elections** were another anti-party, Progressive era reform designed to weaken the influence of political parties and the lower-status voters, often recent immigrants, whom they relied upon for support. At-large elections were sold as a "good government" reform, in part, for their ability to get working-class ethnics, blacks, and Socialists off of city councils.[46] Because minorities and the poor are often concentrated in specific neighborhoods, and because most white voters usually vote for white candidates,[47] racial and ethnic minority candidates often have a better chance of being elected from small districts than at large when they run for a citywide

office.[48] Districted contests facilitate the election of minority candidates, but if districts are drawn to be heavily homogeneous (that is, safe for a minority group), districted elections may also limit competition.

The Effect of Place

People who live in smaller communities tend to participate more. Across a wide range of American towns and cities, people are more likely to contact public officials and attend board meetings, for example, if they live in a place with a smaller population.[49] Voter turnout in local elections is also higher in places with a lower population, even after accounting for things such as levels of income and the racial-ethnic composition of the cities.[50] People in Vermont are more likely to attend town meetings if they live in less populous communities.[51]

A sense of place, or a sense of community, seems to increase political participation. Many people develop the social skills and networks—the **social capital**—they use in political activity by volunteering with local service clubs and social, fraternal, and religious groups.[52] For example, by organizing a bake sale for a church or an auction to raise money for a soccer team, one might build social networks and learn fundraising skills that carry over to political activity. Where there is more social capital, then there is likely to be more political participation. Social capital

[46] Amy Bridges, *Morning Glories*; Samuel P. Hays, "The Politics of Municipal Reform in the Progressive Era," *Pacific Northwest Quarterly* 55(1964):157–69; and Chandler Davidson and George Korbel, "At-Large Elections and Minority Group Representation," *Journal of Politics* 43(1981):982–1005.

[47] Paul Kleppner, *Chicago Divided: The Making of a Black Mayor* (DeKalb, IL: Northern Illinois Press, 1985). For a thorough review of the literature and critical analysis of this proposition, see Keith Reeves, *Voting Hopes or Fears: White Voters, Black Candidates and Racial Politics in America* (New York: Oxford University Press, 1997).

[48] Davidson and Grofman, *Quiet Revolution in the South* (1992); and Richard Engstrom and Michael D. McDonald, "The Election of Blacks to City Councils," *American Political Science Review* 75(1981):344–54.

[49] Eric Oliver, "City Size and Civic Involvement in Metropolitan America," *American Political Science Review* 94(2)(2000):362–63; also see Robert Dahl and Edward Tufte, *Size and Democracy* (Stanford, CA: Stanford University Press, 1973).

[50] Hanjal and Lewis, "Municipal Institutions and Voter Turnout." Also see Stephen Hansen, Thomas Palfrey, and Howard Rosenthal, "The Downsian Model of Electoral Participation: Formal Theory and Empirical Analysis of the Constituency Size Effect," *Public Choice* 52(1987):15–33.

[51] Frank Bryan, *Real Democracy: The New England Town Meeting and How It Works* (Chicago: University of Chicago Press, 2003).

[52] James Coleman, *Foundations of Social Theory* (Cambridge, MA: Belknap, 1990); and Putnam, *Bowling Alone*.

seems to coexist with trusting other people, and residents of smaller places tend to trust other people more than residents of larger places do.[53] A prominent investigation of social capital found that people in smaller places were much more likely to volunteer in their communities, to work on community projects, and to give to charity.[54]

Personal Barriers

When Americans are asked about the barriers to local participation, lack of information is the barrier most frequently cited as being a serious impediment. As Table 3.5 illustrates, over one-third of Americans agree that not knowing where to begin, or not having enough information, is a serious barrier to becoming involved in local politics. People with no education beyond high school, African Americans, and Hispanics were significantly more likely to share these sentiments.[55] People who work in congested urban areas a few miles from their neighborhood polling places may also be less likely to vote.[56]

Table 3.5	

Public Attitudes as Barriers to Participation in Local Politics

Public Attitudes	%
Lack of information or don't know how to begin	35
Feel can't make a difference	26
Work schedule (too busy)	25
Poor transportation	20
Feel unwelcome	22
Safety concerns	28

Source: Social Capital Benchmark Survey, 2000.

Breaking Down Barriers to Voter Participation

One of the ironies about low rates of political participation in the United States is that for the last several decades, serious efforts have been made to remove barriers to voting and political participation—but participation remains low. Congress passed the Voting Rights Act in 1965, empowering the federal government to take control of local voter registration agencies away from racist state and local governments. Federal anti-poverty "community action" programs of the 1960s also included requirements for the "maximum feasible participation" of community residents in implementing the programs.[57] The participatory elements of community action programs were soon abandoned as being ineffective, but the Voting Rights Act had the dramatic effect of bringing voter participation rates among African Americans to levels equal with those of whites.[58]

Subsequent efforts to boost participation have been less effective. In the 1980s, political parties spent millions on Get Out the Vote (GOTV) drives. In the 1990s, Congress also passed the Motor Voter Act to make registration easier. MTV's Rock the Vote encouraged young people to register and vote. These efforts may have increased registrations, but they seem to have had little effect on getting newly registered voters to actually vote. The hotly contested Bush versus Kerry 2004 presidential race, in contrast, was associated with an increase in voting.

State-Level Reform Efforts

In the past decade, several states have also attempted to make it easier for people to vote.

---

[53] Wendy Rahn and Thomas Rudolph, "A Tale of Political Trust in American Cities," *Public Opinion Quarterly* 69(2005):530–60.

[54] Putman, *Bowling Alone*.

[55] Social Capital Benchmark Survey; and author's calculations.

[56] James Gimpel and J. E. Schuknecht, "Political Participation and the Accessibility of the Ballot Box," *Political Geography* 22(2003):471–88.

[57] Daniel Patrick Moynihan, *Maximum Feasible Misunderstanding: Community Action in the War on Poverty* (New York: Basic Books, 1969).

[58] When the effects of income and education on participation are accounted for, African Americans vote at higher rates than whites. Leighley and Nagler, "Individual and Systemic Influences."

On the West Coast and in a few states in other areas, for example, many people now take advantage of less restrictive rules about absentee voting. These rules allow them to vote permanently by mail without having to provide any reason. Oregon adopted all-mail elections in 1998, and 37 of 39 counties in Washington held all elections by mail as of 2009. Texas, Iowa, and other states implemented "early voting" and set up polling places days before elections in 2008 to make voting easier. Some states have experimented with Internet voting, particularly for overseas military personnel.

Effect of Reforms on Voter Participation

Despite these efforts, participation in American elections remains low compared to most other established democracies. There is some evidence that reforms such as voting by mail might slightly increase turnout, and liberal absentee laws were found to increase turnout among students.[59] Studies suggest that the increased turnout associated with making voting more convenient might exacerbate social bias in the electorate by increasing turnout among white, wealthy, and better-educated voters at a greater rate than turnout among minorities and the less affluent.[60]

Interest Matters

It probably comes as little surprise that participation in state and local politics is largely the domain of those who are most interested in politics. It may be less obvious that having an interest in politics often has a distinct class bias and that some reforms designed to increase turnout might, ironically, magnify this bias. Efforts to increase participation by making it easier to vote can increase turnout do not make elections any more interesting. As noted above, lack of information is the primary reason that people mention when citing barriers to participation— particularly the less affluent, the less educated, and racial and ethnic minorities. Competitive elections, increased campaign activity, and active political parties may increase interest and information about elections. Most current reform efforts focus on making it more convenient for people to vote. The people who take advantage of increased convenience tend to be people who already have some engagement with politics— those with education and higher incomes.[61]

Increasing Citizen Engagement with Competitive Elections

This is not to say that reforms cannot increase participation across the board. Increased electoral competition, and more information about candidates and issues, may significantly increase participation in state and local politics. Partisan local elections, multi-party politics, and even "semiproportional" nonpartisan elections have each been shown to be associated with higher levels of participation.[62]

Some observers suggest that eliminating partisan gerrymandering of electoral districts might also help boost interest in state politics by making more state legislative contests competitive.[63] In presidential, gubernatorial,

[59] Jeffrey Karp and Susan Banducci, "Absentee Voting, Participation, and Mobilization," *American Politics Research* 29(2001):183–95.

[60] J. Eric Oliver, "The Effects of Eligibility Restrictions and Party Activity on Absentee Voting and Overall Turnout," *American Journal of Political Science* 40(1996):498–513; and Jeff Karp and Susan Banducci, "Going Postal: How All Mail Elections Influence Turnout," *Political Behavior* 22(2000):223–39. On Internet voting, see R. Michael Alvarez and Jonathan Nagler, "The Likely Consequences of Internet Voting for Political Representation," *Loyola of Los Angeles Law Review* 34(2001):1115–52.

[61] A full extension of this argument can be found in Adam Berinsky, "The Perverse Consequences of Electoral Reform in the United States," *American Politics Research* 33(4)(2005):471–91.

[62] Andre Blais and Ken Carty, "Does Proportional Representation Foster Voter Turnout?" *European Journal of Political Research* 18(1990):167–81; and Shaun Bowler, Todd Donovan, and David Brockington, *Election Reform and Minority Representation* (Columbus, OH: Ohio State University Press, 2003).

[63] Morris Fiorrina, S. Adams, and J. Pope, *Culture War? Myth of a Polarized America* (New York: Longman, 2006); conversely, see Nolan McCarty, Keith Pool, and Howard Rosenthal, "Does Gerrymandering Cause Polarization?" *American Journal of Political Science* 53(3)(2009):666–80.

congressional, and state legislative races, voter participation is greater in places where the vote gap between the winning and losing candidates narrows. People tend to participate more when elections are close than when they are uncompetitive. Some suggest that voters are more likely to calculate that their participation will be decisive in close races—causing turnout to increase.[64] We suggest that close, competitive elections increase participation, as these races generate more campaign activity and information.

Experiments with Alternative Local Election Systems

Different types of local election systems can also encourage more candidates to run, which increases campaign activity and, as a result, increases participation. Unique experiments with "semiproportional" local election systems in Texas, Alabama, and a few other states demonstrated that **cumulative voting systems** offer minority candidates more opportunities to win than standard at-large elections. There are different forms of at-large elections. Under standard at-large elections, if there are five city council seats, each seat is elected separately by all voters in the city. Cities using standard at-large elections often narrow the field of candidates with a primary contest that determines the two candidates who will contest each position in the general election. The candidate with a majority wins, and if there is a cohesive citywide majority, it sweeps every seat. This means minority-supported candidates have little chance to win. Cumulative voting modifies the at-large system by allowing voters to cast multiple votes for one or more candidates running citywide. This allows some candidates with less than a majority to win and causes minority candidates

to run active campaigns. Cumulative voting has been found to increase campaign activity by local groups and increase turnout in local elections by about 5 percent.[65]

E-Government

City and state governments have also tried to stimulate citizen interest and participation by making it easier for people to follow government through electronic media from the convenience of their own homes. Many states and cities maintain public access cable TV stations to broadcast hearings and meetings and maintain ever-improving websites designed to make it easier to contact public officials.

Voter Choice in State and Local Elections

When people vote in partisan state and local elections, their decision-making process is somewhat similar to the process they use when voting in national elections. Voters who identify with a political party have a strong inclination to pick candidates from their party. Party labels—Democrat, Republican, Libertarian, and so on—act as a cue as to the policies the candidate might pursue. If people know nothing about a candidate except the candidate's party label—as is often the case—the inclination to vote based on party labels may even be stronger because voters have little more to guide their choices. Voters also tend to give incumbents the benefit of the doubt and may also reward or punish candidates for state offices based on the health of the economy.[66] They may also be more likely to punish a governor for the health of the state economy than the national economy.[67] Despite these factors, a voter's party

[64] For a discussion, see Gary Cox and Michael Munger, "Closeness, Expenditures and Turnout in the 1982 US House Election," *American Political Science Review* 83(1989):217–31.

[65] Bowler et al., *Election Reform*.

[66] Lonna Atkeson and Randal Partin, "Economic and Referendum Voting," *American Political Science Review* 89(1995):99–107.

[67] Robert Stein, "Economic Voting for Governor and US Senator," *Journal of Politics* 52(1990):29–53.

affiliation is the main thing driving voter choice in partisan contests.

If candidates must run for office without party labels on the ballot, however, the voter's decision-making process is different. In non-partisan elections, which are quite common at the local level, voters may be more likely to rely on endorsements of slating groups. These groups mimic the role of parties by recruiting and publicizing candidates sympathetic to the goals of the group. Pro-business slating groups have been found to have important influence in low-turnout local elections.[68]

Effects of Voter Participation on Public Policy

Levels of participation in state and local politics are affected by state laws that regulate voter registration, polling place hours, absentee voting rules, representation, and many other factors. As we have shown above, these rules can make it easier or harder to vote and can make elections more or less interesting by limiting or increasing electoral competition, information, and representation. It is important to stress that the effects of these rules are not neutral; many of them filter out minorities and the less affluent or increase participation by the wealthy. In this section, we consider how rules might affect who participates and how this affects who gets represented and who gets what from government.

First, one must consider how different the participating electorate could be under different institutional conditions, all of which can be changed by altering state laws. The first condition we describe below is a recipe for higher participation, and the second is a recipe for lower participation.

High Voter Participation Election Rules

Under one condition, state law could allow cities to have partisan local elections, with state and local contests held in conjunction with an "even year" general election. By holding state and local contests in synch with presidential contests, more people would probably vote in state and local races. New voters could be allowed to register at the polls and vote on the day of the election. If a state used highly competitive districts to elect its legislature, more candidates would campaign, further increasing interest. Ex-felons and legal immigrant noncitizens could be allowed to vote in state and local races. Some elections could also be awarded by proportional representation, further encouraging different candidates to campaign. It is unlikely these sorts of reforms would be adopted without massive public pressure, as incumbent politicians of both major parties typically resist changing the rules that existed when they were elected.[69]

Low Voter Participation Election Rules

Under a second condition, state law could require local elections to be nonpartisan—a rule that limits the information available to the voters. State and local contests could be allowed only in "odd years" when no important federal contests are on the ballot. Voters would have to register at least 30 days in advance, and only citizens without felony convictions could vote. State legislative districts could be gerrymandered to ensure that parties didn't have to compete against each other in a single district, and local council races could be by single-member districts, leaving many incumbents without opposition.

Our point is not that more voter participation is always better but that participation is,

---

[68] Chandler Davidson and Luis Fraga, "Slating Groups as Parties in a 'Nonpartisan' Setting," *Western Political Quarterly* 41(1988):373–90.

[69] Shaun Bowler, Todd Donovan, and Jeffrey Karp, "Why Politicians Like Electoral Institutions: Self-Interest, Values or Ideology," *Journal of Politics* 68(2)(2006):454.

in part, a function of laws that are under state control. State legislatures can make it harder or easier for people to participate, and state laws can make elections more or less competitive. State laws affect not only who can vote but also if the elections will generate interest sufficient to stimulate the participation of a wide range of people. Rules thus shape the composition of the electorate; that is, they determine who ends up making demands on government.

The scope of the differences between participants and nonparticipants is likely to vary across states and is due to state laws as well as the demographic profile of the state's residents. In California, surveys estimate that 70 percent of likely voters in 2006 and 63 percent of likely voters in the 2008 election were white, yet whites were not a majority of the population.[70] Different turnout rates reflect lower participation among young voters and Latinos and the fact that many Latino citizens have not registered to vote. States with larger proportions of recent immigrants have similar gaps between participants and nonparticipants. An estimated 20 million legal, tax-paying immigrant noncitizens—1.3 million in New York City alone—are prohibited from voting in the United States. In a few communities, however, they are allowed to vote in local elections.[71]

Public Policy and Public Opinion

Representation means that elected officials, to some degree, produce laws and policies that their constituents want. Evidence from the 50 states demonstrates that citizens' preferences for public policy generally correspond with the policies that states adopt. States where more people identified themselves as liberals had more liberal public policies, and states

where more people identified themselves as conservatives had more conservative policies.[72] Something must be working to connect public preferences to policy. Elected representatives may reflect the public in response to those citizens who participate in politics, and those who participate may be fairly representative of the public opinion of the state's larger population. That is, representatives may respond to pressure from voters and constituents and do what the voters want. Or politicians may simply anticipate what people want, regardless of whether people participate or not. This distinction presents an important question for democracy: Does active political participation make the actions of government better represent what citizens want? Put differently, does more participation—or less social bias in participation—make state and local policy more representative of public opinion? One study of California found voters and nonvoters had substantially different attitudes about what government should do—with nonvoters much more supportive of higher taxes.[73]

Does Participation Make State and Local Policy More Representative?

It is possible for elected officials to be perfectly representative of the public, even if most people didn't participate in politics. This would require that representatives have a keen sense of what everyone wanted and strong incentives to give people what they want. More realistically, representatives may do things that reflect what the general public wants when there is more pressure on them to do so.

As examples, states with just one dominant political party (such as the U.S. South through

[70] CNN exit poll results for 2008. See also Mark Baldassare, "California's Exclusive Electorate," Public Policy Institute of California (2006).

[71] Alexandra Marks, "Should Non Citizens Vote?" *Christian Science Monitor*, 27 April 2004.

[72] Robert Erikson, Gerald Wright, and John P. McIver, *Statehouse Democracy: Public Opinion and Policy in the American States* (New York: Cambridge University Press, 1993).

[73] Baldassare (2006).

most of the twentieth century) had policies less representative of what the public probably wanted than states where two parties compete for voter support. Competition between parties is expected to force legislators to try to attract support by passing popular policies—including things that are popular with the poor.[74] Primary election systems that allow more people to participate also produce representatives who are more likely to share their constituents' opinions on policy.[75] States with direct democracy (Chapter 4) also adopt some public policies, such as death penalty laws and laws requiring parental notification for abortions, which are closer to the state's public opinion than policies adopted in states that lack the pressure of direct democracy.[76]

Participation Bias

As we illustrated earlier in this chapter, people who participate in politics are different than nonparticipants. But does this mean that nonparticipants want different things from their governments than participants do or that by responding mainly to those who participate, governments are not very representative of the general public? Scholars are divided on this question. A study of a national sample of public opinion in 1972 and another from 1988 found that voters and nonvoters had largely similar policy preferences.[77] These results have been used to support the idea that American governments are largely representative of all citizens, even those who do not vote. If government responds only (or mostly) to those who vote or contribute, participation bias

(the overrepresentation of the wealthy) might mean that state and local policies are not representative of the population. Recent studies of national opinion have found that nonvoters are more liberal on social welfare issues than voters.[78]

Participation is relatively high in national elections, however. Far fewer vote in state and local contests. Given this fact, and given the increased information demands associated with state and local elections, it is possible that there are greater gaps in policy preferences between participants and nonparticipants in local elections than in national contests. If participants are different than nonparticipants, what are the policy consequences of this participation bias?

Effects of Participation Bias

Several scholars provide evidence that the turnout decline in American elections has produced an overrepresentation of upper-middle-class and upper-class people and an underrepresentation of lower- and middle-class citizens.[79] One way to assess if participation bias matters is to look at how differences in state policies across the 50 states correspond with differences in who participates.

Effects on State Policies The magnitude of this "class bias"—the overrepresentation of the wealthy—is larger in some states and smaller in others. A study of the 1980s found the inequality in participation was highest in Kentucky, New Mexico, Texas, Georgia, and Arkansas. These are states with high minority

---

[74] Key, *Southern Politics*, ch. 14, p. 307. Evidence from the contemporary era suggests the poor get more when Democrats are in power rather than when their party is losing in close competition against Republicans.

[75] Elisabeth Gerber and Rebecca Morton, "Primary Election Systems and Representation," *Journal of Law, Economics and Organizations* 14(2) (1998):304–24

[76] Elisabeth Gerber, *The Populist Paradox* (Princeton, NJ: Princeton University Press, 1999); also see John Matsusaka, *For the Many or the Few* (Chicago: University of Chicago Press, 2004).

[77] Raymond Wolfinger and Steven Rosenstone, *Who Votes* (New Haven, CT: Yale University Press, 1980); and Sidney Verba, Kay Schlozman, Henry Brady, and Norman Nie, "Citizen Activity: Who Participates? What Do They Say?" *American Political Science Review* (1993):303–18.

[78] Adam Berinsky, "Silent Voices: Opinion Polls, Social Welfare Policy and Political Equality in America," *American Journal of Political Science* 46(2002):276–87.

[79] Frances Fox Piven and Richard A. Cloward, *Why Americans Don't Vote* (New York: Pantheon, 1989); and Walter Dean Burnham, "The Turnout Problem," in *Elections American Style*, ed. A. James Reichley (Washington, DC: Brookings Institution Press, 1987).

populations—most with legacies of erecting barriers to voter participation (see Figure 3.2). States with the most balanced representation between the rich and poor were New Jersey, Minnesota, Louisiana, Illinois, and Nebraska.[80] The study found that state-level class bias in participation during the 1980s was strongly related to lower state welfare (AFDC) spending. States where the poor were underrepresented among participating voters spent less per person on welfare than states where the poor were better represented. A study of state spending from 1978 to 1990 found similar results, with welfare spending higher where there was higher lower-status-voter turnout.[81]

If bias in participation affects which candidates end up winning elections, then it may also affect what governments do. Despite claims by third-party presidential candidates Ralph Nader (in 2000) and George Wallace (in 1968) that there is no difference between the Democratic and Republican parties, there are clear policy differences at the state level related to which party has more control over the state government. Republican control at the state level means less Medicaid spending; Democrats spend more.[82] Republicans may tax less[83] and use a different mix of taxes and expenditures than Democrats[84] (see Chapter 10).

Elections and Representation

Elections can be thought of as a tool for translating votes into "seats." When a group or party has seats in a state legislature or on a city or county council, they have a form of representation. Election rules have a great effect on which parties or groups have representation. The rules used to conduct elections, like many things examined in this book, are not always (if ever) neutral. They can affect who wins and who loses, and who gets more seats—in short, who ends up being represented.

Number of Representatives per District

The number of representatives elected inside a district's boundaries can also affect who is represented in a legislature. Most states now elect their state legislators from single-member districts (SMDs)—but it hasn't always been this way. In single-member districts, the winning candidate is typically elected with a majority vote, but if three or more candidates divide up the vote enough, whoever has the most support—a simple plurality—wins. Some states have more than one representative per district (just as each U.S. state has two U.S. senators per statewide district or as Australian states elect six federal senators per statewide district). The number of representatives for a specific geographic area is referred to as **district magnitude**.

In the middle of the twentieth century, about half of all American state legislative seats were elected by **multimember districts** (or MMDs), where two or more candidates are elected to represent each district.[85] Many of these older MMDs overrepresented rural areas. A series of U.S. Supreme Court rulings required that states apportion legislative districts equally according to population.[86] Since the 1950s, many states

---

[80] Kim Q. Hill and Jan Leighley, "The Policy Consequences of Class Bias in State Electorates," *American Journal of Political Science* 36(2) (1992):351–65.

[81] Kim Q. Hill, Jan Leighley, and Angela Hinton-Andersson, "Lower-Class Mobilization and Policy Linkages in the U.S. States," *American Journal of Political Science* 39(1)(1998):75–86.

[82] Coleen Grogan, "Political-Economic Factors Influencing State Medicaid Policy," *Political Research Quarterly* 47(3)(1994):589–623.

[83] Brian Knight, "Supermajority Vote Requirements for Tax Increases: Evidence from the States," *Journal of Public Economics* 67(1)(2000):41–67.

[84] DL Rogers and JH Rogers, "Political Competition and State Government Size: Do Tighter Elections Produce Looser Budgets?" Public Choice 105 (1) (2000):1–21; and Timothy Besley and Anne Case, "Political Institutions and Policy Choices: Evidence from the United States," *Journal of Economic Literature* 41(1)(2002):7–73.

[85] Maurice Klain, "A New Look at the Constituencies: The Need for a Recount and Reappraisal," *American Political Science Review* 49(1955):1105–19.

[86] *Baker v. Carr* (1962); *Reynolds v. Sims* (1964); and *Wesberry v. Sanders* (1964).

have abandoned their MMD systems, often as part of their plans to equally apportion districts by population. Those that now use MMDs can no longer give extra representation to rural areas.

There are important differences in how states use MMDs to elect their legislatures. In Washington and Idaho, lower house districts elect two representatives, but candidates run for two separate positions. These elections are largely identical to those held in SMDs because voters cannot vote for more than one candidate per position. In Arizona, however, voters cast two votes to select two representatives from a single list of candidates who will represent their district. The top two candidates win. In Vermont, if there are three representatives per district, voters cast three votes across a single list, and the top three win. Illinois used three-member districts with a semiproportional representation system known as cumulative voting for decades, ending the system in 1980. In MMD systems such as those used in Arizona, Vermont, or Illinois (until 1980), candidates can win a seat with less than a majority and even with less than a plurality. The winning candidates are the first-, second-, and third-place finishers—depending on how many seats are elected from the district. New Jersey, North Dakota, and South Dakota also use MMDs to elect their lower house.

Effects of Multimember Districts on Minority Representation MMD elections can produce different patterns of representation than SMD elections. Some suggest that MMDs hurt the chances of minority candidates, especially in areas where minority vote strength is geographically concentrated—places where a heavily minority SMD might be drawn.[87] Others note that evidence showing MMDs giving advantages to white candidates is dated.

Because MMDs allow candidates to win with a relatively low vote share, MMDs might help minority candidates get elected. Recent studies suggest these systems may have produced more racial and ethnic minority representation in state legislatures from 1980 to 2003 than found under SMDs. African Americans appeared particularly advantaged but Latinos less so.[88]

There is clear evidence that traditional "at-large" MMDs disadvantage minority candidates in local elections.[89] In these systems, candidates file for one position out of several in a district, and only the first-place candidate for each position can win a seat. In *Gingles v. Thornberg* (1986), the U.S. Supreme Court ruled that local MMD at-large elections may be an unconstitutional "dilution" of minority vote influence if the minority group is geographically compact and politically cohesive and there is a history of "bloc voting" by whites that leads to the defeat of minority candidates. If these conditions exist, a judge may order the jurisdiction to switch to SMD elections or some alternative that will allow the minority group to elect a representative of their choice. However, in *Shaw v. Reno* (1993), a 5–4 Court decision also ruled that it would not tolerate district maps that maximize minority representation by drawing majority-minority districts based exclusively on where minority voters live.

District Type and Ideological Polarization MMDs and SMDs may also create different representation of ideologies in state legislatures. Winner-take-all rules mean that just one candidate is ever elected for any position or just one representative per district (i.e., an SMD). One influential theory predicts that when only one candidate can win and most voters are centrists, all candidates seeking the office have incentives to take positions near the

[87] Malcolm E. Jewell, *Representation in State Legislatures* (Lexington, KY: University of Kentucky Press, 1982); and Gary Moncrief and Joel Thompson, "Electoral Structure and State Legislative Representation," *Journal of Politics* 54(1992):246–56.

[88] Lilliard Richardson and Christopher Cooper, "The Mismeasure of MMD: Reassessing the Impact of Multi-Member Districts on the Representation on Descriptive Representation in the United States". Paper presented at the State Politics and Policy conference. Tucson, AZ (2003).

[89] Engstrom and McDonald, "The Election of Blacks to City Councils."

"center" of the political spectrum.[90] In contrast, when two or more candidates are elected to represent the same district, candidates may have incentives to position themselves closer to one or the other end of the ideological spectrum. If they can get elected with fewer votes by placing second or even third, they don't need to appeal to most voters in order to win. This means that candidates further from the ideological center may have more chances to win under MMD elections. There is evidence of more ideological extremism in the Arizona House, which is elected by MMDs, than in the Arizona Senate, which is elected by SMDs.[91] Another study found the same thing in Illinois when its house was elected by MMDs.[92]

Campaign Spending

Politicians campaign to tell voters about themselves (and their opponents). These campaigns cost money, and politicians spend a significant amount of their time raising campaign funds.[93] Money clearly matters at all levels of American politics: Candidates who spend more in state and local races typically do better in elections than those who spend less.[94] Campaign spending may be particularly important for candidates challenging incumbents. Because challengers are less well known than incumbents, challenger spending may produce more "bang for the buck" than incumbent spending. Challenger spending disseminates information about a lesser-known candidate, so any dollar spent can increase information about the candidate. Incumbents may be so well known prior to an election that their spending may have less effect on their vote share.[95]

Spending on campaigns transmits information to citizens—through television, radio, direct mail, and other modes of advertising. Because the information is meant to cast candidates in a good light (and their opponents in a bad light), the quality of this information may be dubious. A survey of voters in one state found that 81 percent believed campaign advertising was "misleading." A slightly higher proportion of politicians in the state agreed.[96] Nonetheless, voters use the information they get from political ads. People are more likely to be aware of state-level elections as spending increases,[97] and spending may cause skeptical voters to seek out additional information. Spending may also cause increased media coverage. Although turnout in elections is mostly structured by larger socioeconomic and institutional forces already discussed in this chapter, higher levels of spending in state-level races can also increase voter turnout.[98] One study of spending in state legislative races concluded that for every dollar spent per eligible voter, turnout increased by 1.2 percent.[99]

[90] Anthony Downs, *An Economic Theory of Democracy* (1957); and Gary Cox, "Centripetal and Centrifugal Incentives in Electoral Systems," *American Journal of Political Science* 34(1990):903–35.

[91] Lilliard Richardson, Brian Russell, and Christopher Cooper, "Legislative Representation in Single Member versus Multi Member District Systems: The Arizona State Legislature," *Political Research Quarterly* 57(2004):337–44.

[92] Greg Adams, "Legislative Effects of Single-Member vs. Multi-Member Districts," *American Journal of Political Science* 40(1996):129–44.

[93] Peter Francia and Paul Herrnson, "Begging for Bucks," *Campaigns and Elections* (April 2001).

[94] Kedron Bardwell, "Campaign Finance Laws and the Competition for Spending in Gubernatorial Elections," *Social Science Quarterly* 84(4) (2003):811–25; and Robert K. Goidel, Donald A. Gross, and Todd G. Shields, *Money Matters: Consequences of Campaign Finance Reform in U.S. House Elections* (Lanham, MD: Rowman & Littlefield, 1999).

[95] Gary Jacobson, "The Effects of Campaign Spending in House Elections: New Evidence for Old Arguments," *American Journal of Political Science* 34(1990):334–62; and Donald Philip Green and Jonathan S. Krasno, "Rebuttal to Jacobson's 'New Evidence for Old Arguments,'" *American Journal of Political Science* 34(1990):363–72.

[96] Todd Donovan, Shaun Bowler, and David McCuan, "Political Consultants and the Initiative Industrial Complex," in *Dangerous Democracy?* eds. Larry J. Sabato, Howard R. Ernst, and Bruce A. Larson (Lanham, MD: Rowman & Littlefield, 2001), 127.

[97] Shaun Bowler and Todd Donovan, *Demanding Choices* (Ann Arbor, MI: University of Michigan Press, 1998), p. 152.

[98] Robert Hogan, "Campaign and Contextual Influences on Voter Participation in State Legislative Elections," *American Politics Review* 27(4) (1999):403–33.

[99] Francia and Herrnson, "Begging for Bucks."

Finance Regulations State laws also determine who can contribute to state and local candidates; how much individuals, groups, or political parties may give; and how contributions must be disclosed to the public. Some states, such as Massachusetts and Oregon, have a broad range of restrictions on contributions. Others, including Idaho, Texas, and Virginia, have minimal regulations.[100] Defenders of these regulations note that they give the public more information about whom the candidates might be beholden to and that these rules limit the influence of money in politics. Critics argue that limits on spending might make it harder for lesser-known challengers to unseat incumbents and that spending limits may make elections less competitive. There is some evidence that these rules do reduce spending in state races and that they might also limit electoral competition if limits are set too low.[101]

Clean Money A handful of states and cities provide full or partial public financing for state candidates in exchange for candidates promising to reject all private contributions. Maine and Arizona became the first states to do this in 2000. Vermont, Connecticut, New Mexico, and North Carolina have also adopted **clean money** programs, and other states, such as Minnesota, provide partial public funding of candidate campaigns in exchange for candidates limiting the total amount that they raise from private sources. A proposal to provide public funds for elections of the Secretary of State was rejected by California voters in 2010.

One major idea behind these clean money laws is to ensure candidates are not beholden to their donors. Advocates of publicly financed campaigns also hope it will broaden the pool of people who seek office and cut down the amount of time politicians spend raising money. Jesse Ventura, a professional wrestler turned city mayor, was elected governor of Minnesota under the Reform Party banner with the help of public campaign funds. One study found that state legislative candidates do spend less time raising money in states with public financing of campaigns.[102]

Representation of Parties

Every American state is now—more or less—a two-party system: 99.9 percent of state legislative seats are held by Democrats or Republicans. There have been brief periods of multi-party politics in a few states and long periods of one-party rule in many southern states. These are exceptions, however, and not the rule. Nearly every partisan office in the United States is elected on a winner-take-all basis. Second-, third-, and lower-place candidates win nothing. If a party rarely does better than second place in most contests, it will win few offices and likely disappear. The near total, oligopolistic control that Democrats and Republicans have over elected offices overstates the level of support these parties have among the public.[103] Winner-take-all election rules, combined with the ballot access laws discussed above, essentially predetermine that only two parties will ever be represented.

Despite this, third-party and independent candidates have had more success in state and local elections than in congressional and federal races over the last several decades. Since 1990, a few were elected as governor (Angus King in Maine, Jesse Ventura in Minnesota, and Lowell Weicker in Connecticut).[104] As of 2010,

[100] John Pippen, Shaun Bowler, and Todd Donovan, "Election Reform and Direct Democracy: Campaign Finance Regulation in the American States," *American Politics Quarterly* 30(6)(2002):559–82.

[101] Donald Gross, Robert Goidel, and Todd Shields, "State Campaign Finance Regulations and Electoral Competition," *American Politics Research* 30(2)(2002):143–65.

[102] Peter Francia and Paul S. Herrnson, "The Impact of Public Finance Laws on State Legislative Elections," *American Politics Research* 31(5)(2003):520–39.

[103] Depending on the year, about one-third of Americans fail to identify with either major party, and less than 40 percent of Americans support the idea of maintaining the two-party system (NES data, 2000–2002).

[104] Howard J. Gold, "Explaining Third-Party Success in Gubernatorial Elections," *Social Science Journal* 42(2005):523–40.

minor parties and independent candidates held just 21 seats in state legislatures (out of 7,333 positions in the 49 states with partisan legislatures).[105] Several of these minor-party and independent candidates served in Vermont (which uses MMD elections and clean money for campaign finance). Minor-party and independent candidates have also won seats in Arizona and Massachusetts under clean money rules. Some of the remaining handful of candidates who are not affiliated with a major party are southern Democrats who defected from their party as their state's population grew more conservative.

Representation of Women

States differ substantially in terms of the number of women who are elected to office. As of 2010, 24.3 percent of state legislators were women—far more than in the U.S. Congress and double the levels of women in state legislatures back in 1981. Although this is still modest representation given that most of the population is female, the growth of representation of women in the past 30 years has important implications. A growing number of women in state-level posts means that the pool of women with elected experience who seek higher-level positions has grown.

In seven states (Arizona, Colorado, Hawaii, Minnesota, New Hampshire, Vermont, and Washington), one-third of all state legislators were women as of 2010. States with the lowest rates of women representation were South Carolina (10 percent), Oklahoma (11 percent), and Alabama (12 percent). Why do some states have three times more representation of women than others? Some have noted that three of the seven states with the most women in their legislatures (Arizona, Vermont, and Washington) use MMD elections.[106] One problem with this logic, however, is that Washington does not use "pure" MMD elections; candidates actually run for individual positions, where the winner takes all. Other explanations for the differences in levels of women's representation emphasize the role of political parties and regional (or cultural) effects. Some parties have made greater efforts to recruit candidates to seek office.[107] There are clear regional differences. Women are less represented in the South and more represented in the West and New England.

Representation of Racial and Ethnic Minorities

African Americans, Latinos, Asians, and Native Americans are underrepresented in state legislatures relative to their share of U.S. population, as illustrated in Table 3.6. The pattern for minority representation at the local level is similar. Although 11 percent of all state legislative seats are held by minorities, some groups are better represented than others. Minority populations are not evenly distributed across the nation or within states such as Hawaii,

Table 3.6

Minority Representation in U.S. State Legislatures

	White (%)	African American (%)	Latino (%)	Asian or Pacific Islander (%)	Native American (%)
U.S. population	66	13	15	4	1
All state legislators	86	9	3	1	1

Source: Samantha Sanchez, "Money and Diversity in State Legislatures, 2003" (Institute on Money in State Politics, 2005); National Conference of State Legislatures, "Legislature Demographics" (2010).

[105] Data from National Conference of State Legislatures, "2009 Partisan Composition of State Legislatures," http://www.ncsl.org/default.aspx?tabid=19488. Nebraska has a nonpartisan legislature.

[106] Wilma Rule and Joseph F. Zimmerman, *United States Electoral Systems: Their Impact on Women and Minorities* (Westport, CT: Greenwood Press, 1992).

[107] Miki Caul, "Women's Representation in Parliament: The Role of Political Parties," *Party Politics* 5(1999):79–98.

California, and New Mexico, where various minority groups combine to form a majority of the state's population. This means that there are great differences across the United States in minority representation at the state and local levels.

Hawaii (80 percent "minority" legislators), New Mexico (45 percent), California (33 percent), New York (26 percent), Florida (26 percent), Illinois (24 percent), Alabama (23 percent), and Texas (22 percent) had some of the highest levels of minority representation in their states' legislatures. States with few minorities, not surprisingly, elect few minorities. The Iowa legislature, for example, was 97 percent Caucasian in 2010. Yet, even relatively high levels of minority representation in such places as California and New Mexico are deceptive. These states, along with Arizona, lead the nation in the gap between the proportion of state residents who are minority and the proportion of their representatives who are. In contrast, minorities in Alabama, although still underrepresented, are much more represented relative to their share of the population than minorities in New York, Florida, and Texas.[108]

Why are large populations of minorities better represented in some places than others? The answers, in part, are race and single-member districting. In state and local elections, African Americans benefit from the use of **majority-minority districts** drawn with boundaries that ensure the district's population is heavily African American. This guarantees

that the district will elect an African American, and it has led to near proportional representation of African Americans in many local elections. It also explains relatively high levels of minority representation in Deep South states, where African Americans are the predominant minority group.[109] In western and southwestern states, however, the largest minority group is Latino. Latinos turn out at lower rates than African Americans and are not as segregated as African Americans in the South.[110] Latinos, moreover, are a less ethnically cohesive group than African Americans. All of these factors combine to make it more difficult to design districts at the state or local level that are certain to produce Latino representation.[111] At the local level, Latinos win more seats via SMDs than they do under "at-large" arrangements,[112] but they may not win as many seats as African Americans.

Majority-minority districts present a paradox. They clearly increase the numbers of minorities holding state and local offices, and they offer people **descriptive representation**, that is, the ability to see people like themselves serving as their representative. When minority candidates win seats, moreover, they are able to affect the substance of public policy in ways that benefit their constituents and affect whether minorities are hired to implement policies approved by cities and school boards.[113] Descriptive representation of minorities at the local and congressional level may also increase minority trust and

[108] Samantha Sanchez, *Money and Diversity in State Legislatures, 2003* (Helena, MT: Institute on Money in State Politics, 2005).

[109] Engstrom and McDonald, "The Election of Blacks to City Councils."

[110] Douglas Massey and Nancy Denton, "Trends in Residential Segregation of Blacks, Hispanics and Asians," *American Sociological Review* 52(1987):802–25.

[111] Jerry Polinard, Robert Wrinkle, and Tomas Longoria, "The Impact of District Elections on the Mexican American Community," *Social Science Quarterly* 17(3)(1991):608–14; Delbert Taebel, "Minority Representation on City Councils: The Impact of Structure on Blacks and Hispanics," *Social Science Quarterly* 59(1978):142–52; A. Velditz and C. Johnson, "Community Segregation, Electoral Structure and Minority Representation," *Social Science Quarterly* 67(1982):729–36.

[112] David Leal, Ken Meier, and Valerie Martinez–Ebers, "The Politics of Latino Education: The Biases of At-Large Elections," *Journal of Politics* 66(4) (2004):1224.

[113] J. L. Polinard, Robert Wrinkle, Tomas Longoria, and Norman Binder, *Electoral Structure and Urban Policy: The Impact of Mexican American Communities* (New York: M. E. Sharpe, 1994); and Kenneth J. Meier, Eric Gonzalez Juenke, Robert Wrinkle, and J. L. Polinard, "Structural Choices and Representation Biases: The Post-Election Color of Representation," *American Journal of Political Science* 49(4)(2005):748–49.

participation and reduce political alienation among minority citizens.[114]

Some suggest that there may be a trade-off between descriptive representation and the substantive representation of minority interests. By packing large proportions of a minority group into one safe district, the group may have less overall influence in a legislature than they may have had if they were a swing group electing representatives across a larger number of districts.[115] Almost 95 percent of minority state legislators were Democrats in 2005, so we might assume that people in these districts find their substantive policy interests advanced by Democrats more than Republicans. A majority-minority district can help elect a minority Democrat representative, but this may also weaken other Democrats' chances of winning in surrounding districts. The minority district gains descriptive Democratic representation locally, but Democrats may elect fewer seats statewide, making it more difficult to advance the substantive policy goals of minority voters in the majority-minority district.

Summary

A healthy democracy depends, at least in part, on having citizens who are engaged with each other and with politics. Participation in local voluntary groups is one way that people learn the skills required to be citizens. As important as local democracy is, this chapter illustrates that there are substantial barriers to participation at the state and local levels. Elections are often designed to be uncompetitive, a situation that may only serve incumbents well.

Nonpartisan races, uncompetitive elections, and other barriers may depress interest in state and local politics.

But this need not be the case. One theme of this book is that institutions matter and institutions can change. Race-based barriers to voting have been reduced substantially over the last 100 years. This is evidence that the rules can change and that political participation can become more inclusive.

Key Terms

At-large elections

Cumulative voting

Descriptive representation

District magnitude

Efficacy

Grandfather clause

Literacy tests

Majority-minority district

Multimember district

Participation bias

Poll tax

Social capital

Voting-age population

Voting-eligible population

Winner-take-all

---

[114] Lawrence Bobo and Frank Gilliam Jr., "Race, Sociopolitical Participation and Black Empowerment," *American Political Science Review* (1990):377–93; Adrian Pantoja and Gary Segura, "Does Ethnicity Matter? Descriptive Representation in Legislatures," *Social Science Quarterly* 84(2003):441–60; and Susan Banducci, Todd Donovan, and Jeffrey Karp, "Minority Representation, Empowerment and Participation," *Journal of Politics* 66(2004):534.

[115] David Lublin, *The Paradox of Representation: Racial Gerrymandering and Minority Interests in Congress* (Princeton, NJ: Princeton University Press, 1997).

Discussion Questions

(1) Which demographic groups are most likely to participate in local political activities? What effect does this have on policy making?

(2) Discuss the terms and effects of voting rights legislation. What barriers have been overcome and what barriers remain?

(3) How do levels of citizen participation and political efficacy in local elections compare to those in national elections?

(4) Do people have more influence when participating in local or in national politics?

(5) Why are minorities better represented in some districts than others? What effect does this have on their influence in legislatures?

Suggested Readings

Berkman, Michael, and Eric Plutzer. 2006. *Ten Thousand Democracies: Politics and Public Opinion in America's School Districts.* Washington, DC: Georgetown University Press.

Browning, Robert, D. Rodgers, and D. Tabb. 1984. *Protest Is Not Enough: The Struggle of Blacks and Hispanics for Equality in Urban Politics.* Berkeley: University of California Press.

Erikson, Robert, Gerald Wright, and John McIver. 1994. *Statehouse Democracy: Public Opinion and the American States.* New York: Cambridge University Press.

Gimple, James, J. Celeste Lay, and Jason Schuknecht. 2003. *Cultivating Democracy: Civic Environments and Political Socialization in America.* Washington, DC: Brookings Institution Press.

Oliver, J. Eric. 2001. *Democracy in Suburbia.* Princeton, NJ: Princeton University Press.

Putnam, Robert. 2000. *Bowling Alone: The Collapse and Revival of American Community.* New York: Simon and Schuster.

Rosenthal, Alan. 1998. *The Decline of Representative Democracy: Process, Participation, and Power in State Legislatures.* Washington, DC: CQ Press.

Websites

Center for Voting and Democracy (http://www.fairvote.org): The center promotes election systems that increase voter turnout, fair representation, inclusive policy, and meaningful choices. It conducts research, analysis, education, and organizing to ensure all Americans can exercise their right to vote and elect representatives who reflect our racial and political diversity.

Public Campaign (http://www.publicampaign.org): Public Campaign is a nonpartisan organization dedicated to reforming how elections are financed. It provides details on state and local efforts to promote publicly financed campaigns.

National Association of Secretaries of State (http://www.nass.org): The association offers information about election administration, voter participation, and electronic or e-government services administered by secretaries of state. It also has links to state-specific sites for voter registration and the location of local polling places.

Bowlingalone.com (http:www.bowlingalone.com): The site promotes a book on social capital by Robert Putnam. The site provides access to the public opinion data used in this chapter and information about how the United States can "civicly reinvent itself again."

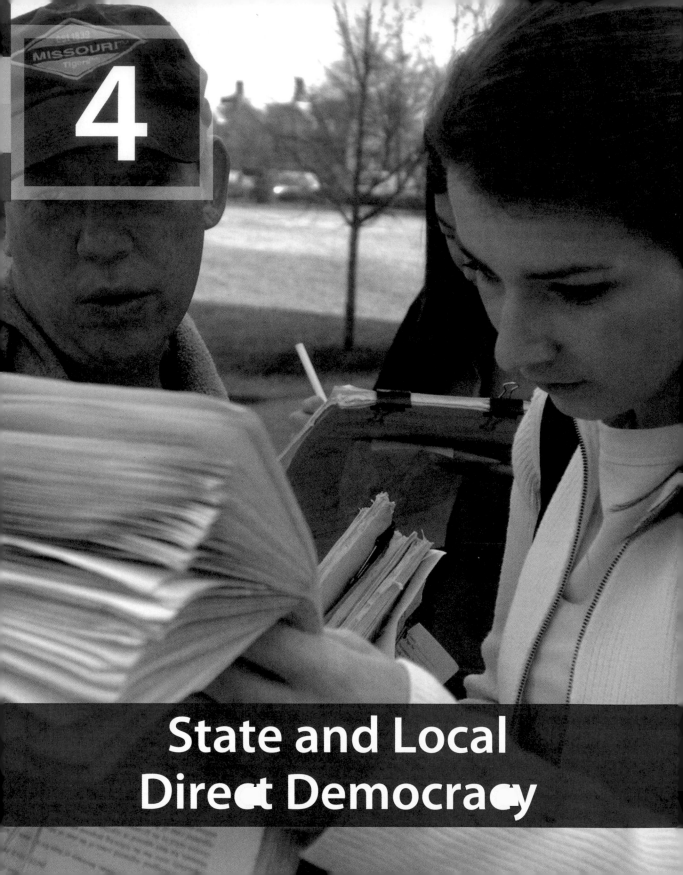

4

State and Local
Direct Democracy

INTRODUCTION

The link between citizens and their government can be quite different at the state and local levels than at the national level. State legislators and local governments regularly refer matters to voters for their approval; in fact, most states require that amendments to state constitutions ultimately be approved by voters. In nearly half the states, people can draft their own legislation and petition to have a public vote to approve or reject it. Additionally, many local governments, including those in states that do not allow the usage of direct democracy at the state level, permit this process. Some of our biggest cities—including Baltimore, Columbus, Dallas, Denver, Detroit, Houston, Jacksonville, Los Angeles, Miami, Milwaukee, New York, Phoenix, Portland, San Antonio, San Diego, San Francisco, Seattle, and Washington, DC—permit citizens to propose charter amendments to be placed on the ballot for fellow citizens to either adopt or reject. In fact, a majority of Americans reside in cities and towns where they can vote directly on matters of public policy.[1] Processes of direct democracy can leave elected representatives with limited influence over public policy. It is difficult to understand state and local politics in much of the nation without considering the effects of direct democracy.

In many American states and communities, citizens have more ability to affect what their governments do than other people in almost any other political system in the world. Apart from areas in Switzerland, no other places with such freewheeling democratic arrangements exist. In its most extreme form, direct democracy gives people outside the corridors of power the potential to cut taxes, propose tax hikes or new spending programs, veto most laws passed by elected representatives, and even remove elected officials from office. This contrasts dramatically with how American citizens participate in national politics. Although the United States is one of the few advanced democracies to have never put a question of national policy or constitutional design up for a public vote, these questions are commonly decided by voters at the state and local levels. Americans regularly decide on matters such as local school funding, land-use rules, social policy, or how much their state should borrow for specific long-term projects. The scope of direct democracy varies widely across the states and thus provides one of the key features distinguishing politics in some states and cities from that in other places.

In this chapter, we consider American direct democracy as a grand democratic experiment that allows us to consider, in effect, whether more democracy is "better." That is, does democratic politics work "better" when citizens are given more direct control over their government? As we shall see, no consensus exists among political observers, pundits, journalists, scholars, or politicians about these questions. We also illustrate that each state has a unique set of rules defining how direct democracy works, and these rules affect how much the process is used. Politics and policies can be fundamentally different in states with freewheeling forms of direct democracy.

[1] John Matsusaka, *For the Many or the Few: The Initiative, Public Policy, and American Democracy* (Chicago: University of Chicago Press, 2004).

Institutions of Direct Democracy

Three main features of direct democracy are the referendum, the initiative, and the recall. Almost every state uses some form of referendum. As Figure 4.1 reveals, 24 states have some form of a statewide initiative, 24 allow a statewide popular referendum (most of which also provide the initiative), and 18 states have provisions for the recall of state officials.

Referendum

A referendum is a public vote on a statute or a constitutional amendment that has already been considered by a state legislature or local government. The most widely used instrument of direct democracy in the American states (and localities) is the legislative referendum. In the case of the **legislative referendum**, elected officials have control over the question that voters will consider, although legislators are often bound to place certain items on state ballots. Use of legislative referendums at the national level is quite widespread, with nearly every advanced democratic nation other than the United States using the process.[2] Every American state has some provision for a legislative referendum—particularly for state constitutional matters. Most state constitutions require that voters approve constitutional amendments via referendum, and some require that voters approve when a state issues debt. Legislators may also choose to defer to the wisdom of voters and

Figure 4.1

States with Statewide Initiative, Popular Referendum, and Recall

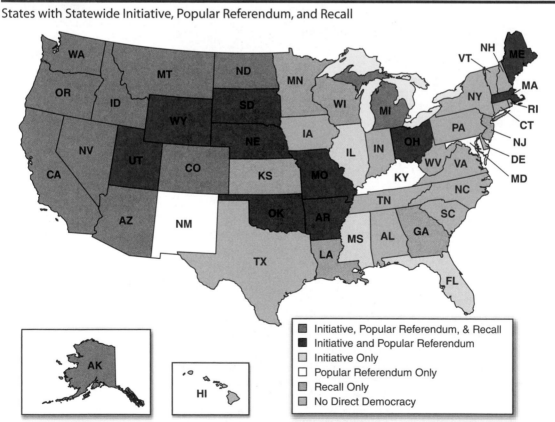

Legend:
- Initiative, Popular Referendum, & Recall
- Initiative and Popular Referendum
- Initiative Only
- Popular Referendum Only
- Recall Only
- No Direct Democracy

[2] David Butler and Austin Ranney, eds., *Referendums around the World: The Growing Use of Direct Democracy* (Washington, DC: AEI Press, 1994).

allow them to have the final say over controversial issues, such as tax increases.

The **popular referendum**, by way of contrast, allows a person or group to file a petition to have a public vote on a bill that the legislature has already approved. Every state with the initiative process (except Florida, Illinois, and Mississippi) also allows citizens to propose popular referendums.[3] The popular referendum is effectively a public veto of a law. Proponents may qualify popular referendums for the ballot by collecting a certain percentage of signatures in a set amount of time following the passage of the legislation in question.

Initiative

The two types of initiative process in the United States are the direct initiative and indirect initiative. The **direct initiative** allows a person or group to file a proposed bill with a state office and then collect signatures from voters to qualify the measure for a spot on the state ballot. If the initiative qualifies, voters have a direct say on approving or rejecting the proposal. If voters approve the measure, it becomes law.[4] An **indirect initiative** functions as a petition to have the legislature consider a bill proposed by citizens. This is similar to the Swiss system. If the indirect initiative qualifies by its proponents collecting enough signatures, the legislature can adopt or reject the bill. If it is rejected by the legislature, it must be placed on the ballot to give voters a chance to approve or reject the proposal.

Direct and indirect initiatives appear on the ballot if sufficient signatures are collected. Rules for qualifying initiatives vary across the states, but the number of signatures on petitions required to qualify is typically set as a fixed percentage of votes cast in a previous election, or

as a fixed percentage of all registered voters. Most states with any sort of initiative process only have direct initiatives; however, a few (Alaska, Maine, Massachusetts, and Wyoming) have indirect initiatives only. Five additional states (Michigan, Nevada, Ohio, Utah, and Washington) allow both direct and indirect initiatives. Depending on the state, a legislature may submit to voters an indirect initiative that it rejected, along with its own alternative proposal; alternatively, the legislature may simply take no action.

Recall

The **recall** allows a person or group to file a petition for a public vote to remove an elected official from office prior to when the official's term expires. The first place in the United States to adopt the recall was Los Angeles in 1903. Many cities and 18 states now have rules allowing for the recall of elected officials, although the process is rarely used at the state level. In most states that allow the recall process, the signature requirement for qualification is much greater than that required for the initiative and referendum.[5] Only two governors have been recalled: Lynn Fraiser of North Dakota in 1921 and Gray Davis of California in 2003.[6] Recall efforts against mayors, city councilpersons, and school boards are more common. There is some controversy about whether there should be narrow grounds for having a recall, or if a recall should be allowed simply because an elected official becomes unpopular. In 2009, the mayor of Toledo, Ohio, was subjected to a recall for allegedly mismanaging the budget (it failed to qualify). Dissatisfaction with economic conditions, taxes, and public services led to recall efforts that year against the mayors of Akron, Ohio, and Kansas City, Missouri.[7]

[3] David Magleby, *Direct Legislation: Voting on Ballot Propositions in the United States* (Baltimore, MD: Johns Hopkins University Press, 1984).

[4] A simple majority is usually required for approval, although some states require more. See Richard Ellis, *Democratic Delusions: The Initiative Process in America* (Lawrence, KS: University Press of Kansas, 2002).

[5] Magleby, *Direct Legislation*.

[6] Shaun Bowler and Bruce Cain, eds., *Clicker Politics: Essays on the California Recall* (Englewood Cliffs, NJ: Prentice Hall, 2005).

[7] Kevin Friedl, "Mayors Face Tough Times," *National Journal Online*, 29 June 2009. Available: http://www.nationaljournal.com/njonline/no_20090626_9048.php.

Some states require that proponents of either a state or local recall establish compelling grounds to have a vote to remove an elected official (such as criminal misconduct), whereas other states' rules are less restrictive or have no formal requirement that substantial misconduct be established in order to proceed with a recall. States also differ in how recalls are conducted. In some situations, voters are given two choices on one ballot: First, they decide if the official should be removed; then they may decide who should replace the official. This was the case with the California recall, where, after deciding on Governor Davis's fate, voters then had 135 candidates to choose from (including actor Arnold Schwarzenegger, porn publisher Larry Flint, ex–child actor Gary Coleman, and at least two adult "entertainers," Angelyne and Mary Carey. In other cases, voters are only asked the question about the recall. In these cases, the office is left vacant until the next election, a replacement is appointed, or a special election is conducted later to fill the vacancy.

More Responsible and More Representative Government?

Part of the difficulty in assessing the merits and pitfalls of direct democracy lies in how we define what a "better" democratic system might look like. One way to consider this task is to ask if direct democracy in the states makes politics more responsible and more representative.[8] Early advocates of direct democracy claimed that it could do both.

The Promise of Direct Democracy

Direct democracy has its roots in the Populist and Progressive movements of the late nineteenth century and early twentieth century, respectively. In the early 1900s, campaign contributions were largely unregulated, and bribery and graft were not uncommon in state legislatures. State and local elected officials were paid poorly, and, with few laws regulating political corruption, they were subject to influence by firms seeking favorable treatment from government. As one observer of the 1880s Oregon legislature noted, it consisted of "briefless lawyers, farmless farmers, business failures, bar-room loafers, Fourth-of-July orators [and] political thugs."[9] Many elected officials had little enthusiasm for social, economic, and political reforms that may have had widespread support among the general public.

To Populist and Progressive reformers of that era, representative government alone could not be trusted to serve the public interest. Their goal was to give the public greater influence over the behavior of elected officials. Reformers were suspicious of the power that wealthy economic interests had over elected representatives. In this context, then, reformers argued that by giving people the ability to write their own laws and veto unpopular laws passed by legislators, public policy would be more representative of public opinion. Likewise, it was assumed, then, that elected officials would often work to protect powerful economic interests by doing such things as granting monopolies, giving away public resources, blocking health and safety regulations, and blocking anticorruption laws. If the public could use direct democracy as an end run around these elected officials, reformers assumed that public policy would become more responsible.

Defending Direct Democracy

Before he was elected president in 1912, Woodrow Wilson offered a pragmatic defense of the instrumental use of the initiative. Wilson argued that if a state legislature was unable or

---

[8] Todd Donovan and Shaun Bowler, "Responsible and Representative?" in *Citizens as Legislators: Direct Democracy in the United States,* ed. Shaun Bowler, Todd Donovan, and Caroline Tolbert (Columbus, OH: Ohio State University Press, 1998).

[9] David Schuman, "The Origin of State Constitutional Direct Democracy: William Simon Uren and the Oregon System," *Temple Law Review* 67(1994):947–63, 949.

unwilling to pass popular legislation, citizens could directly propose and adopt laws themselves to correct any legislative "sins of omission." Even indirectly, the mere threat of an initiative—the "gun behind the door," as Wilson called it—could pressure recalcitrant legislators to take action. For Wilson, direct legislation was not a radical solution; he foresaw the device being used sparingly. The initiative would serve as a stopgap mechanism—a benign tool that would "restore," not "destroy," representative government. The expedience of direct legislation, according to Wilson, could bring "our representatives back to the consciousness that what they are bound in duty and in mere policy to do is represent the sovereign people whom they profess to serve." As a prodding instrument, then, the initiative had the potential of directly or indirectly bringing forth substantive policy changes in the American states.[10]

This was, in part, the promise of direct democracy 100 years ago. In considering how direct democracy works in American states and communities today, it is important to consider the adoption of direct democracy in its historic context. We assess how it might make politics more representative of public opinion and consider whether it makes policy more responsible. The latter quality, of course, is much more difficult to assess.

Populist Origins of Direct Democracy

Although states in New England have practice with town meeting forms of local government that provide for direct citizen voting on policy questions, direct democracy did not exist at the state level prior to the late 1890s. Eighteen of the 24 states that currently have the initiative

process adopted it between 1898 and 1914. Many of the early initiatives reflected the agenda of groups that agitated for the adoption of direct democracy. Issues such as women's suffrage, Prohibition, labor laws, and electoral reforms were common in the first decade that direct democracy was in use.

The initiative process at the state level was first adopted in South Dakota in 1898, but it was first used statewide in Oregon in 1904. Several political movements that included organized labor, disaffected farmers, proponents of the so-called single tax, Prohibitionists, and women's suffrage advocates pressed their states to adopt the initiative, recall, and referendum. These direct democracy tools were part of a larger set of reforms advocated by the **Populist Party** in the 1890s, including direct election of U.S. senators, direct election of the president, direct voter control candidate nominations, direct primary elections, and the income tax.[11] Recall that Figure 4.1 illustrates how direct democracy is more common in the West, in part because minority parties had greater political influence and some of these states were just forming their first constitutions when Populists and Progressives were most influential.[12]

Although short-lived on the political scene, the Populists were one of the most influential third parties in American history. Their attack on the disproportionate influence of powerful economic interests (railroads, banks, mining firms, and monopolies) had great appeal to laborers, western farmers, and miners. Democrat William Jennings Bryan, who ran for president on the Populist ticket in some states in 1896, was soundly defeated, but he ran very strong in western states, sweeping Populist and "Fusion" Democrats into Congress and state legislatures. Bryan spent part of his career in the 1890s promoting direct democracy in states

[10] Daniel A. Smith and Caroline J. Tolbert, *Educated by Initiative: The Effects of Direct Democracy on Citizens and Political Organizations in the American States* (Ann Arbor, MI: University of Michigan Press, 2004).

[11] Eric D. Lawrence, Todd Donovan, and Shaun Bowler, "Adopting Direct Democracy: Tests of Competing Explanations of Institutional Change," *American Politics Research* 37(2009):1024–47.

[12] Daniel A. Smith and Dustin Fridkin, "Delegating Direct Democracy: Interparty Legislative Competition and the Adoption of the Initiative in the American States," *American Political Science Review* 102(2008):333–50.

where Populists had political success.[13] Even though Populists were largely dead as a political party by 1900, states where Bryan had his greatest electoral appeal, as well as states where Socialist presidential candidate Eugene Debs ran strongest early in the twentieth century, were most likely to amend their state constitutions to allow some forms of direct democracy by 1914.[14] Direct democracy is more common in the West, in part because Populists and Socialists had greater political influence there and because Progressive era reformers gained influence in these states in the first decades of the twentieth century. Direct democracy was part of a broad set of **Progressive era reforms** that included attempts at weakening political parties, improving public health and working conditions, and regulating business.

Adopting Direct Democracy during the Progressive Era

Whereas the Populists set the stage for U.S. direct democracy in the 1890s, most states actually adopted institutions of direct democracy during the Progressive era of the next two decades. Populists and Progressives differed in their critiques of American representative government. As such, the Populists saw that common people were trustworthy and competent and that elected legislators were neither. The Populists' goal was to take power away from incumbent politicians, vested interests, and party machines and give it to voters. Progressives, on the other hand, were more sympathetic to the legislative process but wanted to "liberate representative government from corrupt forces so that it might become an effective instrument for social reform."[15] The Progressive model aimed to use direct democracy to improve representative government rather than replace it. Early advocates of direct democracy envisioned a process that allowed regular citizens to resolve a particular grievance. But modern direct democracy may have evolved into a process where professional politicians and wealthy interests use initiatives and referendums to advance their own agendas.[16]

The Ebb and Flow of Ballot Initiatives

From the 1930s to the 1960s, as legislatures became more professional and anticorruption laws took hold, direct democracy was used less. It made a comeback, however, as groups again began to use the initiative process to promote public votes on policy questions. There was a steady increase in the number of ballot measures qualified in all states since the 1960s. After a decline in the 1940s and 1950s, use of initiatives reached a new peak in the 1990s, when there were nearly 400 initiatives on statewide ballots—far more than in any other decade.[17] The annual use of initiatives remained relatively high by historic standards after 2000. It is important to remember that roughly 60 percent of all initiatives that qualify for state ballots are rejected by voters; however, measures that pass can have a powerful effect on the design of state political institutions and on the political agenda.[18]

---

[13] Steven Piott, *Giving Voters a Voice: The Origins of the Initiative and Referendum in America* (Columbia, MO: University of Missouri Press, 2003).

[14] Shaun Bowler, Todd Donovan, and Eric D. Lawrence, "Introducing Direct Democracy" (paper presented at the annual meeting of the American Political Science Association, Washington, DC, August 2005).

[15] Bruce Cain and Kenneth Miller, "The Populist Legacy: Initiatives and the Undermining of Representative Government," in *Dangerous Democracy? The Battle over Ballot Initiatives in America*, ed. Larry Sabato, Bruce Larson, and Howard Ernst (Lanham, MD: Rowman & Littlefield, 2002).

[16] Daniel A. Smith, *Tax Crusaders and the Politics of Direct Democracy* (New York: Routledge, 1998); Todd Donovan, Shaun Bowler, David McCuan, and Ken Fernandez, "Contending Players and Strategies: Opposition Advantages in Initiative Elections," in Bowler, Donovan, and Tolbert, *Citizens as Legislators*.

[17] Ellis, *Democratic Delusions*.

[18] David Magleby, "Direct Legislation in America," in Butler and Ranney, *Referendums around the World*.

Studies find a large degree of stability in terms of the subjects of ballot measures on which voters have been asked to decide over most of the last 100 years. The most common initiatives since 1980 have been governmental reform measures, such as term limits and campaign finance regulation (23 percent) and taxation questions (22 percent). Social and moral issues (17 percent) and environmental measures (11 percent) are the next most common questions.[19] Some attribute the revival of direct democracy in recent decades to a new generation of citizens who demand more say in politics but who are less interested in traditional forms of participation via representation by political parties.[20] Others note that the rise of initiative use in the United States corresponded with the proliferation of new interest groups[21] and with the maturation of a sophisticated industry of campaign professionals promoting the use of initiatives.[22]

Direct Democracy and National Politics

Battles over several state initiatives from the later decades of the twentieth century have set the stage for major policy debates at the national level. Contemporary initiative efforts in the states sometimes become part of larger campaigns that shape the issues discussed by politicians in Washington and those trying to win election to federal office. Antitax initiatives from the late 1970s—most notably, California's Proposition 13 in 1978—foreshadowed the enthusiasm for the Reagan-era federal tax cuts of the early 1980s.[23] Initiatives in California and Washington targeting affirmative action set the tone for national debate on the policy in the late 1990s. That same decade, voters in over a dozen states decided the fate of proposals to limit state legislative terms. Popular enthusiasm for term limits may have led some aspiring candidates for Congress to take positions in favor of short tenure in office (although several years later, many of those same members had less enthusiasm for limiting how long they should serve).

State initiatives and referendums proposing to ban gay marriage in 2004 had effects that spilled into the presidential election. Voters were more likely to evaluate George W. Bush and John Kerry in terms of the gay marriage issue if they lived in one of the 13 states where there was a gay marriage ban measure on the state's ballot.[24] Initiative activists with an eye on the national stage have gotten their proposals on the ballot in multiple states to promote their causes and set the national agenda.[25] As a result, measures backed by national groups advocating such things as increasing the minimum wage, eminent domain, school choice, nuclear freeze,

[19] Caroline J. Tolbert, "Cycles of Democracy: Direct Democracy and Institutional Realignment in the American States," *Political Science Quarterly* 118(2003):467–89.

[20] Russell Dalton, Wilhelm Burklin, and Andrew Drummond, "Public Attitudes toward Direct Democracy," *Journal of Democracy* 12(2001):141–53; and Ian Budge, "Political Parties in Direct Democracy," in *Referendum Democracy: Citizens, Elites and Deliberation in Referendum Campaigns,* ed. Matthew Mendelsohn and Andrew Parkin (New York: Palgrave, 2002).

[21] David Magleby, "Direct Legislation in America," in Butler and Ranney, *Referendums around the World*.

[22] David Broder, *Democracy Derailed: Initiative Campaigns and the Power of Money* (New York: Harcourt Brace, 2000); and Sabato, Larson, and Ernst, *Dangerous Democracy?*

[23] Smith, *Tax Crusaders and the Politics of Direct Democracy*.

[24] Todd Donovan, Caroline J. Tolbert, and Daniel A. Smith, "Priming Presidential Votes by Direct Democracy," *Journal of Politics* 70(2008):1217–31; David Campbell and J. Quinn Monson, "The Religion Card: Gay Marriage and the 2004 Presidential Election," *Public Opinion Quarterly* 72(3):399–419; Gregory B. Lewis, "Same-Sex Marriage and the 2004 Presidential Election," *Political Science and Politics* 38(2005):195–200; Daniel A. Smith, Matthew DeSantis, and Jason Kassel, "Same-Sex Marriage Ballot Measures and the 2004 Presidential Election," *State and Local Government Review* 38(2)(2006):77–90; Alan Abramowitz, "Terrorism, Gay Marriage, and Incumbency: Explaining the Republican Victory in the 2004 Presidential Election," *Forum* 2 (2004):art. 3, http://www.bepress.com/forum/vol2/iss4/art3; Barry Burden, "An Alternative Account of the 2004 Presidential Election," *Forum* 2 (2004):art. 2, http://www.bepress.com/forum/vol2/iss4/art2.

[25] Steven P. Nicholson, *Voting the Agenda: Candidates Elections and Ballot Propositions* (Princeton, NJ: Princeton University Press, 2005).

term limits, the repeal of affirmative action, and tax cuts have each gotten their measures on the ballot in several different states.

Nonetheless, most of the initiatives and referendums to reach a state's ballot are homegrown proposals. This does not mean that most initiatives are the product of the "average" citizen who rallies the grassroots to challenge an established order. The initiative process is also used by a wide array of interest groups, corporations, and political parties. Ballot initiatives targeting the use of public services by illegal immigrants have been used by the Republican Party in attempts to mobilize supporters or drive a wedge through the rival party's base.[26] Democrats have made similar attempts to mobilize likely Democratic voters with minimum wage initiatives.[27] Incumbent politicians, candidates for office, and wealthy individuals also promote their pet causes with initiatives.[28] In states where expensive petition campaigns are required to qualify for the ballot, many of the same powerful interest groups that dominate legislative politics—trial lawyers, teachers' unions, nurses, insurance companies, and casinos and Indian tribes—also fund campaigns promoting and opposing initiatives.[29]

Sometimes the primary goal of interest groups promoting ballot measures is not to win on Election Day. For example, in the 1990s, pro-business interest groups, including Americans for Tax Reform, promoted "paycheck protection" ballot measures in Oregon and California to require individual union members to give their leaders prior approval for dues to be used for political purposes. A leader of ATR hoped that their initiatives would force organized labor to spend millions of dollars in campaign funds on efforts to defeat the measures—money that unions would not be able to contribute to Democratic candidates. They turned out to be right—unions spent some $24 million to narrowly defeat the measure in California.[30]

Groups also use initiatives to pass policies that they cannot get through the legislature. Large membership interests, such as teachers' unions, have been successful in promoting initiatives designed to benefit their members. The California Teachers' Association, for example, sponsored the successful Proposition 98 in 1988, mandating that a fixed percentage of state general fund revenues support K–12 education. More recently, Washington's teachers' union also promoted two successful initiatives: Initiative 728 mandated smaller class sizes, and Initiative 732 mandated pay raises for the state's public school teachers. Interest groups also use ballot initiatives to send signals to legislators, or to force legislators to come up with an alternative.

The Explosion Continues

Nationally, the most initiatives qualifying for statewide ballots in one year was 87 (in 1914 and 1996). In the 2008 general election, there were 59 statewide initiatives and two popular referendums on statewide ballots; two years earlier, there were 74 initiatives and five popular referendums.[31] In both elections there also were hundreds more local referendums and initiatives on the ballots of all 50 states. Substantively, ballot propositions cover a remarkable range of issues; some of the issues involved are complex, whereas others are relatively straightforward. Some measures make

[26] Daniel A. Smith and Caroline Tolbert, "The Initiative to Party: Partisanship and Ballot Initiatives in California," *Party Politics* 7(2001):781–99; and Richard Hasen, "Parties Take the Initiative (and Vice Versa)," *Columbia Law Review* 100(2001):731–52.

[27] Jeanne Cummings, "Wedge Issue: Minimum Wage," *Wall Street Journal,* 1 May 2006, p. A4.

[28] Ellis, *Democratic Delusions.*

[29] Shaun Bowler and Todd Donovan, *Demanding Choices: Opinion, Voting, and Direct Democracy* (Ann Arbor, MI: University of Michigan Press, 1998).

[30] Smith and Tolbert, *Educated by Initiative.*

[31] National Conference of State Legislatures, "Ballot Measure Database," 2009, http://www.ncsl.org/default.aspx?tabid=16580.

national headlines; others remain obscure in terms of public or media attention. Voters have cast ballots dealing with issues as diverse as banning gay marriage, punishing negligent doctors, prohibiting the confinement of pregnant pigs, limiting the taxation and spending powers of state governments, funding stem cell research, and ending affirmative action programs and social welfare benefits to illegal immigrants. In many states, virtually no subject matter is off-limits.

Looking back at the November 2008 ballot, three states featured initiatives targeting immigrants (two of which failed), and three had measures that proposed banning abortion (all of which were rejected). Arizona, California, and Florida voters approved measures banning same-sex marriages. Arkansas voters approved an initiative that prohibited gay couples from adopting children. Coloradoans had 14 measures on their ballot, and rejected several proposals that would have made it easier for the state to tax and spend. Twelve measures appeared on ballots in Oregon and California. Californians approved billions of dollars in bond sales (for hospitals, veterans, and a high-speed train), and approved an initiative prohibiting the confinement of pregnant pigs and other farm animals.[32]

In 2009, Oakland, California, voters approved taxation of medical marijuana. Voters in Washington state approved a referendum extending the rights of marriage to same sex couples in "domestic partnerships," while Maine voters narrowly approved a referendum that overturned a state law that authorized same-sex marriages. The seven million dollar campaign was the most expensive ballot measure ever in Maine, with the largest contributions ($1.1 million) coming from the National Organization for Marriage (NOM), and the Catholic Diocese of Portland Maine ($550,000). The anti-gay marriage group NOM was found to be in violation of Maine's campaign finance law after refusing to release information about the source of their funding.[33]

Differences across Initiative States

States differ with regard to how directly democratic their direct democracy processes are in practice. In most of the United States, direct democracy is limited to legislative referendums used at both the state and local levels. Most western states that adopted the initiative early have rules that allow citizens to draft **constitutional initiatives** as well as **statutory initiatives**. Statutory initiatives are more readily amended or repealed by the legislature in some states (such as Colorado, Maine, Idaho, and Missouri), whereas others require waiting periods, supermajorities, or both before a statutory initiative may be amended. California is the only state where the legislature may neither amend nor repeal an initiative statute.

In states where rules for direct democracy were put in place when Populists and Progressives were still influential (such as Arizona, California, Colorado, and Oregon), provisions for the initiative and popular referendum are more radically democratic than what exists in states that adopted the initiative process later in the twentieth century. States that adopted the direct initiative and popular referendum in the early 1900s have rules that make it relatively easy to qualify for the ballot. Most early-adopting states have a relatively low threshold of signatures required to qualify initiatives as well as other requirements to qualify ballot measures.[34]

---

[32] Ballot Initiative Strategy Center, "2008 Ballot Election Results," 13 November 2008, http://www.ncsl.org.

[33] The group faced similar charges in Iowa and California. A federal judge ordered NOM to submit the information to Maine officials by June 1, 2010. U.S. District Court of Maine, "Memorandum Decision and Order." *National Organization for Marriage v. McKee*, May 23, 2010.

[34] Shaun Bowler and Todd Donovan, "Measuring the Effect of Direct Democracy on State Policy: Not All Initiatives Are Created Equal," *State Politics and Policy Quarterly* 4(2004):345–63.

Using the Initiative

As Figure 4.2 reveals, Oregon and California—two early adopters—lead the pack in initiative use, with both states averaging close to 6.3 initiatives per each two-year election cycle. Over 300 initiatives have appeared on Oregon ballots since that state adopted direct democracy, with California having nearly as many. The six states with the most frequent use of initiatives (Arizona, California, Colorado, North Dakota, Oregon, and Washington) have averaged more than three initiatives per general election since the Progressive era.[35] Roughly 60 percent of all initiative activity has taken place in these six states.[36] Few states, however, look like California or Oregon in terms of the ease of qualifying initiatives for the ballot and the difficulty that legislatures face when it comes to amending voter-approved initiatives.

The handful of states that adopted direct democracy long after the demise of the Populists and Progressives have much more restrictive rules on how it can be used. Alaska included the initiative in its constitution when it was admitted to the union (1959), but only Florida and Wyoming (1968), Illinois (1970), and Mississippi (1992) have adopted the initiative process since that time. Three of these states (Florida, Illinois, and Mississippi) only allow constitutional initiatives. Illinois and Mississippi place severe restrictions on the subject matter that may appear on the ballot, and both states have strict provisions for qualification. As such, initiatives are rarely used in these two states—only one initiative has ever appeared on the Illinois ballot, and only two have qualified in Mississippi.[37]

Limits on Initiative Content

Most any topic is a potential initiative subject. A few states, however, prohibit measures dealing with the judiciary, bills of rights, or

Figure 4.2

Historic Statewide Initiative Use (year of adoption through 2008)

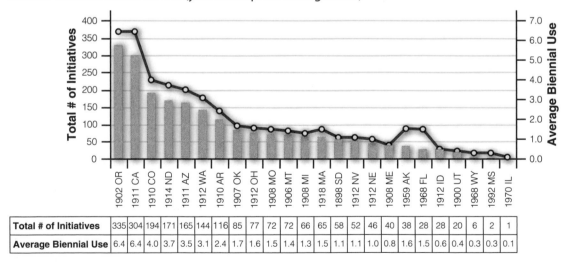

	1902 OR	1911 CA	1910 CO	1914 ND	1911 AZ	1912 WA	1910 AR	1907 OK	1912 OH	1908 MO	1906 MT	1908 MI	1918 MA	1898 SD	1912 NV	1912 NE	1908 ME	1959 AK	1968 FL	1912 ID	1900 UT	1968 WY	1992 MS	1970 IL
Total # of Initiatives	335	304	194	171	165	144	116	85	77	72	72	66	65	58	52	46	40	38	28	28	20	6	2	1
Average Biennial Use	6.4	6.4	4.0	3.7	3.5	3.1	2.4	1.7	1.6	1.5	1.4	1.3	1.5	1.1	1.1	1.0	0.8	1.6	1.5	0.6	0.4	0.3	0.3	0.1

Note: Bars represent the total number of initiatives that have qualified in a state since its adoption of direct democracy, with values plotted along the left-side axis. The line represents the average number of initiatives in a state every two years, with values plotted on the right-side axis.

[35] Caroline Tolbert, Daniel Lowenstein, and Todd Donovan, "Election Law and Rules for Using Initiatives," in Bowler, Donovan, and Tolbert, *Citizens as Legislators*.

[36] Ballot Initiative Strategy Center, "Election Results 2004."

[37] National Conference of State Legislatures, Initiative and Referendum in the 21st Century: Final Report and Recommendations of the NCSL I&R Task Force (Denver, CO, 2000), http://www.ncsl.org/default.aspx?tabid=16571.

tax questions. The major constraints on initiatives are constitutionality and single-subject laws, both of which are typically evaluated by state courts after a measure has been approved by voters. Some states allow elected officials or courts to amend or revise the language of propositions without the proponent's consent. Of the 24 states, only six have much of a preelection review at all. Four states—Colorado, Idaho, Montana, and Washington—have an advisory preelection certification process.

Half of the initiative states have rules that limit initiatives to one subject. Most state courts have been fairly tolerant of individual proposals with sweeping breadth, as long as their component parts could be seen as reasonably germane to one subject. State legislatures originally adopted the **single-subject rule** to ban egregious attempts at building coalitions of supporters by rolling many attractive features into a single measure in the hope of expanding potential support for it. One famous yet unsuccessful initiative proposal from California linked the regulation of margarine, voting rights for Native Americans, gambling, fishing, mining, and apportionment of the state senate into a single initiative question.[38] This sort of "log-rolling" proposal is prohibited by single-subject laws. Only Florida's State Supreme Court has been known to regularly nullify initiatives on single-subject grounds, even after proponents have collected hundreds of thousands of valid signatures to qualify their measures for the ballot. The Florida State Supreme Court is also the only court to overtly declare that single-subject evaluations should be applied more rigorously to initiatives than legislative bills.[39] Since 2000, however, state courts in California, Colorado, Nevada, and Oregon have become more rigid in the application of their state's single-subject rule. At times, this has meant that a single initiative must be split into several questions that are put before voters simultaneously.[40]

Qualifying for the Ballot

Initiatives and referendums, when they qualify for the ballot, are usually placed on a ballot whenever the next regularly scheduled general election occurs. This means direct democracy votes typically occur in even-numbered years. Some states (including Maine, Ohio, and Washington) have initiative votes annually in November, and a few (such as California) place initiatives and referendums on general and primary ballots every two years, so voters decide on an array of initiatives and referendums at least twice a year in even years. California and a handful of other states also allow either the governor or the legislature to schedule special statewide elections in odd years for votes on initiatives and referendums.

States that allow the initiative have considerable variation regarding how easy it is for citizens to use the process. Most states share four basic steps.[41] First, the proposal is drafted by proponents. Next, it is forwarded to a state office that issues an official title and summary of the measure. Proponents may then circulate petitions—usually within a fixed time period, often 90 or 180 days—for voters to sign. Finally, the state verifies whether a valid number of signatures were collected. If so, the proposal is placed on the ballot.

Rules for qualification vary across direct democracy states. In some states, petitioners have less time than in others. Some states also require that a certain proportion of signatures be collected in specific geographical areas, such as congressional districts. States also differ in the proportion of voters' signatures required to qualify for the ballot. Differences in these

[38] Winston Crouch, *The Initiative and Referendum in California* (Los Angeles: Haynes Foundation, 1950).

[39] Daniel Lowenstein, *Election Law: Cases and Materials* (Durham, NC: Carolina Academic Press, 1995), p. 282.

[40] Ellis, *Democratic Delusions*, pp. 144–46.

[41] For a more detailed discussion of California's initiative process, see California Secretary of State, http://www.ss.ca.gov/elections/elections.htm.

rules, and in the population of a state, affect how costly it is to get on a ballot. The difficulty of collecting hundreds of thousands of signatures means that many proponents hire people to collect signatures. Qualification is more difficult, and more costly (see Table 4.1), when a higher proportion of signatures must be collected in a shorter time period.[42]

Amateurs or Professionals?

In many states, it is difficult to place a measure on the ballot unless professional petition firms are paid to collect some or all the signatures required for qualification. In large states like California and Florida, where nearly 700,000 valid signatures are required to qualify a constitutional amendment initiative for 2010, few measures reach the ballot without proponents resorting to hiring firms that use paid petition gatherers to collect signatures. Some of these signature-gathering firms will have their subcontractors carry multiple petitions for the various groups that have hired them to gather signatures. For instance, in Missouri in 2006, employees of National Voter Outreach, a paid signature-gathering firm based in Carson City, Nevada, were carrying petitions for three separate measures: a measure tightening the state's eminent domain law, a measure limiting the taxing and spending authority of the state, and a measure increasing the tax on cigarettes to pay for health care costs for people receiving Medicaid. In states that have fewer voters, it is easier to collect the required signatures. In Colorado, for example, 76,000 valid signatures were needed to qualify either a statutory or constitutional amendment initiative in 2010. A hundred years ago, when there were far fewer people voting, fewer signatures were required to qualify a measure for the ballot, which may have helped to simplify the logistics of qualification.

Today, few citizen-based groups have the resources to collect signatures equal to 12, 8,

Table 4.1	

Ease of Qualifying Ballot Initiatives Index

State	Qualification Difficulty Index
Oregon	0
California	1
Colorado	1
North Dakota	1
Arkansas	2
Ohio	2
Michigan	2
South Dakota	2
Idaho	2
Arizona	3
Washington	3
Oklahoma	3
Montana	3
Missouri	3
Massachusetts	3
Utah	3
Nebraska	4
Maine	4
Nevada	4
Florida	4
Illinois	4
Alaska	5
Mississippi	5
Wyoming	6

Note: Higher scores indicate more difficulty; states with lower scores have the least burdensome rules for qualification.

Source: Shaun Bowler and Todd Donovan, "Measuring the Effect of Direct Democracy on State Policy: Not All Initiatives Are Created Equal," *State Politics and Policy Quarterly* 4(2004):345–63.

or even 5 percent of a state's voting population. The use of paid signature gatherers and professional campaign staff has been part of the process in some states since early in the

---

[42] Susan Banducci, "Direct Legislation: When Is It Used and When Does It Pass?" in Bowler, Donovan, and Tolbert, *Citizens as Legislators*.

twentieth century.[43] In the early 1900s, paid petition gatherers in some states were earning upwards of $0.03 a signature.[44] As the raw number of signatures required to qualify has increased, fewer voluntary, "grassroots" measures appear on state ballots.[45] In California, for example, volunteer petition campaigns are rarely successful. Those who wish to get a constitutional initiative amendment onto the ballot have to gather signatures equivalent to 8 percent of the number of votes for governor. This means gathering close to 1 million signatures in just 150 days, as a large percentage of signatures will surely be found to be invalid. Petition management firms in the state offer proponents a guarantee of qualification but at a price that runs close to $2 million for each initiative to be qualified. Paid signature gatherers in California have been known to earn up to $5 per valid signature, although the $1 to $2 range is more typical. In less populous states, the cost to qualify an initiative ranges anywhere between $50,000 and $400,000.

Champions of the Populist-Progressive vision of direct democracy have long argued that if the process is to combat the power of wealthy established interests, petition efforts should rely on volunteers only. In this spirit, several states passed laws banning the use of paid signature gathering. In the early 1900s, several states, including Ohio, South Dakota, and Washington, passed laws banning paid petition-gatherers. In the 1930s and 1940s, Oregon and Colorado also passed laws banning the practice, with Idaho and Nebraska following suit in the late 1980s.[46] The U.S. Supreme Court eventually overturned these laws in a 1988 decision, *Meyer v. Grant*, reasoning that the 1st Amendment protected paid petitioning, as it was a form of political speech.[47] This ruling, and the difficulties of qualifying measures, means that wealthy groups (unions, corporations, business organizations, professional associations, and trade groups) and wealthy individuals play a prominent, if not dominant, role in affecting what gets put to a public vote. Roughly a dozen states have responded by passing laws requiring circulators to disclose if they are being paid or not, and Oregon and North Dakota prohibit paid signature gathers from being compensated on a per-signature basis, requiring them instead to be paid a fixed salary or an hourly wage.[48]

Millionaires' Amusement?

Wealthy individuals, such as Microsoft cofounder Paul Allen, Hollywood actor-director Rob Reiner, billionaire financier George Soros, and even actor Arnold Schwarzenegger (in his pregovernor, *Terminator* days), have all bankrolled the qualification of successful ballot initiatives. For his part, Allen convinced taxpayers to subsidize a new stadium for his then mediocre football team, the Seattle Seahawks, but Washington voters rejected the school reform initiative he funded. In 1998, Reiner sponsored an initiative to create early childhood development programs, and in 2006, he sponsored a tax on wealthy individuals to expand preschool education. In the 1990s, Soros, along with a couple of other wealthy individuals, helped finance

[43] Charles Beard and Birl Shultz, eds., *Documents on the State-Wide Initiative, Referendum and Recall* (New York: Macmillan, 1912); and David McCuan, Shaun Bowler, Todd Donovan, and Ken Fernandez, "California's Political Warriors: Campaign Professionals and the Initiative Process," in Bowler, Donovan, and Tolbert, *Citizens as Legislators*.

[44] Daniel A. Smith and Joseph Lubinski, "Direct Democracy during the Progressive Era: A Crack in the Populist Veneer?" *Journal of Policy History* 14(4)(2002):349–83.

[45] Broder, *Democracy Derailed*; Peter Schrag, *Paradise Lost: California's Experience, America's Future* (New York: New Press, 1998); John Haskell, *Direct Democracy or Representative Government? Dispelling the Populist Myth* (Boulder, CO: Westview, 2001); and Ellis, *Democratic Delusions*.

[46] National Conference of State Legislatures, *Initiative and Referendum in the 21st Century*.

[47] *Meyer v. Grant* 486 U.S. 414 (1988).

[48] Todd Donovan and Daniel A. Smith, "Identifying and Preventing Signature Fraud on Ballot Measure Petitions," in Michael Alvarez, Thad E. Hall, and Susan D. Hyde, eds., *Election Fraud: Detecting and Deterring Electoral Manipulation* (Washington, DC: Brookings, 2008).

nearly a dozen initiatives legalizing the medical use of marijuana. In 2002, Schwarzenegger funded an initiative that bulked up spending on his state's after-school programs (and helped to burnish his image as a budding policy wonk). After making millions from his medical marijuana business, Richard Lee succeeded in qualifying a marijuana legalization initiative for the 2010 California ballot.

Financing Direct Democracy Campaigns

The large sums of money spent on ballot measure campaigns gave rise to concerns about the presence of an "initiative industrial complex."[49] From this perspective, paid political consultants are seen not just as "guns for hire" but also as actors who create the demand for their services by advocating their own proposals for ballot measures. Their services include contracting petition work, polling, crafting TV ads, and purchasing airtime for the ads.

The public clearly has concerns about the campaign side of direct democracy. Despite being overwhelmingly in favor of the initiative process, people claim that initiative campaigns are misleading, that campaigns are too expensive, and that "special interests" dominate the process.[50] Longtime and persistent critic of the initiative process, *The Los Angeles Times* editorialized in 2003 that "Direct democracy is running amok" in California. Critics in other states agree, such as the former president of the Florida Senate, who has warned of the potential "Californication" of Florida resulting from the rash of expensive initiative campaigns.[51]

One critical question about direct democracy is whether the initiative process is driven by citizens or by political consultants.[52] Some note that consulting and initiative marketing firms "sometimes test market issues for their feasibility . . . and then shop for a group to back them" and that petition firms may try to drum up business after pitching issues to potential sponsors.[53] However, few examples of this have occurred in California or elsewhere. The claim is likely overreaching, as one is hard-pressed to find evidence of this type of practice, save for a single campaign professional promoting a lottery initiative in 1988.[54]

Nonetheless, the amount of money spent on initiative politics can be staggering. In 2008, over $800 million was spent nationally on state-level initiative and referendum campaigns, nearly $300 million more than was spent on ballot measures in the 2006 election cycle.[55] In several states, more money was spent on ballot initiative campaigns than for all other races for political office combined. In California alone, proponents and opponents of eight initiatives on the November ballot spent more than $300 million in an effort to qualify the measures and sway voters on the merits of their arguments.

Direct Democracy Campaigns and the Supreme Court

These enormous expenditures are possible because the U.S. Supreme Court views initiative campaigns differently than candidate

[49] Schrag, *Paradise Lost*; and David Magleby and Kelly Patterson, "Consultants and Direct Democracy," *Political Science and Politics* 31(1998):160–62.

[50] Shaun Bowler, Todd Donovan, Max Neiman, and Johnny Peel, "Institutional Threat and Partisan Outcomes: Legislative Candidates' Attitudes toward Direct Democracy," *State Politics and Policy Quarterly* 1(2001):364–79.

[51] Smith, "Initiatives and Referendums."

[52] Magleby and Patterson, "Consultants and Direct Democracy."

[53] Schrag, *Paradise Lost*, p. 16.

[54] Todd Donovan, Shaun Bowler, and Dave McCuan, "Political Consultants and the Initiative Industrial Complex," in S. Bowler, T. Donovan, and C. Tolbert, eds., *Citizens as Legislators* (Columbus, OH: Ohio State University Press, 1998).

[55] Spending data reported by http://www.followthemoney.org.

contests. The Court recognizes that large contributions to candidates may create either the appearance or the actuality that a candidate for office may become corrupted.[56] This ruling has allowed Congress and state legislatures some limited ability to regulate the size of contributions given to candidates. Contributions to initiative campaigns, in contrast, are seen as attempts at direct communication with voters rather than attempts to influence elected officials. In *Bellotti v. First National Bank of Boston*, the Court reasoned in 1978 that there was no possibility of corruption or appearance of corruption because a ballot measure cannot provide illicit political favors to a donor of a campaign. In its *Bellotti* decision, the Court reasoned that states thus have no compelling reason to limit the 1st Amendment right of donors contributing to initiative campaigns.[57] The 1978 decision was also the Court's first effort to explicitly extend free speech rights to corporations.[58] Put simply, no limits exist on what sources can be used, or the amount spent, in ballot initiative campaigns.

"Special Interests" and Initiative Campaigns

As noted, one common critique of direct democracy is that well-financed campaigns trick voters into passing policies that they actually do not prefer. The argument that "special" interests dominate the initiative process is a plausible one. After all, if it can take up to $1 million to simply ensure a proposal gets on the ballot, playing initiative politics obviously requires significant resources. Ordinary citizens are likely to lack such funds, but established, well-funded groups

are not so disadvantaged. Powerful special interests, the argument goes, can afford to get any issues they want onto the ballot, and once the initiative is on the ballot, they buy enough spin doctors, campaign managers, and TV ads to get voters to vote for things they do not want or for things that harm the public interest.[59]

We can assess this argument by breaking it into two questions: first, do "special" economic interests dominate the initiative process (as opposed to broad-based, citizen concerns); and second, are voters readily swayed by expensive TV campaigns? One way to assess these questions is to ask whether narrowly focused economic interests (for example, banks, trade and industry groups, corporations, and professional associations) outspend other, broader-based kinds of citizens' groups. Another way is to ask whether these economic groups tend to win the initiative contests they finance.

Which Groups Dominate Direct Democracy? One major study of the role that interest groups play in the initiative process defines economic groups as those whose members and donors are almost exclusively business firms and professional organizations rather than individual citizens. Examples include the Missouri Forest Products Association, the California Beer and Wine Wholesalers, the Washington Software Association, and businesses such as casino operators and tobacco giant Philip Morris.[60] This study of eight states found that 68 percent of campaign contributions came from such narrowly based economic groups. It also found that ballot measures with more financial backing from economic interests were more likely to fail.[61] A similar study found

[56] *Buckley v. Valeo* 424 U.S. 1 (1976).

[57] *First National Bank of Boston v. Bellotti* 435 U.S. 765 (1978); and Daniel A. Smith, "Campaign Financing of Ballot Initiatives in the American States," in Sabato, Larson, and Ernst, *Dangerous Democracy?*

[58] Tolbert, Lowenstein, and Donovan, "Election Law and Rules for Using Initiatives."

[59] For variants of this argument, David Broder, *Democracy Derailed*; Schrag, *Paradise Lost*; and Smith, *Tax Crusaders and the Politics of Direct Democracy*.

[60] Elisabeth Gerber, *The Populist Paradox: Interest Group Influence and the Promise of Direct Legislation* (Princeton, NJ: Princeton University Press, 1999), pp. 69–71.

[61] Gerber, *The Populist Paradox*, p. 110.

that wealthy economic interests in California regularly outspent broadly based "citizen" groups, and 80 percent of campaign spending by these economic groups was directed against citizen group proposals that threatened business interests. However, when economic interest groups spend in favor of their own initiatives, they usually lose.[62]

In short, most of the big money in direct democracy comes from "special" interests defending themselves or, as with the case of the malpractice initiatives in Florida, fighting each other. A battle over a 1988 automobile insurance regulation in California provides an extreme example: Insurance companies and trial lawyers' groups spent over $82 million promoting four competing initiatives and spending heavily against a fifth proposal placed on the ballot by Ralph Nader's consumer group. Voters rejected all four well-financed initiatives but approved the fifth insurance measure (the one endorsed by consumer activist Nader).[63]

Record Expenditures In 2008, over half of the $800 million spent on ballot measures was associated with a handful of campaigns. As Table 4.2 shows, initiative campaigns in California, Colorado, and Ohio spent over $0.5 billion to convince voters to accept or reject measures on the ballot. The most expensive campaign was an effort to convince California voters to approve a package of measures that expanded gambling (and tax revenues from gambling) on tribal lands. As in other years, spending advantages were often associated with the success of a campaign. But this is not always the case. Well-funded opponents of a same-sex marriage ban were not able to prevail in California. The "payday loan" industry outspent opponents promoting regulations on the industry by nearly 40 to 1 in Ohio, yet were defeated. That industry also outspent opponents by 14 to 1 in Arizona, where they were also defeated.

Table 4.2

Most Expensive Ballot Initiative Campaigns, 2008

State	Ballot No.	Subject	Side	Expenditure
CA	94, 95, 96, 97	Tribal gambling compacts	**Yes**	**$108 million**
			No	$64 million
CA	8	Ban same-sex marriage	**Yes**	**$42 million**
			No	$64 million
OH	6	Allow state's first casino	Yes	$26 million
			No	**$39 million**
CA	7	Utilities buy 20% clean energy	Yes	$9 million
			No	**$30 million**
CA	16	Limit publicly owned electricity	Yes	$46 million
			No	**$80,000**
CO	47, 49	Prohibit closed shop, no paycheck deductions (antiunion)	Yes	$6 million
			No	**$31 million**
CA	93	Revise term limits	Yes	$17 million
			No	**$9 million**
CA	98, 99	Eminent domain	Yes	$7 million
			No	**$17 million***
CA	10	Bonds for alternative fuel vehicles	Yes	$23 million
			No	**$0.2 million**
OH	5	Limit payday loan businesses	**Yes**	**$0.5 million**
			No	$21 million

Bold: indicates winning side.
*Groups spent across multiple campaigns to defeat a proposal while advocating alternative measure that voters approved.

High levels of expenditure listed in Table 4.2 reflect the high costs of campaigning in populous states like California and Ohio. When the costs of campaigns and number of voters are considered, spending on ballot measures is much higher in other states. One Alaska campaign over adding new regulations to mining saw $61 spent per vote cast in 2008. The same year, over $12 was spent per vote cast on a

---

[62] Elisabeth Gerber, "Interest Group Influence in the California Initiative Process," Public Policy Institute of California Report, November 1998.

[63] Arthur Lupia, "Shortcuts versus Encyclopedias: Information and Voting Behavior in California Insurance Reform Elections," *American Political Science Review* 88(1994):63–76.

South Dakota abortion measure. In each case, most of the spending was on the "no" side, and the measures were defeated.

Does Money Matter in Initiative Campaigns?

Money spent to defeat initiatives can be quite effective. Some research shows that a dollar spent by the "no" campaign has almost twice as much impact on the eventual vote share than a dollar spent by the "yes" side.[64] This may explain why narrow economic groups regularly defeat initiatives such as environmental or business regulations that enjoy substantial majority support in preelection polls, but they can have trouble advancing their own interests.[65] There is some evidence that measures supported by broad-based and grassroots citizens' groups pass at rates a bit higher than average, regardless of campaign spending.[66] But wealthy interests may avoid wasting their money when defeat is certain. When this is accounted for, money spent by both the "yes" and "no" sides appears to have similar effects on support for ballot measures.[67]

Although exceptions do exist, wealthy economic interests aren't usually successful at using initiatives to "buy" public policy that directly benefits them. California's wealthiest power company, Pacific Gas and Electric, spent $46 million pitching what it called a "Taxpayer's Right to Vote" initiative in 2010. It would have protected PG&E's monopoly by making it harder for cities to establish public utilities. Despite PG&E outspending opponents by 575 to 1, voters rejected the proposal.

Heavy spending can also mobilize opposition spending by other wealthy interests. This was the case with the 2008 Ohio casino initiative listed in Table 4.2. It generated massive opposition spending from the owners of a casino in a neighboring state who feared losing customers. Most initiatives that do pass can be seen as things, for better or worse, that tap into the preferences and concerns of the broader public, such as social and moral questions.[68] Many measures that pass, such as tougher criminal-sentencing laws, animal protection laws regulating hunting, or even somewhat peculiar measures—such as a 1998 California initiative that banned the slaughter of horses for human consumption and a 2002 Florida initiative that amended the state's constitution to prohibit the confinement of gestating pigs in crates—pass despite having relatively little campaign spending by the proponents.

Dumber Than Chimps? Voting on Ballot Questions

A voter's ability to make reasonably informed choices on ballot measures depends on what sort of information is available. Few suggest that voters study the details of the laws they are voting on. Rather than using exhaustive research, they decide on the basis of information shortcuts that are easily available.[69] Information about who is in favor or against a proposal may be the primary shortcut many people use.[70] Partisanship is one of the most reliable predictors of voting

[64] Banducci, "Direct Legislation."

[65] Magleby, *Direct Legislation*; and Bowler and Donovan, *Demanding Choices*.

[66] Gerber, *The Populist Paradox*, pp. 18-19; and Donovan, Bowler, McCuan, and Fernandez, "Contending Players and Strategies," 90.

[67] Thomas Stratmann, "Is Spending More Potent for or against a Proposition?" *American Journal of Political Science* 50(2006):788–801.

[68] Bowler and Donovan, *Demanding Choices*.

[69] Arthur Lupia, "Dumber Than Chimps? An Assessment of Direct Democracy Voters," in Sabato, Larson, and Ernst, *Dangerous Democracy?*

[70] Arthur Lupia and Matthew McCubbins, *The Democratic Dilemma: Can Citizens Learn What They Need to Know?* (New York: Cambridge University Press, 1998); Lupia, "Shortcuts versus Encyclopedias"; and Bowler and Donovan, *Demanding Choices*.

on ballot measures.[71] If, for example, voters see a prominent Democrat support a proposition, then loyal Democratic voters are likely to support the proposition and Republicans oppose it.

Where do voters find these cues to help them make informed decisions on ballot questions? In many states, an official state agency mails every registered voter a pamphlet that lists each ballot proposal and includes arguments for and against the proposition. Other sources include media coverage and paid ads. The availability of information shortcuts may explain why so few examples of initiatives pass that are later found to be unpopular with the voters who approved them.

The Role of the Media in Initiative Campaigns

A survey of voters found that just 20 percent claimed to make use of TV ads. A follow-up question found that only 13 percent of this group thought the information in the ads was "very important" in affecting their decisions. In contrast, 85 percent of consultants saw TV and radio as "very important" information for voters. Consultants see TV and radio ads as the most influential, whereas voters themselves see ads as one of the least important sources of information. Similarly, consultants afford the advertising mailers produced by the campaigns a much larger degree of importance than do voters.

These differences between what voters say they use when deciding on ballot measures and what consultants think they use may come as little surprise. Most people probably have little wish to claim being dupes of advertising, whereas consultants believe in their own importance. Thus, if these responses contain

bias, it is probably for voters to underestimate the effects of ads and for consultants to overestimate their effects. However disparate and inconsistent the results, they could be accurate: It may be that a relatively small group responds to information in TV ads, but these might be the voters who consultants are trying to reach with their ads.

Despite these differences in perceptions of information sources, some similarities emerge. Both consultants and voters, for example, recognize the importance of the news media. Voters see news media as more important than advertisements, and the consultants' evaluations of the importance of news are similarly high. Consultants and voters also have similar perceptions of the state-provided voter's guide in terms of importance. The voter's guide is seen by voters and consultants as an especially important piece of campaign information provided to voters. This is consistent with our idea that it provides a convenient and easy source of endorsements.

TV ads may actually provide useful cues to voters. One study of initiative campaign TV ads from several states found the ads often provide cues, such as names of sponsors or opponents, as well as name prominent groups, newspapers, and politicians who have taken positions on the measure. High levels of spending on initiative TV ads probably increase public awareness of initiatives[72] and may increase public attention to campaign issues. This may explain higher levels of general knowledge about politics in states with prominent initiative campaigns.[73] Relatedly, another study found voters more likely to have heard about initiatives when more was spent on the campaigns and that more citizens voted on initiatives that had higher campaign spending.[74]

[71] Regina Branton, "Examining Individual-Level Voting Behavior on State Ballot Propositions," *Political Research Quarterly* 56(2003):367–77. Smith and Tolbert, "The Initiative to Party."

[72] Shaun Bowler and Todd Donovan, "Do Voters Have a Cue? TV Ads as a Source of Information in Referendum Voting," *European Journal of Political Research* 41 (2002): 777–93; Stephen P. Nicholson, "The Political Environment and Ballot Proposition Awareness," *American Journal of Political Science* 47(2003):403–10.

[73] Mark Smith, "Ballot Initiatives and the Democratic Citizen," *Journal of Politics* 64(2002):892–903.

[74] Bowler and Donovan, *Demanding Choices.*

Direct Democracy and Electoral Politics

Initiative and referendum campaigns can alter a state's political context. Several examples of ballot measures affect the agenda and tone of candidate elections.[75] In 1998, for example, Republican Party operatives in Colorado tried to link Democratic candidates to positions on state ballot initiatives that Republicans expected voters to find unpopular. Democrats did the same and ran campaign ads linking the Republican gubernatorial candidate to two antiabortion measures. The Republican had been trying to distance himself from the social conservatives. During their 2004 Florida campaign, the rival U.S. Senate candidates attempted to craft their campaign themes to fit with initiatives on the state's ballot. Republican nominee Mel Martinez, for example, worked several ballot issues into his standard campaign speech and at candidate debates. In California, numerous candidates for governor, including Arnold Schwarzenegger, have sponsored initiatives to promote their candidacies.[76]

Political party organizations also use initiatives to promote **wedge issues**—measures they hope will divide the opposing party's candidates and weaken the opposition's base of support. Two major examples of wedge issues from the past decade are affirmative action and immigration initiatives. In 1996, Republicans promoted a California initiative to restrict affirmative action and another measure restricting services to illegal immigrants, hoping that Democrats across the nation would be forced to adopt policy positions that would harm their chances for reelection. Republican governor

Pete Wilson of California, as well as Democratic candidate John Van de Kamp, raised money to put several policy questions on the ballot when they sought office.[77]

Anecdotes and academic studies also suggest that different ballot measures can mobilize different elements of the electorate at different times.[78] A classic example is the 1982 California gubernatorial election. The Democratic mayor of Los Angeles, Tom Bradley, led narrowly in polls conducted immediately prior to the November vote, but Bradley ended up losing to Republican George Deukmejian. In this case, polls may have had difficulty estimating how an initiative would shape the participating electorate. The same ballot included a highly contested gun control measure, Proposition 15, which the National Rifle Association (NRA) opposed. The NRA spent over $5 million against the measure and rallied pro-gun voters to the polls.[79] Deukmejian probably benefited from these voters being drawn to the polls.

Spillover Effects of Ballot Measures in Candidate Races

Direct democracy's effect on candidate races may be indirect. One prominent study found that various state and local ballot measures advocating a freeze on the development of nuclear weapons in 1982 affected how voters evaluated candidates in U.S. Senate elections, in some U.S. House races, and even in some gubernatorial contests. In places where voters were presented the nuclear freeze question, they were more likely to evaluate candidates in terms of the nuclear proliferation measure. There were similar effects with California's Proposition 187 in 1994, which restricted social services

---

[75] Nicholson, *Voting the Agenda*; Donovan, Tolbert, and Smith, "Priming Presidential Votes by Direct Democracy"; Sunshine Hillygus and Todd Shields, "Moral Issues and Voter Decision Making in the 2004 Presidential Election," *Political Science and Politics* 38(2005):201–10; Burden, "An Alternative Account of the 2004 Presidential Election."

[76] Smith and Tolbert, *Educated by Initiative.*

[77] Smith and Tolbert, "The Initiative to Party."

[78] Caroline J. Tolbert, John Grummel, and Daniel A. Smith, "The Effect of Ballot Initiatives on Voter Turnout in the American States," *American Politics Research* 29(2001):625–48.

[79] John Allswang, *The Initiative and Referendum in California, 1898–1998* (Stanford, CA: Stanford University Press, 2000), pp. 125–26.

to illegal immigrants, and Proposition 209 in 1996, which ended affirmative action in the state. Both ballot questions shaped the issues voters used to evaluate candidates.[80]

One need only point to the 2004 presidential election to understand the potential ramifications of ballot measures on candidate elections. Assessing George W. Bush's narrow victory in Ohio, which tipped the electoral college balance in his favor, journalists and political analysts were quick to credit the mobilizing effects of Issue 1, a statewide antigay marriage measure on the ballot that year. *The New York Times* speculated that "state constitutional amendments banning same-sex marriage increased the turnout of socially conservative voters in many of the 11 states where the measures appeared on the ballot," with the measures appearing "to have acted like magnets for thousands of socially conservative voters in rural and suburban communities who might not otherwise have voted."[81] Although scholars have questioned the actual turnout effects of the statewide same-sex marriage ballot measures, the margin in Ohio was so close that if the initiative had even a minor effect on turning out pro-Bush voters, it may have been decisive.[82]

Direct Democracy and Turnout in Elections

As the 2004 Ohio example suggests, statewide ballot initiatives may affect politics by bringing voters to the polls who wouldn't otherwise

turn out. In 1978, more Californians cast votes for a critical antitax measure (**Proposition 13**) than cast votes for the governor's race on the same ballot. Studies of voting prior to the 1990s concluded that ballot measures did not affect voter turnout. Political scientist David Magleby concluded in 1984 that "turnout is not increased by direct legislation," although occasionally, a highly salient measure, such as California's Proposition 13 in 1978, "might encourage" higher turnout.[83]

Recent studies of initiative use, however, have produced evidence that initiatives can increase turnout by 0.5 percent per initiative in midterm elections and 0.3 percent in presidential elections, all else being equal.[84] Initiatives receiving substantial media attention have the greatest effect on turnout, particularly in "off-year" (non–presidential election year) state elections.[85] In municipal races, evidence has shown that at the local level, cities that use the initiative process have higher voter turnout than cities that don't allow their citizens to place measures directly on the ballot.[86]

The Effects of Direct Democracy on Citizens

Some propose that frequent voting on ballot measures may make people feel more as if they "have a say" in politics.[87] Evidence of this is mixed. Some studies show that people in states with initiatives are more likely than people in noninitiative states to think government is

[80] Nicholson, *Voting the Agenda*, pp. 111, 124.

[81] Jame Dao, "Flush with Victory, Grass-Roots Crusader against Same-Sex Marriage Thinks Big," *The New York Times*, 26 November 2004, p. A28.

[82] Sunshine Hillygus and Todd Shields, "Moral Issues and Voter Decision Making in the 2004 Presidential Election," *Political Science and Politics* 38(2005):201–0; Smith, DeSantis, and Kassel, "Same-Sex Marriage Ballot Measures"; Burden, "An Alternative Account of the 2004 Presidential Election"; and Abramowitz, "Terrorism, Gay Marriage, and Incumbency."

[83] Magleby, *Direct Legislation*, p. 197.

[84] Caroline Tolbert, Todd Donovan, Bridgett King, and Shaun Bowler. "Election Day Registration, Competition and Voter Turnout." In B. Cain, T. Donovan and C. Tolbert (eds.), *Democracy in the States* (Washington: Brookings Institution Press, 2008).

[85] Mark Smith, "The Contingent Effects of Ballot Initiatives and Candidate Races on Turnout," *American Journal of Political Science* 45(2001):700–706.

[86] Zoltan Hajnal and Paul Lewis, "Municipal Institutions and Voter Turnout in Local Elections," *Urban Affairs Review* 35(2003):645–68.

[87] Shaun Bowler and Todd Donovan, "Democracy, Institutions, and Attitudes about Citizen Influence on Government," *British Journal of Political Science* 32(2002):371–90.

responsive,[88] and that initiative use corresponds with people believing they can make a difference in politics.[89] It is difficult to determine if this is due to something else about states that use initiatives, and scholars have been unable to replicate results linking initiative use to opinions about government responsiveness.[90] Other studies have found that people have higher levels of factual knowledge about politics in places where initiatives are used more frequently, perhaps because initiatives stimulate media attention.[91] Still others have linked the use of direct democracy to happiness, at least in Switzerland.[92] Another found that people in initiative states are more likely to engage in political discussion, have greater political knowledge, and contribute to interest groups.[93] None of this means that initiatives make people more likely to trust government. Initiatives, many with antigovernment themes, may create an environment that encourages people to distrust government.[94]

Other research suggests that the initiative process may actually stimulate greater interest group activity, increasing the number of broad-based interest groups in a state. Interest groups in initiative states tend to have more members than those in noninitiative states, because the process provides potential groups with yet another incentive to become mobilized and engaged in the political process. States with the initiative, studies have found, have more registered citizens and nonprofit groups than those states without the process.[95]

Direct Democracy and Minorities

As noted, one of the original concerns about direct democracy is the potential it has to allow a majority of voters to trample the rights of minorities. Many still worry that the process can be used to harm gays and lesbians as well as ethnic, linguistic, and religious minorities.[96] Those who worry about repressive majorities point to a series of antiminority measures approved by voters. A majority of voters have supported initiatives repealing affirmative action protections in California, Michigan, Washington, and Nebraska, but in 2008, voters in Colorado bucked the trend, and narrowly defeated an anti–affirmative action ballot initiative. The battle over illegal immigration has been a perennial issue on the ballot in Arizona. Voters have approved propositions repealing bilingual education in Arizona, California, and Massachusetts (though Coloradoans rejected such an initiative in 2002). Initiatives declaring English an "official language" have been approved in

[88] Bowler and Donovan, "Democracy, Institutions and Attitudes"; Smith and Tolbert, *Educated by Initiative*.

[89] Bowler and Donovan, "Democracy, Institutions and Attitudes."

[90] Joshua Dyck and Edward Lascher, Jr., "Direct Democracy and Political Efficacy Reconsidered," *Political Behavior* 31(2009):401–27.

[91] Mark Smith, "Ballot Initiatives and the Democratic Citizen"; Matthias Benz and Alois Stutzer, "Are Voters Better Informed when They Have a Larger Say in Politics?" *Public Choice* 119(2004):31–59.

[92] Bruno Frey and Alois Stutzer, "Happiness, Economy and Institutions," *The Economic Journal* 110(2000):918–38.

[93] Caroline J. Tolbert, Ramona McNeal, and Daniel A. Smith, "Enhancing Civic Engagement: The Effect of Direct Democracy on Political Participation and Knowledge," *State Politics and Policy Quarterly* 3(2003):23–41.

[94] Joshua Dyck, "Initiated Distrust: Direct Democracy and Trust in Government," *American Politics Research* 34(2009):539–68.

[95] Frederick Boehmke, "The Effect of Direct Democracy on the Size and Diversity of State Interest Group Populations," *Journal of Politics* 64(2002):827–44.

[96] See, for example, Lydia Chavez, *The Color Bind: California's Battle to End Affirmative Action* (Berkeley: University of California Press, 1998); Barbara Gamble, "Putting Civil Rights to a Popular Vote," *American Journal of Political Science* 41(1998):245–69; Rodney Hero and Caroline Tolbert, "A Racial/Ethnic Diversity Interpretation of Politics and Policy in the States of the U.S.," *American Journal of Political Science* 40(1996):851–71; and Donald P. Haider-Markel, Alana Querze, and Kara Lindaman, "'Win, Lose or Draw?' A Reexamination of Direct Democracy and Minority Rights," *Political Research Quarterly* 60(2007):304–14. Conversely, see Bruno Frey and L. Goette, "Does the Popular Vote Destroy Civil Rights?" *American Journal of Political Science* 41(1998):245–69.

numerous states.[97] Scores of measures dealing with gay rights and gay marriage have appeared on state and local ballots,[98] and many cities have held referendums on whether to abolish low-income housing.[99] This presents a critical question: Does direct democracy harm minorities?

Recent scholarly research shows that the initiative process "is sometimes prone to produce laws that disadvantage relatively powerless minorities—and probably is more likely than legislatures to do so."[100] State and local ballot initiatives have been used to undo policies—such as school desegregation, protections against job and housing discrimination, and affirmative action—that minorities have secured from legislatures where they are included in the bargaining process. But most initiatives probably do not produce divisions between majorities of white voters and minority voters. Studies of support for ballot initiatives across different groups of voters show that minority voters were no more likely to support the losing side in an initiative contest than white voters. This may reflect that most initiatives do not pit the interests of racial and ethnic minorities against those of the majority or perhaps that minorities and whites have similar issues and concerns addressed by the initiative process. It is important to note, however, that on issues dealing with racial and ethnic matters, studies show that racial and ethnic minorities do end up more on the losing side of the popular vote.[101]

The issue of gay rights has been one of the more contentious areas of initiative politics where minority interests are frequently put to a vote. Majorities have, in some cases, voted to restrict the extension of some civil rights to gays and lesbians. Until recently, with the rash of anti–same-sex marriage amendments on state-wide ballots, voters in a number of states had refused to pass most measures that would deny gays and lesbians protections against discrimination. A 1992 anti-gay measure in Colorado, Amendment 2, which changed the state constitution to expressly prohibit local laws aimed at protecting gays and lesbians against discrimination, was a major exception.[102] The Colorado measure was eventually overturned by the U.S. Supreme Court in 1995 for being an unconstitutional denial of equal protection before the law.[103] Voters, however, have been much less tolerant of granting equal rights to marriage. By 2010, citizens in at least 27 states had voted to ban same-sex marriage. About half of these proposals reached the ballot via the initiative process, but most were referred to voters by state legislatures.

The record of direct democracy for minority interests is a mixed bag then. Racial and ethnic minorities may agree with majority voters on most ballot measures, but there have been some critical initiatives where minority rights have been lost when put to a public vote. Yet, in nearly every instance where the initiative process has been used to limit minority rights to fair housing, desegregated schools, public services, and protections against discrimination, courts have stepped in to overturn initiatives and uphold minority rights.[104] But regardless of whether antiminority ballot

[97] Jack Citrin, Beth Reingold, Evelyn Walters, and Donald Green, "The 'Official English' Movement and the Symbolic Politics of Language in the United States," *Western Political Quarterly* 43(1990):535–60.

[98] Donald Haider-Markel, "AIDS and Gay Civil Rights: Politics and Policy at the Ballot Box," *American Review of Politics* 20(1999):349–75; and Todd Donovan, James Wenzel, and Shaun Bowler, "Direct Democracy Initiatives after *Romer*," in Craig Zimmerman, Ken Wald, and Clyde Wilcox, eds., *The Politics of Gay Rights* (Chicago: University of Chicago Press, 2000).

[99] Roger Caves, *Land Use Planning: The Ballot Box Revolution* (Newbury Park, CA: Sage, 1992).

[100] Cain and Miller, "The Populist Legacy," in Sabato, Larson, and Ernst, *Dangerous Democracy?* p. 52.

[101] Zoltan Hajnal, Elisabeth Gerber, and H. Louch, "Minorities and Direct Legislation: Evidence from California Ballot Proposition Elections," *Journal of Politics* 64(2002):154–77.

[102] Donovan, Wenzel, and Bowler, "Direct Democracy Initiatives after *Romer*."

[103] *Romer v. Evans* 517 U.S. 620 (1996).

[104] Kenneth Miller, "Constraining Populism: The Real Challenge of Initiative Reform," *Santa Clara Law Review* 41(2001):1037–84; and Bowler and Donovan, *Demanding Choices*.

Comparisons Help Us Understand

DEMOCRACY AND MINORITIES

Are minorities worse off when policies are decided by representative democracy or directly by voters? History shows that both can produce anti-minority outcomes. State legislators have approved laws allowing slavery, racial segregation, laws excluding Chinese from owning land, the internment of Japanese in concentration camps during World War II, and laws advanced by the Ku Klux Klan designed to strip Catholics of their rights. None of these discriminatory laws needed direct democracy to flourish. But representative democracy, with its opportunities for minority representatives to participate while laws are being crafted, may have a better record of advancing civil rights.

In recent years, voters and legislators have been making decisions about the nature of rights that are extended to gays and lesbians.

A recent study compared minority rights decisions produced by representative democracy to those produced by direct democracy. It found that most civil rights bills affecting gays and lesbians in state legislatures were "pro-gay" (for example, banning job discrimination) and that slightly more pro-gay than anti-gay bills (for example, rules against being a foster parent) were approved by state legislators. With direct democracy, most civil rights proposals were anti-gay, and anti-gay measures were more likely to pass. Overall, representative democracy produced pro-gay outcomes 44 percent of the time, compared to 39 percent for direct democracy. The difference between outcomes across these institutions is subtle, because most pro- or anti–minority rights proposals failed. But the authors note that minority rights suffer more under direct democracy, especially when the policy is anti-minority in intent.[1]

[1] Donald P. Haider-Markel, Alana Querze, and Kara Lindaman. 2007. 'Win, Lose or Draw?' A Reexamination of Direct Democracy and Minority Rights." *Political Research Quarterly* 60:304–14.

measures pass or fail, they may still have effects on people they target. By targeting a minority group with an initiative, for example, public attitudes about the group (or about policies that benefit the group) can be changed, with mass opinion becoming less tolerant of the targeted minority group.[105]

The Effects of Direct Democracy on Public Policy

By this point, it should be clear that there are many reasons to expect that direct democracy can make a state's political environment and its public policies different than if there were no initiative process. When voters are allowed to make direct choices on policies, they sometimes make decisions that their elected representatives would not. An obvious example of this is term limits. Voters in many states have placed limits on time their representatives may serve. Absent the initiative process, elected representatives rarely, if ever, adopt such a policy.[106] But besides term limits and some forms of campaign finance reform, states that use the initiative are no more likely than states without the process to adopt other ethics and lobbying reform measures.[107] It is unclear, then, whether direct democracy systematically makes policy more representative of what people want or if it leads to "better" public policy.

[105] Donovan, Wenzel, and Bowler, "Direct Democracy and Minorities."

[106] The exception is Louisiana. Caroline Tolbert, "Changing Rules for State Legislatures: Direct Democracy and Governance Policies," in Bowler, Donovan, and Tolbert, eds., *Citizens as Legislators*; and Bowler and Donovan, "Measuring the Effect of Direct Democracy on State Policy."

[107] Daniel A. Smith, "Direct Democracy and Election and Ethics Laws," in Bruce Cain, Todd Donovan, and Caroline Tolbert, eds., *Democracy in the States: Experiments in Elections Reform* (Washington, DC: Brookings, 2008).

Some scholars and practitioners have proposed that the mere presence of the initiative process can affect public policy by changing how legislators behave. If legislators anticipate that there is a threat that someone might pass a law by initiative, then legislators may have greater incentives to pass some version of the law so they can maintain influence over what the final law looks like.[108] Initiatives can also send signals about the sort of policies the public wants.[109] Several studies show that certain public policies—including abortion regulations, death penalty laws, some civil rights policies, and spending on some state programs—more closely match public opinion in states with initiatives than in states without initiatives.[110] As an example, states with liberal public opinion and initiatives may have relatively liberal abortion rules, whereas states with conservative opinions and initiatives may have conservative policies. Absent the initiative, policies may be less likely to reflect the state's opinion climate. Studies that examine a wide range of state policies, however, find no such effects; some initiatives may make policy more reflective of public opinion with some policies but not others.[111]

The biggest effects of direct democracy on policy may be in the realm of what Caroline Tolbert calls "governance policy"—policies that set the rules about how government can function. Voters in initiative states can, and do, pass measures that amend rules that structure the political system itself. These include initiatives that may run counter to the interests of elected officials. States with the initiative process are more

likely to have adopted term limits and tougher rules for adopting new taxes and increasing spending[112] and were quicker to adopt some campaign finance regulations.[113] Examples of tax limitation measures include California's Proposition 13 of 1978, Oregon's Measure 5 in 1990, and Colorado's Taxpayers Bill of Rights (TABOR) amendment of 1992. If given a chance via direct democracy, voters often place constraints on what their representatives can do, especially when it comes to fiscal matters.

Long-Term Effects of Direct Democracy

Direct democracy can alter state policy directly by providing an additional point of access for citizens and interest groups. Advocates of decriminalization of drugs, campaign finance reforms, physician-assisted suicide, and many other policies have successfully used direct democracy to do an "end run" around state legislatures that did not turn their ideas into policy. As noted, some suggest this threat of the "gun behind the door" makes state policy more representative of state opinion. But what are the major long-term consequences of direct democracy on state policy?

In addition to promoting specific policy ideas, the initiative process allows those outside of the legislature, and those outside of the traditional corridors of power, the ability to permanently change rules that define institutions of government. As examples, initiatives have been used to rewrite state rules about how judges sentence

---

[108] Gerber, *The Populist Paradox.*

[109] Thomas Romer and Howard Rosenthal, "Bureaucrats versus Voters: On the Political Economy of Resource Allocation by Direct Democracy," *Quarterly Journal of Economics* 93(1979):563–87.

[110] Kevin Arceneaux, "Direct Democracy and the Link between Public Opinion and State Abortion Policy," *State Politics and Policy Quarterly* 2(2002):372–87; Elisabeth Gerber, "Legislative Response to the Threat of Popular Initiatives," *American Journal of Political Science* 40(1996):99–128; Gerber, *The Populist Paradox*; Matsusaka, *For the Many or the Few*; and Bowler and Donovan, "Measuring the Effect of Direct Democracy on State Policy."

[111] Michael Hagen, Edward Lascher, and John Camobreco, "Response to Matsusaka: Estimating the Effect of Ballot Initiatives on Policy Responsiveness," *Journal of Politics* 63(2001):1257–63; and John Camobreco, "Preferences, Fiscal Policies, and the Initiative Process," *Journal of Politics* 60(1998):819–29.

[112] Tolbert, "Changing Rules for State Legislatures."

[113] John Pippen, Shaun Bowler, and Todd Donovan, "Election Reform and Direct Democracy: The Case of Campaign Finance Regulations in the American States," *American Politics Research* 30(2002):559–82.

criminals, how much a state may collect via existing taxes, and how much the legislature may spend in a given year. Initiatives have been used to change rules about future tax increases and have placed limits on how often legislators may run for reelection. As we note in Chapter 10, these tax and expenditure limits (TELs) adopted by direct democracy may have important long-run effects on state and local finances.

The long-term effect of policy passed by direct democracy is probably more consequential in states that allow constitutional initiatives. When initiatives constraining taxing and spending are embedded in a state's constitution, it is difficult for elected officials to amend budgeting rules. This complicates their budgeting tasks. This means that voters can place things in their constitution that limit property taxes, increase tobacco taxes, guarantee a certain share of general funds for education, or authorize teacher pay raises and smaller class sizes. Even statutory initiatives can complicate the task of crafting long-term budgets. A single ballot may present voters with choices about cutting some taxes, raising others, issuing bonds for specific projects, and increasing spending on specific programs. When legislatures pass their budgets, their choices about increasing spending or cutting taxes need not be linked to specific revenue sources and programs. Voters, deciding on individual initiatives, face no such constraints.

Despite all of this, there are reasons to expect that the long-range effects of direct democracy are not that dramatic. Once an initiative is approved by voters, proponents often do not have the resources or political clout to maintain pressure on legislators over time to ensure that their law is implemented as the proponents would like. Elected officials can eventually rewrite rules, amend what voters approved (in most states), or stall implementation. The end result may be that "the policy impact of most initiatives reflects a compromise between what electoral majorities and government actors want."[114] This means that governing is quite different in initiative states, yet direct democracy has not replaced the role of the legislature.

Majority Tyranny and Judicial Review

The potential effects of initiatives on policy are further muted when we consider judicial review.[115] Initiatives, like any other law, must be consistent with the U.S. Constitution and state constitutions and must abide by a state's regulations on the initiative process, such as subject matter constraints. State and federal courts tend to treat initiative laws just like laws passed by legislatures, regardless of how popular they may have been with voters. Courts have been very willing to strike down voter-approved initiatives. One study of several states found that most state initiatives ended up being challenged in court, with 40 percent overturned in whole or in part.[116] People challenging voter-approved initiatives in court may increase their odds of success because they are able to "venue shop": They can file cases in different districts of either state or federal courts in order to find judges most likely to grant them a favorable ruling.

Assessments of Direct Democracy

When some of the most careful observers of American politics turn their attention to the process of direct democracy, their assessments of it are rather negative. Alan Rosenthal, a preeminent scholar of state legislatures, suggests

[114] Elisabeth Gerber, Arthur Lupia, Mathew McCubbins, and Roderick Kiewiet, *Stealing the Initiative* (Upper Saddle River, NJ: Prentice Hall, 2001), p. 110.

[115] Todd Donovan, "Direct Democracy as Super Precedent?" *Political Constraints of Citizen-Initiated Laws* 43(2007):191–234.

[116] Kenneth Miller, *Direct Democracy and the Courts* (Cambridge, MA: Cambridge University Press, 2009).

that growing enthusiasm for direct democracy—in the form of growing use of opinion polls that influence representatives as well as use of initiative and referendum—has a corrosive effect on representative government. Rosenthal suggests that a demise of representative government has occurred in American states over recent decades, leaving legislators with less responsibility for government and leaving states more difficult to govern.[117] Some blame direct democracy for shattering the fiscal health of some states, then leaving elected officials to pick up the pieces. Initiatives are also blamed for promoting confrontational (and unconstitutional) policies that target minority groups, such as immigrants and gays and lesbians.

David Broder, an insightful U.S. journalist, echoes this sentiment. Broder spent weeks on the West Coast observing the initiative campaigns being waged in California in 1998. The nearly $200 million spent in California initiative campaigns was nearly as much as taxpayers spent on the public financing of the national presidential campaigns that year. Broder's experience in California led him to conclude that wealthy special interests and political parties were driving the process, spending millions to place their measures on ballots and then spending heavily on deceptive advertising to convince voters to approve their schemes.[118]

Public Approval of Direct Democracy

Despite its flaws, the public remains quite supportive of the initiative process in states where it is used rather frequently. Average citizens look at direct democracy quite differently, and more positively, than many political observers and elected officials. Even voters who have experienced California's high-stakes, high-cost ballot initiatives remain generally supportive of the process. Americans give widespread support to expanding direct democracy nationally. Roughly two-thirds of Americans say they favor having a national vote on important matters of policy.[119]

Surveys of elected officials find much less enthusiasm about direct democracy. For their part, legislators in direct democracy states would like to change things so that they have more say over what ends up going to a public vote and also have more ability to amend laws after voters approve them. Voters in these states, for their part, are unwilling to let their representatives have such discretion.[120] Recent proposals for expanding initiative use to additional states appear sensitive to critics of California's process and are less sweeping than the early twentieth-century models. An initiative plan considered by the New Jersey legislature in 2002, for example, would limit subject matter and only permit petitions for statutory measures that would first be evaluated by the legislature.[121] Recently, the Minnesota and Alabama state legislatures each considered bills to create a scaled-down version of the initiative, and Rhode Island used an advisory referendum in 2008 to ask voters whether they would like to have the initiative process.

Despite this public enthusiasm and the support of some states' governors, voters have little reason to expect that direct democracy will expand to additional states in the near future. This is due to the fact that state legislators

---

[117] Alan Rosenthal, *The Decline of Representative Government* (Washington, DC: CQ Press, 1998).

[118] Broder, *Democracy Derailed*; also see Schrag, *Paradise Lost*.

[119] Shaun Bowler and Todd Donovan, "Reasoning about Institutional Change: Winners, Losers and Support for Electoral Reform," *British Journal of Political Science* 37(2007):455–76; see also Daniel A. Smith, Caroline J. Tolbert, and Amanda Keller, "Electoral and Structural Losers and Support for a National Referendum in the U.S.," *Electoral Studies* 29 (2010): 509–20.

[120] Bowler, Donovan, Neiman, and Peel, "Institutional Threat and Partisan Outcomes."

[121] Craig Holman, "An Assessment of New Jersey's Proposed Limited Initiative Process," Brennan Center for Justice at New York University School of Law, 2002, http://www.iandrinstitute.org/New%20IRI%20Website%20Info/I&R%20Research%20and%20History/I&R%20Studies/Holman%20-%20Review%20of%20Proposed%20NJ%20Initiative%20Process%20IRI.pdf.

largely control whether their state will change rules to allow direct democracy. Legislators are reluctant to adopt rules that weaken their control over the political agenda.[122] Absent heightened interparty legislative competition and another social movement pushing for major political reform similar to the Populist and Progressive movements a century ago, elected representatives are unlikely to adopt or expand direct democracy.[123] Voters have probably even less reason to expect adoption of the initiative, referendum, or recall at the national level.

Summary

Direct democracy is a curious American institution. It plays a large role in the politics of some states and communities but much less of a role in other places. The initiative, referendum, and recall were adopted in an era when overt corruption among state legislators and local elected officials was common. Rather than thwarting the political influence of wealthy interests, however, direct democracy may give powerful, established interests an additional tool they may use to shape public policy. It represents one of the major institutional differences between states like California and New York or between Arizona and Connecticut.

This chapter illustrates that direct democracy—specifically, the initiative process—has important effects where it is used. It can change the rules that affect how elected officials govern, and may alter participation levels and the issues voters use when evaluating candidates. There is also some evidence that direct democracy may lead state policies to be more representative of what voters in a state prefer. Furthermore, as we discuss in more detail in Chapter 10, direct democracy can affect state and local fiscal policy. In short, few similar institutions in the United States are associated with as many differences between the states. Whether direct democracy makes politics better is often left to the eye of the beholder.

Key Terms

Constitutional initiative

Direct initiative

Indirect initiative

Legislative referendum

Popular referendum

Populist Party

Progressive Era reforms

Proposition 13

Recall

Single-subject rule

Statutory initiative

Wedge issues

---

[122] Shaun Bowler, Todd Donovan, and Jeffrey Karp, "Why Politicians Like Electoral Institutions: Self-Interest, Values, or Ideology?" *Journal of Politics* 68(2006):434–46.

[123] Smith and Fridkin, "Delegating Direct Democracy."

Discussion Questions

(1) Why is the initiative process called the "gun behind the door"? Provide examples of how this process has been used effectively.

(2) Discuss some of the criticism of financing ballot initiatives. How has the U.S. Supreme Court ruled when it comes to spending money on ballot initiatives?

(3) What is the general public's view of direct democracy? Discuss the merits and pitfalls of the process. Would direct democracy work at the national level?

(4) How have minorities been affected by direct democracy measures? What minority groups have been on the front line of initiative battles, and how have they faired?

(5) What is the future of direct democracy in the states? If you live in a state that permits statewide ballot initiatives, is direct democracy under fire? If you live in a state that does not permit statewide ballot initiatives, is there a push to adopt the process? What are the politics behind the adoption, or regulation, of direct democracy?

Suggested Readings

Boehmke, Frederick. 2005. *The Indirect Effect of Direct Legislation: How Institutions Shape Interest Group Systems*. Columbus, OH: Ohio State University Press.

Bowler, Shaun, and Todd Donovan. 1998. *Demanding Choices: Opinion, Voting, and Direct Democracy*. Ann Arbor, MI: University of Michigan Press.

Broder, David S. 2000. *Democracy Derailed: Initiative Campaigns and the Power of Money*. New York: Harcourt.

Ellis, Richard. 2002. *Democratic Delusions: The Initiative Process in America*. Lawrence, KS: University of Kansas Press.

Gerber, Elisabeth R. 1999. *The Populist Paradox: Interest Group Influence and the Promise of Direct Legislation*. Princeton, NJ: Princeton University Press.

Magleby, David B. 1984. *Direct Legislation: Voting on Ballot Propositions in the United States*. Baltimore, MD: Johns Hopkins University Press.

Matsusaka, John. 2004. *For the Many or the Few: The Initiative, Public Policy and American Democracy*. Chicago: University of Chicago Press.

Nicholson, Stephen P. 2005. *Voting the Agenda: Candidates, Elections and Ballot Propositions*. Princeton, NJ: Princeton University Press.

Schrag, Peter. 1998. *Paradise Lost: California's Experience, America's Future*. New York: New Press.

Smith, Daniel A. 1998. *Tax Crusaders and the Politics of Direct Democracy*. New York: Routledge.

Smith, Daniel A., and Caroline Tolbert. 2004. *Educated by Initiative: The Effects of Direct Democracy on Citizens and Political Organizations in the American States*. Ann Arbor, MI: University of Michigan Press.

Websites

Ballot Initiative Strategy Center (http://www. ballot.org): In addition to coordinating a national strategy to use ballot initiatives to strengthen progressive politics across the states, BISC tracks initiatives circulating for qualification to statewide ballots.

Initiative and Referendum Institute (http:// www.iandrinstitute.org): In addition to tracking initiatives and referendums on the ballot, the I&R Institute provides a historical database that dates back to 1904.

National Conference of State Legislatures (http://www.ncsl.org): Although generally critical of direct democracy, NCSL does an excellent job of tracking ballot initiatives and popular referendums and also provides a historical database.

Centre for Research on Direct Democracy (http://www.c2d.ch/): C2D, based in Geneva, Switzerland, provides an international online library and several direct democracy data sets.

5

Political Parties and Interest Groups

INTRODUCTION

Political parties and interest groups are critical players in the electoral process, governance, and policy making of the states. For two longtime observers of state politics, "the single most important factor in state politics is the political party."[1] You will get a sense in this chapter that not all parties at the state and local level are equally powerful. Parties come in all kinds of shapes, sizes, and political flavors, and their respective influence within a state varies widely. At their most rudimentary level, parties allow individuals to come together periodically to articulate a political viewpoint. Parties also help to cultivate and nurture the ambitions of political leaders, mobilize citizens to vote, organize governments, and formulate public policy.[2]

Interest groups, on the other hand, are often portrayed in the media as detriments to the common good or general welfare. "The popular perception," according to one interest group scholar, "is that interest groups are a cancer spreading unchecked throughout the body politic, making it gradually weaker, until they eventually kill it."[3] Like political parties, though, organized interests play an indispensable role in state politics. Organized interests not only help protect the interests of those who join them; belonging to an organization can help to cultivate democratic values and enhance the capacities of individuals and the communities in which they live. As we shall see, both political parties and interest groups are essential political players in states and localities.

[1] Sarah Morehouse and Malcolm Jewell, *State Politics, Parties, and Policy*, 2nd ed. (Boulder, CO: Rowman & Littlefield, 2003), p.15.

[2] David Hedge, *Governance and the Changing American States* (Boulder, CO: Westview, 1998); Joseph Schlesinger, "The New American Political Party," *American Political Science Review* 79(1985):1152–69; and John Aldrich, *Why Parties? The Origin and Transformation of Party Politics in America* (Chicago: University of Chicago Press, 1995).

[3] Jeffrey Berry, *The New Liberalism: The Rising Power of Citizen Groups* (Washington, DC: Brookings Institution Press, 1997), p.19.

Understanding Political Parties

Political parties serve multiple functions. Parties may be rightly understood as one of the principal agencies for "aggregating and mobilizing the interests of vast numbers of citizens, enhancing voters' capacity to hold public officials accountable, acting as agents of political socialization, and organizing the decision-making institutions of government."[4] Parties recruit candidates running for office, oversee the nominations of those candidates, and provide a durable link between citizens and their governments. Less clear is whether a party needs to be ideologically coherent or merely functional in order to truly be understood as a party.[5]

Some scholars view parties from a normative perspective, offering a prescriptive ideal of what parties ought to strive to become. According to this **responsible party model**, parties should be ideologically consistent, in that they should present to voters a clear platform and set of policies that are principled and distinctive. Voters are expected to choose a candidate based on whether or not they agree with the proposed programs and policies of that candidate's party. Once in office, the candidate (and his or her party) is to be held responsible for implementing the party's program and policies.[6] However, because of institutional constraints (as discussed in Chapter 3)—such

as single-member, winner-take-all elections, direct and open primaries, and federalism—the two major political parties tend to operate as "big tents," allowing considerable disagreement over their principles and policies in an effort to win elections.[7]

Sometimes, though, it is quite rational for parties to try to broaden their coalitions in their search for the elusive median voter, even if it means compromising on their core convictions. After all, parties are self-interested organizations, striving to maximize votes for their candidates in order to win elections.[8] Emphasizing the pragmatic character of American parties, some scholars have advanced a **functional party model**, which defines a party as "any group, however loosely organized, seeking to elect governmental officeholders under a given label."[9] This functional definition captures the primary goal of parties in the United States: winning and maintaining control of political office.[10]

Regulating Parties as Quasi-Public Entities

Political parties are "quasi-public" entities, meaning that they not only are regulated by the states but also carry out official functions conferred upon them by the states. As such, they are more akin to public utilities than private associations.[11] Until the 1950s, for example, many Democratic parties in the South were permitted

---

[4] Thomas Holbrook and Ray La Raja, "Parties and Elections," in Virginia Gray and Russell Hanson, eds., *Politics in the American States: A Comparative Analysis*, 9th ed. (Washington, DC: CQ Press, 2007).

[5] John Coleman, "Responsible, Functional, or Both? American Political Parties and the APSA Report after Fifty Years," in *The State of the Parties: The Changing Role of Contemporary American Parties*, 4th ed., ed. John Green and Rick Farmer (Lanham, MD: Rowman & Littlefield, 2003).

[6] Edmund Burke, *Select Works of Edmund Burke: A New Imprint of the Payne Edition*, vol. 1 (Indianapolis, IN: Liberty Fund, 1999), 150; and Richard Hofstadter, *The Idea of a Party System: The Rise of Legitimate Opposition in the United States, 1780–1840* (Berkeley: University of California Press, 1969).

[7] John Gerring, *Party Ideologies in America, 1828–1996* (Cambridge: Cambridge University Press, 2001); Geoffrey C. Layman, Thomas M. Carsey, and Juliana Menasce Horowitz, "Party Polarization in American Politics: Characteristics, Causes, and Consequences," *Annual Review of Political Science* 9(June 2006):67–81; and Gary Miller and Norman Schofield, "Activists and Partisan Realignment in the United States," *American Political Science Review* 97(May 2003):245–60.

[8] Anthony Downs, *An Economic Theory of Democracy* (New York: Harper, 1957), p.25.

[9] Leon Epstein, *Political Parties in Western Democracies* (New York: Praeger, 1967).

[10] Leon Epstein, *Political Parties in the American Mold* (Madison: University of Wisconsin Press, 1986), p.25.

[11] Epstein, *Political Parties in the American Mold*, pp.155–99.

by state law to hold discriminatory "white-only" primaries that excluded blacks from participating in the party nomination process. These "Jim Crow" laws, which codified racial segregation far beyond electoral politics and were designed specifically to restrict black suffrage, included such barriers to voting as poll taxes, literacy tests, and an array of complex voter registration laws.[12] In 1964 the 24th Amendment was ratified, outlawing the poll tax in federal elections. The next year, Congress enacted the Voting Rights Act, outlawing state election laws that discriminated against minorities, immigrants, and the poor.

Today, party registration, party nomination, and ballot access laws vary greatly across the states. Although federal law establishes that the voting age is 18 and over, that federal elections are held on the first Tuesday after the first Monday in November, that there may be no poll taxes or literacy tests to determine voter eligibility, and that all polling places must be accessible to people with disabilities, within these broad parameters every state is permitted to establish its own set of laws that regulate voting and political party status.[13] As such, state regulations governing political parties differ considerably.

In a series of rulings, the U.S. Supreme Court provided broad contours of what is permissible when it comes to the rights of political parties and their members as well as the kinds of regulations the states may place on political parties.[14] In general, the high court has upheld the associational rights of the major parties, but it has also reaffirmed the rights of states to regulate state parties in the name of maintaining and preserving political stability.[15] Although hardly constitutive of a coherent jurisprudence,

several important high court rulings concern the associational rights and state regulations of state political parties.[16]

Primaries and Caucuses

Parties have broad discretion in determining how candidates running on their party labels are to be nominated. By defining who may participate in their nomination process, the parties are essentially able to define who belongs as a party member. At the same time, state legislatures make the rules governing elections, including whether the state will have a primary election or a caucus in which the nominees running on party labels are determined. Primaries and caucuses are held weeks or months ahead of the general election to determine who will appear on the general election ballot. In a **direct primary** election, voters select one candidate affiliated with a political party for each elected office; the party nominees later face one another in a general election.

Caucus A few states use a party **caucus**, or even a series of party caucuses, to nominate candidates. At a caucus, party members informally meet, deliberate, and then cast votes for their preferred candidates. Party members not only discuss the candidates and the pressing issues but also elect delegates to the party's county conventions. These, in turn, elect delegates to the party's congressional and state conventions, which (in presidential election years) elect national convention delegates. In Iowa, for example, a caucus participant must be registered with a party as well as a resident of the precinct in which the caucus is being held (often in a school, a town hall, or even a private home). Iowa has no absentee voting, as the citizen must attend a caucus meeting to have his or her voice heard and counted.

[12] V. O. Key, *Southern Politics in the State and Nation* (New York: Knopf, 1949).

[13] Thomas Holbrook and Raymond J. La Raja, "Parties and Elections," in *Politics in the American States*, eds. Virginia Gray and Russell L. Hanson (Washington, DC: CQ Press). "Parties and -Elections."

[14] David Ryden, *The Constitution, Interest Groups, and Political Parties* (Albany: State University of New York Press, 1996).

[15] Sandy Maisel and John Bibby, "Power, Money, and Responsibility in the Major American Parties," in *Responsible Partisanship? The Evolution of American Political Parties since 1950*, ed. John Green and Paul Herrnson (Lawrence: University Press of Kansas, 2002).

[16] Lisa Disch, *The Tyranny of the Two-Party System* (New York: Columbia University Press, 2002).

Closed and Open Primaries A **closed primary** system is one in which voters must register with a political party prior to Election Day and can only vote for candidates of the party for which they are registered. Independent or unaffiliated voters may not vote in a party's primary. A **semiclosed** primary system allows those who are registered with the party or who are registered as independents to vote in a party's primary. In an **open primary**, by contrast, voters are not required to register their party affiliation with the state and may freely and secretly choose the ballot of any party's primary in which they wish to vote. Some states use a **semiopen primary**, which permits registered voters to vote in any party's primary, but voters must publicly declare on Election Day the party primary in which they choose to vote.

Today, as Figure 5.1 displays, 26 states currently have closed or semiclosed primaries, 21 have open or semiopen systems, and three

(California, Louisiana, and Washington) have variations of a **top-two blanket primary**. These categories are not definitive, as a few states use a mix of open and closed primaries. In these states, the parties are permitted to choose for themselves their own type of primary election. For example, in Alaska, two or more political parties may decide jointly to hold a primary, whereby all the candidates that have opted in are on the same ballot. The candidate from each party who wins the most votes advances to the general election. In contrast, a party may hold a semiclosed primary if it so desires, closed only to voters registered to that party.

Top-Two Blanket Primaries In 2008, the U.S. Supreme Court weighed in on the side of the associational rights of the major political parties. The court handed Republican and Democratic state political parties a defeat when it ruled that a successful 2004 ballot initiative

Figure 5.1

States with Closed Primaries, Open Primaries, and Top-Two Blanket Primaries

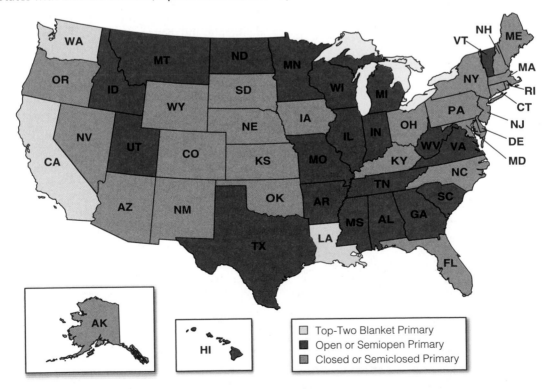

☐ Top-Two Blanket Primary
■ Open or Semiopen Primary
▨ Closed or Semiclosed Primary

in Washington calling for a top-two blanket primary system was constitutional. In its decision, *Washington State Grange v. Washington State Republican Party*, the court ruled that the top-two blanket primary, in which the two candidates for an office—regardless of their party affiliations—who receive the most votes in the primary are to face off in the general election, did not deprive state parties of their associational rights to choose their party nominees. The Court's ruling on Washington's top-two blanket primary took some by surprise. Eight years earlier, in *California Democratic Party v. Jones*, the court struck down as unconstitutional a top-two primary system that had been approved by California voters in a 1996 ballot initiative. Not to be deterred, in June 2010, voters in California adopted Proposition 14, a top-two primary system whereby candidates for state and congressional office each run in a single primary open to all registered voters; the top two finishers, regardless of their party, face off in the general election. Candidates for each political office decide for themselves if they wish to have their party affiliation appear on the ballot, and the parties may endorse a candidate of their choosing.

Washington and California join Louisiana as having very different primary systems than other states. Louisiana continues to use its own unique top-two blanket primary system. Primaries for state and local offices (but not federal offices) in the Bayou State are nonpartisan, with all candidates, regardless of their party label, facing off in a single primary. A candidate wins the election outright if he or she wins more than 50 percent of the vote in the primary election. If no candidate wins a majority of votes in the primary, the top two candidates—irrespective of their party—then run against one another in the general election. Louisiana's primary system has enabled extremist candidates to qualify for the general election, even though they have combined for substantially less than 50 percent of the primary vote. In the 1991 gubernatorial election, Louisiana's blanket primary system

received national attention when David Duke, the former head of the state's Ku Klux Klan and a Republican state legislator, qualified for the runoff election after a former governor (and the eventual general election winner), Edwin Edwards, failed to win 50 percent of the vote in the primary.

The Effect of Primary Systems on Representation Primaries vary with regard to how much voters are permitted to participate in the nomination process. In theory, open primaries should encourage more participation among the electorate, as all voters, even independents (sometimes referred to as *unaffiliateds*), may cast a ballot in the election. The costs associated with voting are much less in blanket and open primary systems than in closed systems. Yet, analyses of voter turnout levels across states with open versus closed primary systems do not reveal any significant differences in rates, as the mobilization of citizens goes well beyond the particularized costs or benefits of an individual's decision to vote. Because open primaries diminish the control that parties and candidates have over who participates in the nomination process, parties and candidates may have less incentive to bolster turnout.[17]

Party Fusion

States may prohibit the name of a candidate running for a political office from appearing more than once on a ballot, a practice known as **party fusion**. Fusion permits two or more parties to nominate the same candidate for office. In a 1997 ballot access case, *Timmons v. Twin Cities Area New Party*, the U.S. Supreme Court affirmed the regulatory power of state legislatures by affirming Minnesota's law banning fusion—the listing of a candidate on the ballot under two or more political parties. The Court ruled 6–3 that the state's anti-fusion law was constitutional, as it did not severely burden the associational rights of the members of the New Party. In the words of the majority decision,

[17] Rebecca Morton, *Analyzing Elections* (New York: Norton, 2006).

the ruling upheld the right of the states to avoid "voter confusion," protect political stability in the state, and protect the integrity of the ballot by prohibiting candidates to be cross-listed as two or more parties' nominee for a given elective office.

Of the 10 states (Arkansas, Connecticut, Delaware, Idaho, Mississippi, New York, South Carolina, South Dakota, Utah, and Vermont) that currently allow party fusion, only minor parties in New York continue to use it with considerable frequency. The Conservative, Independence, and Working Families parties in New York are usually not strong enough to have their candidates win against Republicans or Democrats. Instead, these minor parties routinely cross-endorse Republican or Democratic candidates running for office. If the cross-endorsed candidate wins, the minor party can claim that it had a hand in the victory—pointing to the votes cast for the candidate on its minor party label.[18]

Party Ballot Access

States have been granted wide latitude by the U.S. Supreme Court to determine what parties and their candidates must do to qualify for the ballot. In some states, the rules are fairly restrictive; in others, they are less so. Democrats and Republicans are, by state law, usually given "major-party" status and are entitled to permanent space on the ballot. A minor party may have to collect a certain number of signatures or register some percentage of the state's voters with their minor party before being granted ballot access. A candidate wishing to run as an independent or as the nominee of a new political party usually has to collect thousands of signatures in order to qualify for the ballot.

In other states, candidates wishing to run for office need only pay a nominal filing fee.[19] In most states, parties typically retain their ballot access as long as one of their candidates collects a minimum percentage of votes cast in a state election.

Many states continue to have very onerous ballot qualification standards. In the 1970s, Arkansas lawmakers required minor parties to collect signatures equal to 7 percent of votes cast in the last election in order to qualify for the ballot. The U.S. Supreme Court subsequently ruled the requirement could not exceed 5 percent. But it is still illegal in Arkansas for minor parties to nominate candidates by conventions. Not surprisingly, no third-party candidate for governor has ever reached the Arkansas ballot. In Virginia, candidates running as independents for statewide office are required to collect 10,000 signatures from registered voters to have their names placed on the ballot; at least 400 of those signatures must come from each of Virginia's congressional districts.[20]

Party-in-the-Electorate

Parties are often understood as tripartite social structures composed of three integrated components: party-in-the-electorate, party organization, and party-in-government.[21] Although somewhat limited and overly schematic, the three-pronged framework can serve as a heuristic, allowing us to isolate and appreciate the various dimensions of political parties.[22] We begin our discussion with party-in-the-electorate, which refers to ordinary citizens—eligible voters as well as nonvoters—who identify with and share some sense of loyalty to a particular party.

---

[18] Joel Rodgers, "Pull the Plug," *Administrative Law Review* 52(2000):743–68; and David Dulio and James Thurber, "America's Two-Party System: Friend or Foe?" *Administrative Law Review* 52(2000):769–92.

[19] Richard Winger, "The Importance of Ballot Access," 1994, http://www.ballot-access.org/winger/iba.html.

[20] Richard Winger, "What Are Ballots For?" 1988, http://www.ballot-access.org/winger/wabf.html.

[21] V. O. Key, *Politics, Parties, and Pressure Groups*, 5th ed. (New York: Thomas Y. Crowell, 1964), 163–65.

[22] J. P. Monroe, *The Political Party Matrix: The Resistance of Organization* (Albany: State University of New York Press, 2001).

Partisan Identification

The strength of an individual's attachment to a political party is measured by **party identification,** or PID. A person's PID usually forms early in adulthood and is largely conditioned by one's family. Party identification is a genuine form of social identity that is affected in part by sociopsychological influences; a person is often initially drawn to a political party because of his or her sense of belonging and allegiance.[23] As people age, though, they often make retrospective and prospective cognitive evaluations (or running tallies) of how the parties are doing.[24] Because some people are continually adjusting their PID in response to political and economic change, evidence at the macro level reveals that the average PID in some states has been slowly changing.[25] For example, in the 1980s, many white Southerners who were ideologically conservative but still loyal to the Democratic Party began identifying more with the Republican Party. As a result, southern states began turning redder, as the party-in-the-electorate became more aligned with the GOP.

Political Ideology

Not all Democrats and Republicans have the same political ideology or a consistent and coherent belief system concerning the principles of political rule. When individual political ideologies are aggregated, political ideologies found across the states vary considerably. Cultural, economic, demographic, and sociological dissimilarities may lead states to have more liberal or more conservative electorates.[26]

Because national public opinion polls tend not to survey a representative number of respondents from all 50 states, there are relatively few direct measures of state-level political ideology. As such, scholars have tried to derive indirect measures of a state's political ideology by using election returns and interest groups' ratings of members of Congress from each state, pooling data from national polls and estimating state public opinion, and using data from national election surveys designed to study U.S. Senate races.[27] Regardless of the method, these studies show that southern states—such as Alabama, Arkansas, and Oklahoma—tend to be the most ideologically conservative, and northern states—such as Massachusetts, Maryland, and New York—tend to be the most liberal in the country.

Does a state's political ideology predict the kinds of public policies it adopts? Usually, but not always. You may recall from Chapter 1 that state policies tend to reflect the median ideological preferences of the states' citizens. However, Democratic-controlled legislatures tend to produce policies that are more conservative than their more liberal citizens.[28] The reason for this divergence between citizen ideology and public policy is often rational; parties

---

[23] Donald Green, Bradley Palmquest, and Eric Schickler, *Partisan Hearts and Minds: Political Parties and the Social Identities of Voters* (New Haven, CT: Yale University Press, 2002).

[24] Morris Fiorina, *Retrospective Voting in American National Elections* (New Haven, CT: Yale University Press, 1981).

[25] Robert Erikson, Michael MacKuen, and James Stimson, *The Macro Polity* (New York: Cambridge University Press, 2002); and Alan Abramowitz and Kyle Saunders, "Ideological Realignment in the U.S. Electorate," *Journal of Politics* 60(1998):634–52.

[26] Andrew Gelman et al., *Red State, Blue State, Rich State, Poor State: Why Americans Vote the Way They Do* (Princeton: Princeton University Press, 2008).

[27] See Jeffrey Lax and Justin Phillips, "Gay Rights in the States: Public Opinion and Policy Responsiveness," *American Political Science Review* 103(2009): 367–86; William Berry et al., "Measuring Citizen and Government Ideology in the American States," *American Journal of Political Science* 42(1998):327–48; Gerald Wright, Robert Erikson, and John McIver, "Measuring State Partisanship and Ideology with Survey Data," *Journal of Politics* 47(1985):469–89; Barbara Norrander, "Measuring State Public Opinion with the Senate National Election Study," *State Politics and Policy Quarterly* 1(2001):111–25; Paul Brace et al., "Public Opinion in the American States: New Perspectives Using National Data," *American Journal of Political Science* 46(2002):173–89; and Thomas Carsey and Geoffrey Layman, "Party Polarization and 'Conflict Extension' in the American Electorate," *American Journal of Political Science* 46(2002):786–802.

[28] Wright, Erikson, and McIver, "Measuring State Partisanship and Ideology."

often pursue public policies to win future elections rather than passing public policies that are reflective of their ideology.[29]

Are a State's Partisan Identification and Political Ideology Related?

A state's partisan identification leanings and its political ideology are not always correlated, or linked together. States populated with citizens having strong Republican ties—Utah, South Dakota, Idaho, and Kansas, for example—are not inhabited solely by citizens who are ideologically conservative. Some states with heavy Republican PID are actually less ideologically conservative than states with high percentages of Democratic identifiers. Likewise, several states with strong Democratic PID are considerably more ideologically conservative than states with high proportions of Republican identifiers. Only a functional understanding of political parties can accommodate the tremendous diversity of political ideology and partisanship found across the American states.

For example, states with more ideologically liberal populations are not necessarily more Democratic, and states more ideologically conservative are not necessarily more Republican. Massachusetts, for instance, lives up to its reputation as being one of the most liberal states in the union. Yet seven states, including Oklahoma, a state ranked as one of the most conservative in the country, have stronger levels of Democratic PID than the Bay State. According to one study, two of the most conservative states—Arkansas and Alabama—do not even register in the top 30 of Republican-leaning states with respect to their PID.[30]

From an institutional perspective, there are several reasons why a state's political ideology and partisanship are not always correlated. As mentioned in Chapter 3, states have differing registration laws, making it alternatively easier

or more difficult for citizens to initially register with a political party or subsequently switch their party registration. Most states require voting-age citizens to register their party affiliation with the state at least 30 days prior to an election, although under the National Voter Registration Act passed by Congress in 1993, all states must allow voters to register to vote by mail and when applying for a driver's license. Nine states (Idaho, Iowa, Maine, Minnesota, Montana, New Hampshire, North Carolina, Wisconsin, and Wyoming) have same-day registration, allowing eligible citizens to register to vote on Election Day. North Dakota has no voter registration requirements; all voting-age citizens may cast ballots. These differences can affect partisan identification, irrespective of political ideology. Residents in states with strict registration laws, for example, might be more inclined to identify with a political party because they are required by state law to register with a party if they want to participate in the electoral process. Variations in state registration laws may also help to explain why the percentage of voters who are registered with a party in a state is not always a reliable indicator of the level of partisan identification within a state.

Party Organization

Over the years, state and local party organizations have shown their adaptability by responding to changing regulatory and electoral conditions. In the early 1970s, state and local political parties—along with their national brethren—were often given up for dead because they were seen as dinosaurs of a bygone era. Today, most state and many local political parties are vibrant organizations, carrying out essential campaign activities, such as mobilizing voters and raising campaign funds in support of their candidates. Party organization refers

---

[29] Downs, *An Economic Theory of Democracy*; Thomas Dye, "Party and Policy in the States," *Journal of Politics* 46(1984):1097–116; Charles Barrileaux, Thomas Holbrook, and Laura Langer, "Electoral Competition, Legislative Balance, and American State Welfare Policy," *American Journal of Political Science* 46(2002):415–27.

[30] Norrander, "Measuring State Public Opinion with the Senate National Election Study."

to the network of elected and appointed party officials; paid staffers; national, state, and local committees; and volunteer workers.[31] Some political scientists have reduced the organizational role of parties to a single function—that of electing candidates. In today's "candidate-centered era," a party is designed primarily as a "party-in-service" to candidates.[32]

The level of party organization across the 50 states varies considerably. State parties are typically composed of a state central committee, congressional district committees, county committees, and ward or precinct committees. The structure of state parties, though, can be far more complex. The California Democratic Party has what can only be described as a Byzantine organizational flowchart. Each level of the state party has members who are either elected or appointed to their positions. Almost all party officials at the local level are volunteers, although most state parties now have permanent, paid staff at the central committee level.[33] Most state parties convene annual conventions that are attended by party delegates and the party's elected officials. Most states hold primaries to choose a party's nominee for the general election, but a few states use party conventions to vet and select party nominees.

At a minimum, if a party organization is to be successful, it must be able to overcome barriers to collective action. The organizational configuration a party selects, though, may be tight or loose. A functional definition of a political party accommodates variation in party organizations found across the country—from urban party machines, to well-financed and professionally staffed state party committees, to the underfinanced and disorganized bands of volunteers running some local party organizations. Recall that a functional definition of parties is not concerned with a party's organizational hierarchy but rather its preoccupation with contesting elections. As rational actors, then, state and local parties have been able to adapt their organizational structures to the changing regulatory and electoral environment, thereby ensuring their continued relevance.[34]

The Rebirth of Party Organizations

For much of the twentieth century, state and local political party organizations were mere shadows of their former selves. It was not until the 1970s that many state and local party organizations began to strengthen themselves organizationally, expanding their bureaucratic and programmatic capacities. Research conducted during the 1970s and 1980s highlighted the institutionalization of state parties, depicting the integration of new party professionals and the bureaucratization of what were once often parochial, unsophisticated organizations. Most state parties during that period began to establish permanent headquarters and hire specialized staff to raise contributions and direct campaigns.[35] The parties transformed themselves from provincial party machines into service vendors ready to recruit, train, and support candidates in their run for office.[36] Although the labor-intensive parties of the nineteenth century are in the past, state and local party organizations have reinvigorated themselves as service providers. By the turn of the millennium, scholars generally

[31] John Bibby, "Party Networks: National-State Integration, Allied Groups, and Issue Activists," in *The State of the Parties: The Changing Role of Contemporary Parties*, 3rd ed., ed. John Green and Daniel Shea (New York: Rowman & Littlefield, 1999).

[32] Schlesinger, "The New American Political Party."

[33] Raymond La Raja, "State Political Parties after BCRA," in *Life After Reform*, ed. Michael Malbin (Boulder, CO: Rowman & Littlefield, 2003).

[34] Monroe, *The Political Party Matrix.*

[35] Cornelius Cotter, James L. Gibson, John F. Bibby, and Robert J. Huckshorn, *Party Organizations in American Politics* (New Brunswick, NJ: Eagleton Institute of Politics, Rutgers University, 1984).

[36] Paul Herrnson, "Do Parties Make a Difference? The Role of Party Organizations in Congressional Elections," *Journal of Politics* 48(1986):589–613; and Xandra Kayden and Eddie Mahe, *The Party Goes On: The Persistence of the Two Party System in the United States* (New York: Basic Books, 1985).

agreed that state political parties were as strong and fiscally sound as they were anytime in recent history.[37]

Measuring Party Organizational Strength

There are several comparative studies of the 50 state organizations that measure party organizational strength. Unfortunately, the methodologies scholars have utilized to measure party organizational strength have varied widely, leading to some inconsistent findings.[38] Many of the studies gauging state party organization have measured the number of staff and other party assets. Party organizations, of course, are much more than their staff. They can also be understood as a complex web of political consultants and campaign specialists and elected officials in national, state, and local offices as well as their respective staff. A recent study finds that party organization strength influences the ideological tenor of the party, with more top-down, hierarchical structures being more moderate, and those with more open structures being more polarized.[39]

State Party Financing

As with any organization, the capacity and relative power of state party organizations are directly affected by their money-raising prowess. Considerable variation in state campaign finance laws exists across the states when it comes to restricting contributions and expenditures of political parties. Thirteen states (Arkansas, Florida, Georgia, Idaho, Illinois, Maine, Missouri, Nebraska, Nevada, New Mexico, Oregon, Utah, and Virginia) allow unlimited contributions from virtually any source to be made to state political parties. Roughly the same number have similarly lax contribution regulations, except that they prohibit donations from corporations and labor unions; eight other states prohibit contributions from corporate entities but allow union donations. Alabama, for instance, allows individuals, labor unions, **political action committees (PACs)**, and national party committees to contribute unlimited sums to the state political parties, but limits corporations to donations up to $500 per election. Campaign finance laws in Arizona are similar to Alabama's, except that corporations and unions may not make contributions to state parties with money drawn from their own treasuries. Montana and Oklahoma prohibit corporate contributions to state parties, but Montana allows unlimited union contributions, whereas Oklahoma limits them to $5,000 per year. Connecticut, on the other hand, allows individuals to contribute up to $5,000 per year to state parties, but it completely bans corporations and unions from making contributions from their treasuries, permitting them only to make limited PAC contributions.[40]

Many of these state campaign finance regulations are new. Between 1990 and 2000, more than 30 states adopted campaign finance laws that directly or indirectly affected state parties. Going through state legislatures, but also

[37] John Aldrich et al., "Challenges to the American Two-Party System: Evidence from the 1968, 1980, 1992, and 1996 Presidential Elections," *Political Research Quarterly* 53(2000):495–522; and Morehouse and Jewell, *State Politics, Parties, and Policy.*

[38] See, for example, James Gibson et al., "Assessing Party Organizational Strength," *American Journal of Political Science* 27(1983):193–222; James Gibson, John Frendreis, and Laura Vertz, "Party Dynamics in the 1980s: Changes in County Party Organizational Strength 1980–1984," *American Journal of Political Science* 33(1989):67–90; Robert Huckshorn et al., "Party Integration and Party Organizational Strength," *Journal of Politics* 48(1986):976–91; David Mayhew, *Placing Parties in American Politics: Organization, Electoral Settings, and Government Activity in the Twentieth Century* (Princeton, NJ: Princeton University Press, 1986); and Sarah Morehouse, *The Governor as Party Leader: Campaigning and Governing* (Ann Arbor: University of Michigan Press, 1998).

[39] Daniel Coffey, "Measuring Gubernatorial Ideology: A Content Analysis of State of the State Speeches," *State Politics and Policy Quarterly* 5(2005):88–103. See also John Coleman, "Party Organizational Strength and Public Support for Parties," *American Journal of Political Science* 40(1996):805–24.

[40] Center for Responsive Government, "Contributions Limits on State Party Committees" (2002), http://www.publicintegrity.org/partylines/overview.aspx?act=cl; National Conference of State Legislatures, "Limits on Contributions to Political Parties" (2009), http://www.ncsl.org/programs/legismgt/ABOUT/contrib_pol_parties.htm.

circumventing politicians who were the beneficiaries of weak campaign finance restrictions, good government public interest groups placed more than two dozen initiatives on statewide ballots dealing with campaign finance issues during the decade.

The capacity of state parties to raise campaign contributions ranges tremendously. The disparity across states in party fundraising has less to do with the organizational strength of state Democratic or Republican parties and more to do with the kind of campaign finance laws that are on the books and the competitiveness of state and federal elections.[41] In 2008, the state parties in the 50 states raised more than $440 million for state elections (which excludes contributions raised by the state parties for federal elections). Overall, state Republican parties raised roughly $222 million, just a few million more than the combined total for state Democratic parties.

Party-in-Government

Party-in-government refers to candidates running for elective office as well as officeholders at the local, state, and national levels who are elected under the party label. With the exception of Nebraska (because of its nonpartisan, unicameral legislature), Republicans and Democrats dominate the governmental structure of every state. As you will see in Chapter 6, political parties structure state government, especially state legislatures. Of course, because of winner-take-all elections and restrictive ballot access laws, the two-party dominance of state legislatures and statewide elected officials exaggerates the level of popular support for the two parties in the electorate. Due to these structural barriers, it is difficult for citizens who are displeased with the two-party system to articulate their dissatisfaction with the status quo.[42]

Party Competition in State Legislatures

Although political parties may be inevitable, their mere existence is not sufficient to guarantee a democratic form of governance. Rather, competition *between* the parties is said to be essential for democracies to function. Competition forces the parties to become more internally cohesive and disciplined, giving citizens a real choice at the polls.[43]

Partisan control of state legislatures has ebbed and flowed over time. Between 1950 and 2000, a clear majority of legislative seats across the states were held by Democrats; by 2000, the partisan split in legislative seats had become dead-even between the parties, as Republicans gained a larger share of legislative seats. Since that time, Democrats slowly regained their advantage at the aggregate level, only to lose their edge in the 2010 mid-term elections—a GOP tsunami—in which Republicans regained nearly 700 legislative seats in both chambers. Figure 5.2 shows the overall trend over time in the number of legislative seats held by the two major parties between 1938 and 2010. Following the 2010 general election, Democrats controlled 3,369 (45.9 percent) of the 7,333 House and Senate seats in the 49 states that use partisan elections (which excludes Nebraska). Republicans held 3,921 (53.4 percent) seats, with Independents and third-party candidates controlling the balance.[44]

Figure 5.2 can be somewhat deceptive, as states vary considerably with respect to the degree of legislative party control. In addition, some states historically have had intense two-party competition, whereas others have had

[41] Raymond La Raja, Susan Orr, and Daniel A. Smith, "Surviving BCRA: State Party Finance in 2004," in John Green and Daniel Coffey, eds., *The State of the Parties*, 5th ed. (Boulder, CO: Rowman & Littlefield, 2006).

[42] Theodore Lowi and Joseph Romance, *A Republic of Parties? Debating the Two-Party System* (Lanham, MD: Rowman & Littlefield, 1998).

[43] V. O. Key, *The Responsible Electorate: Rationality in Presidential Voting*, 1936–1960 (Cambridge, MA: Harvard University Press, 1966).

[44] National Conference of State Legislatures, "2009 Partisan Composition of State Legislatures," http://www.ncsl.org/statevote/partycomptable2009.htm.

Figure 5.2

Republican and Democratic Share of Legislative Seats, 1938–2010

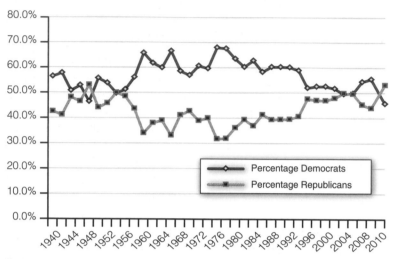

Source: National Conference of State Legislatures, "2009 Partisan Composition of State Legislatures," http://www.ncsl.org/statevote/
partycomptable2009.htm.

a tradition of single-party dominance. Many of the social and economic conditions as well as numerous institutional rules that helped to ensure one-party dominance have eroded or have been eliminated, making two-party competition more common throughout the country. This is particularly true in the South, as the Republican Party over the past 30 years has become more competitive, and even dominant, in some states. Today, two-party competition exists in every state, although to different degrees.

Party Control and Interparty Competition

There are numerous ways to measure the party control and interparty competition of a state's party system. One of the most popular methods was first developed by Austin Ranney and has become known as the "Ranney Index."[45] The index averages four measures of party competition: the proportion of the gubernatorial vote

won, the proportions of the state senate and state house seats won, and the proportion of time (over a given period) the governorship and the two legislative chambers are controlled by a party. Ranney's measure of state party control ranges from 0 (complete Republican control) to 100 (complete Democratic control), and his measure of interparty competition ranges from 50 (no party competition) to 100 (a perfectly competitive two-party system).

In terms of party control, 19 states over a 20-year period (1980–2000) had solid Democratic control, and another 12 leaned Democratic. In contrast, there were only eight solidly Republican states, with another ten that leaned Republican. The most Democratic state during this period—in terms of the control of the governor's office and the state legislature—was Maryland (with a score of 80.8), followed closely by Arkansas and Hawaii. Utah, with a score of 25.1, was by far the most Republican state, with South Dakota and Idaho also solidly in the hands of the GOP.

[45] Austin Ranney, "Parties in State Politics," in *Politics in the American States*, ed. Herbert Jacobs and Kenneth N. Vines (Boston: Little, Brown, 1965). See also James King, "Inter-Party Competition in the American States: An Examination of Index Components," *Western Political Quarterly* 42(1989):83–92; and Thomas Holbrook and Emily Van Dunk, "Electoral Competition in the American States," *American Political Science Review* 87(1993):955–62.

Ranney's interparty competition scores give us a sense of where the battles between the two major parties were taking place over this time period. The states with the highest scores—Delaware (98.5), followed closely by Wisconsin, Michigan, and New York—had intense interparty competition. Maryland, with a score of 69.2 and dominated by the Democratic Party, was by far the least competitive state over the time frame. Utah, with the strongest Republican Party control score of any state, interestingly had a higher interparty competition score (75.1) than seven states controlled by the Democrats.

Increasing Interparty Competition

Since the 1970s, across a range of indicators, there has been a gradual increase in interparty competition in the American states. Much of this increase has occurred in the South, where there has been a wholesale transformation of solid Democratic Party control giving way to the rise of the Republican Party. Between 1980 and 2000, Democratic Party control declined precipitously as the twentieth century came to a close. When comparing the averages of the last five years with those of the first five years of the period, 40 states shifted from being less Democratic to being more Republican, and nearly all the states that were classified as Republican became even stronger under GOP control.[46]

Why Interparty Competition Matters

State governments produce different kinds of public policies depending on the dynamics of party strength and interparty competition. Evidence shows that heightened interparty competition leads to public policies that are more representative of the whole population of a state rather than just its elites. In his classic work, *Southern Politics in the State and Nation*, V. O. Key argued that the lack of party competition in southern states from the 1880s through the 1950s enabled the "haves" in society to run roughshod over the "have-nots," as the dominant Democratic Party had no fear of reprisal at the polls. Key argues that because they were unlikely to be defeated at the next election, the majority southern Democrats did not have to respond to the concerns and needs of all the people residing in their states. Others have formally tested Key's proposition that lack of party competition leads to worse redistributive policy outcomes, finding some support.[47] More recently, as interparty competition has increased across the country, scholars have found that increased party competition in a state tends to lead to the passage by state legislatures of more liberal public policies. Specifically, Democratic-controlled legislatures in states with tough electoral competition from Republicans tend to pass more liberal public policies, whereas the reverse holds for Republican-controlled state legislatures facing stiff Democratic electoral challenges.[48]

There is also scholarly evidence that heightened interparty competition leads to greater levels of participation by citizens. General election voter turnout in the 11 southern states from 1960 to 1986 averaged less than 40 percent, well below the national average. With the decline of the Democratic Party's lock on state government and the advent of greater interparty competition, average turnout among these states increased to nearly 43 percent between 1990 and 1996. Comparing the two periods, Alabama

---

[46] Morehouse and Jewell, *State Politics, Parties, and Policy*, 109.

[47] James Garand, "Partisan Change and Shifting Expenditure Priorities in the American States, 1945–1978," *American Politics Quarterly* (October 1985):355–91; and Morehouse and Jewell, *State Politics, Parties, and Policy*, 50.

[48] Holbrook and Van Dunk, "Electoral Competition in the American States"; Charles Barrilleux, "Party Strength, Party Change, and Policymaking in the American States," *Party Politics* 6(2000):61–73; Charles Barrilleux, "A Test of the Independent Influences of Inter-Party Electoral Competition and Party Strength on State Policy," *American Journal of Political Science* 41(1997):1462–66; Charles Barrilleux, Thomas Holbrook, and Laura Langer, "Electoral Competition, Legislative Balance, and American State Welfare Policy," *American Journal of Political Science* 46(2002):415–27; and James Alt and Robert Lowry, "Divided Government, Fiscal Institutions and Budget Deficits: Evidence from the States," *American Political Science Review* 88(1994):811–28.

had an eight point increase, and Louisiana experienced a double-digit jump in turnout.[49]

Whither Third Parties?

Nearly every state is dominated by a two-party system. As we discuss in greater length in Chapter 6, nearly all state legislative seats are held by either Democrats or Republicans, with third-party organizations in most states virtually nonexistent. Although some scholars point to the historical or cultural bias for having two dominant parties in the states, the primary reason for the two-party duopoly is institutional. There are many constraints that limit the possible success of third parties. Some of these barriers are constitutional, such as the single-member district electoral systems used in most states. Other hurdles are statutory, such as ballot access restrictions, which are often very onerous for third parties and their candidates.[50]

Third parties at the state and local levels have not always been weak. The adoption in most states of the Australian ballot (or secret ballot) in the late nineteenth century initially gave a boost to third parties. The Australian ballot placed governments—rather than the parties themselves—in charge of printing ballots and administrating elections, making voting a private rather than a public act. The secret ballot diminished the power of the party bosses, who could no longer directly monitor the vote choices of citizens and also made split-ticket voting possible. Furthermore, many states during this period switched from a **party-column ballot** (sometimes known as the Indiana ballot), which listed all the candidates running for separate offices by their political party and had the effect of strengthening the parties, to an **office-block ballot**, which made split-ticket voting easier,

thereby weakening the major parties.[51] Today, 17 states still use party-column ballots, which encourage straight-party voting (see Figure 5.3). With the push of a single button, voters are able to support all the candidates running for office of a given party.[52]

Third parties, such as the Libertarian, Green, and Natural Law parties, have been hampered by both the direct primary system and ballot access laws adopted by the states. The direct primary system of nominating congressional and state officials has hurt the prowess of state-level third parties in the states. Because party bosses no longer overtly control the nomination processes of the two major parties, Republican and Democratic party dissidents are able to act as "outsiders" while remaining within the two parties. As such, the major parties are able to absorb dissidents and broader protest movements, which in the past often led to the rise of third parties.

Ballot access laws also ensure that the two major parties are guaranteed a place on the ballot, whereas minor parties—if they do not win a certain percentage of the vote in a previous election—are required to collect signatures to qualify for the ballot. In some states, this barrier to access is relatively easy to overcome. Colorado lawmakers in 1998 made it easier for minor parties to win recognition as actual political parties and not just as political organizations; all a third party needs to be recognized is to have 1,000 registrants and run at least 10 candidates for statewide or legislative seats. If a minor party fails to meet this requirement, it must either collect 10,000 signatures on petitions or have one of its candidates win at least 5 percent of a statewide vote.

Third parties and their candidates face a host of psychological barriers, too. At the individual level, citizens who vote regularly (likely voters)

---

[49] Calculations derived from Morehouse and Jewell, *State Politics, Parties, and Policy*, Table 2.1.

[50] John Bibby and Sandy Maisel, *Two Parties—or More?* 2nd ed. (Boulder, CO: Westview, 2002).

[51] Richard Niemi and Paul Herrnson, "Beyond the Butterfly: The Complexity of U.S. Ballots," *Perspectives on Politics* 1 (2003):317–26.

[52] David Kimball, Chris T. Owens, and Katherine M. Keeney, "Residual Votes and Political Representation," in Robert Watson, ed., *Counting Votes: Lessons from the 2000 Presidential Election in Florida* (Gainesville: University Press of Florida, 2004).

Figure 5.3

Party-Column and Office-Block Ballots

Source: Alex Peterman, *Elements of Civil Government* (New York: American Book Company, 1916). Available: http://www.gutenberg.org/files/15018/15018-h/images/img-187.jpg and http://www.gutenberg.org/files/15018/15018-h/images/img-186.jpg.

tend to have a strong allegiance to one of the two major parties. In addition, citizens who are alienated from the political system, and who therefore might be likely suspects to vote for a third-party candidate, are much less likely to vote. Because of the winner-take-all nature of most state and local elections, third parties often have a difficult time convincing contributors to give them money. Because candidates running on third-party tickets have little chance of winning, the media tend not to cover them. It becomes a self-fulfilling prophecy that because their candidates rarely win, third parties have a difficult time recruiting qualified candidates to run on their ticket.

Every blue moon, of course, third-party candidates do win elective office at the state or local level. A study of voting patterns for presidential candidates found three factors have motivated citizens to vote for third-party candidates: majority party deterioration, an influx of new voters with weak allegiance to the two major parties, and, most importantly, attractive third-party candidates who present viable alternatives to major nominees.[53] The same factors are often in place at the state level. Since 1930, eight third-party and independent candidates have been elected governor, including four since 1990. Most recently, in 1998 in Minnesota, former professional wrestler Jesse "The Body" Ventura, running as a Reform Party candidate, won with 37 percent of the vote.

Understanding Interest Groups

Like parties, interest groups are essential components of the democratic process. They serve a basic function of aggregating different points of view and pushing policy agendas in the public sphere. By linking the public to elected officials, interest groups encourage individuals to participate in state and local affairs, allowing their voices to be heard. Without a collective voice, citizens would have relatively little direct power over their elected officials. Casting ballots, after all, happens infrequently, every two years or so. And most people have limited access to their elected officials or political party operatives. If individuals are to be heard and represented by elected officials, they often require a vehicle to collectively convey their concerns. As countervailing forces, interest groups can apply pressure on public officials, educate them about the issues, and push them to adopt or defeat a public policy. They can even serve as **governmental watchdogs**, monitoring government programs and sounding a public alarm if they uncover inefficient or mismanaged programs or corruption.

Of course, interest groups do not always promote the values and desires of the public interest; regularly, they attempt to promote their own agendas and sway public officials. Some groups have more clout—some might say too much—in state and local politics, influencing who governs.[54] It will also become apparent to you that interest groups are not randomly distributed throughout society but reflect an inherent upper-class bias, with corporate interests and wealthier individuals having greater representation in state and community interest group systems.[55]

Defining Interest Groups

What are interest groups, and how do they differ from merely having an interest? As you might expect, interest groups come in all shapes and sizes, advancing a seemingly infinite number of political causes. Nearly every one of you will belong to at least one—if not several—interest groups during your lifetime. An interest group is a formally organized body of individuals, organizations, or enterprises that

---

[53] Steven Rosenstone, Roy Behr, and Edward Lazarus, *Third Parties in America: Citizen Response to Major Party Failure*, 2nd ed. (Princeton, NJ: Princeton University Press, 1996).

[54] Robert Dahl, *Who Governs?* (New Haven, CT: Yale University Press, 1961).

[55] Peter Bachrach and Morton S. Baratz, "Two Faces of Power," *American Political Science Review* 56(1962):947–52.

shares common goals and joins in a collective attempt to influence the electoral and policy-making processes. Simply put, an interest group is any organization that attempts to influence the electoral process or governmental policy making. Unlike political parties, interest groups do not nominate or run a slate of candidates for political office and do not take over the reins of government. Many interest groups are heavily involved in the electoral process; others focus on lobbying elected officials and policy makers.

If we are to adhere strictly to this definition, "farmers," for example, would not constitute an interest group. Because different farmers have different interests, they fail to meet the definitional standard of sharing common goals. For example, dairy farmers in Wisconsin have interests that are quite dissimilar from those of alfalfa, soybean, and corn growers in Iowa and Illinois or even other dairy farmers in California and Vermont. Wisconsin dairy farmers want to keep down the cost of the feed for their herd, prevent California milk producers from expanding their agribusiness operations, and ensure a fair milk-pricing system. Some may want to increase state and federal subsidies to set aside land for conservation easements protecting wetlands; limit price supports for small, organic dairies in Vermont; and even allow the injection of bovine growth hormone into their cows to increase milk production. Indeed, there are even several competing interest groups representing milk producers in Wisconsin, including the National Milk Producers Federation, the Dairy Farmers of America, the Wisconsin Dairy Business Association, and the State Dairymen's Association. It is important to keep in mind that an interest is categorically different from an organization or a group. Individuals may (and often do) share common concerns with one another without ever belonging to a group.

Types of Interest Groups

The universe of interest groups is not limited to membership organizations or groups of like-minded individuals sharing common social, economic, or political goals joining together to advance them. Membership organizations bring together individuals—such as the myriad farmer organizations mentioned above—to pursue their collective goals. Some well-known membership organizations with an active presence in the states include the Chamber of Commerce, the Sierra Club, the National Rifle Association, the American Federation of Teachers, Common Cause, and the American Association for Justice (formerly known as the Association of Trial Lawyers of America).

In addition to membership organizations, the definition also includes associations. Associations do not have individuals as members; rather, their members are composed of individual businesses, unions, or even other associations from the public and private spheres. The Texas Petroleum Marketers and Convenience Store Association, the Michigan Beer and Wine Wholesalers, and the Association of Washington Business are all examples of associations, which are also known as "peak associations."

Finally, under this broad definition of interest groups, enterprises—from corporate and family-owned banks to hospitals to insurance companies to colleges and universities—are also included. Enterprises are not membership based and do not have individuals as members. Employees of an enterprise are usually not involved or even consulted when it pursues a policy or electoral outcome. Publicly traded corporations, for example, do not need to obtain shareholder approval before pursuing political and electoral goals. As such, an enterprise is permitted to support issues and candidates that may be at odds with the preferences of its employees or shareholders.

Madison's "The Federalist No. 10"

Interest groups are not new. Although the term did not become part of the political vernacular until the late nineteenth century, interest groups are rooted in the fabric of American political life and were heavily involved in the founding of the nation. Interest groups, or what Founder James Madison called "minority factions" in his classic essay, "The Federalist No. 10," are inevitable in a free society. The causes of both majority and minority factions, Madison argued, are "sown into the nature of man." Although a "necessary evil," Madison realized that factions were essential to liberty. If citizens lacked the ability to form factions, they could potentially be tyrannized by government, squandering their fundamental liberties in the process. Madison's solution was to create an institutional framework of checks and balances to control the baneful effects of factions.[56]

Some scholars have been critical of Madison's solution, what political scientists often refer to as **pluralism**. Not all interests, they claim, can be organized, and some are structurally more advantaged than others. E. E. Schattschneider, for instance, argued that the pressure group system is limited to those groups that are private and that are organized. As a result, "The flaw in the pluralist heaven is that the heavenly chorus sings with a strong upper-class accent," in that the pluralist system has a **mobilization of bias** benefiting private, organized interests.[57] Because the distribution of interests participating in the interest group system is uneven and "far from isomorphic with the distribution of interests in society," for-profit and business organizations are likely to dominate.[58]

Interest Groups and Their Members

Why do people join interest groups, and how do they maintain themselves organizationally? Scholars have taken two very different approaches—one grounded in social dynamics and group theory, and the other in microlevel

economics—in an effort to gain some leverage on these questions.

How Do Interest Groups Form?

In the 1950s, David Truman advanced what has become known as **disturbance theory**.[59] Focusing on macrolevel shifts that cause groups to emerge in response to a change in the status quo, Truman argued that voluntary associations would form naturally out of the desire of humans to satisfy their needs. Various interests, including even **potential interests**, would galvanize collectively, according to Truman, when their common interests were marginalized or threatened. When macrolevel societal or environmental disturbances in society occur—such as changes in demographic shifts, changes in the economy, advances in technology, or crises or societal disruptions, such as those resulting from plagues and disease, war, or even natural disasters like hurricanes or earthquakes—new patterns of interaction are created. With such occurrences, nascent groups will emerge in response to the change in the status quo. The resulting new groups help restore the larger "social equilibrium" of the interest group system. For Truman, it was rational for individuals to voluntarily join groups to further their own interests.

Barriers to Collective Action

Other social scientists were not so sure about the natural proclivity of individuals to voluntarily join groups. For some, disturbance theory seemed too easy. Problematizing the logic of collective action, economist Mancur Olson turned his attention to microlevel, transactional reasons why an individual may—or may not—choose to join a group. Olson began by tackling the **free-rider problem**, that is, the

[56] James Madison, "The Federalist No. 10," 1788, http://www.constitution.org/fed/federa10.htm.

[57] E. E. Schattschneider, *The Semisovereign People* (New York: Holt, Rinehart & Winston, 1960).

[58] David Lowery and Virginia Gray, "Bias in the Heavenly Chorus: Interests in Society and before Government," *Journal of Theoretical Politics* 16(2004):5–30.

[59] David Truman, *The Governmental Process* (New York: Alfred A. Knopf, 1951).

assumption that individuals will try to benefit from **public goods** without paying for them. Contra Truman, Olson contended that there are many costs associated with an individual joining a group. If given a choice, rational actors would generally not join groups, choosing instead to benefit from the actions of the groups without bearing any of the attendant costs.[60]

Flipping many of the assumptions of pluralism on its head, Olson pointed out that individuals usually join groups for three reasons: peer pressure, coercion, or receipt of some type of **selective benefit**. By keeping itself small, a group can exert peer pressure on potential free-riders, embarrassing them to join the group. When small, it is easy for a group to determine who is benefiting from its actions without bearing the costs of membership. Individuals, too, have an easier way of calculating the costs and benefits of becoming a member when a group is small. People might also join groups when they are coerced to do so. For example, say you just graduated from law school and want to become a practicing attorney in the State of North Carolina. You first must pass the state bar exam. Once you do, you must pay annual dues to the North Carolina State Bar and complete mandatory continuing legal education course requirements every year.

For some, an important incentive to join a group is to receive a selective benefit that is only provided to members of the group. For example, some retirees join the American Association of Retired Persons (AARP) for the various benefits it provides to its 30 million–plus members, such as discounts on group health insurance, lower rates on hotels and car rentals, or price-reduced tickets to the theater and the movies. Like Truman's macrolevel perspective, Olson's rational choice microlevel framework does not provide a complete picture of group activity. Some people, of course, decide to join groups even if no overt peer pressure, coercion, or selective benefits exist. We do not necessarily think any worse of these people—call them altruistic—but Olson's rational choice framework sees them largely as acting irrationally by not taking advantage of free-ridership.

Interest Group Techniques

In their concerted effort to represent their constituencies, interest groups use different tactics to shape public policies and elections. What do interest groups do, how do their techniques differ, and which groups are most active at the state and local levels? From classic insider techniques, such as lobbying policy makers, to outsider techniques, such as issue advocacy, electioneering, and litigation, interest groups are increasingly using multiple strategies to maximize their effectiveness.[61]

Although interest groups do not typically engage in every type of activity, there are many common patterns across the states and across interests. One study has detailed the various insider and outsider techniques that some 301 state-level organizations surveyed in three states (California, South Carolina, and Wisconsin) use to shape public policy. Nearly all state-level interest organizations report using insider techniques, such as lobbying state legislators, testifying at legislative hearings, contacting government officials, helping to draft legislation, and meeting with government officials. Interest groups also report using several outsider tactics, including grassroots campaigns to mobilize supporters, letter-writing campaigns, and having influential constituents contact elected officials. Less than half report they contribute money to candidates, and still fewer say they work on campaigns or endorse candidates.

---

[60] Mancur Olson, *The Logic of Collective Action* (Cambridge, MA: Harvard University Press, 1965).

[61] Kay Lehman Schlozman and John Tierney, *Organized Interests and American Democracy* (New York: Harper & Row, 1986); Thomas Gais, *Improper Influence: Campaign Finance Law, Political Interest Groups, and the Problem of Equality* (Ann Arbor: University of Michigan Press, 1986); and Ken Kollman, *Outside Lobbying: Public Opinion and Interest Groups Strategies* (Princeton, NJ: Princeton University Press, 1998).

Two of every five organizations claim they use litigation as a strategy, but only one in five runs issue ads or engages in protest activities.[62] Although activities of interest groups operating at the local level are similar, because many community-based groups lack necessary resources, they tend to use more reactive—as opposed to proactive—strategies when trying to influence public policy.[63]

Lobbying

Lobbying is an integral part of the state and local policy-making process, as it is the systematic effort to influence public policy by pressuring governmental officials to make decisions that comport with the interests of the group pursuing the desired action. The advocacy community in every state capital now consists of hundreds or even thousands of people being paid to alter public policy. It should come as no surprise to you that lobbying is big business. In 2004, nearly $1 billion was spent on lobbying activities in the 42 states that require lobbying

Lobbyists and lawmakers crowd "The Rail" outside the Illinois House of Representatives chambers at the Illinois State Capitol in Springfield.

Photo by AP Photo/Seth Perlman

expenditure reports. In some states, lobbyists—not citizens—have become known sardonically as the "True Constituency."[64]

The growth of the lobbying industry is indicative of its importance. As one keen observer of state legislatures notes, "Any group that can be touched by state government cannot afford to be without representation. If groups do not realize the need for a lobbyist at the outset, they soon learn their lesson."[65] This was certainly the case regarding Native American tribes. Since the passage of the Indian Gaming Regulatory Act in 1988, which opened the way for casino-style gambling on tribal lands, the lobbying efforts of Indian tribes have skyrocketed, as they have used their newfound wealth to pursue traditional insider strategies.[66] As with other groups, the lobbying efforts of the tribes have helped ensure their collective voice is heard by state and local policy makers.

What Do Lobbyists Do? Lobbyists try to influence policy making by marshaling information and communicating it to policy makers.[67] Lobbyists regularly monitor pending legislation, communicating directly with policy makers and their staff about the potential substantive and political impacts of policy choices. Lobbyists need to know not only how but also when to communicate information and to whom. In addition to meeting with policy makers, lobbyists provide information to officials about issues and give testimony before committee hearings. In states with less professional legislatures, elected officials often do not have the resources to stay informed on every issue, so they take cues from lobbyists. Lobbyists even help draft legislation. Testimony provided by

[62] Anthony Nownes and Patricia Freeman, "Interest Group Activity in the States," *Journal of Politics* 60(1998):86–112.

[63] Christopher Cooper and Anthony Nownes, "Citizen Groups in Big City Politics," *State and Local Government Review* 35(2003):102–11. We examine local power structures and land-based growth coalitions in more detail in Chapters 11 and 12.

[64] Martin Dyckman, "It's Fla. Voters vs. the True Constituency," *St. Petersburg (Fla.) Times*, 3 April 2005.

[65] Alan Rosenthal, *The Third House: Lobbyists and Lobbying in the States* (Washington, DC: CQ Press, 1993), 5.

[66] Richard Witmer and Fredrick Boehmke, "American Indian Political Incorporation in the Post–Indian Gaming Regulatory Act Era," *Social Science Journal* 44(2007):127–45.

[67] Anthony Nownes, *Pressure and Power: Organized Interests in American Politics* (Boston: Houghton Mifflin, 2001).

lobbyists, of course, is heavily biased, despite claims from the lobbying industry that they are simply providing impartial, objective information.

Types of Lobbyists Lobbying may be conducted by in-house, contract, government, or voluntary lobbyists. Roughly 40 percent of all the lobbying done in state capitals is conducted by **in-house lobbyists,** with individuals who are employees of a membership group, association, or institution representing their own organization. The Kentucky Distillers' Association, the Montana Mining Association, the Texas Association of Business, the California Nations Indian Gaming Association, the Iowa Corn Growers Association, and the Nevada State AFL-CIO all use in-house lobbyists to maintain a foot in the doors of state lawmakers and policy makers. According to one survey of interest group activity in the states, roughly 75 percent of in-house lobbyists are male.[68]

In contrast, **contract lobbyists** work either independently or for a lobbying firm. They typically work for multiple clients and charge their clients an hourly fee. Many contract lobbyists—who are predominantly male—are former legislators, elected or appointed state officials, or staff. Contract lobbyist extraordinaire Frank L. "Pancho" Hays (who sold his Colorado lobbying firm Hays Hays and Wilson in 2003 but remains a registered lobbyist) was legendary in Denver for his self-effacing, ever-professional demeanor. The son of a former lieutenant governor, Hays represented business interests as diverse as the Denver Broncos professional football team, tobacco giant Philip Morris, the Wine and Spirits Wholesalers of Colorado, Colorado Ski Country USA, the Colorado Association of Realtors, and the Cherry Creek School District. Roughly 20 percent of the lobbying

corps in state capitals is composed of contract lobbyists, depending on the professionalization of the state legislature.[69]

Lobbying done by government employees, who are sometimes referred to euphemistically as governmental relations personnel or legislative liaisons, is also quite common. Roughly 30 percent of all lobbyists in the states are government lobbyists, a figure that is difficult to exactly determine, as many states do not require government personnel to register when they lobby. Municipal, county, and regional governments as well as special districts, fire and police forces, and municipal and county hospitals and agencies all have business before the state.[70]

Finally, about 10 percent of state lobbying communities are composed of individuals who give their time and expertise without compensation.[71] These individuals are known as volunteers or, in some instances, as hobbyists. Volunteer lobbyists tend to assist public interest groups—retirees helping out the League of Women Voters of Ohio or the Gray Panthers of Metro Detroit, college students interning with Colorado Common Cause and Georgia Public Interest Research Group (GeorgiaPIRG), or high school students earning civic education credit that is part of a class requirement by putting in 10 hours a week working with Arizona Rock the Vote or the Maine chapter of Mothers Against Drunk Driving. Others are regular gadflies who like hanging around state legislatures and partaking in the action. As one public interest group jokes, volunteer lobbyists are the only ones left worthy of the name lobbyists, as contract and in-house lobbyists do not need to hang out in the lobbies anymore; their campaign contributions and influence enable them to be ushered directly in the front door of legislators' offices.[72]

[68] Clive Thomas and Ronald Hrebenar, "Interest Groups in the States," in Gray and Hanson, *Politics in the American States.*

[69] Nownes and Freeman, "Interest Group Activity in the States."

[70] Thomas and Hrebenar, "Interest Groups in the States."

[71] Nownes and Freeman, "Interest Group Activity in the States."

[72] Center for Lobbying in the Public Interest, "Ten Immutable Paradoxes of Public Interest Lobbying," http://consumerillinois.com/documents/Ten%20Immutable%20Paradoxes%20of%20Public%20Interest%20Lobbying.doc

The Rise of the Statehouse Lobbying Corps

In the 1980s, the number of firms and individuals registered to lobby state governments skyrocketed. By 1990, the average number of interest groups in a state registered to lobby a state legislature was 587, up from an average of only 196 in 1975. The total number of registered lobbyists also increased exponentially over the time period. In 1990, there were nearly 29,352 lobbyists registered in the 50 states, up from just 15,064 in 1980.[73] Today, there are nearly 40,000 registered lobbyists in the states.[74]

State lawmakers are far outnumbered by lobbyists. On average, there are roughly six lobbyists for every one state legislator. In New York, there were 4,145 lobbyists registered in Albany in 2008, enough for each lawmaker to have nearly 20 lobbyists to call his or her own. There are more than 10 registered lobbyists for each Colorado, Florida, Illinois, and Ohio lawmaker. In contrast, only two states, Maine and New Hampshire, have more lawmakers than registered lobbyists.[75] Although the "old bulls"—large corporations—still tend to dominate the lobbying corps in state legislatures, much turnover occurs in the corridors of state capitols. The annual turnover of registered lobbyists working for businesses is actually higher than it is for those working for membership groups and associations.[76]

Regulating Lobbyists State ethics laws and registration requirements for lobbyists have been on the books for years.[77] New York instituted the first comprehensive governmental ethics law in 1954. Since that time, states have passed a patchwork of ethics legislation, resulting in a "Byzantine array of public integrity rules and regulations that vary tremendously from state to state."[78] Currently, 12 states regulate only legislative lobbying, 20 regulate the lobbying of both legislative and executive officials, and 18 regulate the lobbying of all government officials.

Every state requires lobbyists to register with a state regulatory agency or the state legislature, although limitations and disclosure requirements on lobbying activities vary considerably. Several states do not require a fee to register as a lobbyist. In contrast, the annual fee to lobby in Massachusetts is $1,000. Thirty-seven states currently require lobbyists to report their expenditures, 24 have independent ethics commissions to launch investigations and enforce lobbying regulations, and 22 have a "cooling-off" period before government officials or legislators can become lobbyists. Another 38 states ban lobbyists from accepting payment that is contingent upon the defeat or enactment of a piece of legislation or administrative action and another four limit the practice. Several states, including Indiana, South Carolina, and Wisconsin, prohibit public employees from accepting "anything of value" that could be reasonably expected to influence a government employee's official action. In Wisconsin, this includes items as seemingly innocuous as a cup of coffee. Many states also ban gifts from lobbyists when the legislature is in session.

The relative effectiveness of lobbyists is conditioned by institutional constraints existing within a state. State lobbying restrictions on gifts to lawmakers and prohibitions on campaign finance activities by lobbyists can diminish the clout of lobbyists. Term limits on state legislators can affect the behavior

---

[73] Jennifer Anderson et al., "Mayflies and Old Bulls: Organization Persistence in State Interest Communities," *State Politics and Policy Quarterly* 4(2004):140–60.

[74] National Institute on Money in State Politics, "Total Lobbyists for 2007," http://www.followthemoney.org/database/graphs/lobbyistlink/lobbymap.phtml?p=0&y=2007&l=0.

[75] John Broder, "Amid Scandals, States Overhaul Lobbying Laws," *The New York Times,* 24 January 2006.

[76] Anderson et al., "Mayflies and Old Bulls."

[77] Rosenthal, *The Third House*; and Beth Rosenson, "Against Their Apparent Self-Interest: The Authorization of Independent State Legislative Ethics Commissions, 1973–1996," *State Politics and Policy Quarterly* 3(2003):42–66.

[78] Peggy Kerns and Ginger Sampson, "Do Ethics Laws Work?" *State Legislatures*, July–August 2003, 40–43.

and relative influence of lobbyists.[79] Term limits tend to weaken the long-standing ties and social networks that lobbyists work tirelessly to cultivate over time with government officials. Studies have shown that states with term limits have more lobbyists who report having to work harder to do their jobs. Yet, term-limited states also have worse ethical behavior among lobbyists, which might be tied to lobbyists in these term-limited states wielding more influence in the legislative process than they do in states where incumbents may keep their office interminably.[80]

Issue Advocacy

Rather than having their lobbyists directly press lawmakers and public officials to take action that benefits their members, some interest groups use indirect tactics to influence the making of public policy. Although fewer interest groups report regularly engaging in outsider strategies rather than insider strategies, many groups do engage in issue advocacy. **Issue advocacy** is a form of political speech that mentions issues and the positions taken on those issues by elected officials or candidates but stops

Comparisons Help Us Understand

REPRESENTING THE AMERICAN DREAM

We represent the American dream. That's why we win these things. It's about housing… [but] the other stuff helps." The "other stuff," according to Mike Toalson, the chief lobbyist and executive vice president of the Home Builders Association of Virginia, is the extensive campaign contributions and gifts his group has lavished on members of the Virginia General Assembly. Over the past decade, his association, with its 6,400 dues-paying members and its powerful political action committee (PAC) known as Build-PAC, has pumped in excess of $1 million into the coffers of the 14 senators who sit on the Local Government Committee and the 22 members of the House of Delegates who sit on the Counties, Cities and Towns Committee. The association has been an equal-opportunity donor, contributing roughly the same amount to Republican and Democratic committee members. Prior to his retirement in 2009, former Minority Leader, Franklin P. Hall (D-Richmond), raked in more than $145,000 from the home builders during his 30-plus-year career in the legislature. Several other

members have received over $100,000 from building and construction PACs during their tenures in office. Only one member of the House committee—Republican Robert Marshall, an ardent opponent of sprawl—has never taken a penny from the association. The powerful lobby has virtually guaranteed that bills seeking to limit development or rein in sprawl will die in committee. Delegate Marshall, who regularly sponsors bipartisan slow-growth bills, refers somewhat ruefully to his own committee as "a funeral pyre for all those bills."[81]

For close observers of state lobbying laws, the influence of home builders in Virginia should not come as a surprise. Virginia has some of the weakest lobbying regulations in the country, and the laws on its books are substantially weaker than they were 20 years ago. According to a recent composite index of state lobbying regulations, Virginia is tied for third, behind North Dakota and Wyoming, for the most lax lobbying requirements in the country. On the other end of the continuum, South Carolina has the toughest laws, followed by Alaska and Maine.[82]

[79] John Carey, Richard Niemi, and Lynda Powell, *Term Limits in State Legislatures* (Ann Arbor: University of Michigan Press, 2000); and Marjorie Sarbaugh-Thompson et al., *The Political and Institutional Effects of Term Limits* (New York: Palgrave Macmillan, 2004).

[80] Christopher Mooney, "The Impact of State Legislative Term Limits on Lobbyists and Interest Groups" (paper presented at the Fifth Annual State Politics and Policy Conference, East Lansing, Mich., May 2005).

[81] Michael Shear, "Va. Growth Bolstered by Well-Funded Voting Bloc," *The Washington Post*, 30 January 2006, p. B1.

[82] Adam Newmark, "Measuring State Legislative Lobbying Regulation," *State Politics and Policy Quarterly* 5(2005):182–91.

short of expressly advocating the support or defeat of those elected officials or candidates. Issue ads themselves may be articulated in any type of media—TV and radio broadcasts, newspaper ads, billboards, placards, banners strung behind airplanes, handbills, and fliers—with some costing millions, and others just a few dollars. Each state regulates issue advocacy differently, though most take cues from the federal government's regulations.

Interest groups may employ several issue advocacy strategies, including boycotts, sit-ins, mass rallies, and marches, that give their issues visibility and engender public support. Although done with less frequency today than in the past, interest groups sometimes sponsor boycotts, sit-ins, rallies, mass rallies, and marches to give their issues visibility and engender public support. For example, hundreds of supporters of Georgia death-row inmate Troy Davis, who was scheduled to be executed for the 1989 murder of an off-duty police officer, regularly rallied on the steps of the Georgia state capitol in Atlanta to put pressure on the Georgia parole board to consider granting Davis clemency. Supported by members of anti-death penalty interest groups, such as Amnesty International, as well as judges and former state prosecutors convinced of his innocence after several witnesses recanted their statements fingering Davis, members of his family and friends wore blue t-shirts proclaiming "I am Troy Davis" and carried placards during the choreographed demonstrations. Perhaps in part due to the international attention Davis' supporters generated by their mass rallies, the U.S. Supreme Court in 2009 ordered a federal trial court to hear new testimony in the case.[83]

Other groups, most notably liberal- and conservative-leaning public interest groups and labor unions, provide their members (and the broader general public) with information about incumbents and candidates running for office. These educational efforts—the groups do not actually endorse candidates—are nevertheless quite political. Some groups produce scorecards reporting the voting records of incumbents. For example, New Yorkers against Gun Violence is a nonprofit advocacy group that publicizes the destructive effects of gun violence in New York and advocates gun legislation. The group regularly compiles and distributes a legislative voting scorecard detailing whether members of the legislature supported or opposed key bills dealing with guns.

Electioneering

Interest groups not only try to shape the public policy debate through their lobbying and issue advocacy. Organized interests can also actively participate in the electoral process in a variety of ways. Many become engaged in candidate campaigns in an effort to influence who will be elected and thus have a hand in making public policy. The practice of explicitly supporting candidates or political parties is known as **electioneering**. Working on campaigns or financing candidates and parties helps to solidify the relationships that interest groups have with winning candidates and the parties in control of the state legislatures. Not all electioneering comes in the form of financial contributions. Some interest groups provide candidates and political parties with nonmonetary, in-kind contributions. Such contributions include sharing data from public opinion polls, giving out membership lists for fundraising, and lending staff and field operations for support during the campaign. Other groups will publicly endorse their support or opposition for candidates. Of course, many groups give monetary contributions directly to candidates and political parties. For these groups, state laws vary considerably with regard to what kinds of contributions they are permitted to give, how much they may give, and to whom they may give.

Regulating Campaign Contributions In 2010, the U.S. Supreme Court ruled in *Citizens*

[83] Adam Liptak, "Supreme Court Orders New Look at Death Row Case," *New York Times*, 17 August 2009. Available: http://www.nytimes.com/2009/08/18/us/18scotus.html.

United v. FEC that the federal government's restrictions on corporate and union direct spending on independent ads in candidate races were unconstitutional. By extension, similar laws in two-dozen states were deemed to be invalid too. Yet, the Court has continued to allow the states (and federal government) to have wide latitude in regulating and limiting the amount of money that interest groups may give directly to candidates and political parties.[84] Countless municipal and county governments and all but a handful of states have laws restricting the amount of campaign contributions that can be made by interest groups to candidates and political parties. The effort by states to limit spending in candidate campaigns has largely stemmed from the perception that special interests—predominantly corporations and business associations—have had undue influence in candidate races.

Similar to the regulation of elections, there exists a tremendous amount of variation across the states in the amount of regulation in the campaign finance activities of interest groups. Roughly 20 states prohibit corporations from making contributions to state parties and candidates from their general treasuries; another dozen states ban unions from contributing to campaigns using their general treasury funds. Close to another 20 states permit state parties to receive unlimited contributions from political action committees (PACs), legal entities that allow like-minded individuals who belong to a corporation, labor union, or virtually any other organization to pool their money and contribute directly to candidates and political parties. About a dozen states allow interest groups to give directly from their corporate or union treasuries to candidates. And a few states, including Florida, Illinois, and Virginia, permit virtually any interest group to make unlimited contributions to state political parties.[85]

PAC Contributions PAC contributions made to candidates running for office depend largely on the type and ideology of the interest group that controls the PAC. Some interest groups give according to their principles; others have more pragmatic giving patterns. Liberal PACs affiliated with local and state chapters of unions such as the Service Employees International Union and the American Federation of Teachers as well as pro-choice groups, such as NARAL and Planned Parenthood, give nearly all their contributions to Democrats. Conservative PACs affiliated with single issues, such as the National Rifle Association (NRA) and state affiliates of the National Right to Life, give nearly exclusively to Republicans. In contrast, many corporate-controlled PACs are equal-opportunity givers, writing checks to both Republican and Democratic candidates—as long as they are incumbents. Rather than ideology, these pragmatic PACs use their campaign donations as a means to purchase continued access to lawmakers and policy makers. According to one study, the energy industry—primarily oil and gas companies and their peak associations—pumped more than $134.7 million into candidate committees and state parties between 1990 and 2004. Nearly 70 percent of those contributions went to incumbents, irrespective of their political party.[86]

In 2008 alone, state-level candidates (running for governor, legislatures, and state supreme courts) and other political committees raised over $2.6 billion, up $0.5 billion from 2004, but down from the $3.5 billion brought in by the same entities in 2006. (There are many more statewide and legislative elections in midterm presidential election years.) As in previous years, most of the money flowed from special interests in the form of PAC contributions. General business and labor organizations both gave more than $200 million to candidates running for state offices in 2008, lawyers and lobbyists

[84] *Nixon v. Shrink Missouri Government PAC* (2000); but see the Supreme Court's decision, *Vermont Republican State Committee, et al. v. William Sorrell, et al.* (2006), for limits on expenditures and how low states can regulate contributions to candidates.

[85] Edward Feigenbaum and James Palmer, *Campaign Finance Law 2002* (Washington, DC: Federal Election Commission, 2003).

[86] Edwin Bender, "Energy Companies Build Power Base in Statehouses," Institute on Money in State Politics, http://www.followthemoney.org/press/Reports/200410061.pdf.

greased the campaign coffers of candidates to the tune of $142 million, and the combined financial, insurance, and real estate sector contributed over $108 million. Single-issue groups, which usually are more ideological, contributed nearly $112 million to candidates running for state offices.[87]

Money, it is often said, is like water. It is hydraulic, leveling itself and circumventing any barriers placed in its way. It can swamp the democratic process. A survey conducted in 2002 of some 1,300 interest groups operating in 38 states found that state contribution limits affect the contribution strategies that groups make. States with laws severely restricting interest group contributions to candidates tend to increase groups' spending in other electioneering areas. Interest groups operating in those states tend to increase their expenditures on issue advertising and independent expenditures in candidate elections.[88]

Litigation

Some interest groups turn their attention to state and federal courts when doing battle. As interpreters of laws and constitutions, courts are important venues for interest groups if they have been stymied by policy makers or administrators charged with implementing a law. One survey of state organizations finds that roughly half of all interest groups report that they either often or sometimes use litigation, or legal action, as a tactic.[89] For some groups, a lawsuit may be easier, less expensive, and more effective than paying lobbyists to advance their cause through the legislative process. This might be especially true for groups with small memberships, little political influence in the state or community, or less than stellar reputations.

When pursuing a litigation strategy, interest groups tend to use one of two tactics. Some

groups will seek out laws that they view as unconstitutional and file what is known as a "test case" on behalf of an aggrieved individual. One of the best-known test cases is *Brown v. Board of Education of Topeka* (1954). The National Association for the Advancement of Colored People (NAACP) had filed a suit on behalf of the parents of an eight-year-old elementary student, Linda Brown, who was forced to attend an all-black school in Kansas even though an all-white elementary school was only a few blocks from her home. In 1954, the U.S. Supreme Court struck down the practice of racial segregation in public schools ("separate but equal"). The court ruled that the 14th Amendment of the U.S. Constitution prohibited states from denying equal protection of the laws to persons within their jurisdiction.[90] Following the success of *Brown*, many other liberal organizations turned to the courts in the 1950s and 1960s, as many judges were seen as more progressive on social issues than were many state and local governments. In addition to civil rights associations like the NAACP, consumer rights advocacy organizations, women's and pro-choice groups, and environmental organizations all used lawsuits—especially pursued in federal courts—to advance their causes.

Beginning in the 1970s, many conservative groups started pushing lawsuits to advance their agendas, in part because they had more sympathizers sitting on the federal and state benches. Perhaps most notably, the National Right to Life Committee, founded in 1973 following the U.S. Supreme Court's *Roe v. Wade* ruling legalizing abortion, has relied on litigation as a key strategy to challenge state statutes protection a woman's right to an abortion. The increase in litigation by interest groups has been well documented: Between 1953 and 1993, the number of U.S. Supreme Court cases drawing

[87] National Institute on Money in State Politics, "Total Dollars for Candidates and Committees," 2008, http://www.followthemoney.org/database/nationalview.phtml.

[88] Robert Hogan, "State Campaign Finance Laws and Interest Group Electioneering Activities," *Journal of Politics* 67(2005):887–906.

[89] Nownes and Freeman, "Interest Group Activity in the States."

[90] *Brown v. Board of Education of Topeka*, 347 U.S. 483 (1954).

interest group attention increased from just 13 percent to 92 percent of all cases.[91]

The Dynamics of State Interest Group Systems

How do state interest group systems evolve over time, how are they comparatively different from one another, and which groups tend to hold the upper hand in a state's system? As studies on the dynamics of state interest group systems make evident, the concern voiced by critics of pluralist theory—that the system is biased in favor of economic interests—appears to be supported by empirical data.

The Advocacy Explosion

Paralleling the trend in Washington, DC, the number and types of interest groups in the American states greatly expanded during the 1960s and 1970s.[92] The rise of public interest groups in the American states and communities was not limited to newfangled nonprofit public interest groups pushing postmaterialist values. The rise of liberal-leaning citizen groups in the 1960s and 1970s helped to fuel a conservative backlash. During the 1970s and 1980s, conservative public interest groups, such as the Eagle Forum, with over 30 state chapters; National Right to Life; and the Christian Coalition established themselves as key political actors in many of the states. As countervailing forces, these groups continue to serve as foils to the liberal groups that emerged out of the social changes begotten from the 1960s.

There was a simultaneous backlash in the business community. In response to the strengthened public interest lobby as well as to the prowess of organized labor, which had

reached its zenith of influence in the 1950s, businesses began forming their own peak associations.[93] Today, corporate interests dominate the universe of state interest group systems. According to the most recent survey of interest groups registered in the states, enterprises comprise nearly three-fifths of all registered groups, with associations accounting for an additional 22 percent. Membership-based groups only account for 19 percent of all registered interest groups, down from 31 percent of all groups in 1980.[94]

The number of professional associations registered in the states, particularly ones representing business and trade interests, also rose in the 1970s and 1980s. The sharp rise was fueled in part by the surge in the number of white-collar jobs and women entering the workforce. By one count, the number of professional associations nationally increased from just 6,500 national organizations in 1958 to more than 23,000 by 1990.[95] Whereas some of these professional associations are well established and have active chapters in the states, others such as the Montana Bed and Breakfast Association, the Mid-Atlantic Alpaca Association, and the Oregon State Beekeeper's Association are relatively new.

Density and Diversity of State Interest Group Systems

The explosion of interest groups has not been consistent across all states, policy domains, or types of interests represented in a state's interest group system. The states have considerable variation in terms of the composition of interest groups. Interest group power, in turn, is not distributed evenly across the systems. So, why are state interest group systems different from one another?

[91] Andrew Koshner, *Solving the Puzzle of Interest Group Litigation* (Westport, CT: Greenwood Press, 1998).

[92] Nownes, *Pressure and Power*.

[93] Jeffrey Berry, *The Interest Group Society*, 3rd ed. (New York: Longman, 1997).

[94] Anderson et al., "Mayflies and Old Bulls."

[95] Theda Skocpol, Marshall Ganz, and Ziad Munson, "A Nation of Organizers: The Institutional Origins of Civic Voluntarism in the United States," *American Political Science Review* 94(2000):527–46.

Following the pluralist logic that groups emerge when a disturbance in the status quo occurs, the number and types of interest groups will grow as a society becomes more complex. There are considerable differences in the size, strength, and dynamics of state economies. As a state's economy grows, so does the number of interest groups operating in that state.[96] States with the largest economies invariably have the most interest groups. In 1997, for instance, Texas and California both had over 2,000 interest groups with registered lobbyists, Illinois had over 1,500, and Pennsylvania, Minnesota, New York, Ohio, Missouri, Florida, Michigan, and Massachusetts all had more than 1,000. At the other end of the spectrum, five states—Rhode Island, Wyoming, New Hampshire, Delaware, and Hawaii—all had fewer than 300 interest groups with registered lobbyists.

As competition for resources among registered organizations in the states increases, however, interest group systems gradually become denser and the expansion rate of the system slows down.[97] A state's **interest group system density** refers to the number of functioning groups relative to the size of the state's economy. Wealthier states tend to have more interest groups, in part because governments are able to attract new businesses by increasing their expenditures. In states with fairly dense interest group systems, the relative power of each group is lessened. A state's **interest group system diversity**, in contrast, refers to the spread of groups across various social and economic realms. Interest group diversity is positively related to a state's economic diversity.[98]

There is a tremendous amount of diversity in terms of the kinds of interest groups that have representation in a given state. In some states, such as New Mexico, California, Montana, and

Wyoming, nearly one out of every three interest groups with a registered lobbyist is a nonprofit organization. In New Jersey, by way of contrast, only 14 percent of all groups are in the nonprofit sector. The Dakotas, followed closely by Montana, lead the way with the highest percentage of membership organizations, with roughly 30 percent of their interest group systems composed of groups with individuals as members. Less than 14 percent of all groups are membership based in Pennsylvania and New Jersey, with Texas having the fewest, at only 11.7 percent. Texas is the state with the highest percentage (71.5 percent) of interest groups that are enterprises; in Wisconsin, less than 40 percent of all groups with a registered lobbyist are enterprises. At 31.6 percent, North Carolina has the highest percentage of associations, with Idaho a close second; the percentage in Utah, by contrast, is roughly half that amount.

Several factors seem to contribute to the density and diversity of a state's interest group system. States with more competition among the parties also tend to have denser interest group systems, as the lack of single-party rule perhaps exacerbates policy uncertainty and, thus, more intergroup competition. The legislatures of states with denser interest group systems tend to be less productive, as measured by the proportion of all bills introduced that are passed. Interestingly, states that have the initiative process also tend to have an increased number and a greater diversity of active interest groups. One study finds that states that allow the initiative process had on average 17 percent more interest groups between 1975 and 1990, after controlling for other factors that might lead to interest group growth, than states without the process.[99] A parallel study finds that actual initiative use by a state leads to a general

[96] David Lowery and Virginia Gray, "The Density of State Interest Group Systems," *Journal of Politics* 55(1993):191–206.

[97] Virginia Gray and David Lowery, *The Population Ecology of Interest Representation: Lobbying Communities in the American States* (Ann Arbor: University of Michigan Press, 1996).

[98] Virginia Gray and David Lowery, "The Expression of Density Dependence in State Communities of Organized Interests," *American Politics Research* 29(2001):374–91; and Virginia Gray and David Lowery, "The Institutionalization of State Communities of Organized Interests," *Political Research Quarterly* 54(2001):265–84.

[99] Frederick Boehmke, "The Effect of Direct Democracy on the Size and Diversity of State Interest Group Populations," *Journal of Politics* 64(2002):827–44.

increase in the number of membership groups, associations, and nonprofit organizations that have registered lobbyists in the state, indicating that the institution of direct democracy can increase the aggregate size as well as the diversity of state-level interest groups.[100] Finally, states with more diverse interest group systems tend to adopt public policies that are more distributive and progressive.[101]

In states with dense and diverse interest group systems, it is difficult for a single interest to dictate the overall policy agenda of state government. But even in these states with more diversified economies, interest groups are often able to carve space for themselves within a policy domain that is central to their policy objectives, where they become a dominant force. The number of participants in these policy niches tends to be limited in scope, with the vested interests holding considerable influence. In ensuring its survival, a successful interest group is able to stake out its own niche within a given policy domain.

Interest Group Competition: Who's Got Clout?

Today, most states and many communities have much more diversified economies than they did a half century ago. This economic change has led to a robust competition among a variety of private and public sector interest groups that battle over the making of public policy. Yet, private economic interests tend to dominate interest group systems. For example, the oil industry remains king in Alaska and Louisiana, the agriculture lobby reigns supreme in Iowa and South Dakota, ranching interests continue to be a strong force in Nebraska, and the tourism industry holds an upper hand in Florida, Nevada, and

Hawaii. Although the company town, communities literally built by firms to house their employees, disappeared from the local landscape long ago,[102] some towns—Bentonville, Arkansas, the corporate headquarters of Wal-Mart, comes to mind—are still dominated by a single industry.

An interest group's clout, or relative influence, is largely determined by its own internal resources, but it is bounded by external conditions. Internal resources include a group's political, organizational, and managerial skills as well as its finances, the size and geographical distribution of its membership, its political cohesiveness, and its long-term relations with public officials. A group's policy goals are also conditioned by external factors, such as the political climate of the state or community, including partisan identification, political culture, issues and events, and public opinion. Although it is difficult, if not impossible, to precisely measure a group's "clout," these internal and external factors affect the ability of an interest organization to wield influence and power within a state or community. When lacking in clout, some groups opt to team up with other organizations to build coalitions. Rather than acting independently and going it alone, it sometimes makes strategic sense for an organization to form alliances with other like-minded groups, especially if competition increases among groups in the system.[103]

Most Influential Interests in the 50 States
Is it possible to rank the most powerful interests in the 50 states? Based on survey responses from political scientists working in all 50 states, Table 5.1 categorizes interest organizations by their effectiveness, listing the 20 most influential interests in the states in 2007 (with comparison rankings from 1985). The table reveals how some sectors of interest organizations are

[100] Daniel Smith and Caroline Tolbert, *Educated by Initiative: The Effects of Direct Democracy on Citizens and Political Organizations in the American States* (Ann Arbor: University of Michigan Press, 2004).

[101] Sarah Morehouse and Malcolm Jewell, *State Politics, Parties and Policy*, 2nd ed. (New York: Rowman & Littlefield, 2003).

[102] John Gaventa, *Power and Powerlessness: Quiescence and Rebellion in an Appalachian Valley* (Champaign-Urbana: University of Illinois Press, 1980).

[103] Clive Thomas and Ron Hrebenar, "Who's Got Clout?" *State Legislatures*, April 1999, 30–34; Kevin Hula, *Lobbying Together: Interest Group Coalitions in Legislative Politics* (Washington, DC: Georgetown University Press, 1999); and Michael T. Heaney, "Outside the Issue Niche: The Multidimensionality of Interest Group Identity," *American Politics Research* 32(2004):1–41.

Table 5.1

The 20 Most Influential Interests in the 50 States in 2007 Compared to 1985

2007 Ranking (1985 ranking in parentheses)	Interest Organization	Number of States in 2007 in Which Interest Ranked Among		
		Most Effective	Somewhat Effective	Less/Not Effective
1 (2)	General business organizations (state chambers of commerce, etc.)	39	14	5
2 (1)	Schoolteachers' organizations (NEA and AFT)	31	17	2
3 (6)	Utility companies and associations (electric, gas, water, telephone/telecommunications)	28	22	9
4 (4)	Manufacturers (companies and associations)	25	18	14
5 (17)	Hospital/nursing home associations	24	18	10
6 (13)	Insurance: general and medical (companies and associations)	22	16	14
7 (11)	Physicians/state medical associations	21	16	14
8 (22)	Contractors, builders, developers	21	12	27
9 (9)	General local government organizations (municipal leagues, county organizations, elected officials)	18	18	15
10 (8)	Lawyers (predominantly trial lawyers, state bar associations)	20	13	18
11 (14)	Realtors' associations	20	10	20
12 (10)	General farm organizations (state farm bureaus, etc.)	14	17	19
13 (3)	Bankers' associations	15	14	21
14 (19)	Universities and colleges (institutions and employees)	14	14	23
15 (5)	Traditional labor associations (predominantly the AFL-CIO)	15	11	24
16 (15)	Individual labor unions (Teamsters, UAW)	13	11	26
17 (36)	Gambling Interests (race tracks, casinos, and lotteries)	13	9	28
18 (7)	Individual banks and finance institutions	11	11	28
19 (29)	State agencies	10	13	30
20 (23)	Environmentalists	8	17	25

Source: Clive Thomas and Ronald Hrebenar, "Interest Groups in the States," in Virginia Gray and Russell Hanson, eds., *Politics in the American States*: A Comparative Analysis, 9th ed. (Washington, DC: CQ Press, 2008), p. 117.

influential interests across many states, whereas others are only effective in a few states.[104]

General business organizations, most notably the Chamber of Commerce, and teachers' associations, such as the American Federation of Teachers and the National Education Association,

are powerful interest groups in most of the 50 states today, just as they were in 1985. Interest groups representing energy utilities, insurance companies, hospitals, lawyers, and manufacturers are also forces to be reckoned with in most states. Although liquor, wine, and beer interests

[104] Totals for a category interest may exceed 50, as some interest groups within a category sometimes were reported to be in separate categories by the political scientists who were surveyed. See Clive Thomas and Ronald Hrebenar, "Interest Groups in the States," in Virginia Gray and Russell Hanson, eds., *Politics in the American States: A Comparative Analysis*, 9th ed. (Washington, DC: CQ Press, 2008), pp. 117–18.

are not nearly as powerful (the industry was 28th most influential according to the 2007 rankings), the lobby has a presence in all 50 states. The brewer Anheuser-Busch, for instance, employs lobbyists in all 50 states because alcohol policy is largely regulated by the states. On the other hand, groups representing senior citizens, forest products, mining companies, and tobacco companies have a strong presence in only a handful of states.

Overall, the relative power of interest groups across the 50 states has remained fairly constant over time. Table 5.1 reveals little change between 1985 and 2007 in terms of the relative strength and weakness of interest organizations. In addition to the aforementioned economic interests, groups representing physicians, general farm organizations, and realtors have retained their strength through the years. Although minimal, some change has occurred across some of the sectors: hospital and nursing home associations, the insurance industry, gaming, and contractors, builders, and developers have all become relatively stronger (including the venerable NRA), whereas energy corporations and their associations, banks, and other financial enterprises have become weaker players.

Despite some flux in the relative strength of the different sectors represented in state interest group systems, economic groups remain powerful players in most states, just as they were back in the 1950s when the first survey of interest groups was conducted.[105] This has led some observers, following the pioneering work of Schattschneider and Lindblom, to again ask whether a corporate bias in the interest group systems of the states exists. One recent study—which finds that 77 percent of the total universe of state interest groups is made up of for-profit organizations—seems to confirm Schattschneider's prediction that private interest organizations will dominate the interest group system.[106] Yet, the dominance of business interests is not hegemonic. Business interests do not control all policy niches. As state economies increase in size, business interests tend to fragment to some degree.[107] As interest group systems become more and more crowded and complex, it is possible that powerful groups—including business associations and firms—may lose their "clout."[108]

Relative Impact of Interest Groups Interest group strength can also be measured with a five-fold typology that assesses the overall impact of interest groups relative to other actors (most notably political parties) in a state's political system. Last updated in 2007, a survey of the 50 states reveals that the power of interest groups compared to other actors can be considered dominant in four states, dominant/complementary in 26 states, complementary in 15 states, complementary/subordinate in five states, and subordinate in no states.[109] Table 5.2 provides the overall impact of interest groups in the 50 states. The number of states found in each category today has changed since the survey was first conducted in the early 1980s; roughly half of the states are still classified in the same category as they were in 1985, with the remainder shifting categories. Slightly more than half of the states today are categorized as dominant/complementary. Why are interest group systems in some states more dominant than others? Although it's difficult to precisely answer this question, states with less robust economies tend to have political systems with more dominant interest groups. Conversely, in states with larger economies, interest groups were weaker or more complementary relative to other actors, such as parties.[110]

---

[105] Belle Zeller, *American State Legislatures*, 2nd ed. (New York: Thomas Y. Crowell, 1954).

[106] Anderson et al., "Mayflies and Old Bulls."

[107] Lowery and Gray, "Bias in the Heavenly Chorus."

[108] Schattschneider, *The Semisovereign People*; and Schlozman and Tierney, *Organized Interests and American Democracy*.

[109] John Heinz et al., *The Hollow Core* (Cambridge, MA: Harvard University Press, 1993); and Thomas and Hrebenar, "Interest Groups in the States."

[110] Heinz et al., *The Hollow Core*; and Mark Smith, *American Business and Political Power* (Chicago: University of Chicago Press, 2000).

Table 5.2

Classification of the 50 States According to the Overall Impact of Interest Groups in 2006–2007, Compared with Previous Classifications

Dominant (4)	Dominant/Complementary (26)	Complementary (15)	Complementary/ Subordinate (5)
Alabama	–Alaska, Arizona	Colorado	--Kentucky
Florida	Arkansas, California	+/–Connecticut	–Michigan
+/– Hawaii	++Delaware,	Indiana	Minnesota
+ Nevada	Georgia, Idaho	Maine	–South Dakota
	+Illinois, +Iowa	Massachusetts	Vermont[a]
	+Kansas, –Louisiana	+/–Montana	
	+Maryland, –Mississippi	New Hampshire	
	+Missouri, Nebraska	New Jersey	
	–New Mexico, Ohio	New York	
	Oklahoma, Oregon	North Carolina	
	–South Carolina	North Dakota	
	–Tennessee, Texas,	Pennsylvania	
	Utah[a], Virginia	+Rhode Island	
	–West Virginia,	–Washington	
	Wyoming	Wisconsin	

Source: Clive Thomas and Ronald Hrebenar, "Interest Groups in the States," in Virginia Gray and Russell Hanson, eds., *Politics in the American States: A Comparative Analysis*, 9th ed. (Washington, DC: CQ Press, 2008), p. 121.

Note: The symbols +/–, ++, and – indicate that a state has moved across adjoining categories since the first survey in 1985. If a state has moved up and down, it is designated with a +/–; if it has moved up only, it is designated with ++; and if it has moved down only, it is marked by –. The symbols + and – indicate movement of one category only, up or down, since the 1985 survey.

[a]Utah and Vermont are in the same categories they occupied in 1985, but both states have moved twice since 1985—into the complementary category and then back to their original categories.

Summary

Political parties and interest groups hold different levels of power in states and localities, and these levels can vary over time. Sometimes interest groups are subservient to parties; at other times, the relationship appears to be reversed. Regardless of whether they are understood as responsible or functional organizations, the two major political parties are essential players in state and local politics. Parties help to structure the electoral and governing environments in states, which in turn affect the parties. The partisan identification and political ideology of a state's electorate, which are not always synonymous, help to shape the organization and the governance strategies of the parties. Furthermore, the strength of state parties is ever shifting in terms of their electoral, organizational, and governance strength, with considerable differences across the states. Like parties, interest groups are political institutions that operate as rational actors. Some employ lobbyists to place pressure on public officials. Others use issue advocacy, electioneering, and litigation to advance their collective goals. Whatever their tactic, interest groups are constantly fighting to shape the political terrain, molding it to reflect their image. Because economic and political resources are not distributed evenly across society, some interests are more easily articulated and aggregated than others. As such, not all societal interests are equally represented in states and communities by organized interests, nor are they all heard by elected officials and policy makers.

Key Terms

caucus

closed primary

contract lobbyist

direct primary

disturbance theory

electioneering

free-rider problem

functional party model

governmental watchdog

in-house lobbyist

interest group system density

interest group system diversity

issue advocacy

lobbying

mobilization of bias

office-block ballot

open primary

party-column ballot

party fusion

party identification

pluralism

political action committee (PAC)

potential interest

public good

responsible party model

selective benefit

semiclosed primary

semiopen primary

top-two blanket primary

Discussion Questions

(1) James Madison, during the Founding, and David Truman during the 1950s, discussed the formation of interest groups as "necessary evils." What were their arguments? What were their recommended solutions to the supposed "evils" of interest groups?

(2) Discuss the differences between the responsible party model and the functional party model. Use examples from your own state to explain why parties in the United States tend to be more "functional" than "responsible."

(3) What are the differences between open and closed primary systems? How have Supreme Court rulings affected primary system laws? Which kind of primary system do you think is the fairest, and why?

(4) Why do candidates running on third-party tickets have such difficult time winning office? Discuss various barriers to third-party candidates, and make suggestions on how third parties might be able to garner more success at the polls in state elections.

(5) How is interest group strength measured, and what are the strongest interest groups in the 50 states? What is the overall impact of interest groups in your state, compared to other states? Do you agree with the ranking? Why or why not?

Suggested Readings

Aldrich, John H. 1995. *Why Parties? The Origin and Transformation of Party Politics in America*. Chicago: University of Chicago Press.

Baumgartner, Frank, and Beth L. Leech. 1998. *Basic Interests: The Importance of Groups in Politics and in Political Science*. Princeton, NJ: Princeton University Press.

Berry, Jeffrey. 1999. *The New Liberalism: The Rising Power of Citizen Groups*. Washington, DC: Brookings Institution Press.

Gelman, Andrew, et al. 2008. *Red State, Blue State, Rich State, Poor State: Why Americans Vote the Way They Do*. Princeton: Princeton University Press.

Gray, Virginia, and David Lowery. 1996. *The Population Ecology of Interest Representation: Lobbying Communities in the American States*. Ann Arbor, MI: University of Michigan Press.

La Raja, Raymond. 2008. *Small Change: Money, Political Parties, and Campaign Finance Reform* (Ann Arbor: University of Michigan Press.

Masket, Seth E. 2009. *No Middle Ground: How Informal Party Organizations Control Nominations and Polarize Legislatures*. Ann Arbor: University of Michigan Press.

Olson, Mancur. 1965. *The Logic of Collective Action*. Cambridge, MA: Harvard University Press.

Rosenthal, Alan. 2001. *The Third House: Lobbyists and Lobbying in the States*. Washington, DC: CQ Press.

Schattschneider, E. E. 1960. *The Semisovereign People*. New York: Holt, Rinehart & Winston.

Truman, David B. 1951. *The Governmental Process*. New York: Alfred A. Knopf.

Websites

American League of Lobbyists (http://www.alldc.org): The American League of Lobbyists is an association devoted to enhancing the professionalism, competence, and ethical standards of lobbyists.

Ballot Access News (http://www.ballot-access.org): A treasure trove of information on state ballot access laws, primary systems, and barriers to third parties.

Project Vote-Smart (http://www.vote-smart.org): A nonprofit organization that provides a wealth of information on all candidates running for state and federal office.

National Institute on Money in State Politics (http://www.followthemoney.org): Provides comprehensive and up-to-date campaign contribution data for state political parties and candidates.

6

State Legislatures

INTRODUCTION

Legislatures and legislators have the tough job of dealing with the public problems of the state with limited resources. Sometimes their job is harder than others—like today, when most states dealing with the worst fiscal crisis in years—but it is never easy. The way that state legislative institutions are set up makes the job especially difficult, with the large numbers of decision makers, frequent elections, two chambers, and more. Some institutions have evolved to help make these bodies run better, like legislative committees and leadership, but they do not solve all the difficulties. Because public problems outstrip public resources, compromise is always needed in lawmaking, leading to dissatisfaction and frustration.

In the 15 states that have them, state legislative term limits have undoubtedly complicated lawmaking by reducing institutional knowledge and shifting influence to other actors in the process. The part-time nature of service in most state legislatures further exacerbates the difficulties. Since most lawmakers need an external source of income, conflicts of interest can arise, even if they rarely rise to the level of outright graft and corruption. Regardless, the recent well-publicized cases of legislative corruption in several states have shaken the public's faith in their representatives. Various ethics laws and regulations have been advocated, and sometimes adopted, but none of them is a panacea. But despite all the problems with the legislative process, and no matter what its outcomes in a given state in a given year, two things are guaranteed: The legislature's actions will have important effects on all the residents of the state, and lawmakers will do it all over again next year.[1]

AP Photo/Mike Groll

[1] This is except for those five state legislatures (in Montana, Nevada, North Dakota, Oregon, and Texas) that meet biennially. These state legislatures will do it all over again in two years.

State legislatures provide a vital link between a state's citizens and its government—they are the "engines of democracy."[2] State legislators have the smallest constituencies of any type of state or federal official, and they best reflect America's diversity. It is common for women and members of minority groups not only to serve in state legislatures but also to hold the highest leadership positions there, something that couldn't be said of legislatures in the past or in many other political even bodies today. State legislatures are richly diverse in other ways, too. For example, in the New Hampshire House of Representatives, the nation's youngest (Jeff Fontas, 21) and oldest (Angeline Kopka, 92) state lawmakers serve side by side, and many of the nation's 7,382 state lawmakers are openly gay or lesbian (e.g., Minnesota Representative Karen Clark and Utah Senator Scott McCoy).[3] Furthermore, since lawmaking is not a full-time job for most state legislators, and since they therefore live and work in and among their constituents most of the time, people are far more likely to know them than, say, their governor or representatives in Congress.

Serving as a state legislator is service, indeed. The pay is low, the hours are long, and the conditions are poor,[4] but their work is essential in the process of translating the wishes and needs of a state's citizens into public policy. Every law that exists in a state, every change in any state law, and every penny that a state spends must be approved by the state legislature in a long and complicated process much like that of the U.S. Congress. It is impossible to over-emphasize the importance of legislatures for their states.

If state lawmaking is such a tough job under such tough conditions, why do people actively and aggressively run for these positions? Plain ambition is one reason. Being a state legislator is excellent training for higher office, and lawmakers often move up the political ladder.[5] Almost half of those serving in Congress today are former state legislators; even President Barack Obama served in the Illinois Senate not that long ago (from 1997 to 2004). In fact, some (including Obama himself) have argued that what the president learned in the Illinois Statehouse about the details of public policy, how to work with people of all stripes, the skills of compromise, debate, and perseverance, and more were even more important to his success at the national level than what he learned in the U.S. Senate.[6]

Beyond self-aggrandizement, the work of public service in state legislatures is truly important and satisfying—and it simply fascinates many people.[7] State lawmakers work to solve problems in every area of life, from helping poor people get health care to improving a state's business climate, from reducing city traffic to building roads and bridges, from educating preschool children to searching for a cure for Alzheimer's disease. Just ask Fred Risser. After 52 years representing Madison in the Wisconsin House and Senate, in November 2008, he was elected to another four-year term.[8]

[2] Alan Rosenthal, *Engines of Democracy: Politics and Policymaking in State Legislatures* (Washington, DC: CQ Press, 2009).

[3] Donald Haider-Markel, *Gay and Lesbian Candidates, Elections, and Policy Representation* (Washington, DC: Georgetown University Press, 2010); Morgan Cullen, "He's 21. She's 92," *State Legislatures* (July/August 2008):52–54.

[4] For example, see: Jennifer Mock, "Lawmakers Share Apartment during Session: Homes away from Home Vary for Legislators with One Even Staying in a Travel Trailer," *The Oklahoman*, 28 March 2007, online edition; Nicholas K. Geranios, "Police: Legislator Target of Extortion," *The Seattle Times*, 31 October 2007.

[5] Michael B. Berkman, "State Legislators in Congress: Strategic Politicians, Professional Legislatures, and the Party Nexus," *American Journal of Political Science* 38(1994):1025–1055.

[6] Alan Ehrenhalt, "Barack's Chops," *Governing* (July 2008):7–9; Beth Fouhy, "Obama Tackles Questions about His Experience: Senator Touts Background as State Lawmaker," *State Journal-Register* (Springfield, IL), 22 April 2007, p. 63; Michael D. Shear and Cesi Connolly, "In Illinois, a Similar Fight Tested a Future President," *The Washington Post*, 9 September 2009, online edition.

[7] Tom Loftus, *The Art of Legislative Politics* (Washington, DC: CQ Press, 1994).

[8] Morgan Cullen, "The Long View," *State Legislatures* (May 2009):33–34.

State Legislatures: The Basics

After 250 years of constant tinkering and practice, U.S. state legislatures have evolved to the institutions we see today. As lawmaking bodies, they are similar to one another and to the U.S. Congress. This should not be surprising, since their ancestors are the same—the seventeenth- and eighteenth-century legislative assemblies of the British colonies on the eastern seaboard, such as Virginia's House of Burgesses, where many of our founders served, including George Washington, Thomas Jefferson, and Patrick Henry. The writers of the U.S. Constitution did not copy the British Parliament, that "mother of Parliaments," in designing the U.S. Congress. Rather, they looked to the states, many of which had over 100 years of legislative experience.[9] In particular, the **bicameral** arrangement that exists in 49 states (Nebraska's legislature is a **unicameral** body) arose from colonial arrangements wherein one chamber would consist of the king's appointed representatives and the other would consist of representatives of "freemen" living in the colony. In today's bicameral state legislatures, one chamber is called the Senate and the other chamber is usually called the House of Representatives, although some states use other names, such as the House of Delegates in West Virginia and the Assembly in New York. For a piece of legislation to become law, it must be approved by at least a majority of the members of each chamber in exactly the same form.

In a given state, the House has more members than the Senate, typically about two or three times as many, and so their districts are proportionally smaller. Senators are most commonly elected to four-year terms from **single-member districts (SMDs)**, that is, districts from which they are the only senator; House members are usually called representatives and elected to two-year terms from SMDs.[10] Some legislators (about 13 percent nationwide) are elected from districts with more than one member serving in them, like members of the U.S. Senate (two of whom serve each state). These arrangements are called **multimember districts (MMDs)**. MMDs were once more common because they are easier to draw (since fewer districts need to be drawn). But they have been used less in recent years because of their adverse impact on the fair representation of racial minorities.[11]

Whereas state legislatures have similar structures and the same governance role in their respective states, they vary dramatically in their **legislative professionalism**. States with larger, more urban, growing, and diverse populations, such as Massachusetts, Illinois, and especially California, tend to have the most professionalized legislatures.[12] These bodies meet most of the year, are well staffed, and pay their members a wage on which they can live without the need for another job, if they so choose.[13] On the other hand, smaller, more rural, and more homogeneous states, such as New Hampshire, Wyoming, and Arkansas, have what are sometimes called **citizen-legislatures,** where lawmaking is a part-time job, with legislatures meeting 30 to 90 days a year, earning less than $20,000 per year, and having very few staff to help them. Of course, there are many states that hold the middle ground on these characteristics and whose legislatures also take the middle ground on professionalism, such as Colorado, Missouri,

---

[9] Peverill Squire and Keith E. Hamm, *101 Chambers: Congress, State Legislatures, and the Future of Legislative Studies* (Columbus, OH: The Ohio State University Press, 2005), pp. 22–25.

[10] In 12 states, senators have two-year terms, and in five states, representatives have four-year terms.

[11] Bernard Grofman and Lisa Handley, "The Impact of the Voting Rights Act on Black Representation in Southern State Legislatures," *Legislative Studies Quarterly* 16(1991):111–28.

[12] James D. King, "Changes in Professionalism in U.S. State Legislatures," *Legislative Studies Quarterly* 25(2000):327–44; Christopher Z. Mooney, "Citizens, Structures, and Sister States: Influences on State Legislative Reform," *Legislative Studies Quarterly* 20(1995):47–68.

[13] H.W. Jerome Maddox, "Opportunity Costs and Outside Careers in U.S. State Legislatures," *Legislative Studies Quarterly* 29(2004):517–44.

and Delaware.[14] Whereas once all state lawmakers had another job to help them make a living, today one out of six of them consider lawmaking to be their only job.[15] About the same number consider their main occupation to be an attorney, a proportion that is much lower than even just 30 years ago. More than one in four state legislators own or work in private business, while most others are retired, farm, or are teachers or medical professionals. In addition, a smattering of today's state lawmakers pursue other types of professional activities.

Another central feature of many state legislatures is **term limits**. Term limits are specific and reasonably low ceilings on the number of times an officeholder can be reelected. In the 1990s, 21 states adopted limits for their state lawmakers, although they were repealed or struck down in six of these. In the 15 states that now have the reform, the restrictions on lawmakers' service range from 6 to 12 consecutive years.[16] The impetus for this reform movement in the 1990s was a frustration with the lack of competition in state legislative races (as you will read about below).[17]

State Legislative Elections

There are 7,382 men and women serving in the 50 state legislatures, from 20 in the Alaska Senate to 400 in the New Hampshire House of Representatives, and each of these legislators was elected to his or her seat.[18] To understand state legislatures and state legislators well, you must first understand state legislative elections.

The Paradox of Competition in State Legislative Elections

A healthy representative democracy requires vigorous electoral competition. When any candidate could win a given race, each one works hard to appeal to voters. Energetic campaign activity raises voters' interest in and understanding of the race, the office being contested, and the candidates. Probably more important, elected officials who anticipate a tough reelection fight will make every effort to serve and represent their constituents well. When a race is not competitive—that is, when only one candidate has a real chance of winning—neither the voters nor the candidates take much interest in it and elected officials have little electoral incentive to work hard for their constituents. Of course, elected officials also serve their districts out of a sense of professional responsibility, but the fear of losing the next election is a strong institutional motivation for good representation.

Are state legislative elections competitive? The data from recent elections suggest a paradoxical answer to this question. First, considering the macro-level, or overall, picture, there seems to be relatively strong competition in state legislative elections. As mentioned in Chapter 5, elections since 1992 have yielded remarkably similar total numbers of Democratic and Republican state legislators nationwide. For example, after the 2004 elections, there were 3,640 Republican and 3,655 Democrat state legislators in the country—a difference of about one-fifth of 1 percent of

---

[14] Peverill Squire, "Measuring Legislative Professionalism," *State Politics and Policy Quarterly* 7(2007):211–27.

[15] "Working Full-Time in State Legislatures," *State Legislatures*, July/August 2009, p. 6.

[16] State legislative terms limits are in place in: Arkansas, Arizona, California, Colorado, Florida, Louisiana, Maine, Michigan, Missouri, Montana, Nebraska, Nevada, Ohio, Oklahoma, and South Dakota.

[17] Thad Kousser, *Term Limits and the Dismantling of State Legislative Professionalism* (New York: Cambridge University Press, 2005); Karl T. Kurtz, Bruce Cain, and Richard G. Niemi, eds., *Institutional Change in American Politics: The Case of Term Limits* (Ann Arbor, MI: University of Michigan Press, 2007); Rick Farmer, Christopher Z. Mooney, Richard J. Powell, and John C. Green, eds., *Legislating without Experience: Case Studies in State Legislative Term Limits* (Lanham, MD: Lexington, 2007); Christopher Z. Mooney, "Term Limits as a Boon to Legislative Scholarship," *State Politics and Policy Quarterly* 9(2009):204–28.

[18] All legislators are elected to their seats except for the few at any given time who have been appointed to serve out the remainder of a term for an elected legislator who died or resigned.

the total.[19] This reflected the very close partisan competition at the national level that year, with George Bush beating John Kerry by only a 50.7-to-48.3 percent margin. State legislative elections since then have continued to track national trends, with Democrats picking up 322 seats in 2006 and another 98 in 2008. Following a small pick-up in the 2009 elections, Republicans added over 675 more state legislative seats in 2010's big year for the GOP. They now hold about 53 percent of all legislative seats, the most since 1928.

This swing from Democrats' 55 percent lead to the Republicans' 53 percent advantage reflects well the national trend. This happened because Democratic gains in the elections of 2006 and 2008 were achieved in the small number of legislative seats that are closely contested by the parties, the so-called swing seats. The fact that the Democrats gained only 98 seats in 2008 (as opposed to their 322-seat gain in 2006), a year that brought them great success nationally, demonstrates how little of the "low-hanging fruit" there was left for the party to pick at the state legislative level.[20] If historical trends continue (and if the economy improves), odds are that many of those swing seats will go back into Democratic hands in 2012.

Another way to look at political competition on the macro level is to think about party control of state legislative chambers. As we discuss later in this chapter, the party that has a majority of seats in a chamber has a huge advantage in pursuing its policy agenda there. Recent elections have shown that the two major parties vie closely for control of many state legislative chambers. For example, of the 84 chambers that had partisan elections in 2008,[21] 11 changed party control. In other words, 2008 saw major partisan change in 13 percent of those state legislative chambers with elections that year. In 2010, 19 chambers switched from Democratic to Republican control, one went from Democratic control to being tied, and one went from being tied to Republican.

That's a lot of significant political change in two succeeding elections. In addition, every election sees several other chambers come very close to changing their partisan control. For example, in 2008 if a mere 10 people (out of over 40,000 people casting votes) had switched their votes from the Republican to the Democratic candidate in the 105th Texas House of Representatives district in Dallas, that chamber would have changed party control, too.[22] Certainly, there are chambers with lopsided partisan distributions, such as in Hawaii, Idaho, Massachusetts, and Kansas, but these distributions reflect well the lopsided electorates in those states. All this swinging back and forth between majority party control demonstrates that there is considerable macro-level political competition in state legislative elections.

On the other hand, if we look at these elections on the micro level, that is, if we look at individual state legislative races, we actually find precious little political competition. This is exhibited in various ways. First, whether you measure competition as the percentage of races with more than one candidate, the percentage where the incumbent lost, or the winner's share of vote, competition has been declining in primary elections for state legislative seats at

[19] *Book of the States 2006*, op cit. In addition to these Democrats and Republicans, there were 58 Independents, 22 vacancies, six Progressives, and one Green.

[20] Michael D. McDonald and Robin Best, "Equilibria and Restoring Forces in Models of Vote Dynamics," *Political Analysis* 14(2006):369-92; Tim Storey, "The Perils of Success," *State Legislatures* (September 2008):15-18.

[21] In 2008, six states (Alabama, Louisiana, Maryland, Mississippi, New Jersey, and Virginia) did not have legislative elections, none of the senators in Minnesota or Michigan were up for reelection, and Nebraska's legislature is nonpartisan.

[22] Or at least the chamber would have gone from Republican control to being tied. See Daniel C. Vock, "Dems Take Full Control in 3 More States," *Stateline.org*, 7 November 2008; Brandon Formby, "GOP Keeps Control of Texas House after Heated Race Decided," *Dallas Morning News*, 11 November 2008, online edition.

a steady pace for almost 80 years.[23] Likewise in general elections, when an **incumbent**—the current state legislator—runs, he or she wins approximately 93 percent of the time; many state legislative races are routinely won by 10 or 20 percent or more.[24] In fact, 33 percent of the winners of state legislative general elections in 2008 did not even have an opponent. Thus, while having two candidates in a race, that is, **contestation**, is the minimum requirement for any competition at all, even this is not occurring in over one-third of general election races. Even in California, where contestation is high and state legislative **term limits** have been imposed to enhance electoral competition, when an incumbent state senator was defeated in a primary in 2008, it made statewide news, because she was the first senator to lose a primary in 12 years.[25] Connecticut couldn't even encourage contestation by paying candidates to run. In 2008, when the state started a public financing program for state legislative races, contestation actually declined compared to the previous election.[26] And remember that Texas House election, where a 10-vote switch in one district would have changed the chamber's partisan control in 2008? In that same election, less than a quarter of the general election races had even as few as 20 percentage points

between the winner and loser.[27] The other three-quarters of the seats were uncompetitive by anyone's definition, with the winners getting 60 percent of the vote or more—often, a lot more. In fact, more races had no contestation at all than had its winner get less than 60 percent of the vote. And the Texas House actually has above average general election contestation when compared to other state Houses.

This lack of micro-level competition in state legislative races and incumbents' high reelection rate has not gone unnoticed. Indeed, it inspired the most significant state legislative reform movement in recent years—the drive for state legislative term limits. Advocates thought that term limits would increase competition in state legislative elections by forcing out incumbents every so often, and one early study suggested that this might be true.[28] But several more recent studies have now shown that they have not increased competition; in fact, the reform may even reduce micro-level competition.[29] More incumbents seem to be running unopposed under term limits. Potential candidates simply wait for their legislator's limit to be reached, at which time they all join in the fray for the open seat. But term limits do seem to stir the political pot generally, with termed-out lawmakers running more frequently for local offices and Congress,

[23] Stephen Ansolabehere, John Mark Hansen, Shigeo Hirano, and James M. Snyder Jr., "The Decline of Competition in U.S. Primary Elections, 1908–2004," in Michael P. McDonald and John Samples, eds., *The Marketplace of Democracy: Electoral Competition and American Politics* (Washington, DC: Brookings Institution, 2006).

[24] Richard G. Niemi, Lynda W. Powell, William D. Berry, Thomas M. Carsey, and James M. Snyder Jr., "Competition in State Legislative Elections, 1992–2002," in Michael P. McDonald and John Samples, eds., *The Marketplace of Democracy* (Washington, DC: Brookings Institution, 2006); Robert E. Hogan, "Institutional and District-Level Sources of Competition in State Legislative Elections," *Social Science Quarterly* 84(2003):543–60.

[25] Aurelio Rojas, "Migden's Senate Loss Is Rare for Incumbent," *The Sacramento Bee*, 4 June 2008, online edition.

[26] Mark Pazniokas, "Despite Public Financing, More State Races Unopposed," *The Hartford* (CT) *Courant*, 3 June 2008, online edition. On the other hand, a recent study has shown that, more generally, setting campaign contribution limits low can increase contestation: Keith E. Hamm and Robert E. Hogan, "Campaign Finance Laws and Candidacy Decisions in State Legislative Elections," *Political Research Quarterly* 61(2008):458–67.

[27] "2008 Election Coverage: State House—Texas," *USA Today*, 5 November 2008, online edition.

[28] George F. Will, *Restoration: Congress, Term Limits, and the Recovery of Deliberative Democracy* (New York: Free Press, 1993); John H. Fund, "Term Limitation: An Idea Whose Time Has Come," in Gerald Benjamin and Michael J. Malbin, eds., *Limiting Legislative Terms* (Washington, DC: Congressional Quarterly Press, 1992); Mark P. Petracca, "The Poison of Professional Politics," *Policy Analysis* 151(1991), online edition; Kermit Daniel and John R. Lott Jr., "Term Limits and Electoral Competition: Evidence from California's State Legislative Races," *Public Choice* 90(1997):165–84.

[29] Marjorie Sarbaugh-Thompson, Lyke Thompson, Charles D. Elder, John Strate, and Richard C. Elling, *The Political and Institutional Effects of Term Limits* (New York: Palgrave-Macmillan, 2004); Scot Schraufnagel and Karen Halperin, "Term Limits, Electoral Competition, and Representational Diversity: The Case of Florida," *State Politics and Policy Quarterly* 6(2006):448–62; Seth Masket and Jeffrey B. Lewis, "A Return to Normalcy? Revisiting the Effects of Term Limits on Competitiveness and Spending in California Assembly Elections," *State Politics and Policy Quarterly* 7(2007):20–38.

while local officials seek slots opened up by term limits.[30]

So the paradox is this: While macro-level state legislative election results at the national level reflect the close competition between the political parties seen in recent national elections (and at the state level, they reflect the partisan balances in their states), races for most individual state legislative seats are uncompetitive, indeed. What causes this odd situation? The answer has to do with how people vote for state legislators, and how our electoral institutions translate these votes into state legislative seats, especially how state legislative districts are drawn.

Party, Incumbency, and Voting Decisions in State Legislative Elections

To understand the paradox of competition in state legislative elections, we must first understand the nature of these elections. First, the size of legislative districts varies dramatically from state to state based on the number of seats in a chamber and the number of people living in the state, from California Senate districts with 919,916 people to New Hampshire House districts with only 3,290 people.[31] The average state's House district has about 56,000 people in it, and the average state's Senate district has about 154,000. Thus, even compared to members of the U.S. House (each with about

697,000 constituents), state lawmakers have very small districts. Because Americans tend to live near those who are like themselves racially, socially, and economically, these small districts are also relatively homogeneous.[32] That is, while a congressional district may stretch hundreds of miles and encompass farms, small towns, suburbs, and urban areas, a state legislative district may cover as little as a few square miles in a heavily populated city or a dozen sparsely populated counties full of farmers and small-town residents.

The small size of these districts works against voters getting information about state legislative races. These districts usually do not include an entire **media market,** so TV and radio advertising is too expensive, because many viewers are outside of the district where the ad airs.[33] Local TV news rarely covers state legislative elections, largely for the same reason—any given legislative race is not meaningful to very many viewers.[34] As a result, because Americans tend to get their political information from mass media advertisements and news, these races are often invisible to most voters. Furthermore, state legislative races are typically overshadowed by candidates "up the ticket" for Congress, governor, and president.[35] Most people have a limited attention span for politics, so state legislative races are largely irrelevant to them. While voters may have a pretty good idea about how they will vote in those more visible races, they typically have

[30] Christopher Z. Mooney, "The Effects of Term Limits in Professionalized State Legislatures," in Rick Farmer, Christopher Z. Mooney, Richard J. Powell, and John C. Green, eds., *Legislating without Experience: Case Studies in State Legislative Term Limits* (Lanham, MD: Lexington, 2007); Richard J. Powell, "The Impact of Term Limits on the Candidacy Decisions of State Legislators in U.S. House Elections," *Legislative Studies Quarterly* 25(2000):645–61; Rebecca A. Tothero, "The Impact of Term Limits on State Legislators' Ambition for Local Office: The Case of Michigan's House," *Publius* 33(2003):111–22; Jeffrey Lazarus, "Term Limits' Multiple Effects on State Legislators' Career Decisions," *State Politics and Policy Quarterly* 6(2006):357–83; Jennifer A. Steen, "The Impact of State Legislative Term Limits on the Supply of Congressional Candidates," *State Politics and Policy Quarterly* 6(2006):430–47.

[31] Based on the U.S. Census Bureau's 2008 population estimates.

[32] Matthew S. Levendusky and Jeremy C. Pope, "Measuring Aggregate-Level Ideological Heterogeneity," *Legislative Studies Quarterly* 35(2010):259–282; Bill Bishop, *The Big Sort: Why the Clustering of Like-Minded America Is Tearing Us Apart* (New York: Houghton Mifflin, 2008).

[33] Gary F. Moncrief, Peverill Squire, and Malcolm E. Jewell, *Who Runs for the Legislature?* (Upper Saddle River, NJ: Prentice Hall, 2001), ch. 4.

[34] Jeff Venezuela, "Midwest Local TV Newscasts Average 36 Seconds of Election Coverage in Typical 30-Minute Broadcast," press release (Madison, WI: UW NewsLab, University of Wisconsin–Madison, 2006).

[35] Richard G. Niemi and Lynda W. Powell, "Limited Citizenship? Knowing and Contacting State Legislators after Term Limits," in Rick Farmer, John David Rausch Jr., and John C. Green, eds., *The Test of Time* (Lanham, MD: Lexington, 2003).

given little thought to their vote for the state legislature.

This all means that voters usually enter the voting booth with little information about the specific state legislative candidates on their ballot. But once in the booth, they always have one important piece of information on which to base their vote.[36] This information is written on the ballot next to or below each candidate's name—the candidate's party affiliation. The candidates' party affiliations, then, in conjunction with voters' own party leanings, determine most people's votes in state legislative races in general elections. When you know nothing else about a candidate, why not vote for the one from the party with which you most often agree? That person is more likely than the other candidate to have values and beliefs about politics and policy that are most in line with your own values and beliefs. Otherwise, why would you identify with that party? Such party-based voting is perfectly rational in our political system. But when it is the norm for races in small and politically homogeneous districts, like those for the state legislature, it generates very limited two-party competition in general elections. If a district is full of Democratic (or Republican) voters, then the Democratic (or Republican) state legislative candidate is most likely to win.

Another effect of voters' lack of information about state legislative races is that if one simply recognizes a name on the ballot in a contest, he or she is more likely to vote for that candidate.[37] Why might a voter have heard more about one candidate than another? Incumbency is the single biggest reason. The sitting state legislator has campaign experience, has appeared

in newspapers for legislative accomplishments, has been visible at public events, and has mailed information to the voter. This information has probably been positive, because the incumbent controlled most if it, but even if it is negative, research shows that bad publicity can turn into positive name recognition in low-information races like those for the state legislature.[38] As time passes, people are likely to forget why they remember a candidate's name and just assume it was something good. Thus, all things being equal, the effect of name recognition tends to work to the incumbent's advantage.

Campaigns can also increase name recognition; this is, in fact, their primary purpose. State legislative campaigns have traditionally been down-home affairs, run from a kitchen table and a home computer, with a small group of the candidate's friends and neighbors going door to door, distributing campaign brochures, putting up yard signs, and so forth.[39] But even a down-home campaign can cost money for those yard signs and brochures, doughnuts and coffee for volunteers, and so on. Research shows that campaign spending is generally effective; all things being equal, the more money a candidate spends on the campaign, the more votes he or she receives.[40]

The effects of incumbency and campaign spending are quite intertwined. Interest groups may try to gain access to lawmakers by giving them campaign contributions. Thus, incumbents' electoral chances are improved both by the name recognition they earn from serving in the legislature and by having more money to spend on campaigns than their challengers.

Actual state legislative election results confirm this line of thinking—incumbents who

[36] Except Nebraska, where state legislative elections are nonpartisan.

[37] Marsha Matson and Terri Susan Fine, "Gender, Ethnicity, and Ballot Information: Ballot Cues in Low-Information Elections," *State Politics and Policy Quarterly* 6(2006):49–72.

[38] Barry C. Burden, "When Bad Press Is Good News—The Surprising Benefits of Negative Campaign Coverage," *Harvard International Journal of Press—Politics* 7(2002):76–89.

[39] Loftus, op cit.; Moncrief, Squire, and Jewell, op cit.; Ralph G. Wright, *Inside the Statehouse: Lessons from the Speaker* (Washington, DC: CQ Press, 2005).

[40] Anthony Gierzynski and David Breaux, "Legislative Elections and the Importance of Money," *Legislative Studies Quarterly* 21(1996):337–57.

run for reelection win overwhelmingly.[41] For example, in 2008, in the 133 races for the Texas House where there was an incumbent on the general election ballot, 128 of them won. That 96.2 percent incumbent success rate is about par for state legislative general elections in recent years.[42] However, this success rate is inflated by the fact that if an incumbent foresees defeat, he or she may not run for reelection.[43] Incumbents also are occasionally challenged successfully in their party's primary.[44] In Texas in 2008, 17 general election House races had no incumbent on the ballot, and most of these were voluntary retirements. But even with all this, out of all 150 districts in the entire election season, 128 incumbents, or 85.3 percent, were reelected.

On the other hand, the fact that voters know so little about state legislative candidates—even current officeholders—can have its disadvantages for incumbents. In particular, one bad piece of information that catches voters' attention may be enough to turn even a long-term legislator out of office. For example, after Pennsylvania lawmakers voted themselves a pay raise in 2005, the state's media wrote stories about the various perks of office that they enjoyed, such as generous pension benefits and lobbyist wining, dining, and providing tickets to Steelers and Eagles games, among other things. Perhaps as a result, in 2006, Pennsylvania voters threw incumbents out in record numbers, including some top legislative leaders.[45]

Incumbents can also be vulnerable to well-funded activist groups, or even wealthy individuals, who want to affect the makeup of state legislatures. Officeholders must cast many votes, and these can sometimes annoy such groups. State legislators are more vulnerable to this sort of attack than are congressional or statewide officeholders, because the costs of their campaigns are low enough that sometimes $100,000 (or even $10,000) can make a real difference. In 2008, for example, wealthy gadflies from across the political spectrum in Michigan, New York, and Montana threw millions of dollars into state legislative races with some effect.[46]

Furthermore, during those elections, like that of 2010, where voters seem to have a "throw the bums out" attitude, just being an incumbent officeholder can add a hurdle to overcome. But even in elections when the electorate is in this type of mood, the advantages of being an incumbent typically outweigh any transient disadvantages. And state legislators have a special advantage here. Being less visible than governors or even members of Congress, they seldom arouse the ire of anti-incumbent activists. And the forces that work for them in ordinary elections—name recognition, party identification advantages—continue to lead to incumbent success. The result was that while incumbents had a somewhat rougher time than normal in 2010, over 90 percent of those running for reelection were returned to their state capitols.[47]

Thus, most state legislative races are usually decided by incumbency and/or the partisan

[41] Robert E. Hogan, "Challenger Emergence, Incumbent Success, and Electoral Accountability in State Legislative Elections," *Journal of Politics* 66(2004):1283–1303; David Breaux, "Specifying the Impact of Incumbency on State Legislative Elections," *American Politics Quarterly* 18(1990):270–86.

[42] Niemi et al., op cit.

[43] Gary W. Cox and Jonathan N. Katz, *Elbridge Gerry's Salamander: The Electoral Consequences of the Reapportionment Revolution* (New York: Cambridge University Press, 2002).

[44] Robert E. Hogan, "Sources of Competition in State Legislative Primary Elections," *Legislative Studies Quarterly* 28(2003):103–26; Robert E. Hogan, "Campaign War Chests and Challenger Emergence in State Legislative Elections," *Political Research Quarterly* 54(2001):815–30.

[45] Alan Greenblatt, "Perks That Kill," *Governing* (July 2006):18.

[46] Nicholas Confessore, "Billionaire's Albany Reform Group Puts Its Money behind 39 Incumbent Senators," *The New York Times*, 26 August 2008, online edition; Tom Lutey, "3 Targeted, Lose Re-Election Bids," *Billings* (MT) *Gazette*, 6 June 2008, online edition; Charlie Cain, "Stryker Plans Assault on Key Republicans," *Detroit News*, 16 May 2008, online edition.

[47] "The People Speak: In This State's Primary, Their Voices Defy the Mood," *Pittsburgh Post-Gazette*, 20 May 2010, online edition.

alignment of the district. These forces go a long way toward explaining the dearth of district-level competition in state legislative races. But another crucial part of the explanation has to do with political institutions—the processes by which state legislative districts are drawn.

State Legislative Redistricting

Each state legislator is elected from a specific, legally defined subsection of the state—his or her legislative district. For a given legislative chamber, its state is cut up into districts that neither overlap nor leave any area of the state out of a district.[48] The map defining these mutually exclusive and exhaustive districts is written into a state's law, with the boundaries precisely drawn so that every square inch of the state is placed into exactly one Senate and one House district.[49] Precisely where each of these boundaries runs is determined by policy makers using various criteria, some of which are written into law and some are just custom or preference.[50] Because of these criteria and the way people are distributed around the state, districts are not simply neat, geometric figures, nor are they shaped only by geography (e.g., rivers and mountain ranges) or other political boundaries (e.g., city or county boundaries). What is more, the U.S. Supreme Court requires that legislative districts be redrawn every 10 years to reflect changes in a state's population. How these districts are drawn is another big factor in explaining the lack of political competition in state legislative races.

"One Person, One Vote" Before the early 1960s, most states rarely redrew their legislative district boundaries, because **redistricting** causes great political conflict. Redrawing district boundaries means moving some of a lawmaker's old constituents to a new district and bringing in new people to take their place. You might think that legislators would appreciate gaining constituents who would vote for them and losing constituents who would not, but they can never be sure which voters are which. So in this situation, as in many other aspects of elections, legislators generally favor the status quo. The current arrangements got them elected, so why would they want to change them? And before the 1960s, they didn't—sometimes for many decades.

The problem was that while the legislative district boundaries remained the same, the states' populations were constantly shifting. In particular, people were driven from the countryside to the cities in the early to mid-twentieth century by the Great Depression, two world wars, and the mechanization of agriculture. Most Americans lived in rural areas in 1900, but by 1960, most of them lived in the cities and suburbs. Because of this migration, districts that were equal in population in 1900 were very unequal by 1960. Some states suffered from extreme legislative **malapportionment**, that is, the unequal representation of people living in different districts. For example, Connecticut's districts were so malapportioned in 1960 that a party controlling districts containing as little as 12 percent of the state's population could have had a majority of seats in its state House.[51] Ironically, the worse this situation got, the more politically difficult it was for state policy makers to do anything about it. Those lawmakers and voters who benefited from malapportionment had strong incentive to block any changes.

But in a series of landmark decisions beginning in 1962, the U.S. Supreme Court changed all this by ruling that the Equal Protection Clause of the 14th Amendment to the U.S.

---

[48] But districts for different chambers in a state—its House and Senate—will overlap.

[49] MMDs might be thought of as containing more than one "district," one for each legislator elected from it.

[50] Richard Forgette, Andrew Garner, and John Winkle, "Do Redistricting Principles and Practices Affect U.S. State Legislative Electoral Competition?" *State Politics and Policy Quarterly* 9(2009):151–75; Jason Barabas and Jennifer Jerit, "Redistricting Principles and Racial Representation," *State Politics and Policy Quarterly* 4(2004):415–36.

[51] Richard K. Scher, Jon L. Mills, and John J. Hotaling, *Voting Rights and Democracy* (Chicago: Nelson-Hall, 1997).

Constitution required that districts in the same legislative chamber[52] had to be "substantially equal" in population.[53] Thus, the Court established the principle of "one person, one vote,"[54] meaning that all votes in a state must be of equal value. With malapportioned districts, a person's vote in a smaller district is worth more than a person's vote in a larger district. For instance, a person in a district of 5,000 people would have three times the influence in an election as a person in a district of 15,000 people for the same chamber—1/5,000 versus 1/15,000. And influence in elections translates into influence in policymaking.

These Supreme Court decisions forced the states to spend the rest of the 1960s undertaking the gut-wrenching task of completely redrawing their state legislative (and congressional) districts so that they would be equal in population based on the 1960 U.S. census.[55] Most state legislatures were required to draw their own districts, which made the process particularly painful since everyone involved knew that these changes would lead to many legislators losing their next reelection bids. Where legislatures were not able to get the job done, the courts intervened to force it. By the end of the 1960s, however, one way or another, every state had redrawn its legislative districts to comply with the Supreme Court mandates. This eliminated the rural bias in state legislatures, shifting political power to the urban and suburban areas where most people lived.[56]

Comparisons Help Us Understand

CONTRASTING REDISTRICTING PROCESSES—THE RIDICULOUS (TEXAS) AND THE SUBLIME (IOWA)

While the states use different processes for legislative redistricting, the resulting politics of redistricting vary even more dramatically among the states. These dramatic differences can tell us much about the overall politics and political culture of the states. Compare what happened in Iowa and Texas in the 2000s, for example.

The 2000 U.S. census ignited what can only be called "the Redistricting Wars" in Texas.[57] Republican Congressman Tom DeLay of Sugarland was the majority leader in the U.S. House in the early part of the decade, and he didn't like the way that the Democrat-controlled Texas legislature had drawn the state's congressional districts in 2002 (recall that state government is responsible for redrawing congressional districts, too). DeLay was outraged by the political gerrymander he said was responsible for giving Democrats 17 U.S. House seats from Texas as compared to the Republicans' 15 seats following the 2002 election, even though the state had given favorite son, George Bush, 59.3 percent of the

[52] This principle applies only within a given chamber. So, for example, South Dakota House districts may have more people in them than North Dakota Senate districts, but all South Dakota House districts must be equal in population.

[53] The pivotal cases on state legislative redistricting in this period were *Baker v. Carr*, 369 U.S. 186 (1962); *Reynolds v. Sims*, 377 U.S. 533 (1964); and *Lucas v. 44th General Assembly of Colorado*, 377 U.S. 713 (1964).

[54] The principle was originally referred to as "one man, one vote," but we prefer the nonsexist phrasing.

[55] Gordon E. Baker, *The Reapportionment Revolution* (New York: Random House, 1966).

[56] Stephen Ansolabehere and James M. Snyder Jr., "Reapportionment and Party Realignment in the American States," *University of Pennsylvania Law Review* 153(2004):433–57.

[57] Layla Copelin, "DeLay and His Legacy Are Both on Trial," *Austin* (TX) *American-Statesman*, 18 December 2005, p. A1; David Espo, "Top Court Rules States Free to Redistrict," *Sacramento Bee*, 28 June 2006, online edition; and Tim Storey, "Supreme Court Tackles Texas," *State Legislatures* (April 2006):22–24.

vote in the presidential contest of 2000. So when Republicans took control of the state legislature in 2002, DeLay had a novel idea—why not *re-redistrict*? That is, he convinced the legislature to draw a new set of congressional districts that would be more favorable to Republicans. No state had ever tried to redistrict more than once a decade, and opponents of the plan fought it unsuccessfully all the way to the U.S. Supreme Court.[58] After a superheated political battle—including the spectacle of Democratic state legislators twice fleeing the state to deprive the legislature of a quorum—the Republicans succeeded in passing a districting plan that yielded a 21–11 Republican-Democrat margin in Texas's U.S. House delegation following the 2004 election.

Iowa, on the other hand, has a unique redistricting system that aims to eliminate political gerrymandering and incumbent protection altogether.[59] In the Hawkeye State, nonpartisan legislative staffers are assigned to draw state legislative and congressional districts based almost solely on simple population data, with an eye toward not splitting political units (like cities and counties) between different districts, when possible. By law, these redistricters are not even allowed to consider where incumbent legislators live. As a result, the final 2001 map put 64 (of 150) incumbent state legislators in districts with at least one of their colleagues; two of their five members of Congress were likewise paired with co-partisan incumbents. And there was no partisan slant to these pairings. For instance,

the two members of Congress placed in the same district were both Republicans, the party that controlled both chambers of the Iowa General Assembly. While Iowa's lawmakers must officially approve the district maps drawn by their staffers, and these legislators may ask their staff to redraw the plan, public and media pressure to keep the process nonpartisan usually leads the General Assembly to accept the first or second plan. The result is that Iowa has legislative and congressional districts that are more competitive than those in most other states, and there have been no lawsuits over their redistricting plans since the 1970s—another rarity.

There is no starker difference between the Texas-sized political conflict and institutional innovation in the name of partisan advantage in the Lone Star State and Iowa's technocratic, bloodless redistricting institution assiduously designed to avoid any taint of political unfairness. This tells us quite a bit about what is acceptable political behavior in these two states, and it also shows the impacts of political institutions. In the Texas experience, we see that merely moving around district lines (an institutional change) radically changed its congressional map from an outrageous Democratic gerrymander to only a modestly bad Republican one. In Iowa, we see that its unique redistricting institution can truly be said to enhance political competition; with only 1 percent of the U.S. population, Iowa's maps yielded 10 percent of the competitive congressional races in the country in the early 2000s.[60]

Drawing New Districts Since Americans are always on the move, districts that start off equal in population do not stay that way for long. The U.S. Supreme Court requires that states maintain the one person, one vote standard by going through the redistricting process after each national census to adjust to the population shifts that will have occurred

over the previous decade. But if redistricting in the 1960s was like an 8.0 earthquake on the Richter scale, the regular decennial redistricting is generally only like a 6.0 trembler. Yes, it causes a significant political battle in every state every decade, but policy makers have developed the processes and skills required to fight those battles in a rather orderly way.

[58] *League of Latin American Citizens v. Perry,* 548 U.S. 399 (2006).

[59] Alan Greenblatt, "Monster Maps: Has Devious District-Making Killed Electoral Competition?" *Governing* 19(1)(2005):46–50; Paul Chesser, "Iowa Offers Redistricting Lessons," *Carolina Journal*, 23 January 2004, online edition.

[60] Brian O'Neill, "The Case for Federal Anti-Gerrymandering Legislation," *University of Michigan Journal of Law Reform* 38(2005):683–96.

The result is that the changes made each decade are not nearly as large as those that were required in the 1960s, when policy makers had to make up for generations of neglect.

Each decade in each state, new maps are adopted either through the regular legislative process or through a nonpartisan or bipartisan commission.[61] The Supreme Court requires that every redistricting plan meet two criteria to be constitutional: (1) Districts in a given chamber must be "substantially equal" in population, as of the most recent census, and (2) each district must be geographically **contiguous**.[62] Beyond these national legal minimums, there is considerable variation among the states in the criteria redistricters use to draw maps, and there is considerable disagreement among scholars, policy advocates, and policy makers about which criteria ought to be used. Some argue that districts should be compact, follow local government boundaries, or reflect "communities of interest," that is, groups of people with common cultural or economic values.[63] Some of these criteria are embodied in various state statutes and constitutions, while some are mere desiderata; others fall somewhere in the middle, as more or less vague goals defined by various courts.

Racial and ethnic representation is one criterion that has long been important in legislative redistricting. Multimember districts were once used to dilute minority voters' power, but this use of MMDs was banned by the national **Voting Rights Act of 1965**.[64] Then in the 1980s, the Supreme Court seemed to encourage drawing "majority-minority" districts wherever possible, that is, including enough people of a given race or ethnicity—generally, African Americans or Latinos—so that they might be able to elect one of their own.[65] However, in the 1990s, the Court appeared to change its mind, ruling that race could not be the primary consideration in drawing a district.[66] But race and ethnicity continue to be considerations for redistricters because (1) it is illegal to draw maps that deliberately disenfranchise minority voters; (2) partisanship and race are closely intertwined in the United States and it is legal to draw maps for partisan advantage; and (3) all things being equal, many people believe that representing different racial and ethnic groups fairly is simply the right thing to do. Furthermore, since the Court continues to weigh in on the subject,[67] race will likely be a consideration in the 2011 round of redistricting that follows the 2010 census.

Three general forces shape the politics of legislative redistricting: conflicts of interest among those charged with drawing the maps (in most cases, state legislators and political parties); and the general public's lack of concern with, or simply knowledge of, the redistricting process; The lack of agreed-upon criteria for redistricting.

The politics that follow from these three forces yield districts that have at least two general characteristics.[68] First, they tend to be electorally safe for most incumbent legislators and their parties. A lawmaker has a strong and direct interest in precisely how his or her district is drawn. Those boundaries can mean political life or death. So the price of a legislator's

[61] Michael P. McDonald, "A Comparative Analysis of Redistricting Institutions in the United States, 2001–02," *State Politics and Politics Quarterly* 4(2004):371–95.

[62] The U.S. Supreme Court allows the largest and smallest districts in a state legislative chamber to vary by as much as 10 percent.

[63] Barabas and Jerit, op cit.

[64] Grofman and Handley, op cit.

[65] *Thornburg v. Gingles*, 478 U.S. 30 (1986).

[66] *Shaw v. Reno*, 509 U.S. 630 (1993); *Miller v. Johnson*, 515 U.S. 900 (1995).

[67] For example, the Supreme Court decided a new redistricting case in 2009: *Bartlett v. Strickland* 556 U.S. ___ (2009).

[68] McDonald, op cit.

vote for an overall districting plan may be a favorable district for him or her. The result is that the typical state legislative map is full of with **incumbent-protection districts, districts with** lopsided partisan balances incorporating as much of an incumbent's previous district as possible. This means that incumbent legislators are even more difficult to defeat than normal and the overall partisan balance in the legislature is reinforced. This incumbent-protection dynamic mutes the potential of this process to shake up a state's political system every 10 years.[69]

The second effect of the politics of redistricting is that when one party controls the process, whether by having unified government or by controlling the redistricting commission, partisan **gerrymandering** may occur. That is, the party in control may try to draw districts that improve its chances of winning more seats. A party can do this both by dispersing some of its opponent's voters so that they are less than a majority in many districts—so-called **cracking**—and by **packing** many of the others into a few seats so as to "waste" the votes they get over 50 percent. Such machinations often lead to irregular, if not downright bizarre, boundaries as district-drawers search for just the right balance of partisan votes. Gerrymandering is named after the nineteenth-century Massachusetts political boss and U.S. vice president, Elbridge Gerry, who attempted to maximize his party's legislative advantage by drawing such weirdly shaped districts that a famous political cartoon caricatured one of them as a salamander.

With today's detailed census and voter databases and geographic information system (GIS) software, redistricters can now easily outdo Gerry in their pursuit of political advantage (see Figure 6.1). Surprisingly, perhaps, the U.S. Supreme Court has held that it is perfectly legal for those drawing these districts to pursue partisan advantage, so long as they break no other state or federal laws in the process.[70]

Certain forces limit the amount of blatant partisan or incumbent-protection gerrymandering that can occur in state legislative and congressional redistricting. Some states have institutionalized some more-worthy redistricting criteria by putting them into law, and studies show that even the most determined "gerrymanderers" have a hard time getting around them.[71] For instance, 21 states require that county or municipal boundaries be followed, 19 require that districts be compact, and 10 require efforts to preserve old districts, all of these to the extent possible while meeting the one person, one vote mandate. Not only can such institutions increase electoral competition and reduce gerrymandering, but the U.S. Supreme Court has also recently given them strong legal status.[72] Second, the clashing interests among map makers, whether between the two political parties or between individual legislators and their parties, mitigate the mischief that they can do.[73] Finally, despite all the data and high-tech equipment at the disposal of today's redistricters, they still cannot predict the future. The census data they use are two and a half years out of date by the time even the first general election they are used in takes place.[74] Because

---

[69] John N. Friedman and Richard T. Holden, "The Rising Incumbent Reelection Rate: What's Gerrymandering Got to Do with It?" *Journal of Politics* 71(2009):593–611.

[70] *Easley v. Cromartie*, 532 U.S. 234 (2001).

[71] Barabas and Jerit, op cit.; Forgette, Garner, and Winkle, op cit.; Jonathon Winburn, *The Realities of Redistricting: Following the Rules and Limiting Gerrymandering in State Legislative Redistricting* (Lanham, MD: Lexington, 2008); David Butler and Bruce Cain, *Congressional Redistricting: Comparative and Theoretical Perspectives* (New York: Macmillan, 1992).

[72] *Bartlett v. Strickland*.

[73] Brian F. Schaffner, Michael W. Wagner, and Jonathon Winburn, "Incumbents Out, Party In? Term Limits and Partisan Redistricting in State Legislatures," *State Politics and Policy Quarterly* 4(2004):396–414.

[74] So, for example, the next redistricting process will use census data collected on 1 April 2010, to draw districts first used for a general election on 6 November 2012.

Figure 6.1

Consider these four current Mississippi House of Representatives districts (Districts 23, 62, 80, and 95). Although they are admittedly extreme examples, they are by no means the only odd-shaped state legislative districts in use today. Why might these districts been drawn as they were? If you were a political cartoonist, what objects or animals could you make out of them?

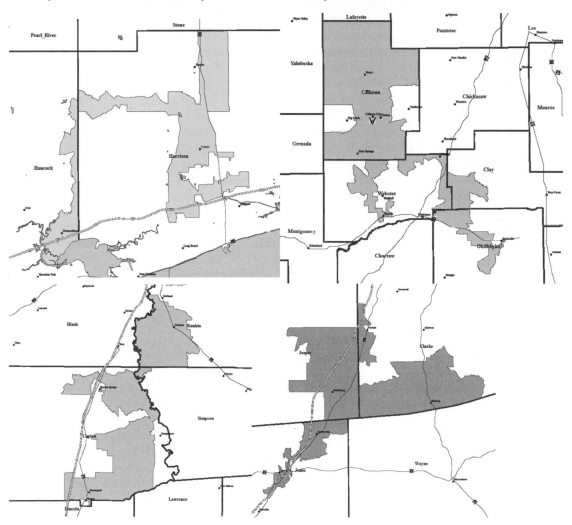

Source: Mississippi Legislative Reapportionment Committee, 2002 (Ben Collins, Coordinator).

Americans are so mobile, major demographic changes can occur in these districts over the decade in which they are used, especially in suburban areas around large cities. Thus, gerrymandering has a less significant impact on legislative elections than one might think given that lawmakers get to draw their own districts.

Revisiting the Paradox of Competition in State Legislative Elections

In the end, the way people vote and the way state legislative districts are drawn go a long way toward explaining why we find close competition between the parties in the aggregate (or at least a good reflection of the state or national electorate's partisan balance) but little of it in individual races. State legislative districts tend to be homogeneous due to their relatively small size and Americans' increasingly segregated living patterns, and they are further homogenized and manipulated during the redistricting process. This results in near certainty about which party will win each seat in the general election. For example, in California's 2004 general election, of the 153 congressional and state legislative seats up for election, none of them changed parties—and this is in a state where legislative term limits was supposed to decrease incumbents' dominance in elections.[75] On the other hand, when averaged out at the state or national level, state legislative elections do a good job of reflecting the balance between the two major political parties today.

State Legislators: Who Are They?

Those who win state legislative races barely have time to celebrate before they must meet in their respective state capitols to begin work. State legislators make big decisions about public policy and the allocation of resources that affect your life every day, so who they are makes a difference. Although any generalization about these 7,382 unique individuals glosses over many differences, looking at them in broad strokes can help us begin to understand how well the legislature represents the residents of the states.

Like most American political elites, state legislators are unrepresentative of the diversity of the country's population in many ways. The average state legislator is a 56-year-old white man, either in business or a lawyer, who is married and has lived in the same area most of his life.[76] Non-Latino whites make up only about 66 percent of Americans, a bit more than half are women, most are not lawyers or businessmen, and the typical person moves house every five years or so.[77] But if we look past simple averages, we find that state legislators are actually much more varied than any other set of state or national elected officials. In particular, the descriptive representativeness of state legislatures, that is, the extent to which their members look like the people they serve, has been improving steadily in recent years. But as we have seen on many other state-level characteristics, there is wide variability in this representation among the states.

Women in the State Legislature

Women were the first major underrepresented group to make headway in state legislatures. The first of these, Representatives Carrie Clyde Holly, Frances Klock, and Clara Cressingham, were all elected to the Colorado General Assembly in 1894, but for the next 80 years, women made little steady progress in this regard.[78] By 1971, at the beginning of the modern women's movement in this country, only 4.5 percent of state legislators were women. Since then, however, women have made solid, if not spectacular, gains. Today, 24.2 percent of state legislators are women. To put this in context,[79] only 14.0 percent of governors (see Chapter 7) and 16.8 percent of members of Congress are women; 25.4 percent of elected statewide executive officials (such as lieutenant governors and

[75] Alan Greenblatt, "Monster Maps: Has Devious District-Making Killed Electoral Competition?" *Governing* (January 2006):46–50.

[76] National Conference of State Legislatures, "Legislator Demographics," http://74.125.95.132/search?q=cache:afgUnnxedKsJ:www.ncsl.org/%3Ft abid%3D14850+%22legislator+demographics%22&cd=1&hl=en&ct=clnk&gl=us.

[77] Morgan, Kathleen O'Leary, and Scott Morgan, eds. *State Rankings 2010: A Statistical View of America*. Washington, DC: CQ Press, p. 466.

[78] Kathleen A. Bratton, Kerry L. Haynie, and Beth Reingold, "Gender, Race, and Representation: The Changing Landscape of Legislative Diversity," in Audrey S. Wall, ed., *The Book of the States 2008*, vol. 40 (Lexington, KY: Council of State Governments, 2008).

[79] To put these numbers in international perspective, consider that out of 187 countries ranked in 2009 by the Inter-Parliamentary Union, women's representation in the U.S. Congress ranked eighty-fifth ("Women in National Parliaments," http://www.ipu.org/wmn-e/classif.htm#2). The states' 24.2 percent would place it 46th, between Liechtenstein and Singapore.

attorneys general) are women.[80] While women made steady progress in state legislatures from 1971 to 1993, increasing one or two percentage points per year nationwide, that progress has slowed since then. Regardless of the speed of their recent progress, remarkably, there has never been a year since 1972 when, nationwide, fewer women served as state legislators than in the previous year. Just as important, more women are assuming state legislative leadership positions.[81] Although it was not until the 1980s that the first women assumed the top leadership positions of House speaker and Senate president, as of 2010, 44 women from 22 states had done so.[82]

Even though women have made steady progress in their state legislative representation nationally, if we break the data down a bit, we see considerable variation here. And as it does with so many characteristics, that variation can help us better understand state legislatures and American politics more generally. First, women are not represented equally well in all states. At the extremes in 2010, women's representation ranges from the New Hampshire Senate, the first state legislative chamber ever to have a majority of women (13 of 24 senators are female), to the South Carolina Senate, which, following the 2008 elections, became the first chamber since 1991 to have no women among its members. Figure 6.2 shows how women's legislative representation, combined in both chambers, varies among the states. The West and Northeast tend to have more women legislators, while the Southeast tends to have fewer.

State legislative women are not equally well represented in the two major parties, either.[83] After the 2008 elections, a record 30.9 percent of Democratic state legislators were women, while they made up only 15.8 percent of Republican lawmakers. Just as important, the proportion of women in the Republican legislative ranks has been decreasing somewhat, so that today's representation is lower than at any time in the last 20 years. This discrepancy did not always exist. Until 1992, the vaunted Year of the Woman,[84] when the electoral success of women candidates across the country took a great leap, the proportions of women state legislators in the parties were largely equivalent; if anything, women were even better represented in the Republican Party. But starting with the 1992 election, women's representation among Democratic legislators has been progressively greater, while among Republicans, it has been flat or even decreasing. Today, a Democratic state legislator is almost twice as likely to be a woman as is a Republican legislator.

Why has women's representation in state legislatures increased so dramatically since the 1970s? Why is there so much variation in this representation across the states and parties? Why is it still far below a fair level of representation that would reflect women's proportion in society? Although we do not yet have complete answers to these questions, recent scholarship can give us certain insights. For example, state legislatures with lower pay and shorter sessions and those that use MMDs have traditionally tended to have more women.[85] The standard explanation for this has had to do

[80] Center for Women and American Politics, "Women in Elective Office 2009," http://www.cawp.rutgers.edu/fast_facts/levels_of_office/documents/elective.pdf.

[81] Garry Boulard, "It's Different at the Top," *State Legislatures*, July/August 2009, pp. 20–22.

[82] Center for American Women and Politics, "Women State Legislators: Leadership Positions and Committee Chairs 2009," http://www.cawp.rutgers.edu/fast_facts/levels_of_office/documents/leglead.pdf.

[83] Linda Fieldmann, "Why GOP Is Trending Away from Women in State Legislatures," *Politico.com*, 20 July 2009, online edition.

[84] Michelle Swers, "Whatever Happened to the Year of the Woman: Lessons from the 1992 and 2002 Elections," *PS: Political Science and Politics* 37(2004):61–62.

[85] James D. King, "Single-Member Districts and the Representation of Women in American State Legislatures: The Effects of Electoral System Change," *State Politics and Policy Quarterly* 2(2002):161–75; and Peverill Squire, "Legislative Professionalization and Membership Diversity in State Legislatures," *Legislative Studies Quarterly* 17(1992):69–79.

Figure 6.2

Representation of Women in State Legislatures

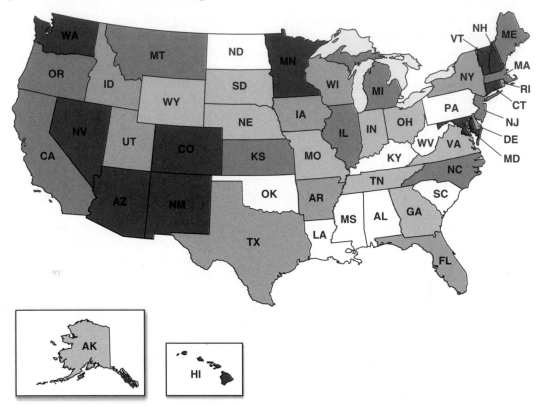

Note: These are the rankings of the states on the percentage of women in both chambers of their state legislature after the 2008 elections. This ranges from 13.7 percent in South Carolina to 40 percent in Colorado. The darker the state, the more representation women have in its legislature.

Source: National Conference of State Legislatures, "Women in State Legislatures: 2009 Legislative Session," http://www.ncsl.org/LegislaturesElections/WomensNetwork/WomeninStateLegislatures2009/tabid/15398/Default.aspx.

with the bias against women serving in elective office, a carryover from the prefeminist period. This story goes like this: Seats in high-paying, professionalized legislatures with single-member districts appear more valuable, generating more competition for them and the tendency to fill them with men. Supporting this explanation is more recent scholarship that has found that when a state's electorate and party leaders hold more traditional attitudes toward religion and gender roles, women are less well represented in its legislature.[86] This would also help explain the upward trend in women's overall representation since 1971, a time when women began moving in large numbers into many nontraditional professions, and attitudes toward their role in society were changing. Studies show that voters are no longer especially sexist in their choice of candidates.[87] Thus, most of the remaining inequities have been attributed to

[86] Kevin Arseneaux, "The 'Gender Gap' in State Legislative Representation: New Data to Tackle an Old Question," *Political Research Quarterly* 54(2001):143–60; John F. Camobreco and Michelle A. Barnello, "Postmaterialism and Post-Industrialism: Cultural Influences on Female Representation in State Legislatures," *State Politics and Policy Quarterly* 3(2003):117–38.

[87] Barbara Burrell, *A Woman's Place Is in the House: Campaigning for Congress in the Feminist Era* (Ann Arbor, MI: University of Michigan Press, 1994); Robert Darcy, Susan Welch, and Janet Clark, *Women, Elections, and Representation* (Lincoln, NE: University of Nebraska Press, 1994).

residual gender biases held by political elites[88] and attitudes of potential women candidates themselves who appear to underestimate their chances of winning and therefore are more hesitant to enter political races than men.[89] The differences between the parties have not yet been studied in depth, but they could be related to the gender gap in political ideology and policy preferences.[90]

Racial and Ethnic Minorities in the State Legislature

State legislative representation for people whose racial or ethnic heritage is in the minority in the United States has also improved in recent decades, but for different reasons than for that of women. For example, in 1969, there were only 172 African American state legislators nationwide (2.3 percent), but today there are 623 (8.4 percent).[91] One way to look at this is that since African Americans make up 12.8 percent of the U.S. population, they are now better represented in state legislatures than are women. Why has African American representation in state legislatures improved? The Voting Rights Act (VRA) of 1965 had a lot to do with it.[92] Focusing mainly on the states of the old Confederacy, which have the highest proportions of African American residents, the VRA banned practices that discouraged blacks from voting, eliminated the MMDs that diluted their votes, and encouraged the drawing of majority-black political districts where possible.

As a result, the number of African American state legislators in these states increased from only 3 in 1965, to 176 as early as 1985, and to 320 in 2010. Efforts to draw majority-minority districts in the 1980s and 1990s also helped increase African American representation in legislatures outside the South, especially in urban areas.

In addition to African Americans, there are now 178 Latinos serving in state legislatures nationwide (2.4 percent), according to the National Association of Latino Elected Officials. This is very disproportionate with Latinos' 15.1 percent share of the U.S. population, making them perhaps the most underrepresented major demographic group today. This is due largely to their low political participation, which stems from the disproportionately large number of children, first-generation citizens, and noncitizens among them today.[93] As time passes, their political participation and state legislative representation may well increase. Latino political representation has already been helped somewhat by the VRA and the drawing of majority-minority districts, but the biggest reason for their recent gains in state legislatures is simply the growing number of Latinos in the population.

Nationally, there are also 85 Asian American legislators (1.2 percent, as compared to 4.4 percent in the population) and 78 Native American legislators (1.1 percent, as compared to 1.0 percent in the population).[94] Most Asian American state legislators serve in Hawaii and California,

[88] Kira Sanbonmatsu, *Where Women Run: Gender and Party in the American States* (Ann Arbor, MI: University of Michigan Press, 2006).

[89] Shannon Jenkins, "A Woman's Work Is Never Done? Fund-Raising Perception and Effort among Female State Legislative Candidates," *Political Research Quarterly* 60(2007):230–239; Richard L. Fox and Jennifer L. Lawless, "Entering the Arena? Gender and the Decision to Run for Office," *American Journal of Political Science* 48(2004):264–80.

[90] Barbara Norrander and Clyde Wilcox, "The Gender Gap in Ideology," *Political Behavior* 30(2008):503–23.

[91] Samantha Sanchez, *Money and Diversity in State Legislatures, 2003* (Helena, MT: Institute on Money in State Politics, 2005); updated by the authors with data from the Joint Center for Political and Economic Studies.

[92] Grofman and Handley, op cit.; Janine A. Parry and William H. Miller, "'The Great Negro State of the Country?' Black Legislators in Arkansas, 1973–2000," *Journal of Black Studies* 36(2006):833–72.

[93] Rodney Hero, F. C. Garcia, J. Garcia, and H. Pachon, "Latino Participation, Partisanship, and Office Holding," *PS: Politics and Political Science* 33(2000):529–34.

[94] National Conference of State Legislators, "Number of Native American Legislators 2009," http://www.ncsl.org/LegislaturesElections/LegislatorsLegislativeStaffData/NativeAmericanLegislators2009/tabid/14762/Default.aspx; National Conference of State Legislators, "Number of Asian American Legislators 2009," http://www.ncsl.org/LegislaturesElections/LegislatorsLegislativeStaffData/AsianAmericanLegislators2009/tabid/14762/Default.aspx.

states with many people of Asian heritage. For the same reason, Montana and Oklahoma have the most Native American legislators.

As with women, the percentage of racial and ethnic minorities in state legislative chambers varies dramatically across the states, but unlike with women, much of the cross-state variation in minority representation is easy to explain. The percentage of African Americans or Latinos in a state's legislature is largely a function of their presence in the state's population.[95] But these numbers alone tell us little about how well racial and ethnic minorities are represented. As discussed in Chapter 1, the proportion of people of different races and ethnicities varies widely from state to state, while gender is distributed much more evenly.[96] A better way to assess the racial and ethnic representation of a state legislature is to compare the percentage of its members who are minorities to the percentage of the state's population who are minorities. A ratio of 1.00 shows that a state's percentages of minority lawmakers and residents are equal, a score below 1.00 shows the extent to which a lawmaking body is unrepresentative in this respect, and a score above 1.00 shows the extent to which minorities are overrepresented.

Minority legislative representation is not easy to explain at first glance. Non-Hispanic whites, or Anglos, make up the majority of Americans (66.1 percent), so those who are non-Anglo (African Americans, Hispanics, Asians, Native Americans, those of mixed heritage, and others) constitute those who are traditionally defined as "minorities" in this country. In two states, however, Anglos are actually in the minority—Hawaii (24.8 percent Anglo) and New Mexico (42.5 percent Anglo). As it

happens, the legislatures in these states are the most representative, with Hawaii's having a representation ratio of 1.05 and New Mexico's of .88. More generally, there is an imperfect tendency among the states for representation to be positively related to the percentage of racial and ethnic minorities in a state.[97] That is, the higher the proportion of non-Anglos in a state, the better they are represented in the state legislature. This is not the same as saying that there are simply more minority legislators in states where more people of those heritages live. It is saying that the higher the proportion of non-Anglos in a state, the more equal are the population and legislative proportions of race and ethnicity.

This relationship between minority proportion and representation helps demonstrate the "Matthew 25:29" principle at work in political districts in the winner-take-all elections that are most common in the United States.[98] This principle derives its name from the Christian Bible, in the 25th chapter of the Gospel of Matthew, verse 29: "For everyone who has will be given more, and he will have an abundance. Whoever does not have, even what he has will be taken from him." That is, the political institutions of our system cause majorities—whether party, racial, ethnic, economic interest, or whatever—to tend to win majorities in legislatures that are disproportionately larger than their majorities among voters.[99] For instance, suppose that Republican voters accounted for 51 percent of the voters in a state and Democrats accounted for 49 percent. If these partisans were distributed evenly around the state so that every legislative district had a 51–49 voter split, then the GOP would win 100 percent of the legislative seats. Such a legislature

---

[95] For example, in 2010, the simple correlation between the percentage of African Americans in states' legislatures and their populations is .96; for Latinos, it is .92.

[96] The percentage of men in a state ranges from 54 percent in Alaska to 47.5 percent in Rhode Island. See: Morgan and Morgan, op cit., p. 464.

[97] This correlation is .70.

[98] This is as opposed to proportional representation systems, in which minorities can receive a more proportionate level of seats in a legislature.

[99] Of course, this does not explain the poor representation of women in state legislatures. This can be blamed on our cultural history of sexism, for the most part.

would certainly not be representative of partisans in the state. Since voters are not distributed evenly, with likes tending to live near likes, this force toward unrepresentativeness is mitigated, but it continues to work to some extent, and the smaller a minority, the stronger this force is.

States in the South and those in the North with large urban centers have high proportions of African Americans, and they rank high on descriptive representation. States with many Latinos, like California, Florida, and New Mexico, or Native Americans, like Montana and Oklahoma (and, again, New Mexico) also have better minority representation in their legislatures. On the other hand, highly homogenous states, such as Maine, North Dakota, and West Virginia, tend be to less representative. But some states defy this trend. For example, Delaware ranks low on representation even though its minority population is similar to that of Alabama and South Carolina, and Ohio ranks high even though it has relatively fewer non-Anglos than Oregon or Kansas. Some of this discrepancy can be explained by living patterns in these states; the more concentrated ethnic groups are among themselves, the more likely they will be to elect a person of their own heritage. Of course, all this discussion is based on the assumption that people are more likely to vote for those of their own racial and ethnic heritage than others, clearly a more questionable assumption today than in years gone by.

Finally, scholars are just beginning to study two other aspects of descriptive representation in state legislatures: the intersection of gender and racial representation, that is, the presence of women of color in state legislatures, and sexual orientation representation. First, early findings suggest that representativeness for women of color cannot be explained by simply extending theories of the representation of minority men or white women. For example, since at least 1976, gender representation has been better for African Americans and Latinos than for Anglos. One study found that in 2003, while women made up 21 percent of white legislators, 35 percent of black lawmakers were women, as were 29 percent of Latino lawmakers.[100] Equally interesting, scholars are beginning to find that the explanations for why the representation of women of color varies among the states are subtly different than those of either non-Anglo men or Anglo women.[101] And second, a recent study of openly gay state lawmakers suggests that their representation may be about on par with that of this sexual minority in the population.[102] This is especially surprising because experimental research suggests that voters tend to view a generic openly gay person as less politically viable than a generic straight person.[103] This may suggest that when confronted with an actual gay person, rather than a hypothetical, Americans are more open-minded than they once were. Ongoing scholarship in both these areas holds great promise for expanding our understanding of lawmaking and representation.

The Impact of Broader Representation

Assessing racial, gender, and sexual orientation descriptive representation in state legislatures is relatively easy to do, but it is much harder to say with certainty what difference it makes. Seeing people like ourselves in political office gives us an emotional lift, a sense of attachment to our government, and increases our political efficacy.

---

[100] Becki Scola, "Women of Color in State Legislatures: Gender, Race, Ethnicity and Legislative Office Holding," *Journal of Women, Politics & Policy* 28(2006):43–69; see also: Wendy G. Smooth, "African American Women and Electoral Politics: Journeying from the Shadows to the Spotlight," in Susan J. Carroll and Richard L. Fox, eds., *Gender and Elections: Shaping the Future of American Politics* (New York: Cambridge University Press, 2006); Robert Darcy and Charles D. Hadley, "Black Women in Politics: The Puzzle of Success," *Social Science Quarterly* 69(1988):629–45.

[101] Beth Reingold, Kathleen A. Bratton, and Kerry L. Haynie, "Descriptive Representation in State Legislatures and Intersections of Race, Ethnicity, and Gender," presented at the American Empirical Series, Stanford Institute for the Quantitative Study of Society (May 2009).

[102] Haider-Markel, op cit.

[103] Rebekah Herrick and Sue Thomas, "Gays and Lesbians in Local Races: A Study of Electoral Viability," *Journal of Homosexuality* 42(2001):103–26.

President Obama's 2008 election spawned much discussion of this, and being represented by a person of one's own gender or heritage even in the state government can have such salutary effects.

But beyond this sort of psychological impact, does better descriptive representation make a difference in public policy and governance? Political scientists have begun to study this difficult question. The most straightforward way of doing this is to assess the degree to which women and minority lawmakers differ from their white male colleagues. The idea here is that if non-Anglo and female lawmakers are different in policy-relevant ways, then more of them serving in the statehouse will have policy impacts. If so, then better descriptive representation is positive even beyond its symbolic value, since it would mean that the values and preferences of those other than white men would be reflected better in policy. For example, African American male and white female legislators each tend to be more interested in education, social welfare, and health care policy,[104] with African American women lawmakers having an especially high interest in progressive legislation.[105] Latino legislators have a special interest in immigration and bilingual education.[106] These preferences are seen in the types of committees they serve on, the bills they introduce, and how they vote on legislation. Certainly some of these differences reflect the values of the constituents who send them to the statehouse, but there is evidence that lawmakers' race and gender have independent effects on their preferences.[107] Not surprisingly, scholars have also found evidence that as non-Anglos and women become better represented in state legislatures, their preferences become better reflected in public policy.[108] On the other hand, there is also disturbing evidence that there can sometimes be a backlash against them and their interests,[109] but this effect seems to be short-lived.[110]

Because of their greater numbers in state legislatures, scholars have been able to study women lawmakers more and longer than minority lawmakers. In the 1970s and 1980s, when women were making their first inroads into public office, there were pretty clear differences between the average female and male lawmaker. Aside from having somewhat different policy agendas, these women tended to be older, have fewer children, be more often unmarried or divorced, be social workers or teachers rather than lawyers, and be less politically ambitious than their male colleagues.[111] In recent years, however, as women have become commonplace in legislatures, most of these demographic differences between the genders in the statehouse have vanished. On the other hand, the ideological gender gap seen among American voters is exaggerated in the statehouse, with

---

[104] Kerry L. Haynie, *African American Legislators in the American States* (New York: Columbia University Press, 2001); Kathleen A. Bratton and Kerry L. Haynie, "Agenda Setting and Legislative Success in State Legislatures: The Effects of Gender and Race," *Journal of Politics* 61(1999):658–79.

[105] Bryon D'Andra Orey, Wendy Smooth, Kimberly S. Adams, and Kisha Harris-Clark, "Race and Gender Matter: Refining Models of Legislative Policy Making in State Legislatures," *Journal of Women, Politics & Policy* 28(2006):97–119.

[106] Kathleen Bratton, "The Behavior and Success of Latino Legislators: Evidence from the States," *Social Science Quarterly* 87(2006):1136–57.

[107] Sarah Poggione, "Exploring Gender Differences in State Legislators' Policy Preferences," *Political Research Quarterly* 57(2004):305–14.

[108] Jocelyn Elise Crowley, "Moving beyond Tokenism: Ratification of the Equal Rights Amendment and the Election of Women State Legislatures," *Social Science Quarterly* 87(2006):519–39; C. T. Owens, "Black Substantive Representation in State Legislatures from 1971–1994," *Social Science Quarterly* 86(2005):779–91; Robert R. Preuhs, "The Conditional Effects of Minority Descriptive Representation: Black Legislators and Policy Influence in the American States," *Journal of Politics* 68(2006):585–99.

[109] Haider-Markel, op cit.; Matthew C. Fellowes and Gretchen Rowe, "Politics and the New American Welfare States," *American Journal of Political Science* 48(2004):362–73; Joe Soss, Sanford F. Schram, Thomas P. Vartanian, and Erin O'Brien, "Setting the Terms of Relief: Explaining State Policy Choices in the Devolution Revolution," *American Journal of Political Science* 45(2001):378–95; Caroline J. Tolbert and Gertrude A. Steuernagel, "Women Lawmakers, State Mandate, and Women's Health," *Women and Politics* 22(2001):1–39.

[110] Robert R. Preuhs, "Descriptive Representation as a Mechanism to Mitigate Policy Backlash," *Political Research Quarterly* 60(2007):277–92; Preuhs, 2006, op cit.

[111] Anne Marie Camissa and Beth Reingold, "Women in State Legislatures and State Legislative Research: Beyond Sameness and Difference," *State Politics and Policy Quarterly* 4(2004):181–210.

the average female legislator being more liberal on social issues, the environment, gun control, and abortion regulation than her male colleague. Interestingly, there is far more of this sort of difference between Republican lawmakers of different genders than there is between male and female Democratic lawmakers.[112] That is, while male and female Democrats are similarly liberal, Republican women tend to be significantly to the left of their male counterparts. In addition, women may also engage in more constituent service and be more cooperative, consensus-building, and egalitarian in the legislative process.[113]

As you will read later, legislative committees play a critical role in lawmaking. Early research on women's legislative committee membership found that they were more likely to be on "women's issues" committees, like those dealing with families and children, education, health care, and so forth, and less likely to be on "power committees," like those dealing with taxes and the budget. This effect was especially pronounced for African American and Latino legislators who were female.[114] The question was then raised whether this difference was caused by the preferences of the women lawmakers or by some bias of (presumably male) legislative leaders. The fact that these differences have diminished in recent years seemed to support the bias explanation. But a new survey of state lawmakers has found that while women are now just as likely as men to be on power committees, they frequently prefer to be on social service and education committees.[115] This is powerful evidence of a true difference between the policy agendas of men and women lawmakers, and thus, it is strong support for the importance of gender representation.

Of course, for any underrepresented group, achieving its political goals requires more than just winning some seats in the legislature. In particular, as we shall see, real policy making requires developing legislative majorities. This means that even if a legislature is representative of racial and ethnic minorities, they will still be at a disadvantage. But numerical minorities can influence lawmaking even in a process that puts a premium on majorities. First, lawmakers in committee or chamber leadership positions have disproportionate influence in their chambers, and committee chairs have been filled increasingly by women and minorities in recent years, largely in proportion to their numbers in their chambers.[116] In addition, lawmakers from these underrepresented groups have also begun to take chamber leadership positions. Forty-four women from 22 states have held the very top leadership position in a state legislative chamber, as have 12 African Americans and eight Latinos.[117] The 2009 legislative session began with 10 of the 99 state legislative chambers being led by women and five by African Americans, a new record in both cases.[118] In 2008, Colleen Hanabusa

[112] Poggione, op cit.

[113] Lyn Kathlene, "Power and Influence in State Legislative Policy-Making: The Interaction of Gender and Position in Committee Hearing Debates," *American Political Science Review* 88(1994):560–76.

[114] Luis Ricardo Fraga, Valerie Martinez-Ebers, Linda Lopez, and Ricardo Ramirez, "Representing Gender and Ethnicity: Strategic Intersectionality," in Beth Reingold, ed., *Legislative Women: Getting Elected and Getting Ahead* (Boulder, CO: Lynne Reinner, 2008).

[115] Susan J. Carroll, "Committee Assignments: Discrimination or Choice?" in Beth Reingold, ed., *Legislative Women: Getting Elected and Getting Ahead* (Boulder, CO: Lynne Reinner, 2008).

[116] Byron D'Andra Orey, L. Marvin Overby, and Christopher W. Larimer, "African-American Committee Chairs in U.S. State Legislatures," *Social Science Quarterly* 88(2007):619–39; Robert R. Preuhs, "Descriptive Representation, Legislative Leadership, and Direct Democracy: Latino Influence on English Only Laws in the States, 1984–2002," *State Politics and Policy Quarterly* 5(2005):203–24; and Cindy S. Rosenthal, *When Women Lead: Integrative Leadership in State Legislatures* (New York: Oxford University Press, 1998).

[117] In addition, several Latino and Asian Americans have served as the top leader in Arizona, New Mexico, and Hawaii, where people of these heritages are well represented. Center for American Women and Politics, "Women State Legislators: Leadership Positions 2009," http://www.cawp.rutgers.edu/fast_facts/levels_of_office/documents/leglead.pdf.

[118] One of these five African American leaders started, but did not finish, the 2009 session as presiding officer. Peter Groff, president of the Colorado State Senate, resigned to head up President Obama's faith-based initiative center in the U.S. Department of Education. Malcolm Smith, Majority Leader in the New York State Senate, lost his position as presiding officer temporarily in June 2009 during a battle over the chamber's majority (see Danny Hakim and Jeremy W. Peters, "Door Is Locked, and Senate Is in Gridlock," *The New York Times*, 11 June 2009, online edition).

became the first woman of color to preside over a state legislative chamber when she became President of the Hawaii State Senate, and later that same year, Karen Bass of California became the first African American woman to become a house speaker.[119] Another way that women and minorities have gained significant influence in state legislatures is by forming informal legislative groups, such as a Black Legislators' Caucus or a Conference of Women Legislators. Such groups provide training and mentoring for new lawmakers, a sense of group cohesion among its members, and a vehicle with which to mobilize blocs of votes that can be used to gain support from other legislators on issues important to the group.[120]

The Job of the State Legislature

Within a few weeks of each general election, state legislators head to their respective state capitols to begin the job they were elected to do. As an institution, the state legislature has three basic jobs: to help make and revise the state's laws; to oversee the executive branch's implementation of the state's laws; and to represent the interests of the state's citizens to the state government.

While these jobs have some overlap, it is useful to discuss them separately.

Lawmaking

First and foremost, the state legislature's job is to deliberate on the public problems of the state and then make or modify state law to address them—a huge undertaking, to say the least.

Each state's legal code consists of thousands of laws touching on every facet of life and business, and every one of these laws has been passed by the legislature over the years.[121] Everything that a state or local government official does must be authorized by the legislature. Roads, bridges and mass transit, education from preschool to the postdoctoral level, parks, prisons and police, hunting, haircutting, and health clubs— all these and much more may be considered in depth in a state legislature each year. Then each year in every state, all this deliberation about public problems results in thousands of pieces of legislation, or **bills**, formal proposals to change state law. For example, in their 2009 legislative session, members of the Connecticut House and Senate considered 3,936 bills and passed 266 of these into law. Lawmaking is a big job for state legislators, and they take this important responsibility very seriously.

The process of making law is complex and difficult—and for a good reason. Mark Twain once said, "No man's life, liberty, or property is safe while the legislature is in session."[122] Like all jokes, this one holds a large measure of truth. Americans tend to be suspicious of government, so we make the legislative process slow and difficult to reduce the risk of unwise or dangerous state government action. In the end, only about 20 percent of the bills considered by state legislatures actually become law.[123] To do so, a bill must be approved by both chambers by at least a majority vote in exactly the same form and then be signed by the governor.[124]

The basic legislative process in the states is quite similar to that of Congress. First, someone says, "There ought to be a law!" Since this is their main business, legislators are always on

---

[119] In fact, the lower chamber in California is called the Assembly.

[120] Michelle G. Briscoe, "Cohesiveness and Diversity among Black Members of the Texas State Legislature," in Charles E. Menifield and Steven D. Shaffer, eds., *Politics in the New South* (Albany, NY: SUNY Press, 2005); Tracy Osborn, "Women Representing Women: Pursuing a Women's Agenda in the States" (Ph.D. diss., Indiana University, 2004).

[121] This is true except for those relatively very few laws that are passed through the initiative process (see Chapter 4).

[122] Tommy Neal, *Learning the Game: How the Legislative Process Works* (Denver, CO: National Conference of State Legislatures, 2005), p. 33.

[123] This varies quite a bit across the states. For example, in 2007, Colorado legislators passed 73.5 percent of its bills, while Connecticut passed only 7.8 percent. See Wall, op cit., p. 130.

[124] Alternatively, the governor's veto may be overridden by the legislature.

the lookout for good ideas for bills. They get many of these ideas from their constituents, the news, and their personal experiences, but the main sources of legislative ideas are interest groups and their lobbyists since their members can be affected directly—positively or negatively—by state policy. Regardless of the source of the idea, once a legislator files a bill with the clerk of his or her chamber, he or she becomes the **bill's sponsor,** at which point the legislative process formally begins. Next, the bill is assigned to a **standing committee** of the legislature for consideration. This committee may hold a public hearing to gather information about the bill's potential effects and its political support. The sponsor is typically the first, and often the only, person to speak at the hearing, giving his or her rationale for the necessity and efficacy of the bill. Constructing a pleasing story about the bill can be critical to convincing colleagues to approve it. Opponents, if any, also try to tell a story about the bill that supports their position. So, for example, a bill giving in-state college tuition to the children of undocumented immigrants might be described as a way to "educate kids and promote the American dream" or as "coddling criminals."[125] In addition, a person from the state agency that would be assigned to implement the bill sometimes weighs in, especially if it is an important bill or one with significant budgetary implications. Given the bureaucrat's expertise and at least relative objectivity, this person's perspective usually carries considerable weight. Furthermore, since the committee specializes in the bill's policy area, the lawmakers that serve on it will already have at least a bit of expertise on the subject.

After hearing these arguments, the committee deliberates. If the problems raised about the bill are sufficiently worrisome, the committee may simply not report it back to the full chamber (or report it unfavorably), and it will not become law in the current legislative session. One of the central functions of standing committees is to screen out bad, weak, or politically unpalatable bills. There is no reason to waste the full chamber's time considering bills that have obvious problems. But state legislative committees tend to be weaker at screening bills than their congressional counterparts.[126] In many states, if a sponsor really wants to get a bill passed in committee, he or she can do so.

The other major function of legislative committees is to **amend** bills, if and as needed, in light of any political or policy weaknesses that might be raised in the hearings and deliberations. If the committee agrees with the general idea of a bill, such amendments may improve both its effectiveness in dealing with the policy problem and the bill's chances of becoming law. In the end, if the committee is convinced of the bill's merit, amended or not, it will vote to report the bill to the full chamber for further consideration.

At this point in the process, the majority party leader (whether the speaker of the house, president of the senate, or a person with some other title) has a critical opportunity to affect the bill's fate in most chambers, particularly if he or she opposes the bill. Standing committees report out far more bills than their full chambers can reasonably consider, creating a bottleneck in the process. One of the majority party leader's central functions is to manage the process by selecting which bills will be considered on the **chamber floor.**[127] How do they make this choice? First, legislative leaders dislike controversial bills because they consume too much of the chamber's precious floor time. Less commonly, majority party leaders will kill bills they do not want to see debated on the floor for political reasons. Perhaps the debate would expose rifts among legislators of their own party, or

[125] Gary Reich and Alvar Ayala Mendoza, "'Educating Kids' versus 'Coddling Criminals': Framing the Debate over In-State Tuition for Undocumented Students in Kansas," *State Politics and Policy Quarterly* 8(2008):177–97.

[126] Wayne Francis, *The Legislative Committee Game: A Comparative Analysis of Fifty States* (Columbus, OH: Ohio State University Press, 1989).

[127] A few states, like Colorado, limit the majority leader's power to do this, requiring a floor vote on every bill that comes out of committee. This weakens the power of the majority leader and reduces the amount of deliberation any given bill has on the floor.

perhaps voting on the bill would be politically damaging for some majority party legislators facing tough reelection campaigns.[128] Even less frequently, a majority party leader may have policy preferences (either personal preferences or, more commonly, those of his or her party) that would be advanced by killing or passing a particular bill, and the leader uses his or her **gatekeeping** power to do so.

Once a bill gets to the floor of the full chamber, lawmakers first consider whether to amend it. Various legislators, especially the bill's sponsor and members of the committee that reviewed it, may speak to describe its intent, support, and opposition (if any). Sometimes suggestions for changes are offered, and to reduce controversy and increase the chances of passage, sponsors tend to agree to amendments unless they think that they go too far in changing the bill's original intent. Even though the norm in most chambers is to defer to sponsors when possible, at this stage of the process, the full chamber is responsible for the bill, and it will pass or fail on its own merits.

Finally, the chamber votes on the bill, and a majority vote passes it in that chamber.[129] Since the goal of the legislative process prior to the floor **roll call** vote is to screen out bills that are flawed or lack political support, most bills that survive to the chamber floor not only pass, but pass by a wide margin. A legislator's default floor vote is "aye"; that is, legislators typically need a reason to vote against a bill on the floor rather than for it. Usually, a legislator will only vote against a bill if it somehow hurts his or her district and, in the long run, his or her chance at reelection. Generally speaking, a lawmaker will vote against

a bill if voting for it could be made to look bad in an opponent's campaign brochure. Because lawmakers vote on hundreds of varied, technical, and arcane bills every year, on most of them, they usually know only the bare minimum when they cast their roll call votes. Therefore, to avoid casting "bad" votes, legislators routinely take **voting cues** from their colleagues.[130]

Cue-taking is informal, and it can happen in a variety of ways, but it often happens like this for roll call votes. Most state legislative chambers have a large electronic "tote board" showing each lawmaker's vote during the roll call.[131] Lawmakers with some knowledge of a bill—such as members of the reviewing committee, the bill's sponsor and co-sponsors, and key opponents (again, if any)—will not only speak about the bill, but they also will vote immediately as the vote is called, with the aye or nay lights flashing by their names. Legislators who are uninformed about that bill then check the votes of members of their own party and those from similar and neighboring districts. Lacking other information, voting with their colleagues who are similarly situated helps legislators avoid casting votes that may hurt their districts (and perhaps come back to haunt them in a reelection campaign). The result of this process is that a lawmaker generates a remarkably consistent voting record that reflects his or her party's ideology and is aligned with his or her district's interests.[132]

A bill that manages to overcome these difficult hurdles in its chamber of origin is then sent to the other chamber, where the entire process is repeated—introduction, committee evaluation and amendment, and floor consideration

[128] John H. Aldrich and James S. Battista, "Conditional Party Government in the States," *American Journal of Political Science* 46(2002):164–72.

[129] Certain types of bills require a supermajority vote, such as bills for borrowing money or votes to override a governor's veto.

[130] This process is best described in the context of congressional roll call voting in John W. Kingdon, *Congressmen's Voting Decisions*, 3rd ed. (Ann Arbor, MI: University of Michigan Press, 1989).

[131] Senates tend to have tote boards less often than houses, since they have fewer members. In chambers without tote boards, members have more informal ways of keeping track of who is voting aye or nay on a bill.

[132] Shannon Jenkins, "Party Influences on Roll Call Voting: A View from the U.S. States," *State Politics and Policy Quarterly* 8(2008):239–62; Gerald C. Wright, "Do Term Limits Affect Legislative Roll Call Voting? Representation, Polarization, and Participation," *State Politics and Policy Quarterly* 7(2007):256–80; but sometimes lawmakers can adapt their voting to situations; e.g., see Thad Kousser, Jeffrey B. Lewis, and Seth E. Masket, "Ideological Adaptation: The Survival Instinct of Threatened Lawmakers," *Journal of Politics* 69(2007):828–43.

and voting. As in its chamber of origin, if the bill fails to pass any of the hurdles in the second chamber, it does not become law, at least that year. Even if the bill passes the second chamber, it may be amended there. Remember that a bill must pass both chambers in identical form before it can become law. For example, in a recent legislative session in Texas, a proposal was derailed when a house member pointed out that the bill that her chamber passed had a comma where the Senate-passed bill had a semicolon.[133] If the second chamber passes an amended bill, to become law, the different versions must be reconciled and then voted on again in each chamber. This may be done by one chamber simply accepting the other chamber's version, or if neither chamber acquiesces, a temporary **conference committee** with members of both chambers may convene to craft a bill that can pass both chambers. Typically, conference committee members are appointed by the leaders of each party in each chamber and include the bill's primary sponsor in each chamber and the leaders of the standing committees that heard the bill. If the conference committee can reach a compromise, it reports it out to each chamber floor (if no agreement can be reached, the bill dies). There, legislators are only allowed to vote aye or nay on the compromise bill, with no amendments being allowed. In the end, even more often than regular bills, conference committee bills usually pass on the floor. By this point in the process, most concerns raised about the bill have been worked out. Besides, too much effort will have been put into it for it to fail.

Once both chambers pass the bill in identical form, it is sent to the governor for consideration. Usually, the governor approves of the bill by signing it, thus completing the process—the bill becomes state law on its effective date, as specified in the bill. Alternatively, the governor

can **veto** the bill, sending it back to the legislature for further deliberation. As described in Chapter 7, veto powers of the governor vary significantly among the states, with most governors having a much more powerful veto than that of the president. Regardless of the type of veto used, the legislature has the opportunity to **override** it, usually through a **supermajority** vote in each chamber. But a governor's veto is very hard to override. Governors do not veto bills lightly or often, so when one does, he or she takes it seriously and uses considerable political resources to make sure not to be overridden.[134]

Overseeing the Executive Branch

Although it is neither as formal, nor as well publicized, nor anywhere near as time consuming as lawmaking, legislatures also oversee the state executive branch's **implementation** of laws and programs. In this way, the legislature acts like the board of directors of a large corporation, setting general policy for the organization and then checking occasionally to make sure that the agencies are executing that policy as originally intended.

First, and most effectively, the legislature can control policy implementation simply by stating clearly in its original legislation what an agency is supposed to do. The more detailed the legislation, the less discretion an agency has and, therefore, the more likely that **legislative intent** will be followed. For example, if the legislature passes a law that just reads, "The Board of Higher Education (BHE) shall offer high-quality postsecondary education," the BHE has tremendous leeway in determining how higher education will be offered in the state.[135] It might decide to emphasize liberal arts education, by providing resources for state colleges to hire plenty of professors of ancient Greek history,

---

[133] Polly Ross Hughes, "Comma Kills Journalists' Shield Law in Texas House," *The Houston Chronicle*, 22 May 2007, online edition.

[134] Carl E. Klarner and Andrew Karch, "Why Do Governors Issue Vetoes? The Impact of Individual and Institutional Influences," *Political Research Quarterly* 61(2008):574–84; Vicky M. Wilkins and Garry Young, "The Influence of Governors on Veto Override Attempts: A Test of Pivotal Politics," *Legislative Studies Quarterly* 27(2002):557–76.

[135] A recent study on the relationship between state legislatures and the higher education bureaucracy is Michael K. McLendon and James C. Hearn, "The Enactment of Reforms in State Governance of Higher Education: Testing the Political Instability Hypothesis," *Journal of Higher Education* 78(2007):645–63.

foreign languages, and philosophy, reducing class sizes, and eliminating engineering and business schools. But state legislators may have an entirely different idea in mind, perhaps thinking that technical training and practical education should be emphasized, focusing on community colleges and professional graduate degree programs. Had these legislators been more specific in their original legislation, the BHE probably would have given them at least much more of what they wanted. Indeed, legislators often write specific legislative language when they want to force a recalcitrant agency or governor to implement legislation a certain way.[136]

But most of the time, lawmakers writing legislation simply cannot anticipate the many details and uncertainties involved in running an agency or enforcing a law. Therefore, they give agencies great flexibility to make the multitude of specific, but important, policy decisions needed to fill in these details. Arguably, these decisions are best made by people with specialized training and experience, such as those working in the executive agencies. For example, who would you rather see set the requirements for a medical degree, state legislators or medical professionals? Furthermore, these detailed decisions can often be made only after bureaucrats and policy makers see how a new law actually works in practice.

Another way for the legislature to oversee an agency is to check occasionally to be sure the agency is following legislative intent, an action called **ex post oversight**, which can take either a "fire alarm" or a "police patrol" approach.[137] Fire alarm oversight occurs in response to problems that are brought to lawmakers' attention somehow, often as a result of their helping constituents having some difficulty with state

government. Such constituent **casework** can sometimes call attention to systematic problems with an agency that need to be addressed by the legislature. For example, perhaps some of a lawmaker's constituents are unable to get into the area's community college because the BHE has reduced its course offerings. This could alert the lawmaker to the BHE's emphasis on liberal arts, perhaps contrary to legislative intent (or at least, perhaps, contrary to *her* legislative intent).

The most effective control, however, may result from the fact that agency officials know that the people with whom they work *could* complain to their state legislators if they have a problem. This encourages these bureaucrats to implement policy conscientiously and to provide good public service. The media provide another important source of fire alarm oversight. The dramatic reduction in state news coverage in recent years has reduced the media's importance here, thus reducing the effectiveness of legislative oversight.[138]

Other oversight techniques are more systematic and ongoing, more like police patrols than fire alarms. Perhaps the most important of these is the legislature's annual review of the proposed state budget. A chamber's budget committee typically has the most experienced and influential lawmakers sitting on it, legislators who specialize in specific agency budgets and, over time, learn the ins and outs of these agencies. Their in-depth knowledge allows them to question agency officials in detail about what they are doing and why, with the threat of budget cuts (and the hope of budget increases) keeping them well attentive to lawmakers' needs and desires. Likewise, **administrative rules review committees**, legislative institutions that review

[136] Sean Gailmard, "Discretion Rather Than Rules: Choice of Instruments to Control Bureaucratic Policy Making," *Political Analysis* 17(2009): 25–44; Jason A. McDonald, "Agency Design and Postlegislative Influence over the Bureaucracy," *Political Research Quarterly* 60(2007):683–95; Christopher Reenock and Sarah Poggione, "Agency Design as an Ongoing Tool of Bureaucratic Influence," *Legislative Studies Quarterly* 29(2004):383–406; John D. Huber, Charles R. Shipan, and Madelaine Pfahler, "Legislatures and Statutory Control of Bureaucracy," *American Journal of Political Science* 45(2001):330–45.

[137] Mathew D. McCubbins and Thomas Schwartz, "Congressional Oversight Overlooked: Police Patrols versus Fire Alarms," *American Journal of Political Science* 28(1984):165–79.

[138] Jennifer Dorroh, "Statehouse Exodus," *American Journalism Review* (April/May 2009), online edition; AJR Staff, "AJR's 2009 Count of Statehouse Reporters," *American Journalism Review* (April/May 2009), online edition.

the myriad regulations that agencies issue each year in implementing policy, can provide effective oversight.[139] In most states, the **state auditor** also works for the legislature, and when it does, this can be another powerful institution of legislative police patrol oversight.[140] The state auditor is a high-ranking official who heads a unit that conducts financial and program evaluations of state agencies, both routinely and in response to legislative requests. Finally, legislatures can build oversight into programs they establish, such as by requiring periodic reports by an agency or including a "sunset clause" that requires the program to be reauthorized by the legislature after a certain period of time.[141]

However, state legislatures do not oversee their executive branches very well or very often, for a number of reasons. First, the state executive branch is large and complex; by comparison, the state legislature is quite small. Even the best-staffed legislatures in the largest states do not have enough resources to examine every state agency closely all the time. Even if they had the resources, legislators are simply far more interested in lawmaking. Regardless of which is more important to a state's government and residents, most legislators get more electoral, professional, and psychological payoff from introducing bills and working on legislation that their districts favor, even if those bills fail, than from spending countless hours trying to understand the intricacies of an executive agency and how well it is following legislative intent.

Representation

The third major duty of a state legislature is to represent the interests of the state's residents to its government.[142] Like electoral competition, we can think about representation at the macro or micro level. At the macro level, studies show that despite all the other forces on state government—especially those of interest groups (see Chapter 5)—a state's overall public policy follows its residents' general values and ideology remarkably well.[143] This good representation is largely due to state legislatures, the institutions that make state law and strongly influence all other state policy. To understand how this good macro-level representation happens, we must look at micro-level representation, that is, how and why each state lawmaker represents his or her constituents. Because their districts are relatively small, because they spend most of their time living in their districts, and because they face reelection frequently, representing their districts comes as natural to state legislators as breathing, and they do it in a variety of ways.

First, legislators sponsor bills and vote on legislation to benefit the people and businesses residing in their districts. Sometimes, a legislator's personal ideology or party allegiance will have a small independent effect on how he or she votes on a bill, but these usually overlap so closely with the district's interests (or at least with the legislator's perceptions of those interests) that these other effects are hard to see.[144] Indeed, a state legislator voting against his or her district's interests is among the rarest of political

[139] Brian J. Gerber, Cherie Maestas, and Nelson C. Dometrius, "State Legislative Influence over Agency Rulemaking: The Utility of ex Ante Review," *State Politics and Policy Quarterly* 5(2005):24–46.

[140] Edward M. Wheat, "The Activist Auditor: A New Player in State and Local Politics," *Public Administration Review* 51(1991):385–92.

[141] Carolyn Bourdeaux and Grace Chikoto, "Legislative Influences on Performance Management Reform," *Public Administration Review* 68(2008):253–65.

[142] Michael A. Smith, *Bringing Representation Home: State Legislators among Their Constituencies* (Columbia, MO: University of Missouri Press, 2003); Ronald E. Weber, "The Quality of State Legislative Representation: A Critical Assessment," *Journal of Politics* 61(1999):609–27; Malcolm E. Jewell, *Representation in State Legislatures* (Lexington, KY: University Press of Kentucky, 1982).

[143] Robert S. Erikson, Gerald C. Wright, and John P. McIver, "Public Opinion in the States: A Quarter Century of Change and Stability," in Jeffrey E. Cohen, ed., *Public Opinion in State Politics* (Stanford, CA: Stanford University Press, 2006); Robert S. Erikson, Gerald C. Wright, and John P. McIver, *Statehouse Democracy: Public Opinion and Policy in the American States* (New York: Cambridge University Press, 1993).

[144] Jenkins, 2008, op cit.; Poggione, op cit.; Shannon Jenkins, "The Impact of Party and Ideology on Roll-Call Voting in State Legislatures," *Legislative Studies Quarterly* 31(2006):235–57.

events, regardless of that lawmaker's ideology, party, district, or anything else. Legislative party leaders rarely want legislators to do this, even if it means voting against the party on a particular bill. Leaders know that voting against his or her district's interests imperils a member's reelection chances, thereby threatening the party's legislative influence. For example, take Georgia State Representative Amy Carter, from Valdosta. Rep. Carter is certainly not going to support a gun control bill, even if it is one of her party's main agenda items. Gun control may be thought of as a public safety issue to Atlanta Democrats, but her constituents in rural areas and small towns in the southern part of the state see it as a threat to hunting and their traditional way of life.

State legislators also represent their constituents' interests by pursuing what are sometimes called **"pork barrel"** projects for their districts.[145] These are specific public construction and economic development ventures whose benefits accrue largely to a specifically defined geographical area—like a legislative district or some part of it. Even conservative legislators who are ideologically opposed to most government spending typically pursue such projects for their districts. In addition to their commitment to representation, legislators "bring home the bacon" because they believe that it helps their reelection chances.[146] Indeed, legislative leaders shower the districts of lawmakers from their party who are facing closely contested reelection races with such "worthy projects," as they are called in North Carolina, or "pet projects," as they are called in New York, in hopes of avoiding a party switch in those districts.[147]

Legislators also represent their constituents by doing casework and whatever else

they can do to keep the lines of communication open with their voters. For example, in 2008, Pennsylvania lawmakers sent out nearly 300,000 calendars to state residents—with the appropriate lawmaker's name emblazoned on each one. Upon receiving a little political heat for what some saw as self-promotional fluff, the Keystone State Senate majority leader said that the calendar was only "one of many informational materials made available to constituents."[148] Lawmakers never miss an opportunity to connect with the voters; they are the original social networkers. This is why they have embraced Web 2.0 social media so heavily, despite their advanced average age (56). In 2009, as many as half of legislators in some states used Facebook, LinkedIn, and MySpace.[149] Many have their own well-designed websites and blogs, and some were among the first to get involved with Twitter soon after its appearance in 2006. For example, at press time, Missouri Senator Jolie Justus had 1,375 followers on Twitter (http://twitter.com/joliejustus), and she wasn't even the most followed legislative tweeter. These are all ways that lawmakers can reach out to their constituents to learn their needs, desires, and opinions, and given their strong reelection incentive to give their constituents what they want, they help representation. Of course, these representation activities also advertise lawmakers, thus increasing incumbents' electoral advantages, for good or ill.

Finally, some state legislators feel a special responsibility to represent certain classes of people more broadly, regardless if they are constituents. This may be because a legislator is in a certain business or profession, such as real estate or law enforcement, and watches out

---

[145] Smith, 2003, op cit.; Michael C. Herron and Brett A. Theodos, "Government Redistribution in the Shadow of Legislative Elections: A Study of the Illinois Member Initiative Grants Program," *Legislative Studies Quarterly* 39(2004):287–312.

[146] Smith, 2003, op cit.

[147] Joel A. Thompson and Gary F. Moncrief, "Pursuing the Pork in a State Legislature: A Research Note," *Legislative Studies Quarterly* 13(1988):393–401; Ronald Smothers, "It's Pork. It's a Pet Project. It's a Christmas Tree," *The New York Times*, 5 March 2007, online edition.

[148] John L. Mick, "Lawmakers Spent $131,500 to Send Calendars to Constituents," *The Morning Call* (Allentown, PA), 9 January 2008, online edition.

[149] Pam Greenberg, "New Surveys Provide Snapshot of Legislators' Use of Social Media," *The Thicket at State Legislatures*, 23 October 2009, online edition.

for these interests in the state legislature. This type of representation is especially important for legislators who are women or of a minority racial or ethnic heritage. These lawmakers often assume a responsibility to watch out for other members of their group, regardless of where they live in the state.[150]

The Collective Action Problem

Lawmaking, oversight of the executive branch, and representation would be hard jobs to accomplish in the most efficient institution, but the unwieldy and complex legislative structure that our state constitutions establish for state legislatures make their three duties especially difficult. Imagine it. A state legislature populated by dozens of people from every part of the state, with a wide range of interests, ambitions, and goals, who come together under the capitol dome often for only a few months each year to try to solve the state's amazing array of complex problems. None of these people can be forced out by anyone else in the group,[151] and they all have an equal say in any final decision. Two parallel groups (senators and representatives) work at the same time on the same problems, and both groups must agree in the end on the exact details of any decision. Plus, all these people work on very short-term contracts—contracts that most of them would like to see renewed—and all their deliberations and decisions occur in full public view (or at least in view of the media). The final kicker is that although they must work together to accomplish their job, they are held accountable in elections only as individuals. If you have ever worked on a group project for a class, you understand the tricky social dynamics involved with this sort of situation.

This institutional arrangement established by a state's constitution gives lawmakers a serious **collective action problem.**[152] That is, they have to figure out how to get their group to work together to accomplish common goals. You see these difficulties everywhere, from the local chapter of Delta Tau Delta trying to run a fundraiser to Ford trying to build and sell cars. Different kinds of organizations solve their problems in different ways. In a small group, like the fraternity, it can often be done by informal consensus building or by a single person just doing all the work. But in a large operation, like Ford, institutions must be set up to accomplish its collective tasks. Businesses do this by establishing command-and-control structures and dividing the work among different units, such as product development, production, and sales. Because of its constitutional arrangements, however, a state legislature's job is unique. In particular, no one can order another person to perform a job; thus, state legislatures use a variety of techniques—both institutions and informal norms—to overcome their collective action problem. The resulting processes and systems are complex and rarely pretty, but they can work. Of course, there is always room for improvement, and the states continually tinker with their legislative institutions to improve their performance.

The basic strategy that legislatures use to solve their collective action problem is to divide themselves on two dimensions along which state policy varies—policy type and policy preference—and then assign some of its members the responsibility of organizing lawmakers in these subgroups. Three sets of institutions are used to do this—committees, party caucuses, and leaders. By distributing policy problems among their standing committees, giving representation to both parties at each stage of the process, and assigning leadership responsibilities to some of its members, state legislatures

---

[150] Camissa and Reingold, op cit.; Haynie, op cit.; Osborn, op cit.

[151] Most legislatures have some method of expelling members, usually for malfeasance, but such expulsions are very rare.

[152] Lawrence Becker, *Doing the Right Thing: Collective Action and Procedural Choice in the New Legislative Process* (Columbus, OH: Ohio State University Press, 2005).

help solve their collective action problem and get their jobs done for the state.

Committees

From preventing birth defects to regulating cemeteries, legislatures deal with a vast range of public issues, and to do so, they must have access to information and expertise on all of them. Like Congress, each state legislature arranges its members into various committees to accomplish the tasks at hand. Each committee specializes in a policy area, such as agriculture, transportation, or K–12 education, so its members can gain knowledge and experience, becoming sort of a quasi-expert on that subject.[153] As we have seen, legislatures use these committees to screen and modify bills before they get to the chamber floor, and then on the floor, other legislators typically look to members of a bill's committee for guidance in roll call voting. Both parties are represented on each committee, so different policy perspectives are represented in the preliminary review of bills and a variety of members are available to help non–committee members make decisions later in the process.[154]

In comparison to standing committees in the U.S. House of Representatives, state legislative committees tend to have much less control over bills relative to a chamber's leaders.[155] In the U.S. House, committees are the center of most policy-making activity, but in the typical state legislature, party caucuses, leaders' offices, and chamber floors also have considerable influence. Furthermore, whether as a cause or an effect of this, most state legislatures don't have the seniority norm that automatically determines the chairs and continuing membership of congressional committees. Party leaders in state legislatures typically have a very strong say in, and often total control over, committee chair and member assignments. As a result, state legislative committees are much less stable than those in Congress, frequently changing memberships and sometimes even forming and disbanding completely from session to session. All this combines to make committees in most state legislatures much weaker and less important as instruments of information gathering and policy making than those in Congress, especially the U.S. House, although this varies among the states.[156]

Party Caucuses

If committees are institutions that help legislatures develop at least a little expertise in all the policy areas they must consider, then political parties are institutions that help legislatures consider at least most major points of view in every policy area. If these views are not represented and considered, the legislature loses legitimacy as a policy-making institution. Democrats and Republicans have somewhat different perspectives in most he areas of state policy, so organizing the legislature by party also organizes it by policy preference, even if in a general and imperfect way.

The importance of party as an organizing principle in state legislatures cannot be overstated. Besides those in Nebraska's nonpartisan **unicameral** body, 99.7 percent of today's state legislators were elected as either a Democrat or Republican, and that percentage has rarely been lower in modern times.[157] A **party caucus** is made up of all the members of a party in a

---

[153] Jesse Richman, "Uncertainty and the Prevalence of Committee Outliers," *Legislative Studies Quarterly* 33(2008):323–47; Brian F. Schaffner, "Political Parties and the Representativeness of Legislative Committees," *Legislative Studies* Quarterly 32(2007):475–97; James Coleman Battista, "Re-Examining Legislative Committee Representativeness in the States," *State Politics and Policy Quarterly* 4(2004):135–57; Nancy Martorano, "Balancing Power: Committee System Autonomy and Legislative Organization," *Legislative Studies Quarterly* 31(2006):205–34; Francis, op cit.

[154] However, the majority party typically has a disproportionate share of seats on committees; see Ronald D. Hedlund, Kevin Coombs, Nancy Martorano, and Keith E. Hamm, "Partisan Stacking on Legislative Committees," *Legislative Studies Quarterly* 34(2009):175–92.

[155] Richard Clucas, "Improving the Harvest of State Legislative Research," *State Politics and Policy Quarterly* 3(2003):387–419.

[156] James Coleman Battista, "Why Information? Choosing Committee Informativeness in U.S. State Legislatures," *Legislative Studies Quarterly* 34(2009):375–98.

[157] National Conference of State Legislatures, "2010 (Post-Election) Partisan Composition of State Legislatures" (http://www.ncsl.org/default.aspx?tabid=19488.)

chamber; thus, there are four party caucuses in each legislature (the Senate Democrats, the House Republicans, and so forth). Many party caucuses meet frequently to discuss strategy and policy; in some chambers, the most crucial policy decisions are made in the majority party caucus, rather than in committees or on the chamber floor. Members of each party usually have their floor desks arranged together on the floor, with members of the other party on "the other side of the aisle," literally. Members of the same caucus may have their offices near one another, share staff, and even play softball on the same team against their chamber's other caucus. Of course, all members of a party do not always agree on every policy—far from it, in some chambers. But a legislator's party affiliation is the single most important predictor of how he or she will vote on a bill, even more important than his or her general political ideology.[158] Their similarity in roll call voting is the result of shared policy preferences, a sense of common cause against the other party in the chamber, and caucus members taking voting cues from one another.

The party distribution of a state legislative chamber greatly affects the activity inside it, both in its policy output and the way it does its work. The party that has a majority of the members of a chamber is said to "control" that chamber, and for good reason. A majority of members must vote in favor of a bill in committee and on the floor for it to pass, so the party in the majority can pretty much do whatever it wishes—if its members vote together.[159] A majority vote can often even change a chamber's institutions and rules,

determine who gets power and who doesn't, stop the proceedings or move them in a different direction, among other things. As a longtime staffer in the West Virginia legislature once stated, "If the majority wants to paint its chamber polky dot, you'd better buy the paint because we're going to paint it polky dot."[160] Recall also that, just as in elections, a majority can have influence far out of proportion to its representation in the chamber; recall the Matthew 25:29 Effect.[161] In essence, a majority party that sticks together can win close to 100 percent of a chamber's decisions even if it has only 51 percent of the seats in it. Because of this inordinate power, gaining a majority in a chamber is the Holy Grail of state legislative parties.

While a close majority can sometimes be broken by a defector or two,[162] perhaps surprisingly, the larger the majority a caucus has, the less its members tend to stick together and the less overt control the party can exert over legislative decision making.[163] When the difference between the number of seats the two parties have in a chamber is small—say, the five seats (out of 203) that divided the parties in the Pennsylvania House following the 2008 election—the majority party must work diligently to maintain control over legislation and to maintain their majority in the next election. The minority party smells success just a few votes away, so it scrambles to gain whatever advantage it can, whether to win passage of legislation or to position bills and votes to use as future campaign issues. When a minority party caucus faces a lopsided partisan split—like the Democrats' 20 percent of the seats in the Idaho Senate or the Republicans' 10 percent

---

[158] Jenkins, 2006 and 2008, op cit.

[159] This generalization is most often true. Sometimes votes require a supermajority, sometimes the result needed is in relation to those voting or those present or those elected, and so forth. But generally, if they stick together, majorities can control a chamber's behavior and decisions.

[160] This comment was made to one of the authors by this West Virginia legislative staffer.

[161] Hedlund et al., op cit.

[162] Consider what happened in the New York Senate in 2009 with party defections—Jeremy W. Peters and Danny Hakim, "Republicans Seize Control of State Senate," *The New York Times*, 8 June 2009, online edition; Fredric U. Dicker, "GOP Pols Dangling $6M to Lure Dems," *New York Post*, 25 November 2008, online edition. But because a legislator's party affiliation is such an integral part of his or her political persona, full-blown party switching is extremely rare.

[163] Hedlund et al., op cit.; Nancy Martorano, "Cohesion or Reciprocity? Majority Party Strength and Minority Party Procedural Rights in the Legislative Process," *State Politics and Policy Quarterly* 4(2004):55–73; Aldrich and Battista, op cit. On the other hand, California is a state where something like the opposite happened, with close partisan competition failing to yield strong parties, both in the legislature and out. This may have something to do with the extremism of the parties in the Golden State; see Seth E. Masket, *No Middle Ground: How Informal Party Organizations Control Nominations and Polarize Legislatures* (Ann Arbor, MI: University of Michigan Press, 2009).

of the Massachusetts House—it knows the only way it will ever manage to pass a bill is with the help of many majority party members, so it tries to avoid partisan conflict. Because the majority party caucus is not threatened by the minority in such unbalanced chambers, they don't mind working with them from time to time. In fact, a majority party that isn't disciplined by the threat of a large minority often crumbles into regional, ethnic, or economic factions, making partisan conflict less relevant.[164] In such legislatures, political party is not a useful organizing principle, making the collective action problem more difficult to overcome.

Legislative Leadership

State legislatures have two fundamental problems of collective action that corporations and the executive branch of government lack: All members of the group (legislators) are constitutionally equal, and no one has responsibility for achieving its common goal. To address these problems, legislators select from their membership various leaders in whom they invest special powers and the responsibility to see that the groups' collective tasks are accomplished.

The two basic types of leaders reflect the organizing principles of a state legislative chamber: committee chairs and party leaders. Committee chairs call committee meetings, decide which legislation is to be heard and voted upon, and have what can often be significant procedural powers to organize and structure committee hearings and votes. These chairs are typically members of the majority party. While each committee usually has a minority party leadership position, that position has far less power than the chair. Of course, because most state legislative committees are less powerful

AP Photo/Nevada Appeal, Kevin Clifford

Nevada Assembly Speaker Barbara Buckley (D- Las Vegas) speaks on the chamber floor in Carson City.

than those of Congress, state committee chairs are correspondingly less powerful.

Conversely, party leaders are usually much more important in state legislatures than in Congress. Most party leadership in state legislatures is focused on a single office for each party in each chamber—the majority and minority party leaders. The majority party leader is the most powerful person in a chamber, serving as the presiding officer in all 49 state Houses[165] (usually called the "speaker") and in 24 state Senates (usually called the "president").[166] The lieutenant governor presides over the Senate floor in 26 states, but in most of these, the real power still rests in the hands of the majority party's leader (usually called something like the "Senate president pro tempore"). Minority party

[164] Matt Viser, "Democratic Infighting Escalates: Murray Calls Governor 'Irrelevant,'" *Boston Globe*, 22 May 2009, online edition; V. O. Key Jr., *Southern Politics* (New York: Vintage, 1949).

[165] There are only 49 state Houses of representatives, since the unicameral Nebraska legislature only has a Senate.

[166] Keith E. Hamm and Gary F. Moncrief, "Legislative Politics in the States," in Virginia Gray and Russell L. Hanson, eds., *Politics in the American State*, 9th ed. (Washington, DC: CQ Press, 2008). Note that in certain unusual political circumstances, a minority party member may become a chamber's presiding officer, as is currently the case in the Tennessee House, and was the case in 2008–2009 in the Louisiana House and in 2007–2008 in the Pennsylvania House. See Alan Greenblatt, "Austin's Surprise Speaker," *Governing* (March 2009):12–13.

leaders are important players in the legislative process, but most have far fewer formal powers and responsibilities than do majority leaders. Each party caucus also has several lower-level leadership positions, often appointed by the top leader, who as a group make up its leadership team.

State legislative party caucus leaders often dominate legislative proceedings, as suggested by the informal names they sometimes acquire, like the "Four Tops" in Illinois and the "Big Five" in California (including the governor).[167] In particular, state legislative majority party leaders have an especially strong hand in the process.[168] These leaders usually appoint committee chairs and members, and to the extent that they can do so, these leaders can have leverage over the output and proceedings of those committees and, therefore, the chamber as a whole.[169] Being a committee chair or on the party leadership team usually boosts a legislator's pay, power, and prestige, so these positions are coveted and those lawmakers holding them are beholden to the party leader who appointed them. Party leaders often negotiate among themselves and with the governor, representing their caucuses on important bills, especially the budget. Party leaders may also control much of the legislature's staff, offices, parking spaces, and other resources. In short, party leaders, especially majority party leaders, typically run state legislatures.

These leaders cannot do whatever they wish, of course. Majorities still make decisions in legislatures, and these leaders do not constitute a majority by themselves—far from it.

As a result, there is an interesting dynamic between leaders and **rank-and-file** legislators that is related to what political scientists call the "principal–agent problem."[170] A legislature's rank-and-file members (the principals) need their leaders (the agents) to help lawmakers to meet their personal goals and the chamber to fulfill its collective duties. Therefore, the rank-and-file members give their leaders considerable power. Without that power, not only couldn't a leader help the legislature overcome its collective action problem, but also no one would take the job of leader in the first place. Being leader is hard work, so legislators have to make the job both feasible and attractive to competent lawmakers. The appeal of these positions comes largely in the power that leaders have over legislative outcomes, personal aggrandizement, extra pay, and other perks. So the principal–agent *problem* is how legislators can get their leaders to meet their (the rank-and-file legislators') individual and collective goals without having to give leaders too much control over rank-and-file legislators and legislative output.

Typically, the harder the problems they need to solve, the more power that rank-and-file members must give their leaders, both to get the job done and to make the job attractive. As with legislative professionalism, since urban, diverse, and heavily populated states have more problems, they tend to have stronger legislative leaders.[171] Furthermore, where the parties are more ideologically polarized and/or partisan competition is greater, lawmakers give their leaders more power.[172] "The heathens are at

---

[167] Kent D. Redfield, "What Keeps the 4 Tops on Top? Leadership Power in the Illinois General Assembly," in David A. Joens and Paul Kleppner, eds., *Almanac of Illinois Politics: 1998* (Springfield, IL: Institute of Public Affairs, 1998); and Andy Furillo, "'Big 5' Put a Range of Issues on the Table," *Sacramento Bee*, 25 August 2005, online edition.

[168] Richard A. Clucas, "The Contract with America and Conditional Party Government in State Legislatures," *Political Research Quarterly* 62(2009):317–28; Richard A. Clucas, "Legislative Professionalism and the Power of State House Leaders," *State Politics and Policy Quarterly* 7(2007):1–19.

[169] Kristin Kanthak, "U.S. State Legislative Committee Assignments and Encouragement of Party Loyalty: An Exploratory Analysis," *State Politics and Policy Quarterly* 9(2009):284–303.

[170] Richard A. Clucas, "Principal-Agent Theory and the Power of State House Speakers," *Legislative Studies Quarterly* 26(2001):319–39.

[171] Clucas, 2001, 2007, op cit.

[172] Clucas, 2009, op cit.

the gates," so to speak, in these legislatures, so each party needs all the help it can get to hold the other one back. In terms of lawmakers' personal goals, where their salaries are higher and politics is more of a career for them (i.e., in professionalized legislatures), they care more deeply about getting reelected, so they need stronger leaders to help them do so. Table 6.1 shows the variation in the power of House speakers across the states based on their formal appointment and procedural powers. For the most part, you can see that larger states with strong two-party competition and professional legislatures are near the top of the list and smaller states with one-party citizen-legislatures are near the bottom, despite a few exceptions (such as West Virginia, Rhode Island, Ohio).

Because leaders are elected by their caucuses, if they fail to help their co-partisans meet their goals, then they may not be reelected to their leadership positions in the next legislative session. This gives leaders strong incentive to help meet their colleagues' goals. On rare occasions, leaders can even be dumped mid-session, as in Wisconsin in 2007, when Senate Democrats were so dissatisfied with the outcome of their state budget bill that they replaced Majority Leader Judy Robson with another member of their caucus whom they thought could do a better job for them.[173] Leaders can also lose their positions when a coalition of members of both parties is able to generate a majority of votes in the chamber and elect a new presiding officer. This is relatively rare, but it has occurred often enough recently to raise the question of whether some chambers are moving toward a "postpartisan politics."[174] A bipartisan coalition has controlled the Alaska Senate since 2008, and in the last full legislative session, the New Mexico Senate and the Texas, Louisiana, and Tennessee Houses had presiding officers elected with votes from each party.

Any overthrow of a top legislative party leader, however, is quite rare because most of them work very hard to help their caucuses meet their goals. First and foremost, this means that these leaders help their caucus members attain their primary personal goal—reelection.[175] This not only helps individual lawmakers, but it also helps the party's principle collective goal of gaining or retaining a majority, from which the policy and personal benefits of being in the majority flow to the caucus. Traditionally, legislative leaders have helped their caucus members' reelection efforts in a variety of ways, from making sure that they don't cast "bad" roll call votes that could be used against them by election opponents to helping them pass "good" bills and get projects that they can tout in their campaigns. Leaders help train new members about constituent service and media relations, and they even work to draw legislative districts to the advantage of their caucus's members (as discussed earlier in the chapter).

In recent years, many caucus leaders have begun to take a more active role in their rank-and-file colleagues' actual campaigns, using a strategy of **electoral targeting**.[176] Through polling, social and election data, and long experience, legislative leaders identify perhaps half a dozen districts that are most likely to have close races in the general election. These races may lack an incumbent or have changing demographics or simply have an even distribution of party voters. In these races, and perhaps only these, extra campaign effort might

---

[173] Steven Walters and Patrick Marley, "State Democrats Oust Robson, Pick Decker as Senate Majority Leader," *Milwaukee Journal Sentinel*, 25 October 2007, online edition.

[174] Greenblatt, 2009, op cit.

[175] The classic book on legislators' reelection goal was written about members of Congress, but the logic applies very well to state lawmakers; see: David Mayhew, *Congress: The Electoral Connection* (New Haven, CT: Yale University Press, 1974). The classic book on state legislative leadership is: Malcolm E. Jewell and Marcia Lynn Whicker, *Legislative Leadership in the American States* (Ann Arbor, MI: University of Michigan Press, 1994).

[176] Bill Boyarsky, *Big Daddy: Jesse Unruh and the Art of Power Politics* (Berkeley, CA: University of California Press, 2008); Richard A. Clucas, *The Speaker's Electoral Connection: Willie Brown and the California Assembly* (Berkeley, CA: IGS Press, 1995); Anthony Gierzynski, *Legislative Party Campaign Committees in the American States* (Lexington, KY: University Press of Kentucky, 1992); Loftus, op cit.; and Ralph Wright, op cit.

Table 6.1

Legislative Leadership Strength—The Formal Powers of the Speakers of State Houses of Representatives

State	Index of Majority Leadership Strength
NY	4.75
IL	4.67
WV	4.50
FL	4.36
IA	4.25
MN	4.08
MD	4.05
GA	4.00
OK	3.86
CA	3.83
CT	3.83
RI	3.82
KS	3.75
NC	3.75
OR	3.75
PA	3.75
TN	3.75
VT	3.75
NH	3.67
AZ	3.58
ME	3.58
MI	3.50
NJ	3.50
CO	3.37
TX	3.33
AL	3.25
ID	3.25
IN	3.25
MO	3.25
UT	3.25
VA	3.25
MA	3.17
DE	3.00
MS	3.00
MT	3.00
NM	3.00
SC	3.00
LA	2.92
SD	2.75
WI	2.75
AR	2.33
WA	2.17
WY	2.08
AK	2.00
HI	1.75
ND	1.25
OH	1.25
NV	1.08
KY	0.25

Note: This is a summative scale of the formal powers of speakers of state Houses of Representatives based on six equally weighted items: powers to appoint committee chairs, to appoint party leaders, to make committee assignments, to refer bills to committee, to control staff, and the amount of extra income a speaker earns. These data are for the 2003–2004 sessions, the most recent data available. Nebraska is not included because it has no House.

Source: Christopher Z. Mooney, "Modeling Legislative Leadership Power: Principals, Agents, Tools, Influence, and Comparative Legislative Analysis in the U.S. States," presented at the meeting of the American Political Science Association, Washington, DC (September 2010).

be the difference between a win for either party. Unlike rank-and-file lawmakers, caucus leaders' statewide perspective allows them to make the hard decisions about which candidates would and would not benefit from extra campaign help. By concentrating the party's resources in a few targeted districts, these leaders use them efficiently. Throughout the period since the previous election, and often over many years prior to this, these leaders will have used their powerful positions in the legislature to attract considerable campaign contributions from all over the state (and the nation, sometimes), and they can use that money in these targeted races. They hire, train, and coordinate top-flight campaign personnel and inundate these races with massive campaign spending in an effort to swing them to their party.

Of course, both leaders of a chamber's two caucuses are more or less equally adept at this targeting strategy, which leads to legislative campaign activity that is very uneven across a state. As we have seen, most state legislative races are blowouts in general elections, and as such they generate a minimal amount of campaign activity and spending. Only a handful of targeted races scattered around the state will see intense campaign battles, with perhaps 10 times the amount of campaign spending as in nontargeted races. In effect, these targeted races for the legislature are proxy battlegrounds for the statewide parties, with the candidates themselves being almost irrelevant. Few of these

candidates complain (at least very loudly), however, because the leaders are trying win these races for them. These targeted races will decide which party has a majority of legislators in the chamber in the next session. As such, they are too important to be left in the hands of mere candidates.

Thus, state legislators solve the collective action problem posed by their states' constitutions by using their internal rules and informal procedures to establish institutions: standing committees, party caucuses, and committee and party leaders. Without such institutions, state legislatures would not be able to accomplish any of their three jobs. The strength of these institutions varies among the states in relation to the level of the collective action problem in a state legislature.

Summary

American state legislatures are nuts and bolts institutions where democracy is up close and personal. Because of their small districts and more or less part-time responsibilities, these officials live, work, and play in and among their constituents on a regular basis. As a group, state lawmakers are demographically more like their constituents than any other group of state or federal elected officials, and their representativeness is getting better with every election. While redistricting, the homogeneity of their districts, and other forces have reduced the competitiveness of individual state legislative races, when taking the statewide or national view, we see that these elections are often very competitive or at least reelect the partisan makeup of voters.

State legislatures are complex institutions charged by their states' constitution and traditions to do three major tasks: set the state's public policy, oversee its executive branch, and represent its citizens' values and interests before the government. However, by giving lawmakers equal power and electing them frequently, and by setting up a bicameral process and otherwise making lawmaking complicated, these constitutions make it difficult for legislatures to accomplish their duties. As a result, lawmakers have developed a variety of institutions and processes to help overcome these obstacles and serve the state. Standing committees, political parties, and legislative leaders help legislatures solve their collective action problem. Never content with these arrangements, the states continually tinker with their legislatures' institutions to improve their performance.

Key Terms

Administrative rules review committee

Amend

Bicameral

Bill

Bill Sponsor

Casework

Chamber floor

Citizen-legislature

Collective action problem

Conference committee

Contestation

Contiguous

Cracking

Divided government

Electoral targeting

Ex post oversight

Gatekeeping

Gerrymander

Implementation

Incumbent

Incumbent-protection district

Legislative intent

Legislative professionalism

Malapportionment

Media market

Multimember district

Override

Packing

Party caucus

Pork barrel

Rank-and-file legislator

Redistricting

Roll call

Single-member district

Standing committee

State auditor

Supermajority

Swing seat

Term limits

Unicameral

Voting cue

Voting Rights Act of 1965

Discussion Questions

(1) What are the major factors that influence voters' choices in state legislative elections? What barriers exist to voters receiving accurate information on these races?

(2) Discuss the reapportionment revolution and the Supreme Court's role in changing legislative districts. What were the causes and effects of this "revolution"?

(3) How well are women and racial and ethnic minorities represented in state legislatures? How and why does this representation vary among states? How has this changed—and continues to change—over time?

(4) Discuss the role of parties, leaders, and committees in the legislative process. Why do they exist and why and how do they vary among the states?

Suggested Readings

Hamm, Keith E., and Gary F. Moncrief. 2008. "Legislative Politics in the States," in Virginia Gray and Russell L. Hanson, eds., *Politics in the American States*, 9th ed. Washington, DC: CQ Press.

Haynie, Kerry L. 2001. *African American Legislators in the American States*. New York: Columbia University Press.

Kurtz, Karl T., Bruce Cain, and Richard G. Niemi, eds. 2007. *Institutional Change in American Politics: The Case of Term Limits*. Ann Arbor, MI: University of Michigan Press.

McDonald, Michael P., guest ed. 2004. "Special Issue: Electoral Redistricting," *State Politics and Policy Quarterly* 4:369–490.

Moncrief, Gary F., Peverill Squire, and Malcolm E. Jewell. 2001. *Who Runs for the Legislature?* Upper Saddle River, NJ: Prentice Hall.

Rosenthal, Alan. 2009. *Engines of Democracy: Politics and Policymaking in State Legislatures*. Washington, DC: CQ Press.

Rosenthal, Cindy Simon. 1998. *When Women Lead: Integrative Leadership in State Legislatures*. New York: Oxford University Press.

Squire, Peverill, and Gary Moncrief. 2009. *State Legislatures Today: Politics under the Domes*. Upper Saddle River, NJ: Prentice Hall.

Squire, Peverill, and Keith E. Hamm. 2005. *101 Chambers: Congress, State Legislatures, and the Future of State Legislative Studies*. Columbus, OH: Ohio State University Press.

Winburn, Jonathon. 2008. *The Realities of Redistricting: Following the Rules and Limiting Gerrymandering in State Legislative Redistricting*. Lanham, MD: Lexington.

Wright, Ralph G. 2005. *Inside the Statehouse: Lessons from the Speaker*. Washington, DC: CQ Press.

Suggested Media Resources

The Redistricting Game (http://www.redistrictinggame.org/): The Annenberg School for Communications has designed this online game "to educate, engage, and empower citizens around the issue of political redistricting." The game lets players act as redistricters trying to maximize various criteria and goals, and in the process shows them see how simply moving district lines can have big political impacts.

Wiseman, Frederick. 2007. *State Legislature: A Documentary*, Zipporah Films. This film (3 hours, 37 minutes) follows the Idaho legislature through its 2005 session. Directed by the famed documentarian and self-described "staunch social reformer," Frederick Wiseman, this critically acclaimed film is an unvarnished, unscripted, and unnarrated look at the complex world of lawmaking in the states.

Websites

American Legislative Exchange Council (http://www.alec.org): ALEC is a national association of conservative state legislators whose goal is to advance the Jeffersonian principles of free markets, limited government, federalism, and individual liberty.

Center for American Women and Politics (http://www.cawp.rutgers.edu): The CAWP is a unit of Rutgers University that conducts research and training about and for women in elective office in the United States. Women in state legislatures are a major focus of the CAWP.

National Black Caucus of State Legislators (http://www.nbcsl.org): The NBCSL is a bipartisan national organization that conducts research and training designed to enhance the effectiveness of its members, African American state legislators.

National Conference of State Legislatures (http://www.ncsl.org): The NCSL is a national, bipartisan organization that provides state legislators and their staff with research, technical assistance, and opportunities to exchange ideas on the most pressing state issues.

Progressive States Network (http://www. progressivestates.org): The PSN is a liberal organization website that conducts and publishes research, tracks state legislation, and coordinates and networks like-minded policy makers and citizens.

7

Governors

INTRODUCTION

Today's state governor is typically a young, energetic, capable, and experienced politician looking to make a difference in the world, and he or she is working in an office that is one of the most powerful in the country. As the eight-year administration of President George W. Bush moved to its denouement, with the country mired in two wars and a miserable economy, and the federal government's reputation at home and abroad at a low ebb, the allure of Washington was not strong.[1] This led many of the best and brightest people in the country to look to the state capitals to carve out a meaningful career in public service. And besides, there is only one chief executive job in Washington, and for the past two decades, it has been filled by someone very much like today's new breed of governors. Today, the states are run by people like Louisiana's Bobby Jindal, Minnesota's Tim Pawlenty, Michigan's Jennifer Granholm, California's Arnold Schwarzenegger, Arkansas's Mike Beebe, and Washington's Christine Gregoire, among many others, people with vision and energy who have shown that the very tough job of governing a state during bad economic times is the sort of challenge that brings out the very best in people.[2] A few governors showed early promise but failed to pan out, some—like Illinois's Rod Blagojevich and South Carolina's Mark Sanford—very publicly so. But these are the exceptions. Many have said that being governor is the best job in American government today—and that it may also be the hardest. In particular, in these tough times, with people suffering and the states' budgets severely out of whack (see Chapter 10), a state's residents, businesses, and public officials look increasingly to the governor to solve their problems. Fortunately for Americans, the talent pool filling governors' offices around the country has never been deeper.

The governor is the single most visible and powerful person in state government. As the official **head of state** (like the president of the United States or the queen of England), the governor is the symbol of the state to people, organizations, and other governments, in and out of the state. So when West Virginia's Joe Manchin held vigil with family members of those lost in the Upper Big Branch Mine disaster in April 2010, he demonstrated the concern of all Mountaineers for the plight of those affected, just as Louisiana's Jindal did when he stood on the coast of the Gulf of Mexico the following month and called for more federal help to clean up the Deepwater Horizon oil spill. On a more positive note, when Alabama Governor Bob Riley traveled to Australia, France, and Singapore in July 2009, he was singing the praises of

[1] The hope engendered in the early days of the administration of Barack Obama seems to have put some luster back into federal government service

[2] Louis Jacobson, "First-Term Govs Largely Successful," *Stateline.org*, 25 July 2008, online edition.

AP Photo/Jeff Gentner

the workers and business opportunities in the Heart of Dixie state, trying to drum up business for its aerospace and shipbuilding industries. Governors meet with schoolchildren and sports champions, business and community leaders, delegations of foreign dignitaries, and many others, showing these people that their state is interested in them and the people they represent.

Also like the president, in addition to being the head of state, a governor is the state's chief executive officer and policy maker, taking a major role in formulating, enacting, and implementing a wide range of public policy. Given the size and complexity of state governments today, few administrative jobs in the world compare to being the governor of even the smallest state. Only a handful of countries are as big and complex as California or New York, and even medium-sized states, like Wisconsin and Maryland, are about the size of smaller, but important, countries, like Denmark and Sierra Leone. Governors are sometimes compared to the CEOs of Fortune 500 companies, but this comparison is not exactly apt. On the one hand, only about half of the states have budgets that would put them among the 500 largest corporations in the world. While California's $200+ billion annual budget would certainly place it among the 10 largest corporations, the budgets of about 20 percent of the states are under $10 billion, much smaller than even Nike or Amazon.com. On the other hand, the multiplicity of functions, and especially the public function, of state governments make them at least as great a managerial challenge as a multinational corporation, regardless of their size. And there is one place that governors and Fortune 500 CEOs certainly do not compare—their salaries. While California's Schwarzenegger's annual salary of $206,500 may sound lucrative to most of us, even companies on the bottom of the Fortune 500 list typically pay their CEO's much more than this. For example, Nike's William Perez earns a salary about 10 times that of Schwarzenegger, not to mention Perez's benefits and stock options.

Thus, being governor is a big job with big responsibilities, and people are clearly not doing it for the money. So why do they do it? Why are there always candidates for these offices, candidates who spend millions of dollars and stake so much of their time, energy, and reputation to win them? Three reasons stand out. First, a governor has the ability to have a major impact on politics, policy, and people's lives in a state. In virtually no other job can a person have such a large effect. Second, the challenge of doing such a complex and visible job well draws highly motivated and skilled people to it. In this way, governing a state is like working on a massive Sudoku puzzle—but one whose result is important to millions of people. Third, the governor's office is highly prestigious, and furthermore, those who do it well have used it as a stepping stone to other important and attractive jobs. For example, more presidents had previously been governor than any other type of office or position. In 50 of the 57 presidential elections in U.S. history, at least one of the major party candidates for president or vice president had been a governor; often, more than one governor was on the ticket. More generally, governors regularly go on to fill a wide variety of other positions that are among the most interesting and significant in the country, including key federal-level cabinet positions, seats in the U.S. Senate, and top executive positions in business, education, and the arts.

Gubernatorial Elections

Gubernatorial races are the most important elections on any state's political calendar, often drawing even more interest in a state than presidential elections. Forty-eight states hold gubernatorial elections every four years,[3] with 34 of these being held in the even-numbered year without a presidential election (for example, 2010, 2014, etc.).[4] Nine states elect their governors to four-year terms during presidential election years, and five states hold their gubernatorial elections in odd-numbered years. While all governors are now elected directly by a state's voters, this was not always the case. In the early days of the U.S., six state legislatures elected their governor; the last such election was in South Carolina in 1864. In fact, the Vermont and Mississippi constitutions still provide for legislative election of their governor if no candidate in the general election receives a majority of the vote. While rare, this last happened in 1999, in Mississippi.[5] Some states, mostly in the South, use a run-off election if no candidate gets a majority in the general or a first-round election. In these states, a run-off is needed about one-third of the time.

Unlike with state legislatures, term limits for governors have existed in most states for a long time, and they have rarely been controversial. There has long been a tradition in this country of chief executives at the state and federal levels serving only for a relatively short period of time. Perhaps long-serving executives

look too much like despots to Americans. But for some reason this doesn't seem to be a problem for mayors, many of whom have served several terms. For example, while voters in the 15 states with legislative term limits have never repealed them, when New York Mayor Michael Bloomberg bumped up against a two-term limit in 2008, he was able to get it repealed with a minimum of fuss.[6] Thirty-seven governors are limited in the number of terms they can serve, with most being limited to two four-year terms, like the U.S. president. In the early days of the country, many states limited their governors to a single term; today, Virginia is the last state to do so.[7] But even in those states without gubernatorial term limits, it is rare for a governor to serve more than two terms. For example, only one governor has done so in Illinois since its new constitution was adopted in 1970.[8]

Voting for Governor

How do people make their choice when voting for governor? Think about our discussion of voting in state legislative races (Chapter 6), and then apply that logic to voting for governor. The central difference between voting for these offices is that, for several reasons, voters have much more specific information about gubernatorial candidates than they do about legislative candidates.[9] Campaigning has economies of scale that allow gubernatorial candidates to transmit more sophisticated messages to voters more frequently. Since the race is run statewide,

---

[3] New Hampshire's and Vermont's governors still serve two-year terms, although there has been a push in the Granite State to move to a four-year gubernatorial term. See Josh Goodman, "A Four-Year Term for New Hampshire Governors?" *Governing*, January 2009, p. 7.

[4] Audrey S. Wall, ed., *The Book of the States: 2008*, vol. 40 (Lexington, KY: Council of State Governments, 2008), Table 4.1.

[5] Michael J. Dubin, *Party Affiliations in State Legislatures* (Jefferson, NC: McFarland and Co., 2007).

[6] Josh Goodman, "The Limits of Limits," *Governing*, April 2009, p. 14.

[7] As with New Hampshire's two-year term, there has been discussion in Virginia about allowing governors to serve more than a single term. See Rob Gurwitt, "Gubernatorial Term Limits: The Last One-Term Governor," *Governing*, October 2005, pp. 17–19.

[8] Of course, the last two Illinois governors have been chased from office with corruption charges, but the previous Illinois governor, Jim Edgar, served only two terms even though he left office in 1999 with one of the highest gubernatorial public opinion ratings in the country.

[9] Randall W. Partin, "Campaign Intensity and Voter Information: A Look at Gubernatorial Contests," *American Politics Research* 29(2001):115–40; and E. Freedman and F. Fico, "Whither the Experts? Newspaper Use of Horse Race and Issue Experts in Coverage of Open Governors' Races in 2002," *Journalism and Mass Communication Quarterly* 81(2004):498–510.

gubernatorial candidates can also advertise on television and radio more cost effectively than can those running for the legislature. But most important, political parties, interest groups, and the general public all recognize the governor's office as a uniquely important position in the state. As a result, gubernatorial candidates can raise more money to get their messages out to the public, groups will make their preferences in the race widely known, and voters will simply spend more time and energy paying attention to the race than they do for virtually any lower-level office.

Not surprisingly, incumbency has a big impact on voting for governor. But unlike with state legislators, gubernatorial incumbency is a mixed blessing. Of course, all else being equal, it is better to be the incumbent than the challenger, even in a gubernatorial election. Since their constituencies are so much larger, governors cannot generate goodwill by doing the sort of personal constituent service that lawmakers can do. But governors often have their names and faces associated with many positive things in the state, like on "Welcome to State X!" signs on highways and parks, on roadmaps, and so forth. They frequently attend ribbon-cutting ceremonies throughout the state for public works projects and even for new factories or businesses that the state had a hand in attracting to the state.[10] A governor has much more staff than a given lawmaker, and they work continually to make him or her look good. And like with those in the state legislature, these staffers can easily switch from governing work to campaign work when reelection time comes. All governors can also correctly claim to have had at least some broad and positive impacts on public policy and on a state in general.

As a result of these advantages, governors win reelection more often than they lose. From 1970 to 2009, 321 incumbent governors sought

reelection, and 76.9 percent were successful. Of the 36 incumbent governors who ran for reelection from 2005 to 2009, only three were defeated. In 2009, when New Jersey Governor Jon Corzine was defeated by Chris Christie in a close, hard-fought battle, his deep unpopularity was in large part due to the severe recession and the anti-incumbent feeling in the electorate nationwide that year. The two other incumbent governors to lose since 2005—Alaska's Frank Murkowski (2006) and Kentucky's Ernie Fletcher (2007)—were embroiled in scandal. In fact, governors who are seen as successful in their office can overcome big obstacles. Pennsylvania Governor Ed Rendell was so popular in 2006 that he was able to raise taxes significantly and still beat handily a well-loved Pittsburgh Steelers Hall of Famer (Lynn Swann) for reelection. A successful incumbent governor's goodwill can even rub off on the candidate of his or her party when he or she is not running for reelection.[11]

But while incumbency is helpful for governors, compared to the much higher rates of reelection for state legislators, members of the U.S. House, and state supreme court justices, incumbent governors are relatively vulnerable. U.S. senators have prestige and a constituency that parallel those of governors, thus attracting equally strong challengers and dealing with equally tough electoral terrain, but even they have a higher reelection rate than governors. Much of this vulnerability is due to the fact that, as chief executives, governors are held accountable for a state's problems to a much greater degree than are legislators at any level.[12] In fact, the only major office with a worse reelection rate in recent decades is that other chief executive of a large and complex government—the president of the United States. As chief executives, governors have to make tough choices that can anger some of their constituents, such

[10] Robert C. Turner, "The Political Economy of Smokestack Chasing: Bad Policy and Bad Politics?" *State Politics and Policy Quarterly* 3(2003):270–93.

[11] James D. King, "Incumbent Popularity and Vote Choice in Gubernatorial Elections," *Journal of Politics* 63(2001):585–97.

[12] Adam Brown and Gary C. Jacobson, "Party, Performance, and Strategic Politicians: The Dynamics of Elections for Senator and Governor in 2006," *State Politics and Policy Quarterly* 8(2008):384–409; David R. Mayhew, *Congress: The Electoral Connection* (New Haven, CT: Yale University Press, 1974).

as when Michigan's Granholm was forced to get involved with the mayor of Detroit's legal trouble in 2008 or when Arizona Governor Jan Brewer had to fight for a tax hike and budget cuts to address her state's recent budget mess.[13] Indeed, the recession has caused most governors to make unpopular choices lately. As the chief executive and most visible policy maker in a state, voters tend to hold their governor responsible for their state's condition, even for things that he or she might not reasonably be expected to control.

As it turned out, Corzine's loss in 2009 was the prelude to a particularly bad round of reelection bids for governors in 2010. First, Nevada's Jim Gibbons lost the GOP primary in is reelection bid, the first Silver State governor to ever do so. The losses of these sitting governors was clearly a result of the general dissatisfaction with government and incumbents among voters in 2010, but governors were hit to an even greater degree than were members of the U.S. Congress, the focus of much media commentary. Of course, it is difficult to know how many incumbents decided to retire than to run for reelection, but any way you look at it, 2010 was a bad year for incumbents, and incumbent governors had it worse than other major officeholders.

Fair or not, governors get the blame when things are going poorly and the credit when things are going well. In particular, studies show that voters tend to hold an incumbent governor accountable for his or her state's economy.[14] And these studies have discovered that the effect of a state's economy on gubernatorial voting is quite nuanced, suggesting that voters are making some fairly sophisticated voting decisions for this office. For example, by studying many gubernatorial elections over many years, scholars have found that voters tend to hold a governor accountable for the state's economy especially when the governor's party controls the legislature (when he or she could be expected to influence policy making more),[15] in election years (when campaigning makes getting information about the governor's performance easier),[16] and when voters know something about the structure of the state's economy (when they understand what the governor can and cannot do regarding the economy).[17] All this shows the importance of information in the voting process. When voters know more, they use this information thoughtfully; since they know more about governors than other state-level elected officials, voters evaluate them more thoughtfully. On the other hand, there is evidence that voters don't always use this increased information rationally. For example, one recent study found that, when the economy is good, voters tend only to give governors credit who are members of the voters' own party, and when the economy is bad, they tend only to blame those governors of the opposing party.[18] Furthermore, this public stage and informed voting gives governors the opportunity to slip up very visibly, such as when Missouri Governor Matt Blunt got into trouble for purging his e-mail system or when Massachusetts Governor Deval Patrick was called to task by the media for pursuing a book deal in Las Vegas during a crucial

[13] Charlie Cain and Mark Hornbeck, "Ouster Request Called a No-Win for Governor," *The Detroit News,* 14 May 2008, online edition; Scarpinato, "Redo Budget, Brewer Tells Lawmakers," *Arizona Daily Star* (Tucson), 2 July 2009, online edition.

[14] John E. Chubb, "Institutions, the Economy, and the Dynamics of State Elections," *American Political Science Review* 82(1988):133–54; and Lonna Rae Atkeson and Randall W. Partin, "Economic and Referendum Voting: A Comparison of Gubernatorial and Senatorial Elections," *American Political Science Review* 89(1995):99–107.

[15] Kevin M. Leyden and Stephen A. Borrelli, "The Effect of State Economic Conditions on Gubernatorial Elections: Does a Unified Government Make a Difference?" *Western Political Quarterly* 48(1995):275–90.

[16] Jason A. MacDonald and Lee Sigelman, "Public Assessments of Gubernatorial Performance," *American Politics Quarterly* 27(1999):201–15.

[17] Michael Ebeid and Jonathan Rodden, "Economic Geography and Economic Voting: Evidence from the US States," *British Journal of Political Science* 36(2006):527–47.

[18] Aaron Strauss, "Partisan Bias and Gubernatorial Approval: The Quest for Asymmetries," presented at the 8th Annual State Politics and Policy Conference, Temple University, 2008.

legislative debate.[19] And of course the fact that he was governor made South Carolina's Sanford's secret rendezvous with his Argentinean lover national front page news rather than a private concern for his family.

Not surprisingly, while gubernatorial voting is affected more by information about candidates and issues than is voting for state legislator, it is not the only factor influencing gubernatorial elections. As with other races, voters use various shortcuts that allow them to make a reasoned vote with the minimum amount of effort. The most important of these shortcuts is political party; people tend to vote for the gubernatorial candidate of the party to which they feel closest. And unlike his or her public record and policy positions, in practice, a candidate has little control over his or her party affiliation. Gubernatorial candidates have even less control over certain other factors that affect voting in these races, such as national-level forces, like the country's economy and the popularity of the president.[20] But as gubernatorial campaigns have become more costly, sophisticated, and personality-based, the link between gubernatorial voting and presidential approval has weakened, with people voting more on party, the issues in the state, and the candidates in the race.[21]

Strategic Behavior, Political Competition, and Gubernatorial Campaign Spending

The growing importance of governors and state government has caused gubernatorial campaigns to become increasingly costly and competitive.[22]

For example, when Indiana Governor Robert Orr ran for reelection in 1980, he spent $4.2 million.[23] But in 2008, when Governor Mitch Daniels ran in a very comparable reelection race in the Hoosier State, he spent $27.7 million—and this is adjusted for inflation.[24] In 2010, total spending in the primary and general gubernatorial election races in California exceeded $200 million—a new national record. A serious gubernatorial campaign even in a small state now costs millions of dollars. For instance, North Dakota's John Hoeven's 2008 cake-walk to reelection cost him $1.8 million, even though he had no primary opponent and ended up receiving almost three-quarters of the votes cast in the general election. Total spending on gubernatorial races almost doubled between the 1977–1980 and 2005–2008 election cycles, again, even controlling for inflation.

The biggest and simplest reason that gubernatorial campaign spending varies so dramatically from state to state is population. Gubernatorial races are more expensive in larger states because in those states, candidates must communicate their message to more people. In 2006, for example, in California, candidates spent a total of $129.0 million running for governor, while those in Wyoming spent only $1.4 million. In other words, spending in the California race—which, while high, was not a record amount—was almost 100 times as high as that in the Wyoming race. While this sounds crazily high, remember the huge difference in the populations of these two states. But since California has nearly 70 times as many residents as Wyoming, population explains only some of this variation.

[19] Frank Phillips and Matt Viser, "Patrick Chased Book Deal during Vote," *The Boston Globe*, 28 March 2008, online edition; Eric Kelderman, "Govs' E-Mail Purges Raise Hackles," *Stateline.org*, 6 December 2007, online edition.

[20] Chubb, op cit.

[21] Kenneth Dautrich and David A. Yalof, "The State of State Elections," in Carl E. Van Horn, ed., *The State of the States*, 4th ed. (Washington, DC: CQ Press, 2006).

[22] Thad Beyle, "Gubernatorial Elections, Campaign Costs and Powers," in *The Book of the States: 2008*, vol. 80 (Lexington, KY: Council of State Governments, 2008).

[23] This figure is adjusted for inflation to make the comparison appropriate.

[24] Our source for these campaign spending figures is: Thad Beyle and Jennifer M. Jensen, "The Gubernatorial Campaign Finance Database," www.unc.edu/~beyle/guber.html.

In order to understand the other forces driving spending in gubernatorial races, you must realize that the behavior of candidates and donors in these contests, like that of candidates and donors in most other races, tends to be strategic.[25] That is, these candidates and donors act differently depending on the situation in which they find themselves. And the most general principle of strategic behavior in gubernatorial elections is that when a race is close, these actors will put in their greatest efforts to win it. As an analogy, think about a game of recreation league basketball. When one team is beating its opponent handily, the coach may send in the second-stringers and the players on both sides take it a little easy. It becomes a sort of Kabuki dance, where everyone knows the outcome, but they go through the motions for the sake of form. But if the score is close, and especially if it is in the league title game, everyone plays as hard as he or she can, even if all that is at stake is a little plastic trophy and bragging rights. The same dynamic is at work in gubernatorial elections. When polling or experience or simply a gut feeling makes it obvious to everyone who is likely to win a race, both sides continue to campaign, but they try not to break a sweat doing it. But when the race is tight, when either candidate could win, all parties and candidates spend every dollar they have and exert every bit of their energy. No one wants to lose an important race like that for governor for want of just one more public appearance or one more round of TV ads.

While unlike in basketball, where the coach controls the level of competition by bringing in the second-string or keeping in the starters, in elections, this is done largely through the strategic behavior of donors (how much money are they willing to contribute?) and challengers (are the best challengers willing to take the risks involved in entering the race?). But the result is the same. In general, all things being equal, more money is spent in close races for governor than in blowouts.

So the next question is, What factors influence the level of competition in a gubernatorial race? Like with legislative races, the first thing to consider in this regard is whether an incumbent is running for reelection. While incumbent governors are more likely to lose than are incumbent state legislators, they still have a leg up in their races. They have run and won in the state before, they are well known, and they have the resources of their office to help their public image. If the incumbent governor is not in the race, no single candidate usually has such a large advantage. As a result, an open race will attract more candidates and is more closely competitive, in general.

Why are potential gubernatorial candidates so strategic in deciding whether to run? First, realize that running for any office is costly. Of course, it takes time and money, but candidates also have to do unpleasant things like ask people for campaign contributions and speak to endless groups and events. And just as important, the potential of losing is always there. To lose a race is not only embarrassing, but it can also end a political career.[26] Most potential candidates for governor are elected officials currently in office, and they may need to choose been running for governor and running for reelection in a relatively safe race. This is especially true for state legislators, members of Congress, and other statewide elected executive officials, like lieutenant governors and attorneys general. Therefore, these highly qualified and experienced candidates are most likely to run for governor only when they have a good chance of winning. And again, the first consideration here is whether there is an incumbent in the race. Incumbents will usually only be challenged by quality opponents if they are especially unpopular and, therefore, seen as "beatable."

[25] Jeffrey Lazarus, "Incumbent Vulnerability and Challenger Entry in Statewide Elections," *American Politics Research*, 36(2008):108–29; Adam Brown, "Gubernatorial Elections Reconsidered: Challengers, Donors, and Governors in the 2006 Campaign," working paper, Brigham Young University, 2009; Brown and Jacobson, op cit.

[26] David L. Leal, *Electing America's Governors: The Politics of Executive Elections* (New York: Palgrave Macmillan, 2006).

Unlike with state legislative races, where so many are uncontested, the opposing major party will almost always find someone to run against even a very popular incumbent governor, but occasionally that person is little more than a sacrificial lamb filling a place on the ballot. Such candidates are doing their duty for their party, and they may neither put much energy into the campaign nor get many campaign contributions to spend. In response, the popular incumbent needs to spend relatively little to win the race. For instance, in 2008, when the West Virginia Republican Party needed someone to run against Governor Joe Machin, one of the country's most popular incumbents in a strongly Democratic state, the best they could come up with was a former one-term state senator and head of a right-to-life group. The result was not surprising, if you think about strategic political behavior—that GOP candidate's campaign managed to spend only $44,000 and get 25.7 percent of the general election votes. But since the office of governor is so much more powerful and important in American politics these days than seats in the state legislature, the U.S. House, or, some might say, the U.S. Senate, there are fewer true sacrificial lambs in gubernatorial races than in these other races. But the principle still applies—the less competitive the race, especially when there is an incumbent running for reelection, the less money will be spent on both sides.

In addition to the presence of an incumbent in a race, potential candidates' strategic choices also hinge on the distribution of party voters in the state.[27] Why would a quality candidate who was an otherwise successful politician or businessperson risk losing a gubernatorial race where the state's partisan deck is stacked heavily against him or her? For example, while a Democrat may hold a safe congressional seat in Alabama, the current statewide electorate is such that he or she would have a hard time being elected governor, even running in an open race. On the other hand, this strategic consideration is less important for potential

gubernatorial candidates than it is for those for the legislature due to the difference in the level of information voters have about candidates for these two offices. Unlike legislative candidates, the extensive campaigning, news coverage, and advertising of gubernatorial candidates give voters considerable specific information about them. So while legislative voting is often driven only by party, gubernatorial voting is less so. Therefore, it is not unusual for the "minority party" to win a gubernatorial election with a good candidate, a good campaign, and a little luck. For example, two of the most Democratic states in the country—Rhode Island and Connecticut—have not had a Democratic governor since 1995 and 1991, respectively.

The strategic behavior of gubernatorial candidates and donors leads to a circular situation whereby many strong candidates are attracted to races without a clear front runner, and with more strong candidates in the race, the competition gets extremely fierce. And when conditions are right—when there is no incumbent in the race (or an unpopular one), when there is no one who is the obvious heir-apparent to the office, and when the statewide electorate is such that a candidate of either party could win—many well-qualified candidates may be attracted to the race. Because of their qualifications and expertise, such candidates are able to raise plenty of campaign money, and as the battle intensifies, more contributions come in on all sides. As a result, when competition is closest, no incumbent is running, and the partisan balance is even, gubernatorial campaign spending can be astronomical, largely as a result of strategic candidate and donor behavior.

In recent years, a certain type of gubernatorial candidate has appeared on the scene that is less than strategic in his or her behavior—the **self-financing candidate**. Apparently, some multimillionaires worry very little about spending $10 million or more pursuing a challenging and prestigious opportunity for public service. Two such men spent a total of over $75 million in the New Jersey governor's race in 2005; in

[27] Peverill Squire, "Challenger Profile and Gubernatorial Elections," *Western Political Quarterly* 45(1992):125–42.

2010, former eBay CEO Meg Whitman spent almost that much just to win the California Republican *primary* for governor.[28] In general, these self-financing candidates are not as strategic in choosing their races and spending their money as are more experienced politicians.[29] That is, their electability appears to have less influence on their electoral behavior. For candidates who are not self-financed, strategic campaign contributors act as a reality check, so that even if the candidates themselves think they can win, when potential donors do not, their contributions will be low. Self-financing candidates, undeterred by either internal or external strategic checks, tend to spend more than is "rational." In the 2002 New York race, Tom Golisano, the billionaire founder of Paychex, Inc., running on the Independence Party ticket, set the standard for non-strategic behavior in a gubernatorial race, spending $76.3 million, almost all of it thought to be his own money.[30] In the general election Golisano received only 654,016 votes, or 13.9 percent of those cast in the race. Put another way, he spent $116.33 per vote—not very strategic and certainly a record that will stand for some time to come.

Today's Governors: Who Are They?

Who are today's governors? What types of people are attracted to the governor's office, and, more important, what types of people are successful in the tough election battles for these prestigious offices? Where do they come from and where are they going? Although each governor has his or her own personal history, experiences, and background, we can make some generalizations about today's breed of state

chief executive. First, as a group, they are a long way from the political hacks who often occupied governors' mansions before the 1960s.[31] Today's governors are younger and better educated than those in years gone by, but they have also been highly successful in their chosen fields before becoming governor. Because they are young and successful when they enter the governor's office, they often move on to important and powerful careers after leaving office. Governors fight hard to win their jobs, and while in office, they pursue their vision of the state and its government energetically. In both their demographics and their professional experiences, today's governors are also a much more diverse group, although they are not nearly as diverse a group as are state legislators. It's hard to know whether it has been the increasing importance of the governor's office that has attracted this new generation of governors or whether their skills, experience, and energy have caused the states and governors to come increasingly to the forefront of American politics and government. Most likely, both of these processes are at work to some extent. But regardless of the direction of causality here, governors are among the most competent and important political actors in the country today.

Governors and Their Careers

Prelude to the Governorship What does the résumé of the typical governor look like? As has long been the case, the most common career path to the top political job in a state is through considerable progressive experience in state and local government. They typically start their public service careers in the local or state legislature or in law enforcement, often as a local prosecutor. These days, governors have almost always been to college, and they

[28] Juliet Williams, "Wealthy Businesswomen Energize Calif. GOP Voters," *The Chicago Tribune*, 8 June 2010, online edition.

[29] Adam Brown, "What Money Can't Buy: Self-Financed Candidates in Gubernatorial Elections," presented at the 9th Annual State Politics and Policy Conference, University of North Carolina at Chapel Hill, 2009.

[30] Delen Goldberg and John O'Brien, "Meet Tom Golisano, the Man Who Flipped Control of the New York State Senate," *The* (Syracuse, NY) *Post-Standard*, 10 June 2009, online edition.

[31] Larry Sabato, *Good-Bye to Good-Time Charlie: The American Governorship Transformed*, 2nd ed. (Washington, DC: CQ Press, 1983).

usually have a postgraduate education, especially in law. Specifically, the highest degree attained by the crop of governors in office before the 2010 election is: PhD—2, doctor of veterinary medicine—1; law degree—23, master's degree—8, bachelor's degree—14; and some college—2.[32] Most governors have been interested in politics, policy, and government from an early age, and their careers reflect this.

You can see the progressive nature of the state political career ladder by examining the jobs the 50 governors in office in 2010 held just before coming into office. Most commonly, these governors came from statewide elected positions, like lieutenant governor or secretary of state (see Table 7.1). As such, these governors had already faced the same voters as in their gubernatorial race, and they had already served and were known among that constituency. For example, Governors Jim Doyle (Wisconsin) and Bob McDonnell (Virginia) were attorneys general just before becoming governor, while Beverly Perdue (North Carolina) was lieutenant governor and Chet Culver (Iowa) was secretary of state. In fact, because of the movement of so many governors up (and out) in the middle of their terms recently, just before the 2010 elections, six sitting governors were finishing terms they had succeeded to, mostly from lieutenant governor (such as Illinois's Pat Quinn and Alaska's Sean Parnell) but also from other offices in states without a lieutenant governor, such as Jan Brewer succeeding from the Arizona secretary of state's office. In addition, Connecticut's Jodi Rell, Nebraska's Dave Heineman, and Texas's Rick Perry succeeded from the lieutenant governorship before being elected in their own rights. Thus, the most recent previous job of fully 18 percent of this recent crop of governors was lieutenant governor, and for another 24 percent, it was some other elected statewide office.

Much further down the list, the next most common "last job" for governors in the public

Table 7.1

Before and After the Governorship

Job	Number of Governors
Statewide Elected Official	
Lieutenant Governor	9
Attorney General	7
Secretary of State	3
Treasurer	2
State Legislature	
State Senate	3
State House	1
Congress	
U.S. House	7
Other	
Private Business	7
Mayor	3
Criminal Justice	4
Federal executive agency director	2
State executive agency director	1
State political party official	1

Note: These reflect the job held by governors serving in October 2010 immediately before taking office, based on information on the governors' official websites and that of the National Governors Association.

Type of Job	Number of Former Governors
Private Activities	
Business	21
Retired	10
Public Service	
President	1
Federal cabinet secretary/Ambassador	5
U.S. Senate	2
U.S. House	1
State senate	1*

(continued)

---

[32] This information was gathered by the authors and Pat McConnell at the University of Illinois at Springfield from these governors' professional web pages. This is the last year for which these data were available at press time. The latter caveat holds for much of the information gathered on these governors that is discussed in this section.

Type of Job	Number of Former Governors
Other	
Federal prison	3
College professor	3
Presidential candidate	2
DNC chair	1

*As president of the New Jersey State Senate, when then-Governor James McGreevey resigned on November 15, 2004, Richard J. Codey succeeded to the governorship. At the end of McGreevey's term, he returned to the senate.

Note: These numbers represent our best understanding of the first post-gubernatorial job, profession, or activity of the last governor (as of October 2009) in each state, based on the personal web sites of these former governors and media searches on LexisNexis.

sector is as a member of the U.S. House of Representatives. This shows that being governor is a step up from the House on today's informal political career ladder.[33] Idaho's Butch Otter and Ohio's Ted Strickland took this route to the governor's mansion. In most states, congressional districts cover just a portion of the state, so members of Congress running for governor have the disadvantage of having to introduce themselves to new constituents. The same problem confronts local government officials trying to move into the governor's office, but three recent governors have done so from big-city mayors' offices, like Tennessee's Phil Bredesen (Nashville) and Pennsylvania's Ed Rendell (Philadelphia). But the mayoral path is less common than one might think, given the parallels between the two jobs (Sarah Palin's well-known path from Wasilla to Juneau notwithstanding). It seems that even popular mayors have a hard time appealing to voters outside of their home cities. For example, the last four mayors of Charlotte—the largest city in North Carolina—have run for statewide office and lost.[34] No mayor of New York, Chicago, or Los Angeles has become

governor for more than a century, although not for want of trying.

Four recent governors, such as South Dakota's Mike Rounds and Georgia's Sonny Perdue, moved up straight from the state legislature. But as the governor's office has become more attractive in recent years, this path is less common than it used to be. Today, state lawmakers usually need to work their way up through more prominent positions, especially in large states where there are more business leaders, members of Congress, and big-city mayors to challenge for governor. A few recent governors came straight from positions in the criminal justice system, such as Oregon's Ted Kulongoski, who was a state supreme court justice, and Colorado's Bill Ritter, who was Denver's district attorney. Other recent governors had been working in an assortment of jobs just prior to taking the state's helm, such as Hawaii's Linda Lingle's job as head of the state Republican Party and Indiana's Daniel's position as head of President George Bush's Office of Management and Budget.

As already discussed, the power and prestige of the governor's office also hold considerable cachet for those who have been successful in the private sector. While it seems more common today, outsiders have won governorships throughout our history, such as in 1911, when Woodrow Wilson moved from the presidency of Princeton University to New Jersey's governor's mansion (on his way to the White House). Running a state appears to many people to be quite similar to managing a large private business, and extraordinarily successful businesspeople often take their first step into politics by running for the governor's office, some of them successfully (on the other hand, remember New York Governor-wannabe Golisano). Some of these business-to-governor stories are well known, like those of Governors George W. (Texas) and Jeb (Florida) Bush, California's

[33] Likewise, the fact that more members of the U.S. Senate are former governors (12) than governors who were previously a senator (0) seems to indicate that the Senate is seen as a step up from the governor's office on the political ladder. But this pattern of succession is also affected by the fact that many governors are term limited and, as such, are forced to move on to another position, should they decide to stay in politics.

[34] Alan Greenblatt, "Charlotte's Curse," *Governing*, March 2008, p. 18.

Arnold Schwarzenegger, and Minnesota's Jesse Ventura.[35] Other governors with perhaps a lower national profile have also moved straight from the private sector, including North Dakota's Hoeven and Montana's Brian Schweitzer. But while business experience may help a governor, the differences between the public and private sectors can sometimes be baffling. For example, while Jon Corzine was a smashing success running the preeminent investment bank on Wall Street, governing New Jersey proved puzzling to him.[36] Several recent governors, such as New Hampshire's John Lynch and Delaware's Jack Markell, had successful business careers but went into the governor's office only after serving in another, less demanding, government position. This two-stage business-to-governor career path seems to be increasingly popular, and it might well be beneficial for all concerned. It could help the state by weeding out those unsuited to government service and giving those who do become governor valuable public sector experience, and it could help the candidates by giving them a less risky and less expensive first step into politics.

After the Governor's Mansion If the governor's office is at the top of a state's political ladder, what can a governor do for an encore? This is an especially important question for those many people in recent years who have been elected governor in their 30s and 40s, giving them the prospect of a long career after leaving the governor's office. Table 7.1 also shows the first "post-gubernatorial" job or activity for those most recently leaving the office in each state.[37] As you can see, the most common thing former governors today continue to do is what former governors have always done— put together a lucrative portfolio of business activities that can include legal work, lobbying, public speaking, corporate board service, and public relations work. Twenty-one of these 50

recent former governors have done this. One might say that these governors are cashing in on their years of experience and many contacts made in state government. But who can blame them? Being governor is an extremely demanding job without an extremely high level of compensation, and as we have seen, it is often the pinnacle of a long career of public service. Former governors who work primarily in the private sector also often serve part-time on various important public commissions and boards at the state and national levels, such as the National Commission on Terrorist Attacks Upon the United States, or the "9/11 Commission," 30 percent of whose membership were former governors, including its chair, New Jersey's Thomas Kean.

Many of today's former governors want to continue in public service full-time, and 12 of those tracked in Table 7.1 found a way to do so. Of course, the position that is most clearly above the governorship in the American political career ladder is president of the United States. The fact that these two positions are more similar to one another than any other two positions also makes voters, political operatives, and governors themselves think of the states' chief executives as a natural talent pool for presidential candidates. This has been true throughout U.S. history; former governors have served as president for 108 years of the nation's 223-year history under the U.S. Constitution—almost 50 percent of the time. While we often think of the U.S. Senate as a natural training ground for presidents, the 2008 election of Barack Obama was the first time a sitting senator was elected to the presidency since John F. Kennedy in 1960; between these two presidents were governors-turned-presidents George W. Bush, Bill Clinton, Ronald Reagan, and Jimmy Carter. Talk about 2012 challengers to Obama centers around governors and former governors, such as Florida's Charlie Crist, Minnesota's Pawlenty, and Louisiana's Jindal.

---

[35] Ventura had also served a stint as the mayor of a small Minneapolis suburb.

[36] Alan Greenblatt, "Tougher Work than Wall St," *Governing*, December 2007, pp. 32–38.

[37] These data are for the last person to leave the governor's as of October 2009.

Of course, while only a small percentage of former governors actually become president, just as important is the idea that any given governor *could* become president. When governors are thought of as "presidential timber" by the media, the political parties, and, just as importantly, by governors themselves, it burnishes the image of both governors and their offices. This attracts higher-quality candidates to run for the office and gives sitting governors more influence, both within and outside of their states. And a governor's presidential aspirations may even be good for a state, as he or she strives to perform well to gain favorable publicity. For example, the performance of Massachusetts' Governor Mitt Romney in managing Boston's "Big Dig" highway reconstruction in 2006 was seen by many as having implications for his 2008 presidential bid, giving him an incentive to do the job well.[38] Furthermore, running a state is a great way both to improve a future president's skills and to weed out those unfit or unwilling to do a good job as president. For example, Alaska's Palin, South Carolina's Sanford, and even Illinois's Blagojevich had at one time been touted as promising presidential aspirants, but their actions as governor demonstrated that perhaps they were best suited to other work. Without that test by fire, perhaps if they had served in a less demanding position, like in the U.S. Senate, their deficiencies might not have become apparent before they entered the Oval Office.

But far more commonly than either the presidency or the Senate, former governors fill many appointive public service jobs, primarily at the national level, especially on presidents' cabinets and as ambassadors to other countries. Currently, four of 14 members of President Obama's cabinet are former governors—Iowa's Tom Vilsack (Secretary of Agriculture); Washington's Gary Locke (Secretary of Commerce); Kansas's Kathleen Sebelius (Secretary of Health and Social Services); and Arizona's Janet Napolitano (Secretary of Homeland Security). Historically, this is not unusual. Several former governors have served on the U.S. Supreme Court in U.S. history, although none has done so since California Governor Earl Warren became chief justice in 1953. The vice presidency is another national position for which governors are routinely considered. But despite Alaska's Palin's highly visible candidacy in 2008, only two governors have actually served in the position in the past 90 years.[39] And regardless of the outcome, virtually any discussion of a presidential appointment for such high positions regularly includes the names of at least one governor, such as the buzz around Michigan's Granholm and Washington's Christine Gregoire as potential Supreme Court appointees in 2010 or the incessant media chatter about a whole list of governors as potential vice presidential candidates for both parties in 2008.[40]

Governors' appointments to such positions, and the talk about them, often have as much to do with political considerations for the president as they do with the qualifications that governors bring to these positions. Traditionally, cabinets are formed by balancing the interests of various factions and parts of the country. For example, picking a governor from a farming state, like Iowa's Vilsack, to serve as Secretary of Agriculture is a tried and true way for a president to show he has concern for rural America. Sometimes more strategic, or some might say, Machiavellian, considerations may be at play. For example, President Obama was said to have co-opted a strong potential opponent for his 2012 reelection bid by appointing Utah Governor Jon Huntsman to the prestigious ambassadorship to China.[41] But politics aside,

[38] Glen Johnson, "Gov. Romney's Future May Hinge on Big Dig," *Sacramento Bee*, 18 July 2006, online edition.

[39] These former governors were New York's Nelson Rockefeller (who was appointed, rather then elected, after President Richard Nixon's resignation) and Maryland's Spiro Agnew.

[40] Daniel C. Vock, "Govs Rarely Picked for VP Slot," *Stateline.org*, 20 August 2008, online edition.

[41] Charles Mahtesian, "Stealth War: Obama Sabotages GOP," *Politics.com*, 3 June 2009, online edition.

there is no doubt that the qualities that have caused governors to be elected and the experience they gained running their states make them a powerful and skilled talent pool for any high-level position.

Women and Minorities as Governor

Until 1975, almost every governor in U.S. history had been an Anglo man. But since then, especially in the past two decades, significant progress has been made in electing governors who, as a group, are more representative of Americans' sex and race,[42] just as progress has been made in electing more diverse state legislators (see Chapter 6).

The most sweeping change in American governors' demographics has been the election of 22 women to the post in the past third of a century. Only three women had ever served as governor before 1975, and these were spouses of former governors who had been term limited, banned from office for official malfeasance, or had died. These first women governors were clearly elected as surrogates for their husbands. One even ran under the slogan "Two governors for the price of one," and another used the slogan "Let George [her husband] do it."[43]

In 1974, Connecticut's Ella Grasso, a former state legislator, secretary of state, and member of the U.S. House, became the first woman elected governor on her own merits. Grasso's success, along with changing values about sexual roles in the American politics, helped Washington State's Dixy Lee Ray follow her in 1977. Three more women were elected to governorships in the 1980s, and six more in the 1990s. This exponential acceleration in women's gubernatorial representation continued with

11 women being elected governor in the 2000s. Indeed, six women were elected or reelected in 2006 alone—fully 17 percent of those winning gubernatorial elections that year. In addition to those women who have been elected governor, since 1982, eight women have succeeded to the governorship when the elected governor died, resigned, or was impeached, serving anywhere from several days to three years. Two of these, Jane Dee Hull of Arizona and Jodi Rell of Connecticut, were later elected to a full term as governor in their own right.

A total of 31 women have now served as governor. While most of them have been Democrats, the balance has not been overly lopsided (19 Democrats and 12 Republicans). Just as important, 23 different states have had a woman governor, and these states represent the country very broadly, from New Hampshire and New Jersey to Texas and Louisiana, from Alaska and Arizona to Michigan and North Carolina. Clearly, the rise of the woman governor is not a regional, partisan, or ideological phenomenon.[44] And as women continue to serve as governors and receive high marks for their performance,[45] Americans will become accustomed to seeing women in powerful executive positions in government, allowing candidates to be judged more on their qualifications than their sex. This levels the playing field for female candidates and may lead to better sexual representation in all public offices. Just as the increasing numbers of women in state legislatures in the 1970s and 1980s encouraged the flourishing of women in the U.S. Senate in the 1990s and 2000s, Hillary Clinton's strong run for president in 2008 was probably helped significantly by the rise of woman governors in the 1990s and 2000s—or, more accurately, the old bias against electing women to executive office

---

[42] As to sexual orientation, no openly gay person has ever been elected governor. In 2004, New Jersey's Governor Jim McGreevy came out as a gay man during his term.

[43] Quoted in Susan J. Carroll, "Women in State Government: Historical Overview and Current Trends," in *The State of the States*, vol. 36 (Lexington, KY: Council of State Governments, 2004).

[44] Jason Windett, "State Effects and the Emergence and Success of Female Gubernatorial Candidates," presented at the 9th Annual State Politics and Policy Conference, University of North Carolina at Chapel Hill, 2009.

[45] Pamela M. Prah, "Report: Women Govs Get High Marks," *Stateline.org*, 30 November 2007, online edition.

Table 7.2

Governors with Minority Racial or Ethnic Heritages

Name	State	Party	Dates of Service	Racial or Ethnic Heritage
Ezequiel Cabeza De Baca	NM	D	1917[a]	Latino
Octaviano Ambrosio Larrazolo	NM	R	1919–1921	Latino
George Ryoichi Ariyoshi	HI	D	1974–1986	Asian American
Jerry Apodaca	NM	D	1975–1979	Latino
Raul H. Castro	AZ	D	1975–1977	Latino
Toney Anaya	NM	D	1983–1987	Latino
John Waihee	HI	D	1986–1994	Hawaiian
Robert Martinez	FL	R	1987–1991	Latino
L. Douglas Wilder	VA	D	1990–1994	African American
Benjamin J. Cayetano	HI	D	1994–2002	Asian American
Gary Locke	WA	D	1997–2005	Asian American
Bill Richardson	NM	D	2003–2011	Latino
Deval Patrick	MA	D	2007–	African American
Bobby Jindal	LA	R	2008–	Indian American
Susana Martinez	NM	R	2011–	
Brian Sandoval	NV	R	2011–	
Nikki Haley	SC	R	2011–	
Successors				
Pinkney B. S. Pinchback	LA	R	1872–1873	African American
David A. Paterson	NY	D	2008–2011	African American

[a] Died in office.

Source: We have identified these governors' heritages based on their biographies on the National Governors Association website, media reports, and other online sources. But like Americans generally, the racial and ethnic heritage of many politicians in this country is not clear cut or easy to identify from documentary sources.

was likely reduced by these governors' success. It is very likely that first woman in the White House will get there through a governor's mansion.

Racial and ethnic gubernatorial representation has improved more slowly and unevenly in the states than has sexual representation. Studies continue to show that voter bias disadvantages non-Anglo candidates in gubernatorial races.[46] But some governors with minority heritages have been elected in recent years, especially in those states with smaller proportions of Anglos than the nation as a whole.[47] Hawaii, with its polyethnic society, has elected two Asian American governors and one of native Hawaiian ancestry. New Mexico has the country's highest proportion of Latinos, and it has elected five Latino governors, including its last head of state, former U.S. Energy Secretary and presidential candidate, Bill Richardson. New Mexico's neighbor, Arizona, also elected a Latino governor, as has Florida, two other states with sizable Latino populations. In 1990, Virginia's L. Douglas Wilder became the first African American to be

[46] Gary M. Segura and Luis R. Fraga, "Race and the Recall: Racial and Ethnic Polarization in the California Recall Election," *American Journal of Political Science* 52(2008):421–35; Christina Bejarano and Gary Segura, "What Goes Around, Comes Around: Race, Blowback, and the Louisiana Elections of 2002 and 2003," *Political Research Quarterly* 60(2007):328–37.

[47] We have identified minority governors based on their biographies on the National Governors Association website, media reports, and other online sources. Of course, like Americans generally, the racial and ethnic heritage of many politicians in this country is not clear cut or easy to identify from documentary sources.

elected a state governor. Since only 20 percent of Virginia's population at that time was African American, this clearly demonstrated that even in the South, significant numbers of white people will vote for a black person. While seven other states with higher proportions of black residents have never elected an African American governor, at least one poll suggested that even in Alabama, where gubernatorial candidates used to compete to by holding the virulent of racist positions, a black person could be elected governor in the near future.[48]

Especially promising in this regard is the fact that three non-Anglo men have been elected governor recently in states where people with their racial heritage made up only a very small proportion of voters. Washington State's Gary Locke, an Asian American, Massachusetts's Deval Patrick, an African American, and Louisiana's Jindal, an Indian American, were obviously elected with mostly white votes, since in none of these states did people of their heritage make up more than 7 percent of the population. In addition, in March 2008, New York Lieutenant Governor David Paterson succeeded to the governorship when Governor Eliot Spitzer resigned as a result of a prostitution scandal. Paterson is not only African American, but he is also legally blind. While no one has studied or even tracked the number of disabled governors,[49] Paterson's succession to the governorship of the second largest state in the country was seen as an inspiration for blind people as well as African Americans.[50] Thus, while racial and ethnic minorities are much underrepresented in the ranks of the nation's governors, the recent elections of Locke, Patrick, and Jindal—and the election of Paterson and many other non-Anglos to a other statewide executive offices—in states where people of their own heritage are in the distinct minority suggest that more governors of color may be elected in the coming years.

The Duties of the Governor—Manager, Policy Maker, and Intergovernmental Liaison

Once in office, what does a governor do and how does he or she do it? The answers to these questions are not as clear as you might think, nor are they as clear as they seem to be for officials of the other two branches of state government. Legislators pass laws, and judges interpret and enforce them in court, but what exactly do governors do? We see them on TV giving speeches, meeting with various officials and members of the public, touring disaster areas, and so forth, and we are vaguely aware that they somehow "run state government," but what does that mean?

In general, governors have three basic duties—managing the state government **bureaucracy**, helping make public policy for the state, and acting as the liaison for the state government with local governments, other state governments, the national government, businesses, and even foreign countries. Each of these is a demanding and complicated task that requires all of a governor's institutional and informal powers, as well as all of his or her personal knowledge, skills, and abilities. We will talk about the powers that governors can use to accomplish these tasks later in this chapter, but first, here is a brief description of their duties.

Chief Executive Officer: Managing the Bureaucracy

Although the republican values of our country's founders led many of them to value the

[48] Charles J. Dean, "Black Governor Now Possible in State, 53% Say in Survey," *Birmingham (Alabama) News*, 12 August 2008, online edition.

[49] At least one governor is known to have been paraplegic. Franklin D. Roosevelt served as governor of New York from 1929 to 1933, before being elected president. However, in that pre-YouTube era, his disability was not widely known to voters.

[50] Lisa W. Foderaro, "The New Governor Also Serves as an Inspiration for the Blind," *The New York Times*, 18 March 2008, online edition.; Verena Dobnik, "Black Pride Surges with Paterson's Rise to N.Y. Governor," *State Journal-Register (Springfield, IL)*, 16 March 2008, p. 7.

legislative over the executive function of government, it was clear to those writing the early states' constitutions that at the very least, an administrator was needed to implement the policies passed by the legislature. Thus, the original job of the governor was simply to do this, supervising various agencies staffed by government workers to provide the minimal services that the states then provided their residents, collect taxes to pay for these services, and pay the state's bills. In this sense, the governor is like the chief executive officer of the state who tries to carry out the wishes of the legislature, which acts, in turn, like a very hands-on board of directors. In the early years of the republic, these duties and workers were few, but as the nation and its need for public services grew, so did the responsibilities of the executive branch of state government. Today, state government is the single largest employer in almost every state. At last count, 4.3 million people worked for state governments nationwide, including over 100,000 each in 11 states.[51] Even the states with the fewest state employees—Vermont, Wyoming, and the Dakotas—each has over 10,000 of them. All but a small percentage of these workers serve in the states' executive branches, and most of these are under the governor's control. As these state executive agencies have grown, so has the importance of the governor's job of managing them.

Given the importance of policy implementation and the size and complexity of the bureaucracy, it should not be surprising that most governors spend a good deal of time trying to impose their will on the executive branch. The state bureaucracy is a mammoth operation, and the governor is but one person, perhaps with several dozen staff. The agencies are like battleships, moving along relatively smoothly in one direction, doing their duty as they have always done it. Despite common misperceptions and biases, the people who work in state agencies tend to be highly skilled,

well educated, and dedicated professionals who come to work every day proud to do what they think of as important work. The generally high level of competence of these people helps governors tremendously by making the huge ship of state run smoothly on a daily basis.

A governor's management duties are much like those of a CEO of a large corporation or non-profit organization, with their problems typically consisting of two types. First, sometimes problems arise with an agency's standard operating procedures so that its ongoing tasks and goals are not being accomplished correctly. Whether it is a morale problem or a goal misplacement issue, governors and their staff need to keep an eye on the various agencies to anticipate and solve such problems. Second, and more problematic, sometimes governors want to change the goals and behaviors of an agency significantly. Inertia, professional pride, and perhaps even the policy preferences of these state workers can make it difficult for a governor to make quick and significant changes. Like a battleship, the agencies will turn, but they do so slowly. Sometimes, a governor just needs to communicate his or her preferences clearly; often, bureaucrats are happy to do what the governor wants, as long as they know what that is and if it fits with their professional norms. Sometimes more forceful actions must be taken, especially those involving a governor's budget powers or executive orders.

Chief Policy Maker: Charting the Course

The original idea of the governor simply as an errand boy for the policy-making legislature quickly gave way both to the realities of state government's daily duties and to Americans' disenchantment with an entirely legislature-driven government.[52] In particular, as you read about in Chapter 6, lawmakers sometimes have a parochial view of public policy, focusing

[51] Morgan and Morgan, op cit., p. 359.

[52] Nelson C. Dometrius, "Governors: Their Heritage and Future," in Ronald E. Weber and Paul Brace, eds., *American State and Local Politics: Directions for the 21st Century* (New York: Chatham House, 1999).

only on their respective districts and the next election coming up in the very near future. The governor can take a broader view and, sometimes, a longer view. The governor is positioned as the single best person to understand the overall problems of the state and the competing interests at play regarding them. It's not that governors are perfect in these respects; it's just that, as an institution, no official in state government is better placed to do so. Today, the general public, the media, and the legislature all expect the governor to propose at least the broad parameters of state government policy. Of course, governors are no more dictators of state policy than they are dictators of the state bureaucracy—less so, really. But the governor is expected to set the tone for state policy making.

In general, the governor's job as chief policy maker involves defining for the legislature and other relevant political actors which public problems are most important and which solutions are most feasible and effective. The state could address countless problems at any given time, but policy makers must ration its limited resources, choosing carefully which problems are most pressing and where the state can do the most good. Every state capital is swarming with people and organizations trying to interest policy makers in their pet problems, whether it is deteriorating highway bridges, ineffective pre-K education, overcrowded prisons, or what have you. The person who can define which issues are most important has tremendous power.[53] Wise governors use their powers judiciously to do just that.

Once the most important public problems have been identified, their potential solutions need to be prioritized. Every public problem could be dealt with in many different ways. These various alternatives are not likely to work equally well, and neither are they equally economically or politically feasible. As chief policy maker, the governor's job is to develop, weigh, and modify the various alternatives, and then to work for the adoption of the ones he or she thinks are best. As you know, the legislative process is so complex that it requires strong leadership to pass the laws that help determine state policy. But even though the governor has only a small formal role in this process (at the signing or vetoing stage), and even though lawmakers are sensitive about breaching the constitutional boundaries between the branches,[54] all those in and around the process expect the governor to use his or her powers to engage informally in the process at all stages. In addition, governors use their powers to set policy formally and informally in the administration of state government every day by establishing rules, plans, and norms in the bureaucracy.

Intergovernmental Relations Manager: Working Well with Others

An increasingly important job for governors has been acting as the point person for relationships between their states and other governments, including local governments, other state governments, the national government, and even foreign governments and Indian tribal governments.[55] The globalized economy, instant communications, and fast transportation mean that people, businesses, and governments interact with one another constantly and repeatedly, as you read about in Chapter 2. Commerce, social problems, and crime move freely across state borders, as they do, perhaps a little less freely, across international borders. Four states border Mexico, 10 border Canada, 16 others have ocean coastlines, 33 have federally recognized Native American tribes, and every state has at least one international airport. In addition, each

---

[53] John W. Kingdon, *Agendas, Alternatives, and Public Policies* (Glenview, IL: Scott, Foresman, 1984).

[54] Alan Rosenthal, *Heavy Lifting: The Job of the American Legislature* (Washington, DC: CQ Press, 2004), ch. 9.

[55] Thad Beyle, "Governors: The Middlemen and Women in Our Political System," in Virginia Gray and Herbert Jacob, eds., *Politics in the American States*, 6th ed. (Washington, DC: CQ Press, 1996).

state has hundreds or thousands of local governments. As the central coordinating figure in state government, governors have by necessity taken on the role of intergovernmental relations (IGR) manager.

Many of these IGR interactions are financial, especially those related to the federal grants coming to the states and state and federal grants going to local governments.[56] This net of financial transactions has drawn the three levels of American government so close that it is often hard to tell where one leaves off and another begins. Governors play an important role in coordinating these financial relationships, but their IGR duties go far beyond this. They work with representatives of other governments in negotiations over mutual and competing interests in much the same way that presidents do in international relations. Governors work with national governments and international corporations to attract business to a state, as when Tennessee's Bredesen traveled to China, Japan, Switzerland, Germany, and Poland in the summer of 2009 to help bring jobs to a new mega-business park near Brownsville in western Tennessee, or when the governors of California, Texas, and New Mexico went to Mexico City in 2008 to discuss the explosion of drug violence in the borderlands with Mexican President Felipe Calderon.[57]

Governors regularly work with other governors to deal with mutual problems. Sometimes these are ad hoc issues between a small number of states, like when Missouri's Jay Nixon and Illinois's Quinn worked together to promote building a high-speed rail corridor between Chicago and St. Louis.[58] More generally, the **National Governors Association (NGA)** is a 100-year-old nonpartisan institution that provides a vehicle for governors to consult one another about their common problems.[59] The NGA has significant staff resources and structured meetings and agendas through which governors both learn what other states are doing and how to work with them. Furthermore, the NGA works as an interest group for governors and the states, allowing them to speak with a single voice to Washington when they can agree to do so.

While it has become increasingly important in recent decades, the gubernatorial job of IGR manager is made more difficult by the fact that it is both newer and less well defined than the job of either chief policy maker or manager of the bureaucracy. Therefore, governors must use their powers creatively to be successful IGR managers.

The Powers of the Governor

How do governors accomplish the three jobs that we have just outlined? This is not an easy question to answer, perhaps since governors seem to work more idiosyncratically than do other political actors in the states, such as legislators, judges, lobbyists, and so forth. Perhaps the fact that there is only one governor per state at any given time just makes their idiosyncrasies more obvious. Their personal governing styles, skills, and experiences sometimes make it hard for scholars to draw useful generalizations about gubernatorial behavior. Certainly scholars who study U.S. presidents have this problem in the extreme.[60] But those studying

---

[56] Timothy J. Conlan and Paul L. Posner, eds., *Intergovernmental Management for the Twenty-First Century* (Washington, DC: Brookings Institution, 2008).

[57] Associated Press, "Tenn. Governor Plans Trade Mission to Japan, China," *Boston Globe*, 30 June 2009, online edition; Juliet Williams, "Border Governors Head to Mexico as Violence Rises," *Arizona (Tucson) Daily Star*, 2 June 2008, online edition.

[58] Jake Wagman, "Jay Nixon, Pat Quinn on Board High-Speed Rail Plan," *St. Louis Post-Dispatch*, 27 June 2009.

[59] Pamela M. Prah, "Govs Celebrate Past, Look to '09," *Stateline.org*, 7 November 2008, online edition; Pamela M. Prah, "Governors Hopeful after Obama Meeting," *Stateline.org*, 3 December 2008, online edition.

[60] Gary King and Lyn Ragsdale, *The Elusive Executive: Discovering Statistical Patterns in the Presidency* (Washington, DC: Congressional Quarterly Press, 1988).

American governors tried to address this question by analyzing, comparing, and generalizing about various **gubernatorial powers**.[61] While it is true that, like with presidents, gubernatorial power is largely the power to persuade,[62] governors have a variety of tools—both formal and informal—that, when used skillfully, can make them a more "persuasive." We talk here about governors' formal and informal "powers," but keep in mind that they each define a continuum of power or control over a given situation. These are tools that vary a great deal from state to state, so that the office of governor is more or less strong from state to state and even, especially in the case of informal powers, from governor to governor.

Formal Powers—A Governor's Institutional Tools

The formal powers that states give their governors, largely in their constitutions and statutes, are institutions that would be available to any governor working under a given legal arrangement. These are powers that a state's policy makers have explicitly decided to give to their governors. In recent decades, the states have increased their governors' formal powers in each of these areas, but significant variation among the states remains.

Control over the Budget The number-one problem facing governors and states in the last few years has been balancing their states' budgets. But as you will see in Chapter 10, the budget is always the central concern of state policy makers because it is perhaps the most concrete expression of a state's public policy. Almost everything a state does, from providing needy children with health care to housing prisoners to building and maintaining roads, requires spending money, and the budget plans and authorizes all the state's spending, as well as laying out the sources of its revenue.

Although a state's budget must pass through the regular legislative process each year,[63] states give the governor special institutional powers in the budget process that they do not have in regular lawmaking. To begin with, most governors have the responsibility to estimate the revenues for the coming year and to propose spending for most agencies. This gives them a great advantage over the legislature and bureaucracy in determining where and how state money will be spent.[64] A budget bill[65] is extremely technical, detailed, and complex, so the legislature often can only review and edit it around the edges, with most of the governor's proposal usually being adopted.

Of course, in bad economic times, having their special budget responsibility is a mixed blessing for governors, at best. Even Democrats like North Carolina's Perdue and Maryland's Patrick O'Malley are ordering massive budget cuts and Republicans like Arizona's Brewer and Utah's Huntsman have pushed for tax hikes.[66] In 2009, several Republican governors tried to

[61] Thad Beyle and Margaret Ferguson, "Governors and the Executive Branch," in *Politics in the American States*, 9th ed. (Washington, DC: CQ Press, 2008)

[62] Richard E. Neustadt, *Presidential Power and the Modern Presidents* (New York: Free Press, 1990).

[63] For those few states that still do biennial budgeting, the budget bill(s) must pass through the legislature every two years.

[64] William Ewell, "Measuring Institutional Political Power in the American States," presented at the 8th Annual State Politics and Policy Conference, Temple University, 2008; Doug Goodman, "Determinants of Perceived Gubernatorial Budgetary Influence among State Executive Budget Analysts and Legislative Fiscal Analysts," *Political Research Quarterly* 60(2007):43–54; James W. Douglas and Kim U. Hoffman, "Impoundment at the State Level: Executive Power and Budget Impact," *American Review of Public Administration* 34(2004):252–58; Dall W. Forsythe, *Memos to the Governor: An Introduction to State Budgeting*, 2nd ed. (Washington, DC: Georgetown University Press, 2004); Charles Barrilleaux and Michael Berkman, "Do Governors Matter? Budgeting and the Politics of State Policymaking," *Political Research Quarterly* 56(2003):409–17.

[65] Some states use a series of bills for the budget, but the principle here is the same.

[66] Mark Binker, "Perdue Mandates Furlough for State Workers," *(Greensboro)News-Record*, 29 April 2009, online edition; Daniel Scarpinato, "Brewer: Fix Deficit by Raising Sales Tax," *Arizona* (Tucson) *Daily Star*, 2 June 2009, online edition; Robert Gehrke, "Huntsman Wants to Push Cigarette Tax to $3," *The Salt Lake Tribune*, 7 January 2009, online edition; Laura Smitherman, "O'Malley Calls for 5% Cuts in State Agencies' Budgets," *Baltimore Sun*, 26 September 2008, online edition.

make political hay by rejecting some of the federal stimulus money—the so-called "Obama Bucks"—that was being sent to the states to fight the recession. While these governors also had some legitimate policy concerns with this program,[67] their opposition to this seemingly "free" money during hard times became a public relations problem for most of them. South Carolina's Sanford was even sued successfully by a high school student to accept the money.[68] On the other hand, sometimes a smart governor can use budget crises to eliminate waste, cut old programs that have out-lived their usefulness, and otherwise craft public policy more in line with his or her vision for the state.[69]

Veto Powers As discussed in Chapter 6, a governor's only institutional role in the state's legislative process is after both chambers have passed a bill in identical form, when the governor must choose whether to sign it into law or to veto it. Legislatures have the opportunity to override a veto by voting again in favor of the bill in both chambers, usually by a supermajority vote. For example, during his 14-year tenure in Wisconsin in the 1980s and 1990s, Republican Governor Tommy Thompson made 1,937 legislative vetoes, and the predominantly Democratic Wisconsin legislature failed to override a single one of them. However, conflict over tough questions of government cutbacks appears to have led to more veto overrides during the current period of economic hardships. For example, South Carolina's Sanford issued 243 vetoes in a recent budget bill—and the legislature overrode 228 of them; Connecticut's Rell was overridden on seven bills in a single day.[70]

Governors in different states have different levels of veto power. All governors can execute a full, or "package," veto on bills; this is the same veto power the president has. But in most states, the governor's veto power is even stronger than this. First, 44 governors have the **line-item veto,** the ability to veto one or more specific lines in a bill while letting the rest of it pass into law.[71] In 30 of these states, the governor can only line-item veto **appropriations bills,** and budget bills are where governors most often use the item-veto. Indeed, the item veto is used so that the legislature cannot hold an entire bill hostage for a single part of it that the governor finds objectionable. Twelve states also give their governors the **reduction veto** on appropriations bills, allowing them to reduce the amount that is authorized to be spent on a budget item. In addition, six states give their governors even greater power with the **amendatory veto,** a power that allows them to send a bill back to the legislature with a message asking for a specific change.[72] The legislature can then either override the veto by passing the original bill or item with a supermajority vote or pass the governor's suggested language with a simple majority. Because it is often much easier to generate a simple majority to agree with the governor than to generate a supermajority to oppose him or her, the amendatory veto can be a powerful tool.

These types of veto vary in their effectiveness in their level of surgical control to legislation. The implied threat of the veto gives lawmakers strong incentive to craft bills with the governor's wishes in mind. Legislators do not want to do the hard work of passing a bill

[67] Peter A. Harkness, "When the Well Runs Dry," *Governing*, May 2009, pp. 18–19.

[68] Rich Brundrett, "S.C. High Court Orders Sanford to Accept Money," *The State* (Columbia, SC), 7 June 2009, online edition.

[69] Raymond C. Scheppach, "The Economic Downturn: An Opportunity for Governors?" *Stateline.org*, 2 April 2008, online edition.

[70] Andy Brack, "Policy Vetoes Go over Better Than Ideological Ones," *South Carolina Statehouse Report.com*, 1 July 2007; Christopher Keating. "Historic Day for Legislature as Seven Vetoes Are Overridden," *Hartford* (CT) *Courant*, 13 August 2009, online edition.

[71] For the details on which governors have which type of veto power, see Wall, op cit., pp. 185–86.

[72] In addition to Alabama, Illinois, Massachusetts, Montana, New Jersey, and Virginia, South Dakota gives its governor the amendatory veto when the legislature is in session, and Wisconsin does so on budget bills; see: Daniel C. Vock, "Govs Enjoy Quirky Veto Power," *Stateline.org*, 24 April 2007, online edition.

in their chambers only to have it vetoed at the governor's desk.

Appointment Powers Governors vary considerably in their ability to make appointments to positions in government. These include such things as appointments to judgeships and various boards and commissions, but the most important gubernatorial powers of appointment tend to be those to top posts in the executive branch. Governors who can put their own people into most of the policy-making and upper-management positions in the executive branch can better control the bureaucracy and policy implementation.[73] Governors can also reward their supporters with positions of prestige and power, and such appointments can even be used as bargaining chips for a governor in dealing with state legislators or others in the policy-making process. Ohio Democrat Strickland used some appointments in a creative—and very political—way in Ohio in 2008 when he appointed some Republican legislators from swing districts to administrative positions, thus giving his party a better chance of winning those seats in the next election.[74] On the other hand, when a governor's appointee does something embarrassing, the governor is often held responsible, at least politically. But overall, a governor is stronger if he or she appoints more rather than fewer state government officials.

Beyond merely the number of appointments governors get to make, their appointment powers vary in two important ways among the states. First, some states allow for the direct and independent election of various top-level executive branch officials, including the lieutenant governor, attorney general, secretary of state, treasurer, and others. The impact on gubernatorial power of this is that when these officials are elected independently, not only can governors not control them or their agencies directly, but they may also actually be rivals for power. Remember that many governors held one of these positions themselves before moving up to the governor's mansion.

The states also vary in how far up into the managerial positions of the bureaucracy a state's **civil service system** reaches. At one time, some governor would gain political power from handing out as many as 20,000 **patronage jobs** to political supporters and their families. Although no one begrudges a governor the power to appoint the top managers of state government so as to hold the bureaucracy accountable and set public policy, many of these positions—such as workers on road construction crews and driver's license examiners—clearly had no policy-making power. How might such appointments increase a governors' power? Consider, for example, that while a state legislator might not be persuaded to vote for a governor's bill by the offer of a road crew job for him or herself, getting one of these jobs for a constituent or supporter might make the lawmaker more amenable to a gubernatorial request. States with extensive civil service systems hire more workers through merit testing, giving governors less power over the bureaucracy and fewer political bargaining chips. But sometimes patronage appointments can be more trouble than they are worth. Not only does a strong, merit-based civil service system help the governor give the state high-quality public service, it also helps him or her avoid scandals in the bureaucracy that can be tied to back to the governor.

Term Length and Term Limits A governor is more powerful if those with whom he or she deals in the political process believe that he or she may be around for a long time. Governors who will soon be leaving office have less to threaten anyone with or offer those with whom they negotiate. State bureaucrats, interest groups, and legislators (at least where no legislative term limits are in place) may be able just to wait out a governor who will soon be replaced, giving them little incentive to compromise. Of course, how long a governor serves

---

[73] Thad Beyle, "Being Governor," in Carl E. Van Horn, ed., *The State of the States*, 4th ed. (Washington, DC: CQ Press, 2006).

[74] Jim Siegel, "Strickland to Hire GOP Incumbents," *The Columbus (OH) Dispatch*, 23 July 2008, online edition.

depends in large part on voters, but two institutions also affect a governor's tenure potential: term length and term limits.

Institutional reforms in recent decades seem to have been inconsistent with respect to gubernatorial tenure. First, many states lengthened their governors' terms in the 1960s and 1970s, changing from two-year to four-year terms. Today, only governors in Vermont and New Hampshire have two-year terms, and even these states continue to consider moving to four-year terms. On the other hand, the states have also been moving quietly toward term-limiting their governors, with fully 37 states now doing so in some way. As a result of these diverging patterns, 32 states now allow only two consecutive four year terms, just as the 22nd Amendment does for the U.S. president.

Executive Orders Governors, like presidents, can issue **executive orders**, official pronouncements that mandate certain government actions.[75] Executive orders are public documents, typically filed with the secretary of state or some other official for public access. They have the force of law, but their scope is usually limited and they can be overturned by the current or future governors simply with another executive order. The power of governors to make executive orders varies as to whether they are authorized by statute, constitution, or simply tradition; by the areas of policy in which a governor is authorized to make such orders; and whether they can be reviewed by the legislature or are subject to any other restrictions.[76] Governors are typically authorized to make executive orders in four policy

areas: to reorganize or control the bureaucracy; to call out the National Guard to respond to emergencies or crises; to set up commissions to study particularly vexing public problems; or to respond to federal rules, regulations, and initiatives. The stronger the legal basis for these executive orders, the broader the scope of their power, and the fewer restrictions or less oversight of them, the more potent a tool they become for a governor.

Tools to Influence the Legislative Agenda

Governors have two institutional powers that help them influence the legislature's **policy agenda**. First, at the beginning of each legislative session, governors give a **State of the State (SOS) address** to the legislature,[77] a major speech much like the president's annual State of the Union address. The SOS address provides an opportunity for governors to identify the public problems that they think their legislatures should tackle in the coming session and to offer a list of proposals to address those problems.[78] As the symbolic kickoff of the legislative session and an important set-piece event on a state's political calendar, governors imbue their SOS addresses with rhetoric that reflects the state's values and interests as well as their own personalities.[79] Of course, the legislature is not in any way bound to follow the agenda the governor lays out in the SOS address, but traditionally, these proposals receive serious consideration. Indeed, legislators will complain of a lack of leadership if the governor's SOS address does not offer them clear guidance.

The other institutional power that lets governors set the legislative agenda is their ability

---

[75] Margaret R. Ferguson and Cynthia J. Bowling, "Executive Orders and Administrative Control," *Public Administration Review* 68(2008):S20–S28.

[76] Wall, op cit., pp. 187–88.

[77] In some states, this is called a budget address; in some states, governors will give both a SOS address and a budget address; sometimes during a governor's first term, his or her inaugural speech serves this function. Regardless of what it is called, all governors have some official way to communicate at the beginning of a legislative session what they want lawmakers to consider during it.

[78] Margaret R. Ferguson, "Gubernatorial Policy Leadership in the Fifty States" (Ph.D. diss., University of North Carolina at Chapel Hill, 1996).

[79] Barbara Ferrara, "The Effect of Gender on a Governor's Policy Agenda" (D.P.A. diss., University of Illinois at Springfield, 2010); J. Cherie Strachan, "Does Gubernatorial Rhetoric Matter? An Analysis of Gubernatorial Inaugural Rhetoric in Three Distinct States," presented at the 10th Annual State Politics and Policy Conference, University of Illinois at Springfield, 2010 ; Margaret R. Ferguson and Jay Barth, "Governors in the Legislative Arena: The Importance of Personality in Shaping Success," *Political Psychology* 23(2002):787–808.

to call the state legislature into **special session** once its regular session has been adjourned. Just the threat of a special session can be a potent weapon against part-time legislatures because it would require these members to sacrifice extra time from their full-time jobs and professions. Lawmakers may quickly acquiesce to the governor's legislative demands to avoid this overtime work, for which they do not receive extra pay.[80] Special sessions are especially important tools in those six states where the legislature only holds a regular session once every two years and those many other states where the length of their regular sessions is otherwise severely limited by law. Special sessions allow legislatures to deal with policy problems as they arise rather than waiting perhaps many months to reconvene.

What can make the power to call a special legislative session an effective tool for a governor is that, more than simply assembling legislators in a special session, governors are empowered to set a limited agenda for that session, in effect forcing lawmakers to consider specific issues. For example, in the summer and fall of 2009, governors in Indiana, California, West Virginia, and many other states called special sessions to force their state legislatures to deal with recession-related budget crises. Calling a special session not only shows the legislature that the governor really cares about an issue, but it also puts the media's spotlight on their deliberations, increasing pressure on lawmakers to act. On the other hand, while the governor can force the legislature into special session on a particular issue, he or she cannot force it to pass anything. A recalcitrant legislature can simply adjourn a special session without taking any action. Occasionally, a tug-of-war ensues as the governor keeps calling the legislature into special session and the legislature keeps adjourning itself without

acting.[81] But this sort of brouhaha is rare because the media, the public, and rank-and-file legislators quickly get fed up with the spectacle and the expense, giving both lawmakers and the governor strong incentive to settle their differences.[82]

Informal Powers—Unofficial, but Potent

In addition to the formal, institutional powers that states give their governors as a matter of official public policy, the circumstances surrounding the office, the state, and the incumbent him or herself also help determine how effective a governor can be in running the state. These informal powers are not as easy to see or compare as are the institutional powers, but that does not make them any less important in understanding how a given state's governors, or any given governor within a state, does the job. Like formal powers, their potency can vary among states, but they can also vary among governors within a state, sometimes even over the term of a single governor. Some informal powers are hard to study. For example, some governors are just more charismatic or intelligent than others. While these characteristics can certainly affect a governor's performance, assessing them systematically would be difficult. But several important dimensions of a governor's informal power are comparable across the states and across time and are based on the office itself rather than on the person holding it. Of course, just as with institutional powers, the effectiveness of informal powers in helping governors manage a state and achieve their policy agendas depends in large part on the skills of the governor in using them, perhaps another informal power, itself.

Head of State As mentioned earlier, the governor is a state's symbolic "head of state,"

[80] Legislators usually receive expense money for these special sessions to cover their meals, hotels, and so on, but they do not typically receive extra salary for them.

[81] Doug Finke, "Under Pressure: Groups Push Jones on Budget Cuts Vote," (Springfield, IL.) *State Journal-Register*, 4 October 2007, p. 1.

[82] Greg Bluestein, "Special Sessions on Budgets Costly," *State Journal-Register* (Springfield, IL), 25 July 2009, p. 7.

representing the state to people both within and outside of the state, just as the queen of England does for her country and the president does for the United States as a whole. Using this symbolic role, governors can gain **political capital** by undertaking largely ceremonial duties that expose them to people around the state in a positive way. Greeting school children, giving commencement speeches, cutting ribbons on public projects, and so forth allow people to see a governor in a favorable, nonpolitical light. As head of state, governors also gain influence because modern-day Americans want executive leadership from our government. When we think about government acting to help us, we

Surrounded by state legislators and some of those affected by the legislation, North Carolina Governor Beverly Perdue signs a bill into law.

Comparisons Help Us Understand

THE INSTITUTIONAL POWER OF THE GOVERNORS

Figure 7.1 shows how governors' formal, institutional powers vary around the country. This index of gubernatorial powers is made up of indicators based on the number of independently elected executives in a state and a governor's appointment power over leaders of state agencies, term length and term limits, budget control, veto strength, and executive order strength. These powers are all based on state laws and constitutional provisions that states have adopted primarily as a way of establishing a governorship with the level of power and control over the state bureaucracy and policy making that their policy makers and residents think appropriate. Like all indicators of social science concepts, this one is not perfect, but it gives us an idea about the types of people and places that think their governors should be more or less powerful.[83]

First, you see that some of the states in the South have weaker governorships. This is a legacy of the reaction to the strong **Reconstruction era** governors in the post–Civil War era. Another apparent pattern is that more populous and urban states tend to have more powerful governorships, whereas smaller, rural states tend to have weaker ones. This might be a case of states equipping their governors with just the level of power they need to deal with the forces at work in their states. Governors in large or urban states must contend both with more diverse public problems and with a broader range of actors in the policy-making arena, such as big-city mayors, strong unions, major industries and corporations, and so forth. Perhaps these governors need greater formal power just to do their jobs as well as those governors with less formal power can do their jobs in the small, rural states where they are big fish in a small pond. What other patterns do you detect in this figure? What state-level characteristics have you read about in earlier chapters that might be relevant here? For example, how might legislative professionalism factor in here? What other historical, institutional, or demographic features might lead a state to want or need a stronger governor or a weaker one? Try both to develop hypotheses in this regard and to test those arguments by looking at the data in Figure 7.1

[83] Beyle and Ferguson, op cit.; Pamela M. Prah, "Massachusetts Gov Rated Most Powerful," *Stateline.org*, 9 March 2007, online ed.

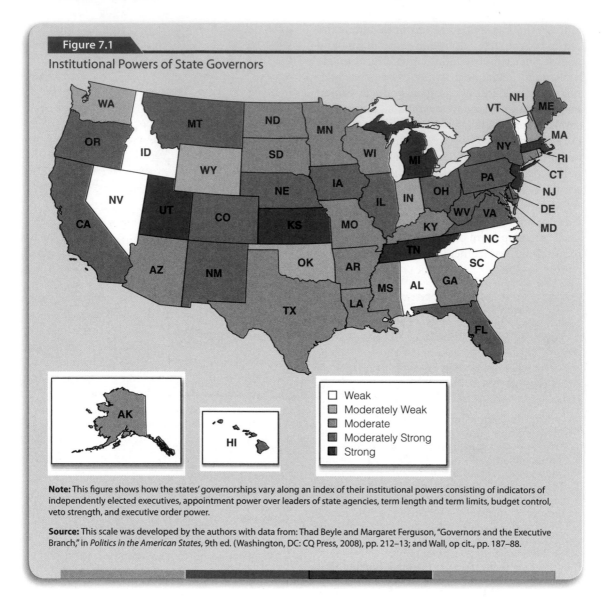

Figure 7.1

Institutional Powers of State Governors

Legend:
- □ Weak
- Moderately Weak
- Moderate
- Moderately Strong
- Strong

Note: This figure shows how the states' governorships vary along an index of their institutional powers consisting of indicators of independently elected executives, appointment power over leaders of state agencies, term length and term limits, budget control, veto strength, and executive order power.

Source: This scale was developed by the authors with data from: Thad Beyle and Margaret Ferguson, "Governors and the Executive Branch," in *Politics in the American States*, 9th ed. (Washington, DC: CQ Press, 2008), pp. 212–13; and Wall, op cit., pp. 187–88.

often think about the governor, the president, or the mayor rather than the state legislature, the Congress, or the city council. Governors can benefit from this attitude by stepping into the role forthrightly, pursuing an active policy agenda in the legislature and taking a strong hand with the executive agencies. Although other actors in the political system may sometimes chafe under such an "imperial" governor, like the general public, they too expect the governor to lead and will complain if such leadership does not materialize. Indeed, one study found that even in a highly partisan state legislature, bills advocated by the governor were regularly supported even by members of the opposite party—except during election years.[84]

Besides the ceremonial duties that governors use to burnish their image, they often

[84] Thad E. Hall, "Changes in Legislative Support for the Governor's Program over Time," *Legislative Studies Quarterly* 27(2002):107–22.

take symbolic actions as head of state to demonstrate sympathy with their constituents in a politically useful way. In 2009, for example, governors frequently demonstrated that they were aware of and working to fix the economic recession and states' budget crises. Delaware's Markell was among many who cancelled their inaugural balls in January 2009 to show fiscal responsibility and concern. As an alternative, Markell led a "Weekend of Service" to help those in need.[85] Other governors, like Connecticut's Rell and Kentucky's Steve Beshear, very publicly took pay cuts and furlough days right along with other state workers.[86] In 2010, governors of states on the Gulf of Mexico frequently made themselves visible on the beaches and at sea demanding action from British Petroleum and the federal government to clean up the oil spill from the Deepwater Horizon disaster. These heads of states were not only trying to solve the problem, but they were also demonstrating to their constituents that their state governments felt their pain and were working to help them. No other state government official has as much right to this role as the governor. Such empathy and outrage can also be good politics for governors seeking reelection or pursuing higher office.

But being the head of state can also backfire if things do not go well. A governor who is not a strong and visible leader may lose influence with the people and state officials. Louisiana's Bobby Jindal likely took a lesson from the failures of former Governor Kathleen Blanco, who was roundly chastised for being a weak head of state during the aftermath of Hurricane Katrina in 2005. Jindal gave many angry press conferences from the beaches of the gulf during the 2010 crisis. In an earlier example, some have argued that his failure in the head of state role in his state's severe budget crisis, rather than objections to any specific actions that he took, was in large part what led to California Governor Gray Davis's recall ouster in 2003.[87] Their symbolic role as head of state also leads governors to bear the brunt of the blame for any state actions that people don't like, whether or not they had much to do with them. A quaint example of this from the 1950s and 1960s was a reaction in many states to their initial adoption of the sales tax. Upset with the increased paperwork and expense, shopkeepers would often ring up the price of an item at the cash register, adding, "...and a penny for the governor."[88]

Public Opinion Related to the power of being head of state is the effect of public opinion on a governor's informal power. Governors have long used the argument that their statewide electoral mandate gives them the backing of the state's people for whatever they want to do. Since the advent of public opinion polling, a governor's support in the state can be assessed more frequently and followed as it changes throughout the term.[89] A governor riding high in the polls will be quick to point out this fact to obstinate legislators, bureaucrats, or the media. Lawmakers, in particular, are much more susceptible to the blandishments of a popular governor because they have to face the voters themselves. On the other hand, a governor's sliding poll numbers may embolden opposition lawmakers.

Governors monitor their ratings closely through their own private polls (sometimes run through their campaign offices to avoid any suggestion of impropriety) and do what they

[85] Emily Bazar, "Many Governors Cut Glitz from Inaugurations," *USA Today*, 9 December 2008, online edition.

[86] Mark Pazniokas, "Governor Takes Symbolic Step to Reduce State Deficit," *The* (Hartford, CT) *Courant*, 14 January 2009, online edition.; Jack Brammer, Jim Warren, and Beth Musgrave, "Beshear Takes 10% Pay Cut," *Lexington Herald-Leader*, 9 December 2008.

[87] Michael Lewis, "The Personal Is the Antipolitical," *New York Times Magazine* 153(2003):40–130.

[88] Philip J. Roberts, *A Penny for the Governor, a Dollar for Uncle Sam: Income Taxation in Washington* (Seattle: University of Washington Press, 2002).

[89] Richard G. Niemi, Thad Beyle, and Lee Sigelman, "Gubernatorial, Senatorial, and State-Level Presidential Job Approval: The U.S. Officials Job Approval Ratings (JAR) Collection," *State Politics and Policy Quarterly* 2(2002):215–29.

can to keep them high, such as using their head of state role to appear at popular, nonpolitical functions, like county fairs and state championship sporting events. Some governors go even further, like when California's Schwarzenegger executed an extensive and sophisticated public image "makeover" after his poll numbers began to drop in his first term.[90] But much of a governor's popularity is beyond his or her immediate control. As a governor's term progresses, he or she will have to make choices that disappoint and anger some members of the public, causing his or her popularity to decline over time, just as it does for presidents. But while one study found that this leads to governors having lower popularity than, for example, U.S. senators when a reelection campaign begins, unlike senators, governors can use their other formal and informal powers to improve their popularity substantially during the campaign.[91]

Other factors beyond a governor's control can also affect his or her popularity. For example, governors of large states tend to have lower ratings than governors of less populated states. Larger and densely populated states tend to have more, bigger, and more complex public problems than other states, making the job of governor more difficult. The national economy is another strong influence on gubernatorial popularity that is largely out of a governor's hands.[92] On the other hand, the state economy also has an impact here, and governors probably have at least some control over this.[93] Governors' actual or perceived handling of major state crises can also affect their popularity. West Virginia's Joe Manchin saw his popularity rise dramatically when he was seen as handling a coal-mining disaster effectively

in 2006. And on the other hand, a scandal, whether caused by a governor or his or her appointees, can reduce gubernatorial popularity quickly.[94]

Mass Media Attention The governor's office is especially well positioned to gain political capital from the effective use of print, broadcast, and online media, and the special attention they get from the media relative to other state policy makers is one of their primary informal powers. Of course, the governor is clearly an important and well-known person whose actions are significant to a lot of people. But governors attract special media attention simply because it is just much easier to report on and understand state government by focusing on the governor. The governor is a single, authoritative news source. Who speaks authoritatively for the legislature, the courts, or the bureaucracy? No one. Who seems more reliable and unbiased on any given issue, the governor or an interest group spokesperson? Often, it is the former. Certainly, significant, thoughtful, and honest people work in all those other institutions, but in none is there a single, recognizable news source that a reporter can go to time and again for the final word on that institution's position on an issue.

News organizations make money by attracting readers, viewers, or listeners. It is easier to do this by discussing a familiar person rather than a more obscure official—like the speaker of the state house—who, although important, would need to be introduced to the media consumer before getting to the heart of the story. Americans' attention span for political news is extremely short, especially for news about state politics.[95] The governor is just

[90] Gary Delsohn, "Governor Embarks on Image Change," *Sacramento Bee*, 26 July 2005, online edition.

[91] Brown and Jacobson, op cit.

[92] James D. King and Jeffrey E. Cohen, "What Determines a Governor's Popularity?" *State Politics and Policy Quarterly* 5(2005):225–47.

[93] Jeffrey E. Cohen and James D. King, "Relative Unemployment and Gubernatorial Popularity," *Journal of Politics* 66(2004):167–82.

[94] Jay Barth and Margaret R. Ferguson, "American Governors and their Constituents: The Relationship between Gubernatorial Personality and Public Approval," *State Politics and Policy Quarterly* 2(2002):268–82.

[95] G. Patrick Lynch, "The Media in State and Local Politics," in Mark J. Rozell, ed., *Media Power, Media Politics* (Lanham, MD: Rowman & Littlefield, 2003).

easier to understand than the legislature—both for media consumers and for reporters. The governor is like the boss of the state or the parent of the family; people are familiar with this role, even if it does distort reality. Legislatures are complex, mysterious, and unfamiliar, so it is harder to write a relatively short, understandable news story about them. It is also no accident that governors' power and prestige rose in the 1960s and 1970s just as television became the main source of political news for Americans.[96] Governors are particularly attractive for television news, where stories are much shorter than in newspapers and rely more on pictures. A governor speaking at a press conference or giving a speech makes pretty good television; a governor touring a disaster site makes even better television. On the other hand, the state legislature in session makes bad television (except as a background shot while the reporter speaks); legislative negotiations and discussions are even worse.

Governors also work hard to make the reporters' job easy. They hire professional media relations staff (many of whom are former statehouse reporters themselves) to develop effective press releases and manufacture television-friendly media events at times convenient for news deadlines. Some governors even send out prepackaged video clips of themselves making brief comments on current issues. This allows those TV stations without the resources to have their own statehouse reporter—which is most stations, these days—to air footage that looks like their own reporter actually interviewed the governor. Of course, governors are not likely to send out footage that makes themselves look bad, so while they help the station get good video for the nightly news, they present themselves in a good light without fear of any tough questions from reporters. Of course,

while this can only help a governor's popularity, it raises serious questions about the quality and ethics of journalism about state government.

Gubernatorial Staff Each governor employs a sizable body of personal staff who work directly for him or her in whatever way the governor wishes to arrange them.[97] Their staff includes press spokespeople, legislative liaisons, and deputy governors to coordinate policy areas that spread out over a variety of agencies, such as education or drug enforcement. Unlike cabinet secretaries and other official managerial appointees, these staff members are solely responsible to the governor and should have no mixed loyalties. They have no agencies or interest groups to appease, and their appointments typically are not subject to legislative approval. Their staff serves as the governor's extra eyes, ears, feet, and hands, greatly extending his or her reach and information-gathering ability and acting as a proxy for the governor.[98]

The size of a governor's staff varies dramatically across states, from a dozen close aides and secretaries to an extended office of well over 100 staffers working in a variety of roles. Not surprisingly, the largest governor's offices are in the more populous states.[99] In some states, the budget office is considered part of the governor's staff. This unit has the primary responsibility for developing the governor's budget proposal and monitoring the budget's execution throughout the fiscal year. As governors have gained more budgetary authority in recent decades, these offices have been increasingly shifted to governors' direct control rather than being independent units. For many governors, the state budget office now acts as one of the main tools for controlling the bureaucracy and guiding policy, much

[96] Dometrius, op cit.

[97] National Governors Association, *Governor's Office Operations: The Many Roles of the Governor's Chief of Staff.* (Washington, DC: National Governors Association, 2006).

[98] Robert J. Dilger, "A Comparative Analysis of Gubernatorial Enabling Resources," *State and Local Government Review* 26(1995):118–26.

[99] Margaret R. Ferguson, *The Executive Branch of State Government* (Santa Barbara, CA: ABC-CLIO, 2006), pp. 176–79.

the same way that presidents now use the federal Office of Management and Budget.[100]

The Governor in the State's Political Environment

Although the governor is the head of state, chief executive, and the single most important political figure in most states most of the time, he or she is only one actor in a large and complex political system. Therefore, a governor's effectiveness not only depends on his or her formal and informal powers, it is also affected by the political environment of the state. Elsewhere in this book, you read in detail about many of these other actors and aspects of the state political environment, but in this section, we discuss two aspects of the environment that have very special impacts on a governor's ability to govern: the partisan balance in the legislature and other rivals for power. Like governors' formal and informal powers, these vary among the states in relatively clear and observable ways.

Partisan Balance in the State Legislature

A governor's ability to make public policy, and the ways in which a governor goes about trying to make public policy, depends in large part on the partisan balance in his or her state legislature. Lawmakers of the governor's party are often thought of, and often think of themselves, as loyal lieutenants of the governor. In particular, an important job of the legislative leaders of the governor's party is to marshal the party's members behind the governor's bills.[101] Therefore, governors whose party is in the majority in both legislative chambers, a situation known as **unified government,** can get their bills passed more easily—if their party sticks together. Of course, this is not always as simple as it sounds, since the legislature is an independent branch with its own interests and great pride in its role in the policy-making process. For example, in 2007, when Massachusetts's Patrick became the first Democratic governor in the Bay State in 16 years, the dashed expectation for a less rancorous legislative-executive relationship left some longing for the good old days of **divided government,** when at least one chamber of the legislature is not controlled by the governor's party.[102]

But in reality, **divided government** usually makes it more difficult for a governor to pass his or her legislative agenda.[103] Governors are less aggressive in pursuing their legislative agendas, more conciliatory, and more open to compromise when facing a legislature controlled by the other party,[104] and each of these reduces his or her ability to control policy. Under divided government, not only does the legislative majority have basic ideological differences with the governor, but the party also has an electoral incentive at least to offer alternative positions on key issues, if not to sabotage the governor's efforts actively. Of course, when the legislature and the governor are at loggerheads publicly, the governor's advantage with the media really helps in the battle over public opinion, if he or she handles the press skillfully. Sometimes the legislature can work against the governor so subtly that the public does not

[100] Forsythe, op cit.

[101] Malcolm E. Jewell and Marcia Lynn Wicker, *Legislative Leadership in the American States* (Ann Arbor, MI: University of Michigan Press, 1994).

[102] Edward L. Glaeser, "Blessings of a Divided Government," *The Boston Globe*, 1 May 2009, online edition.

[103] Cynthia J. Bowling and Margaret R. Ferguson, "Divided Government, Interest Representation, and Policy Differences: Competing Explanations of Gridlock in the Fifty States," *Journal of Politics* 63(2001):182–206; Ferguson, 2006, op cit., pp. 195–96.

[104] Chad Murphy, Martin Johnson, and Shaun Bowler, "Executive Speeches and Divided Government: Is There Common Ground in a House Divided?" presented at the 8th Annual State Politics and Policy Conference, Temple University, 2008.

recognize its obstructionism. Divided government has become much more common in recent decades, encouraged by legislative professionalism and the personalization of gubernatorial campaigns.[105]

Rivals for Power

Finally, a governor can be more influential in state politics and government if a state has fewer other heavyweight political actors who can act as rivals. A major factor here is the number and importance of independently elected statewide executives in state government, and we'll discuss these at some length in the next section. But outside of state government, other potential gubernatorial rivals may exist. In states with large urban centers, major corporations, or a large federal government presence, state government can be pushed from the front page by mayors, business leaders, and federal officials who are significant actors in the political process. Governors with less competition for political attention and power in their state typically have more informal influence. Thus, the governors of New York and Illinois are often less well known and less influential in their states than are the mayors of New York City and Chicago, respectively.

On the other hand, these offices give rising politicians a place to learn the trade of executive management and politics where the stakes aren't as high and the media spotlight isn't as bright as in the governor's mansion. In this way, independently elected statewide offices act as a training ground for future governors, senators, and members of Congress. Notably, many of the women who have become governor in recent years came up through these offices, such as former attorneys general Granholm of Michigan and Gregoire of Washington and former lieutenant governor Perdue of North Carolina.[106]

Indeed, the existence of these offices in a state tends to formalize the political career ladder, reducing confusion (and perhaps opportunity) in state elections, for good or ill.[107]

The State Bureaucracy

The bureaucracy of the executive branch is the quiet giant of state government. Although the media often report about the legislature, the governor, and even the courts, it is the bureaucracy that does most of the day-to-day work of state government, from teaching college students, to testing people for their driver's licenses, to guarding people convicted of crimes, to caring for patients in public hospitals, to regulating cemeteries and carnivals, and so much more. A generic term for the people who work in the executive branch agencies is "bureaucrat," but the disparaging connotations of that word does a disservice to the people who, with an incredible array of talent and great dedication to public service, bring you state government services every day. State workers are hired for their specific expertise to carry out the work that voters and policy makers want done. They are accountants, doctors, engineers, teachers, carpenters, social workers, police officers, and virtually every other profession and trade you can think of.

In high school civics, you learned that bureaucrats simply execute policy set by policy makers, and this certainly is mainly what they do. But because of their expertise and experience, and because of the realities of government in action, bureaucrats also determine, or at least influence, much public policy in the process of doing their work, both formally and informally. Formally, high-level administrators write **administrative rules** to implement state law. By necessity, legislation is written in general language. Legislators have neither the time

[105] Morris P. Fiorina, *Divided Government*, 2nd ed. (Boston: Allyn & Bacon, 1996).

[106] Judith R. Saidel, Xiaolei Chen, and Alison C. Olin, "Women in State Policy Leadership, 1998–2005: An Analysis of Slow and Uneven Progress," a report of the Center for Women in Government and Civil Society, University at Albany, State University of New York (Winter 2006).

[107] Alan Ehrenhalt, "A Deep Bench," *Governing*, 9–10 July 2009.

nor the expertise to go into detail about, say, how a college engineering curriculum ought to be written or how deer hunting ought to be regulated. The agencies charged by the legislature with carrying out these general policies use their training and experience, and their highly skilled staff, to write these detailed rules and regulations. Formal administrative rules have the force of law, although the legislature has the power to countermand them before or after they go into effect.[108] But in practice, because those who write these rules generally try hard to follow legislative intent and because lawmakers simply don't have the time, motivation, or expertise to scrutinize every proposed rule, most administrative rules go into effect without much oversight.

Bureaucrats, even **street-level bureaucrats**, also make policy informally through the decisions they make every day that have the power of the state behind them.[109] So, for example, when Officer Caroline Tolbert of the Iowa State Patrol chooses between giving you a warning or writing you a ticket when she catches you driving five miles per hour over the speed limit on Interstate 80, it may matter greatly to you personally, but it isn't public policy.

Summary

American state governors are among the most powerful and important public officials in the country today. The 50 governors are an impressive bunch, with extensive training and experience behind them and jobs as cabinet secretaries, ambassadors, corporate and not-for-profit CEOs in front of them, In fact, at any given time, the chances are good that one of them will become president or vice president. Governors today are also a more diverse group than ever before. Because the office is so significant in American politics and government, it is much prized by ambitious political actors, which has led to skyrocketing campaign spending. In state government, governors have three basic roles—manager of the bureaucracy, chief policy maker, and intergovernmental relations manager. To do these jobs, the states provide their governors with more institutional power than at any other time in history, and their informal power can be tremendous if used skillfully. A state's political environment, including the partisan balance in the legislature and the existence of other centers of political power, also influences a governor's effectiveness. Besides governors, most states elect several other statewide executive officials, and the governor divides up the state's policy making and implementation duties with these officials. The state government's bureaucracy, those tens of thousands of expert public servants who do the day-to-day jobs of government, also have a major role both in policy implementation and in policy making.

---

[108] Brian J. Gerber, Cherie Maestas, and Nelson C. Dometrius, "State Legislative Influence over Agency Rulemaking: The Utility of Ex Ante Review," *State Politics and Policy Quarterly* 5(2005):24–46.

[109] Norma M. Riccucci, *How Management Works: Street-Level Bureaucrats and Welfare Reform* (Washington, DC: Georgetown University Press, 2005).

Key Terms

Administrative rules

Amendatory veto

Appropriations bill

Bureaucracy

Civil service system

Divided government

Gubernatorial powers

Head of state

Line-item veto

National Governors Association

Neutral competence

Patronage job

Policy agenda

Political accountability

Political capital

Progressive era

Reconstruction era

Reduction veto

Self-financing candidate

Special session

State of the State address

Street-level bureaucrats

Unified government

Discussion Questions

(1) What factors are responsible for the dramatic rise in the cost of gubernatorial campaigns?

(2) What is the typical profile of a governor? What sorts of jobs do they have before and after serving as governor, and why do we see the patterns we do in a state's political career ladder?

(3) How important is a governor's veto power? How do these powers vary across the states? What factors affect a state's need or desire for a strong governor?

(4) How do the formal and informal powers of governors differ?

(5) What effect does the partisan balance in a state's legislature have on gubernatorial power?

(6) How do the values of **neutral competence** and **political accountability** influence the debate over a governor's and legislature's control over the bureaucracy? How might these values be prized differently for different policy areas?

Suggested Readings

Beyle, Thad, and Margaret Ferguson. 2008. "Governors and the Executive Branch." In Virginia Gray and Russell L. Hanson, eds., *Politics in the American States*, 9th ed. Washington, DC: CQ Press.

Carsey, Thomas M. 2000. *Campaign Dynamics: The Race for Governor*. Ann Arbor, MI: University of Michigan Press.

Ferguson, Margaret Robertson. 2003. "Chief Executive Success in the Legislative Arena." *State Politics and Policy Quarterly* 3:158–82.

Ferguson, Margaret R., ed. 2006. *The Executive Branch of State Government: People, Process, and Politics*. Santa Barbara, CA: ABC-CLIO.

Forsythe, Dall W. 2004. *Memos to the Governor: An Introduction to State Budgeting*. Washington, DC: Georgetown University Press.

Klarner, Carl E., and Andrew Karch. 2008. "Why Do Governors Issue Vetoes? The Impact of Individual and Institutional Influences." *Political Research Quarterly* 61(4):574–84.

Leal, David L. 2006. *Electing America's Governors: The Politics of Executive Elections*. New York: Palgrave Macmillan.

Merriner, James L. 2008. *The Man Who Emptied Death Row: Governor George Ryan and the Politics of Crime*. Carbondale, IL: University of Southern Illinois Press.

Morehouse, Sarah McCally. 1998. *The Governor as Party Leader: Campaigning and Governing*. Ann Arbor, MI: University of Michigan Press.

Niemi, Richard G., Thad Beyle, and Lee Sigelman, eds. 2002. "Special Issue: Approval Ratings of Public Officials in the American States: Causes and Effects." *State Politics and Policy Quarterly* 2:213–316.

Sabato, Larry. 1983. *Goodbye to Good-Time Charlie: The American Governorship Transformed,* 2nd ed. Washington, DC: Congressional Quarterly Press.

Sinclair, Upton. 1994 [1935]. *I, Candidate for Governor: And How I Got Licked*. Berkeley, CA: University of California Press.

Weintraub, Daniel. 2008. *Party of One: Arnold Schwarzenegger and the Rise of the Independent Voter*. Sausalito, CA: PoliPointPress.

Suggested Media Resources

American Governors (http://www.globalcomputing.com/GovernorsContent.htm): Private website that is conveniently linked to the website of each U.S. state governor.

State of the State speeches (http://www.stateline.org/live/ViewPage.action?siteNodeId=1 52&languageId=1&contentId=-1): Stateline.org has linked all governors' state of the state speeches since 2000 to this page.

Websites

Border Governors Conference (http://www.bordergovernorsconference.com/): The BGCis an example of groups of governors organized around a common interest. It is an annual meeting of the four U.S. governors whose states border the Mexican border and their six counterparts in Mexico. The BGA also conducts research and holds bimonthly discussion groups among gubernatorial staff.

Democratic Governors Association (http://www.democraticgovernors.org/) and Republican Governors Association (http://thegopcomeback.com/): The DGA and the RGA are voluntary political organizations designed to support the reelection of governors, and the election of new governors, of their respective parties. These organizations raise money, develop strategy, and develop press releases and some research to help shape the policy agenda and for partisan political purposes regarding U.S. governors' races. They are not affiliated with the nonpartisan National Governors Association.

National Governors Association (http://www.nga.org/portal/site/nga): The NGA is a bipartisan organization of the nation's governors, which shares best practices, conducts research, holds conferences, and lobbies Congress and the president for the common interests of the states and the governors. The NGA website has lots of information on individual governors and links to their sites.

8

The State Court System

INTRODUCTION

S tate court systems dispense the vast majority of justice in the United States, and these state court systems are in a state of flux. Big issues about the implementation of justice and the selection of judges are facing the states. In this chapter, we describe the wide variation of courts and judicial activity among the states and consider the effects of these differences. Understanding state courts and how they work can have a significant impact on your life—especially when it's your day in court. Beyond this, studying the state courts can tell us much about the states and the people and politics in them.

Some people think they know a good deal about the legal system, but these beliefs are often mistaken. Courtroom and law enforcement dramas have long been television staples, and now we can even see the "real" criminal justice system in action on *Cops*, *Judge Joe Brown*, and the like. The long-term popularity and variety of these shows—dramas, comedies, "reality" shows—show Americans' great interest in crime and the criminal justice system. But perceptions of the judicial system acquired from television often give a distorted view of this important branch of government.

The administration of justice has been an aspect of government with which people have been deeply concerned throughout history, because those who interpret and enforce the law—judges and the police—literally have life-and-death power over us and the force of the government behind them. Not surprisingly, the American states have spent considerable effort over the years trying to get their judicial systems right. As a result, the three themes of this book—institutions, reform, and comparison—become thoroughly intermingled when discussing the courts. Because it seems to be so much harder to get our judicial institutions right, because the social conditions surrounding the courts change so often, and because the courts must do so many different jobs, the institutions of the states' judicial branches vary far more than those of either their executive or legislative branches. In this chapter, we explore both the causes and the effects of this institutional variation in an attempt to understand the *real* reality of our state court systems.

The Two Dimensions of the American Legal System: Federal versus State Courts and Civil versus Criminal Law

There are two basic dimensions that characterize the American judicial system: state versus federal courts and criminal versus civil law. Much of the confusion about state court systems can be clarified by understanding these dimensions.

State Courts and Federal Courts

As you learned in Chapter 2, much of American politics and government is determined—and complicated—by federalism, and the judicial system is no different. While most people can easily distinguish between their state legislature and Congress and between their governor and the president, the distinction between federal and state courts is often harder for people to understand.

Every state is served by parallel systems of state and federal courts. That is, each state has its own court system, and the federal court system also covers each state. The court system that a case is dealt with in depends primarily on the nature of the crime or conflict involved. Most simply, if the crime or conflict is about a federal law, then the case goes into the federal court system; if it is about a state law, then it goes into the state court system. But whether a law is a state law or a federal law is somewhat idiosyncratic, depending on the actions of Congress and the state legislatures over the years. However, we can make some generalizations.

First, it is important to understand that, by far, most legal cases in the United States are

handled in state courts, including almost all civil cases (except bankruptcies, all of which are handled by the federal courts). For example, in 2006 (the last year for which these data are available), while 88,094 criminal cases went through federal courts, fully 9,312,716 went through the state courts.[1] Most of the crimes that you have heard of—assault, murder, robbery, and so forth—as well as almost all traffic infractions, are violations of state laws or local ordinances. Federal crimes typically involve federal officials (like assassinating the president), interstate activity (like taking a stolen car across a state border), or activities that were outlawed by Congress for some historical reason (like bank robbery and kidnapping). The proportion of state versus federal cases is even more lopsided for civil cases (which we discuss in the next section).

For some cases, it is not obvious whether state or federal law is at issue. In such cases, the state and federal prosecuting authorities usually negotiate which of them will pursue the charges, with the decision often being based on the resources and interests of the arresting authorities and, especially, who made the initial arrest. Sometimes state and local law come into direct conflict. Courts usually hold that federal law trumps any conflicting state law, but sometimes political considerations change this. For example, federal drug laws ban the possession and sale of marijuana, but the Obama administration has chosen not to prosecute people in the 14 states that allow the use of the drug for medicinal purposes.[2]

Criminal Law and Civil Law

The distinction between criminal and civil law is also central to understanding the state court system, since state courts deal with both types of law.[3] Criminal cases involve the government prosecuting a person for violating a criminal

---

[1] See the National Center for State Courts (http://www.ncsconline.org) and the Bureau of Justice Statistics (http://www.ojp.usdoj.gov/bjs/).

[2] These states are: Alaska, California, Colorado, Hawaii, New Jersey, Maine, Michigan, Montana, Nevada, New Mexico, Oregon, Rhode Island, Vermont, and Washington. See *State-by-State Medical Marijuana Laws* (Washington, DC: Marijuana Policy Project, 2008).

[3] Lawrence Baum, *American Courts Process and Policy*, 6th ed. (Belmont, CA: Cengage, 2007), ch. 7.

When federal laws and state laws conflict, federal law is supreme. However, sometimes the federal government informally defers to state law in such circumstances, such as the Obama administration's decision not to prosecute people who possess medically prescribed marijuana in states that allow it.

statute. The person may be charged with doing something that is prohibited (like breaking into a house) or not doing something that is required (like paying taxes). The idea is that if a person (or corporation or some other entity) has violated a criminal statute, he or she or it has committed an offense against the people of a jurisdiction. Criminal complaints are therefore initiated by government prosecutors in the name of "the people." The head prosecutors tasked with bringing such complaints have different titles in different state court systems, usually something like "district attorney" or "state's attorney," and they are typically elected at the county level.[4] These officials supervise an office of sometimes dozens of assistant prosecutors, depending on the size of their jurisdiction. Their duties include following up on the criminal investigations of the police, deciding which cases are worth bringing to trial, negotiating with defense attorneys, and acting as the people's lawyer in cases that go to trial.

Civil cases involve noncriminal legal conflicts between people, corporations, or even governments or governmental units. Such cases can arise out of a dispute over a contract, where one party to the contract feels that another

party has not lived up to his or her obligations, or a dispute where one party claims to have been injured (whether bodily, psychologically, or monetarily) by another party, such as in an automobile accident. Civil cases are brought by the **plaintiff**, the party that feels he or she (or it, in the case of a corporation or governmental unit) has been injured, against the **defendant**, the party that allegedly has done the injury. The case is all about the plaintiff trying to get the defendant to redress the injury, usually by giving the plaintiff a certain amount of money. Lawyers in civil cases make arguments based on case law, or **common law**, a traditional legal system about disputes over contracts and injuries that has evolved case by case over the last 500 years or so, first in England and then in the United States.[5]

Thus, although civil and criminal cases differ from one another, they have one fundamental commonality: They both involve a conflict between two parties that is (or may be) brought before a judge for an authoritative resolution. The role of the courts regarding both civil and criminal law is to resolve specific disputes between specific people or groups by applying the law to the facts of the case as presented by the disputants. This role is the same whether the dispute is over an accusation of murder or an accusation that the landlord failed to fix a leaky faucet.

The Organization of State Court Systems

Different states organize their court systems in different ways, and these institutional differences can affect the efficiency, and perhaps even the fairness, of the administration of justice. In general, however, most state court systems have the same basic hierarchical structure, with each level having its unique role in the process. Figure 8.1 shows this generic state court system structure. In very broad strokes, **trial**

[4] In a few states, these head prosecutors are appointed by the governor or another executive official.

[5] Lawrence M. Friedman, *A History of American Law* (New York: Touchstone, 2005).

Figure 8.1

The Structure of a Generic State Court System

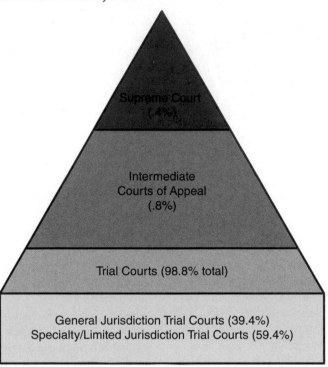

Supreme Court
(.4%)

Intermediate
Courts of Appeal
(.8%)

Trial Courts (98.8% total)

General Jurisdiction Trial Courts (39.4%)
Specialty/Limited Jurisdiction Trial Courts (59.4%)

Note: The figures given were the percentage of the total number of cases disposed of in all state court systems across the country by each type of court in 2006, the most recent year for which these data are available.

Source: Shauna M. Strickland, Chantal G. Bromage, Sarah A. Gibson, and William Raftery, *State Court Caseload Statistics, 2007* (Williamsburg, VA: National Center for State Courts, 2008).

courts establish the facts of a case and apply the law, **intermediate courts of appeal** evaluate questions of fairness about the trial, and the **supreme court** decides whether a law or legal procedure is allowable under the state's constitution. The pyramidal structure of Figure 8.1 reflects both the fact that these courts' authority flows hierarchically from the top to the bottom and the fact that the number of cases handled by these courts drops dramatically as you move up the pyramid.

Trial Courts

If you have ever seen *Law & Order*, *Judge Judy*, or almost any other courtroom drama or reality show, you have been watching a trial court. Television shows focus on trial courts because that is really the only level of court that anyone would really want to watch. The proceedings of intermediate courts of appeal and supreme courts are exciting only to those involved in the cases themselves and to legal scholars. It is also appropriate that trial courts get the most public attention because the vast majority of cases begin and end there. Indeed, virtually every case starts in a trial court, and only about 1 percent[6] of them get any farther than that (see Figure 8.1).

For both civil and criminal cases, trial courts have two basic functions: to establish

[6] Shauna M. Strickland, Chantal G. Bromage, Sarah A. Gibson, and William Raftery, *State Court Caseload Statistics, 2007* (Williamsburg, VA: National Center for State Courts, 2008).

the facts of the case, and to apply the relevant law to those facts. As straightforward as this may sound, the process contains considerable room for judgment—and sometimes, for error.

Procedures and Decision Making The fundamental job of any court system is to resolve disputes between parties and to back that resolution with the authority of the state. Trial courts are the first—and usually last—formal step in this conflict resolution process.

Trial courts determine the facts of a case and apply the law to it. Case facts are often the subject of dispute between the parties, making this no small task. For example, a prosecutor claims that Pat McConnell stole a specific Nokia cell phone from a 2003 Ford Taurus with Kansas license plate number XCJ 420 in the early morning hours of October 24, 2010, in front of 5504 Joe Sayers Avenue. By pleading not guilty, McConnell disputes this claim of fact—he did not take that phone from that car on that day. The court may then be asked to make a definitive resolution of this question.

The parties may also disagree about which specific statute or case law applies to these facts. So even if McConnell indeed took that phone from that car on that night, should this action fall under the category of burglary or breaking and entering? Questions of the application of law are also debated and decided in trial court.

Like all courts in the American system of justice, trial courts resolve legal disputes between two parties through a process of **adversarial argument** and **adjudication** by a neutral third party. Both sides make their best argument in court, usually with the help of a trial lawyer, an attorney who specializes in working with clients going through trials. Each side makes its case through legal and logical analysis, by questioning witnesses to help establish the facts of the case, and by presenting any documents and physical evidence that support their side of the disputed story. This process will sound familiar to viewers of courtroom dramas; but unlike on television, real trials have almost no surprises during the trial.

This adversarial approach gives both sides a strong incentive to develop their best arguments and evidence. A neutral third party then resolves the conflict by deciding which version of the facts and the law to accept. In a trial court, there are two possibilities for this neutral third party—a jury or a judge. In a **jury** trial, the final resolution of facts and the application of the law is made by about a dozen people, selected randomly from the voter rolls, driver's license lists, and other broad-based lists of residents of the court's jurisdiction.

The jury's job is to listen to both sides' arguments and the judge's instructions and then to render a verdict—an authoritative decision—about the dispute. A judge presides over the trial so it is conducted fairly, in accordance with the relevant rules and laws. A judge can influence the jury's verdict by how he or she runs the trial, decides on procedural questions, and instructs the jury before its deliberations. But the final decision about the dispute is done by the jury.

Trials are unpredictable and can have big impacts on the parties' lives. Juries are especially unpredictable. For good or ill, they may be swayed by factors other than objective facts and a strict interpretation of the law. Trial lawyers may even appeal to jury members' emotions, in addition to the law or facts. We have all seen media reports of runaway juries awarding seemingly outrageous sums in lawsuits or freeing "obviously guilty" defendants.[7] But the magnitude of the consequences of most trial outcomes encourage most defendants, plaintiffs, and prosecutors to minimize the unpredictability of their trial as much as possible.

The result is that most trials do not use juries, but are **bench trials**, in which a single judge not only runs the trial but also makes the final decision on the facts and the law. Judges are far more predictable than juries because

---

[7] Eric Helland and Alexander Tabarrok, "Runaway Judges? Selection Effects and the Jury," *Journal of Law, Economics, and Organization* 16(2000):306–33.

they usually follow standard legal practice and interpretation closely.

Although juries add considerable uncertainty to judicial decision making, trial court judges are certainly not legal robots who make decisions in a sort of "mechanical jurisprudence."[8] A case probably wouldn't even get to court if there was no uncertainty about the facts or the law, since a **plea bargain** or **out-of-court** civil settlement would be in the best interests of the guilty or negligent party. Strong professional norms restrain judges from letting their personal preferences color their decisions, but political scientists have found evidence that judges' backgrounds and values can sometimes influence them. Although judges—especially trial court judges—probably don't consciously let these factors color their decisions, unconscious bias may creep in when ambiguity about the facts and law in a case gives a judge discretion.

All of this demonstrates how different trial court decision making is from decision making in the legislative and executive branches. First, while governors and legislators can consider a wide variety of information and opinion, a trial court judge or jury can only consider whatever comes through the formal adversarial process. In fact, any communication by either party in the case with the judge or jury outside of the regular courtroom procedures is both inappropriate and illegal. Second, the courts are passive decision makers. While a governor or legislator can to some extent choose which public problems they want to work on, judges can only make decisions only about questions that are brought to them in a formal case. Finally, judges decide on specific disputes about specific facts and law in specific cases. Legislatures (and governors) make policy decisions that apply equally to everyone. Although state courts—especially supreme courts—sometimes make broader policy in an informal way (as we will see later), the main focus of judicial decision making is always on the individual case at hand.

Courts of Limited Jurisdiction Every state has **general jurisdiction** trial courts, that is, courts where virtually any type of criminal or civil case can be tried. At least 40 states also have various trial courts of **limited jurisdiction** specializing in particular types of cases. Such courts are an institutional way to increase the efficiency of the court system.

Some courts of limited jurisdiction simply handle minor matters. For example, traffic courts deal mainly with processing motor vehicle violations and assessing fines, with only the occasional dispute over a ticket. On the civil side, **small claims courts** handle suits claiming limited amounts of damages, often with the parties presenting their own arguments to an **adjudicator** without lawyers. Many states also use courts with very limited jurisdictions to deal with special populations or special crimes, such as drug crimes, family law, or people with mental health issues. Such **specialty courts** and **problem-solving courts** have become popular reforms in recent years, with the thinking being that judges and other professionals in the legal system may need to specialize to mete out justice fairly under some circumstances.

Courts of limited jurisdiction are used heavily in the states that have them. In fact, in 2006, the last year for which these data were compiled, of all the cases taken up by a trial court, 67 percent came before a court of limited jurisdiction.[9] This is not to say that these courts handle the most important cases; clearly, the opposite is true. But courts of limited jurisdiction are an institutional reform that does a very good job of helping implement justice fairly and efficiently in the states.

Intermediate Courts of Appeal

Trial courts establish the facts of a case and apply the law to those facts, arriving at an authoritative decision about a dispute. Trial courts are not perfect, however, so American court systems

[8] Melinda Gann Hall, "State Courts: Politics and the Judicial Process," in Virginia Gray and Russell L. Hansen, eds., *Politics in the American States* (Washington, DC: CQ Press, 2008), p. 230.

[9] Richard C. LaFountain et al., eds., *Examining the Work of State Courts, 2007* (Williamsburg, VA: National Center for State Courts, 2008).

establish procedures and institutions for people to "appeal" their cases. Appellate courts are the institutions that handle these appeals.

Perhaps surprisingly, the legitimate grounds for an appeal in either civil or criminal law have nothing to do with the facts of the case. An appeals court almost never deals with questions of facts, which are determined by the trial court. A person cannot appeal a trial court decision simply because he or she doesn't like the verdict. A case can be appealed based only on questions about either of two things: the fairness of the trial or the constitutionality of the law involved. Most state court systems today have two levels of appellate courts designed to handle these issues: intermediate courts of appeal and the supreme court. Although it is overgeneralizing a bit, it is not far off to say that intermediate courts of appeal decide questions about a trial's fairness and supreme courts decide questions of constitutionality.

The Role of Intermediate Courts of Appeal

Intermediate courts of appeal (ICAs) have jurisdiction over those cases that are appealed from trial courts of general jurisdiction. In essence, ICAs act as a check to ensure that trials are carried out fairly. Without this oversight, trial judges could act arbitrarily and tyrannically, something that the nation's founders feared. The Fifth Amendment to the U.S. Constitution gives Americans the right to a fair trial, and the ability to appeal a trial court's decision plays a large part in maintaining that right.

State supreme courts originally had the job of directly overseeing the fairness of state trial courts. But by the mid-twentieth century, as states' populations grew, many of their supreme courts became overloaded with relatively routine appeals, denying them the time they needed to consider the deeper issues of law raised only occasionally by certain important cases. ICAs are an institutional reform designed

to relieve this burden on state supreme courts. ICAs decide on appeals that do not raise general points of law, allowing the supreme courts to consider only the most significant cases, as we will discuss later. Fifty years ago, only 13 states had ICAs; today, 40 states do. Those 10 states without ICAs tend to be sparsely populated states with less complex economies. Among the 11 smallest states, only Hawaii and Alaska—states admitted to the union after ICAs were an accepted institution—and North Dakota have them, and North Dakota's ICA is only set up as an experimental, "temporary" institution.

In fact, North Dakota's ICA provides an example of how and why these courts have been used. Founded in 1987, North Dakota's Temporary Court of Appeals (TCA) was explicitly established to take the load off its supreme court.[10] The North Dakota Supreme Court assigns various retired and active judges and attorneys to the TCA for one-year terms as needed to cover the caseload. In some years there are so few appeals that no cases at all are assigned to the TCA, and the North Dakota Supreme Court simply handles all of the appeals itself. On the other hand, the supreme courts of West Virginia and Nevada, the two largest states without an ICA (although they are among the least populous states overall), routinely have problems with overload, resulting in perennial talk of judicial reform in those two states.

By relieving the supreme court of the burden of routine appeals, an ICA helps the state court system make fair, timely, and consistent decisions.[11] ICAs promote fairness by reviewing trials where proper procedures may not have been followed. They promote timeliness by reducing the backlog that an overworked supreme court can generate.[12] They promote consistency by ensuring that trial judges and juries throughout the state apply legal procedures and law the same way.

[10]"The North Dakota Judicial System" (Bismarck, ND: North Dakota Supreme Court, 2007).

[11] Roger A. Hanson, *Appellate Court Performance Standards and Measures* (Williamsburg, VA: National Center for State Courts, 1999).

[12] Megan Callahan, "Influences on the Cases of the State Courts of Last Resort." Presented at the annual meetings of the 2007 Midwest Political Science Association, Chicago, IL.

Procedures and Decision Making The procedures and decision making of ICAs differ markedly from those of trial courts. First, all appeals are heard only by judges, never by a jury, and they are usually heard by more than one judge, perhaps three to five of them. No witnesses testify, and no physical evidence is presented. Witnesses and evidence are used in trials to determine the facts of the case, and these case facts are generally accepted as true in an appeal. This is why a person cannot appeal simply because he or she wanted the decision in the trial to go the other way; the facts that are established in the trial are the facts used by all levels of the court system. Rather than arguing the facts of the case, the parties simply offer arguments about the trial's fairness. These arguments are made in **legal briefs**, documents in which the parties point out what they see as the problems with the trial and respond to the arguments made in the other party's brief. Typically, the actual parties to the case don't even attend ICA hearings (whereas they almost always attend the trial). Instead, only their lawyers appear before the ICA to represent their interests, and these are not usually the same lawyers who argued the trial, but rather specialists in appeals.

ICAs also differ from trial courts in their decision making. After hearing or reading both sides' arguments, the panel of judges votes on the appeal, with the majority determining the verdict. Of course, this means that there can be disagreement among the panel of judges—that's why there is usually an odd number. Typically, the panel hearing an appeal does not consist of all the state's ICA judges. The judges are divided, usually geographically, into panels to cover their large caseloads more efficiently. For certain very important or controversial cases, all of a state's ICA judges sit together *en banc*, that is, as a whole.

The final decisions of trial courts and ICAs also have an important, fundamental difference. In a trial court, case facts are determined and the conflict is resolved through the application of law. That is, in criminal cases, people can be found guilty and sentenced to jail, and in civil cases, fault can be assigned and judgments awarded. But in an ICA, the judges' decision is about the original trial itself—was it fair or not? If the ICA decides that the trial was fair or, more specifically, if it fails to accept the exact arguments of unfairness brought in the appeal, the decision of the trial court is upheld. On the other hand, if the ICA accepts the argument that the trial was flawed, either it can order the lower court to correct the sentence or judgment or it can overturn the entire decision, necessitating a completely new trial. Sometimes, after a trial's verdict has been overturned on appeal, the prosecutor or the party to the lawsuit that won the original trial decides not to pursue a new trial. Perhaps the ICA rules that a piece of evidence can't be used because it was illegally obtained by the police, and without it, the prosecutor may decide to drop the case. But that would be the prosecutor's decision; ICAs only make decisions about the procedures of the trial, not the facts of a case or its verdict.

Supreme Courts

Once upon a time, "things were so quiet on the … State Supreme Court that you could hear the justices' arteries clog,"[13] but that is anything but true today. In the twenty-first century, state supreme courts regularly make decisions that have momentous impacts on their states' residents, businesses, and local governments. Many of their decisions have significant impacts far beyond the borders of their home state, as well. On all matters of a state's law, its supreme court is the final arbiter, that is, it is the **court of last resort** in that state.[14] State supreme courts

[13] Shirley S. Abrahamson, "Homegrown Justice: The State Constitutions," in Bradley D. McGraw, ed., *Developments in State Constitutional Law* (St. Paul, MN: West, 1985), p. 315.

[14] The U.S. Supreme Court may overturn a state supreme court's decision but only based on some aspect of the U.S. Constitution, not state law. In another example of institutional variation among the states, Texas and Oklahoma each have two supreme courts, one for civil cases and one for criminal cases, but each of these has the last word for the cases it hears.

also have important administrative duties, usually running their states' entire court system and regulating their legal professions. Thus, a state's supreme court dominates its entire legal system.

Jurisdiction Trial courts have **original jurisdiction** over the vast majority of cases in a state's judicial system, and ICAs handle appeals of trial court decisions on issues of procedural fairness. So, what is a state supreme court's jurisdiction? In part, this depends on whether the state has an ICA. In the 10 states without an ICA, the supreme courts' **dockets** mostly consist of the same sort of routine fairness appeals that occupy the time of ICAs. In states with the three-tiered system (as shown in Figure 8.1), however, supreme courts have significant discretion over which cases they hear, making them especially important actors in state government and policy.

In the 40 states with ICAs, the state supreme courts handle three types of cases. First, they hear cases about the balance of power in state government at the highest levels. These cases are few and far between, but their consequences can be extensive. In particular, when the state legislature and the governor have a conflict over their constitutional powers, the supreme court can be called on in its role as the final arbiter of the state's constitution. For example, in 2009, South Carolina's governor and legislature battled over accepting federal economic stimulus funds, and its state supreme court was called on to sort things out. The Palmetto State's high court ruled against Governor Mark Sanford, stating that "under the constitution and laws [of South Carolina], the General Assembly is the sole entity with the power to appropriate funds."[15] This was a case of a dispute over the institutional powers of the legislative and executive branches; acting as a neutral third party, the judicial branch resolved it. Likewise, when the Ohio General Assembly complained that Governor Ted Strickland overstepped his veto

powers, it was the Ohio Supreme Court that settled the matter.[16] The parties to these cases can bring suit directly in the state supreme court because they usually don't involve disputes of fact and so no trial is needed. Everyone agreed about what Sanford and Strickland did; they just disagreed on whether their actions were constitutional.

Second, in some states, the supreme court is required to hear appeals of certain criminal convictions. For example, most trials resulting in a death sentence must be reviewed by the supreme court regardless of the facts of the case, what happened in the trial, or even the defendant's wishes. The states vary greatly on which other appeals their supreme courts are required to hear and the percentage of the supreme court's docket that is made up of such cases. For example, all of the cases handled by five state supreme courts (in Iowa, North Dakota, Nevada, Delaware, and Wyoming) are mandatory, while in two states (West Virginia and New Hampshire), none of them are.[17]

This leads naturally to the other category of cases that state supreme courts hear—discretionary cases. Most supreme courts, especially in those 40 states that use ICAs, get to choose whether or not to hear certain appeals of trial court and ICA decisions. That is, part of their docket is discretionary. So, why do these supreme courts decide to hear some appeals but not others? What are their decision criteria in selecting cases to hear? Simply put, these high courts pick cases to review, not because of any intrinsic issue of fairness or fact with the specific cases involved, but because of *their potential implications for public policy and state law more generally.* Thus, where ICAs exist, the development of a state supreme court's docket is a significant decision-making process in itself, and one in which political scientists are quite interested. In this respect, state supreme courts are much like the U.S.

[15] Rick Brundrett, "S.C. High Court Orders Sanford to Accept Money," *The State* (Columbia, SC), 5 June 2009, online edition.

[16] Reginald Fields, "Ohio Supreme Court Voids Strickland Veto of Liability Bill," *The Cleveland Plain Dealer*, 7 August 2007, online edition.

[17] Richard C. LaFountain et al., eds., *Examining the Work of State Courts, 2007* (Williamsburg, VA: National Center for State Courts, 2008), p. 63.

Supreme Court. If a party in a case does not feel that the trial was fair and the ICA decision went against him or her anyway, or if the case involves a dispute over the state constitutionality of a law or procedure, then that party may officially **request** the supreme court to hear the case. However, nationwide, state supreme courts grant only 7 percent of these requests, suggesting just how selective these courts are in setting their dockets.[18] On the other hand, in a recent year, an average of only 29.2 percent of a state supreme court's case-load was discretionary across all states.[19]

State supreme courts grant these requests for discretionary hearings very carefully, with the aim of clarifying the interpretation of state law. Trial courts and ICAs follow the lead of their supreme court closely in applying state statutes and case law both because of judicial norms and because a supreme court can overturn lower court decisions. So, supreme courts choose to hear cases on which their decisions can be used as examples, or **precedents**, for lower courts facing similar cases.

Supreme courts try to identify cases that raise ambiguous legal questions that are common to a class of cases. This ambiguity often leads to inconsistency in trial court and ICA decisions. Without clear guidance on a point of law raised in cases facing them, lower court judges must use their own best legal reasoning in arriving at decisions. If different judges' reasonings vary, however, decisions on similar cases will not be consistent across judges. Because the consistent administration of justice is a hallmark of a fair legal system, and because the state supreme court has the responsibility to maintain a fair legal system in the state, supreme courts agree to hear cases that allow them to clear up these ambiguities.

State law on a subject may be ambiguous for at least two reasons. First, when a statute is new, its practical implications sometimes need to be worked out, and the supreme court may have to interpret it for judges, the police, lawyers, and the public. For example, in recent years, 12 states have passed statues banning or regulating aggressive driving, or "road rage," in response to the deaths, injuries, and property damage it can cause.[20] Because these statutes are the result of the legislative process, they typically do not define "aggressive driving" clearly. This leaves it up to police officers and trial court judges to decide whether a person's specific behavior in a case violates the law of a state. If conflict over, or inconsistency in, how these officials interpret such a state law arises, a representative aggressive-driving case will make its way to the state's supreme court for clarification. Because each state's statute and constitution are unique, such clarification needs to be done by each state's high court.

Legal ambiguity can also arise due to changes in society, the economy, or even technology. For example, suppose that state statutory and case law have traditionally given visitation rights to noncustodial parents in divorce cases.[21] So what about if an unmarried, live-in couple has a child and one of the partners moves out? Should that person be given visitation rights? This is so similar to the traditional divorce situation that trial judges have for many years ruled consistently that traditional divorce case law applies. What if a couple had a child but never lived together and simply stopped being romantically involved? Can the divorce analogy be applied here for child custody? Still pretty close, you say? What about a couple (married or not) who had a child using a sperm donor? Is the man in the relationship entitled to visitation

---

[18] National Center for State Courts, *Examining the Work of State Courts, 2003* (Williamsburg, VA: National Center for State Courts, 2004).

[19] LaFountain et al., op cit.

[20] Governors' Highway Safety Association, "Aggressive Driving Laws," August 2009 (http://www.ghsa.org/html/stateinfo/laws/aggressivedriving_laws.html); Victor E. Flango and Ann L. Keith, "How Useful Is the New Aggressive Driving Legislation?" *Court Review* 40(3–4)(2004):34–43.

[21] Related to this example, consider the way the legal definition of "parent" evolved in the following cases before the California Supreme Court: *In re Nicholas H.* (6 June 2002) 28 Cal. 4th 56; *In re Jesusa V.* (16 April 2004) 97 Cal.App. 4th 878; and *Elisa B. v. Superior Court* (22 August 2005) 118 Cal.App. 4th 966.

rights after a breakup? Looked at from another perspective, is the sperm donor (or egg donor) responsible to support the child financially? The Pennsylvania Supreme Court recently weighed in on this issue when a lower court muddied that water by requiring child support from a sperm donor.[22] What if a lesbian couple has a child through sperm donation? What about a couple who used both sperm and egg donation to produce a child? The Maryland Court of Appeals recently decided that a certain set of twins had no mother at all—they were conceived with their father's sperm from a donated egg and carried by a surrogate mother.[23]

When they see a murky area of the law, supreme courts do not shy away from even the most baffling new issue. It is a supreme court's duty to clarify the law for all the courts below it in its state. As the facts in these cases move farther from those in established case law, the legal questions become more ambiguous and court decisions become less consistent. By hearing a representative case of this type, a supreme court can make a definitive legal interpretation and bring consistency and fairness to them.

Procedures and Decision Making

State supreme court decision making is similar to that of ICAs. There are no juries, witnesses, or physical evidence, only lawyers making oral arguments and filing detailed and lengthy legal briefs that describe and support the parties' arguments. Supreme courts are also made up of multiple judges (typically called "justices"), but unlike ICAs, supreme courts decide almost all cases en banc. Decisions are made with a majority vote; supreme courts have an odd number of justices (usually five to nine) to avoid ties.

Because a supreme court's decisions serve as precedent for its lower courts, they are usually supported by elaborate written opinions explaining the legal reasoning behind them,

especially for its discretionary cases. The **majority opinion** is the official report giving the rationale behind the majority decision on the case. This is the ruling legal reasoning for future cases of this type in the state.

However, because supreme court justices have sharp legal minds and strong opinions, and because their discretionary cases are typically on debatable points of law, by definition, disagreement arises more often on supreme courts than it does on ICAs. When one or more justices dissent from a case's majority opinion, he or she can write a dissenting opinion. A dissenting opinion can establish the arguments for future legal debate on a point of law, perhaps even signaling that the court might change its mind in the future if it has a personnel change. And even if a justice agrees with the majority, he or she may do so for reasons other than those stated in the majority opinion. If so, and if the justice feels strongly enough to do so, he or she may write a concurring opinion, outlining alternative reasons for voting with the majority. In fact, sometimes even justices in the minority write multiple dissenting opinions, outlining their various reasons for voting against the majority. Thus, supreme courts are the most intellectual of state government institutions; a state supreme court sometimes seems more like an advanced seminar in a law school than a government agency—sometimes. From a public policy perspective, the more fractured a court's voice, the less clear guidance it gives to lower courts. But state supreme courts are typically less fractious than the U.S. Supreme Court, with state justices more often deferring to one another's legal expertise than fighting tooth and nail along ideological lines.[24]

The Administrative Duties of the State Supreme Court

In addition to making authoritative decisions on state law, most state supreme

---

[22] Mark Scolforo, "Pa. Sperm Donor Ruled Liable for Child Support," *The Philadelphia Inquirer*, 11 May 2007, online edition.

[23] Andrea F. Siegel, "Ruling Alters Idea of Mother," *The Baltimore Sun*, 17 May 2007, online edition.

[24] Rick A. Swanson, "Judicial Perceptions of Voting Fluidity on State Supreme Courts," *Justice System Journal* 28(2007):199–218; Kevin T. Arceneaux, Chris W. Bonneau, and Paul Brace, "On Consensus in State Supreme Courts." Presented at the 2007 annual meeting of the Midwest Political Science Association, Chicago, IL.

courts also administer the entire court system and regulate the legal professions in their state. These duties make supreme courts much more influential in state government and policy than they would be if they had only judicial powers.

The supreme court is responsible for the smooth operation of the entire state court system. This involves hiring and supervising clerks, court bailiffs, court reporters, and others; buying supplies; and dealing with the budget, and running the system's website, among other duties. Each supreme court

employs a **director of state courts** to do most of this day-to-day administrative work. A court director is a major state administrator, on the same level as a secretary of a cabinet-level state executive agency (see Comparisons Help Us Understand box).

In most states, the state supreme court also regulates the legal and judicial professions. Often in collaboration with the state bar association, the court runs training courses for new judges, regulates the bar examinations that prospective lawyers must pass before being allowed

Comparisons Help Us Understand

STATE SUPREME COURT PROFESSIONALISM

Throughout this book, we have discussed the institutional capacity of state and local government. Some governments have strong, professional institutions, and some are more part-time, "citizen" institutions. Americans have mixed emotions about the propriety of strong, professional government. On one hand, professionalized government institutions allow (at least in theory) for effective and efficient administration of policy; on the other hand, some people think that they can threaten our liberty. The way that states and communities balance these concerns and desires in developing their institutions can tell us a lot about the values of the people living there and what they think about the institutions involved.

Political scientist Peverill Squire recently developed an approach to evaluating the professionalism of state supreme courts based on his work on state legislatures.[25] His state supreme court professionalism scale uses data on judges' salaries, docket control and staff. (See the figure on the back inside cover of this book for a graphic display of this index.).[26]

First, what hypotheses can you develop about why a state would want to have a more or less professional supreme court? What would a more professional supreme court *give* a state? What type of state (or what type of people) would *prefer* more or less of this? What would a professional supreme court *cost* a state? Might anything about the political ideology or economics of state have an impact here? What about a state's social or cultural characteristics—how might they come into play? Look at the map of this index on the inside back cover. Do your hypotheses appear to be correct?

Next, consider how the professionalism of state supreme courts compares to that of other institutions. First the professionalism of state supreme courts is much higher and more uniform than that of state legislatures. The differences here are stark; many state supreme courts are almost as professional as the U.S. Supreme Court; state legislatures are far less professional than Congress and they vary dramatically on this characteristic. Why are so many states so willing to support a professional state supreme court, while few do so for their legislature? What does this tell you about legislative and judicial, institutions, the jobs they do, and people's attitudes toward them?

[25] Peverill Squire, "Measuring the Professionalization of U.S. State Courts of Last Resort," *State Politics and Policy Quarterly* 8(2008):223–38.

[26] Squire actually presents four highly correlated scales. We make a single scale by averaging these, and then we break that scale down into quintiles in the map of this characteristic in back endpages.

to practice law, and establishes professional and ethical standards for the state's lawyers and judges.

It also establishes procedures for investigating and sanctioning judges and lawyers accused of unethical conduct. Charges of impropriety or incompetence against lawyers are common, largely because so many lawyers are in practice and they often deal with expensive and sensitive disputes. Because there are far fewer judges than lawyers and because judges usually seem to hold themselves to a higher ethical standard than do lawyers, such **judicial review** and sanction are relatively rare. Of course, lawyers and judges are subject to criminal and civil law like everyone else; these special procedures and institutions are designed to deal with behavior that, if not illegal, might violate professional standards and ethics. For example, although it may not be illegal for a judge to direct profanity at a defendant, it is not the sort of behavior that is conducive to the proper administration of justice and so a judicial review board might punish a judge for it.

Policy Making in the Courts

In your high school American government class, you learned that the legislative branch makes law, the executive branch implements it, and the judicial branch interprets it. But as you saw in the previous chapter, while the legislative branch certainly does make policy, the executive branch (especially the governor) does, too. Does the state judicial branch also make policy? In the narrowest sense that legislatures and governors establish statutes and official rules and regulations, no, judges do not make policy; but if we think of policy making a little more broadly, then the state judicial branch—especially the supreme court—is very much involved in policy making.

Although the advisability and propriety of judicial policy making are hotly debated,[27] the nature of law and the role the supreme court plays in the state legal system make it inevitable. In writing law, legislators cannot consider every eventuality, so statutes often have gray areas. But the courts must enforce laws in specific cases based on specific factual circumstances, so they must decide on the exact meaning of the relevant law. State supreme courts have their clearest judicial policy-making power when they make the definitive interpretation of state law. Of course, this power is limited to ambiguously worded constitutional provisions, statutes, and rules, the decisions can be overturned if the legislature clarifies the law or changes the constitution, and the decisions can be made only on points of law that are brought before a court in specific cases. While these are serious limitations, in practice, the interpretation of state law by the supreme court frequently has a significant impact on public policy.

When a supreme court determines the specific meaning of a law for a category of legal situations its decision is applied and reified in policy by becoming legal precedent. That is, the lower courts in that state must then interpret that law similarly in that category of legal situation or risk getting their decisions overturned upon appeal, whether by an ICA or the supreme court. And some supreme court decisions can even influence legal decisions—thereby influencing public policy—outside of the court's own state. While they are not legally binding past their state's borders, if lawyers and judges elsewhere find those legal arguments compelling and use them in their own legal briefs, then the force of the court's own good thinking can affect public policy elsewhere in the country.

State supreme courts can also affect public policy through **judicial review**. Just as the U.S. Supreme Court assesses whether state and federal statutes are allowable under the U.S.

---

[27] For example, consider the different opinions of two groups over the Massachusetts Supreme Judicial Court's decision that the state cannot ban same-sex marriage: Andrea Lafferty, "Massachusetts Supreme Judicial Court Legalizes Same-Sex Marriage!," Traditional Values Coalition, 2004, and National Organization for Women (NOW), "NOW Leaders Applaud Massachusetts Supreme Court Ruling Favoring Same-Sex Marriage Rights," 2004, http://www.now.org/issues/lgbi/020604marriage.html.

Constitution, state supreme courts have the power to judge whether a state statute violates its state's constitution and, if so, to nullify that law.[28] For example, the power of judicial review is what allowed the Iowa Supreme Court to strike down that state's law limiting marriage to one man and one woman in April 2009, effectively establishing same-sex marriage in the Hawkeye State.[29] In recent decades, state supreme courts have been especially active in using judicial review, although their propensity to do so varies over time and among the states.

Of course, the influence of these decisions goes well beyond those directly involved in the case being reviewed, applying to everyone potentially affected by that law. This gives considerable staying power to this sort of court-made constitutional law.

Judicial review brings together the judicial and legislative branches of state government in the policy-making process, sometimes in a very uncomfortable way, since it allows the court to deposit the legislature's work in the legal trash can. The legislature can reverse such nullification by initiating a change in the state constitution and then passing the law again, but this is difficult. Lawmakers generally don't like to be rebuked in this way, but sometimes they have political reasons for passing a law that they think will probably be thrown out by the courts. A legislator running for reelection can then say, "At least I *tried* to do something, but the supreme court circumvented the will of the people!" (i.e., the will of the legislature). Consider Iowa's same-sex marriage law. But usually, lawmakers want to see their laws pass constitutional muster and be implemented in the state. As such, legislators try to anticipate what their high court's thinking on the constitution and craft legislation that meets constitutional standards.[30]

On the other hand, several factors work against the courts having a strong and direct policy-making role. Perhaps most important, the judicial branch has little policy-making legitimacy in popular American political culture.[31] We don't believe that judges' values should enter into their decisions; they are just supposed to apply the law to the facts of the case. Judges are also supposed to evaluate each case individually, while policy making is about setting general rules. Furthermore, unlike legislatures and governors, courts are passive decision makers, simply deciding on those cases that have been brought before them. Consequently, even if judges wanted to make policy, their agenda would be set by events and outsiders to a much greater degree than are the policy agendas of legislatures and governors.

Judicial Selection

Unique among major classes of American public officials, state judges are selected in a variety of ways among the states, sometimes even varying between different levels of court in the same state. Whereas all governors and state legislators are elected and all federal judges are appointed by the president, depending on the state and the level of the court, state judges may ascend to the bench in any of five very different ways: appointment by the governor or state legislature, partisan or nonpartisan election, or a hybrid of election and appointment known as the **Merit Plan**. Another unique aspect of judicial selection in the states is that virtually no other judges in the world are selected by any type of election, while a great majority of state judges have to face the voters in some way at some point in their career. This variety of judicial selection method demonstrates Americans' evolving attitudes and ambivalence about the role of the

---

[28] Laura Langer, *Judicial Review in State Supreme Courts: A Comparative Study* (Albany: State University of New York Press, 1999).

[29] Monica Davey, "Iowa Court Voids Gay Marriage Ban," *The New York Times*, 4 April 2009, online edition.

[30] Teena Wilhelm, "Strange Bedfellows: The Policy Consequences of Legislative-Judicial Relations in the American States," *American Politics Research* 37(2009):3–29; Elizabeth A. Stiles and Lauren L. Bowen, "Legislative-Judicial Interaction: Do Court Ideologies Constrain Legislative Action?" *State and Local Government Review* 39(2007):96–106.

[31] Hall, 2008, op cit.

judiciary in the political process. It also offers political scientists a unique opportunity to examine how the institutions by which officials gain office affect their behavior in office.

Judicial Selection Methods

Let's start with a basic description of these judicial selection methods. Figure 8.2 shows how the states select their supreme court justices, but remember that some states use different selection methods for different courts. Indiana has the most diverse system, using three of the five selection methods for some of its trial courts alone. In addition, the details of some states' systems vary idiosyncratically. For example, in Illinois, Pennsylvania, and New Mexico (only its supreme court), judges are initially elected in partisan elections, but they can run for reelection through a **retention election**. Although classifying judicial selection methods can be a little tricky, important distinctions can be drawn. The following are the five most commonly used categories of state judicial selection method.[32]

Figure 8.2

State Supreme Court Selection Mechanisms

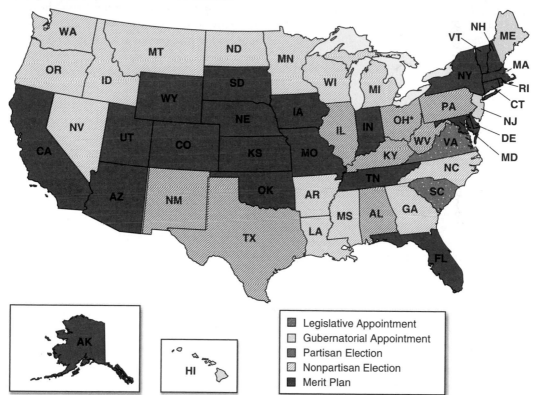

Legend:
- Legislative Appointment
- Gubernatorial Appointment
- Partisan Election
- Nonpartisan Election
- Merit Plan

*In Ohio, party affiliations do not appear on the ballot, but candidates are chosen through partisan primaries.

Source: Audrey S. Wall, *The Book of the States 2008*, vol. 40 (Lexington, KY: Council of State Governments, 2008), pp. 277–78. See the source for details.

[32] These five categories are the ones most commonly used by political scientists studying judicial selection. For more details, the best general source is the most recent edition of *The Book of the States* (Wall, 2008, op cit., pp. 286–93). The website of the National Center for State Courts (http://www.ncsconline.org/) is another good source. The best place to find the exact details of selection and retention for each class of judges in a given state is that state's supreme court own website.

Legislative Appointment Under the earliest state constitutions, just after American independence, most states' judges were appointed by their legislatures, reflecting the faith that the founders had in those representative assemblies. Today, only South Carolina and Virginia continue to select their judges this way. In these states, a legislative committee or commission screens candidates and reports its findings to the full legislature for a vote. These judges are appointed for a fixed term and subject to reappointment by the legislature.

Gubernatorial Appointment Three states—Hawaii, Maine, and New Jersey—continue to use the second-oldest method of selecting judges: gubernatorial appointment. In these states, the governor has almost unfettered discretion in appointing judges to a fixed term (with the caveats that judges can serve only until age 70 in New Jersey and legislative approval is needed for appointees in Maine and New Jersey).

Partisan Elections In 12 states, judges for at least some state courts are elected on a partisan ballot. Just like governors and state legislators, those wishing to become a judge in these states must earn a party's nomination through a primary election, a party convention, or a party slating process, and then they must face an opponent from the other party (or parties) in a general election. Among the six states that use partisan elections for only some of their judges, all but New Mexico use them for trial courts, using other methods for judges on their supreme courts and ICAs.

Nonpartisan Elections The second-most common method of state judicial selection is nonpartisan election, with 21 states using this method for at least some of their courts. These elections are usually held in the spring, often coinciding with nonpartisan municipal elections, rather than during the November general election.

Merit Plan The Merit Plan (also called the Missouri Plan, after the first state to adopt it) is the most widely used judicial selection method,

with 24 states using some variant of it for at least some of their courts. Three steps define this selection method. First, a nominating commission is formed to recruit and evaluate potential judges. The composition of this commission varies from state to state, but it generally includes representatives of key government institutions (such as the state legislature, governor, and state supreme court) and the legal establishment (perhaps leaders or appointees of the state bar association). When a specific judicial vacancy arises, the commission identifies a small number of qualified candidates (usually three) and sends their names to the governor. Next, the governor appoints one of the nominees to the vacancy for a short term, typically of one to three years. Finally, once a new judge has served this probationary term, he or she faces the voters in a retention election. In a retention election, the question on the ballot is not which candidate the voter prefers, as in a regular election, but whether this judge should be allowed to be retained for another (usually much longer) term. In other words, only one name is on the retention ballot (that of the incumbent judge), and voters choose to retain him or her or not. This probationary term and retention election are the hallmarks of the Merit Plan.

To a political scientist, especially one who has learned the craft by studying the states, all this variation in these selection institutions raises two obvious questions: (1) Why have different states chosen different methods? and (2) How do the different methods of judicial selection affect the administration of justice (or anything else) differently? That is, what are the causes and effects of these institutions? We turn to these questions next.

Why Do States Select Their Judges Differently?

We establish institutions for selecting a class of public officials based on the functions that we believe these officials should perform and the values that we hold about these functions. So, for example, we want lawmakers to represent the values of a jurisdiction's residents,[33] so we elect them, and we want bureaucrats who have professional expertise, so we select them through a civil service system of tests and knowledge-based criteria. But since the colonial era, Americans have debated what we want out of our state judges, and the current variation in judicial selection methods reflects in large degree the evolution of Americans' values about our courts.[34] While this debate is a subtle one, the current variation in state judicial selection roughly follows the historic and geographic distribution of Americans' beliefs about the proper role of the courts.

What is the proper role of judges in our representative democracy? This is not an easy question. Consider how you think judges should make decisions. As we have discussed, legal culture and norms hold that their decisions should be based only on the law and the facts of the case—this is the fair administration of justice that we prize. But what should be done when the fair administration of justice conflicts with public opinion? Such conflicts are more common than you might think, and simple, universal resolutions to them are sometimes elusive. For example, an angry mob might want to lynch a person who they think got a too-lenient sentence for a certain crime. Most Americans would agree that the judge was right to ignore the wishes of this community and apply the law as passed by the state legislature. But what about when a law is passed by a state legislature that conflicts with the fundamental rules of governance or human rights set out in the state's constitution? Should a state supreme court override the current will of the people (the statute) in favor of the constitution, which represents the will of the people at

a previous time? In the federal court system, judges are appointed for life so that they can protect constitutional rights and values against the heat of current popular opinion. They have done this to protect the rights of minorities of all types, from African Americans trying to vote in the South to the Ku Klux Klan and neo-Nazi groups trying to hold rallies in predominantly Jewish neighborhoods,[35] but in the states, most judges must face the voters at some point, and they can be thrown out of office if voters don't like their decisions. This makes standing up for an unpopular minority riskier for state supreme court judges than those in the federal system.[36]

This issue becomes an especially pointed one when a supreme court rules that a law passed through the initiative process is unconstitutional. Supreme courts in several direct democracy states have recently come under attack for frustrating the "will of the people" in this way. For example, in 2008, the California Supreme Court held that a 2000 initiative banning same-sex marriage was unconstitutional. The public outcry was loud and swift, resulting in the narrow passage later in 2008 of a new initiative, Proposition 8, that actually changed the state's constitution in order to implement the ban. The retention of supreme court justices in California has been seen to be threatened by these actions,[37] but is this right?

Even if you agree that the judiciary should protect certain basic rights against popular opinion, consider other legal situations where the law and the facts are not clear-cut, giving a judge room for interpretation. To what extent should judges decide such cases using their professional judgment based on their years of legal training and experience, and maybe even their ideological and political values and

---

[33] Of course, this is an oversimplification of our expectations of lawmakers, as we discussed in Chapter 6.

[34] Charles H. Sheldon and Linda S. Maule, *Choosing Justice: The Recruitment of State and Federal Judges* (Pullman: Washington State University Press, 1997).

[35] Donald A. Downs, *Nazis in Skokie: Freedom, Community and the First Amendment* (South Bend, IN: University of Notre Dame Press, 1985).

[36] Brian DiSarro, "Judicial Accountability or Majority Tyranny? Judicial Selection Methods and State Gay Rights Rulings." Presented at the 2007 State Politics and Policy Conference, Austin, TX.

[37] Bill Ainsworth, "Same-Sex Marriage: Law-and-Order Appointee Now Known for Greater Rights," *Union-Tribune* (San Diego, CA), 13 June 2008, online edition.

biases, and to what extent should they reflect the values and preferences of the communities they serve? Another related question about judicial selection is whether there is a difference between the ability of voters to understand the job of a judge, on one hand, versus the job of a governor or legislator, on the other, such that we can trust the average person to know who would make a good governor or legislator but not who would make a good judge?

These are difficult questions, and the debate surrounding them is reflected in the institutions the states use to select their judges.[38] The earliest state legislatures embodied what was seen as the only legitimate source of political power— the people. The British had used the colonial courts as instruments of oppression and thus the founders were suspicious of them, just as they were suspicious of governors. Therefore, the first state governments subordinated their courts to their legislatures by giving the latter the power to appoint judges. As state legislatures fell out of favor in the early nineteenth century, states embraced executive leadership, including giving governors the power to appoint judges. Thus, in keeping with the strongly elitist tone of early American democracy, state judges were almost all appointed for the country's first half-century.

With the rise of Jacksonian democracy in pre–Civil War America, the states began electing many more of their officials directly, including judges. In 1832, Mississippi became the first to elect its judges, and by 1900, about 80 percent of the states did likewise. Like all officials in this era, judges were elected on partisan ballots, with the idea being that the party label would give voters an indication of the candidates' values and preferences. Thus, judges would reflect voters' values in the same way that legislators or governors would.

By the early twentieth century, the good-government reformers of the Progressive Era began to advocate for nonpartisan judicial elections. The Progressives valued judges who would decide cases fairly and impartially based on the law and the facts of the case. They felt that partisanship and political ideology should have nothing to do with the administration of justice, so it made no sense to select judges using those criteria. Nonpartisan elections would force voters to select judges on more job-related criteria, like their training and experience. North Dakota established the first nonpartisan judicial elections in 1910, and by 1952, 15 other states had done so.

Finally, in 1940, Missouri adopted the first Merit Plan, that hybrid of appointment and election. The values reflected by this institution were also a hybrid. The first part is the notion that judicial selection is best made by experts (the selection committee and the governor) because the job is highly technical and voters know little about it. But the retention election reflects the democratic impulse to give voters a way to evaluate their judges once in office. In this way, the Merit Plan is a scientific management approach to good government, an effort to appoint a qualified person to the post based on technical merit and then letting voters review that person based on his or her subsequent performance on the job.

Thus, the diversity among the states in judicial selection reflects the diversity of our values about the role of judges over time and around the country. New states adopted the institution that reflected the values in vogue at the time of their statehood. For example, from 1846 to 1900, every state admitted to the union initially elected its judges on a partisan ballot.[39] Likewise, when states made major changes to their constitutions, they tended to adopt the method that best reflected the contemporary values about the judiciary. In recent decades, Rhode Island, Delaware, New Hampshire, New York, Tennessee, and South Dakota all changed

---

[38] Chris W. Bonneau and Melinda Gann Hall, *In Defense of Judicial Elections* (New York: Routledge, 2009); F. Andrew Hanssen, "Learning about Judicial Independence: Institutional Change in the State Courts," *Journal of Legal Studies* 33(2004):431–73.

[39] Kermit L. Hall, "Progressive Reform and the Decline of Democratic Accountability: The Popular Election of State Supreme Court Judges, 1850–1920," *American Bar Foundation Research Journal* 2(1984):345–63.

to the Merit Plan; since 1992, Mississippi, Arkansas, and North Carolina all moved in this direction by changing from partisan to nonpartisan elections. Often, these changes are instigated by a scandal or some other problem with their system. For example, in 2010, Nevada voted to change from a nonpartisan election system to the Merit Plan. The Silver State's legislature called for this referendum after an elected judge's "volatile, angry, paranoid and bizarre behavior" led the supreme court to assign her an armed security detail and question her competence.[40] The thinking was that someone as problematic as that judge could have risen to the bench only through elections—a Merit Plan would have screened her out very early on in the process. Although a state can—and often does—tolerate a rogue or incompetent state lawmaker, for example, the damage such a judge can do to the lives of those whose cases come before him or her could be intolerable.

Why have some states retained their older systems of judicial selection? This can often be explained simply by inertia and the difficulty of changing a state's constitution. For example, Article VI, Section 7 of Virginia's state constitution requires judges to be selected by the legislature; this provision has not been changed since the constitution was adopted in 1776. In other states, even when the opportunity to change their selection method arose, it was not taken because the existing system reflected the values of the state well. For example, even though Illinois adopted a completely new constitution in 1970, it continued to elect its judges on a partisan basis due to the highly partisan and individualistic political culture of the state. However, even in the Prairie State, recent

high-priced and nasty election campaigns for the Illinois Supreme Court have raised calls for reform.[41]

What Difference Does a Judicial Selection Method Make?

The variation in how states select their judges has given political scientists a unique opportunity to assess the impact of these selection methods and the impact of political institutions more generally. One way to start this analysis is to consider the criticisms of the various selection methods.

Appointments are criticized for reducing the independence of the courts and shifting political power to the appointing institution, whether the governor or legislature.[42] One of the central principles of American government is the separation of powers among the three branches, and elite appointment may upset that balance.[43] Judicial elections also have critics, with the American Bar Association (ABA) being foremost among them.[44] Given the widespread use of elections and the extensive debate about them over the past 100 years, these arguments are more extensive and multifaceted than those regarding judicial appointment.

First, judicial elections have long been criticized for being low-turnout, low-information affairs.[45] Few voters seem to know anything about candidates for state judgeships, especially below the supreme court level. Without such information, voters can't cast an informed vote for a judge. People tend either to skip judicial races on ballots or to fall back on voting cues that may be weakly related to their preferences, completely irrelevant, or even misleading.

[40] Jeff German, "Lawmakers Pave Way for Vote on Appointing Judges," *The Las Vegas Sun*, 6 June 2009, online edition.

[41] Editorial, "Change Way Judicial Races Are Financed," *State Journal-Register* (Springfield, IL), 10 June 2009, p. 6.

[42] Kermit Hall, "The Judiciary on Trial: State Constitutional Reform and the Rise of the Elected Judiciary, 1846–1860," *The Historian*, 45(1983):337–54.

[43] Of course, because all federal judges are appointed by the president, the same argument could be made about the federal judiciary.

[44] James Sample, "Justice for Sale," *The Wall Street Journal*, 25 March 2008; American Bar Association, "Independence of the Judiciary: Judicial Elections Are Becoming More Politicized," 2006.

[45] David Klein and Lawrence Baum, "Ballot Information and Voting Decisions in Judicial Elections," *Political Research Quarterly* 54(2001):709–28.

In partisan elections, the party label may provide some information about a candidate's political values and policy preferences, but it says nothing about his or her fairness and judicial competence; and in nonpartisan elections and primaries, voters do not have even this limited information.

Traditionally, one of the reasons that voters have been so ill informed is judicial candidates' professional norm that they should not use anything in their campaigns beyond basic résumé data. In essence, judicial candidates were able to tell voters only where they went to law school and what jobs they held. This information may be useful to voters who are familiar with the legal profession, but not to the general public.

In particular, the legal profession frowns on judicial candidates offering the sort of information that we expect from candidates for other offices—their opinions on the important issues that might face them. This norm against policy-oriented information in judicial campaigns is a natural extension of the belief that judges should administer the law based only on the specific facts and the established law involved in each case. Governors and legislators are expected to have opinions on public policy and discuss them in their election campaigns; judges are expected to face all decisions before them with an unbiased mind. Some states have tried to codify these norms in law, with varying impacts;[46] but beginning with the important 2002 U.S. Supreme Court case, *Republican Party of Minnesota vs. White*, the federal courts have begun to strike down these regulations as unconstitutional infringements on free speech.[47]

Many people are also concerned with the dramatic increases in judicial campaign spending, especially in supreme court races.[48] Lawyers and law firms have long been the major donors in these races, raising concerns about judicial fairness when a donor subsequently appears in court. Perhaps even more worrisome is the recent trend of interest groups becoming involved in state supreme court races because of the broad judicial issues that are decided there.[49] These groups have been contributing money and airing independent TV ads for the judicial candidates they favor, with no judicial norms constraining the content of such ads. Nasty, independently funded commercials have been pivotal in some races, implying that judges are soft on crime, in bed with certain economic interests, or even friendly with child molesters.

States with partisan elections for their supreme courts have been particularly hard hit with these expensive and bitter campaigns—Ohio, Alabama, Illinois, Texas, and West Virginia, in particular. Even some nonpartisan election states (e.g., Mississippi, Michigan, and Wisconsin) have begun having expensive and bitter races for their high courts.[50] Even retention elections have sometimes been heated, as in California Supreme Court races following hot-button decisions on capital punishment and same-sex marriage.[51]

In addition to simple **conflicts of interest**, some worry that expensive and bitter judicial campaigns may hurt the legitimacy of the court system itself. If judges—or even just their surrogates—are involved in unseemly campaigns, will that reduce the appearance of fairness for

[46] C. Scott Peters, "Canons of Ethics and Accountability in State Supreme Court Elections," *State Politics and Policy Quarterly* 9(2009):24–55.

[47] *Republican Party of Minnesota v. White*, 536 US 765 (2002); U.S. Eighth Circuit Court, *Dimick v. Republican Party of Minnesota* (No. 05–566).

[48] Chris W. Bonneau, "What Price Justice(s)? Understanding Campaign Spending in State Supreme Court Elections," *State Politics and Policy Quarterly* 5(2005):107–25; Brendan Kirby, "Alabama Had Costliest (But Not the Nastiest) Court Race," *The Press-Register* (Birmingham, AL), 11 November 2008, online edition.

[49] Kathleen Hale, Ramona McNeal, and Jason Pierceson, "New Judicial Politics? Interest Groups in State Supreme Court Races." Presented at the 2008 meeting of the Midwest Political Science Association, Chicago, IL.

[50] Steven Walters, Stacy Forster, and Patrick Marley, "After Bitter Race, Calls for Reform," *The Journal/Sentinel* (Milwaukee, WI), 2 April 2008, online edition; Greg Giroux, "Negative Ad Trend in Judicial Campaigns Draws Objections," *Politics.com*, 24 May 2007, online edition.

[51] Traut and Emmert, op cit.; "John H. Culver and John H. Wold, "Rose Bird and the Politics of Judicial Accountability in California," *Judicature* 70(1986):81–89.

the general public? One of the bedrocks of the criminal and civil justice system is that if people think it is fair, they are willing (if not happy) to accept its judgments, even if they don't like them. Some argue that this is even more important for the judicial branch than the executive and legislative branches, since they can be replaced more frequently. And in fact, recent studies have shown that elections, especially those with bitter, expensive, and highly publicized battles, can reduce the court's legitimacy in the public's eyes.[52] But political scientist James Gibson finds that only large amounts of campaign contributions from interest groups reduce the public's opinion of these courts; judicial candidates talking about policy positions and even running attack ads do not cause people to think less well of them. Especially interesting, Gibson also finds that this pattern of effects on state supreme courts' legitimacy is no different than those for state legislatures. In other words, he finds evidence that, at least in these respects, the public holds its judges to no different standard than their legislators. Furthermore, absent such costly and nasty races, other studies find that a court's legitimacy doesn't seem to be affected at all by how its judges rise to the bench.[53] That is, if the election campaigns are not too bitter and expensive, Americans do not seem especially troubled by selecting their judges like they select other state policy makers.

So, after considering some of these arguments against judicial election and elite appointment, the Merit Plan probably sounds like a pretty good alternative, doesn't it? After all, who could argue against picking judges based on merit? Indeed, this hybrid of expert evaluation and voter double-checking through a retention election has been by far the most frequently selected approach by the states that have changed their judicial selection method since

World War II. Most would agree that judges need certain technical expertise and training; not just anyone can be a judge. Going back to Thomas Jefferson, Americans have strongly believed that the average citizen could serve well as a legislator; even the executive skills needed of a governor are probably more evenly distributed in the population than those skills needed to be a judge. Furthermore, the average person probably cannot determine who has the specialized skills that a judge needs. Would you want your doctor or car mechanic to be selected by popular vote or would you rather have them picked (or at least certified) by experts in their fields? The Merit Plan also reduces the temptation in appointment systems for judicial selection to be made on criteria other than pure technical merit, such as party affiliation or returning a political favor.

On the other hand, as we have seen time and again in this book, all institutions have a variety of effects, not all of them good or even intended by their advocates. And we have to be careful not to take labels like "Merit Plan" at face value. If you stop to think about it, it sounds like the sort of marketing slogan that could have been cooked up over martinis on *Mad Men*.

What exactly does *merit* mean in this context? In practice, merit is defined for this reform based on the values of a state's legal establishment. Old, established law firms, the state bar association, and their political allies tend to dominate Merit Plan nomination committees. For example, Oklahoma's Judicial Nominating Commission is made up of six members of the Oklahoma Bar Association elected by their fellow bar members, six nonlawyers appointed by the governor, and one member elected by the other 12.[54] These people know—and really care about— the difference between the University of Texas School of Law and the Texas Tech University

[52] James L. Gibson, "Challenges to the Impartiality of State Supreme Courts: Legitimacy Theory and 'New-Style' Judicial Campaigns," *American Political Science Review* 102(2008):59–75; James L. Gibson, "Campaigning for the Bench: The Corrosive Effects of Campaign Speech? *Law and Society Review* 42(2008):899–928; Damon A. Cann and Jeff Yates, "Homegrown Institutional Legitimacy: Assessing Citizens' Diffuse Support for State Courts," *American Politics Research* 36(2008):297–329.

[53] James P. Wenzel, Shaun Bowler, and David J. Lanoue, "The Sources of Public Confidence in State Courts: Experience and Institutions," *American Politics Research* 31(2003):191–211; Sara C. Benesh, "Understanding Public Confidence in America Courts," *Journal of Politics* 68(2006):697–707.

[54] Oklahoma Bar Association, "2009 Judicial Nominating Commissions Elections," (http://www.okbar.org/news/news09/jnc/default.htm).

This ad for attorneys Fetman and Garland may generate significant name recognition—and business—that could help them should they someday decide to run for an elective judgeship. However, it will not likely impress the legal establishment who control nominations in the Merit Plan judicial selection process.

School of Law. So they may well be the best people to evaluate judicial merit. Some states at least try to expand their pool of potential judges more broadly. For example, in 2009, New Hampshire's Judicial Selection Commission began its work in filling a Supreme Court vacancy by running an online ad for applicants;[55] but where the NHJSC placed this ad is telling—on the website of the New Hampshire Bar Association.

The informal social hierarchy that exists in the legal profession also suggests certain differences in the types of lawyers selected to be judges through the Merit Plan and through elections or appointment. Consider the "See a Lawyer for 10 Bucks" guy who advertises on afternoon television and on city buses. He is not likely to attain a judgeship through the Merit Plan because he likely does not impress the legal establishment. On the other hand, he might have a pretty good chance of winning a judicial election since his TV and bus ads may generate considerable name recognition. The background, values, and clients of establishment lawyers can be quite different

than those of lawyers who advertise on buses. Think about who gains and loses when these values are reflected in judicial decision making.

So far, we have mainly considered reformers' arguments about the effects of these different judicial selection methods, but what has objective research told us about them? Scholars have used the institutional variation among the states in judicial selection method to test a variety of theories about their effects, both those espoused by reformers and others that reformers had not considered. First, scholars have looked at the effect of selection method on the demographic characteristics of judges. This is difficult due to the homogeneity among judges; even compared to other public officials, state judges are overwhelmingly middle-aged, middle class, white, and male. This has been changing somewhat in recent years, in particular with many more women coming to the bench, as a reflection of improvements in gender balance in the legal profession.[56] For example, whereas in 1980, only 3 percent of state supreme court justices were women, today that figure is 29 percent.[57] This parallels improvements in women's representation in state legislatures closely. More people of minority heritages are becoming judges, too.[58] But both socially and educationally, the bench is a very homogeneous place. Given the educational and training requirements for the job, it is probably not surprising that, more than any other class of public officials, judges' professional backgrounds are very similar.

Political scientists have found that elections lead to less racial and ethnic diversity among judges and that Merit Plans and appointment systems tend to increase it.[59] Why? First, because elections are decided on a majority-rule principle; if people tend to vote for those of their own racial or ethnic group (an arguable

[55] Kathryn Marchhocki, "Online Ad Seeks NH Supreme Court Justice," *Union-Leader* (Manchester, NH), 6 January 2009, online edition.

[56] Jennifer M. Jensen and Wendy L. Martinek, "The Effects of Race and Gender on the Judicial Ambitions of State Trial Court Judges," *Political Research Quarterly* 62(2009):379–92; Margaret S. Williams, "Ambition, Gender, and the Judiciary," *Political Research Quarterly* 61(2008):68–78.

[57] McCall, 2008, op cit.

[58] Kaitlyn L. Sill, "Judicial Selection and Racial Diversity: The Selection of African Americans to State Supreme Courts." Presented at the 2007 meeting of the Midwest Political Science Association, Chicago, IL.

[59] Barbara L. Graham, "Do Judicial Selection Systems Matter? A Study of Black Representation on State Courts," *American Politics Quarterly* 18(1990):316–36; Mark S. Hurwitz and Drew Noble Lanier, "Explaining Judicial Diversity: The Differential Ability of Women and Minorities to Attain Seats on State Supreme and Appellate Courts," *State Politics and Policy Quarterly* 3(2003):329–52; Sill, op cit.

assumption, of course), only candidates from majority groups will win for each slot. On the other hand, with an appointment system or Merit Plan, the appointing officials may look at the totality of the bench and purposefully seek diversity, whether because they think that it is the right thing to do or as a way of rewarding various constituencies. But if this is so, why do we find that women judicial candidates do worse in election systems, even though they constitute a slight majority in most states?[60] Attribute this to a lingering gender bias in the electorate, something that affects elections for almost all offices. As with the changing demographics of governors and legislators, this argument is supported by judges' increased gender diversity in recent decades as norms about women's roles in our society have changed.

Most political scientists studying the effects of judicial selection have focused on judicial decision making because of its potential to affect the administration of justice and public policy. The general conclusion of these studies is that judicial selection does not affect judges' decisions much, if at all.[61] This is good—we hope that judges' decisions are driven by the law and the facts of the cases before them. The norm that judges should be impartial arbiters of justice appears largely to override any institutional differences among selection methods. But political scientists have found various

marginal impacts of selection method on judicial decision making (especially at the supreme court level), primarily differences between elected judges on one hand and appointed and Merit Plan judges on the other.

First, as democratic theory suggests and as elections' critics fear, elected judges' decisions tend to reflect the ideology and values of their state's citizens, especially in competitive elections and on issues that are in the public eye, like capital punishment.[62] Perhaps even more worrying for those critics, elected judges tend to adjust their decisions as elections approach (even retention elections), reflecting their state's ideology ever more closely and issuing harsher criminal sentences.[63] Elections also lead to more plea bargaining, fewer trials, fewer dissenting opinions on controversial issues decided by supreme courts, and closer adherence to U.S. Supreme Court precedent.[64] These suggest an effort by elected judges to reflect their constituents' values and reduce conflict, both of which might help their reelection chances. Partisan elections seem to result in judges who vote in ways that reflect their partisanship[65] and, in civil cases, who grant higher awards to injured parties, despite their party affiliation.[66] Finally, as reformers hoped, two current studies have found that judges elected on nonpartisan ballots are more responsive to their constituents than those elected on partisan ballots.[67] At least

[60] Nicholas O. Alozie, "Selection Methods and the Recruitment of Women to State Courts of Last Resort," *Social Science Quarterly* 77(1996):110–26; Kathleen A. Bratton and Rorie L. Spill, "Existing Diversity and Judicial Selection: The Role of the Appointment Method in Establishing Gender Diversity in State Supreme Courts," *Social Science Quarterly* 83(2002):504–18; Hurwitz and Lanier, op cit.

[61] Henry R. Glick and Craig F. Emmert, "Selection Systems and Judicial Characteristics: The Recruitment of State Supreme Court Justices," *Judicature* 70(1987):228–35.

[62] Paul Brace and Brent Boyea, "State Public Opinion, the Death Penalty, and the Practice of Electing Judges," *American Journal of Political Science* 52(2008):360–72; Traut and Emmert, op cit.; Elisha Carol Savchak and A.J. Barghothi, "The Influence of Appointment and Retention Constituencies: Testing Strategies of Judicial Decisionmaking," *State Politics and Policy Quarterly* 7(4):394–415., op cit.; Brace and Hall, 1997, op cit.

[63] Melinda Gann Hall, "Constituent Influence in State Supreme Courts: Conceptual Notes and a Case Study," *Journal of Politics* 49(1987):1117–24; and Melinda Gann Hall, "Electoral Politics and Strategic Voting in State Supreme Courts," *Journal of Politics* 54(1992):427–46; McCall, 2008, op cit.; Huber and Gordon, op cit.

[64] Scott A. Comparato and Scott D McClurg, "A Neo-Institutional Explanation of State Supreme Court Responses in Search and Seizure Cases," *American Politics Research* 35(2007):726–54; Melinda Gann Hall, "State Supreme Courts in American Democracy: Probing the Myths of Judicial Reform," *American Political Science Review* 95(2001):315–30; Harold W. Elder, "Property Rights Structures and Criminal Courts: An Analysis of State Criminal Courts," *International Review of Law and Economics* 7(1987):21–32.

[65] Paul Brace and Melinda Gann Hall, "Justices' Response to Case Facts," *American Politics Quarterly* 24(1996):237–61; and Stuart S. Nagel, *Comparing Elected and Appointed Judicial Systems* (Beverly Hills, CA: Sage, 1973).

[66] Alexander Tabarrok and Eric Helland, "Court Politics: The Political Economy of Tort Awards," *Journal of Law and Economics* 42(1999):157–88.

[67] Caldarone, Canes-Wrone, and Clark, op cit.; Brandice Canes-Wrone and Kenneth W. Shotts, "Do Elections Encourage Ideological Rigidity?" *American Political Science Review* 101(2007):273–88.

on highly salient cases, like abortion questions in supreme courts, nonpartisan ballots give judges no cover from unpopular decisions.

While political scientists research the various causes and effects of judicial selection reform, for Americans and state policy makers, the question is a normative one—which method is best? Although researchers don't have a definitive answer to this question, they have done a good deal to focus it down to one of basic values. Most scholars working on this question, especially legal scholars, find themselves siding with the institution that enhances the value of the independence and experts, that is, the Merit Plan. Given the values of those who devote their lives to the study of the law, it should not be a surprise that this is the approach that appeals to them. In fact, the ABA believes that there are so many problems with any kind of judicial election that it has recently eliminated its support even for the retention elections of the Merit Plan, favoring instead direct appointment by the governor.[68] Since the ABA is the epitome of the legal establishment in this country, their interests would be maximized by this process.

Today's debate on judicial selection is not just between scholars advocating the Merit Plan (or direct appointment) and political party hacks advocating partisan elections. Some political scientists take the normative view that highlights a different set of values than those of legal scholars. In particular, Michigan State University

political scientist Melinda Gann Hall, often with her colleague, University of Pittsburgh's Chris Bonneau, has weighed into the debate about judicial elections as one of their strongest champions.[69] Mainly studying state supreme elections and decision making, Hall builds her argument by first demonstrating that judicial races are no less competitive than most other comparable races, like those for Congress and most statewide offices.[70] The information that voters have about judicial races, as reflected in the factors that influence their votes, is not much different than for those other races, either.[71] Hall and Bonneau also take a completely different tack on the issue of campaign spending, negative ads, and partisan labels than do the ABA and judicial elections' other critics.[72] They find that each of these increases the interest of, and the information available to, voters in judicial races, resulting in increased voter participation, a judicial branch that is more responsive to public values, and victories for better qualified candidates. Another set of studies of ICA elections finds largely supportive evidence.[73]

Hall and Bonneau have managed to focus the debate over judicial selection, demonstrating that competing values are at play, rather than simply a matter of which method is objectively superior. One view considers judges to be public officials who, while following professional norms and rules and using their training and experience, should be thought of like

[68] American Bar Association Commission on the 21st Century Judiciary, *Justice in Jeopardy* (Chicago: American Bar Association, 2003).

[69] Bonneau and Hall, 2009, op cit.

[70] Melinda Gann Hall, "State Supreme Courts in American Democracy: Probing the Myths of Judicial Reform," *American Political Science Review* 95(2001):315–30.

[71] Melinda Gann Hall and Chris W. Bonneau, "Predicting Challengers in State Supreme Court Elections: Context and the Politics of Institutional Design," *Political Research Quarterly* 56(2003):337–49; Melinda Gann Hall and Chris W. Bonneau, "Does Quality Matter? Challengers in State Supreme Court Elections," *American Journal of Political Science* 50(2006):20–33.

[72] Bonneau and Hall, 2009, op cit.; Melinda Gann Hall, "Voting in State Supreme Court Elections: Competition and Context as Democratic Incentives," *Journal of Politics* 69(2007):1147–59; Chris W. Bonneau, "The Effects of Campaign Spending in State Supreme Court Elections," *Political Research Quarterly* 60(2007):498–99; see also Brent D. Boyea, Victoria Farrar-Myers, Chris Bonneau, and Damon M. Cann, "Contributor Decisions in Judicial Elections: Explaining the Impact of Partisan and Nonpartisan Election Formats." Presented at the 9th Annual State Politics and Policy Conference, Chapel Hill, NC.

[73] Matthew J. Streb, Brian Frederick, and Casey LaFrance, "Voter Rolloff in a Low-Information Context: Evidence from Intermediate Appellate Court Elections," *American Politics Research* 37(2009):644–69; Matthew J. Streb and Brian Frederick, "Conditions for Competition in Low-Information Judicial Elections: The Case of Intermediate Appellate Court Elections," *Political Research Quarterly* 62(2009):523–37; Brian Frederick and Matthew J. Streb, "Paying the Price for a Seat on the Bench: Campaign Spending in Contested State Intermediate Appellate Court Elections," *State Politics and Policy Quarterly* 8(2008):410–29.

any other public officials in a democracy, with *responsiveness* to the voters being a value we should prize. The other view considers judges to be a special type of public official, one whose *independence* from all forces not related to the case, the law, and their professional standards we should value. These values parallel those that we hold for legislators, governors, and mayors (responsiveness), on the one hand, and for bureaucrats (independence) on the other. If you value responsiveness in judges, then Hall and Bonneau's research suggests that we should forgo all the middle-of-the-road reforms, like nonpartisan elections and Merit Plan retention elections, and use only partisan elections, since that is the selection method that generates the most interest in, and information about, judicial selection and, thereby, is the most responsive to the public. On the other hand, if you value judicial independence, the ABA's advocacy of a pure appointment process makes sense, since it would guarantee the judiciary's independence from any influence of public opinion. Of course, such appointments do not guarantee independence from the appointing entity.

So while scholars have recently learned much about the impacts of judicial selection processes, two things continue to make designing the perfect system difficult: (1) Each approach involves trade-offs and requires value judgments, and (2) the values involved—responsiveness to the public and the independence of experts, or rather, democracy versus technocracy—are not easily resolved in our political culture. It should be no wonder, then, that these institutions continue to vary widely among the states and that calls for reform continue everywhere.

Reform and the State Courts

The history of American state courts and the civil and criminal justice systems has been one of institutional experimentation and reform. From partisan and nonpartisan elections to the Merit Plan, from intermediate courts of appeal to family and **drug courts**, from directors of state courts to boards that review attorney and judicial misconduct, the states have been trying to get the administration of justice right for over 200 years. The lack of an accepted vision about what we want from our courts makes this a difficult and ongoing task. Certainly, we want fair and impartial adjudication of cases based on the facts and law, but we also want our courts to reflect the basic values and principles that our citizens hold dear. Furthermore, we want the courts to guard the basic rights of minorities because, besides being the right thing to do according to Americans' basic political values, we know that each of us will be in the minority sometimes, and we want our rights protected then.

Doing all of these jobs is a tall order for the courts, so it should be no surprise that we never get them exactly right. Consider the following reforms that have been touted recently and how they speak to the values we want our courts to reflect.

- **Tort reform**—Bringing a civil suit against a person, government, or corporation that we feel has injured us is an old way of settling disputes in the Anglo-American tradition of common law. Such an injury is known as a **tort**. Some argue that tort actions are occasionally abused, whether through excessive awards for damages or outright fraud. Business groups, medical groups (because doctors are the target of many tort suits), and their political allies (often Republicans) have led the fight for reforms that limit the right to sue or the amount that can be awarded in a lawsuit.[74] Trial lawyers, consumer and victims' rights groups, and their political allies (often Democrats) oppose tort reform, arguing that the ability to sue for damages not only compensates those who have suffered such damages, but also encourages manufacturers and

[74] Jefferey O'Connell and Christopher J. Robinette, *A Recipe for Balanced Tort Reform: Early Offers with Swift Settlements* (Durham, NC: Carolina Academic Press, 2008); Eric Helland and Alexander Taborrok, *Judge and Jury: American Tort Law on Trial* (Oakland, CA: The Independent Institute, 2005).

other businesses to avoid inflicting damage in the first place.

- **Criminal court reforms**—Criminal courts have also been the target of procedural reform efforts recently in an effort to make justice both fair and efficient there. Some of the most experimental of these reforms have struck at our oldest and most established courtroom traditions. For example, Oregon and Louisiana criminal trials tend to be shorter than in other states because they don't require a jury's unanimous agreement to convict.[75] As of 2008, judges in Florida can allow jurors to ask questions of witnesses, something that has never been allowed before in our legal system.[76] In another break from the past, the Virginia Court of Appeals (the Old Dominion's ICA) recently granted the first ever "Writ of Actual Innocence" after DNA evidence exonerated a person wrongly convicted of a crime.[77]

- **Prison reforms and alternatives**—The United States incarcerates a far greater proportion of its population than any other industrialized country. With a prison population of over 2 million, greater than 1 percent of adult Americans are imprisoned today, a record even for this country.[78] This prison population explosion has both strained state budgets and led many to question the efficacy, fairness, and humanity of our criminal justice system.

Drug courts, mental health courts, and veterans courts are all, in part, meant to address this crisis. States have also tried other reforms, including the greater use of parole and probation for nonviolent offenders. By one estimate, it costs a state $79 per day to keep a person in prison, while it costs $3.50 per day to monitor that person on probation or parole.[79] Some reforms are aimed at reducing **recidivism** rates, which are both a cause and an effect of prison overcrowding. For example, a new law in Kansas gives prisoners a better shot at parole if they complete educational and drug-treatment programs.[80] Other reforms try to deal directly with the costs of prison, such as instituting telemedicine capacities in prisons, charging convicts for their medical care, and even, in one drastic and controversial move tried in Ohio and Georgia, cutting back on prisoners' meals.[81]

- **CourTools**—CourTools are a set of 10 performance measures developed by the National Center for State Courts in an effort to make courts more user friendly and efficient.[82] Aimed at evaluating court systems rather than specific judges, CourTools use both objective court data and surveys of those who have participated in the judicial system as parties to a case, jurors, witnesses, and family members.

---

[75] Adam Liptak, "Guilty by a 10–2 Vote: Efficient or Unconstitutional?" *The New York Times*, 7 July 2009, online edition. The U.S. Supreme Court has recently agreed to hear a case (*Bowen v. Oregon* No. 08-1117) that challenges the constitutionality of non-unanimous juries, so this reform may not be an option soon.

[76] Colleen Jenkins, "Change Lets Jurors Submit Questions for Trial Witnesses," *The St. Petersburg* (FL) *Times*, 4 January 2008, online edition.

[77] Maria Gold, "Va. Court Grants First-Ever Innocence Writ," *The Washington Post*, 13 August 2008, online edition.

[78] Jenifer Warren, *One in 100: Behind Bars in America* (Philadelphia, PA: Pew Center for the States, 2008).

[79] Keith B. Richburg, "State Seek Less Costly Substitutes for Prison," *The Washington Post*, 13 July 2009, online edition.

[80] John Gramlich, "States Seek Alternatives to More Prisons," *Stateline-org*, 18 June 2007, online edition.

[81] Kurt Erikson, "Illinois Prisons Seek Medical Cost Savings," *Quad-City* (Rock Island, IL) *Times*, 23 April 2009, online edition; Associated Press, "Perdue OKs Charging Inmates for Health Care," *The Atlanta Journal-Constitution*, 22 April 2009, online edition; Associated Press, "Prison Blues: States Slimming Down Inmate Meals," *The Atlanta Journal-Constitution*, 5 June 2009, online edition.

[82] See the National Center for State Courts' website for more details on CourTools: http://www.ncsconline.org/D_Research/CourTools/tcmp_courttools.htm.

Summary

State justice systems are both complex and diverse, and the central themes of this book—the importance of institutions, reform, and comparisons—become thoroughly intermingled when discussing them. Because a court can have a significant and direct impact on a person's life, and because we have ambiguous expectations for our courts, Americans have continuously reformed these institutions. This has led to the substantial state-to-state variation we see among them today. Despite this complexity, we can identify clear patterns and use this variation to understand how the states' institutions of justice work.

State courts settle civil and criminal disputes among people, corporations, and government entities. These courts work as a self-contained system within each state, working parallel to, rather than in competition with or as inferior to, the federal court system. State trial courts, intermediate courts of appeal (ICAs), and supreme courts each have an important and unique role in administering justice. Roughly speaking, trial courts see disputes first, determine case facts,

and apply the law. ICAs examine the appeals about the fairness of trial proceedings. The supreme court assesses the constitutionality of state laws and legal procedures; it is the final arbiter of disputes over the state's constitution and law. Although their explicit job is just to interpret and apply the law in specific disputes, by doing so, the courts have a major impact public policy.

Unlike most other American public officials, state judges gain their positions through a variety of methods, depending on the state and the level of the court. These judicial selection methods include appointment by the governor or legislature, partisan and nonpartisan election, and the Merit Plan. There is perpetual call for the reform of judicial selection, with different methods being touted by those who hold different values about the courts. Although scholars have found some significant impacts of the ways in which judges are selected, little evidence exists that judges selected in different ways behave radically differently from one another on the bench.

Key Terms

Adjudication

Adjudicator

Adversarial argument

Bench trial

Common law

Conflict of interest

Court of last resort

Defendant

Director of state courts

Docket

General jurisdiction

Intermediate courts of appeal

Judicial review

Jury

Legal brief

Limited jurisdiction

Majority opinion

Merit Plan

Original jurisdiction

Out-of-court settlement

Plaintiff

Plea bargain

Precedent

Problem-solving courts

Recidivism

Recuse

Retention election

Specialty court

Supreme court

Tort

Trial court

Trial transcript

Discussion Questions

(1) Discuss the differences between criminal and civil law.

(2) What is the difference between a jury trial and a bench trial? What are the advantages and disadvantages of each type of trial?

(3) Why do states have intermediate courts of appeal, and what is their role in the judicial process?

(4) How and why do state supreme courts influence public policy?

(5) What are the different methods states use for selecting judges? Why is there such variance across the states?

Suggested Readings

Baum, Lawrence. 2007. *American Courts: Process and Policy*, 6th ed. Belfmont, CA: Cengage.

Bonneau, Chris W., and Melinda Gann Hall. 2009. *In Defense of Judicial Elections*. New York: Routledge.

Hall, Melinda Gann. 2001. "State Supreme Courts in American Democracy: Probing the Myths of Judicial Reform." *American Political Science Review* 95:315–30.

Hall, Melinda Gann. 2008. "State Courts: Politics and the Judicial Process," in Virginia Gray and Russell L. Hanson, eds., *Politics in the American States*, 9th ed. Washington, DC: CQ Press.

James L. Gibson. 2009. "'New-Style' Judicial Campaigns and the Legitimacy of State High Courts." *The Journal of Politics* 71(4):1285–304.

Langer, Laura. 2002. *Judicial Review in State Supreme Courts: A Comparative Study*. Albany, NY: SUNY Press.

Lessenger, James E., and Glade E. Roper, eds. 2007. *Drug Courts: A New Approach to Treatment and Rehabilitation*. New York: Springer.

Peters, C. Scott. 2009. "Canons of Ethics and Accountability in State Supreme Court Elections." *State Politics and Policy Quarterly* 9(1):24–55.

Sheldon, Charles H., and Linda S. Maule. 1997. *Choosing Justice: The Recruitment of State and Federal Judges*. Pullman, WA: Washington State University Press.

Squire, Peverill. 2008. "Measuring the Professionalization of U.S. State Courts of Last Resort." *State Politics and Policy Quarterly* 8(3):223–38.

Streb, Matthew J., ed. 2007. *Running for Judge: The Rising Political, Financial, and Legal Stakes of Judicial Elections*. New York: New York University Press.

Suggested Media Resources

CourTopics (http://www.ncsconline.org/WC/CourTopics/topiclisting.asp): This is an information database website run by the National Center for State Courts that provides in-depth information on court-related topics. CourTopics has links to resource guides, overviews, FAQs, state profiles, and other types of information.

Justice Case Files (http://www.ncsconline.org/D_Comm/OrderGrphNovel.asp): These are graphic novels developed by the National Center for State Courts to teach people about various issues facing the state courts.

Benched: The Corporate Takeover of the Judiciary, Wayne Ewing Films, Inc. This 2005 advocacy documentary tells the story of the 2004 Illinois State Supreme Court race between Lloyd Karmeier and Gordon Maag, in which advocacy groups on both sides of the "tort reform" issue spent millions of dollars in the most expensive judicial race in history. Directed and produced by Wayne Ewing. Running time: 75 minutes.

Websites

American Bar Association (http://www.abanet.org/): The ABA is the largest professional association of lawyers in the United States, whose activities include accrediting law schools, training lawyers and judges, and advocating for changes in the law and legal system that it feels necessary.

Association of Family and Conciliation Courts (http://www.afccnet.org/): The AFCC is a nonprofit association of all types of professionals who work in family courts and mediation processes. Its members include judges, lawyers, mediators, psychologists, researchers, social workers, court administrators, and others interested in improving this type of specialty court. Other types of specialty courts have similar associations, but since family courts are among the oldest of this type of court,

this association is currently the most well developed.

National Association of Court Management (http://www.nacmnet.org/): The NACM is a professional association for those who manage courts and court systems in the United States. It provides state, local, and federal court administrators information about best practices in running courts efficiently and effectively, and it advocates on behalf of courts and court administrators to the legislative and executive branches of government.

National Center for State Courts (http://www.ncsconline.org/): The NCSC is a professional association for judges that provides them with training, conducts research about law and legal systems, and advocates for judges' interests in the political system.

9

The Structure of Local Governments

INTRODUCTION

The structure of American local governments today is the product of reforms that redesigned political institutions at the beginning of the twentieth century. Some of these reforms have been discussed briefly in other parts of this book: nonpartisan local elections and direct democracy, for example. These are part of a larger package of institutional changes that fundamentally redefined how state and local politics work in much of the United States. Local political party organizations, or "party machines" that controlled public offices in many American cities in the nineteenth century, were the primary target of these reforms. We begin with a brief description of the major forms of local governments in the United States today and then examine the "machine" origins of American cities in order to understand how these local institutions have evolved into what they are today.

Many Americans might take for granted—or resent—the vast array of local governments in the United States. Local governments, including municipalities, counties, school districts, and numerous special service districts, provide a wide array of public services. Many Americans today reside in a town or city that is part of a larger county. Scattered across those two levels of government are school districts and various special districts that provide services to your place of residence. Given all these different types of local governments, your place of residence is likely located in several local governments simultaneously.

Forms of Local Government

Municipalities

Each state has its own unique rules about how municipal governments (cities, towns, and villages) are structured and how new municipalities are incorporated. Municipalities, like all local governments, are limited to doing only what their state says they may do. This concept, commonly known as **Dillon's rule**, means that a state legislature can make different rules about how various municipalities in a state might function. Many states have one set of rules for large cities (or special rules that affect only one city) and other rules for smaller municipalities. As we see below, these rules define what these places do and how they may do it. Larger, older cities often provide a wide range of general services—including police, fire protection, building inspections, water service, and many others. Newer cities may provide fewer services.

Counties

States are divided into geographic areas that perform some of the same functions as municipalities. Most states refer to these as counties, although they are known as boroughs in Alaska and parishes in Louisiana. Municipalities exist within counties,[1] and counties provide general services to portions of the county that are unincorporated (that is, outside city or town boundaries). Some counties contract with smaller cities and towns to provide a service the municipality does not offer. The range of public services provided varies substantially across the 3,000 counties in the United States. Counties are, traditionally, administrative and record-keeping jurisdictions for their states. County governments are thus often responsible for recording property records, conducting property tax assessments, administering elections, law enforcement, running jails, running courts, maintaining roads, and processing birth and death records.

Modern county governments have assumed many of the same responsibilities as large municipalities. In some ways, counties do even more than many large cities. Much of the federal and state money for health programs is spent in county hospitals and through county-administered health programs. Some states rely heavily on counties to regulate land use and development.

Special Districts

Special districts, or single-purpose governments, typically provide one particular service for an area. School districts may be the best-known single-purpose governments, but special districts supply dozens of different services (e.g., flood control, soil conservation, fire protection, and libraries). As of 2009, there were over 37,000 special districts in the United States. The geographic footprint of a special district may cut across city or county lines. As we see in the next chapter, a high density of special districts in an area can reduce the number of functions engaged by a municipality.

The Rise of the Urban United States

As Figure 9.1 illustrates, few people lived in America's urban places before 1850. As late as 1890, barely one-third of Americans lived in places with a population greater than 2,500. Cities continued to be viewed by many as a threat to democracy, whereas agrarian communities were seen as the soul of pure democracy. Yet, despite Jefferson's misgivings, the United States became a nation of large cities as immigration and industrialization fueled their growth after the Civil War.

In 1850, there was only one U.S. city with a population over 500,000 (New York) and just

---

[1] In Virginia, municipalities are jurisdictions independent from the counties they are located in. In Connecticut and Rhode Island, county governments play no functional role.

Figure 9.1

Percentage of Americans Living in Urban Places, 1790–2000

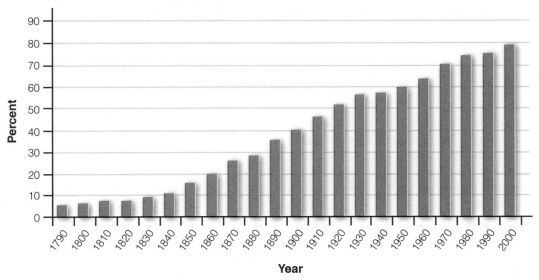

Source: U.S. Census Bureau data. Urban areas are defined as places with a population of over 2,500.

five others with more than 100,000 residents: Baltimore, Boston, Philadelphia, New Orleans, and Cincinnati. Each of these had less than 200,000 inhabitants. By 1870—just 20 years later—there were 14 U.S. cities with over 100,000 people; seven had more than 250,000 people. Chicago grew tenfold between 1850 and 1870, to 299,000. By 1890, America had 28 cities with a population of 100,000 or more, with New York, Chicago, and Philadelphia each having over 1,000,000 people. By 1910, cities like Louisville, Minneapolis, Denver, Seattle, and Portland were all much larger than the second-largest American city was in 1850.[2]

Immigration

Although the United States largely remained a nation of small communities throughout the nineteenth century, its large cities were magnets for European immigrants. Immigrants were pushed from Europe by social transformations that moved peasants from their traditional lands by poverty and, for the Irish, by famine. They were pulled to the United States by the prospect of jobs associated with booming industrialization, by opportunities to farm, and by the prospect of political and religious liberties.

As Figure 9.2 illustrates, millions of Irish and Germans emigrated from their native countries to the United States from 1850 to 1910. In 1890, there were nearly 2 million foreign-born Irish living in the United States, primarily in cities (this was equal to more than half the population of Ireland at the time). The social transformation produced by this immigration was profound. Prior to the 1840s, there was a limited measure of ethnic and religious heterogeneity in the United States. There were few Catholics or Jews and a limited range of Protestant denominations, for example. In 1850, Catholics made up just 5 percent of the U.S. population. With mass emigration from Ireland, Germany, central Europe, Scandinavia, Russia, Italy, and elsewhere, ethnic and religious

[2] Data from Campbell Gibson, "Population of the 100 Largest Cities and Other Urban Places in the United States: 1790–1990," U.S. Census Bureau, Population Division Working Paper no. 27, June (Washington, DC: U.S. Census Bureau. Population Division, 1998).

Figure 9.2

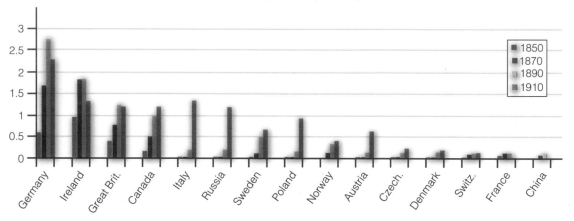

Immigration to the United States, in Millions, by Country of Origin

Legend: ■ 1850 ■ 1870 ▨ 1890 ▥ 1910

Source: U.S. Census Bureau.

Note: Each bar represents the number of immigrants from a nation over the course of one decade.

Dens of Death. New York City's crowded shanties and tenements, circa 1880s; photo by Jacob Riis. Riis's muckraking photography turned public attention toward the problems of crowded, unsanitary housing and urban poverty and helped drive support for reforming city governments.

Hulton–Deutsch Collection/CORBIS

diversity increased dramatically. Millions of Catholics emigrated from Germany and Ireland from 1850 to 1910. Millions more emigrated from Italy, Russia, Poland, and Austria in the first decade of the twentieth century. By 1906, 17 percent of Americans were Catholic, making Catholics the single-largest religious group in the nation.[3] Millions of Jews also immigrated

to American cities between 1880 and 1915—primarily from Eastern Europe (Poland, Latvia, Lithuania, and the Ukraine) and Russia. In 1910, there were 13.5 million people who were foreign born living in the United States, mostly in cities (see Figure 9.3).

The Need for Municipal Government

Multiple governments providing many public services are a relatively modern phenomenon. Governments played little role in providing social services or public services for much of the nineteenth century. No social security, no food stamps, no Medicaid, and no Environmental Protection Agency of the federal government existed at that time. The rapid **urbanization** of the United States largely outpaced the bare minimal levels of basic public services, such as sewerage, street lighting, and garbage collection, as well as any publicly provided social welfare. As cities grew, the need for basic services also grew. Urbanization meant increased fire risks. Cities required sanitation (for humans and horses alike). The growth of manufacturing

[3] Julie Byrne, *Roman Catholics and Immigration in Nineteenth Century America* (Research Triangle Park, NC: National Humanities Center, 2000).

Figure 9.3

Percentage Foreign Born: Large Cities and Rural Areas, 1870–2000

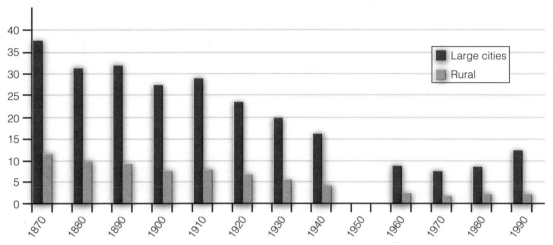

Source: Campbell Gibson and Emily Lennon, "Historical Census on the Foreign Born Population of the United States: 1850–1990," U.S. Census Bureau, Population Division Working Paper no. 29, February (Washington, DC: U.S. Census Bureau. Population Division, 1999).

Note: Bars represent the percentage of residents who are foreign born, for each decade. Large cities are defined as places over 100,000.

industries meant more people were crowded into polluted cities.

The provision of public services in this context was minimal and haphazard. Public and private police forces patrolled cities simultaneously. Fire departments were largely organized by volunteer groups, which often operated as private entities. Although Boston employed paid firefighters as early as 1678, few other U.S. cities followed Boston's lead over the next 200 years. New York City did not have paid firefighters until 1865.[4] A large city could have had multiple neighborhood-based fire brigades that did not cooperate with each other. Nineteenth-century local governments had developed with only minimal powers to regulate building standards, business practices, or public health. As there had never been much need for a public sector prior to the 1870s or for public employees, there were few regulations regarding who city officials could hire or fire. In short, the need for effective local government

outpaced the urbanization and development of U.S. cities.

Origins of Urban Party Machines

Urbanization created new demands for public services and also created new forms of politics. As Figure 9.3 illustrates, immigration built U.S. cities. Many of the new immigrants settled in cities and raised their families in cities. By 1870, 44 percent of New York City's residents were born outside of the United States; 48 percent in Chicago were foreign born, as were 49 percent in San Francisco. The population of the 25 largest U.S. cities outside the South was at least one-quarter to one-third foreign born in 1890.[5]

Growth of the Voting Population At the same time, the use of elections was expanding, although to a much more limited extent than what exists today. In the early 1800s, states placed substantial limits on who could vote. The number of voters in the United States increased

[4] Terry Golway, "Firefighters," *American Heritage Magazine* 56(6)(November/December 2005).

[5] Campbell Gibson and Emily Lennon, "Historical Census on the Foreign Born Population of the United States: 1850–1990," U.S. Census Bureau, Population Division Working Paper no. 29, February (Washington, DC: U.S. Census Bureau, Population Division, 1999).

dramatically after 1824. Several states began extending the right to vote to most white men in the 1820s, and all but one state moved to allow direct voting in presidential elections by 1832. By 1828, when Andrew Jackson was elected, the number of people voting tripled over what it had been in 1824. In the spirit of **Jacksonian democracy,** states were also expanding the range of offices subject to popular election. The first mayor of Chicago was elected in 1837 (he served one year). The first popular election of a Philadelphia mayor was held in 1840. With mass participation in federal, state, and local elections just emerging in the 1830s, there was a need for new methods to recruit candidates, communicate with voters, and earn voter loyalties. Out of this context, modern political parties were born—as institutions designed to meet the challenges of mobilizing regular people who had never before been allowed to play a role in elections.[6]

Early Political Parties A political group (in some cities, they were know as "clubs" before being called parties) seeking to control a city would need to organize support of enough people in enough neighborhoods so they could win elections. Volunteer firehouses provided one base for organizing, as they were distributed in various neighborhoods across a city. Firehouses served as a sort of social center, as did local pubs. By the 1850s, volunteer fire departments were becoming more Irish and more Catholic.[7] Political clubs found the firehouse and pubs places to organize and recruit loyalists, and volunteer fire departments became political forces in large cities like New York, Baltimore, and St. Louis. Firehouses weren't simply a means that parties used to organize support but also provided "an arena in which those who wished to exercise political leadership could win men's loyalty by demonstrating their ability."[8] Machine politicians in several large cities came

up through the ranks of firefighters, as did one of the nation's greatest political operatives, William "Boss" Tweed of New York City's Tammany Hall machine.[9]

Urban Party Machines

Urban political party organizations—known as **machines**—were born out of this nineteenth-century environment of industrialization, urbanization, rapid immigration, expanding democracy, and the absence of basic public services. These local party organizations gained and maintained control of cities by organizing neighborhoods to deliver votes for machine candidates on election day. One observer described machines as "quasi-feudal" because they were very hierarchical. At the top of the hierarchy sat the boss or the core group of leaders. The local boss and local party leaders might control the machine from the position of an elected office, but not every boss held local office. Below the boss and other organization leaders, a city was divided into districts (or **wards**), and each of these was divided into smaller units. Local neighborhoods, divided into **precincts**, were at the bottom of the hierarchy. Voters in neighborhoods remained loyal to the machine leaders when leaders provided them with favors or services. In immigrant neighborhoods where few residents had any political power or English language skills, relatively small favors might be mutually beneficial to party leaders and machine supporters alike. Irish Catholics were the backbone of machines in several, but not all, cities.

Favors that a machine organization provided to supporters could include help with finding a place to live, or assistance with food (a turkey on Christmas), or help with home-heating fuel in winter. Services could include help with the police, help with finding a job, or help with

[6] Richard Gunther and Larry Diamond, "Species of Political Parties," *Party Politics* 9(2003):167–99.

[7] Golway, "Firefighters."

[8] Amy Bridges, *A City in the Republic: Antebellum New York and the Origins of Machine Politics* (Ithaca, NY: Cornell University Press, 1984).

[9] Amy Greenberg, *Cause for Alarm: The Volunteer Fire Department in the Nineteenth Century City* (Cambridge, MA: Harvard University Press, 1998).

making contacts in business.[10] Machines may have also helped immigrants obtain citizenship (so they could vote). Some machine organizations offered illicit businesses protection from law enforcement, thus earning the support of tavern owners, prostitution businesses, and gambling operations. A few city machines had reformist intentions, establishing municipally owned utilities to improve water, sewer, and street-lighting services.

Patronage

Clientele politics involves providing something of value in exchange for political support. Prior to the late nineteenth century, appointment to most government jobs was controlled by elected officials. Winning politicians had the power to fire government employees and replace them with their supporters. For urban party machines, public sector jobs were one of the more lucrative perks that they could use to reward the people who helped keep the machine running. This **patronage** system occasionally had a high cost for politicians. Carter Harrison Sr., the mayor of Chicago, was assassinated in his home in 1893 by a "disappointed office seeker." Some cities such as Chicago retain elements of a patronage-based system to this day.

Precinct-Based Politics

A political machine's ability to organize a city politically depended on its ability to maintain support at the neighborhood level. Many precincts had workers loyal to the party—perhaps led by a **precinct captain**—who provided information about residents' needs and their voting habits to people higher up the party machine hierarchy. Voters might support the machine in response to the patronage and favors it provided or as the result of friendship with party loyalists in neighborhoods or some common social bond with a precinct worker.

Party organizations maintained contacts in neighborhoods by sponsoring picnics, sporting events, dances, and other social events "to keep people in the orbit of the machine."[11] Service as a precinct captain was a potential means for career advancement within the party organization.

District Elections, Large Councils

Given the concentration of different ethnic groups in distinct parts of a city, and given neighborhood-based political loyalties that flowed from this, it was easier for a machine to organize a city on ethnic loyalties when representation on the city council was based on small geographic units. Local councils where each member was elected from a small geographic district helped to transfer ethnic-based neighborhood loyalties into political representation. City councils (or boards of aldermen) with a large number of districts allowed distinct, homogeneous neighborhoods to form the basis of an individual district. A smaller district would be more likely to be ethnically homogenous and thus be easier to organize on the basis of common social bonds or patronage. This helped machine organizations reach out to various ethnic groups concentrated in different parts of a city. As an example, in 1900, the Chicago City Council had 70 members, with two aldermen from each district, elected to two-year terms in partisan elections.

Partisan Elections, Party Ballot Machine control of a city required electing as many machine loyalists as possible to local councils and local offices. The "Democrat" or "Republican" name attached to a party organization provided a banner, or easily communicated brand label, under which the organization's local candidates sought office. Some parties also controlled a newspaper in a city to promote the organization and its candidates.[12] Early American elections

[10] Steven P. Erie, *Rainbow's End: Irish Americans and the Dilemmas of Urban Machine Politics, 1840–1985* (Berkeley: University of California Press, 1988).

[11] Clarence Stone, "Urban Political Machines: Taking Stock," *PS: Political Science and Politics* 29(3)(1996):446–50.

[12] Robert McChesney, *Corporate Media as a Threat to Democracy* (New York: Seven Stories Press, 1997).

were largely unregulated affairs, and secrecy was not always expected in voting. In some places, party organizations printed their own ballots to distribute to voters. Parties gave voters pre-printed ballots listing the party's local candidates, with ballots listing only candidates preferred by the local party organization leaders. This helped the machine control who sought office, and it allowed party poll watchers to observe who voters were supporting. Party ballots printed in party newspapers could be clipped by voters to be cast when they arrived at the polling place. Party-printed ballots meant that there was little secrecy in voting, but it also provided a means of voting for new immigrants and others who were not literate enough to read a ballot and fill in without assistance the names of candidates they preferred. With much of the electorate having limited literacy, party-printed ballots made it possible for parties to communicate easily with voters and made it easier for many voters to participate in elections.

Timing of Elections Local party machines could have substantial influence on state and federal races if local elections were held at the same time as state or national contests. Local party organizations had incentives to bring their supporters to the polls in order to maintain control of the city. When local elections were contested in conjunction with state and federal races using straight-ticket ballots, machine organizations could deliver votes for the party's candidates seeking state and congressional offices, and they could have influence over presidential elections. High-profile state and national races, combined on the ballot with local contests, made it easier for machine organizations to mobilize a larger number of voters. Voter turnout in local elections is higher when local elections are held at the same time as national elections.[13] A local party machine's influence in the state or national party organizations as well as in state capitols and Washington, DC, was enhanced by the local organization's ability to

demonstrate that it could deliver votes for the party's candidates for higher office.

Corruption

Machines maintained voter support with patronage and favors and by building social bonds with their supporters. But some machine organizations also paid their supporters to show up to vote, and in parts of a city where support was weak, they could boost their vote share through electoral fraud—hence the classic machine-inspired slogan "Vote early, and vote often." Stuffing ballot boxes and bribing people for votes were not uncommon, and they were not something limited to big cities.[14] Support at elections—whether earned or bought—was not always enough for a party machine to maintain control of a city. Kickback schemes required people who were given public jobs or awarded lucrative city contracts to pay back part of their salary or revenues to the machine organization. Bribes were offered to judges and other officials who needed to be brought on board. Bribes could also be used to control who won contracts to build city facilities. Alliances with business leaders were important to machine politicians, as business provided resources (money and jobs) for the machine, but machine politicians and machine loyalists also had personal financial interests in private real estate and development businesses and benefited from inside information about where their cities would need to buy land or build bridges and roads.

Who Benefited from the Machines?

It is clear that machines often aided illicit businesses and that many machine leaders enriched themselves personally through their corrupt political activities. Machines also operated cities inefficiently, as they needed an inflated number of public employees to boost their opportunities

[13] Zoltan Hajnal and Paul Lewis, "Municipal Institutions and Voter Turnout in Local Elections," *Urban Affairs Quarterly* 5(2003):645–68.

[14] Loomis Mayfield, "Voting Fraud in Early Twentieth-Century Pittsburgh," *Journal of Interdisciplinary History* 24(1)(1993):59-84; and Genevive Gist, "Progressive Reform in a Rural Community: The Adams County Vote Fraud Case," *Mississippi Valley Historical Review* 48(1961):60–78.

for handing out jobs as patronage. This inflated public sector came at a cost that was borne by taxpayers. When factors like these are considered, it might seem hard to conclude that urban machines provided benefits to anyone but the machine leaders. Machine bosses, like Tammany Hall's George Washington Plunkitt and Richard Croker, made it no secret that they got rich off of politics. As Plunkitt famously stated, "I seen my opportunities, and I took 'em."[15] Likewise, Croker claimed, "I work for my own pocket all of the time."[16]

Despite overt corruption and inefficiencies, however, some argue that machines acted as a humanizing force, making life better for masses of immigrants arriving to the United States.[17] For one thing, the level of corruption, although shocking by contemporary American standards, was not debilitating to local economies. As Chicago Mayor Carter Harrison Sr. noted in the late 1890s, the two major desires of machine politicians and regular Chicagoans were to make money and spend it. Machine corruption and graft—skimming from local contracts and insider trading in real estate markets—probably encouraged machine politicians to boost local economic development and pursue pro-growth strategies. More growth meant more graft, but it also meant more jobs. And because some key businesses could leave a city and move elsewhere if graft and corruption got too bad, there were limits to what machines could extract from businesses.[18]

Whatever their corrupt practices were, machines needed to win elections, and the greater the legitimate voter support they had,

the better were their chances of winning. This meant they had to deliver something to voters—although contemporary studies suggest that machines had few decent-paying jobs to offer supporters.[19] Machines needed far more votes than they had city jobs to be filled. Machines were able to transfer real political power in many cities away from a minority of relatively affluent Protestants to the new Catholic majority. Others credit machines with contributing to the peaceful development of the United States by promoting personality-based and patronage-based politics rather than divisive ideological or radical class-based political divisions.[20] Although urban party machines championed "the little guy," workers, and the immigrant, they rarely flirted with socialist ideology. They also frequently opposed union efforts at organizing workers.[21]

But these latter points open urban party machines to further criticism. By emphasizing personal loyalties and patronage, and by opposing the emergence of organized labor (unions) in the late nineteenth century and early twentieth century, machines may have hampered the upward mobility of the United States' less affluent urban immigrants.[22]

Demise of the Machines

Regardless of whether urban machines served their supporters well, the era of machines came to an end in the twentieth century. Machines thrived when there were large masses of immigrants with limited language skills who lacked economic opportunities and political influence.

[15] William L. Riordan, *Plunkitt of Tammany Hall: A Series of Very Plain Talks on Very Practical Politics* (1905; reprint, New York: Bedford Books, St. Martin's, 1993).

[16] Lincoln Steffens, *The Autobiography of Lincoln Steffens* (New York: Harcourt, 1968).

[17] Clarence Stone, "Urban Machines: Taking Stock," *PS: Political Science and Politics* 29(1996):450; Steffens, *The Autobiography of Lincoln Steffens*.

[18] Rebecca Menes, "Corruption in Cities: Graft and Politics in American Cities at the Turn of the Twentieth Century," NBER Working Paper no. 9990, September (New York: National Bureau of Economic Research, 2003).

[19] Erie, *Rainbow's End*.

[20] Edward Banfield and James Q. Wilson, *City Politics* (New York: Vintage, 1963).

[21] Dennis R. Judd and Todd Swanstrom, *City Politics: Private Power and Public Policy* (New York: Pearson Longman, 2004).

[22] Martin Sheffter, "The Emergence of the Political Machine," in W. Hawley and M. Lipsky, eds., *Theoretical Perspectives on Urban Politics* (Englewood Cliffs, NJ: Prentice Hall, 1976); Bridges, *A City in the Republic*; McCaffery, *When Bosses Ruled Philadelphia*.

As immigrants became more educated and affluent over time, the political base of urban machines weakened. Eventually, as immigrants earned better livings, the relative value of the favors provided by the machines declined. Changes in federal laws produced a dramatic decline in immigration after 1910, further eroding the machine's base of support. Organized labor also became more influential in the early decades of the twentieth century and competed directly with machines for the loyalty (and votes) of working-class people. And as a result of the Great Depression of the 1930s, the federal government became much more active in providing for the basic needs of the poor. All these forces worked to dilute the influence of urban party machines.

Some big-city machines—but not all—can also be faulted for failing to respond adequately to the problems facing cities at the end of the nineteenth century. Many did a poor job of providing public services. Basic functions, such as streetcar service, street lighting, and sewers, were contracted to underfinanced private operators. Some party machines awarded lucrative utility monopolies to their business allies, instead of having the city provide the service or contracting with a firm best suited to providing a service. These private contractors often went bankrupt or defrauded local governments of their investments, leaving cities in debt and with inadequate public services.[23] Public health was also severely neglected. Basic services, such as municipal garbage removal, were sporadic.

The Urban Reform Movement

One reason for the demise of the urban party machines, then, is functional. Machines functioned poorly on several levels. Some functions that they had performed well, such as maintaining personal, ethnic-based loyalties and providing token material rewards for their supporters,

also became less important as society gradually changed. The shortcomings of urban life grew more apparent. Sporadic epidemics made thousands ill, and by the late 1880s, people had knowledge that germs were spread more rapidly in crowded places. **Muckraking journalists** rallied the public against the dangers of crowded, inadequate urban housing and the exploitation of child labor in urban factories and publicized the dangers of slaughterhouses and mass-produced food sources.

But a major reason for the demise of the machines is that rules defining how cities were governed were changed to make it far more difficult for popular political organizations to control city affairs. Industrialization and urbanization happened quite rapidly in the later part of the nineteenth century. By the early 1900s, several social movements were forming in both the United States and Canada to combat the ill effects of industrialization and urban life. In this environment, reformers of various stripes battled party machines to restructure the organization of city governments.

Many reform proposals were attempts to systematically change the rules about how cities could function—to replace the nineteenth-century personal-based style of clientelism with a more impersonal bureaucracy. Urban reformers believed that raw politics as a method for governing cities could be improved with efficient public administration.[24] Efficient administration included depersonalizing politics and replacing party loyalists in city departments with people who served because they had merit and specific job qualifications. Reformers wanted to insulate the functions of local governments from the influence of politicians who ruled because they could win elections.

Who Were the Reformers?

The various groups that worked to redefine local political institutions in the first two decades of the twentieth century are loosely

---

[23] Amy Bridges, *Morning Glories Municipal Reform in the Southwest* (Princeton, NJ: Princeton University Press).

[24] Kenneth Feingold, *Experts and Politicians: Reform Challenges to Machine Politics in New York, Cleveland and Chicago* (Princeton, NJ: Princeton University Press, 1995).

known as the **Progressive era** reformers. They should not be confused with the Populist reform movement discussed in previous chapters, although the goals of these groups often overlapped. The **Populist era** of the late nineteenth century was largely centered in rural and agricultural areas and in western mining regions. Populists believed that government and business were dominated by elites conspiring against common people—particularly against farmers. Populists emphasized reforms that broke up concentrations of political and economic power and favored new rules that nationalized ownership of key industries and empowered common citizens (see Chapter 4). Populists are characterized as having disdain for experts and elites[25] and believed in strengthening the power of popular majorities (voters).

Progressives, in contrast, recognized that the concentration of political and economic power could be dangerous. Their targets of concentrated economic and political power included monopolistic trusts that controlled major industries, including beef, sugar, and oil. Party machines were targeted as concentrations of political power that dominated politics in many cities. Progressives also had a different vision for reform than Populists. Many Progressives believed that society could be improved through scientific study and better administrative practices and by limiting the power that wealthy corporations had in politics. As Wisconsin governor Robert M. Lafollette Sr. said, "My goal is not to smash corporations, but to drive them out of politics."

Progressives, as their name suggests, embraced what they viewed as the positive aspects of progress associated with the modern era: science, technology, and efficiency. Progressives believed that efficiency in business and government could be improved if the proper information was available and the best people were charged with implementing policy.[26] For example, Progressives believed that federal government agencies were needed to regulate private business practices and that local public health agencies were needed to collect data, such as vital statistics, which could be used to improve living conditions. Many Progressives embraced the idea that scientific management practices and practical expertise could replace politics in the administration of local government. They were not antidemocratic, but some Progressives found that popular partisan control of local governments could be a barrier to efficient administration.

Women as a Force for Social Reform

Women's groups were active in promoting Progressive reforms early in the twentieth century. Lacking the power to vote, many politically engaged women sought to improve society and change policy by organizing groups that promoted reform goals.[27] In Chicago, the City Club and Women's City Club of Chicago conducted investigations of urban ills and published recommendations for reforms.[28] The Boston Women's Municipal League performed a similar role in that city. Influential women's clubs organized in most major cities. One study estimates that over 1 million women participated directly in the reform movement under the banner of "municipal housekeeping"—championing reforms that improved sanitation, education, and public health.[29] Women's clubs united under the General Federation of Women's Clubs. Ellen Swallow Richards, an MIT-educated scientist, demonstrated the need for food safety laws. Jane Addams worked with the City of Chicago to improve garbage cleanup, sewers, drinking water, medical care,

---

[25] Richard Hofstadter, *The Age of Reform* (New York: Knopf, 1955).

[26] Samuel Haber, *Efficiency and Uplift: Scientific Management in the Progressive Era: 1885–1930* (Chicago: University of Chicago Press, 1964).

[27] Daphne Spain, *How Women Saved the City* (Minneapolis: University of Minnesota Press, 2000).

[28] Maureen A. Flanagan, "Gender and Urban Political Reform: The City Club and the Woman's City Club of Chicago in the Progressive Era," *American Historical Review* 95(1990):1032–50.

[29] Flanagan, "Gender and Urban Political Reform."

and street lighting.[30] In the early years of the twentieth century, women also organized the backbone of the women's suffrage movement, and women played a major role in promoting reforms to legalize birth control.

Changing the Design of Local Institutions

The urban reform movement was born in this environment as a reaction against party machine dominance of local government. Groups advocating for new political arrangements formed in many American cities in the early years of the twentieth century, and national organizations, including the U.S. Chamber of Commerce and the National Municipal League, provided urban reformers with ideas for reshaping local politics and the administration of local government. Many of these reforms, detailed below, linked improvements in administration with weakening the power of local party machines and made it more difficult for elected officials to affect how cities work.

Class Conflict and Institutional Reform

One influential interpretation of the Progressive era is that reformers were motivated not so much by the goal of fixing the ills of industrialization and urbanization as they were by a reaction to the "status revolution" brought about by industrialism, immigration, and the expansion of mass democracy. Several studies suggest that reform advocates came from the ranks of the wealthy, educated, Protestant classes who had lost political influence to immigrant and working-class groups represented by the machines.[31] Historian Richard Hofstadter notes that industrialization created a new social class of superrich (e.g., Andrew Carnegie, John D. Rockefeller, and Leland Stanford) who dominated business and government with their wealth.[32] At the same time, urban party machines increased the political clout of urban immigrants. Both of those trends shifted power away from the descendants of established, upper-class, patrician Protestant families. These upper-status people may have promoted reforms to reassert their social and political clout over the new superrich "robber barons" and the new, largely Catholic immigrant working class.[33]

Another interpretation argues that the Progressives were largely drawn from a new middle class that was emerging from industrialization: a class of managers, business professionals, and administrators who sought to apply new business models to local politics.[34] Observers have noted that attempts at getting the politics out of city administration with a business model of government meant gutting the representation of lower-status minorities.[35] Some Progressives promoted southern-style Jim Crow laws in order to limit the political influence of racial and ethnic minorities.[36]

How Did Local Institutions Change?

One prominent national advocacy group, the National Municipal League, offered reformers a blueprint for how to rebuild local political institutions so that the influence of mass-based political parties would be weakened and the influence of unelected experts would be increased. The

---

[30] Jane Addams, *Twenty Years at Hull House* (Chicago: The Phillips Publishing Company, 1910).

[31] Samuel P. Hays, *The Politics of Reform in Municipal Government in the Progressive Era* (Indianapolis, IN: Bobbs-Merrill, 1972).

[32] Hofstadter, *The Age of Reform.*

[33] David Morgan and Robert England, *Managing Urban America* (Chatham, NJ: Chatham House, 1999).

[34] Robert H. Weibe, *Businessmen and Reform: A Study of Progressive Movements* (Chicago: Quadrangle, 1968).

[35] Banfield and Wilson, *City Politics,* 170–171.

[36] Glenda Elizabeth Gilmore, ed., *Who Were the Progressives?* (New Haven, CT: Yale University Press, 2002).

National Municipal League publicized its ideas for reform in a **model city charter**. The first model charter was drafted after several years of conferencing among urban reform groups, including the City Club of New York and the Municipal League of Philadelphia.[37] The model charter was an attempt to bring national attention to how various local experiments with new political arrangements "worked" (or "failed") in various cities. Elements of the model city charter were (and continue to be) updated periodically, and the earliest model charters embodied the Progressive reformers' ideal of how local government should function.

Because state laws define how charters for local governments are to be drawn, reform advocates had to lobby state legislatures to change state rules about local government arrangements. Progressive reformers were also able to define (or redefine) rules shaping local charters by electing sympathetic candidates as state legislators and governors. Some states had Progressive wings in both the Democratic or Republican parties, but Progressives were more often associated with the liberal wing of the Republican Party.

In many parts of the United States, there was wide public support for Democrats and Republicans who promoted Progressive reforms. Candidates who adhered to the Progressive reform agenda were elected governor in several states, including Wisconsin, California, Minnesota, Kansas, New York, Utah, and Pennsylvania. Although these governors are often classified as Progressives, some emphasized social reforms (e.g., public health and improved public education) and economic reforms (e.g., regulating monopolies) when in office more than changes to political institutions. Reformers committed to changing the nature of local political institutions also lobbied state governments to grant cities **home rule charters**.

A Menu of Reforms

Prior to the Reform era (another name for the Progressive era), mayors in most large cities had few formal powers, with major decisions controlled by large city councils. Machine organizations exercised their influence over a city by controlling council elections. Some of these institutional arrangements were characterized as **weak mayor–council systems**. Voters elected the mayor and council separately, but weak mayors often had little formal influence over city budgets, city departments, or what the city council did. By the middle of the 1800s, most U.S. cities had a city council and mayor who shared legislative and administrative powers.[38]

It is important to consider that in the early decades of the twentieth century, there were many ideas for changing how local political institutions operated and that these ideas have had a tremendous effect on defining how local governments work today.

Mayor–Council Government Progressives had conflicting views about how powerful a city's mayor should be and what the relationship between the mayor and council should be. Some early reformers believed that strong mayors were needed so that a reformist leader could take firm control of government and check the actions of the city council.[39] And by concentrating control of city administration in one institution (the mayor's office) and legislative and policy-making power in another institution (the city council), reformers hoped that the separation of powers would produce better governance. A mayor with strong powers who was directly elected by the voters could also be held accountable at the ballot box. This idea of a strong, accountable mayor also reflected a business model of government. In a business corporation, for example, shareholders and a board of directors give a chief executive strong

[37] National Municipal League, *Municipal Program* (New York: Macmillan, 1900).

[38] Charles Adrian, "Forms of City Government in American History," *Municipal Yearbook* (Washington, DC: International City Manager's Association, 1988).

[39] Charles Adrian and Charles Press, *Governing Urban America* (New York: McGraw Hill, 1977), p. 160.

authority over the day-to-day operations of a business, and shareholders or the board can remove an executive if they are dissatisfied with the performance of the corporation. At the end of the 1890s, a strong mayor was seen as a cure to municipal corruption.[40]

The National Municipal League's first Model City Charter (of 1900) recommended that mayors be given strong executive powers. Under a **strong mayor–council system,** mayors are directly elected by the voters at the same time that the city council is. Depending on how many powers a city grants its mayor, a strong mayor may interact with a city council in a manner similar to how a governor interacts with a state legislature. A strong mayor can be given executive powers that include hiring and firing heads of city departments (and other staff), drafting budgets, and vetoing acts of the city council. Mayors may have even stronger powers if they are elected to long terms (four years rather than two), if they are not limited in how often they can seek reelection, if they don't

have to share budget powers with the council, and if they have control over city schools. Figures 9.4 and 9.5 illustrate two versions of mayor–council government.

The second edition of the Model City Charter, published in 1915, gave up on the strong mayor plan. Since then, subsequent Model City Charters advocated a council–manager system with an appointed city executive (see below). About one-third of U.S. cities had mayor–council forms of government as of 2002, but many have mayors who have limits on their formal executive powers. About 40 percent of mayor–council cities have mayors with strong powers to affect budgets and appointments of city staff.[41] Most American cities that have a mayor today, particularly in smaller cities, have mayors with weak executive powers. Just 12 percent of U.S. mayors have the responsibility for developing budgets, and just 17 percent of mayors have the power to appoint department heads. Less than 30 percent of U.S. mayors have the power to

---

Figure 9.4

Weak Mayor–Council System

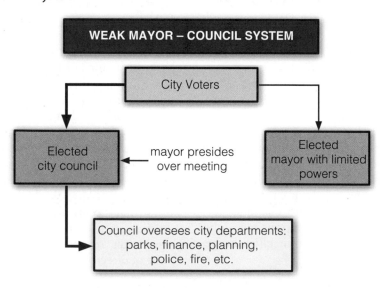

---

[40] Victor S. Desantis and Tari Renner, "City Government Structures: An Attempt at Clarification," *State and Local Government Review* 324(2002):95–104.

[41] International City Managers Association, "2001–2002 Survey" (Washington, DC: International City Managers Association, 2002).

Figure 9.5

Strong Mayor–Council System

veto acts of their city's council. Eighty-five percent of American mayors' jobs are considered part-time positions.[42] As Table 9.1 illustrates, many of the United States' largest cities have mayor–council systems of government today. These cities vary in how the mayor shares power with the city council.

Council–Manager Government After 1915, the National Municipal League began advocating for a **council–manager system** of government.[43] The council–manager system is the epitome of the business model of local government. Under this system, a small (five- to seven-member) council hires a professional administrator to implement its policies. The appointed executive is responsible for preparing the budget, directing day-to-day operations of city departments, overseeing personnel management, and serving as the council's chief policy advisor.[44] City managers supervise city staff, and they recruit, hire,

and fire city employees within the boundaries of civil service rules. Cities with a pure form of the council–manager system either have no mayor or have a very weak mayor who serves on the council. Most U.S. cities have council–manager governments.[45]

Under the council–manager arrangement illustrated in Figure 9.6, the city council may appoint one of its own members to serve as a part-time mayor, but the mayor's role is largely ceremonial (e.g., attending functions, presiding over meetings). About 37 percent of council–manager cities have no elected mayor. Another 47 percent have a mayor elected by voters, but the mayor has no veto power and little executive power. Mayors in council–manager systems may nonetheless act as spokespersons for their community and, despite their limited executive power, may be the most visible representative of the community.

[42] http://www.ncl.org/publications/index.html.

[43] International City Managers Association, *The Council-Manager Form of Government* (Washington, DC: ICMA, 2006).

[44] International City Managers Association, *Form of Government Survey* (Washington, DC: ICMA, 2001).

[45] David Morgan, Robert England, and John Pellissero, *Managing Urban America* (Washington, DC: CQ Press, 2006).

Table 9.1

Largest U.S. Cities with Mayor–Council Systems of Government

City	Population	Pop. Rank	Grade	Council Elections
New York, NY	8,214,000	1st	B	51 districts
Los Angeles, CA	3,849,000	2nd	C	15 districts
Chicago, IL	2,833,000	3rd	B–	50 districts (wards)
Houston, TX	2,144,000	4th	C+	9 districts, and 4 at-large
Philadelphia, PA	1,448,000	6th	B	10 districts, and 7 at-large
Detroit, MI	871,000	11th	B–	9 at-large
Jacksonville, FL	794,000	12th	B–	14 districts , and 5 at-large
Indianapolis, IN	785,000	13th	B+	25 districts, and 4 at-large
San Francisco, CA	739,000	14th	C	11 at-large
Columbus, OH	733,000	15th	C	7 at-large
Memphis, TN	670,000	17th	C+	13 districts
Baltimore, MD	631,000	19th	B–	18 districts
Boston, MA	591,000	22nd	B–	9 districts, and 4 at-large
Seattle, WA	582,000	23rd	B	9 at-large
Milwaukee, WI	573,000	25th	B	17 districts
Denver, CO	566,000	26th	B–	11 districts, and 2 at-large
Louisville, KY	554,000	27th	n/a	26 districts
Nashville, TN	552,000	29th	C+	35 districts, and 5 at-large
Albuquerque, NM	504,000	33rd	n/a	9 districts
Atlanta, GA	486,000	34th	C+	12 districts, and 3 at-large
Fresno, CA	466,000	36th	n/a	7 districts
Cleveland, OH	444,000	40th	C	21 districts (wards)
Omaha, NE	390,000	42nd	n/a	7 districts
Oakland, CA	397,300	44th	n/a	7 districts, and 1 at-large
Tulsa, OK	382,000	45th	n/a	9 districts
Honolulu, HI	377,000	46th	B	9 districts
Minneapolis, MN	372,000	47th	B+	13 districts (wards)

Note: Grade is the overall performance rating for the cities rated by the Government Performance Project, 2000, *Governing Magazine*. 2006 population figures.

A council–manager system gives executive powers and administrative control to the council-appointed administrator, known as a city manager (in some places, the position is called the city administrator, chief executive officer, or chief administrative officer). Executive powers, such as the authority to prepare a budget or hire department heads, are granted to the unelected, professional executive, who serves at the pleasure of the city council. A majority vote is required to fire a manager. Managers are expected to stay clear of political disputes and should not engage in local political activity. Most city managers now have professional academic training (a master's degree), and most serve in their position for about five years

Figure 9.6

Council–Manager System

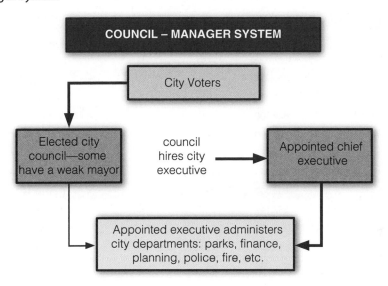

and have about 17 years of job experience in public administration.[46] Many managers move from city to city during their careers, and city managers' salaries average over $160,000 in cities that have between 120,000 and 220,000 residents.[47]

Adoption of the council–manager reform was rapid and widespread. In 1908, Staunton, Virginia, became the first city to pass an ordinance that defined the authority of an appointed executive. In 1912, Sumter, South Carolina, was the first city to define a council–manager system in its charter, and Dayton, Ohio, became the first large city to adopt the council–manager system in 1913.[48] By 1915, 82 cities had adopted the system, and twice as many more had by 1920.[49] The council–manager plan was subsequently adopted throughout the United States and is also used in Australia,

Canada, the Netherlands, and New Zealand. Most U.S. cities and towns—particularly smaller places—now operate with some version of a council–manager system, often with the councils elected in nonpartisan elections. Of the 247 American cities with a population over 100,000, 144 (58 percent) use a council–manager system. Some of the largest cities using this system include Cincinnati, Dallas, Kansas City, Phoenix, and Las Vegas. Over 92 million Americans live in cities governed with a council–manager system.[50]

Table 9.2 lists the largest American cities that use the council–manager system of government today.

Council–Manager and Mayor–Council Blends Cities continue to alter their charters to redefine the separation of powers between

---

[46] ICMA salary survey Worcester Regional Research Board. *Oh Manager, Where Art Thou? Best Practices for Selecting a City Manager* (Worcester, MA: ICMA, 2004).

[47] International City Managers Association, *The Council-Manager Form of Government*.

[48] Stillman, Richard J. (1974). *The Rise of the City Manager: A Public Professional in Local Government*. Albuquerque: University of New Mexico Press.

[49] International City Managers Association, *The Council-Manager Form of Government*.

[50] Adrian, "Forms of City Government in American History."

Table 9.2

Largest U.S. Cities with Council–Manager Systems of Government

City	Population	Pop. Rank	Grade	Council Elections
Phoenix, AZ	1,512,000	5th	A	8 districts
San Antonio, TX	1,296,000	7th	B	10 districts
San Diego, CA*	1,256,000	8th	B	8 districts
Dallas, TX	1,232,000	9th	C+	14 districts
San Jose, CA	929,000	10th	B–	10 districts
Austin, TX	709,000	16th	A–	6 at-large
Ft. Worth, TX	653,000	18th	n/a	9 districts
Charlotte, NC	611,000	20th	n/a	7 districts, and 4 at-large
El Paso, TX	609,000	21st	n/a	8 districts
Las Vegas, NV	552,147	28th	n/a	6 districts (wards)
Oklahoma City, OK	537,000	30th	n/a	8 districts (wards)
Tucson, AZ	518,000	32nd	n/a	7 at-large
Long Beach, CA	472,000	35th	B	9 districts
Sacramento, CA	453,000	37th	n/a	8 districts
Mesa, AZ	447,000	38th	n/a	6 districts
Kansas City, MO	447,000	39th	B–	6 districts, and 6 at-large
Virginia Beach, VA	435,000	41st	B+	7 districts, and 4 at-large
Colorado Springs, CO	369,000	49th	n/a	4 districts, and 5 at-large
Arlington, TX	362,000	50th	n/a	5 districts, and 4 at-large

Note: Grade is the overall performance rating for the cities rated by the Government Performance Project, 2000, *Governing Magazine*, 2006 population figures.

councils, mayors, and appointed city executives. Some mayor–councils adopted rules that borrowed features of the council–manager system in order to increase the autonomy of professional administrators. As an example, San Francisco became the first mayor–council city to hire a professional administrator in 1931, yet it remained a relatively strong mayor–council system.[51]

More recently, some council–manager systems have adopted features from mayor–council systems to increase direct political control by voters.[52] Surveys of cities suggest that over the last 25 years, a large number of cities have been switching from mayor–council systems.[53] In larger cities, however, there may be greater public pressure to have political institutions that make it easier for citizens to hold elected officials directly accountable for how a city operates. This has led some council–manager cities to adopt some of the features of mayor–council systems, such as directly elected mayors, as well as mayors with veto powers over councils.

Mayors in several cities, including Sacramento's Kevin Johnson, have championed charter revisions that give the mayor new powers.

[51] H. George Frederickson, G. A. Johnson, and C. Wood, "The Changing Structure of American Cities," *Public Administration Review* 64(May 2004):320–30.

[52] Desantis and Renner, "City Government Structures."

[53] Frederickson, Johnson, and Wood, "The Changing Structure of American Cities."

Sacramento Mayor Kevin Johnson

at the request of then-mayor Jerry Brown. Four years later, they voted to make the strong-mayor system permanent. In 2009, Mayor Kevin Johnson, a former NBA star, sponsored and qualified a ballot measure asking voters to change from a council–manager to strong-mayor form of government.

Commission System The National Municipal League was initially enthusiastic about a third form of local government: the commission system. The commission system was another attempt to isolate the administration of government from politics. Under this system, voters would select people, rather than a city council, to run city departments. A commission of these elected administrators shared executive and legislative powers.

In some early versions of the commission system, voters elected commissioners who would head specific city departments—for example, a finance commissioner, a public works commissioner, and a public safety (police and fire) commissioner. These commissioners would meet together as a council to pass city budgets (a legislative function), but each individual would be in charge of administering his or her own city department (an executive function). Most of these commission systems soon proved unworkable, as commissioners would promote the interests of their own departments over the general needs of the city, and it was difficult for anyone to coordinate city policy across rival city departments. Portland, Oregon, the 32nd largest U.S. city, is the only remaining large city to use the commission form of government. In Portland, voters elect a nonpartisan mayor and four nonpartisan commissioners, who serve together as a council. The mayor is in charge of assigning the administration of various departments to the four commissioners.

Proponents argue strong mayors can be more effective leaders. In 2009, Johnson asked voters to grant him the power to write the budget, appoint department heads, and veto acts of the city council. Dallas voters rejected a strong-mayor proposal in 2005.

Other council–manager cities have abandoned their council–manager systems. As examples, in 1999, Cincinnati voters approved a charter amendment that added a directly elected mayor to their council–manager system. The Cincinnati mayor has some elements of strong-mayor powers, can veto the council, and has a role in selecting the city manager, but a city manager remains in charge of administering Cincinnati's city departments and implementing policies approved by the council. Voters in San Diego, a council–manager city, approved a referendum in 2004 to have a four-year experiment with a strong mayor–council system. The experiment began in 2006. Oakland, California, voters approved a similar experiment in 1998

At-Large Elections In addition to altering the powers of mayors and city councils, many of the Progressive reforms from the early 1900s were aimed at changing how councils represented a city and how local elections were conducted.

Councils elected by individual districts increase opportunities for a political group or candidate to win support based on the social or ethnic bonds of specific neighborhoods. In district elections, only voters in the district vote for their representative. This meant that various ethnic minority groups concentrated in distinct neighborhoods could win council seats. Racial and ethnic minorities are more likely to win seats via districts than under citywide elections (known as at-large elections).[54]

In the early 1900s, Progressive reformers argued that at-large elections would make it more difficult for machines to organize cities from the precinct level up based on ethnic loyalties. In at-large elections, everyone in the city votes for each "position" on the city council. This allows a cohesive majority to sweep every council seat. At-large elections may also produce council representation with more of a citywide focus, whereas representatives elected by districts may have more parochial concerns. Most American cities now have at-large elections, although classic strong-mayor cities, and the 60 largest U.S. cities, are more likely to use district elections (see Tables 9.1 and 9.2). Some cities have representatives on their council elected partly by districts and partly citywide.

Since the 1970s, the U.S. Supreme Court has ruled that at-large elections may illegally dilute the influence of minority groups, and as a result, many larger cities (which have more minorities) have switched from at-large to district elections and other alternative election systems in recent decades (see Chapter 3).

Smaller Councils Large councils elected by district made it easier to organize a city on ethnic and neighborhood lines, as more seats on the council allowed the city to be divided into many distinctive council districts. Reformers promoted smaller councils elected at large as a means to create governments that had a more "citywide" focus.

Nonpartisan Elections Party labels allowed the machines an easy way to inform their supporters whom they should vote for. All they needed to do was select the candidates nominated by the machine organization listed as a Democrat (or Republican) candidate (depending on the city). Progressives and the National Municipal League promoted the idea that elections for local offices did not require partisan labels. This made it more difficult for low-literacy voters to support a party organization's candidate. Most U.S. cities now have nonpartisan elections, especially cities with council–manager forms of government. Ninety percent of council manager cities have nonpartisan elections.[55]

Australian Ballot The urban party machine's ability to communicate with its supporters was also eroded with the introduction of the Australian ballot (also known as the secret ballot). Unofficial, party-printed ballots were favored by machines because they listed only one party's candidates (that of the machine organization). The government-printed Australian ballot, in contrast, listed candidates from all parties and required voters to pick and choose among them in a private voting booth without assistance. Australian ballots also allowed voters to "split their ticket" and vote for candidates from different political parties and weakened the influence of local precinct captains who had printed and distributed ballots.[56] New York adopted the Australian ballot throughout the state in 1890.[57] In the southern and western regions of the United States, Australian ballots were adopted for different reasons. They made it difficult for third parties, such as the

---

[54] Richard Engstrom and Michael D. McDonald, "The Election of Blacks to City Councils," *American Political Science Review* 72(1981):344–54.

[55] Desantis and Renner, "City Government Structures."

[56] Some elite party officials may have allied with reformers in support of the Australian ballot to limit the influence of local precinct captains. John Reynolds and Richard McCormick, "Outlawing 'Treachery': Split Tickets and Ballot Laws in New York and New Jersey, 1880–1910," *Journal of American History* 72(1986):835–58.

[57] Gary Cox and Morgan Kousser, "Turnout and Rural Corruption: New York as a Test Case," *American Journal of Political Science* 25(1981):646.

Populists, to win support from illiterate working-class voters who required party-printed, **straight-ticket ballots**.[58] Nonpartisan elections, contested with Australian ballots, likely made it much more difficult for party organizations to get their supporters to vote for machine candidates.

Off-Year Elections Elections happen in cycles. When local elections are held on separate dates than other elections (presidential, congressional, or gubernatorial), fewer people are likely to take notice. A study of cities in California found that when local elections were held jointly with presidential elections, turnout was 36 percent higher than when elections were held at times when there were not any higher-level offices up for election. Local elections held in synch with a gubernatorial race had 21 percent higher turnout than a "local-only" election, and similar increases in turnout occur when local races are on the same ballot as candidates in a presidential primary.[59]

Voter Registration Prior to the late 1890s, there was little regulation of who could vote. Before then, a voter who arrived at the polls was automatically registered for the next election,[60] and party machines are reported to have created ways to offer immigrants "instant citizenship" to make them eligible for voting.[61] Repeat voting also inflated vote totals. One New York City election produced a reported turnout of 8 percent more than the total city voting population.[62]

By the early 1900s, many states attempted to combat electoral fraud by requiring that voters personally apply for registration before each election. Many early registration statutes applied only to the state's largest cities.[63] In 1908, the New York state legislature passed regulations on voting, requiring that all voters in cities of over 1 million people produce personal identification when voting and sign in when voting. Signatures could be matched to registration applications, and poll workers could query voters. Districts in New York City suspected of fraud-inflated vote totals in 1906 had substantially less voting in 1908.[64] As voter registration spread to other states, voter turnout in American elections fell sharply.[65]

Civil Service–Merit System Many federal government jobs became protected by civil service rules only after President James A. Garfield was assassinated in 1881 by a party activist who did not receive the patronage appointment he expected. The **Pendleton Act** of 1883 established a Civil Service Commission that began to depoliticize (or bureaucratize) the hiring and firing of many federal employees. The modern **civil service** system requires that public employees should be hired only on the basis of merit (that is, based on job-specific qualifications) and that they should not be fired unless employers can prove just cause for doing so. However, the federal civil service system does not apply to state and local governments. States and cities have adopted their own civil service systems, but differences exist across places in

---

[58] J. Morgan Kousser, *The Shaping of Southern Politics* (New Haven, CT: Yale University Press, 1974).

[59] Zoltan Hajnal, Paul Lewis, and Hugh Louch, *Municipal Elections in California: Turnout, Timing and Competition* (San Francisco: Public Policy Institute of California, 2002).

[60] Cox and Kousser, "Turnout and Rural Corruption."

[61] See Fund, "How to Steal an Election"; Kevin Phillips and Paul Blackman, *Electoral Reform and Voter Participation* (Washington, DC: AEI Press, 1975); Gist, "Progressive Reform in a Rural Community"; Mayfield, "Voting Fraud in Early Twentieth-Century Pittsburgh," for dates on introduction of these reforms across states.

[62] Fund, "How to Steal an Election."

[63] Walter Dean Burnham, *Critical Elections and the Mainsprings of American Politics* (New York: Norton, 1970), p. 81.

[64] John Lapp, "Election: Identification of Voters," *American Political Science Review* 3(1)(1909):62–3.

[65] Jerrod Rusk, "Communications," *American Political Science Review* 65(1971):1152–57; Jerrod Rusk, "Comment: The American Electoral Universe," *American Political Science Review* 68(1974):1028–49.

how many public jobs are classified as civil service and in terms of how many public employees serve at the pleasure of elected officials. Public jobs that do not fall under state or local civil service rules can still be awarded by political appointments.

Federal civil service rules did not apply to state and local government employees. Progressive reformers promoted the adoption of civil service rules on a city-by-city basis after 1900. By 1935, at least 450 U.S. cities had adopted some form of a civil service system. At least 200 more had adopted a civil service–merit system by 1938, including 80 percent of cities over 100,000.[66] This transferred the routine, day-to-day tasks of city governments from political loyalists to bureaucrats. By 1939, federal law required that states adopt some form of civil service for state workers, and in the 1960s, many states began requiring that their cities develop civil service–merit systems to depoliticize the hiring and firing of public employees. By the 1990s, most (but not all) states required their cities to adopt merit-based civil services.[67]

Today, cities vary in terms of how many city positions are classified as political appointments or civil service. In most places, only a few "policy advisor" positions are left for elected officials to appoint. In less-reformed cities, a strong mayor may still control numerous appointments to a wide range of city jobs and boards. A contemporary mayor of Chicago is estimated to control the appointment of 900 to 1,200 city positions.[68]

Although patronage-based cities are often linked with corruption, some studies suggest that they may be less expensive to run. Patronage allows local party officials more control over employee wages. In contrast, civil service unions may command higher wages. City workers may also be more accountable to voters in a patronage system than where they are protected by civil service rules.[69]

Corrupt Practices Acts After 1900, several states adopted laws to make it illegal to use bribes in elections and illegal to impersonate someone else when voting. An Oregon Corrupt Practices Act passed by voter initiative in 1908 designated as corrupt "the unlawful expenditure of money for election purposes; which covers the giving of cigars and tobacco; undue influence, including the threat of even a 'spiritual injury,' [im]personation; bribery; betting by a candidate on any pending election, or furnishing money therefore; seeking nomination for a venal motive, and not in good faith." Some states also attempted to regulate elections by limiting campaign expenditures.[70]

Strict Rules for Public Contracts Most states also now require cities to abide by strict rules when spending public money. These rules are designed to limit the ability of public officials to use public funds for their own benefit (or for the benefit of their supporters). These rules govern how public employees can make routine purchases and how contracts for public work shall be put to bid (most require sealed bids that conceal the identity of the firm bidding for the job). Other rules require detailed public records of expenditures and that city departments be subjected to external audits.

Local Direct Democracy Many reform advocates also promoted the adoption of the direct initiative, referendum, and recall for use in cities and counties. We discussed these institutions in Chapter 4. Initiatives were seen as a

---

[66] Pamela Tolbert and Lynne Zucker, "Institutional Sources of Change in the Formal Structure of Organizations: The Diffusion of Civil Service Reform, 1880–1935," *Administrative Science Quarterly* 28(1983):22. Also see H. George Frederickson, Bret Logan, and Curtis Wood, "Municipal Reform: A Well Kept Secret," *State and Local Government Review* 35(1)(2003):7–14.

[67] Frederickson, Logan, and Wood, "Municipal Reform."

[68] Author's personal communication with Ron Michaelson, former executive director of the Illinois State Board of Elections.

[69] Ester Fuchs, *Mayors and Money: Fiscal Policy in New York and Chicago* (Chicago: University of Chicago Press, 1992); Joseph Gyourko, "Looking Back to Look Forward: Learning from Philadelphia's 350 Years of Urban Development," *Brookings-Wharton Papers on Urban Affairs* (2005):1–58.

[70] Leon E. Aylsworth, "Corrupt Practices," *American Political Science Review* 65(1909):50–56.

way to advance reform goals that might not be approved by a city council. In 1893, California changed its law to allow the initiative in every county. Nebraska granted residents of all its cities the right to use initiatives in 1897. By 1911, state laws were changed to allow initiatives in cities in 11 states, mostly in the West.[71]

Municipal Reforms as a Continuum and Constant Process

Research suggests that municipal reform efforts had greater success in places where there were fewer working-class and immigrant voters, as these voters were the major supporters of the urban party machines. This means that some of the reforms discussed above were less likely to end up being adopted in older cities and were more likely to be adopted in smaller communities and in places outside the northeastern states.[72] Cities with high percentages of Irish immigrants were particularly resistant to adopting reforms during the Progressive era, as were northern cities that had a machine presence during the Reform era (e.g., Albany, New York; Baltimore; Boston; Chicago; Cleveland; Hartford, Connecticut; Jersey City, New Jersey; New Haven, Connecticut; Indianapolis; Philadelphia; Toledo, Ohio; and Youngstown, Ohio). Western cities, and cities without established machines, were more likely to adopt several of these reforms during the Progressive era (e.g., Colorado Springs, Colorado; Pasadena, Sacramento, and San Jose, California; and Wichita, Kansas).[73]

The structure of any city's political institutions today can be categorized in terms of a continuum, with cities employing fewer of these reforms at one end of the continuum and many reforms at the other. Cities now show limited variation regarding whether or not they have corrupt practices rules, civil service systems, or strict rules about public spending. But a large amount of variation still exists across cities in terms of how these rules work and in who ultimately administers the city. These rules mean that cities also vary in terms of how much direct control elected officials ultimately have on how their city is administered.

Larger cities, particularly those in eastern states where political institutions were more firmly established before the Progressive Reform era began, are more likely to be located on the less reformed end of the continuum: that is, they are more likely to have partisan elections, council elections by district, large city councils, and nearly all city affairs controlled by elected officials. This does not mean that former machine cities, such as Chicago and New York, have been insulated from the reform movement: both of these mayor–council cities now have some reform institutions (such as civil service). As Table 9.1 illustrates, cities with mayor–council systems are still "less reformed" in that they are more likely to have larger councils (even when population is accounted for), with a high proportion of the council representing individual districts. Mayor–council cities listed in Table 9.1 average 15 seats in size, with 83 percent of seats elected from districts. In contrast, council–manager city councils listed in Table 9.2 average nine seats in size, with 68 percent elected by district.

It is important to remember that city institutions are flexible and change frequently in response to crises and public demands for reform. The reform of municipal institutions is a continuing process. And, as noted above, larger council–manager cities, including some listed in Table 9.2, are also considering changing their institutions to provide for greater political accountability in the form of a strong, directly elected mayor. Many cities and counties periodically appoint or elect **charter review commissions** for the purpose of proposing changes to city institutions that voters might accept or reject.

[71] John Matsusaka, *For the Many or the Few* (Chicago: University of Chicago Press, 2004).

[72] James Weinstein, *Corporate Ideal in the Liberal State, 1900–1918* (Boston: Beacon Press, 1968).

[73] James Gimpel, "Reform Resistant and Reform Adopting Machines: The Electoral Foundations of Urban Politics," *Political Research Quarterly* 46(2)(1993):371–82.

Consequences of Municipal Reforms

One thing that occurred after the Reform era was that reformed cities became more efficient and had less political corruption. The cumulative effect of many of these reforms may be efficient, professional, modern city administration that is more capable of managing the "housekeeping" functions of cities. Building codes and public health standards are now much more likely to be implemented and administered by civil servants following standard operating procedures. Business licenses and lucrative contracts to provide services to a city are more likely to be granted on the basis of standard operating procedures rather than political favoritism. Public works projects are now far more likely to be constructed by qualified contractors who offer the lowest bid. Well-regulated public utilities now provide many cities with water, power, street lighting, and sewerage. Police enforce laws with greater objectivity, and politicians cannot easily enrich themselves by directing the police to "selectively" enforce laws. Of course, it is difficult to prove that reforms themselves made cites more efficient and less corrupt. Since the early 1900s, all U.S. cities, reformed and unreformed alike, are probably governed better today.

Nonpolitical Administration?

The discussion of party machines in this chapter suggests that patronage, corruption, and other inefficiencies may have inflated public spending in unreformed cities. We also might expect public spending to be higher in unreformed cities because classic machines were designed to be responsive to many different groups that might demand city services. Reforms such as at-large, nonpartisan elections and council–manager

systems could insulate city officials from such demands. One influential study did find less taxing and spending in reformed cities,[74] but subsequent research found few differences in city finances in reformed versus unreformed cities.[75] Council–manager systems may limit how much direct influence elected officials have on how city money is spent, but this need not mean that these cities spend less or that their appointed managers are insulated from political pressures. Modern city managers face pressure from elected officials for changes in how (and to whom) services are delivered and for changes in how cities are managed.[76]

Efficiency–Accountability Trade-Off?

Some observers suggest that gains in administrative efficiency may come at the price of less direct control of city government by citizens. With so many administrative functions now supervised by appointed city managers and public employees protected against being fired for political reasons, it may be more difficult for a majority of voters to hold their government accountable at the ballot box for unpopular actions. Rigid bureaucratic rules, civil service protections, and "red tape" may make it difficult for elected officials to put political pressure on city administrators, but these rules ensure that politicians cannot use their position to enrich themselves and their friends. A study of nonpartisan city council members also found that unlike machine politicians, nonpartisan elected officials may care little about getting reelected and thus have little regard for public opinion.[77]

Another side exists to the efficiency–accountability trade-off, however. Cross-national studies show that high levels of political corruption increase cynicism about politics and depress

[74] Robert Lineberry and Edmond Fowler "Reformism and Public Policies in American Cities," *American Political Science Review* (1967):701–16.

[75] David Morgan and John Pellissero, "Urban Policy: Does Political Structure Matter?" *American Political Science Review* 74(1980):999–1006.

[76] James H. Svara, "The Politics-Administration Dichotomy Model as Aberration," *Public Administration Review* 58(1998):51.

[77] Kenneth Prewitt, "Political Ambitions, Volunteerism, and Electoral Accountability," *American Political Science Review* (1970):5–17.

respect for the rule of law.[78] Public corruption causes people to retreat from conventional politics. In contrast, reforms that root out political corruption may increase public confidence in democracy.

Barriers to Mass Participation

Several studies find that the combined effects of reforms, such as off-year elections and nonpartisan elections, act to depress voter participation in reform cities.[79] These reforms make local elections less visible to many people and make it more difficult for many people to evaluate candidates. We provide more discussion of this in Chapter 3. For much of the twentieth century, turnout for local elections was higher in large machine cities than in large reform cities.[80] Lower turnout may lead to substantial

Comparisons Help Us Understand

STRONG VS. WEAK MAYORS

In March 1991, the Los Angeles Police Department's brutal beating of African American motorist Rodney King was captured on video. The tape was played repeatedly on television news, leading many to view the LAPD as a racist organization. The LAPD already had a strained relationship with the black community in south Los Angeles after aggressive responses to gang violence in the area. After the King beating, local politicians, community organizations, and national figures, such as Jesse Jackson and Al Sharpton, called for Gates to be dismissed.

Mayor Tom Bradley, however, had no power to hire or fire his city's police chief. Those decisions were controlled by an independent, five-member police commission designed to function like a corporate board of directors. The Los Angeles Charter gave the police commission little power to discharge the chief. The charter granted the chief "substantial property right" to his job. The intent of the Charter, drafted in 1925, was to remove political control of city affairs from "politicians" and place it in the hands of professional managers. Architects of the city charter expected that city departments would be corrupted if politicians had direct control over them.[1]

Mayor Bradley asked Gates to resign on April 2, 1991, but Gates refused. On April 29, 1992, the officers involved in the beatings were acquitted of all charges by a California jury. Violent riots began shortly after the verdict was announced. Rioting lasted for three days and left 53 dead. Gates remained in office until late June 1992, when he finally resigned.

Mayors in some other cities, in contrast, have far more power to hire and fire city employees. When New York City Mayor Michael Bloomberg saw a city employee playing solitaire on a city computer in 2006, he fired the man on the spot with no warning or severance pay. The mayor of Baltimore fired the head of the city's police force after the chief was accused of beating his girlfriend.[2] Politics in Los Angeles, and similar cities, is shaped heavily by institutional reforms designed to limit political control of municipal functions. Cities like Baltimore and New York City, in contrast, have traditions of unfettered political control of the administration of city departments.

[1] Report of the Independent Commission on the Los Angeles Police Department (Los Angeles: Independent Commission on the Los Angeles Police Department, 1991), ch. 10.
[2] National Briefing, "Mid Atlantic: Maryland: Mayor Fires Police Commissioner," *The New York Times*, 11 November 2004.

[78] Todd Donovan, David Denemark, and Shaun Bowler, "Trust, Citizenship and Participation: Australia in Comparative Perspective," in David Denemark et al., eds., *Australian Social Attitudes: The 2nd Report* (Sydney: University of New South Wales Press, 2007).

[79] Albert Karing and B. Oliver Walter, "Decline in Municipal Voter Turnout: A Function of Changing Structure," *American Politics Quarterly* 11(1983):491–505; Hajnal and Lewis, "Municipal Institutions and Voter Turnout in Local Elections."

[80] Jessica Trounstine, "Dominant Regimes and the Demise of Urban Democracy," *Journal of Politics* (2006):879–93.

reductions in the representation of Latinos and Asian Americans on city councils and in mayors' offices. African Americans win office less often when turnout is depressed by off-year elections.

Class and Racial Bias

Class and racial bias in local politics may be affected by low turnout, itself a product of some reforms. Turnout can be lower than 10 percent in some off-year, nonpartisan local elections. Although there may not be large differences in who votes and who does not vote in high-turnout national elections, very low turnout in local elections may increase the class and racial differences between voters and nonvoters.[81] This may distort democracy because elected officials may be more attentive to the interests of voters than nonvoters. Low turnout rates also result in less representation of Latinos and Asian Americans as mayors and on city councils than they might receive when turnout is higher. At-large elections can further increase the influence of middle-class and upper-class groups in local politics by reducing opportunities for representation of African Americans and ethnic minorities (see Chapter 3). Maintaining lower levels of minority officeholders has consequences for who gets what from city government. Fewer minorities in offices mean fewer minority citizens holding city jobs.[82]

The Scope of Local Governments in America

Cities are one of most visible forms of local government in America, but there are many other types of local governments. Over 80 percent of Americans now reside in a **metropolitan area** that consists of many overlapping local governments, with at least one central city, several other cities, and unincorporated areas governed by a county. A single metro area may consist of multiple central cities, dozens of other suburban cities and several counties. Within a metro area, there are also school districts, plus several other **special districts** that supply one specific service, such as fire protection districts, parks districts, library districts, or hospital districts.

What Do Cities Do?

Today, more Americans live in suburban places than in rural areas or older, traditional central cities such as Chicago, New York, or San Francisco. Many of these suburban places did not exist 60 years ago. Depending on where you live, you are likely to simultaneously be a resident of a county, a city, and numerous special districts. Older, traditional cities tend to provide more public services—such as fire, water, transit, sewer—than newer cities.[83] Given these stakes, local governance in traditional cities may be quite visible to residents, particularly if the city has partisan elections or a strong mayor.

In contrast, some newer cities may not provide a single municipal service other than police. Most cities formed since the 1950s contract for services from other governments, depend on low-visibility special districts to provide services, or have private companies supply services. Most don't provide fire protection, water, sewerage or public transit.[84] This fragmentation, combined with nonpartisan elections and council–manager governments, may make it difficult for residents to be aware of who is responsible for governing their community.

---

[81] Albert Karing and B. Oliver Walter, "Decline in Municipal Voter Turnout: A Function of Changing Structure," *American Politics Quarterly* 11(1983):491–505.

[82] Peter K. Eisenger, "Black Employment in Municipal Jobs: The Impact of Black Political Power," *American Political Science Review* 76(1982):380–390; Lana Stein, "Representative Local Government: Minorities in the Municipal Workforce," *Journal of Politics* 48(1986):694–713; Thomas Dye and James Renick, "Political Power and City Jobs: Determinants of Minority Employment," *Social Science Quarterly* 62(1981):457–86.

[83] Nancy Burns, *The Formation of Local Governments: Private Values in Public Institutions.* (Oxford University Press, 1994)

[84] Burns, *The Formation of Local Governments*, p. 9.

Summary

In this chapter, we examine how the United States began as a rural nation but experienced rapid urbanization in the mid-1800s. The growth of cities outpaced the growth of effective government, and urban machines emerged in this context with a style of politics that thrived for decades. The machine style emphasized personal bonds over substantive government services. The style is well-represented by a machine politician quoted as saying that he wanted to be sure that there has to be someone in every ward of his city that "any bloke can come to—no matter what he's done—and get help. Help, you understand; none of your law and justice, but help."[85]

The personal touch of machine politicians might have helped some people find jobs or fix problems with the law, but it could not ensure that all people were treated equally before the law. The absence of law, justice, and effective municipal services made machines a target for reforms that redesigned local political institutions. The modern bureaucratic city, for all its cold impersonal character, is designed to have routine standards that public employees must follow if everyone is going to be treated the same.

This chapter also illustrates how changes in political institutions can affect who gets what from local government. The reforms adopted during the Progressive era altered how people become engaged with local politics. Some reforms were clearly designed to limit which sort of people would be mobilized. Many of these reforms survive to this day, but others, such as at-large elections, are often challenged and rejected. Overall, the municipal reforms discussed here may have subtle effects on how a modern city is governed. Elected officials in reformed cities have less direct influence over some administrative matters than their counterparts in cities that adopted few reforms. But for all their supposed separation of politics and administration, highly reformed cities may differ from contemporary "unreformed cities" not so much in how efficiently they are governed but in who governs. Institutions that increase participation, increase diversity in representation, and guarantee electoral competition—such as partisan local elections, local elections held during presidential contests, and representation by district—may create a more pluralist form of local politics. By pluralist, we mean a form of politics where more voices are heard and where it is difficult for any single group to consolidate power.

Key Terms

Charter review commission

Civil service

Council–manager system

Dillon's rule

Home rule charters

Jacksonian democracy

Machines

Metropolitan areas

Model city charter

Muckraking journalists

Patronage

Pendleton Act

Populist era

Precinct

---

[85] Martin Lomansy, quoted in Steffens, *The Autobiography of Lincoln Steffens*.

Precinct captain

Progressive era

Special districts

Straight-ticket ballot

Strong mayor–council system

Urbanization

Ward

Weak mayor–council systems

Discussion Questions

(1) What was Jefferson's vision for American communities? What caused this model to see drastic change?

(2) How were cities governed during the nineteenth-century urbanization and industrialization boom?

(3) What ended the urban party machine era?

(4) How did the urban reform movement change the design of local governments?

(5) Discuss the differences between the mayor–council and council–manager systems of government. What are the advantages and disadvantages of each?

Suggested Readings

Bridges, Amy. 1984. *A City in the Republic: Antebellum New York and the Origins of Machine Politics*. Ithaca, NY: Cornell University Press.

———. 1997. *Morning Glories: Municipal Reform in the Southwest*. Princeton, NJ: Princeton Univer sity Press.

Elkins, Steven. 1987. *City and Regime in the American Republic*. Chicago: University of Chicago Press.

Erie, Steven. *Rainbow's End: Irish Americans and the Dilemmas of Urban Machine Politics,* *1840–1985*. Berkeley: University of California Press.

Riordan, William L. 1993. *Plunkitt of Tammany Hall: A Series of Very Plain Talks on Very Practical Politics*. New York: Bedford Books, St. Martin's (Originally published in 1905).

Spain, Daphne. 2000. *How Women Saved the City*. Minneapolis: University of Minnesota Press.

Websites

International City Manager Association (ICMA; http://www.icma.org): The professional and educational organization for appointed city managers, administrators, and assistants. ICMA provides technical assistance, training, and information resources to its members and the local governments. Also publishes the city manager code of ethics. Founded in 1914.

National Civic League (http://www.ncl.org): A nonprofit, nonpartisan group founded in 1894 by Teddy Roosevelt and others to promote municipal reform and community democracy. NCSL serves as a resource for anyone interested in cutting-edge community-building practices. The group was originally known as the National Municipal League and periodically publishes recommendations for government structures (the Model City Charter).

National League of Cities (http://www.nlc.org): Lobby groups for local government interests in Washington, DC. The oldest and largest national organization representing municipal governments throughout the United States.

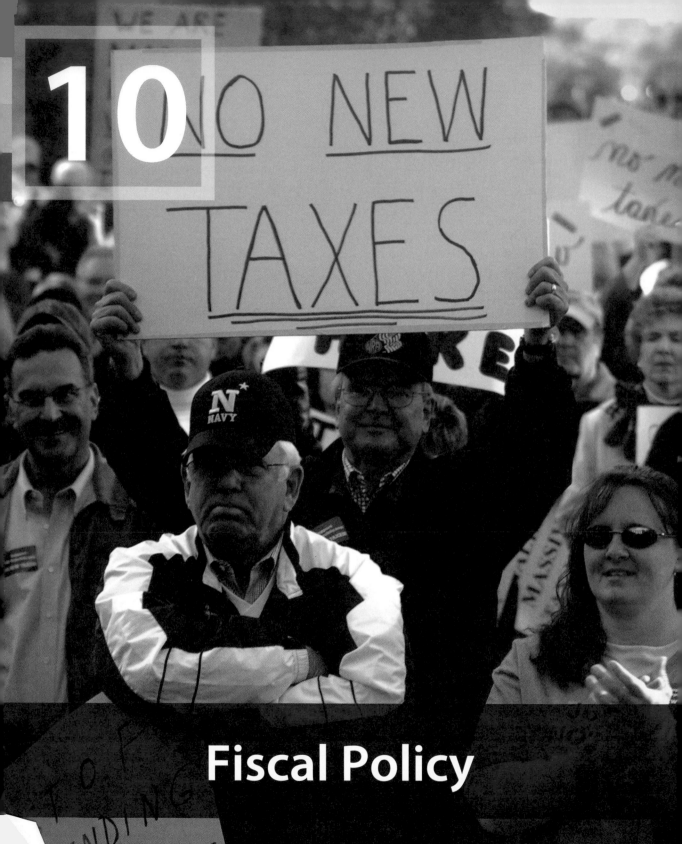

10

Fiscal Policy

INTRODUCTION

Economic boom and bust can have dramatic effects on state and local budgets. Unlike the federal budget, state and local budgets must balance. When the economy is booming, revenues can exceed expectations and provide funds for more public services, for tax cuts, or both. Many states experienced robust growth in the years before 2008. A growing economy, built on consumer borrowing and spending, meant more revenues, and more spending on popular programs such as education and health care for poor children. When things go bust, people stop investing, some lose their jobs, and people consume less. Tax revenues dry up. Painful cuts or unpopular tax increases are needed to make budgets balance.

Things went spectacularly bust in late 2008. In spring, Bear Sterns, one of America's largest investment firms, collapsed. A large California mortgage bank failed in July. By fall, banks quit lending, the real estate market evaporated, and the consumer spending, construction jobs, and business investments that had provided tax revenues dried up. In September 2008, other major financial institutions failed or avoided failure via government take-over. The economy continued to decline, and it became clear that most states' budgets for the 2008–09 fiscal year would end up in deficit. State and local governments had to revise their budgets to make them balance.

Arizona was hit hard. In January 2009, the legislature patched a $1 billion hole with the hope that would balanced the budget by the end of the fiscal year (June 30, 2009). Pac 10 football coaches were given pay cuts, and university budgets were cut heavily. By July 2009, however, the state still faced a projected $2.5 billion deficit (in the 2008–09 budget), equal to 25 percent of the budget. Meanwhile, it also had to plan a 2009–10 budget, and revenue forecasts showed a $3 billion deficit for that budget. The state used spending cuts, one-time federal stimulus funds, and the sale of state House and state Senate buildings to close part of the deficit in September. Entire academic programs were cut at universities, and per student funding was set at the lowest level in years. Spending on social services was cut, and 10,000 families lost state health insurance.[1] Fifteen thousand state employees were furloughed.[2] Arizona's tax collections were 18 percent lower in 2009 than 2008. By 2010 Arizona's revenues shrank to 2004 levels, but the population was larger—more students and an additional 475,000 people on its Medicaid rolls.[3] It cut another $1 billion in spending (from an $8.9 billion budget) by eliminating 350,000 from the state health insurance plan and eliminating full day kindergarten.[4]

[1] Casey Newton, "10,000 Working Parents in Arizona to lose Health Insurance" *Arizona Republic*, 8 September 2009.

[2] *Harper's*, July 2010.

[3] David Von Drehle, "Inside the Dire Financial State of the States," *Time*, 17 June 2010.

[4] Stateline.org, "Dramatic cuts in Arizona," March 17, 2010.

Gail Burton/AP

Arizona was not alone. States collected 9 percent less tax revenue in 2009 than in 2008. The budget blow was softened somewhat in 2009 with an influx of "stimulus" money from the federal government, but much of that was a one-time fix. In 2010, most states faced deficits when planning their 2011 budgets. The weak economic recovery had many states expecting deficits for 2012 as well.[5] Rainy day funds were drawn to near zero in most states. New Jersey's governor proposed cutting his state's budget by 25 percent for the 2011–12 fiscal year.

Such is fiscal politics when a recession eats away revenues. Since states and localities must balance their budgets, officials have less room to hide from tough budgeting choices. This chapter examines how and when states and cities make choices about taxation and spending, and what are possible consequences of these choices.

Raising Revenues

State and local governments provide people with a wide array of services—literally from birth to death. States, counties, and cities run hospitals and health care systems, child care programs, elementary education, and colleges and universities. They provide for public safety by enforcing building codes, inspecting restaurants, maintaining drinking water systems, and operating police and firefighting services. Some jurisdictions even run cemeteries.

One of the most difficult tasks of governing is generating the revenue required to fund the wide range of public services that people expect and demand and then balancing limited revenues with those demands for services and programs. Matters are complicated by the fact that people do not agree on what the government's spending priorities should be and by disagreement over which taxes should be used to fund government. Fiscal politics involves policies and decisions relating to raising and spending public money. Fiscal policy—or

budgeting—is how state and local elected officials figure out who gets what from government, at whose expense.

People generally do not like to pay taxes, but a fundamental trait of a sovereign government is that it has some ability to coerce citizens to pay their taxes. For example, it is very difficult, and typically illegal, to avoid paying taxes that you owe. Whether a tax applies to your income or the purchase of this book, the federal, state, county, or city governments that have the power to tax also have the power to penalize you if you are found to have avoided a tax you owed.

Some taxes are more unpopular than others (few taxes can be called popular), and some levels of taxation are not realistic. As we shall see in this chapter, perceptions of unreasonable taxation can still lead to public revolts that affect what state and local governments can do.

Budgeting is an attempt to deal with scarcity: There's never enough money to fund every possible government program that people might want. States and communities deal with scarcity in different ways.

Criteria for Evaluating Taxes

The public's willingness to pay a particular tax (or a fee or charge) is one criterion we will use in this chapter when evaluating the revenue sources that state and local governments use. Willingness to pay, as we will illustrate, may be a function of how visible a tax is. We also focus on additional features of taxes that are of interest to political scientists, economists, and perhaps most importantly, government officials. As we examine different taxes, we see they differ in terms of **tax equity**—or who bears the burden of paying them. With a **progressive tax**, the wealthier people pay a larger proportion of their total income to cover the tax than the less affluent pay of theirs, whereas a **regressive tax** will have the poor pay a larger proportion of their income than the wealthy do to cover the tax.

Some governments may also be positioned to use taxes that are exportable. Exportable taxes are those mostly paid by people from other places (such as hotel taxes and taxes on natural resources, such as oil). Taxes also differ in their **elasticity**, that is, in how stable (or volatile) revenues from the tax are in times of economic boom and bust. Furthermore, some taxes may be "neutral" in their ability to alter the economic behavior of people and businesses. Others may create odd incentives that distort behavior. All these factors enter into the politics of which taxes governments use to fund public services.

Options for revenues also vary widely due to the economic structure of a state or community, institutional differences, and differences in popular support for taxation. Options for revenues that are available in California and New York, such as increasing the state personal income tax, are not available in, say, Florida or Texas. California and New York have established income taxes and have rather liberal public preferences for government spending. Florida and Texas, in contrast, have voters who may be less sympathetic to public spending, and neither state has adopted a personal income tax. States also vary considerably on what can be taxed. Alaska can rely heavily on revenue from oil extraction, whereas Ohio cannot.

Why Do Some Places Tax and Spend More Than Others?

State and local governments raise and spend about 10 percent of the nation's gross domestic product. When spending of federal money

transferred to states and localities is added in, all state and local governments spend roughly the same amount as the federal government. This reflects that states and localities spend money they collect in taxes, in charges, and fees and also spend hundreds of billions of dollars that the federal government collects each year that is transferred to states and localities.[6] Federal funds, rather than replacing state money, seem to correspond with greater state spending. States that receive more money from the federal government also spend more of their own funds for public services.[7]

States vary in terms of how much revenue they raise and how they raise it. Some rely heavily on traditional taxes, others raise revenue from resource extraction and gambling. This makes it difficult to clearly define which states have the highest taxes. It depends on how we rank the states. The first two columns in Table 10.1 rank states according to how much they tax residents relative to the amount of income in the state per person. This ranking only considers traditional tax revenue sources, not those from fees (e.g., tuition), gambling, and others. Ranked this way, New Jersey, New York, and Connecticut tax the most and Alaska, Nevada, and Wyoming tax the least.

The third column ranks states somewhat differently: according to the total tax dollars collected per resident. Again, this ranking gives priority to traditional tax sources (income, sales, and property), but the rankings express how much is raised regardless of how wealthy the state is. Rankings in columns 2 and 3 differ somewhat because relatively wealthy states like Massachusetts and Illinois, and resource-rich Wyoming, move up in the rankings. Although these states rank near the average in terms of tax levels as a percent of state income, they generate more revenue because there is more wealth being taxed—if even at a lower rate than in less affluent states. When states are ranked this way,

---

[6] States raised $1.56 trillion in 2007 (excluding transfers from the federal government and including insurance revenues), and local governments raised $1.34 trillion in 2007 (excluding transfers). That is a total of $2.9 trillion. Total federal spending in 2007 was $2.7 trillion. States and localities spent 2.7 trillion when transfers are included.

[7] James Garand. "Explaining Government Growth in the U.S. States. *American Political Science Review*. 82(3):837–849, 1988.

less affluent states with average tax rates (e.g., West Virginia) and relatively affluent states with low taxation (e.g., Alaska) rank lowest.

Rankings in column 4 of Table 10.1 look quite different. States are ranked here according to how much total revenue (traditional tax and other sources) is generated per person. Ranked this way, Alaska and Wyoming, sparsely populated states that generate funds from natural resources, top the list. More populous places like Georgia and Arkansas drop in this ranking. These rankings are affected by the state's level of wealth and the size of its population, but they also reflect the political and economic circumstances that shape the mix of taxes used in a state. Big states like New York and California have more wealth to tap *and* have relatively high taxes, so they rate high regardless of how the states are ranked.

As noted, the final column in Table 10.1 ranks states according to their level of per capita personal income, from the wealthiest (Connecticut) to the least affluent (Mississippi). When the first two columns are compared to the final column, we can see that wealthier states tend to tax more than less wealthy states. The relationship is much stronger than suggested in Table 10.1, because these rankings do not illustrate how dollars of tax revenue correspond with dollars of state income. Figure 10.1 illustrates a clear linear pattern: As state per capita (per person) income rises, so does tax revenue collected per person.

Where Does the Money Come From? Major Sources of Revenues

Income Tax

The first state began collecting income taxes in 1911, prior to the constitutional amendment that granted the federal government the power to tax income. The most recent state to adopt an income tax was Connecticut in 1991. Nearly all states (41) tax personal income, and two more states (Tennessee and New Hampshire) tax just personal income from investments. In addition, Alaska and Florida tax corporate income. This

Table 10.1

States Ranked by Tax Revenue and Total Revenue Received, 2008

State	State and local tax revenue as % of per capita income, 2008	Effort Ranked by tax revenues as % of per capita state income, 2008	Effort Ranked by tax revenue received per capita, 2008	Yield Ranked by total revenue received per capita, 2008	Capacity Ranked by income per capita, 2008
New Jersey	11.8%	1	2	9	3
New York	11.7%	2	3	3	4
Connecticut	11.1%	3	1	12	1
Maryland	10.8%	4	4	24	6
Hawaii	10.6%	5	7	15	14
California	10.5%	6	6	4	11
Ohio	10.4%	7	18	16	31
Vermont	10.3%	8	12	17	22
Wisconsin	10.2%	9	17	25	23
Rhode Island	10.2%	10	10	11	19
Pennsylvania	10.2%	11	11	21	20

(continued)

		Effort	Effort	Yield	Capacity
State	State and local tax revenue as % of per capita income, 2008	Ranked by tax revenues as % of per capita state income, 2008	Ranked by tax revenue received per capita, 2008	Ranked by total revenue received per capita, 2008	Ranked by income per capita, 2008
Minnesota	10.2%	12	8	14	16
Idaho	10.1%	13	27	45	42
Arkansas	10.0%	14	37	47	48
Maine	10.0%	15	21	20	34
Georgia	9.9%	16	23	50	38
Nebraska	9.8%	17	19	10	25
Virginia	9.8%	18	9	34	12
Oklahoma	9.8%	19	22	44	33
North Carolina	9.8%	20	28	42	39
Kansas	9.6%	21	20	37	24
Utah	9.6%	22	35	32	45
Massachusetts	9.5%	23	5	5	2
Delaware	9.5%	24	16	6	17
Kentucky	9.4%	25	41	48	47
Oregon	9.4%	26	24	8	27
Michigan	9.4%	27	26	23	28
Indiana	9.4%	28	34	33	40
West Virginia	9.3%	29	48	39	49
Illinois	9.3%	30	14	27	13
Iowa	9.3%	31	31	29	32
Missouri	9.2%	32	33	43	37
North Dakota	9.2%	33	30	19	26
Colorado	9.0%	34	13	22	9
Washington	8.9%	35	15	7	8
Mississippi	8.9%	36	50	31	50
S. Carolina	8.8%	37	45	35	46
Alabama	8.6%	38	44	36	43
New Mexico	8.6%	39	46	13	44
Montana	8.6%	40	43	26	41
Arizona	8.5%	41	40	46	35
Louisiana	8.4%	42	38	18	29
Texas	8.4%	43	32	40	21
Tennessee	8.3%	44	42	38	36
South Dakota	7.9%	45	47	41	30
N. Hampshire	7.6%	46	29	49	10
Florida	7.4%	47	36	28	15
Wyoming	7.0%	48	25	2	5
Nevada	6.6%	49	39	30	7
Alaska	6.4%	50	49	1	18

Source: Tax Foundation (2009).

means that Wyoming, Washington, Nevada, Texas, and South Dakota are the only states that lack taxation of personal or corporate income.[8] A handful of states allow local governments to levy an income tax. The proportion of all states' total personal income collected in state income taxes has increased steadily since the 1960s.[9]

A few states have a **flat rate tax** for their income tax, where everyone pays the same rate, but most state income tax systems place people into one of several brackets defined by how much they earn. Tax rates increase for each bracket, with people in the highest income brackets paying the highest tax rate. Even for people in the top brackets, state income tax rates are far lower than those levied by the federal government. An average state has about five brackets, with the tax rate for people in the lowest income bracket averaging about 2.6 percent, and the rate for people in the highest bracket averaging about 6.8 percent. Hawaii and Oregon (11 percent), New Jersey (10.7 percent), California (10.5 percent), and Vermont (9.4 percent) have the highest rates for top income brackets.[10] In some states (California and New Jersey), the top bracket starts at $1,000,000 in income. In Oregon and Hawaii, an income of $175,000 is subject to the top bracket tax.

Evaluating the Income Tax Supporters of the income tax note several features they find attractive. Advocacy groups note that states making use of an income tax have the most progressive revenue systems overall, whereas the poor pay a much larger proportion of their income in state and local taxes than the

wealthy in states that lack an income tax (such as Washington, Florida, and Texas).[11] Income taxes are relatively easy for governments to collect (through payroll deduction), and revenues collected tend to be more stable in times of economic downturns when compared to sales taxes. Public opinion polls illustrate that voters find state income taxes more politically acceptable than federal taxes and property taxes, at least in states where the income tax already exists.[12] One study of the political consequences of adopting income taxes found that the party in control of the legislature that adopted the tax was usually re-elected. When voters did punish politicians for adopting a state income tax, Republicans were much more likely to suffer than Democrats.[13] This may be due to the fact that Republican voters expect more fiscal prudence from Republicans than Democratic voters expect from Democrats.

Critics point out that income is already taxed by the federal government, and that inflation can drive people who get **cost of living allowances (COLAs)** into higher tax brackets even though their real earning power does not increase. Income taxes may also distort the incentives that people have to work; and by taxing income that people save, it creates disincentives for savings, which makes less money available for investment and economic growth.

Sales Tax

States began taxing the purchase of goods during the Great Depression of the 1930s. At the time, federal social programs were in their infancy and states were searching for resources to deal with massive unemployment and poverty.

---

[8] South Dakota does levy a tax on bank income.

[9] James Garand and Kyle Baudoin, "Fiscal Policy in the American States," in V. Gray and R. Hanson, eds., *Politics in the American States: A Comparative Analysis,* 8th ed. (Washington, DC: CQ Press, 2004).

[10] http://www.taxadmin.org/fta/rate/ind_inc.html; http://www.taxfoundation.org.

[11] 1996 Center for Tax Justice Report: Michael P. Ettlinger, John F. O'Hare, Robert S. McIntyre, Julie King, Neil Miransky, and Elizabeth A. Fray, "Who Pays? A Distributional Analysis of the Tax Systems of the 50 States," Citizens for Tax Justice, http://www.ctj.org/html/whopay.htm.

[12] Shaun Bowler and Todd Donovan, "Public Responsiveness to Taxation," *Political Research Quarterly* 48(1995):79–99.

[13] Susan Hansen, *The Politics of Taxation: Revenue without Representation* (New York: Praeger, 1983).

Mississippi first adopted the sales tax in 1932, and another 11 states had adopted it by 1933.[14] Today all but five states (Oregon, Alaska, Montana, New Hampshire, and Delaware) have a sales tax. About half of all tax revenue collected by state governments comes from the sales tax. California has the highest sales tax (8.25 percent), followed by Indiana, Mississippi, New Jersey, Tennessee, and Rhode Island (at 7 percent).[15] In addition, nearly all states grant their local governments the power to levy an additional increment on top of the state rate. This is the reason why you might pay a different rate as you move from one county to the next inside a state. When local sales taxes are considered, residents in parts of several high-sales-tax states pay over 9 or 10 percent in state and local sales tax on their purchases (e.g., residents of Seattle, Chicago, and parts of Tennessee).

Evaluating the Sales Tax One of the most noteworthy features of the sales tax is its relative political acceptability. Surveys of opinion demonstrate that when compared to other major revenue sources, state sales taxes are the most popular (or usually the least disliked). Taxes are collected at the point of sale on individual purchases, so they may not be as noticeable to the taxpayer as lump sum payments that can come due with property taxes and income taxes. For local governments, sales tax revenue can be particularly attractive because it offers the opportunity to get folks from out of town to bear some of the costs of funding services. As a tax on consumption, sales taxes may also create fewer distortions in people's incentives to work, save, and invest than an income tax does.

Susan Hansen's study suggests that most state governments that adopted a state sales tax between 1911 and 1977 survived the next election, but that they faced a slightly greater threat of defeat than governments that adopted the income tax. Again, Republican governments

that adopted the tax were at a greater risk of defeat than Democratic governments.[16]

The sales tax has two clear weaknesses, however. The first is the elasticity or stability of it as a revenue source. The total amount collected depends on how much people are spending on "big-ticket" consumer goods. When the economy cools, and consumer confidence wanes, the demand for things such as new cars, boats, televisions, computers, and construction materials declines—and so does sales tax revenue. This problem is magnified when the sales tax applies only to goods and not to services.

The second issue is equity. People who earn less usually spend all their income, which means the sales tax applies to most of what they earn. People who earn more are able to save and invest some of what they earn, and the sales tax does not apply to that portion of their income. This means the poor pay much more of their overall income to sales taxes than the rich. It also means that states that rely heavily on sales taxes have the most regressive tax systems. Many states offset the regressive nature of this tax by exempting basic items such as food and medicine from the tax. The definition of basic needs is a political question and must be defined by the legislature.

Due to growing exemptions and shifts in the nature of the economy, the base of what the sales tax applies to has been eroding over time. Over the past several decades, spending has shifted from goods to services (lawyers, health care, advertising, consulting), and purchases are moving from the physical storefront to the virtual store online. Services are not always covered by state sales taxes (in part due to successful lobbying efforts by the affected groups), and states have particular difficulty collecting taxes from sales made via the Internet. As the base of the tax erodes, states are under pressure to raise sales taxes on the remaining items

[14] Richard Winters, "The Politics of Taxing and Spending," in V. Gray and R. Hanson, eds., *Politics in the American States: A Comparative Analysis*, 7th ed. (Washington, DC: CQ Press, 1999).

[15] California's rate includes a 1 percent statewide local sales tax, http://www.taxadmin.org/fta/rate/sales.html.

[16] Hansen, *The Politics of Taxation*.

subject to the tax.[17] If more exemptions are made for "basic" necessities, the remaining base of the sales tax becomes more dependent on big-ticket purchases, making revenues even more volatile.[18] Sales taxes may also distort behavior by creating incentives for people to travel to make purchases where taxes are lower or by encouraging them to shop online in order to avoid paying any sales tax.

Property Tax

Some states collect state property taxes, but for most states, the property tax contributes less than 2 percent to total state taxes collected. However, property taxes are the main source of revenues for local governments. Property taxes are typically levied as a flat rate proportion (1 percent, for example), multiplied by the assessed value of property. These rates are often referred to as mill levies. A 1 percent mill levy is the same as saying the tax is $1 per $1,000 in assessed value of property, or the property value multiplied by .01. The amount one pays in tax is determined as much by the value of the property as by the tax rate. Most homeowners pay the same rate on residential property, with those having more valuable homes paying a higher tax amount overall. For example, a home assessed at $276,000 in Clark County, Washington, is subject to a 1.618 percent annual county property tax (or 0.00161 mill), a 2.766 percent state property tax (0.00276 mill), and various other property taxes. It would owe $446 a year in county property tax and $763 per year in state property tax (most state

Comparisons Help Us Understand

RHODE ISLAND AS A "SIN TAX" MODEL TO EMULATE?

Concerns about social costs have limited the expansion of state-regulated gambling in some states. Others earn substantial revenues from gambling—from both Indian tribe operations and from other state-regulated games. Rhode Island collects a whopping $1,300 per capita in lottery and video lottery terminal (VLT) sales.[1] It is one of only six states that combine a lottery with fast-paced VLTs that allow people to bet a great deal in a short period. Revenues from gambling made the tiny state 8th overall in the United States for total lottery sales. The state lottery program was established in 1974, and thousands of VLTs have been located at racetracks since 1995. A report forecast that over 14 percent of the state's general revenues would come from gambling in 2010, whereas the U.S. average for states with a lottery is just 2 percent of revenues.[2] Delaware, South Dakota, and West Virginia, which also make heavy use of VLTs, are the only states that rival Rhode Island in how much lottery and VLT revenue is generated per capita. Rhode Island also collects another 4 percent of all revenues from cigarette taxes. Rhode Island collects more from smoking and gambling than it does from inheritance taxes and general business taxes combined. Of course, size and location matter. Hardly any place in Rhode Island is more than 10 miles from Connecticut or Massachusetts. Many people from other states pass through Rhode Island, which might make it easy for the state to export its tax burden by selling them lottery tickets and cigarettes.

Notes: 1. State of Rhode Island and Providence Plantations, Revenue Estimating Conference Memorandum, 19 December 2005.

2. Rhode Island 2010: Charting a New Course. Rhode Island Public Expenditure Council, 2005.

[17] Winters, "The Politics of Taxing and Spending."

[18] W. Duncombe, "Economic Change and the Evolving State Tax Structure: The Case of the Sales Tax," *National Tax Journal* (1992):308.

property tax rates are much lower than this).[19] All property taxes are usually collected on a single bill or two bills that arrive six months apart. This means that taxpayers are likely to be highly attentive to the total dollar amount they pay in property taxes (compared to what they pay in sales taxes—imagine if you received one large bill each year for all that you owed in sales taxes rather than paying it at each individual purchase). Depending on where the property is located, the bill may include taxes for the county, the city, the school districts, the state, and other special service districts (that is, library districts, port districts, and water districts).

In the first half of the twentieth century, property taxes accounted for nearly all of municipal revenues. Today, the local government revenue mix is quite different. Because cities, counties, and towns now use a wider range of taxes and fees to raise revenue while also receiving funds from the national government and their state governments, property taxes now contribute less overall to local budgets. Nonetheless, it is still the primary source of revenue for local governments. At the end of the twentieth century, property taxes still generated 79 percent of all local tax revenues.[20] Cities, counties, school districts, and special districts each levy their own property taxes.

The Property Tax Evaluated One traditional rationale for the property tax is that it taxes people who benefit the most from local public services. Property values are increased by public services, such as fire, police protection, and quality schools, so property taxes target people who benefit from these services. Historically, real property (land, homes, and farms) was the place where most Americans held their wealth.

When fewer people owned property and fewer people invested their wealth in stocks and bonds, the wealthy had a greater share of their assets in real property. This made a tax on property relatively progressive.

In the contemporary era, however, home-ownership is no longer something reserved for the wealthy. About two-thirds of American families now own a home. Moreover, for most middle-class families, a home is their primary investment and thus represents most of their wealth. In contrast, the wealthiest people today have much more of their wealth invested in paper assets. Property taxes—a flat rate—thus cost the poor (if they can buy a home) and the middle class a larger share of their wealth than they cost the wealthiest people. Some economists suggest contemporary property taxes are highly regressive.[21]

Property Taxes and Tax Rebellions This may explain why Americans consistently rate property taxes as the most unpopular tax.[22] A 2009 survey found a majority of people reporting that local property taxes were unfair. In contrast, most felt that state cigarette taxes, state income taxes, sales taxes, state motor vehicle taxes, and the federal income tax were fair.[23] Unlike the sales tax, property tax payments are made in a lump sum (unless built into monthly mortgage bills), which may add to the sting of the tax. One of the biggest political liabilities of the tax is that inflation in home values can drive up a person's tax burden much faster than any increase in their income. In booming housing markets, home prices may increase 15 to 30 percent per year. Local governments are often required by law to reassess home values frequently, leading some homeowners to find steep increases in their property tax bills virtually overnight. Tax bills increased

---

[19] State laws also determine what percentage of the assessed value of property is subject to the tax.

[20] National Council of State Legislators, *A Guide to Property Tax: Property Tax Relief* (Denver, CO: National Council of State Legislators, 2002).

[21] Daniel B. Suits, "Measurement of Tax Progressivity," *American Economic Review* 67(4)(1977):747.

[22] Bowler and Donovan, "Public Responsiveness to Taxation."

[23] 2009 Tax Attitudes Study, Harris Interactive, conducted for the Tax Foundation, February.

dramatically, not because elected officials raised the rates but because market demand increased home values.

This dynamic of rising home prices driving tax bills higher fueled a rebellion against property taxes in California (Proposition 13 in 1978) and Massachusetts (Proposition 2½ in 1980) and led to an anti-tax movement[24] that has consequences to this day. Populist anti-tax advocates became fixtures in many states: Howard Jarvis (California), Bill Sizemore (Oregon), Tim Eyman (Washington), and Douglas Bruce (Colorado) rallied the public around anti-tax proposals they promoted via ballot measures. Policies that cut the property tax proved among their most popular proposals.

Other Revenue Sources

Given the political difficulties of relying on traditional tax sources such as income, property, and general sales taxes, states and communities also generate revenues from taxes that are more narrowly targeted as well as direct charges for services. Over the last two decades, state and local governments are relying more heavily on some of these "other" sources of revenues and have been using them more than ever before.[25]

Selective Sales Taxes

General sales taxes, as discussed, apply to most common purchases. Additional sales taxes are often levied on select items, such as fuel, alcohol, tobacco products, and public utilities. Sometimes, these taxes are referred to as excise taxes, or **sin taxes**, because they target behavior—such as drinking or smoking—that many people believe should be discouraged. If higher taxes actually cause people to consume less of the targeted item, the state may benefit. If demand for the item is elastic and responds

to increases in prices, higher taxation will lead to less consumption of the item targeted with the tax. But if the tax applies to something that has **inelastic demand**—that is, something people must have regardless of the cost—a higher sin tax might not lower consumption.

Motor Vehicle Fuel Most of the revenues collected in this category come from state taxes on gasoline and diesel. Gas taxes are charged per gallon, with a state rate added on top of the $0.18 per gallon in tax going to the federal government. Most states add about another $0.20 per gallon—Alaska has the lowest ($0.08 per gallon), with California ($0.466), New York ($0.446), Hawaii ($0.444), Connecticut ($0.419), Illinois ($0.397), and Washington ($0.375) the highest. Several other states have gas taxes over $0.30 per gallon. The political acceptability of gas taxes may be enhanced by the fact that these funds are often dedicated to transportation expenses. Gas taxes, as a share of a state's personal income, were lower in 2000 than they were in the 1960s and 1970s.[26] Several states increased gas taxes in 2009 and 2010.

Tobacco Products The proportion of state revenues from cigarette and tobacco taxes has been increasing recently. In several states that experienced tax rebellions in recent decades, citizens have actually voted to raise their state taxes. Or, at least, they voted to raise taxes on people who smoke.

On average, cigarette taxes increased from $0.21 per pack in 1996 to $0.77 by 2006, and continued to climb. Cigarette taxes have proved popular in part because they target an unpopular minority (smokers), with increases often linked to spending on public health programs. Voters in Washington and California, for example, approved cigarette tax increases that earmarked funds for health care (and anti-tobacco education). As a result of these taxes, cigarette prices

---

[24] David O. Sears and Jack Citrin, *Something for Nothing in California* (Berkeley, CA: University of California Press, 1982); David Lowery and Lee Sigelman, "Understanding the Tax Revolt: Eight Explanations," *American Political Science Review* (1981):963–74; Daniel A. Smith, *Tax Crusaders and the Politics of Direct Democracy* (New York: Routledge, 1999).

[25] Data in this section are from the Federation of Tax Administrators, http://www.taxadmin.org, and the 2009 report of the Tax Foundation, http://www.TaxFoundation.org.

[26] Garand and Baudoin, "Fiscal Policy in the American States."

now vary substantially across states. As of 2010, Rhode Island charged the most: $3.46 tax per pack (on top of federal taxes of $1.01 per pack). Connecticut taxes $3.00 per pack and in July 2011, Hawaii's tax will increase to $3.00 per pack. New York ($2.75), New Jersey ($2.70), Wisconsin, ($2.52), Massachusetts ($2.51), Vermont ($2.24), and Washington ($2.02) were the next highest, respectively. It seems that proximity to Canada—where tobacco taxes are high—and U.S. neighbors with higher tobacco taxes gives states greater ability to raise these taxes without fear that residents can buy their smokes elsewhere. Smoking is a much more affordable habit in the South, particularly in tobacco-producing states. South Carolina ($0.07), Missouri ($0.17), Virginia ($0.30), North Carolina ($0.35), Georgia ($0.37), and Louisiana ($0.36) have the nation's lowest cigarette taxes.[27]

Alcoholic Beverages On average, states charge about $0.25 in tax on a gallon of beer. Alaska, which has no neighboring state to buy from, has the highest rate ($1.07 per gallon) and some of the nation's most expensive beer. Alabama, Georgia, and Hawaii are not far behind. Some of the cheapest beer in the United States can be found in Missouri (the home of Anheuser-Busch/Budweiser—which controls 45 percent of U.S. beer sales), Colorado (the home of Coors—which controls 10 percent of U.S. beer sales), Oregon (center of the U.S. microbrewing industry), and Wisconsin (the home of many thirsty Green Bay Packer fans, Miller, Pabst, and Stroh's Brewing—the latter three control 33 percent of U.S. beer sales). Beer taxes in each of these states, and in Pennsylvania and Wyoming, are under $0.09 per gallon. The distribution of beer taxes suggests that industries are able to avoid sin taxes in states where the industry is a key part of the economy. When Washington state raised its beer tax by 300 percent in 2010,

it exempted microbreweries in an attempt to protect local producers. Wine taxes are also very low in California[28] ($0.20 per gallon), the nation's largest wine-producing state, and highest in Alaska ($2.50 per gallon, or $0.50 per bottle), North Carolina ($2.34 per gallon), and Florida ($2.25 per gallon)—NC actually does produce a fair amount of wine, notably on the Vanderbilt estate in Asheville.

Direct Charges

Some of what state and local governments do can be funded by direct charges to the people who use a service, also known as **user fees**. For every $4 that state and local governments collect in taxes, another $1 is collected in user charges and fees. States generate billions in revenue by charging users of hospitals, highways, higher education, and other services. User charges for hospitals, sewers, garbage collection, airports, and parks contribute tens of billions of dollars to local government revenues. For the most part, none of these services are fully funded by charges to users, but fees reduce the amount of revenue from general taxes that would otherwise be used as funding.

Despite the names, user fees and charges are a source of revenue, just like any other tax. States and local governments have come to rely more heavily on fees and charges in recent years because they make it possible to avoid increasing visible taxes, such as sales or income tax. Critics of direct charges and fees argue that they can be highly regressive because people at all income levels often pay the same flat fee.

Estate and Inheritance Taxes

In 2010, fifteen states collected estate taxes,[29] and eleven collected inheritance taxes[30] (Maryland and New Jersey collected both). Inheritance taxes are levied on what an heir

---

[27] Cigarette tax information is from the Federation of Tax Administrators, http://www.taxfoundation.org. Rates are as of July 1, 2009, unless noted.

[28] In New Hampshire, Pennsylvania, Utah, and Wyoming, states control wine sales and apply different taxes.

[29] These included Connecticut, Delaware, Hawaii, Maine, Maryland, Massachusetts, Minnesota, New Jersey, New York, Ohio, Oregon, Rhode Island, Tennessee, Vermont and Washington.

[30] These include Connecticut, Indiana, Iowa, Kansas, Kentucky, Maryland, Nebraska, New Jersey, Oregon, Pennsylvania, and Tennessee.

(but not a spouse) receives after inheriting something. Estate taxes are levied on the estate of a deceased person before it is distributed. Critics of estate taxes argue that they force "family farms" to be broken up upon the death of a property owner and that they amount to double taxation because the property taxes are already paid by the person accumulating the wealth. Political opponents of estate taxes have successfully rebranded these as "death taxes," although they can be levied on the living person inheriting a person's wealth (rather than the dead person). Federal and state estate tax programs typically made exemptions for family farms, and as of 2010, the minimum value for an estate to owe the federal tax was $3.5 million. This meant that the vast majority of people inheriting money are not affected by the tax.[31] Advocates of the estate tax—including Bill Gates Sr., father of one of the world's richest men—note that the estate tax is fair because it taxes wealth that was not earned by the person receiving it. Estate taxes may also be a way to tax accumulated wealth that has avoided taxation during a person's lifetime. The estate tax is also one of the few instruments of progressive taxation available to government. Gates estimates that the repeal of the estate tax would largely benefit future heirs of the wealthiest estates in this country—several of whom have funded the successful anti–estate tax lobbying effort.[32]

In 2001, President George W. Bush signed a bill that phased down the federal estate tax, and had it disappear in 2010 and reappear in 2011. Until recently, most states didn't set their own estate tax rates but collected an amount based on the federal estate tax. Because most states' estate taxes were linked to the federal tax, those state taxes diminished and then ended when the federal estate tax disappeared. Many states adopted their own, independent estate taxes prior to 2010, and President Barack Obama signed a budget that restored the federal tax on estates valued over $3.5 million in 2011 and beyond.

Lotteries

Lotteries are seen by some as a form of voluntary taxation and have been popular enough to be approved by voters in many states. Lotteries were common in the 19th century, and lottery advocates point out they were used in 1776 to raise money for the Colonial Army.[33]

Widespread corruption and strong opposition on moral grounds led to the elimination of government lotteries. No states had public lotteries again until 1964, when New Hampshire adopted a state lottery. Seven more states had lotteries by the 1973, but the lottery swept the nation after the tax revolts of the late 1970s and 1980s. Modern lotteries were promoted to state legislators and voters (by a corporation that prints the tickets and sells lottery equipment) as a politically painless way to raise revenues that could be earmarked for public education.[34] Although they are classified as a regressive tax,[35] most tickets are purchased by middle- and upper-income people.[36]

Forty-two states now have lotteries. In 2010, 18 states had lottery sales well over $1 billion each, with nearly $59 billion in sales nationally.[37] However, less than $18 billion of that was profit that contributed to state revenues. Most states dedicate their lottery revenues to education. Because only a fraction of sales end up as revenues, lotteries contribute a

[31] Elizabeth McNichol, Center for Budget and Policy Priorities, 2010, http://www.cbpp.org/cms/index.cfm?fa=view&id=3185.

[32] William Gates Sr. and Chuck Collins, "Tax the Wealthy: Why America Needs the Estate Tax," *American Prospect*, 17 June 2002.

[33] National Association of State and Provincial Lotteries, http://www.naspl.org/index.cfm?fuseaction=content&PageID=12&PageCategory=11.

[34] David Broder, *Democracy Derailed: Initiative Campaigns and the Power of Money* (San Diego, CA: Harcourt, 2000), pp. 83–4.

[35] John Mikesell and C. Kurt Zorn, "State Lotteries as Fiscal Saviors or Fiscal Fraud," *Public Administration Review* 46(1986):311–20.

[36] Daniel B. Suits, "Gambling Taxes: Regressivity and Revenue Potential," *National Tax Journal* 30(1977):25–33.

[37] http://www.naspl.org/.

very small percentage to state funds, even to education budgets. One estimate is that states receive only 30 cents in revenue for every dollar wagered and that the yield has been in decline since the 1990s. In California, where profits are dedicated to education, the lottery provides less than 2 percent of all funds for the state's K–12 system.[38] Some evidence reveals that the market for the lottery is saturated: With so many states now running lotteries, and with competition from the growing tribal gambling industries, more places now exist for a limited number of gamblers to risk their money. States respond to declining sales by increasing payouts, which can result in modest revenues.

Gambling

All but two states (Hawaii and Utah) have dropped their prohibitions against all forms of gambling. The recent expansion of legal gambling facilities means that taxes on gross receipts from casino gambling have been one of the faster-growing sources of state revenues. Indian nations are major players in expanding the American gambling industry (the industry prefers to refer to the business as gaming, not gambling). A tribe negotiates a compact with its state government about the scope of casino operations allowed in exchange for a certain share of the casino revenues. As tribes and states become more dependent on each other in this way, tribes have become some of the largest campaign donors for legislators in some states. For Nevada, gambling revenues are a method to export the state's tax burden to people from out of state. Consumers spent $37 billion in non-tribal commercial casinos and racetrack casinos in 2009, generating $8.2 billion in state and local tax revenues.[39]

Severance Taxes

Severance taxes are levied on resources "severed" from the earth or sea and are applied to resource extraction industries, such as fishing, mining, and coal, oil, and natural gas production. Most states lack the natural resources that make severance taxes a significant source of revenues; however, some are blessed with valuable natural resources that provide a major source of revenues. Severance taxes are levied on the volume of the resource extracted. When market prices for the resource are up, these revenues boom. If prices collapse, so do revenues.

The global price of oil spiked dramatically in 2007 and 2008, moving from $60 per barrel to nearly $130 by mid-2008. Revenues were booming in resource-rich states. Alaska generated over 80 percent of state revenues from severance taxes. The economic collapse of late 2008 corresponded with a sharp decrease in demand for oil, and the price dropped to below $50 per barrel in early 2009. As a result, in a two-month period in 2009, Alaska went from a projected budget surplus to having one of the nation's largest projected deficits as tax revenues declined by 41 percent from 2008 to 2009.

Tax and Expenditure Limits

Property tax revolts of the 1970s were followed by more anti-tax and spending-limit ballot measures in many states. Elected officials in still more states embraced various policies designed to curb the growth of taxation and government spending. Known collectively as **tax and expenditure limitations** (or TELs), these policies set formulas that determine by how much revenue and spending can grow. These formulas typically limit growth in spending or future revenues collected from existing sources to some level that keeps pace with inflation or population growth (or some combination). By 2009, 30 states had adopted some form of TELs: 23 had spending limits, 4 had tax revenue limits, and 3 had both.[40] Sixteen states also established

---

[38] California Department of Education, *State Lottery Fact Book 2004* (Sacramento, CA: California Department of Education, 2004).

[39] American Gaming Association, State of the States, 2010.

[40] National Council of State Legislators, http://www.ncsl.org/Default.aspx?TabId=12633. Accessed September 2009.

the **supermajority vote requirement** in order to pass a tax increase.

Substantial academic debate continues over whether TELs actually limit the growth of government expenditure over the long term. Several observers blame (or credit) California's Proposition 13 of 1978 with a dramatic reduction in revenue available for public services, particularly schools.[41] Others note that although property tax limits and spending limits affected which level of government raised revenues (shifting taxation from one level of government to another), overall spending was largely unaffected.[42] The first generation of TELs—particularly those enacted by legislators rather than via ballot initiatives—may not have had much effect on limiting the growth in taxation and spending.[43] It is difficult to evaluate the effects of these policies because the same formula limiting revenue growth (e.g., a limit tied to population growth) might have quite different effects in a state with rapid population growth than in a state with no population growth.[44] A second generation of TELs adopted in the 1990s and more recently may have more teeth than those adopted in the 1970s and 1980s.[45]

Colorado's Taxpayer Bill of Rights (or TABOR) serves as an example. In addition to strict formulas limiting revenue growth, TABOR required a public referendum to approve any tax increase proposed in the legislature. One critical case study of TABOR suggests that it resulted in substantially reduced levels of government spending, with education and health care suffering.[46] But Colorado voters have shown some willingness to tweak TABOR limits by approving proposals that allow school districts and cities to keep revenue collected beyond the TABOR limit.[47]

Fiscal Federalism

State and local governments receive substantial money from the federal government to promote the federal government's goals in areas such as health care, urban renewal, education, and transportation. The relative power of the federal government and the states is often measured in dollars, with the efforts of federal and state governments to exert control over policies limited by their willingness to pay for such authority.

During the 1960s, the expansive social welfare programs under the Lyndon B. Johnson administration's Great Society led the federal government to become involved in virtually every state and local governmental activity.

The federal role in financing state and local government activity abated after the election of Ronald Reagan in 1980. Reagan's annual budgets eliminated or reduced funding for many programs established in the 1960s and 1970s. Welfare reform legislation, passed by President Bill Clinton in August 1996, also changed the federal role in funding state spending. Federal funds made up roughly 40 percent of state and

[41] Peter Schrag, *Paradise Lost: California's Experience, America's Future* (Berkeley, CA: University of California Press, 2004).

[42] Elisabeth Gerber, Arthur Lupia, Mathew McCubbins, and D. R. Kiewiet, *Stealing the Initiative: How State Government Responds to Direct Democracy* (Upper Saddle River, NJ: Prentice Hall, 2001).

[43] Shaun Bowler and Todd Donovan, "Evolution in State Governance Structures," *Political Research Quarterly* (2004):189–96; James Alt and Robert Lowry, "Divided Government, Fiscal Institutions and Budget Deficits: Evidence from the States," *American Political Science Review* 88(1994):811–28.

[44] Ronald Shadbegian, "Do Tax and Expenditure Limitations Affect the Size and Growth of Government?" *Contemporary Economic Policy* (January 1996):22–35.

[45] Michael New, *Limiting Government through Direct Democracy: The Case of State Tax and Expenditure Limitations*, Cato Policy Analysis no. 420 (Washington, DC: Cato Institute, 2001).

[46] Bell Policy Center, *Ten Years of TABOR: A Study of Colorado's Taxpayer's Bill of Rights* (Denver, CO: Bell Policy Center, 2003).

[47] Debbie Bell, "TABOR 101: Expert Explains City Ballot Question," *Canon City Daily Record*, 4 September 2009.

local expenditures in 1980, but by 2006, they made up roughly 34 percent.[48]

Federal transfers increased in 2009 as part of Barack Obama's $737 billion economic stimulus package. It included $140 billion that states and localities could use to maintain programs after the recession ate away at state and local revenues. These funds were one of the major sources many states relied upon to balance their 2008–09 budgets.[49] Since the 2009 stimulus was ostensibly a one-time boost of federal funds, some state and local governments faced tougher decisions about how to balance their budgets for 2010 and beyond.

General Funds Versus Non–General Funds

All of these various revenues may end up in different budgets before they are spent. Revenues collected from the general sales tax, income tax, and property tax often end up in a state or local government's general fund budget. Some states may also put their lottery revenues and other miscellaneous funds in their general budget. General fund revenues can typically be used for any purpose, so politicians have substantial discretion over how such revenues might be spent. Budget battles in the legislature, or between the legislature and the governor, largely center on what should be done with general fund revenues.

Revenues that are collected for a specific purpose or transferred to a state or community for a specific program often end up in a non–general fund budget. For example, most money that comes as transfers from the federal government is allocated to fund health and welfare programs and cannot be spent on other things. Likewise, tuition and fees collected by universities are dedicated to fund universities and cannot be spent on other programs. Gas taxes

are often dedicated to road construction and transportation only, and most states earmark their lottery funds for education. This means that budget writers often have very little discretion over how non–general fund revenues can be spent. More than half of a state's total revenues may end up in a non–general fund budget. In Virginia's 2009–10 budget, for example, 54 percent of all state revenues went into the non–general fund.

Adding It All Up: Variation in State Revenue Packages

Every state and local government has its own unique combination of revenue sources. When state revenue sources are displayed graphically, it's often in the form of a pie, with larger slices depicting the major revenue sources. Unfortunately, there's not one single pie to consider, as the overall mixture of state or local revenue can be expressed at least three ways. The first is to think in terms of the tax revenues a government generates on its own, but state and local taxes are only part of the story—governments also generate substantial revenues by charging for services. This means we must also consider these additional non-tax revenues as part of a government's revenue package. Finally, much of what state and local governments spend comes from funds transferred from other, higher levels of government, so a third way to express a government's revenue mix is to include all "own-source" revenues (taxes and other sources) plus transfers from other levels of government.

The Mix of State Revenues

The 50 states combined had nearly $1.5 trillion in annual revenue in 2008. To put that

[48] U.S. Census Bureau, http://www.census.gov/prod/2004pubs/04statab/stlocgov.pdf.

[49] Center on Budget and Policy Priorities, 2009, http://www.cbpp.org/cms/index.cfm?fa=view&id=2831.

amount in perspective, the federal government collected about $1.6 trillion in annual revenue the same year (excluding Social Security).[50] Figure 10.1 illustrates the sources of all funds available to state governments. Of the $1.5 trillion available, about $1 trillion was generated by states. This includes about $780 billion collected via state taxes, $151 billion in direct charges and fees collected by states, and about $135 billion from miscellaneous state revenue sources. Federal funds and direct charges allow states to spend about twice what they collect in taxes. Direct charges apply to users of state services and include college tuition, road tolls, park fees, and the like. As noted in Chapter 2, the federal government redistributes substantial funds back to the states each year—over $446 billion, mostly to fund health

and welfare expenses shared between the state and federal governments.

About 73 percent of all state-generated (or own-source) revenues come from taxation, with another 14 percent from direct charges for services and 13 percent from interest earned on investments and other miscellaneous sources. Most revenue from direct charges for public services (paid only by those who use the services) comes in the form of tuition for higher education. This is one of the fastest-growing sources of funds for state governments.

Figure 10.2 focuses more narrowly on what the average state's mix of tax revenues might look like: just less than one-third coming from general sales tax (plus another 15 percent from "selective" sales taxes on things like gas, cigarettes, and alcohol), just over one-third from individual income taxes (plus another 7 percent from corporate income taxes), 6 percent from license fees (mostly on vehicles), and the rest from miscellaneous taxes. Taxes bring in most, but by no means all, the revenues that states generate.

States vary tremendously in the mix of revenues they use to fund public services. A balanced package of revenues—like a balanced stock portfolio—helps bring stability to a state's budget process through periods of economic recession. But can states thrive without having both an income and sales tax, the two main pillars of revenue systems? A few states endowed with natural resources or specialized industries avoid having to rely on one of the major taxes (income and sales). Alaska and Texas have generated tremendous revenue from oil and gas. Wyoming has profited from mining, Nevada from gambling, and Florida from tourism. These revenue sources export the burden of state taxes to people in other states, and allow these states to get by without income taxes. However, they may face budget crises when prices of their key commodity crash or if the tourist industry

---

Figure 10.1

Sources of All State Revenue, 2008

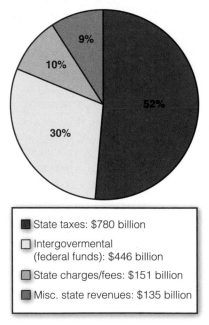

Legend:
- State taxes: $780 billion
- Intergovernmental (federal funds): $446 billion
- State charges/fees: $151 billion
- Misc. state revenues: $135 billion

Note: Total state revenues from all sources = $1.51 trillion (excludes $83 billion in insurance trust revenues).

Source: U.S. Census Bureau, State Government Finances, 2008, http://www.census.gov/govs/state/0800usst.html.

[50] http://www.usgovernmentrevenue.com/yearrev2007_0.html.

crashes (as Florida and Nevada learned after September 11, 2001).

Absent major tourism or natural resources, few states have the luxury of funding their operations without sales and income taxes—which, as mentioned, are the two main pillars of state revenue. Those that have only one must rely heavily on it. Oregon lacks a sales tax, so it collects over 70 percent of state tax revenues from the income tax. Washington lacks an income tax, so it must collect over 75 percent of its tax revenue from the sales tax. New Hampshire has neither a general sales nor a general income tax and manages to balance its budget via frugality and having local governments fund many services. Although no state is average, most have tax revenue packages that look less like Washington, Oregon, Alaska, or

New Hampshire and more like what is shown in Figure 10.2.

The Mix of Local Revenues

When transfers from higher levels of government are factored in, local governments collect about $1.4 trillion in revenues (plus another $122 billion from utilities, and $6 billion from insurance funds). Local governments, including cities, counties, school districts, and other special districts, collect just over $771 billion in locally generated taxes and charges, with the majority of this coming from the property tax.

Figure 10.3 illustrates that local governments collect 39 percent of this $1.4 trillion from local taxes, with a similar proportion of funds coming from transfers (mostly from their

Figure 10.2

Sources of Taxes Generated by State Governments, 2008

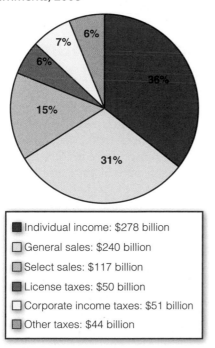

■ Individual income: $278 billion

□ General sales: $240 billion

▨ Select sales: $117 billion

■ License taxes: $50 billion

□ Corporate income taxes: $51 billion

▨ Other taxes: $44 billion

Note: Total state revenues generated from state taxes = $780 billion.

Source: U.S. Census Bureau, State Government Finances, 2008, http://www.census.gov/govs/state/0800usst.html.

Figure 10.3

Sources of All Local Government General Revenue, 2008

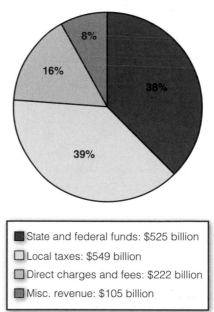

■ State and federal funds: $525 billion

□ Local taxes: $549 billion

□ Direct charges and fees: $222 billion

■ Misc. revenue: $105 billion

Note: Total local revenues = $1.40 trillion. Excludes $6 billion in revenues from insurance trusts and $122 billion from utilities.

Source: U.S. Census Bureau, http://www.census.gov/govs/estimate/.

states). Most of these transfers are state funds dedicated to school districts and to cities and counties to cover their costs of running health programs. Another 16 percent of local funds comes from direct charges, mostly for hospitals, airports, and sewerage.

When we focus only on the revenues that local governments collect themselves, we find that a local government's revenue package looks quite different from a state's revenues. Although most locally generated revenues come from local taxes, local governments rely much more on charges and fees than do states. Sixteen percent of locally generated revenues come from user fees and charges for services, compared to 10 percent for state-generated revenues.

Figure 10.4 breaks down the sources of the $549 billion in taxes generated by local governments. Again, we see a substantially different

Oregon Lottery official checks on state gambling terminal in Salem tavern. There are over 2,000 video poker outlets that provide the state with revenue.

picture when we compare locally generated tax revenue (Figure 10.4) to tax revenue generated at the state level (Figure 10.2). Local governments have a much less diversified tax portfolio compared to states, and they rely heavily on the property tax. School districts and special districts (those that provide services such as fire protection or libraries) rely almost exclusively on property taxes.

Who Bears the Burden of State and Local Taxes?

Other than the income tax, most revenues that states and communities rely on are relatively regressive, compared to the federal tax structure. That is, those who earn less income pay more of their income in state and local taxes. At the same time, the wealthiest people, having far more income, pay more of the total dollars collected. Just as states and cities differ in the revenue packages they use, they also differ in terms of how regressive their taxes are. As Table 10.2 illustrates, the poorest 20 percent of a state's population can pay 9 to 17 percent of their income in state and local taxes, whereas the richest residents in the same state pay as little as 2 or 3 percent of their income in state taxes. In some states (Delaware, Maine, Minnesota, Montana, and New York), all income groups pay about the same share of their income in state taxes.

Figure 10.4

Local Tax Revenues by Source, 2008.

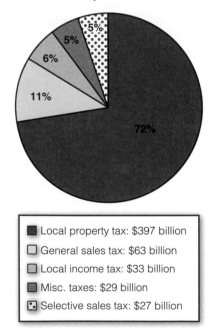

- ■ Local property tax: $397 billion
- □ General sales tax: $63 billion
- □ Local income tax: $33 billion
- ■ Misc. taxes: $29 billion
- ▣ Selective sales tax: $27 billion

Note: Total local tax revenues = $549 billion.

Source: U.S. Census Bureau, http://www.census.gov/govs/estimate/.

| Table 10.2 | | | |

The Ten Most Regressive State Tax Systems (taxes as shares of income for nonelderly residents)

	Taxes as a % of Income		
State	Poorest 20%	Middle	Top 1%
Washington	17.3%	9.5%	2.9%
Florida	13.5%	7.8%	2.6%
South Dakota	11.0%	6.9%	2.1%
Tennessee	11.7%	7.6%	3.3%
Texas	12.2%	7.6%	3.3%
Illinois	13.0%	9.7%	4.9%
Arizona	12.5%	8.5%	5.6%
Nevada	8.9%	6.1%	2.0%
Pennsylvania	11.3%	8.9%	5.0%
Alabama	10.2%	8.6%	4.8%

Note: States listed in bold have no income tax.

Source: *Who Pays? A Distributional Analysis of the Tax Systems in All 50 States.* Institute on Taxation and Economic Policy, November 2009.

Why such differences? States that adopted the income tax early tend to rely on it more heavily, making their tax systems more progressive. A state's economy matters as well. States with larger manufacturing sectors and with wealthier people have more progressive revenue systems. Taxation may also be more progressive in states with strong competition between parties. A party out of power trying to win support from a broad base of voters may have an incentive to propose increased government spending for the poor and middle class, financed by taxes on the rich.[51] Economic growth and Democratic governors are also associated with more progressive taxation.[52] States that never adopted the income tax tend to have the most regressive overall revenue systems.

Since the tax revolt of the late 1970s, states and local governments have begun to rely more heavily on user fees (particularly direct democracy states) and specific sales taxes, such as cigarette taxes—trends that may make revenues more regressive over time.

When Do Taxes Go Up or Down?

Tax "innovation," or the adoption of new taxes, is a function of need and political opportunity. Factors that increase the need for new revenues also increase the likelihood that a government might adopt a new tax or raise an old one. Perhaps the most important thing motivating a state to adopt new taxes is, not surprisingly, fiscal hardship. States have not typically adopted new sales and income taxes during prosperous years. Although such taxes are unpopular, a fiscal crisis may make tax increases more palatable for voters and reduce the risk elected officials face when they increase taxes.[53]

[51] David Lowery, "The Distribution of Tax Burdens in the American States: The Determinants of Fiscal Incidence," *Western Political Quarterly* (1986):137–58; V. O. Key, *Southern Politics in the State and Nation* (New York: Knopf, 1949). This effect may depend on the period being studied. See B. R. Fry and R. D. Winters, "The Politics of Redistribution," *American Political Science Review* 70(1970):508–22.

[52] Neil Berch, "Explaining the Changes in Tax Incidence in the States," *Political Research Quarterly* 48(1995):629–41.

[53] Hansen, *The Politics of Taxation.*

Some research suggests that politicians also wait until after an election year to raise unpopular taxes, but the frequency of tax increases the year after a general election also reflects that some states budget for two years (a biennial budget). Budget that might reflect promises from the previous election are drawn in the first year of the biennium, after a new governor and legislature may have been elected. Less unpopular revenue sources—like the lottery or targeted user fees—may be more likely to be adopted in an election year as politicians try to avoid highly unpopular tax increases. New taxes adopted in one state may also be more likely if a neighboring state has already adopted the tax.[54] Some studies suggest the scope of government spending increases when the same party controls both the legislature and governor's office, particularly when Democrats have unified control outside of the South.[55] Others find evidence that party control of government may not correspond with tax increases.[56] Similarly, politicians are more likely to increase existing taxes when the political costs are lowest, that is, when the next election is far away and the economy is bad.[57]

Taxes also go down. States often implement tax cuts when the economy is strong and revenues are growing. During the boom of the mid- to late 1990s, 44 states enacted tax cuts. Tax cuts are often packaged as a means to stimulate a state's economy, although one think-tank report suggests that states with the largest tax cuts of the 1990s had the biggest fiscal problems and were more likely to have their credit rating downgraded in the next decade. Between 2001 and 2006, states with the largest tax cuts had weaker job growth.[58]

What Are the Effects of Taxes?

Do taxes help or hurt long-run economic development? This is one of the more contentious questions in politics as well as in the academic world of economists and political scientists. Some economic theory assumes that growth depends on the development of physical and human capital, that is, on the amount that machines and people can produce. Human capital includes education, skill, and training. Physical capital can be seen in factories, tools, roads, and equipment. Traditional models of growth assume that taxes are just part of some equilibrium level of capital and that economic growth results from technical changes that increase productivity.

But things are more complex than this. There are different types of taxes—some might discourage the formation of human and physical capital, some might have fewer effects, and other taxes might actually encourage capital formation. Different taxes also have different effects on how people spend their money and invest. In other words, the relationship between taxes and economic growth depends on how the money is raised and varied expenditures. Taxes that are spent on education, for example, can generate positive effects on the formation of human capital—effects that a private market might not produce.[59] However, the personal

[54] Francis Berry and William D. Berry, "State Lottery Adoptions as Policy Innovations," *American Political Science Review* (1990):395–415.

[55] Hansen, *The Politics of Taxation*; James Alt and Robert Lowry, "Divided Government, Fiscal Institutions and Budget Deficits"; W. Robert Reed, "Democrats, Republicans and Taxes: Evidence That Political Parties Matter," *Journal of Public Economics* 90(2006):725–50.

[56] Francis Berry and William D. Berry, "Tax Innovation in the States: Capitalizing on Political Opportunity," *American Journal of Political Science* (1992):715–42; David Primo (2006).

[57] Francis Berry and William D. Berry, "The Politics of Tax Increases in the States," *American Journal of Political Science* (1994):855–99.

[58] Nicholas Johnson and Brian Filipowich, *Tax Cuts and Continued Consequences* (Washington, DC: Center for Budget and Policy Priorities, 2006).

[59] Robert Lucas, "On the Mechanics of Economic Development," *Journal of Monetary Economics* (1988):3–42; Enrico Moretti, "Estimating the External Return to Higher Education," *Journal of Econometrics* (2003):175–202.

income tax might also discourage entrepreneurial activity.[60] Taxes on corporate earnings, on the other hand, might discourage economic growth,[61] but when corporate taxes are low relative to high personal income taxes, entrepreneurial activity might be encouraging because people have greater incentives to incorporate businesses.[62]

Some studies show positive effects of state taxation on state economic growth, and some studies find negative effects.[63] Results are sensitive to the statistical methods used, the time period examined, and the tax or spending patterns that are examined. Studies of state taxing and spending from the 1950s found no relationship between taxes and growth.[64] Some studies from the 1970s and early 1980s found a negative relationship, with one noting that welfare spending harmed economic growth, whereas business taxes increased growth.[65] Further evidence shows that state tax increases used to fund welfare payments depress economic growth;[66] however, state taxes spent on education, highways, and public health and safety have been shown to have favorable impacts on the location decisions of businesses.[67] One overview of these studies concluded that most found "a weak or insignificant relationship between taxes and economic performance" because they failed to account for what taxes were spent on. Taxes dedicated to health, education, and highways were found to have a positive effect on private investment and employment in a state, but welfare spending had a negative effect. The authors concluded that their findings should not be interpreted as a prescription for curtailing welfare spending. They noted, rather, that states face a "vicious cycle" in a prolonged economic slump. They risk crowding out public investment in health, education, streets, and highways if they increase welfare spending alone, but raising taxes to fund public investment and welfare may further depress the economy.[68]

The Growth of State Governments

The size of government can be thought of in terms of the proportion of the total economy that is taxed and spent by government. Whatever the effects of taxing and spending, state governments are now much larger than they were 50 years ago. When the size of the economy is measured as the sum of everyone's personal income, state governments spent about $0.04 of each dollar of personal income in 1950. Today, they spend about $0.16 of each dollar.[69]

[60] William M. Gentry and R. Glenn Hubbard, "Tax Policy and Entrepreneurial Entry," *American Economic Review* (2000):283–7.

[61] Young Lee and Roger H. Gordon, "Tax Structure and Economic Growth," *Journal of Public Economics* (2005).

[62] J. B. Cullen and Robert H. Gordon, "Taxes and Entrepreneurial Activity: Theory and Evidence for the U.S.," NBER Working Paper No. 9015 (New York: National Bureau of Economic Research, 2002).

[63] James Heckman, "A Life-Cycle Model of Earnings, Learning, and Consumption," *Journal of Political Economy* 84(4)(1976):S11–S44; in contrast, see P. A. Trostel, "The Effect of Taxation on Human Capital," *Journal of Political Economy* (1993):327–50.

[64] Clark C. Bloom, *State and Local Tax Differentials and the Location of Manufacturing* (Iowa City, IA: Bureau of Business and Economic Research, 1955); Wilbur Thompson and John M. Mattilla, *An Econometric Model of Postwar State Economic Development* (Detroit:, MI: Wayne State University Press, 1959); Dennis W. Carlton, "Why New Firms Locate Where They Do," in W. Wheaton, ed., *Interregional Movements and Regional Growth* (Washington, DC: The Urban Institute, 1979).

[65] Thomas Romans and Ganti Subrahmanyam, "State and Local Taxes, Transfers, and Regional Economic Growth," *Southern Economic Journal* (1979):435–44; Robert J. Newman, "Industry Migration and Growth in the South," *Review of Economics and Statistics* (1983):76–86.

[66] Romans and Subrahmanyam, "State and Local Taxes"; L. Jay Helms, "The Effect of State and Local Taxes on Economic Growth: A Time Series–Cross Sectional Approach," *Review of Economics and Statistics* 67(1985):574–82.

[67] Helms, "The Effect of State and Local Taxes on Economic Growth."

[68] Alaeddin Mofidi and Joe A. Stone, "Do State and Local Taxes Affect Economic Growth?" *Review of Economics and Statistics* (1990):686–91.

[69] Garand and Baudoin, p. 293.

Nearly all of this growth in the size of state government occurred from 1950 to 1970. Growth was driven by massive state investments in education and highways during this period. Prior to the 1950s, the federal highway system was nonexistent, and states spent much less on infrastructure. This growth period was also when many states were building new public universities. California, for example, spent heavily on public investment in the 1950s and 1960s, building multibillion-dollar water projects, five new University of California campuses, eight new California State University campuses, and dozens of community colleges.

With highway construction on the wane by the late 1960s and the political revolts against taxation taking effect in the late 1970s, the size of state government peaked around 1978 and then declined through the 1980s. After the federal government shifted responsibility for welfare to the states in the 1990s, the size of state government began a steady increase back to levels seen in the late 1970s.[70]

Trends in State and Local Revenues

As states struggled in 2009 to recover from the recession, they approved more new tax revenues than at any time in the past decade. Despite this, new tax revenues approved for fiscal year 2010 budgets still made up only about 17 percent of what states used to fill their budget gaps (the remainder came mostly from cuts, and federal funds). Several states relied on higher personal income taxes. Eight states raised income tax rates on their top brackets, with increases in half of those states adopted as temporary or one-time measures. California and New York approved billions in new tax revenues for 2010. Two states (Vermont and North Dakota) reduced income tax rates. Florida raised its tobacco tax and approved $1 billion in new fees.[71]

Where Does the Money Go? Government Spending

Discussing state and local revenue sources before examining what government spends the money on is a bit like putting the cart before the horse. Revenues are generated in large measure to satisfy public demands for programs and services and to fund budget drivers—the major programs that state and local governments operate.

Figures 10.5 and 10.6 illustrate the major program spending areas for state and local governments, respectively. State and local governments combine to spend about $3.1 trillion: $1.6 trillion by the 50 states and $1.5 trillion by local governments.

Education

The largest area of direct state spending illustrated in Figure 10.5 is education—36 percent of total spending by the states. The amount of state funds spent on education is actually much larger than what is suggested by Figure 10.5, because states transfer hundreds of billions of dollars to local governments to fund K–12 schools. Local schools have their own revenue source (local property taxes), but state funds are used to supplement what schools raise in local taxes. Because these funds are actually spent at the local level, they are included in our picture of the local government spending mix (Figure 10.6). If we had illustrated state spending just as a percentage of state-generated funds (excluding federal funds for social programs), education would be an even larger area of state expenditure. Figure 10.5 illustrates funds that are spent directly by the state, and omits state funds spent by local school districts.

Unlike local K–12 schools, state colleges and universities have no local tax revenues and

---

[70] Garand and Baudoin.

[71] State Budget Update: July 2009, National Conference of State Legislatures; State Tax Update: July 2009, National Conference of State Legislatures.

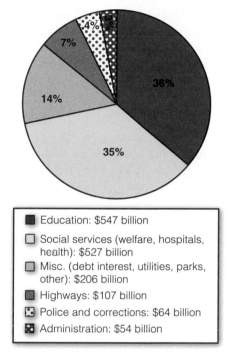

Figure 10.5

Major State Government Spending Programs, 2008

- Education: $547 billion
- Social services (welfare, hospitals, health): $527 billion
- Misc. (debt interest, utilities, parks, other): $206 billion
- Highways: $107 billion
- Police and corrections: $64 billion
- Administration: $54 billion

Note: Total expenditure = $1.50 trillion (excludes $200 billion in insurance benefits payments).

Source: U.S. Census Bureau, State Government Finances, 2008, http://www.census.gov/govs/state/0800usst.html.

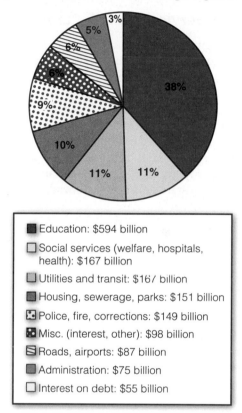

Figure 10.6

Major Local Government Spending Programs

- Education: $594 billion
- Social services (welfare, hospitals, health): $167 billion
- Utilities and transit: $167 billion
- Housing, sewerage, parks: $151 billion
- Police, fire, corrections: $149 billion
- Misc. (interest, other): $98 billion
- Roads, airports: $87 billion
- Administration: $75 billion
- Interest on debt: $55 billion

Note: Total local government expenditure = $1.57 trillion. Excludes $34 billion in insurance trust expenditure.

Source: U.S. Census Bureau, http://www.census.gov/govs/estimate/.

are totally reliant on state funds and tuition they collect from students. The majority of direct state spending on education (80 percent) goes to operate universities, community colleges, and vocational schools. The National Association of State Budget Officials notes that "when the state fiscal picture darkens, higher education often is the first category of spending to cut." Colleges and universities are an easy target because they are one of the largest state services that allow costs, however painful, to be transferred to users (students or their parents). Many states responded to the 2002 fiscal crisis by accelerating the shift toward financing higher education with higher direct charges (fees and tuition), while reducing general fund revenues spent. Over

the decade that ended in 2004, tuition and fees increased 47 percent at public four-year universities.[72] Several states proposed tuition increases of 10 percent or more in 2009 and 2010.

Figure 10.6 illustrates that education is the largest component of local government spending—38 percent of all local expenditures, 94 percent of which is spent on elementary and secondary education (K–12 schools). Most of this money is raised by local property taxes or provided by the states and is spent by local school districts. The largest cost of education is labor: paying salaries for teachers, counselors,

[72] National Association of State Budget Officers, State Expenditure Report (Washington, DC: NASBO, 2003).

school administrators, technology staff, cooks, and so on.

Social Services: Health Care

Thirty-four percent of money spent by states funds social services. Social service spending, the second largest and fastest-growing component of state budgets, is dominated by health care. When looking at Figure 10.5, it is important to remember that a large part of overall state spending is financed by the federal government. Much of the federal dollars going to states are from the **Medicaid** program. Medicaid accounts for most of state social service spending—about 20 percent of all state expenditures.[73] Given the absence of national health care insurance and the high costs for private health insurance, states are left with much of the responsibility for providing health care to the millions of Americans who are uninsured. Federal funds come with standards that define minimal levels of service the states must provide, and federal dollars are given to match state spending on Medicaid. If states want to provide additional health care beyond the minimal standards— for example, offering prenatal care or providing basic health care insurance for the working poor—they must spend more. A growing proportion of social service spending is used to fund prescription drug purchases.

Because spending on hospitals, long-term care for the elderly, mental health, and other health care–related services comprise the single largest part of a state's budget, health care spending is the largest target for cuts in times of economic downturn. Given the size of health care in the overall state budget, it is nearly impossible to reduce spending without rolling back reimbursement rates paid to health care providers (doctors, hospitals, and nursing homes),

freezing reimbursement levels, or cutting back on the number of people eligible for benefits. In times of fiscal crunch, states will cut back on health care, even if it means losing federal Medicaid matching dollars.[74] Nonetheless, the proportion of state spending on health care has been growing. Local governments, in contrast, spend much less on social services, as these programs are largely administered by the states.

Social Services: Aid to the Poor

Assistance to the poor, or welfare programs, works in a similar manner as medical benefit programs. Federal government funds are sent to the states and topped up by a state if it expands services offered or people who are eligible. Cash assistance to the poor represents a much smaller proportion of state spending on social services than health care: less than 20 percent of all social service spending. Social welfare programs include transferring cash to individuals and providing services. In 1996, Congress passed the Temporary Assistance to Needy Families (TANF) block grant program and shifted much of the responsibility for welfare assistance programs from the national government to the states. The TANF program also represented a contraction of total welfare benefits. By 1998, states and communities were spending 20 percent less on cash assistance to the poor than they were in 1992.[75]

Pensions and Unemployment

A major component of state expenditures is payments from insurance and trust funds. States spend about as much on these programs as on higher education, but they are considered "off budget" because they have their own funding sources. States maintain various trust funds to provide unemployment coverage for

---

[73] Kenneth Feingold et al., "Social Program Spending and State Fiscal Crisis," Urban Institute Occasional Paper no. 70 (Washington, DC: Urban Institute, 2003).

[74] Feingold et al., "Social Program Spending and State Fiscal Crisis."

[75] Mark Rom, "Transforming State Health and Welfare Programs," in *Politics in the American States: A Comparative Analysis* (Washington, DC: CQ Press, 2004).

state residents or to provide compensation to residents who cannot work because they were injured on the job. States also maintain pension funds to cover their own employees' retirement payments, some of which provide rather generous benefits. In theory, these can be "pay as you go" programs. Workers pay weekly or monthly contributions into an unemployment insurance fund, for example, and are eligible for benefits if they lose work. Likewise, the state, as an employer, matches public employees' contributions to public pension funds to create a pool of money to cover future retirement benefit costs for state workers and public school teachers. Pension funds may be invested in order to increase their value.

In practice, things do not always work this way. When revenues are low, some states and cities forgo contributing to trust funds or borrow from the funds in order to make it appear that their budgets balance. If pension fund investments go bad, states may also have to make up for losses. States have full responsibility for workers' comp and unemployment programs, so these programs do not factor into the local spending mix. For many state governments and some local governments, obligations to fully fund public employee retirement pension accounts may be a looming crisis. It is easy to forgo collecting revenues to cover the costs of pension funds, but if the deficits in such accounts grow over time, it may be harder to make up lost ground. A 2004 survey of cities found 79 percent reporting that their pension funds' fiscal health was eroding. San Diego's public employee pension fund was nearly $2 billion in deficit in 2004. The city had been providing lavish benefits while reducing payments into the fund. When a stock market crash reduced the value of the fund, the city faced bankruptcy.[76] Many pension funds suffered from the market collapse of 2008. In New York, the state and local governments agreed to higher contributions to employee retirement funds as the state's fund lost 30 percent of its value. This required higher property taxes so governments could meet their pension obligations.[77]

Transportation and Highways

About 7 percent of state spending and 6 percent of local spending are for transportation. Localities also spend more than states on transit systems. Most state expenditures on transportation are funded by earmarked revenues placed in special non–general fund accounts, usually from gasoline taxes. Federal funds are also directed to the states for highway construction and cover about 30 percent of transportation spending. States also finance highways with bonds. Transportation represents the largest part of state spending in capital budgets. States spend more on transportation infrastructure than they do on building prisons, universities, housing, and all other infrastructure combined.

Government Administration and Debt Interest

Four percent of state and 5 percent of local expenditure are used to operate public buildings, run court systems (including paying public defenders, judges, and prosecutors), and fund general administrative costs.

Public Safety, Police, and Prisons

Four percent of state spending and 9 percent of local spending finance public safety programs. At the state level, 66 percent of public safety costs fund corrections operations (mostly salaries for prison guards and other staff); most of the remainder pays for state troopers (highway patrols). The operation of prisons is a growing part of state budgets. At the local level, most spending in this area supports local police forces.

---

[76] John Ritter, "San Diego Now Enron by the Sea," *USA Today*, 24 October 2004.

[77] Adam Sichko, "Pension Fund Increase Could Lead to Local Tax Hikes," *The Business Review* (Albany), 3 September 2009.

Do State and Local Spending Actually Reflect What People Want?

Much of governing involves responding to the popular demands for spending. Thus, if a state's population consistently tells politicians they want more spent on schools and playgrounds, we might expect more spent on schools and playgrounds. Likewise, if voters routinely approve taxes and bonds for parklands, we might expect legislators to interpret this as a signal to spend money on recreation amenities. Other factors, however, may drive spending away from what most voters (or the average voter) want. This raises at least two questions: How much do state and local spending reflect what people really want? How much should they reflect what most people want?

In addition to trying to determine the preferences of the general public, elected officials hear from many different interest groups who each want some unique benefit just for themselves: a tax break here, a new road there, higher salaries for prison guards or professors, more spending on somebody's favorite program—public funds to help all sorts of relatively narrow concerns. In many legislative hearings, representatives of rather narrow constituencies may outnumber everyone else.

Governing involves the need to balance these demands and the ability to anticipate other things that also need to be done. These may include things the public might not be paying much attention to or that they might not want to spend much money on. Courts' interpretations of state and federal constitutions often force states to spend millions to reduce prison crowding. The business climate in part of a state may be threatened by traffic gridlock, forcing politicians to find ways to fund transportation options in that area. Even lightly used bridges, levees, and tunnels will eventually need maintenance or modernization to meet new safety or seismic standards. The fact that these matters may require public investment does not necessarily mean that the public supports such spending.

Budgeting

Deficits and Balanced Budget Requirements

If the federal government decides it wants to spend more than it is collecting in taxes, it can. The federal government can finance its operations by selling long-term U.S. Treasury bonds. Investors buy the bonds and earn interest on their investment over time. This allows for long-term borrowing to finance the annual operations of the federal government. In recent decades the federal budget has been in deficit more years than not, which means a large percentage of each federal budget includes funds to pay interest on bonds that are outstanding. Critics of chronic federal deficits look to state **balanced budget rules** as a model for fiscal reform. In all but one state, these rules require that proposed budgets are projected to balance at the end of the fiscal year. Twenty-seven states also prohibit deficits from being carried into the next fiscal year.[78]

Borrowing

State governments cannot run deficits—at least not in the same way the federal government does. Virtually all states—Vermont is the only exception—have constitutional rules that require annual (or biannual) spending to not exceed revenues. Many states actually write two budgets, with balanced budget rules applying to the state's **operating budget**. Operating budgets cover spending on services, salaries, and purchases of supplies. States might borrow funds in the short term to manage cash flow problems during the year (some tax collections peak in certain months, but government expenses, such as paying salaries, are more constant). Short-term debts are supposed to be repaid by the end of the budget cycle. **Capital budgets** can be a separate matter; states and local governments issue long-term bonds to finance capital investment in roads, bridges, buildings, and other infrastructure. Capital budgets may be funded with long-term borrowing, which is a form of deficit spending. Borrowing, rather than paying costs up front, can be seen as a fair way of paying for infrastructure that will be in use for years. Paying for a road, a bridge, or a sports arena all at once means that some of those who paid for it will die or move away before the project is completed and thus never benefit from it.

In addition to having balanced budget rules, some states require that voters approve the sale of any bonds that will be used to finance long-term borrowing. Some also require a supermajority vote in the legislature before the proposal can go to voters for approval.

Do Budgeting Rules Matter?

But do these budgeting rules really make any difference? Some balanced budget rules have weak provisions for enforcement. Most studies suggest that tough rules do work at preventing deficits when they are combined with limits on government borrowing, but weak rules do not.[79] Some rules simply require the governor to submit a balanced budget to the legislature or require the legislature to enact a balanced budget at the start of the fiscal year. But a state with such rules may still be allowed to run a deficit if revenue or spending estimates end up wrong.[80] Rules that simply require the budget to be balanced when written may be less effective than rules that require it to be balanced

at the end of the year. Likewise, constitutional rules may be more effective than regular laws that politicians can easily amend. Finally, balanced budget rules may be more effective when enforced by an independently elected state supreme court than when enforcement depends on a court appointed by the politicians who write the budget.[81] One study noted that balanced budget rules were more effective when Republicans were in office.[82]

Some rules regulating long-term capital borrowing don't necessarily lead to less state indebtedness. Requiring a supermajority vote in the legislature for transportation infrastructure bills, for example, may create incentives to place a transportation project in every representative's district.[83] Even voters seem more likely to approve state-level borrowing if a project is proposed for their local area.[84]

Budget Surpluses

Independent of whatever these balanced budget rules may produce, states have a fairly predictable record of not only balancing their budgets but also ending with a surplus. In many years, states maintain a surplus "rainy day fund" to be used in times of crisis. When 50 state budgets were considered across a 40-year period starting in 1961 (that is, 2,000 different budgets), 83 percent produced surpluses. Texas and New Mexico ran in the black every single year. Although Massachusetts (52 percent of budgets had a surplus), Hawaii (55 percent), and Rhode Island (60 percent) were least likely to run surpluses, they usually did.[85] With state governments usually running surpluses, they soften the effects that federal deficits might

[79] James Poterba, "Budget Institutions and Fiscal Policy in the U.S. States," *American Economic Review* 86(2)(1996):395–400.

[80] James Poterba, "Balanced Budget Rules and Fiscal Policy: Evidence from the States," *National Tax Journal* (1995):329–7.

[81] Hening Bohn and Robert P. Inman, "Balanced Budget Rules and Public Deficits: Evidence from the U.S. States," NBER Working Paper no. W5533, 1996, http://ssrn.com/abstract=4069.

[82] James Alt and Robert Lowry, "Divided Government, Fiscal Institutions, and Budget Deficits: Evidence from the States," *American Political Science Review* 88(1994):811–28.

[83] D.R. Kiewiet and Kristin Szakaty. "*Constitutional Liminations on Borrowing*" *Journal of Law, Economics & Organizations.* 12(1)(1996):62–97.

[84] Shaun Bowler and Todd Donovan, *Demanding Choices: Opinion, Voting, and Direct Democracy* (Ann Arbor, MI: University of Michigan Press, 1998).

[85] Garand and Baudoin, "Fiscal Policy in the American States."

have on the national economy. States and communities run deficits at their own peril. Lenders charge states more in interest if they have more debt (relative to the size of their economies).[86]

There may be a political risk, however, in maintaining a large "rainy day fund." A large surplus can become a target for anti-tax activists, as it illustrates that government is collecting more revenue than it needs to spend. California's tax revolt of the 1970s occurred when the state was running a multibillion-dollar surplus. Washington voters also slashed their motor vehicle tax in the late 1990s when the state was running a surplus.

Boom to Bust Budgeting

After the national economy faced a crisis in 2008, most states had difficulty balancing their budgets. Budgeting in recession years, however, can encourage great creativity. In addition to cuts in spending and raising taxes, states have responded by delaying payments they owed, raising tuition, offering early retirement programs to lower salary costs, expanding gambling, raiding transportation and pension funds, mortgaging funds awarded in a settlement with tobacco companies, and borrowing money to fund operations. In 2009, eight states used rainy-day funds to help balance their budget. Smokers helped some states balance their books by paying higher cigarette taxes.

The most dramatic case of boom to bust budgeting may be California, where income tax revenues exploded in the 1990s as people cashed in on stock options in the superheated tech industry. During the 1990s, the state increased spending on K–12 education, expanded medical care eligibility, froze tuition, and cut taxes while balancing its budget. A recession began in March 2001, the tech bubble burst, and tax revenues from stock options and capital gains taxes fell from $17 billion to $6 billion between 2001 and 2002. In 2004, California voters approved the sale of $15 billion in bonds to cover part of their deficit. Such gimmicks only worked in the short term. When the national economy went into a deep freeze in 2008, the state was facing another $40 billion deficit for 2009 and 2010. Before reaching a budget deal that included substantial spending cuts and tax increases, California briefly ran out of operating cash in 2009, and was paying people with IOUs.

California's sustained fiscal crisis, although an extreme case, was not unique. The economic decline of 2008 was one of the most severe recessions since World War II. By 2010, the decline had stopped, but the economic recovery was slow. This recession came after a period when many states cut taxes, while maintaining spending via increased charges, fees, and delays in funding pension obligations. By 2010, boom had gone full bust. Most states forecast deficits their fiscal year 2011 budgets, and many expected deficits when planning for 2012.[87] States responded to revenue shortfalls by cutting social services at a time when demand—for job training, education, unemployment insurance, health care—was peaking due to the poor economy.

[86] Tamim Bayoumi, Morris Goldstein, and Geoffrey Woglom, "Do Credit Markets Discipline Sovereign Borrowers?" *Journal of Money, Credit and Banking* 27(1995):1046–59.

[87] Center for Budget Policy Priorities, "Press Release: New Fiscal Year Brings Painful Spending Cuts, Continued Budget Gaps in Almost Every State," 29 June 2009, http://www.cbpp.org/cms/index.cfm?fa=view&id=2853.

Summary

In surveys of state and local fiscal politics from previous decades, the taxing and spending patterns of states and communities were often explained largely in terms of "environmental" factors. That is, wealthy states were said to spend more because they had more. Political factors, such as public opinion, budgeting rules, and other partisan and institutional forces, were largely dismissed because most studies found little effect of politics on fiscal policy.

The dismissal of political and institutional forces was probably a mistake resulting from flawed measures of political influence and from a lack of investigation. We now have detailed measures of state public opinion and decades of research examining the effects that taxing and spending limits (TELs), balanced budgeting rules, direct democracy, and popular opinion have on taxation and spending. Although some debate the magnitude of the effects of such rules, or of public opinion, it is clear that politics matters, perhaps more than anything else, in determining who gets what from government via fiscal policy.

Keywords

Balanced budget rules

Capital budget

Cost of living allowances (COLAs)

Elasticity

Inelastic demand

Medicaid

Operating budget

Progressive tax

Regressive tax

Sin tax

Tax equity

Tax and expenditure limitations (TELs)

Discussion Questions

(1) How does state income tax factor into a state's revenue mix? What are the benefits and critiques of state income taxes?

(2) How do Internet sales influence state and local sales tax collection?

(3) What factors have fueled rebellion against property taxes? What reforms have resulted?

(4) What are the positive and negative effects of state tax and expenditure limits?

(5) How do local revenue mixes differ from state revenue mixes? What are the different key revenue sources for each of these?

Suggested Readings

Beamer, Glenn. 1999. *Creative Politics: Taxes and Public Goods in a Federal System*. Ann Arbor, MI: University of Michigan Press.

Briffault, Richard. 1996. *Balancing Acts: The Reality Behind State Balanced Budgets*. New York: Twentieth Century Fund Press.

Brunori, David. 2005. *State Tax Policy: A Political Perspective,* 2nd ed. Washington, DC: Urban Institute Press.

Crain, W. Mark. 2003. *Volatile States: Institutions, Policy, and State Economies*. Ann Arbor, MI: University of Michigan Press.

Forsythe, Dall W. 2004. *Memos to the Governor: An Introduction to State Budgeting,* 2nd ed. Washington, DC: Georgetown University Press.

Lowry, Robert C. 2008. "Fiscal Policy in the American States," in V. Gray and R. Hanson, eds., *Politics in the American States: A Comparative Introduction*. Washington, DC: CQ Press.

Smith, Daniel A. 1998. *Tax Crusaders and the Politics of Direct Democracy*. New York: Routledge.

Thurmaier, Kurt M., and Katherine G. Willoughby. 2001. *Policy and Politics in State Budgeting*. Armonk, NY: M. E. Sharpe.

Websites

Cato Institute (http://www.cato.org): A conservative organization that provides policy analysis "based on individual liberty, limited government, free markets and peaceful international relations."

Center for Budget Policy Priorities (http://www.cbpp.org): A liberal organization that conducts research on the needs of low-income families and the impact of policies on state budgets. Works with states and nonprofit groups to advocate for the needs of low-income families. Provides analysis of state fiscal policy.

Federation of Tax Administrators (http://www.taxadmin.org): Comparative information on state tax rates and state tax agencies.

National Association of State and Provincial Lotteries (http://www.naspl.org): Represents lottery organizations and provides reports about revenues from state lotteries.

National Association of State Budget Officers (http://www.nasbo.org): Professional organization for all state budget officers. An independent association with membership consisting of the heads of state budget offices and state finance departments. Provides reports on trends in the fiscal condition of the states.

National Council of State Legislators (http://www.ncsl.org): An organization that provides research, technical assistance, and other information to state legislators. Provides reports on state and federal relations and on key policy issues.

U.S. Census Bureau, Census of Governments (http://www.census.gov/govs/www/): Detailed data on state and local expenditures and revenues.

Glossary

Adjudication: To settle a dispute by judicial procedure.

Adjudicator: Legal professional trained in resolving disputes between parties outside of the courtroom.

Administrative rules: Regulations, restrictions, and requirements written by executive agencies and used to implement public policy enacted through the legislature, the courts, or the governor.

Adversarial argument: As in a courtroom, when two parties to a dispute make their best arguments to a neutral third party, who then decides the dispute. This is as opposed to a negotiated settlement, where the parties work back and forth between themselves to resolve the dispute.

Amend: To modify a bill in the lawmaking process.

Amendatory veto: The power of some states' governors to send a passed bill back to the legislature asking for specific changes in it before he or she will sign it.

Appropriations bill: A bill that authorizes a state agency to spend money in specific ways.

Articles of Confederation: The country's first constitution, ratified in March 1781.

At-large elections: Elected officials represent an entire city (or county) rather than a district. All voters can cast one vote for each position on the council.

Balanced budget rules: Rules that require a state's operating budget balance by the end of the year. Some rules also prohibit deficits from being carried into the next fiscal year.

Bench trial: Trial with no jury, where the judge or judges alone decide the outcome.

Bicameral: Having two chambers, such as in 49 state legislatures and Congress, which have a house of representatives (called by another name in some states) and a senate.

Bill: A proposed law that is formally introduced by a legislator for consideration by his or her chamber.

Bill of Rights: The first ten amendments to the U.S. Constitution, ratified in December 1791, which ensure the protection of individuals and the states from the national government.

Bill sponsor: The legislator who proposes that a bill be considered by his or her chamber.

Block grants: Funds provided by the federal government to states and localities with few restrictions on how the money may be spent.

Bureaucracy: The administrative structure of any large, complex organization, like a government, that is characterized by hierarchical control and fixed rules of procedure.

Capital budget: A budget for spending and revenues associated with construction and repairs to infrastructure and facilities such as buildings, schools, and other public facilities.

Casework: The activities of a legislator and his or her staff in helping constituents with specific problems, usually with state government. For example, a legislator may help a constituent solve a problem with getting a driver's license or adjusting a state tax bill.

Categorical grants are issued by the United States Congress and may be spent by state and local governments for narrowly-defined purposes, and usually require matching funds.

Caucus: Used by parties to nominate candidates, with party members informally meeting, deliberating, and casting a vote for their preferred candidate.

Centralization: Empowering a national governing authority with unitary control and authority.

Chamber floor: Where and when the members of one chamber (the house or senate) meet as a group to debate and vote on legislation.

Charter review commission: A representative body selected periodically to serve for a brief period of time to make recommendations for changes to a local government's charter. After public hearings, the commission may place proposals for changing the charter on the ballot.

Citizen legislature: A state legislature that is largely a part-time body, whose members are paid a modest salary, have little staff, meet infrequently, and are expected to have careers and interests other than the state legislature.

Civil service: Public employees are hired on the basis of merit (rather than political loyalties). Civil service rules stipulate non-political processes about how public employees are hired, promoted, and fired.

Civil service system: A system of hiring, promoting, and firing government workers based on job-related criteria rather than on political connections or other biases.

Clientele parties: Political parties that depend upon patronage. A party acts as a patron that serves its supporters (the clients) by providing them personal favors in exchange for votes.

Closed primary: A primary nomination election in which voters registered with a political party are permitted to vote only for candidates of the party with which they are registered.

Coercive federalism: A federalist arrangement whereby the federal government spearheads and funds programs; also referred to as creative federalism.

Collective action problem: The problem of coordinating a group of people to achieve a common goal.

Commerce Clause: Gives Congress the power "to regulate Commerce with foreign Nations, and among the several States, and with the Indian Tribes." Used by Congress to expand its power vis-à-vis the states.

Common law: The system of laws originated and developed in England, based on court decisions, the doctrines implicit in those decisions, and customs and usages rather than on codified written laws.

Comparative method: An approach to political analysis that entails comparing units of analysis (such as states or communities) on more than one characteristic to help understand the relationships among those characteristics.

Confederal system: Also known as a confederacy, a system of governance whereby the national government is subject to the control of subnational, autonomous governments.

Conference committee: A temporary legislative committee made up of equal members of the senate and house who meet to reconcile the differences between the versions of a bill passed by the two chambers and to propose a single version for both chambers to consider.

Conflict of interest: A situation in which a government decision maker may personally benefit from his or her official actions or a judge has a personal interest in the outcome of a case that may bias his or her actions in that case.

Constitution: A document laying out the fundamental law defining the basic political institutions of a government and the fundamental values for which that government stands.

Constitutional initiative: A ballot initiative that amends a state's constitution.

Contiguous: Areas of land that touch (except for islands).

Contract lobbyist: A professional lobbyist who temporarily works on behalf of a client.

Cooperative federalism: A federalism arrangement whereby responsibilities for most governmental functions are interdependent, shared between the federal and state governments.

Cost of living allowances (COLAs): A mechanism where wages or benefits are increased to keep pace with inflation.

Council–manager system: Local government where administrative and executive duties are delegated to a professional city manager. The manager is appointed by an elected council. Some council–manager cities have a mayor, but the mayor will have few formal powers.

Court of last resort: Those courts whose decisions cannot be appealed to another court; these courts have the final word on a given set of laws. Typically called the supreme court (or something similar).

Cracking: Dispersing a party's voters among many districts so it will win fewer district races.

Cumulative voting: Elected officials represent an entire city (or county) rather than a district. Voters can cast all their votes for one candidate, or distribute their votes to multiple candidates.

Decentralization: Devolving to citizens or their elected representatives more power to make decisions, including the formation and implementation of public policies.

Defendant: The person or institution against whom an action is brought in a court of law; the person being sued or accused of a crime.

Descriptive representation: Representation where elected officials share key traits (race, ethnicity) of their constituents.

Devolution: The decentralization of power and authority from a central government to state or local governments.

Dillon's rule: An 1868 ruling by an Iowa judge that defines local governments as legal creations of their state government. The rule has been used widely to define local government powers as narrow, and determined by state laws.

Direct initiative: An initiative that, if qualified with sufficient signatures, is voted on directly by the public.

Direct primary: An election in which voters select one candidate affiliated with a political party for each elected office; the party nominees later face one another in a general election.

Director of state courts: Administrator hired by a court system to handle the bureaucratic chores of the system, including personnel and budget issues.

District magnitude: The number of representatives elected from a district (or from a jurisdiction is not districted).

Disturbance theory: A macrolevel theory that assumes groups emerge in response to societal changes.

Divided government: When two of the three legs of the legislative process (the governor, the house, and the senate) are controlled by different parties.

Docket: A calendar of the cases awaiting action in a court.

Drug courts: Trial courts of limited jurisdiction used in some states and localities to prosecute certain minor drug and related offenses, with a focus on reducing recidivism and drug abuse treatment. Judges and lawyers working in these courts specialize in the issues surrounding drug abuse and addiction.

Dual federalism: A system of federalism whereby governmental functions are apportioned so that the national and subnational governments are accorded sovereign power within their respective spheres; sometimes referred to as "layer cake" federalism.

Efficacy: The sense that one's effort at something can make a difference.

Elastic demand: Demand for something is said to be elastic if it responds to changes in price. If a tax raises the price of something that has elastic demand, such as travel or some luxury items, the tax may reduce consumption of the good.

Elasticity: The relationship between the price of something and its consumption. Demand for a good is elastic if consumption is sensitive to price. Tax revenues are elastic if they are sensitive to changes in how much consumers are purchasing.

Electioneering: Explicitly supporting or opposing candidates or political parties, including recruiting and endorsing candidates, fundraising, phone banking, canvassing, and advertising.

Ex post oversight: When the legislature investigates how well an agency is carrying out the intent of a law.

Exportable tax: A tax that is paid disproportionately by people who live outside of the taxing jurisdiction.

Federal preemption: Federal government taking regulatory action that overrides state laws.

Federalism: The structural relationship between a national government and its constitutive states.

Flat rate tax: An income tax where all taxpayers are subject to paying the same rate of taxation on their income.

Free-rider problem: When the benefit of some valuable good or service cannot be restricted to those who pay for it.

Full Faith and Credit Clause: Enshrined in Article IV, Section 1, a clause that stipulates that the states must mutually accept one another's public acts, records, and judicial proceedings.

Functional party model: A theory that parties are pragmatic, self-interested organizations, striving to maximize votes in order to win elections and control political office.

Gatekeeping: Determining which questions and decisions will and will not be considered.

General jurisdiction: Referring to courts that deal with virtually any type of case.

General Revenue Sharing (GRS): A federal grant-in-aid program that provides financial aid to subnational units but does not prescribe how those units are to allocate the funding.

Gerrymander: The process of drawing governmental district boundaries for political advantage.

Grandfather clause: Granting the right to vote only to men who had ancestors who could vote before the Civil War.

Gubernatorial powers: Institutional and informal tools that a governor can use to develop and promote public policy, manage the state bureaucracy, and act as an intergovernmental relations (IGR) manager, among other duties.

Head of state: The main public representative of a government.

Home rule: The delegation of power from a state government to local governments. Home rule charters define the boundaries of local government autonomy and result in less state control over local government affairs.

Hypothesis: A potential answer to a research question that is based on theory and that will be tested by observing data in the world.

Implementation: The execution by government agencies of laws passed by the legislature.

Incorporation of the Bill of Rights: A legal doctrine whereby parts of the U.S. Bill of Rights are applied to the states through the Fourteenth Amendment's Due Process Clause.

Incumbent: The person currently holding a position.

Incumbent-protection district: A governmental district drawn to give electoral advantage to the incumbent.

Indirect initiative: An initiative that, if qualified with sufficient signatures, is considered by the legislature prior to being voted on by the public. The legislature may adopt it or place it on the ballot for a vote. The legislature may also offer an alternative proposal for a public vote.

Individualistic political culture: The general and informal set of beliefs and attitudes that politics in a state or community is a place where individuals can work to advance their personal economic and social interests largely the same as they would do in private business.

Inelastic demand: Tax revenues are inelastic if they are not sensitive to changes in how much consumers are purchasing.

In-house lobbyist: A professional lobbyist who is a permanent employee of an interest group.

Injunction: A court order prohibiting someone from taking some action.

Interest group: A formally organized body of individuals, organizations, or public or private enterprises sharing common goals and joining in a collective attempt to influence the electoral and policy-making processes.

Interest group system density: The number of functioning groups relative to the size of a state's economy.

Interest group system diversity: The spread of groups in a state across social and economic realms.

Intergovernmental relations: The interactions among the federal government, the states, and local governments.

Intermediate courts of appeal: Courts that hear appeals of trial decisions and are concerned with whether the trial was fair and conducted with proper procedures. ICAs were developed as a way to take the burden of routine appeals off of supreme courts so that supreme courts can focus on the most important cases.

Issue advocacy: A form of political speech focusing on issues of public concern that mentions issues and the positions taken on those issues by elected officials or candidates, but stops short of expressly advocating the support or defeat of those elected officials or candidates.

Jacksonian democracy: Expansion of the number of offices elected, and of the right to vote, that occurred during the late 1820s and 1830s. Political parties became more mass-based and more dependent on patronage.

Judicial review: The power of a supreme court to judge whether a law is in violation of the state constitution and, if so, to nullify that law.

Jurisdiction: Geographical or topical area over which a court, institution, or official has power and authority.

Jury: A randomly selected group of citizens who are sworn by a court to hear and render a verdict and/or set a penalty in a trial.

Land Ordinance of 1785: A law allowing the federal government to sell land west of the original 13 states. Huge tracts of land were divided into 6 mile by 6 mile square sections called townships, which were divided into 36 different square subsections. One subsection in each township was reserved for public education.

Legal brief: A document stating legal facts and arguments.

Legislative intent: What the legislature meant for a piece of legislation to do when it passed it.

Legislative professionalism: When a legislature is established to be largely a full-time body, with members who are paid a living wage, have plenty of staff, and believe that legislating is their primary job.

Legislative referendum: A public vote on a bill placed before the voters by the legislature at the discretion of the legislature.

Libertarianism: A political ideology that values freedom of individual action from government interference, control, or help.

Limited jurisdiction: Referring to courts that handle cases on only certain topics, such as traffic courts or probate courts.

Line-item veto: The power of some governors to block only parts of passed appropriations bills from becoming law, subject to override by a supermajority vote of the legislature.

Literacy tests: Tests that allowed local officials to determine if a person had a proper understanding of some written passage prior to being granted their right to vote.

Lobbying: Communicating with elected officials in general as well as the systematic effort to shape public policy by pressuring governmental officials to make decisions in line with the goals of an organized interest. The term lobbying comes from the fact that representatives were often approached in the lobby of legislative buildings.

Louisiana Purchase: The 1803 purchase by the United States of much of continental North America from France.

Machines: A hierarchical political organization controlled by a boss or a small group. Machine power is based on the ability to control party nominations, and to control elections by mobilizing loyal supporters. Supporters may be rewarded with patronage.

Majority opinion: For courts with multiple judges, like supreme courts, the official decision and rationale of the majority of the court's members on a case.

Majority-minority district: Legislative districts where a racial or ethnic minority makes up the majority.

Malapportionment: When the districts in a legislative chamber are not equal in population.

Media market: Region where the population is exposed to the same (or similar) media offerings, including the same television and radio stations and newspapers.

Medicaid: Publicly funded health insurance program created by the federal government in 1965 for low-income children and adults, and people with disabilities. Each state operates a Medicaid program. Programs are funded jointly by states and the federal government.

Merit Plan: A method used to select at least some judges in 24 states whereby (1) a panel of experts recommends a few candidates for a judicial opening to the governor, (2) who then appoints one person to that position for a trial period, and (3) after which the judge faces a retention election to see whether he or she will earn a full term.

Metropolitan areas: Regions of mostly contiguous population centers, as defined by the U.S. Census Bureau. A large area, such as New York, can include several metropolitan areas (northern New Jersey, Long Island, and Connecticut) consolidated into a larger metropolitan area. Smaller regions, such as Pocatello, Idaho, may include cities and towns in a single county.

Meyer v. Grant: A 1988 U.S. Supreme Court ruling against a Colorado law that made it a felony to pay for the collection of signatures on initiative and referendum petitions. The Court ruled that spending to collect signatures was "core political speech" and that no state could ban campaign spending on signature collection. Since 2005, however, two federal appellate courts (the 8th Circuit and 9th Circuit) have permitted states to ban payment per signature, thus requiring that paid petitioners receive a salary or an hourly wage.

Mobilization of bias: The benefiting of private, organized interests in an interest group system.

Model city charter: A blueprint for reforming the structure of local government published by the National Municipal League.

Moralistic political culture: The general and informal set of beliefs and attitudes that politics in a state or community is intended to enhance the public good and for the uplifting of the have-nots of society.

Muckraking journalists: Journalists who exposed corruption in politics and business in the early twentieth century.

Multimember district (MMD): Legislative districts that elect more than one representative.

National Governors Association: Bipartisan association of the 55 state and territorial governors, supported by research and training staff.

National Supremacy Clause: Stipulates that the U.S. Constitution and national laws and treaties "shall be the supreme law of the land."

Necessary and Proper Clause: Also known as the Elastic Clause, it grants Congress the power to make all laws that shall be "necessary and proper for carrying into execution the foregoing powers"; that is, the other congressional powers listed in Article I, Section 8, of the Constitution.

Neutral competence: The value that a government agency should implement policy based only on original legislative intent and its workers' professional norms and training rather than by nonlegislative political pressure.

Nonpartisan primary: An election to nominate candidates for the general election where candidates have no party labels and all voters can participate. Used in many local elections and at the state level in Nebraska.

Office-block ballot: Groups together all candidates running for a single political office by the political office rather than by their party.

Open primary: A primary nomination election. Any registered voter, including independents, can participate. Voters must decide which party's primary they will participate in and can choose only among that party's candidates.

Operating budget: A budget that plans for spending and revenues associated with the provision of government services (benefit spending, costs of supplies, employee salaries, etc.).

Original jurisdiction: The right of a court to be the first to hear a case; where a case must begin its path through the judicial system.

Out-of-court settlement: An agreement made privately between the parties to a civil suit before a trial court decision.

Outsider gubernatorial candidates: Candidates for governor who are not traditional politicians but who have achieved success in other ways, such as in business or as entertainers.

Override: When the legislature passes a law despite a gubernatorial veto, usually by a supermajority vote in each chamber.

Packing: Concentrating one party's voters into a few districts so as to "waste" those votes over 50 percent, allowing the other party to win more district races.

Participation bias: The difference between the general population of eligible voters and the people who actually participate in elections.

Party caucus: All the legislators in a given chamber from a given party, such as the house Democrats or the senate Republicans.

Party fusion: Permits two or more parties to nominate the same candidate for office, with the candidate's name appearing on the ballot alongside the name of each party by which he or she is cross-endorsed.

Party identification: Also known as PID, it is the strength of an individual's attachment to a political party.

Party-column ballot: Groups together all candidates running for different political offices by their party affiliation, making straight-ticket voting possible.

Patronage: Tangible, material rewards (jobs, housing, assistance with the police, food, government contracts) that a political machine can offer in exchange for support.

Patronage job: A government job obtained at least in part through political connections rather than entirely by personal merit; used by elected officials to reward their political supporters and secure loyalty from the bureaucracy.

Pendleton Act: A federal law enacted in 1883 to establish a federal civil service system.

Petition: To make a formal request.

Plaintiff: The party that starts a lawsuit in a court of law.

Plea bargaining: A deal in which the defendant in a criminal case agrees to plead guilty to a lesser charge if the prosecutor agrees to drop a more serious charge.

Pluralism: A political theory that assumes conflict is at the heart of politics and that the diversity of interests will lead to consensual outcomes through discussion and debate.

Policy agenda: The public problems and solutions that are discussed and addressed by policy makers at a given time.

Political accountability: The value that government agencies should implement law following closely the wishes of current elected officials.

Political action committee (PAC): A legal entity that allows like-minded individuals who belong to a corporation, labor union, or virtually any other organization to bundle their contributions and give them to candidates or political parties.

Political capital: The intangible goodwill or support for an elected official that can be used to influence the actions of other officials informally.

Political culture: What people in a group or region generally believe about government and politics; what they think government ought to do and how people should act toward it.

Political ideology: A relatively coherent and consistent set of beliefs about who ought to rule, what principles ought to be used to govern, and what policies rulers ought to pursue.

Political institution: The rules, laws, and organizations through which and by which government functions.

Poll tax: A tax or fee that must be paid in order to secure the right to register or to vote.

Popular referendum: A public vote on a bill passed by the legislature. Referenda are placed on the ballot as the result of a petition effort.

Populist era: Period from 1890s to early the twentieth century when the Populist Party's political influence peaked. Populists advocated for major economic and political reforms.

Populist Party: A third party that had success electing candidates to state and federal offices in the 1890s. Populists championed numerous political and economic reforms, including direct democracy.

Pork barrel: A derogatory and subjective term referring to government spending that is focused on a single geographic area, such as a bridge or a park, suggesting that such spending is wasteful and politically motivated.

Potential interest: An interest that is yet to be organized but has some latent acceptance in society.

Precedent: A legal decision that serves as a guide to deciding another, later legal decision.

Precinct: Smallest geographic political division in American cities. Parties may organize cites at the precinct level.

Precinct captain: Local party official who works with party to maximize voter support for the party in the precinct.

Privileges and Immunities Clause: Ensures that residents of one state cannot be discriminated against by another state when it comes to fundamental matters, such as pursuing one's professional occupation or gaining access to the courts.

Problem-solving courts: Trial courts of limited jurisdiction whose focus is less on prosecuting crimes or settling lawsuits than on helping the parties in the case work out certain types of especially difficult problems; for example, family court, drug court, and mental health courts can be thought of as problem-solving courts.

Progressive era: The first two decades of the twentieth century. Overlaps with Populist era somewhat. Both the Democratic and Republican parties had influential Progressive factions that promoted economic and political reforms.

Progressive Era reforms: Changes to rules governing public health, working conditions, corporations, and the conduct of elections from the early part of the twentieth century.

Progressive federalism: The Obama administration's early inclination to grant the states the green light to supersede regulations set by the federal government.

Progressive tax: A tax where wealthier people pay a larger proportion of their income as tax than the less affluent pay of their total income as tax.

Proposition 13: A June 1978 ballot initiative in California that froze assessments of property and reduced property tax revenues and required a two-thirds majority for the legislature to raise any taxes.

Public goods: A policy or action providing broad benefits to society, as opposed to an action providing narrow benefits to a specific group.

Racial gerrymandering: Drawing boundaries for legislative districts on the basis of race.

Rank-and-file legislator: Legislator who does not hold a leadership position in his or her chamber.

Reapportionment revolution: The political upheaval in the states in the 1960s following the U.S. Supreme Court's mandate that they redraw their legislative and congressional districts to be equal in size in each chamber.

Recall: A special election, qualified via collecting sufficient signatures, where voters decide if a specific incumbent will remain in office.

Recidivism: The tendency to relapse into a previous pattern of behavior, especially criminal behavior.

Reconstruction era: The post–Civil War era (1865–1877) when government and public policy in the 11 states of the former Confederacy were dominated by the federal government, immigrants from the northern states ("carpetbaggers"), and freed slaves and where those sympathetic with the Confederacy were shut out of the political process.

Recuse: To disqualify from participation in a decision on grounds such as prejudice, personal involvement, or conflict of interest.

Redistricting: The redrawing of political districts, as required after each census to keep them equal in population.

Reduction veto: The power of some state governors to reduce the level of spending authorized in an appropriations bill passed by the legislature, subject to an override by a supermajority vote of the legislature.

Reform: A word referring to a policy or institutional change that connotes a positive, purposeful change.

Regressive tax: A tax that the less affluent pay a greater share of their income to cover than wealthy taxpayers pay.

Responsible party model: A theory advanced by eighteenth-century Irish philosopher Edmund Burke that parties should be ideologically consistent, presenting voters with a clear platform and set of policies that are principled and distinctive. Elected officials are expected to be held responsible for implementing the party's program and policies.

Retention election: An election in which the issue on the ballot is whether an incumbent should be kept in office (yes or no) rather than one that offers a choice between two or more competing candidates.

Roll call: When legislators are required to cast a recorded vote on a bill or motion, whether in a committee or on the chamber floor.

Selective benefit: The provision by a group of some material, purposive, or solidarity incentive that can be enjoyed only by members of the group.

Self-financing candidates: Candidates for office who mainly use their own money for their campaign expenses.

Semiclosed primary: Voting in a party's primary is permitted for voters who are registered with the party or as independents.

Semiopen primary: Registered voters may vote in any party's primary, but they must publicly declare for which party's primary they choose to vote.

Sin tax: A tax that is designed to target behavior that may be deemed worthy of discouraging.

Single-member district (SMD): Legislative district in which only one legislator from the same chamber serves.

Single-subject rule: Rules that limit any single initiative to one general subject.

Social capital: Aspects of social life, such as social networks and trust in other people, that allow people to work together effectively.

Special session: An extraordinary meeting of the legislature after its regular session has adjourned, usually called by the governor to consider a very limited policy agenda.

Special districts: Local governments that are established (under state law) for limited purposes, such as providing a single public service.

Specialty courts: Courts with very limited jurisdictions to deal with special populations or special crimes.

Standing committee: An at least semipermanent legislative committee that evaluates legislation in a particular area of policy.

State auditor: The state auditor is a high-ranking official who heads a unit that conducts financial and program evaluations of state agencies, both routinely and in response to legislative requests.

State of the State address: In most states, the annual address by the governor to the state legislature at the beginning of its session in which he or she describes the condition of the state and presents a policy agenda for the coming legislative session.

Statute: A law passed by a legislative body.

Statutory initiative: A ballot initiative that has the same legal status as statutes passed by a legislature.

Stay of execution: The power of governors in most states with capital punishment to delay temporarily executing a condemned person.

Straight-ticket ballot: A ballot that allowed (or required) a voter to cast votes for every office for candidates from a single political party.

Street-level bureaucrats: Government workers who have direct contact with the public, such as police officers, teachers, and driver's license examiners.

Strong mayor–council system: A system of local government where executive and administrative powers (appointments, budgeting, vetoes) are given to an elected mayor. A council approves budgets and passes ordinances.

Supermajority: A portion of a vote that is greater than one-half, such as two-thirds or three-fifths.

Supermajority vote requirement: The requirement that votes in excess of 50 percent (plus one) are required for a legislature to approve a bill or a new tax.

Supreme court: The highest court in a judicial system, with final appellate jurisdiction over cases of law in that system.

Swing seat: A legislative district where the partisan balance of voters is fairly even, allowing either party to have a good chance of winning it in any given election.

Tax and expenditure limits (TELS): Rules that limit how much a government can increase taxes and/or spending by each year. The annual limit in growth of spending or taxes may not exceed some formula that accounts for population growth and inflation

Tax equity: Judging the fairness of a tax in terms of which income groups bear the cost of paying the tax.

Term limits: The requirement that a person can be elected to a certain office only for a specified number of terms or years.

Top-two blanket primary: Allows eligible voters, irrespective of their party affiliation, to vote in a primary for any candidate running on any party ticket, with the top candidates from each political party squaring off in the general election.

Tort: Damage, injury, or a wrongful act to person or property—whether done willfully or negligently—for which a civil suit can be brought.

Traditionalistic political culture: The general and informal set of beliefs and attitudes that politics in a state or community is the domain of social and economic elites and that the have-nots ought not to get involved in politics.

Trial court: A court before which issues of fact and law are tried and determined for a legal case.

Trial transcript: The official, verbatim, and written record of what was said during a trial.

Unfunded mandate: A public policy that requires a subnational government to pay for an activity or project established by the federal government.

Unicameral: Having only one chamber, such as the Nebraska Legislature, which has a senate but no house.

Unified government: When all three legs of the legislative process (the governor, the house, and the senate) are controlled by the same party.

Unitary system: A system of governance with a strong central government that controls virtually all aspects of its constitutive subnational governments.

Unit of analysis: In scientific research, the generic person, place, or thing being studied.

Urbanization: A process of landscape change characterized by increased scale of human population, increased population density, and increased social heterogeneity.

User fees: Charging people who use a government service a direct fee.

Voting cue: A simple signal about how to vote, in lieu of more detailed information; for example, a candidate's political party.

Voting Rights Act: A law passed by Congress in 1965 designed to remove racial barriers to voting. The original law gave the federal government authority over local voter registration procedures in several southern states. It has been amended and reauthorized by Congress several times since 1965.

Voting-age population: All U.S. residents age 18 and over.

Voting-eligible population: All U.S. citizens age 18 and over who are eligible to vote. Excludes noncitizens and ineligible felons.

Ward: A geographic subdivision in a city, defined for the purpose of representation. Also know as a district.

Weak mayor–council systems: A system of local government where executive and legislative powers are given to the council. The mayor may have mostly ceremonial duties, has few formal powers, and may serve as a member of the council.

Wedge issues: Issues that tap into divisions of opinion among supporters of one party and weaken the base of support for the party's candidates.

Winner-take-all: Also known as first-past-the post. An election system where only one position or one single seat is selected, and the candidate with the most votes wins. A majority is not required to win.

Author Index

A

Abrahamson, Shirley S., 236
Abramowitz, Alan, 93, 106, 121
Adams, Greg, 77
Adams, Kimberly S., 172
Adams, S., 70
Addams, Jane, 270
Adrian, Charles, 271, 275
Ainsworth, Bill, 245
Aldrich, John H., 115, 124, 176, 183
Allswang, John, 105
Alozie, Nicholas O., 251
Alt, James, 127, 315
Alvarez, R. Michael, 70, 99
Anderson, Jennifer, 136, 141, 145
Ansolabehere, Stephen, 156, 161
Arceneaux, Kevin T., 19, 110, 168, 239
Atkeson, Lonna Rae, 49, 71, 197
Aylsworth, Leon E., 280

B

Bachrach, Peter, 130
Baker, Gordon E., 161
Baldassare, Mark, 73
Banducci, Susan, 70, 81, 98, 102
Banfield, Edward, 267, 270
Barabas, Jason, 160, 163, 164
Baratz, Morton S., 130
Bardwell, Kedron, 77
Barghothi, A.J., 251
Barnello, Michelle A., 22, 168
Barrilleaux, Charles, 18, 122, 127, 212
Barth, Jay, 215, 220
Battista, James Coleman, 182, 183
Battista, James S., 176
Baudoin, Kyle, 294, 298, 309, 310, 315
Baum, Lawrence, 230, 247
Bayoumi, Tamim, 316
Bazar, Emily, 219
Beard, Charles, 99
Becker, Lawrence, 181
Beer, Samuel, 28, 40

Behr, Roy, 130
Behrens, Angela, 65
Bejarano, Christina, 207
Bell, Debbie, 302
Bender, Edwin, 139
Benesh, Sara C., 249
Benhabib, Seyla, 45
Benjamin, Gerald, 156
Benz, Matthias, 107
Berch, Neil, 307
Berinsky, Adam, 70, 74
Berkman, Michael B., 152, 212
Berns, Walter, 12
Berry, Francis, 308
Berry, Jeffrey, 115, 141
Berry, William D., 121, 156, 308
Besley, Timothy, 75
Best, Robin, 155
Beyle, Thad, 198, 210, 212, 214, 217, 219
Bibby, John, 117, 123, 128
Binder, Norman, 80
Binker, Mark, 212
Bishop, Bill, 157
Blackman, Paul, 279
Blais, Andre, 70
Bloom, Clark C., 309
Bluestein, Greg, 216
Bobo, Lawrence, 81
Boehmke, Frederick, 107, 134, 142
Bogen, David, 34
Bohn, Hening, 315
Bond, Jon R., 22
Bonneau, Chris W., 22, 239, 246, 248, 252
Borrelli, Stephen A., 197
Boulard, Garry, 167
Bourdeaux, Carolyn, 179
Bowen, Lauren L., 242
Bowler, Shaun, 63, 64, 65, 66, 70, 71, 72, 77, 78, 89, 90, 91, 92, 93, 94, 95, 96, 98, 99, 100, 103, 104, 106, 107, 108, 109, 110, 112, 113, 222, 249, 283, 294, 297, 302, 315
Bowling, Cynthia J., 215, 222

331

Subject Index

Gubernatorial Election Cycle

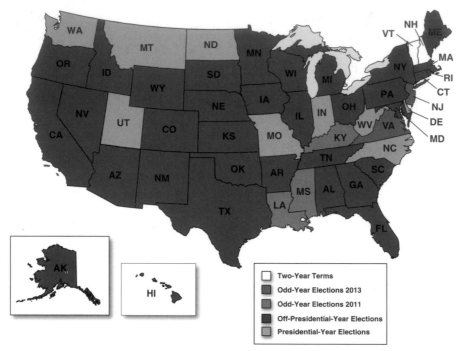

Two-Year Terms
Odd-Year Elections 2013
Odd-Year Elections 2011
Off-Presidential-Year Elections
Presidential-Year Elections

Source: Audrey S. Wall, ed., *The Book of the States: 2008*, vol. 40 (Lexington, KY: Council of State Governments, 2008), table 4.1.

★★★

State Legislative Term Limits

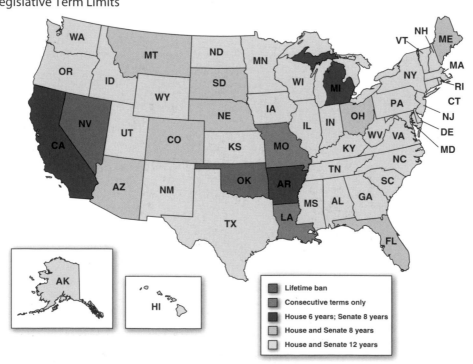

Lifetime ban
Consecutive terms only
House 6 years; Senate 8 years
House and Senate 8 years
House and Senate 12 years

Note: The states that are blank have no state legislative term limits.